READER'S DIGEST GUIDE TO CREATIVE GARDENING

READER'S DIGEST GUIDE TO
Creative Gardening

PUBLISHED BY THE READER'S DIGEST ASSOCIATION LIMITED
LONDON NEW YORK

READER'S DIGEST GUIDE TO CREATIVE GARDENING
was edited and designed by The Reader's Digest Association Limited, London

First Edition Copyright © 1984
The Reader's Digest Association Limited, Berkeley Square House,
Berkeley Square, London W1X 6AB
Reprinted 1990

Printed in Great Britain

ISBN 0 276 35223 8

Front cover *This delightful summer association includes glowing, red
oriental poppies (left) with their deep-cut leaves contrasting with the grey-green
heart-shaped foliage of the hosta (right). Behind, lupins of many hues stand in bold contrast
against a delicate, white-flowered clematis.*
Back cover *The golden blooms of the Modern shrub rose 'Fruhlingsgold' are complemented by the
yellow beards of the blue and purple irises, which stand sentinel over the
deep rose-pink peonies and the silver-leaved lamb's tongue.*

Contributors

The Publishers would like to thank the following people for major contributions to this book

CONSULTANT EDITOR   CONSULTANT PLANTSMAN

Allen Paterson, NDH, MEd, FLS   Kenneth A. Beckett

MAJOR CONTRIBUTORS

Mavis Batey   Lizzie Boyd   Penelope Hobhouse   Christopher Lloyd   Anne Scott-James

Richard Bisgrove   John Brookes   Roy Lancaster   Sheila Macqueen   Kay Sanecki

Beth Chatto   Kenneth Lemmon   Brian Mathew

ARTISTS

Julie Banyard
(THE GARDEN STUDIO)

Richard Bell

Frances Billington

Richard Bonson

Leonora Box
(SAXON ARTISTS)

Wendy Bramall
(ARTIST PARTNERS)

Patricia Calderhead

Lynn Chadwick
(THE GARDEN STUDIO)

Kevin Dean

Brian Delf

Colin Emberson

Shirley Felts

Jane Fern
(THE GARDEN STUDIO)

Sarah Fox-Davies

Delyth Jones

Nikki Kemball
(THE GARDEN STUDIO)

Ann Kirkland

Josephine Martin
(THE GARDEN STUDIO)

Tricia Newell

Annette Robinson

Helen Senior
(GROOM AND PICKERILL)

Sally Smith

Susan Stitt

Jane Tippett

Gill Tomblin

Andrew Vass

Barbara Walker
(SAXON ARTISTS)

Ann Winterbotham
(JOHN MARTIN AND
ARTISTS LTD)

*The Publishers would also like to thank the following organisations
for their help in the preparation of this book*

Cambridge University Botanic Gardens, Cambridge

Greenwich Park, London SE10

Hatfield House, Hertfordshire

Pulbrook and Gould Ltd, London SW1

Royal Botanic Gardens, Kew, Surrey

The Royal Horticultural Society's Garden, Wisley, Surrey

Syon Park, Brentford, Middlesex

Wakehurst Place, Ardingly, W. Sussex

Contents

A GUIDE TO THE BEST PLANTS AND HOW TO USE THEM

SPECIAL FEATURES

Creating a beautiful garden

A LOVE OF FLOWERS seems inborn in most people. Since primitive times, plants have been brought in from the wild to decorate dwellings, while in more recent centuries they have been cultivated for use not only as food and medicine but also as objects of pure beauty. In parallel with this delight in flowers, methods of growing and arranging them have turned gardening at its highest level into something of an art.

However, this does not mean that a beautiful garden can only be created with professional expertise. Indeed, some of the finest gardens of this century were the result of inspired work by gifted amateurs: people such as Victoria Sackville-West and her husband Sir Harold Nicolson who made the garden at Sissinghurst Castle, and Major Lawrence Johnston who planted Hidcote Manor.

So the amateur gardener need not feel inadequate. For in any garden the main ingredients required to lift it above the level of the ordinary are an intelligent choice of plants, care with their arrangement and combination, and a knowledge of their cultivation. These are the subjects of this book.

Many professional gardeners make much about the techniques of plant growing. Of course, there are plants that are difficult to grow successfully, but the majority generally prefer to live than to die, and if treated sensibly will thrive.

Certain facts will add to the gardener's understanding of a plant's needs, such as where it comes from. For example, the genus *Cistus* is a native of hot, Mediterranean hillsides, while *Trillium* originates in the deep, temperate woodlands of New England in the United States. Armed with this knowledge, the gardener can create the right conditions for each of them to flourish. In addition, he can consider other plants, adapted to the same conditions, which will present themselves as associates.

But which of the 250,000 species of flowering plants and which of the similar number of horticultural selections and hybrids should the gardener grow? One famous gardener, William Robinson (1839-1935), was perfectly clear. 'Throw away the weedy kinds,' he said. 'There is no lack of the best.' It is easy to agree, but less easy to define either the weeds or the best.

For instance, species that are highly successful in the wild may be totally useless in the garden. To be 'best', they must earn their keep: it may be the year-round effect of evergreen (or ever-grey) foliage, which may also be aromatic; the flowers may be brilliantly coloured, unusually shaped and exquisitely scented; or the blooms may last for weeks and then be followed by coloured fruits.

All these aspects are subjective when it comes to choice, and the selections made in this book are the personal preferences of the experts who have compiled the sections. To vary and add individuality to the selection the gardener needs to know a wide range of plants. There is no better practical way of doing this than visiting the many great gardens open to the public.

In this book the 'best plants' are not described or illustrated in isolation. They appear as the centrepieces or partners in carefully conceived associations, in which a combination of plants are used to produce a colourful garden scene.

Although emphasis has been given to natural species, the many colourful hybrids have not been ignored, especially where science has improved on nature. However, some of the brilliant colours are less easy to fit harmoniously into the overall garden picture, where colour combination is an important consideration when creating plant associations. Unlike a painting, which is eventually finished, the plants in a garden may grow for centuries or die in a few months. The gardener's pictures are never quite complete; that is their joy.

Annuals and biennials

A treasure chest of summer jewels that needs careful selection and display for best effect

THE SEEDSMEN'S CATALOGUES, arriving in late autumn ready for quiet reading during the dark winter days, promise much for the spring and summer to come. Invariably, they display flowers in a profusion of colours of gem-like brilliance. But like the wearing of rich jewels, the effect of annuals and biennials in the garden is greatest if selection and setting are given careful thought. Annuals do not merely offer colour – they provide foliage, texture and scent as well. The flowers of the castor oil plant (*Ricinus communis*), for instance, have little to commend them, but statuesque plants such as these can often offer more than a bright but boring bed of better-known annuals.

Most of our popular annuals – petunias for example, or lobelias – have their origins in the tropics. These are the half-hardy ones that should not be planted out until the last frost has passed. They are often in flower by this time, so the show begins at once; but they are time-consuming to raise and expensive to buy. Therefore, they must be used with discretion. A tub of petunias at an important focal point can be more effective than ten times the amount dotted about the garden.

Far cheaper are the hardy annuals which can be sown straight from the packet into the ground. Their flowering season may be shorter but such simple, old-fashioned flowers as larkspurs and love-in-a-mist seldom offer any problems in arrangement – most packets of seeds produce a combination of subtle, harmonising colours. Not so the half-hardies – with these, every gardener has a living kaleidoscope in his hands. It must be shaken with care.

Behind a white edging of sweet alyssum sprawling over the stone flags lies an eye-catching array of annuals – verbenas, senecios, pansies, salvias, petunias and marigolds.

Abutilon striatum 'Thompsonii' is skirted by *Salvia splendens*.

Abutilon × hybridum

Growing some 4-6 ft tall, this is a group of vigorous shrubs that root readily from cuttings and can be treated as annuals. The flowers of red, orange or yellow, appearing from May to October, are often attractively veined by a deeper tone; the maple-like leaves are pale green.

Abutilon striatum 'Thompsonii', a variegated form of one of the species from which *A.* × *hybridum* is derived, has orange-veined yellow flowers and leaves that are conspicuously spotted and striped with creamy-yellow. Abutilons are excellent as large pot plants.

HOW TO GROW
For bedding and pot plants, take cuttings from existing stock during summer; root and overwinter under glass. Set out in early summer - as dot plants in borders and beds or as container plants - in ordinary moist soil, and in a sunny, sheltered spot.

Abutilon × *hybridum* is not hardy and needs shelter. Here 'Ashford Yellow' is being grown as a pot plant in a courtyard.

Mauve *Ageratum houstonianum* and yellow ursinias form a summer carpet.

Ageratum houstonianum

This blue-flowered annual (also known as *Ageratum mexicanum*) has been superseded by its garden varieties. The newer ones, such as 'Blue Cap' and 'Blue Danube', make compact cushions, 6-9 in. high, that are splendid for formal bedding schemes. The older, looser cultivars, such as 'Tall Blue' and 'Blue Bunch', 1½-2 ft high, are more versatile: they combine well with other plants and are excellent in cut-flower arrangements.

Ageratum flowers are just like lavender-blue powder puffs. For some reason, they are generally described in seed catalogues as gentian blue, but this is not so.

HOW TO GROW
Sow these half-hardy annuals under glass in early spring. Plant out in early summer, 9 in. apart for dwarf types, 12 in. apart for the taller 'Blue Bouquet'. Both do best in moisture-retentive, ordinary soil, in sun or light shade, with some shelter.

Flowering from early summer until the first hard frosts, *Ageratum houstonianum* 'Blue Danube' erupts with fluffy blooms.

With its larger flowers, 'Milas' is superior to the parent species.

Agrostemma githago 'Milas'

This fine variety of our native corn-cockle comes from Turkey – from just outside the town of Milas. It is a charming annual that bears delicately veined flowers of lilac-pink, deepening slightly at the edges. They are carried from midsummer to autumn on 3-4 ft high stems, above slender leaves.

Actually a tough cornfield weed, the plant has a delicate appearance that belies its hardy constitution. It associates particularly well with *Clarkia elegans* and candytuft (*Iberis umbellata*). Alternatively, 'Milas' can be used in gaps among spring and early summer-blooming perennials to keep up the floral display.

HOW TO GROW
Sow in the open, in spring or autumn, in ordinary, even poor soil. Tolerant of drought and wind exposure, but does best in full sun. Thin seedlings to 6 in. apart. Dead-head to prevent inferior self-sown seedlings.

A glorious riot of colour is produced by pink *Agrostemma githago* 'Milas', scarlet poppies and orange and red nasturtiums.

Althaea rosea (HOLLYHOCK)

Hollyhocks (now classified as *Alcea*), have been favourite garden flowers for centuries, differing little over the years from those depicted in illustrated 'Herballs' of the 16th and 17th centuries. A hundred years ago, until the outbreak of rust disease, they were cultivated as perennials by specialist growers, and in hundreds of named varieties. The disease is kept at bay nowadays by treating hollyhocks either as annuals or as biennials.

Althaea rosea (syn. *A. chinensis*) is a stately plant with large, handsome basal leaves diminishing in size up the stem and interspersed with large flowers of pink, red, dark crimson, yellow or white. Most seedsmen offer only double varieties, such as the old and reliable 'Chater's Double', which has large, full, flower rosettes in various colours. But the single varieties are, with their frail, crumpled petals, just as attractive and well worth growing if they can be obtained. All varieties flower from July and continue well into autumn.

Where space is available for a nursery bed, the best results are obtained by growing the plants as biennials, giving them time to build up magnificent 9 ft high stems. Particularly good plants can be left to flower for several years until rust becomes serious; you can then propagate new plants from seeds. Among the best varieties are 'Summer Carnival', 'Single Mixed', and dwarf 'Majorette'.

Because hollyhocks are so striking, they should not be grown with other tall plants but with plants much lower than themselves. For example, you could interplant them with *Crambe cordifolia*, 4-6 ft high, and a low drift of the 2 ft tall musk mallow, *Malva moschata* 'Alba'. The crambe bears billowing masses of tiny white flowers in early summer, and the musk mallow carries single white flowers from June to September.

HOW TO GROW

As an annual, sow seeds under glass in early spring; prick off singly into 4 in. pots and plant outside in late spring. If the plants are to be retained for a second year, cut flowered stems down to 6 in. above ground level in early autumn.
Crambe cordifolia: see p. 78.
Malva moschata: see p. 104.

Althaea rosea 'Chater's Double' is available in various colours.

In July, the towering spires of single-flowered hollyhocks mingle with the branching stems of *Crambe cordifolia* – seen here in seed – on the right. Beneath them blooms the white musk mallow, *Malva moschata* 'Alba'.

Amaranthus caudatus (LOVE-LIES-BLEEDING)

This dramatic plant derives its common name from the long, drooping, crimson flower tassels that from July onwards gradually turn it into a blood-red cascade. Its light green leaves provide a muted accompaniment until late summer, when they gradually assume a deep bronze tone; in addition, the stems turn crimson in autumn.

The variety 'Viridis', which has become popular for flower arrangements, has flowers of pale lime-green which contrast exquisitely with the red of the species. Though both plants are tall – 3-4 ft – they should still be used at the front of a border where they can be fully appreciated. If carefully dried when young, both red and green forms make excellent winter decorations, and retain their colours for a considerable time.

HOW TO GROW
Sow seeds under glass in spring, harden off in a cold frame, and plant out in late spring, 1½-2 ft apart. Any ordinary soil is suitable, ideally rich and well drained to dry. The plants are best in full sun.

Love-lies-bleeding hangs its glowing tassels above a mixed planting of clarkias, pot marigolds and nasturtiums.

Anchusa capensis

The bright blue blooms of *Anchusa* are among the few truly blue flowers. *Anchusa capensis* closely resembles a forget-me-not, and like that plant it produces its flowers over a long season – throughout July and August. Only at the end of summer do spent flowers so greatly outnumber new that the plant begins to look bedraggled.

The modern standard cultivar, 'Blue Angel', forms a compact dome 9 in. high. Its strikingly beautiful flowers are ideal companions for pale yellow Californian poppies (*Eschscholzia californica*).

HOW TO GROW
Sow in mid-spring, where the plants are to flower, thinning to 9 in. apart. Best in good, fertile, moisture-retentive soil and in full sun. Remove faded flower stems at the base to encourage later blooms.

The vivid blue flowers of *Anchusa capensis* blend attractively with the tall rose-pink plumes of limoniums.

Yellow Californian poppies glow against *Anchusa capensis* 'Blue Angel'.

Arabis caucasica

Very often called *Arabis albida*, this can be grown as a biennial for bedding or as a hardy perennial. Its height is only 9 in., but it spreads up to 2 ft. Being rather invasive, less vigorous cultivars are generally more popular. All have a long flowering season – February to June.

The most attractive cultivar is 'Variegata', white flowered like the species but with compact cushions of white-edged leaves that make a cheering sight all winter long. The pale pink 'Rosea' is more usually grown, however. It is extremely vigorous, and should be sheared close to the ground after flowering to keep it compact.

HOW TO GROW
Set out plants in autumn or spring, 18 in. apart for 'Rosea', 10 in. for 'Variegata'. Both need sharply drained soil and full sun. Propagate by stem cuttings after flowering, division in autumn, or seeds in summer. Trim hard after flowering.

A bed of *Arabis caucasica* intermingles with the similarly shaped rose-lilac flowers of *Aubrieta deltoidea*.

'Variegata', with white-edged leaves, planted beside a pool.

Antirrhinum majus (SNAPDRAGON)

The snapdragon (*Antirrhinum*) is, like the hollyhock, one of our most ancient garden flowers, and, if it were not attacked by rust disease, it would still be one of the most popular. However, plant breeders have managed to raise many cultivars, from low, trailing plants to tall ones suitable for cut flowers, that are rust-resistant.

The range of *Antirrhinum majus* varieties is extremely wide, and includes the splendid large-flowered Tetraploids and Penstemon-flowered group, whose flowers are trumpet-shaped. The colour range of antirrhinums is extensive, and there are bicoloured forms, too. Crimson cultivars usually have dark bronze foliage.

Among the great choice of cultivars, one of the finest for general garden use is the intermediate height group, 18 in. high, with erect spikes of single flowers. Their spires of bright, pure-coloured blooms, delightful when repeated in groups, made them one of the favourite border plants of that great garden designer, artist and writer, Gertrude Jekyll.

White cultivars such as 'White Spire' are particularly lovely grown with the green-flowered form of love-lies-bleeding, the 3 ft high *Amaranthus caudatus* 'Viridis', flowering from July to October, and with the variegated *Hosta fortunei* 'Albopicta'. Such a grouping creates a cool effect that is especially attractive at dusk or seen by artificial light near the house.

Crimson antirrhinums, such as 'Welcome', are ideal for predominantly red-flowered, coppery-leaved associations.

HOW TO GROW

Antirrhinum majus: raise plants under glass in early spring and bed out during late spring and early summer, 10 in. apart for intermediates, 18 in. for larger strains and 8 in. apart for dwarfs. When each plant is well established, pinch out its growing point to induce side branching. Grow in well-drained soil enriched with organic matter, in full sun or very light shade.
Amaranthus caudatus: see p. 14.
Hosta fortunei: see p. 95.

The rust-resistant semi-dwarf snapdragons *Antirrhinum majus* Nanum 'Monarch Mixed' are widely used for bedding.

Nanum snapdragons bloom with green *Nicotiana* and white *Lavatera*.

Subtle shades of green and white fashion a graceful, summer border. Drooping green racemes of *Amaranthus caudatus* 'Viridis' create an unusual background to *Antirrhinum majus* 'White Spire' and vigorous *Hosta fortunei* 'Albopicta'.

Dark 'Atrosanguinea' contrasts with other plants' lighter foliage.

Atriplex hortensis (PURPLE ORACH)

Three cultivars of this annual – 'Rubra', 'Atrosanguinea' and 'Cupreata' – have deep crimson-purple stems and leaves that, when young, are covered in a fine, glistening white powder. The flowers are insignificant, and it is really the foliage that is the plant's true claim for a place in a good ornamental bed. On rich soil, orachs grow rapidly to a height of 3-4 ft and spread at least 2 ft across. If they are left in the ground until late summer, they will obligingly produce an abundant crop of seedlings the following year.

The leaves of the orach plant are sometimes used as a substitute for spinach.

HOW TO GROW
Sow seeds under glass in early spring or outdoors in late spring, with ultimate distances of 16 in. between seedlings. Any well-drained, good garden soil is suitable, in full sun. The plants are wind-resistant and flourish in an open site.

The purple growth of *Atriplex hortensis* 'Cupreata' rises in front of a white form of *Chrysanthemum parthenium*.

Pink *B. p.* Monstrosa and blue *Muscari armeniacum* brighten a spring bed.

Bellis perennis Monstrosa (DOUBLE DAISY)

For some reason, we are forever trying to eradicate the common daisy, *Bellis perennis*, that uniquely attractive fresh-faced flower of British lawns. Its large-flowered forms, however – known as *B. p.* Monstrosa – are favourite garden plants and have been cultivated for centuries. They have double, mop-like flower heads at least 2 in. across, borne on 6 in. high stems, and loose rosettes of evergreen leaves that are much larger than those of the species. They bear a profusion of white, pink or red flowers from April to July. Double miniature varieties are also available.

HOW TO GROW
Sow in early summer, in an outdoor nursery bed, thinning as necessary and transplanting to flowering sites in autumn, 8-10 in. apart. Grow in full sun or partial shade, in good, moist soil. Dead-head to prevent self-seeding, especially plants grown as short-lived perennials.

Bellis perennis miniature varieties have neat, double pompon flowers in rich colours and make fine bedding plants.

A pink × *tuberhybrida* begonia is seen here with *Lobelia erinus*.

Begonia × tuberhybrida (MULTIFLORA GROUP)

A miniature version of the familiar rose-flowered begonias, this dwarf, free-flowering hybrid is about 8-10 in. high, with a wide, bushy, neat habit. It makes an excellent bedding or pot plant.

The many named varieties come in a colourful range of pink, crimson, scarlet, orange and yellow flowers, and some have bronze foliage. 'Tasso' is an excellent double red, while 'Fiesta' and 'Clips F₁' are reliable modern mixtures.

HOW TO GROW
Start the tubers into growth in mid-spring, in moist peat at a temperature of 64°F (18°C). Embed them hollow side up in boxes 3 in. deep. Plant out in early summer, in large pots or baskets containing proprietary potting compost, or as bedding plants, 15 in. apart, in loamy, moist but well-drained soil and in light shade. Give a diluted liquid feed every three weeks to pot-grown plants. Lift the tubers as the foliage withers, dry them and store in a frost-proof place. Propagate from cuttings in spring.

On *Begonia × tuberhybrida* varieties the few single, female flowers are outnumbered by double, male blooms.

Begonia semperflorens (FIBROUS BEGONIA)

The Latin name *semperflorens* means ever-flowering. It well suits this Brazilian plant, which, though a perennial, is more usually grown in this country as an annual for summer bedding; afterwards, however, it can be lifted to make a winter pot plant for a well-lit room. These begonias, generally 6-9 in. tall, carry clusters of white, pink or red flowers from June to early autumn. Their foliage is a succulent glossy green or purple.

The species is now represented by an increasing number of cultivars. Until recently, the white-flowered varieties have always had pale green leaves, the pink-flowered mid-green, and the red-flowered ones, dark, reddish-brown leaves. But it is now possible to obtain, for example, white-blooming plants with deep coppery foliage.

Obviously, so versatile a plant would be marvellous in all kinds of associations. Try a centrepiece of the 12 in. high pink-flowered variety 'Pink Avalanche', which has green leaves, and fringe it with *Lobelia erinus* 'Cambridge Blue' or the compact *L. e.* 'White Lady'.

The association could be rounded off with the 18 in. high perennial *Pyrethrum ptarmaciflorum*, whose principal interest is its dissected grey-silver foliage.

HOW TO GROW
Begonia semperflorens: sow seeds under glass in late winter. In late spring or early summer, bed out home-raised or bought young plants, 8-10 in. apart, in rich, moist but well-drained soil, and in light shade or sun. In autumn, either discard the plants or transfer them to pots for indoor decoration or for stock to supply cuttings for spring.
Lobelia erinus: see p. 40.
Pyrethrum ptarmaciflorum: see p. 52.

Clouds of pink *Begonia semperflorens* and blue *Lobelia erinus*, overflowing from a stone urn in August, are framed by the filigree foliage of *Pyrethrum ptarmaciflorum*. White begonias with copper foliage look elegant in an earthenware pot. Containers filled with begonias cheer any terrace or balcony and these flowers will survive even in exposed areas.

Calceolaria integrifolia

This pretty little half-hardy semi-shrubby perennial will do very well outdoors in the warmer parts of Britain. The proviso is that you find it a snug spot, preferably with a wall at its back. There it may grow to 4 ft high, create a wealth of fresh, pale green, wrinkled leaves and put out a great halo of bright yellow flowers.

A tougher relation altogether is *Calceolaria mexicana*, a slender, lax annual with narrow, toothed foliage. This will self-seed in shady corners, an ideal position to bring out the luminosity of the pale yellow flowers.

HOW TO GROW
Sow seeds under glass in late winter, potting on and hardening off the seedlings before planting out, in early summer, 10 in. apart or in final 5 in. pots for growing under glass. Sow Calceolaria mexicana in situ in spring and thin to 6 in. apart. All bedding calceolarias do best in neutral to acid, light and fertile soil and in a sunny, sheltered site. Discard plants after flowering.

The pouch-like blooms of *Calceolaria integrifolia*, in front of *Phormium tenax*, blaze with colour from July to September.

Left undisturbed, *Calceolaria integrifolia* may become perennial.

Calendula officinalis (POT MARIGOLD)

The pot marigold is one of the easiest to grow of all hardy annuals and, with its glowing orange or yellow flowers, borne on 2 ft stalks, one of the brightest. Medieval cooks used to scatter the petals over food, partly as a decoration and partly to ward off toothache, warts, spots and other ills. Flowers and leaves were, and to some extent still are, widely used in cookery; hence the common name of 'Pot' marigold, and the species name '*officinalis*', indicating that it was used by apothecaries in medicinal preparations.

Double-flowered and dwarf varieties (12 in. tall) are available in colours ranging from pale cream to orange-red. 'Fiesta Gitana' is an award-winning dwarf form in a mixture of pastel hues. To prolong the flowering season – May to autumn – dead-head regularly, otherwise the plant will be finished by early summer.

HOW TO GROW
Sow seeds outdoors, in early autumn or early spring; thin to 12 in. apart. Calendulas thrive in any soil – even a poor one – that is well drained, and in full sun. They are drought and wind-resistant. Shear the plants over after the first flush of bloom, to prevent self-seeding.

A mixed strain of *Calendula officinalis* blazes like miniature suns.

Yellow and orange pot marigolds, framed by lavender-blue catmint and blue *Anchusa azurea*, light up a mixed border.

Callistephus chinensis (CHINA ASTER)

The many varieties of this half-hardy annual have replaced the species in general cultivation. They are popular bedding plants, but are best in a mixed border.

Good dwarf sorts, all less than 12 in. high, include 'Dwarf Queen Mixed' and 'Pinocchio Mixed'. Taller, late-flowering kinds, such as those in the Californian Giants and Super Sinensis groups (which are both 2½ ft tall), rival chrysanthemums in their autumn display.

HOW TO GROW
Sow under glass in spring, and harden off before transplanting. Alternatively, sow directly in the flowering site, thinning to 18 in. apart for tall bedding types, 12 in. for others. Make occasional sowings at regular intervals, to extend the flowering season. Set in well-drained but moisture-retentive soil, and in a sunny, wind-sheltered site. Avoid using the same site in consecutive years, to deter soil-borne diseases.

Dwarf China asters have the intense colouring of a stained-glass window.

The bright yellow centres of these daisy-like, single-flowered China asters show off the strong purple of the petals.

Campanula medium (CANTERBURY BELL)

The Canterbury bell is a typical cottage-garden plant –
easily grown, showy in flower for part of the summer but
contributing nothing at other times. For this reason it is
best planted in small groups throughout the border, which
it will seem to fill with its bell flowers from May to July
but in which it will not leave large gaps when it has
finished blooming.

The large bells, which may be single or double, and
white, pink, mauve or blue, are carried on stems 1¼-3 ft
high. They harmonise well with candytuft (*Iberis*),
Gypsophila or *Nigella*, all of which can be sown in autumn
to flower early the following summer.

HOW TO GROW
*Sow outside in late spring (or summer), transfer to a nursery
bed and move to the flowering site in autumn (or spring), in
groups of at least five spaced 12 in. apart. Any well-drained
soil, in sun or light shade, is suitable.*

Stately, pink Canterbury bells rise out of a
haze of delicate, cornflower-blue *Nigella
damascena* (love-in-a-mist).

A massed planting of Canterbury bells fills a bed with colour.

Canna × generalis

For many years these hybrid perennials, which can be used
for summer bedding, were scarce, but they are now
gradually returning to the catalogues, where they may well
also be listed as *Canna × hybrida* or *C. indica*.

The brightly coloured blooms look like a cross between
an orchid and a gladiolus, and in late summer appear in
vivid clusters at the tops of stems that are often 4 ft tall.
They come in magnificent shades of yellow, orange, red
and pink. The leaves are very large – at least 18 in. long
and up to 12 in. across – and vary in colour from pale
green through deep green to bronze and purple.

Cannas are generally grown with half-hardy annuals and
other bedding plants, but it pays to be more adventurous.
Try either of the two purple-leaved cultivars – 'America',
which has deep red flowers, and 'Wyoming', which is
bronze-orange – in combination with a plant such as
Crocosmia × crocosmiiflora 'Solfatare', an unusual montbretia
with apricot-yellow flowers and broad bronze-tinted leaves.
A yellow bedding dahlia or two will strengthen the yellow
of the montbretia and provide a contrast of form. If you
prefer green-leaved cannas, you could substitute the deep
orange 'Ingeborg' or the vivid scarlet 'President'.

HOW TO GROW
*Canna × generalis: start the rhizomes into growth in early
spring in moist peat, at a temperature of 61°F (16°C). Move
them into containers of potting compost, or bed them out in
early summer, 18 in. apart, in rich, moist soil and in a sunny,
sheltered position. In autumn, lift the rhizomes and dry them
off before storing in a frost-free place. Propagate by division in
spring.*
Crocosmia × crocosmiiflora: see p. 148.

The golden-orange light of the late summer sun is reflected in this
striking cluster of plants. Sheltered by a wall, the dark leaves and
dramatic blooms of *Canna × generalis* 'Wyoming' brood over the delicate
butterfly flowers of *Crocosmia × crocosmiiflora* 'Solfatare' like exotic
creatures. Bobbing cheerfully at the side is a deep yellow bedding dahlia.

Cheiranthus cheiri (WALLFLOWER)

With its dense spikes of richly coloured blooms and its heady fragrance, the wallflower is the queen of spring-flowering biennials. The many cultivars now available, all flowering from April to June, provide an extensive range of colours. 'Fair Lady Mixed' and 'Tom Thumb Mixed' add subtle shades of yellow, apricot, pink and purple to the strong, clear reds, oranges and yellows of such old varieties as 'Blood Red', 'Fire King' and 'Cloth of Gold'.

Other good varieties include 'Primrose Monarch' (primrose yellow), 'Ruby Gem' (velvety ruby-red), and 'Eastern Queen' (salmon).

The individual colours of the mixtures are attractive, but some people feel that, as a medley, they have an insipidly mottled appearance, and that the best way to use wallflowers is to grow them in a mass of one bold colour, set off by another species. Traditionally, they are grown with tulips, but the crimson wallflower 'Vulcan' looks even better with the bronze young shoots of peonies.

Most cultivars are anything up to 2 ft high, and are excellent as cut flowers. But there are also dwarf kinds, only 9-12 in. tall, which can be used in small informal patches in borders near the house, so that their scent will waft through the open windows.

Wallflowers can be used in a thousand combinations, but a particularly charming plan is to interplant dwarf wallflowers such as 'Orange Bedder', 'Scarlet Bedder' and 'Primrose Bedder' – orange, red and yellow – with pink and red tulips. At the front, a wide edging of forget-me-nots (*Myosotis*) helps to create an association both sweetly coloured and fresh.

HOW TO GROW
Cheiranthus cheiri: cultivation as for C. × allionii, with tall cultivars spaced 12-15 in. apart, dwarf types 10 in. Wilting of wallflowers is usually caused by frost damage of foliage infected with grey mould. Minimise this risk by transplanting the seedlings well before the onset of cold weather.
Myosotis sylvestris: see p. 44.
Paeonia: see p. 107.
Tulipa: see pp. 169-171.

'Fire King' blazes beneath yellow *Coronilla* and purple *Aubrieta*.

Beneath a wisteria-covered wall, several varieties of *Cheiranthus cheiri* bloom with tulips and forget-me-nots.

Cheiranthus × allionii (SIBERIAN WALLFLOWER)

The blooms of the Siberian wallflower, usually grown as a biennial, are a solid, bright orange, and even the paler, orange-gold variety 'Golden Bedder' rivals summer-flowering marigolds in its intensity of colouring. These wallflowers, which should be kept well away from pastel varieties of *Cheiranthus cheiri*, are neat 15-18 in. high plants. They bloom from May to July, but sometimes put on an early display in autumn when they are planted out.

A splendid miniature association would be a clump of five or six blue-purple-flowered *Camassia leichtlinii* 'Atroviolacea' which stand about 3 ft high, surrounded by a group of Siberian wallflowers.

HOW TO GROW
Sow outdoors in early summer and transplant to flowering sites in autumn, 12 in. apart, in neutral to limy, well-drained and fertile soil, in full sun. After transplanting, pinch out the growing tips to encourage branching.

Siberian wallflowers and pink stocks fill a border with a broad sweep of colour. Behind them is *Cotoneaster horizontalis*.

Blue *Camassia leichtlinii* tempers the vivid orange of *C. × allionii*.

Centaurea cyanus (CORNFLOWER)

The cornflower is one of our oldest and best-loved hardy annuals, easy to grow and excellent for cutting. Two tall cultivars, 2-3 ft high, are 'Blue Diadem', a large-flowered form, and the Ball strain, which has flowers in white, pink, deep red, purple and blue. The 'Polka Dot' strain, only 12 in. high, is equally colourful.

Just as bright as the cornflower, but much less commonly grown, is the 2 ft high sweet sultan (*Centaurea moschata*), which has larger, more elegant, scented flowers in a softer colour range that includes yellow. Both flower throughout summer.

HOW TO GROW
Sow seeds of Centaurea cyanus in the open in autumn (under cloches) or late spring. C. moschata seeds should be sown under glass in early spring, or in the open in late spring. Thin seedlings to 12 in. apart (dwarf types to 9 in.). Grow in any good, well-drained soil, in full sun.

The cornflower 'Blue Diadem' has larger flowers than the parent species and is sturdier and more wind-resistant.

Cornflowers, marigolds and poppies form a kaleidoscope of colour.

Chrysanthemum carinatum

This annual (also known as *Chrysanthemum tricolor*), has everything to recommend it, being colourful, graceful and hardy. The flat, circular, daisy flowers are delightful. Borne singly at the top of stiff, 2 ft high stems, from June to September, each consists of a dark purple centre surrounded with petals banded with concentric circles of colour. The elegantly lacy, bright green leaves make the plant attractive even before it starts to bloom.

There are many named varieties, among which a new group, Monarch Court Jesters, is outstanding. This has very large blooms and lasts well as a cut flower.

HOW TO GROW
Sow seeds outdoors in spring, or under cloches in late summer for earlier flowering in the following year. Grow in good, light and well-drained soil, in full sun, and thin the seedlings so that they stand 12 in. apart.

Squirrel-tail grass (*Hordeum jubatum*) contrasts softly with the crisp mini-parasols of *Chrysanthemum carinatum*.

A cheerful patch of the chrysanthemum forms part of an annual border.

Chrysanthemum parthenium (FEVERFEW)

Feverfew is a short-lived perennial (also listed as *Matricaria eximia*), but is usually grown as a half-hardy annual that produces a mass of double white flowers, like snowballs, from July to September. Another attraction of this 9-18 in. high plant is its aromatic, pale green leaves. The old herbalists used to prescribe an infusion of these as a cure for migraine.

'White Gem' is a cultivar with pale creamy-yellow double blooms ringed with white petals. 'Golden Ball' has yellow flowers, and 'Aureum' has a charming combination of white flowers and golden-yellow leaves.

HOW TO GROW
Cultivation as for Chrysanthemum carinatum (see p. 21). Sow in spring in the open, thinning plants to 10-12 in. Feverfews also thrive in light shade and seed themselves freely, with variable results.

Snowy *Chrysanthemum parthenium* blooms in a yellow and white border.

All the double and dwarf varieties of feverfew have sprung from the wild species, seen here massed in starry array.

Clarkia elegans

The tall flower spikes of this Californian plant, also known as *Clarkia unguiculata*, provide a valuable contrast to the rounded blooms of most other annuals. There are many cultivars in a whole range of colours – white, pink, salmon, orange, scarlet, purple and lavender – available singly or as assortments, as in 'Mixed'. Blooming from July to September, they link early summer lupins, delphiniums and peonies with autumn asters and chrysanthemums.

The plants, which are 1½-2 ft high, are slender, and so can also be used as an interplanting with groups of June-flowering perennials such as irises and oriental poppies (*Papaver orientale*).

HOW TO GROW
Sow where the plants are to flower, in early spring, and thin to 9 in. apart. Best in light, well-drained, sandy loam, and in full sun. In mild gardens, sow in early autumn under cloches for sturdier, earlier flowering plants.

A pink and mauve sea of *C. elegans* washes over spent irises and poppies.

The brilliantly coloured flower spikes of *Clarkia elegans* are 9-12 in. long and individual blooms are up to 1½ in. across.

Cleome spinosa (SPIDER FLOWER)

The common name spider flower, given to the species of *Cleome*, is derived from the long, slender stamens that protrude from the plants' flower heads. In the half-hardy annual *Cleome spinosa* (syn. *C. pungens* and *C. hasslerana*) the heads are scented, pink-flushed, white globes that open gradually from July to autumn. Good cultivars include the pure white 'Helen Campbell' and 'Pink Queen'.

With the added attraction of elegant leaves divided into many leaflets, *C. spinosa* is a handsome plant – and the discovery that it will tolerate life in windy places has increased its popularity. In a tub it will rarely exceed 2 ft in height, but in well-prepared ground it reaches almost double that.

HOW TO GROW
Sow under glass in early spring, harden off the seedlings and plant in large containers. Alternatively, bed out, 2 ft apart, at the backs of borders, in well-drained fertile soil.

Cleome spinosa can develop into a shrubby plant 4 ft high.

Unlike the parent species, the modern forms of *Cleome spinosa*, such as this mixed strain, are free-flowering.

Coleus blumei

This shrubby perennial, grown as an annual, is valued for its colourful evergreen foliage. Because of the phenomenal ease with which cuttings from it root, it is a popular pot plant; but few gardeners realise that it can also be used outside for summer display. Best for this purpose are cultivars with broad, single-coloured leaves of yellow, orange, red, purple or pink. These make a splendid setting for flowering plants.

Most kinds of *Coleus blumei* varieties are 18 in. high and have a spread of about 12 in. To promote bushy growth – and so yield plenty of cuttings for propagation and thereby create bold groups of plants – the tiny blue and white, tubular flowers should be removed as soon as they appear in bud.

Named coleus with decorative foliage include 'Molten Lava' (carmine to plum-red and black), and 'Milky Way' (dwarf plants with deeply cut leaves in a variety of colours).

HOW TO GROW
Sow in early spring under glass; pot on the seedlings and bed out in early summer, as dot plants or in groups with 10-12 in. between plants. Pinch out the growing tips to encourage sideshoots. Coleus grow in any type of well-drained but moisture-retentive soil, in sun or dappled shade. Propagate exceptional colour forms by 3 in. long tip cuttings of non-flowering shoots in early autumn.

Grown together, the many different varieties of *Coleus blumei* can produce a scintillating display of colour.

Convolvulus tricolor 'Blue Ensign'

The hardy annual *Convolvulus tricolor* has all the beauty of the white-flowered perennial bindweed (*C. arvensis*) with none of its attendant problems. Its funnel-shaped flowers, which are on display from July to September, are a deep blue with a white or yellow throat.

The exceptionally beautiful variety 'Blue Ensign' is a smaller, more compact plant, only 9 in. high. Its rich blue flowers, which have a star-like, yellow-eyed white centre, form a perfect complement with a bed of yellow flowers.

For example, 'Blue Ensign' makes a splendid edging for a bed of yellow roses or when interplanted among pale yellow French and African marigolds (*Tagetes patula* and *T. erecta*).

When the three-zoned flowers of the convolvulus can be echoed by those of its neighbours, the effect is especially good. An edging of orange-yellow *Eschscholzia californica*, for example, and groups of white penstemons would provide a colourful and arresting combination.

HOW TO GROW
Convolvulus tricolor: sow under glass in spring, harden off in a cold frame and plant out in late May, 10-12 in. apart. Alternatively, sow in the open in April and thin out. The plant grows best in well-drained, fertile soil, in a sunny and wind-sheltered site or with twiggy sticks for support. Dead-head to extend the season.
Eschscholzia californica: see p. 28.
Penstemon × gloxinioides: see p. 51.
Tagetes erecta: see p. 57.
Tagetes patula: see p. 56.

The fresh blue, gold and white of *Convolvulus tricolor* 'Blue Ensign' is the starting point for this summer bed. Planted around it are clumps of white *Penstemon × gloxinioides* and golden *Eschscholzia californica*.

Mixed varieties of tickseed make a conflagration of the annual border.

Cosmos bipinnatus bears single bright flowers atop wiry stems.

Steeples of the Giant Imperial strain soar vividly in a herbaceous border.

Coreopsis drummondii (TICKSEED)

Sometimes listed under *Calliopsis*, this annual from Texas has daisy-like, purple-centred, bright yellow flowers on long straight stems. Its rich colouring, the jagged-toothed outline of its flowers, the alert stance of its petals and its deeply cut, dark green leaves all combine to make it a distinctive plant.

It has a branching habit and reaches a height of 2 ft. Flowering profusely from July to September, it has few rivals for supplying a border with a mass of brilliant colour; it also provides excellent cut flowers. A fine companion is the delicate pearl grass, *Briza maxima*, with its dangling clusters of flowers.

HOW TO GROW
Sow outdoors, where the plants are to flower, in succession from early spring to midsummer. Thin seedlings to 10 in. apart. Any good, well-drained soil in full sun is suitable. Cut back early flowered plants to encourage a second blooming.

Tickseed thrives in smoky, industrial areas. *Briza maxima* forms an eye-catching foreground for the blazing flowers.

Cosmos bipinnatus

Most plants produce flowers either in the blue-purple-crimson range of the spectrum or in the scarlet-orange-yellow band. Few combine both as spectacularly as does *Cosmos*. *C. bipinnatus* has finely dissected foliage and elegant flowers of crimson, pale or deep pink or white, on 3-4 ft stems, in August and September. A good companion for it is silver-leaved *Artemisia absinthium* 'Lambrook Silver'

Another species, *C. sulphureus*, has given rise to some outstanding yellow and orange cultivars, of which the best is 'Diablo'. Reaching 2-2½ ft, it flowers when well below its ultimate height and produces loose, semi-double, slightly translucent, fiery orange blooms.

HOW TO GROW
Sow under glass in early spring and harden off before planting out in late May, 18 in. apart, in any ordinary well-drained soil, in full sun. Staking may be necessary.

A white variety of *Cosmos bipinnatus* holds up its crisp blooms, 3-4 in. across, above dense, finely cut foliage.

Delphinium ajacis (ROCKET LARKSPUR)

Rocket larkspur is an annual that definitely repays the care you bestow upon it. Seeds should be sown in autumn – in a cold frame in all but mild areas – and the seedlings transplanted to well-cultivated fertile soil in spring. The result will be magnificent spires, 2-4 ft tall, of blue or mauve flowers in late spring and early summer. Most strains, such as the old Giant Imperial, have branching spires of blooms ideal for garden decoration. For cut flowers, the non-branching Hyacinth-flowered strain is best.

HOW TO GROW
If a cold frame is available, sow as above. If not, sow where the plants will grow, preferably in early autumn (with cloche protection in cold areas), or in spring; thin seedlings, 12-15 in. apart for Giant Imperial strain, less for other varieties. Choose a site with fertile, well-drained soil in full sun or light shade. Twiggy supports may be needed. Cut out faded stems after flowering.

Fern-like leaves surround the blue spikes of *Delphinium ajacis*, a fine plant for early summer flower arrangements.

Dahlia variabilis

The range of dahlia bedding varieties – more modest cousins of the large flower-show favourites – is increasing. The small sorts, 12-20 in. high, are grown as annuals from seeds and are suitable both for bedding and for planting in the foreground of a mixed border. All come in a wide range of colours, including white, yellow, orange, scarlet, crimson and pink, and flower from July to the first frosts.

'Coltness Hybrids' is a long-established, reliable strain with single flowers in several colours. The Collerette group has even larger single flowers, but with an inner collar of small petals sometimes contrasting in colour with the outer ones. A particularly effective Collerette dahlia is the seed-raised strain 'Dandy', which comes in a wide range of colours, each with a white or yellow collar, on stems up to 2 ft tall. 'Rigoletto', a strain of fully double bedding dahlias in various colours, grows to 15 in. in height.

HOW TO GROW
Sow indoors in spring, at gentle heat; transplant in late May/early June, 15-18 in. apart, in any fertile soil that is well drained but moisture-retentive, and in full sun. Staking is generally unnecessary, but dead-head regularly. Water during prolonged dry spells.

'Bishop of Llandaff' dahlias and day lilies blaze in summer splendour.

A border between a climber-covered wall and a clipped edging of box is filled with modern mixed dahlia varieties

Dianthus chinensis (INDIAN PINK)

Annual Indian pink cultivars, derived from the now rarely grown perennial species *Dianthus chinensis*, became popular only a few years ago with the emergence of some eye-catching new forms. One is 'Queen of Hearts', with a profusion of spectacular scarlet blooms. The grassy-green foliage of this compact, 12 in. high plant is a perfect foil for its flowers.

At the same height but in cool contrast are the glistening scarlet and white flowers and grey leaves of 'Snowfire'. This makes an excellent edging for a border given over to grey-leaved plants and is superior as a bedding plant to the overused white-flowered alyssums.

HOW TO GROW
Sow under glass in early spring, or outdoors in April, thinning or transplanting to 6-8 in. intervals. Soil and position as for Dianthus barbatus (see p. 26). Good colour forms can be propagated by cuttings in summer.

Clumps of scarlet and white *Dianthus chinensis* 'Snowfire' catch the eye like red ink blots on white paper.

Dianthus chinensis 'Queen of Hearts' is set off here by gypsophila.

Dianthus barbatus (SWEET WILLIAM)

Sweet william is a versatile plant, as much at home on a modern patio as in the cottage-garden border. It is a short-lived evergreen perennial, 1-2 ft high, that is usually grown as a biennial but that may also be grown as an annual in all except very cold areas. In June and July it bears sweetly scented, single or double flowers in combinations of white, pink and red. Its glossy, green or bronze leaves form compact mats that provide handsome ground-cover in winter. On light soils, especially, it should be sheared after flowering. This will encourage it to maintain its growth for another year or two.

Many people like the cheerful pink, or red and white varieties with their colours marked in concentric circles. But if drama is your aim, go instead for the sumptuous deep crimson ones with dark bronze foliage.

HOW TO GROW
For biennial or short-lived perennial plants, sow in an outdoor nursery bed in early summer and transplant to flowering sites in autumn. For annuals, sow under glass in spring, harden off and plant out in May. In both instances, space plants 8-10 in. apart and grow in ordinary, well-drained soil, in full sun. Shear the plants as soon as flowering is over if they are to be kept for a second year.

With their gaily patterned blooms, sweet williams brighten any border.

After *Spiraea × arguta* has finished flowering, its foliage forms a backdrop for the pink, red and purple sweet williams.

The deep crimson flowers of a variety of *Dianthus barbatus* are here used to fill gaps where young shrubs – white philadelphus, *Rosa glauca* and *Salvia officinalis* – need time to establish themselves.

Digitalis purpurea (COMMON FOXGLOVE)

Our native foxglove is a wonderful combination of strength
and delicacy, growing 5 ft high in good conditions yet
needing no support for its gracefully arching stems. In June
and July these stems, which rise from large rosettes of soft
green leaves, turn into one-sided spires of hanging
bellflowers – rich red-purple or white.

The 'Excelsior' strain provides a wide range of flower
colours, including white, cream, apricot and pink, and in
addition the flowers completely encircle the stem and stand
out horizontally. Many, however, believe that this cultivar
has lost all the charm of the wild species and that the
dwarf varieties, such as 'Foxy', are even less satisfactory.
There certainly remains great scope for the amateur plant
breeder to combine the colour range of the garden
foxglove with the grace of the wild plant.

Foxgloves make excellent border plants, even in winter
when their rosettes of foliage form good ground-cover. For
a rich summer composition of colour and form, you might
try the dark *Rosa rugosa* 'Roseraie de l'Hay', and magenta
Geranium psilostemon with purple foxgloves. A final,
distinctive touch would be to add *Heuchera sanguinea*
'Scintillation', or some other low bronze-leaved plant as a
front edging.

HOW TO GROW
*Digitalis purpurea: sow outdoors in early summer, thinning as
necessary; transplant in autumn, 1½-2 ft apart, in any well-
drained but moisture-retentive soil, and in sun or shade. After
flowering, cut faded stems out at the base.*
Geranium psilostemon: see p. 88.
Heuchera sanguinea: see p. 93.
Rosa rugosa: see p. 239.

Digitalis purpurea 'Excelsior' is the centrepiece of this gorgeous, blushing
cottage-garden border in June. Behind is *Rosa rugosa* 'Roseraie de l'Hay'
and in front *Geranium psilostemon*. Edging the border is *Heuchera
sanguinea* 'Scintillation'.

Dimorphotheca aurantiaca

(STAR OF THE VELDT)

Like so many other dwarf annuals, star of the veldt grows
rapidly and flowers quickly in the wild in order to produce
its seeds before the dry season sets in. In the cooler
summers of this country it lasts longer, producing hundreds
of elegant daisy-like flowers from June to September. Borne
on 12-18 in. stems, the blooms are brilliant orange with a
dark brown eye.

'New Hybrids' is a selection with mixed colours – white,
lemon, yellow, orange and red. Bolder is 'Giant Orange',
with glowing dark-eyed blooms. 'Dwarf Salmon', only
9 in. high but wide spreading, has softly coloured flowers of
the palest orange-yellow.

HOW TO GROW
*Sow under glass in spring, or outdoors when all danger of frost
is past. Thin or transplant to 12 in. intervals, in well-
drained, loamy soil, and in an open sunny site.*

Throughout summer the bright 2 in. wide
flowers of star of the veldt light up the
border with their orange fires.

Dimorphotheca aurantiaca 'New Hybrids' come in a cooler colour range

Everlasting flowers

There are a number of annuals whose flowers are of a papery texture. Many of these, if hung up to dry, will retain their bright colours for months on end, and can therefore be used to make winter decorations that will last through to greet the cut flowers of spring.

Helichrysum bracteatum (syn. *H. macranthum*) provides some of the most brilliant everlasting flowers. They resemble small chrysanthemums with incurving petals, and are available in white, yellow, orange, red and pink. The species grows to 3-4 ft high; but there are several smaller cultivars, including the 15 in. 'Bright Bikini'. Other good flowers for drying are pale pink *Helipterum roseum* (syn. *Acrolinium roseum*), 15 in. high; and *H. manglesii* (syn. *Rhodanthe manglesii*), of the same height, which carries blooms of red or white.

Among the most popular of everlasting flowers are several species of *Limonium* (found in many catalogues as *Statice*). Try the 18 in. high *Limonium sinuatum*, a species that, with its cultivars, ranges across almost the entire spectrum and is perhaps the most popular of all the everlasting flowers. The bold, 2-3 ft high *Xeranthemum annuum* introduces purple to the range.

In a dry, sunny border, drifts of *Helipterum manglesii* could provide the basis of an association of Mediterranean warmth and splendour. Try interplanting them among the silvery-grey *Senecio maritimus*, grown from seeds, and surrounding them with white old-fashioned pinks (*Dianthus*) – for example, 'White Ladies'.

HOW TO GROW

All these everlastings are half-hardy; they thrive in any light, well-drained or dry soil, and in full sun. Sow helichrysums and limoniums under glass and harden off before planting out in late spring, helichrysums 10 in. apart (6 in. for dwarfs), limoniums 9-12 in. apart. Alternatively, sow outdoors in late April, at the same time as helipterums and xeranthemums, neither of which transplant well; thin the former to 6-8 in. apart, the latter to 12 in. For drying, cut all everlastings before the flowers are fully open; strip the foliage from the stems and hang them upside-down in an airy but shaded place until they are dry.

Dianthus: see p. 80.
Senecio maritimus: see p. 56.

Limonium sinuatum shows its gay colours.

Xeranthemum, a native of the Mediterranean, flowers in July.

Between clumps of soft, silvery *Senecio maritimus* lies a glowing mixture of pink *Helipterum roseum* and red and white *H. manglesii*. Completing the graceful effect is an edging of old-fashioned pinks – the variety 'White Ladies'. The group of plants is pictured here in August.

Colourful *Helichrysum bracteatum* 'Dwarf Spangle Mixed' spreads widely.

Echium lycopsis

Brightly coloured flowers, a long flowering season from June until the end of August, and adaptability to almost any soil and climate – these are the factors that make *Echium lycopsis* (sometimes wrongly listed as *E. vulgare*) so well worth growing. The garden cultivars are best; their tubular flowers are larger and clearer-coloured than in the species and they are much more compact plants.

In the splendid 12 in. tall 'Blue Bedder' the flowers are a bright blue with a hint of pink. 'Dwarf Mixed', the same height, come in a mixture of white, pink, red, mauve and blue, though perhaps the colours lack the clarity of those in 'Blue Bedder'.

HOW TO GROW
Sow seeds in the flowering site in spring or early autumn; thin seedlings to 18 in. apart. Most soils give reasonable results but they flower best in light, dry soil, in full sun. They are particularly good plants for seaside gardens.

With its larger, more vivacious flowers, *Echium lycopsis* 'Blue Bedder' is a much superior annual to the parent species.

Echium lycopsis 'Dwarf Hybrids' provide a medley of pastel hues.

Eschscholzia californica (CALIFORNIAN POPPY)

The fragile, delicate charm of poppies is apparent from the moment the conical green hats split open around their buds of crumpled silk, until the petals fall to reveal long, cylindrical seed pods. The Californian poppy glorifies the garden with a bright flower display that lasts from June to October, and complements it, too, with its exquisitely cut, blue-green foliage.

A spectacular cultivar is 'Ballerina', a 12 in. high assortment of double flowers in red, orange, yellow and pink, some with white stripes. More elegant still are the older, single-coloured sorts, such as the translucent, 15 in. tall, 'Orange King'.

HOW TO GROW
Sow outdoors in spring, or in autumn under cloches, thin seedlings to 6 in. apart. The plants thrive in sandy, poor soil and in full sun, seeding themselves freely.

The brilliant, 2 in. wide, cup-shaped blooms of Californian poppies bring sunshine to the border in any weather.

'Mission Bells' is a dwarf form with semi-double flowers in many colours.

Felicia amelloides (BLUE MARGUERITE)

This little-known South African tender perennial (also called *Agathaea coelestis*) is usually grown in Britain as a half-hardy perennial. Its slender-petalled, daisy-like flowers are a delightful pale blue and are borne in great profusion throughout the summer above 18 in. high domes of small, greyish-green leaves.

The kingfisher daisy, *Felicia bergeriana*, is a dwarf species, 6 in. tall, that puts out steel-blue, yellow-eyed daisy flowers above a mat of hairy grey-green foliage from June to September.

HOW TO GROW
Sow under glass in early spring, harden off and plant out in May, 10-12 in. apart for Felicia amelloides, 6 in. for F. bergeriana (as edging and in rock gardens). Both species thrive in ordinary, well-drained to dry soil, in full sun, and are wind-resistant. F. bergeriana is suitable for window-boxes.

Felicia amelloides is one of the few plants with daisy-like flowers that are true blue. It makes an attractive pot plant.

F. bergeriana and white *Lobularia maritima* combine well together.

Fuchsia hybrids

The flowers of *Fuchsia* combine vivid colour with elegance. They are highly distinctive, each consisting of a narrow tube that opens out into four petal-like sepals, below which is a bell of overlapping petals, often differing in colour from the tube and sepals.

The fuchsias described here can all be used for outdoor summer bedding. They flower from midsummer to late autumn and reach a height of about 2 ft.

Since the flowers are so intricate, they look best when they are small and single. Large, double blooms, such as those of 'Texas Longhorn' and 'Tennessee Waltz', tend to look too complex. The old cultivars still include some of the finest of all fuchsias: 'Mrs Popple', which has red sepals and purple petals; 'Hidcote Beauty', pink sepals, creamy-white petals; and the all-white 'Ting-a-ling'. Among newer sorts, double 'Peppermint Stick', which has red sepals and mauve and red petals, and 'La Campanella', with white sepals and violet petals, are outstanding.

For a subtle blending of colours you might try planting 'Mrs Popple' with *Fuchsia magellanica gracilis* 'Versicolor', which has crimson sepals, purple petals and variegated foliage. With the two fuchsias you could grow the annual *Salvia farinacea*, 2-3 ft high, which bears dark blue flowers from midsummer to autumn. The group could be completed with an edging of the dwarf perennial *Campanula portenschlagiana*.

HOW TO GROW
Fuchsia: plant bedding fuchsias in early summer, as accent plants. They need good, fertile soil, well drained but with plenty of moisture in summer to prevent bud drop. Full sun or light shade, with some shelter, is ideal. Before autumn, lift and pot the plants and store them where they will be safe from frosts. Start into growth in spring, and propagate from cuttings for new bedding plants.
Campanula portenschlagiana: see p. 200.
Fuchsia magellanica gracilis: see p. 281.
Salvia farinacea: see p. 54.

Fuchsia 'Ting-a-ling'.

Fuchsia 'Chequerboard' hangs above *Lobelia erinus* 'Cambridge Blue'.

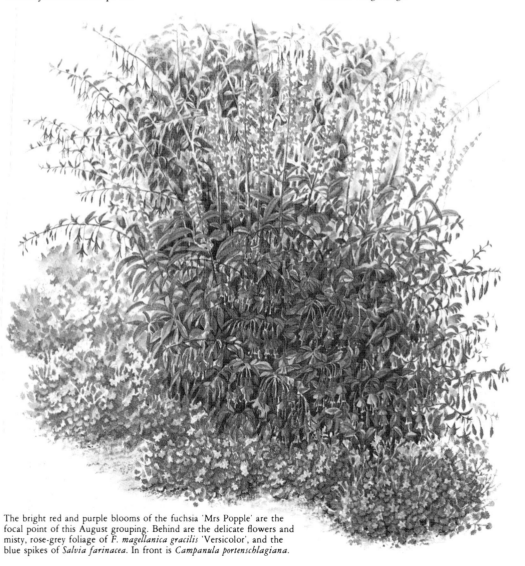

The bright red and purple blooms of the fuchsia 'Mrs Popple' are the focal point of this August grouping. Behind are the delicate flowers and misty, rose-grey foliage of *F. magellanica gracilis* 'Versicolor', and the blue spikes of *Salvia farinacea*. In front is *Campanula portenschlagiana*.

GRASSES

Hardy annual grasses are among the easiest and most rewarding of plants. The fresh, green blades created by thin sowings in a border gradually increase in height as the flower spikes appear and unfold, their colours gradually changing to fawn and grey, bronze, purple or pink, as the seed heads ripen. It is wise to avoid mixtures; the varied heights, forms and colours of the different grasses are best appreciated individually.

The 18 in. high pearl grass (*Briza maxima*), with its silvery-green lockets dancing and rustling on unbelievably slender stems, is deservedly the most popular; but *Agrostis nebulosa*, a 12 in. high mist of tiny florets, is also well worth trying. *Hordeum jubatum*, squirrel grass, that puts out 12 in. high feathery flower heads from June to August, is splendid for giving an original touch to flower arrangements. The hare's-tail grass, *Lagurus ovatus*, grows to 12 in. and produces delightfully fluffy, white inflorescences from which it derives its common name.

Half-hardy grasses are a little more trouble, but are worth growing for their generally bolder and more colourful flower heads. Like the hardy annuals, they are good for garden decoration, and excellent for drying and using for indoor decoration if they are cut before the seeds ripen. A good example is the 2 ft high *Tricholaena rosea*, which has the most graceful, slender, silvery-pink spikelets that deepen to maroon.

HOW TO GROW
Sow hardy sorts in spring, making a thin, shallow sowing where the plants are to grow. A well-drained, fertile, sunny site is best. Thin the seedlings to 4 in. apart each way when they are large enough to handle. In sheltered sites, seeds can be sown in late summer for an earlier display the following year.

Briza maxima, known as pearl grass.

Agrostis nebulosa flutters around a clump of blue *Echium lycopsis*.

Hare's-tail grass here mingles charmingly with rosy *Clarkia elegans*.

The soft plumes of squirrel grass can be used to break up the brilliance of echiums (right) and dimorphothecas (left).

Needing little moisture, *Gazania × hybrida* is ideal for a dry wall.

Gazania × hybrida

Large daisy-like flowers in bright shades of yellow are the principal feature of this mat-forming, 9 in. high South African hybrid. They appear from July until the first frosts, open only in bright sunshine, and even then they are closed again by mid-afternoon. The leaves are deep green, with white, felt-like undersides.

Similar in overall appearance but with a wider colour range, including red and orange, is *Gazania × splendens*. Many of its cultivars have the base of the petals patterned in a variety of contrasting colours. The leaves vary, too, some being hairy and grey, while others are quite smooth.

HOW TO GROW
Sow under glass in early spring, harden off and plant out in June, 12 in. apart. Gazanias thrive in well-drained to dry, sandy loam, and in full sun. They are wind-resistant and excellent for seaside gardens.

G. × splendens has a curious, vivacious patterning at the heart of its flowers, each of which is more than 3 in. across.

Helianthus annuus (SUNFLOWER)

The logical choice of sunflowers for a small garden should be the low-growing cultivars. But these, with their blooms huddled coyly in dense foliage, have none of the appeal of the giant species, with its determination to grow skywards, its pole-like 8-10 ft stem sparsely clad with huge, bristly leaves and its immense, solitary yellow flower gazing down to earth in late summer with a wide brown or purple eye, seemingly astonished at its own success.

Single-flowered sunflowers have the added attraction of a beautifully precise pattern of florets (tiny sub-flowers) in their central disc. These are replaced by large, oily seeds, and the acrobatics of birds as they sample them are a further delight.

HOW TO GROW
Sow outdoors in spring, thinning the seedlings in stages to 2-3 ft apart. Excellent as tall temporary screens, in any well-drained fertile soil, and in sun or light shade. Support giant sunflowers with strong stakes.

Single-flowered giant sunflowers have a dramatic appeal all their own.

Helianthus annuus and *H. × 'Excelsior'* raise their heads majestically behind a group of yellow annual lupins.

Gypsophila elegans (BABY'S BREATH)

The cloud of tiny white or pink flowers that this 2 ft high annual produces from May to September gave rise, so it is said, to its common name; and there is indeed a vaporous effect that persists until the last bloom has withered. The foliage is a soft grey-green that harmonises with the flowers. 'Monarch White', and 'Covent Garden' have white flowers; 'Rosea' is bright rose.

The traditional role of baby's breath is to accompany the gentle shades of sweet peas, but it associates well with any pastel-coloured flowers, such as clarkias, delphiniums and scabious.

HOW TO GROW
Sow at two to four-week intervals, from mid-spring onwards, where the plants are to flower. Thin the seedlings to 8-12 in. It grows best in average-to-poor, limy, well-drained soil and in full sun.

The white or pale pink, yellow-eyed flowers of baby's breath, individually minute, create a vaporous effect when massed.

White *Gypsophila elegans* froths round the stems of *Delphinium ajacis*.

Helichrysum petiolatum

This tender perennial is grown mainly for its soft silver-grey stems and foliage, which are covered in a dense felt of white hairs. It is 1½-2 ft high and spreads widely. There is also a fine lime-green form, 'Aureum'.

The main uses of grey foliage plants in the garden are to show rich reds and purples to full advantage and to blend with pastel-coloured flowers. This second function is shown in the association suggested here. *Helichrysum petiolatum* is planted freely among groups of the 4-5 ft high white rose 'Iceberg', which flowers intermittently from June to October. Some small drifts of blue or white-flowered love-in-a-mist (*Nigella damascena*) will add an exquisite touch to this delicate scheme.

When the first frosts come, the helichrysums and nigellas can be pulled up to allow easy access to the roses for pruning and mulching.

An excellent alternative to *H. petiolatum* is the 18 in. high *H. microphyllum*, which has leaves of a more intense silvery-grey. It is a comparative newcomer to Britain but is already being widely used and can be seen in many public parks and botanic gardens. With smaller leaves than *H. petiolatum*, it makes a deep, attractive carpet from which tall annuals can spring up.

HOW TO GROW
Helichrysum petiolatum: bed out in June, setting it (or H. microphyllum) 18 in. apart, in any soil with good drainage. Grow in full sun, with shelter from strong winds. During summer, take cuttings from sideshoots; overwinter these in pots under glass, for bedding out in summer.
Nigella damascena: see p. 47.
Rosa 'Iceberg': see p. 230.

Cool tones of silver, blue and white create patches of soft focus in a sunny cottage garden in July. 'Iceberg' roses – white with tints of flesh pink – rise out of a cloud of blue *Nigella damascena. Helichrysum petiolatum* tumbles and trails around the base of the roses, encroaching on to the lawn and garden path. It is a fast grower and can spread 2-3 ft in the course of a summer.

Heliotropium arborescens (CHERRY PIE)

These evergreen hybrid heliotropes received their common name because the heavy fragrance from their small forget-me-knot-like flowers resembles that of cherry-pie filling. They bloom from May to October, grow to at least 2 ft tall and have mid to dark green, wrinkled leaves that are oblong and shaped like the head of a lance.

Few cultivars of these half-hardy shrubs grown as annuals are available but this scarcely matters, since one variety, 'Marine' syn. 'Marina', offers everything that could be desired: clusters of deep purple flowers, richly scented, over deep purplish-green velvety leaves. Cherry pies are rather slow to flower, but the foliage is attractive enough to compensate for the wait.

HOW TO GROW
Sow under glass in late winter; pinch out tips of seedlings when well established to induce branching. Harden off and plant out in May/June, 12 in. apart. Heliotropes need fertile, well-drained soil and full sun.

Heliotropium arborescens 'Marine' syn. 'Marina' is in a container with *Begonia semperflorens*, and a fuchsia behind.

'Marine' syn. 'Marina' and pink antirrhinums are here backed by centaureas.

Combining *I. umbellata* with *Clarkia elegans* creates variety of texture.

Sown successively, *Iberis umbellata* will brighten the annual border all summer with its cheerful clusters of flowers.

Iberis umbellata (CANDYTUFT)

Easy to grow and generous in their flowering, candytufts, as *Iberis* is commonly known, are deservedly popular annuals. *Iberis umbellata*, 6-15 in. high, is a spreading plant with compact clusters of flowers in white, pink and lavender. *I. amara*, 15 in. high, bears heads of fragrant white flowers that gradually extend to form spikes that are splendid for cutting.

Candytufts flower in June and July after an autumn sowing, or from June to September if seeds are sown in spring. Except for 'Red Flash', a vivid newer cultivar of *I. umbellata*, they make excellent companions for the similarly coloured but taller *Clarkia*.

HOW TO GROW
Sow outdoors in early autumn, or in spring at one or two-monthly intervals to extend the flowering season. Thin Iberis amara to 6 in., I. umbellata to 9 in. Both species thrive in ordinary soil, in full sun.

Hibiscus hybrids

There are few more exotic-looking plants than *Hibiscus*, with its wide, funnel-shaped, richly coloured flowers, whose short life is compensated for by their splendour. The best of the annual species is *Hibiscus trionum*, commonly called flower-of-an-hour because it opens only briefly. However, some new strains do not have this drawback. The flowers are a lovely cream to pale lemon with a red-brown eye, and they appear throughout August and September.

Most spectacular are some of the new perennial hybrids grown as annuals. 'Southern Belle', 'Dixie Belle' and 'Rio Carnival' all erupt at the end of summer with enormous flowers, 6-10 in. across, in red, deep or pale pink or white. 'Southern Belle' is 4-5 ft tall, the other two half that height.

Despite the advice given in some catalogues, these hybrids do not repay being kept for a second season unless they are grown in a heated greenhouse. All three make excellent pot plants.

If the garden has a suitably sheltered corner, try them with the purple-leaved castor oil plant *Ricinus communis* 'Sanguineus' behind and a blend of crimson *Coleus blumei* and bronze-leaved *Canna × generalis* 'Wyoming' in front for a really tropical effect.

HOW TO GROW
Hibiscus: sow H. trionum outdoors in late spring, in the flowering site, thinning seedlings to 9 in. Sow the large-flowered hybrids under glass, setting the seeds singly in small pots. Best in rich, moist but well-drained soil, in full sun and in shelter.
Canna × generalis: see p. 19.
Coleus blumei: see p. 23.
Ricinus communis: see p. 53.

Sultry and exotic, 'Dixie Belle' is the pink and crimson centrepiece of this sheltered August border. *Ricinus communis* 'Sanguineus' with its red-purple leaves and tall *Canna × generalis* 'Wyoming' intensify the tropical illusion. Encroaching on the stone steps, *Coleus blumei* unites all the colours in a rainbow of crimson, bronze, green and purple.

Impatiens walleriana (BUSY LIZZIE)

The busy lizzies *Impatiens sultanii* and *I. holstii* – both colour forms of *I. walleriana* – were for long used as house plants but, with the recent introduction of good dwarf hybrids between the two species, they have become popular for bedding in sheltered spots.

The mixed colours of 'Cleopatra', 6-9 in. high, can be too much of a good thing. Better are the single-coloured sorts, 9 in. tall, of the Blitz F₁ series. These are available in white, pink, scarlet and orange, from which a harmonious combination can be selected. All bloom from April to October.

HOW TO GROW
Bed out in early June, 14-16 in. apart, in fertile soil, well drained but moisture-retentive, in light shade or sun. Also excellent for container gardening. Propagate by stem cuttings (easily rooted in water) and protect from frost; or sow under glass in spring.

Normally grown in a pot, the exquisite *Impatiens walleriana* 'Variegata' can also be used outside as a bedding plant.

A mixed strain of *Impatiens walleriana* here fills a bed in a lawn.

Scilla sibirica, in a spring carpet of I. acaule, brightens a shady spot.

Ionopsidium acaule (VIOLET CRESS)

With a height of only 2-3 in., this diminutive hardy annual is certainly not a plant for the short-sighted gardener. Its neat tufts of long-stalked, rounded leaves are continually studded with tiny lilac flowers.

Violet cress can be sown thinly in a border and left to grow into a close carpet among other annuals, but these tend to swamp it. It is best grown in moist, shaded parts of the rock garden where it can be closely tended. It will usually produce seedlings in small crevices among the stones. Summer-sown seeds will flower in autumn; autumn-sown ones in winter and spring.

Violet cress looks delightful growing in and around a drift of the electric-blue Scilla sibirica.

HOW TO GROW
Sow seeds thinly outdoors, in rock gardens and raised beds, at intervals, from mid-spring to early summer and again in autumn. Thinning is unnecessary.

Only ¼ in. across, the tiny flowers of *Ionopsidium acaule* need to be emphasised by careful placing in a rockery or paving.

Kochia scoparia (SUMMER CYPRESS)

Untidy forms of this intriguing and lovely foliage plant grow in the wild from southern Europe to Japan, and, with great injustice, it is widely regarded on the Continent as simply a weed. It forms a mass of delightful pale greenery that associates beautifully with the yellow of petunias, marigolds or coreopsis but that will bring a sprightly freshness to so many plantings.

The form *Kochia scoparia* 'Trichophylla', the one usually sold by seedsmen, has the advantage over the species of being neatly symmetrical and rounded – rather like a feathery green busby in fact. In the autumn the whole plant gradually turns a rich crimson-purple – hence its second common name, burning bush. If it is used with violet heliotropes, purple petunias or scarlet salvias, the effect gradually changes from contrast to harmony.

Summer cypress can also be used more informally to fill sunny gaps among shrubs. For a ravishing summer combination try it with the misty blue of *Nigella damascena* and the brilliant gold of *Mentzelia lindleyi*.

HOW TO GROW
Kochia scoparia: sow under glass and harden off before bedding out in May. For low screens and hedges, space plants 18 in. apart; alternatively use as dot and accent plants. Kochias need full sun and do well in any well-drained soil. They are wind-resistant and thrive by the sea.
Mentzelia lindleyi: see p. 43.
Nigella damascena: see p. 47.

Luminous green summer cypresses, 2-3 ft high, with blue *Nigella damascena* and gold *Mentzelia lindleyi* make a showy group in front of a *Weigela florida* 'Variegata'. This delightful summer association is pictured in early August. In autumn, the summer cypresses will turn crimson-purple.

Kochia scoparia 'Trichophylla', changing into flaming autumn colours.

Lathyrus odoratus (SWEET PEA)

The much-loved sweet pea is a hardy annual that is usually grown as a climber. But there are several dwarf cultivars, such as 'Little Sweetheart', 'Cupid' and the small-leaved, tendril-less 'Snoopea', that rival the claims of their tall, climbing relatives. They form neat cushions of growth less than 12 in. high, with spikes of large, scented, white, pink, lavender or red flowers from June to September. The dwarf kinds combine well with such traditional cottage-garden annuals as clarkias, candytufts and cornflowers.

HOW TO GROW
Sow in autumn or spring in a cold frame or under cloches. Transplant or thin out in late spring to 9 in. apart. Pinch out to induce branching. Fertile soil, ideally enriched with plenty of organic matter, and full sun give the best results. Keep the roots cool with a deep, moist mulch, and dead-head to prevent the plants from setting seeds and exhausting themselves.

Free-flowering, with wavy petals: an example of the tall Spencer type.

Lathyrus odoratus 'Knee-high' is one of the dwarf varieties, growing to a height of 2-4 ft.

Layia elegans (TIDY TIPS)

Tidy tips' charm lies in the neat white tips at the ends of the pale yellow petals, which give each flower an attractive fringe. The specific name *elegans* is just as appropriate as the common name. The petals themselves surround a bright yellow, central disc.

Tidy tips is a bushy, well-branched plant, some 18 in. high, with pleasantly scented grey-green leaves suitable for the edge of a border of annuals or perennials. It provides a long succession of flowers – lasting from June through to October – both for garden decoration and for cutting; it looks especially well with an edging of pale blue lobelias, such as 'Cambridge Blue', which will bloom from May until the first autumn frosts cut them back.

A pure white garden cultivar, 'Alba', is available but is not commonly listed.

HOW TO GROW
Sow in spring where the plants are to flower, in beds, borders or window-boxes; thin seedlings to 8 in. apart. The plants thrive in full sun, in any well-drained to dry soil. They are fairly drought and wind-resistant. In sheltered areas in the south and west, September-sown seeds provide flowers in May.

Layia elegans and *Lobelia erinus* 'Cambridge Blue' will produce a profusion of flowers all through the summer.

Yellow *Layia elegans* contrast boldly with scarlet *Tropaeolum majus*.

The clear pink, trumpet-shaped blooms of *Lavatera trimestris* surround purple-leaved *Canna* × *generalis*.

Lavatera trimestris (MALLOW)

Great improvements have recently been made in the cultivars of this annual mallow, known by some nurseries as *Lavatera rosea*. The old, aptly named 'Loveliness', a bushy, 3 ft tall plant that produces rose-pink, hibiscus-like flowers in late summer and autumn, is indeed delightful; but even more attractive is the modern 'Silver Cup', which carries larger, bright pink flowers with darker veining and white shading and blooms a little earlier. For dramatic contrast, combine any one of these pink cultivars of *L. trimestris* with the purple-leaved annual *Canna* × *generalis*.

The even more recent 'Mont Blanc' is similar to 'Silver Cup' in all respects except that its flowers are a dazzling white. It makes an excellent companion for 'Silver Cup' or for pale pink *Cosmos* species and their cultivars; however, it should not be juxtaposed with other white flowers, for they will look dingy by comparison. A less brilliant white than 'Mont Blanc' is 'Splendens Alba'; its flowers, however, are just as large.

Lavateras should not be planted in over-rich soils, as these tend to encourage excessive leaf growth. They flower best in hot, sunny positions where the soil is dry, and make good plants for the back of the border.

L. trimestris seeds itself freely and produces great numbers of plants in the following season if the soil is not disturbed by cultivation.

HOW TO GROW
Sow in the open, in early autumn in mild areas, and in spring elsewhere. Thin the seedlings to stand 15 in. apart. Any well-drained soil of average fertility is suitable. A site in full sun is best, but light shade is tolerated.

Limnanthes douglasii (POACHED EGG FLOWER)

The whimsical common name of this annual from north-west America accurately describes the colour scheme of its flowers – a large yolk-yellow centre surrounded by white – but fails to convey the loveliness of the blooms. These are bowl-shaped, softly waved and delicately fragrant, and are set off to perfection by glossy, pale yellowish-green, deeply dissected foliage. Bees and other nectar-loving insects find them irresistible. The plants do best if grown in a sunny position in a moist soil; they produce excellent flower displays if grown in clumps.

The plant, 6 in. tall and widespreading, produces its many flowers in late spring if seeds are sown in autumn, or from mid to late summer following a spring sowing. It makes a charming edging plant for borders or paths, where seedlings will swiftly colonise the cracks between the paving stones.

HOW TO GROW
Excellent for rock gardens and for edging. Sow in autumn or spring, depending on flowering season desired. Cloche protection may be needed for autumn sowings in cold areas. Thin to 6 in. apart. Ordinary garden soil is suitable, preferably in full sun. These conditions are often found along paths, or between rocks and paving. The plants usually seed themselves prolifically, so sowings for succeeding seasons can usually be left to nature to set in train.

Limnanthes douglasii, seen here with *Hosta sieboldiana* and an *Acer palmatum*, is ideal for brightening up the edge of a bed.

Leptosiphon hybridus

Almost everyone who comes across this unjustly neglected annual is enchanted by it. A good common name for it might be dolly mixtures, since its tiny flowers are scattered in profusion over the plant, and are in a random collection of clear, bright colours: pink, red, orange, yellow, cream and white. They sit pertly, from June to September, on straight, slender stems, just above the very finely divided deep green foliage, which forms a mound 4-6 in. high. Good garden varieties, providing fine mixtures of colour, are 'French Hybrids' and 'Rainbow Mixture'.

Apart from its use in edging borders, this plant can also be sown in earth-filled cracks in paving or in small pockets of soil between rocks or stones.

Leptosiphon hybridus blends especially well with Moroccan toadflax (*Linaria maroccana*), another slim annual with a similar array of colours. The two could be grown mixed fairly densely together to create a multi-coloured mass, and above this could rise the spires of dwarf lupins, in particular *Lupinus hartwegii* 'Pixie Delight', a compact 18 in. tall strain in shades of pink, lavender, blue and white.

HOW TO GROW
Leptosiphon hybridus: sow shallowly outdoors in mid-spring, broadcasting the seeds in ordinary, well-drained soil and in a sunny, open site. Excellent for rock gardens, window-boxes and shallow containers. Thin seedlings to 3-4 in. apart.
Linaria maroccana: see p. 39.
Lupinus hartwegii: see p. 42.

Linaria maroccana: see p. 39.
Lupinus hartwegii: see p. 42.

There is nothing subdued about this border of sparkling, jewel-bright flowers. Colours in the carpet of low-growing *Leptosiphon hybridus* are echoed in the taller *Linaria maroccana* growing among the leptosiphon and the row of *Lupinus hartwegii* 'Pixie Delight' standing behind. The plants are pictured here in July.

A mass of *Linaria maroccana* glows like a fragmented rainbow.

Linaria maroccana (MOROCCAN TOADFLAX)

This annual toadflax is an ideal companion for *Leptosiphon hybridus*, since it has a similar bright colour range of yellows, reds, pinks and mauves, but is very different in form. It is a narrow, upright plant 8-15 in. tall with slender, light green leaves and spikes of narrow, tubular flowers. These, spurred and often blotched with white, look like miniature antirrhinums.

The toadflax, which flowers throughout the summer, is extremely versatile. It can be grown in annual and mixed borders and rock gardens, is suitable for edging a path and makes a fine pot plant.

HOW TO GROW
Sow where the plants are to flower, in early autumn or in spring, making successive sowings to extend the season and thinning to 6 in. spacings. Linarias grow best in full sun, in any kind of well-drained soil, where they usually seed themselves freely.

At the front of a border, the flowers on their bushy stems look well against a background of *Skimmia japonica*.

Lobelia erinus

Across the country there must be many thousands of miles of blue-lobelia edging used for formal beds. The inevitable companion of lobelias in this role is white alyssum; yet the partnership is not a good one, since lobelia is a light, airy, long-flowering plant that thrives in moist soil, while alyssum is dense in growth, short-lived and is best suited to a dry, sunny site. Much better than alyssum in a formal blue-and-white edging is one of the fine, white lobelia varieties now available.

Lobelia erinus, though grown as an annual, is actually a half-hardy perennial. It is a small plant, only 4-9 in. high, that has light green leaves and produces masses of small blue flowers from May to autumn. More popular than the species are the many cultivars, which may be either compact, making neat 4-6 in. high domes, or trailing in a spread at least 12 in. across.

The colour range embraces white, pale blue, deep purplish-blue and wine-red, and they are such attractive plants that they deserve not to be restricted to edging but to be grown also for display.

Red varieties such as 'Rosamund' and 'Red Cascade' associate well with ivy-leaved geraniums (*Pelargonium peltatum*). The deep blue 'Crystal Palace' (with bronze foliage), 'Mrs Clibran' (with white-eyed flowers) or trailing 'Sapphire' look splendid with pale pink petunias. You might also try the pale 'Cambridge Blue' or 'Blue Cascade' with French marigolds (*Tagetes patula*), such as 'Susie Wong', 'Gypsy Sunshine', or 'Goldfinch'. Add white-leaved *Senecio maritimus* for a soft, cool effect.

HOW TO GROW
Lobelia erinus: sow under glass in late winter; harden off and transplant in late May, 6 in. apart for compact edging types and 9 in. apart for trailing lobelias in containers. Fertile, moisture-retentive soil, preferably in a lightly shaded site, gives the best results.
Pelargonium peltatum: see p. 48.
Petunia: see p. 50.
Senecio maritimus: see p. 56.
Tagetes patula: see p. 56.

Clumps of the carmine-red *Lobelia erinus* 'Rosamund' are here planted between light and dark pink pelargoniums.

Linum grandiflorum shown with an ideal neighbour, *Nigella damascena*.

Linum grandiflorum (FLAX)

With their elegant, five-petalled flowers in bright, clear colours and their slender leaves, flaxes of any kind are welcome in the garden. *Linum grandiflorum*, a branched plant 15-18 in. tall, produces a long succession of rose-red flowers from June to August. The 12 in. high 'Rubrum' (scarlet flax) is a particularly brilliant variety; there are also pink and white forms. The common flax, *L. usitatissimum*, with its pale blue flowers, provides softer colouring in June and July. When massed, it looks like a summer sky fallen to earth.

HOW TO GROW
Sow seeds in the flowering site, in autumn or spring, reducing the seedlings to 6 in. apart; make successive sowings, at four-week intervals. Grow in an open, sunny position, in any well-drained soil; though flax flourishes in alkaline soil, it does not mind acid conditions.

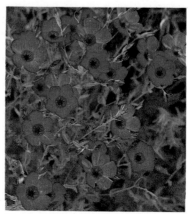

Linum grandiflorum can also be grown as a spring-flowering pot plant. The form illustrated above is 'Rubrum'.

Lobularia maritima (SWEET ALYSSUM)

This alyssum, usually planted with *Lobelia erinus*, is suitable for formal beds, informal border groups, the rock garden or chinks in paving. It is a low, spreading (9-12 in.), densely branched bushy plant with small, thin, somewhat grey-green leaves. From June to September it is smothered with flowers of white or mauve.

The old cultivars are still the best. Two particularly good ones are 'Little Dorrit', 4-6 in. high, and 'Carpet of Snow', 3-4 in. Both are white, sweetly scented and immensely attractive to bees.

The many newer sorts that flower in shades of pink and crimson should be grown by themselves and not intermingled with white varieties; grown together, they detract from each other.

Among the newer, improved cultivars that are now available, the following are recommended: 'Royal Carpet', a compact grower with violet-purple flowers, standing about 4 in. high; 'Wonderland', which is rose-carmine; 'Rosie O'Day' with rose-pink flowers; 'Oriental Night', a splendid and unusual deep purple; and 'Snow Carpet' and 'Snowdrift', both of which are white. These last five are all of flat, spreading habit.

HOW TO GROW
Sow under glass in early spring or outdoors a little later. Space compact forms 8 in. apart, spreading types 12 in. apart, as edgings to beds and borders, and in rock gardens, paving chinks and containers. Shear the plants over after the first early flowering. Best in full sun, in ordinary, well-drained soil. Self-sown seedlings are common.

Sweet alyssum *Lobularia maritima* flowering profusely over paving and steps with *Campanula portenschlagiana*.

Lunaria annua (HONESTY, MOONWORT, MONEYWORT)

Although this honesty (also known as *Lunaria biennis*) can well be grown as an annual, it is naturally a biennial and, grown as such, produces finer flowers. These, borne in loose, fragrant clusters from April to June, are pale lavender in the species and range from rich purple to red in garden forms.

L. a. 'Alba' has pure white flowers of great appeal. They are succeeded in summer by fruits that split to reveal almost transparent, disc-shaped membranes, which can be dried and used for winter flower arrangements. It is these round and silvery seed cases that lead to its Latin name *Lunaria*, derived from *luna* meaning 'moon', and also provided one of its common names, moonwort.

An additional favour conferred by this 2½ ft tall plant is its rosettes of dark green, wavy-margined leaves that last through all but the most severe winter. Since honesty will grow in shady places, the kinds with cream-variegated leaves are useful for lighting up dark corners of the garden. The form 'Variegata' produces crimson flowers.

HOW TO GROW
Sow in an outdoor nursery bed in summer; thin seedlings to 6 in. apart and transplant to the flowering site in early autumn, 12 in. apart. Can also be sown in situ. Any well-drained soil is suitable. For drying, cut stems when the seed pods have changed colour. Self-sows freely.

Lunaria annua adds colour to a shaded area of the garden, beneath a pink Kurume azalea and a *Magnolia kobus*.

Frothy *Gypsophila elegans* reflects the pink in 'Pixie Delight'.

Slender stems carry tiny pink, red and white flowers, ½ in. across.

Fragrant spires of pink *M. incana* blooms adorn the middle of a border.

Lupinus hartwegii (LUPIN)

Best known of the annual lupins, this species is generally available only in its 18 in. high dwarf form, 'Pixie Delight', a mixed strain whose flowers may be white, pink, red, lavender, purple, blue or bicoloured.

'Pixie Delight', producing colourful spikes from July to October and persisting long after perennial lupins have faded, is excellent for producing a band of medium height colour in the border and is extremely easy to grow. Its charms can be highlighted by surrounding groups of it with a pink mist of *Gypsophila elegans* 'Rosea'.

HOW TO GROW
Soak the hard seeds before sowing outdoors in autumn or spring. Thin seedlings to 8-10 in. apart. Best in acid to neutral soil, well drained and of average fertility. Remove faded flower stems. Dig roots and foliage into the soil for a useful source of extra nitrogen.

Lupinus hartwegii 'Pixie Delight' is the familiar, long-lasting dwarf lupin. The colours are mixed.

Malcolmia maritima (VIRGINIAN STOCK)

Delightfully old-fashioned are the flowers of this hardy, easily grown, 8 in. high annual. They are sweetly scented little cross-shaped blooms in white, pink, red, lavender and purple, these colours being mixed in most strains. A succession of sowings from March to July will produce flowers from April right through to autumn.

Sown sparingly, the fragile plants grow into one another to form a drift of soft colour. They make a delightful edging for mixed petunias of a similar colour range, or can be grown in the border with other cottage-garden annuals such as clarkias and candytufts (*Iberis*).

HOW TO GROW
Broadcast seeds thinly in the flowering site, at four-week intervals, from spring to midsummer, raking in the seeds. Do not disturb the seedlings. In a sunny site, in ordinary, well-drained soil, plants seed themselves.

A scattering of Virginian stock seed will fill an out-of-the-way corner with a satisfying mass of flowers.

Matthiola incana (STOCK)

The versatile and heady-scented stock has been developed into a vast range of annual and biennial cultivars and strains to flower in spring, summer or (under glass) in winter. All have felty grey-green foliage that provides a soft setting for the equally soft white, cream, apricot, pink, lavender and red spikes of flowers that appear in June and July. Height varies from 10 to 12 in. for the much-branched bedding types to 2½ ft for the Column strain, which is splendid for cutting.

HOW TO GROW
Raise annual strains under glass, planting out in late spring, but raise others by planting out in autumn. Set out 12 in. apart, in soil as for Matthiola bicornis. Place in sun or light shade. With seedlings of double-flowered strains, discard singles, discernible by their dark green leaf colour. Brompton stocks should be treated as biennials – sown in a nursery bed in summer and transplanted to the flowering site in autumn, 12 in. apart.

A darker red form of *Matthiola incana* gives strength and contrast when dotted around the edge of a shrubbery.

Matthiola bicornis (NIGHT-SCENTED STOCK)

All stocks are fragrant, but night-scented stock has a more heady, widespreading sweetness than any other. It is an easily grown hardy annual, not flamboyant like the more common half-hardy annual and biennial stocks but with a quiet charm all its own.

The plant is 15 in. high, loosely branching and bushy, with narrow, soft grey-green leaves. Slender spikes of greyish-lilac or purple flowers open in July and August. They remain closed for most of the day, opening only in the early evening, when they release their fragrance.

One way of growing night-scented stock is to mingle it with sweet-smelling tobacco plants (*Nicotiana*) and mignonette (*Reseda*), in a sheltered, enclosed part of the garden. This makes a delightful place to sit on a warm summer evening.

A lovely association would be small groups of night-scented stock grown with *Nicotiana alata* (syn. *N. affinis*) 'Dwarf White Bedder' and given a white and silver setting: the white-bloomed sweet william *Dianthus barbatus* 'Giant White', which grows 1½-2 ft tall, and the silver-leaved, 18 in. high lamb's tongue (*Stachys olympica*).

HOW TO GROW
Matthiola bicornis: for early flowering, sow under glass in late winter, transplanting the seedlings 8 in. apart. Alternatively, sow in spring, in a site close to the house. The plants thrive in ordinary soil, neutral to alkaline and moisture-retentive, in sun or partial shade.
Dianthus barbatus: see p. 26.
Nicotiana alata: see p. 46.
Reseda odorata: see p. 53.
Stachys olympica: see p. 122.

Around a stone bench in August heady perfumes mingle. White *Nicotiana alata*, encroaching on the bench, and delicate pink *Matthiola bicornis* will scent the evening air, while white *Dianthus barbatus* and red-tinted *Reseda odorata* attract butterflies and bees during the day. In the foreground is silver-leaved *Stachys olympica*.

The sweetly scented, bright yellow flowers of *Mentzelia lindleyi*, 2½ in. across, lend gaiety to the summer border.

Mentzelia lindleyi

A robust, freely branching, slightly sprawling hardy annual, 18 in. high, *Mentzelia lindleyi* (syn. *Bartonia aurea*) produces a long succession of fragrant, brilliant yellow flowers from June to August. The flowers, which open from gracefully pointed buds, have five broad petals and in the centre a mass of slender golden stamens. The leaves are narrow, pale greyish-green and toothed, and make an attractive background to the flowers.

The plant is a native of California and so does best here in warm summers. If the weather is cool and cloudy, the flowers may fail to open properly.

There is no better foil for the yellow flowers of this vigorous annual than the deep purple-blue spires of larkspur (*Delphinium ajacis*).

HOW TO GROW
Sow under glass in early spring or in the flowering site in late spring, thinning the seedlings to 9 in. apart. Wind-resistant if grown in full sun and in ordinary well-drained soil.

Mesembryanthemum criniflorum make a brilliant show in a sunny garden.

Mesembryanthemum criniflorum

(LIVINGSTONE DAISY)

Originating in South Africa, the Livingstone daisy has astonishingly brilliant pink, lavender, red, orange and yellow flowers and thick, glossy, pale green leaves. The flowers are daisy-like, with slender petals, and put on their dazzling display from June to August, provided they have a sunny, dry position.

Though the plant is barely 6 in. high, it trails and looks out of place among other annuals. Try growing it instead with such attractive foliage plants as *Eryngium variifolium* or *Festuca glauca*.

HOW TO GROW
Sow under glass in early spring; harden off and plant out, 6 in. apart, in late May, when seeds may also be sown in the flowering site (flowering is then later). Full sun is essential, and light, well-drained soil.

Easy to grow in the right conditions, these little flowers are suitable for banks, rock gardens and borders.

Myosotis sylvatica (FORGET-ME-NOT)

All the garden forget-me-not cultivars stem from this parent species, providing a succession of delightful tiny pure blue flowers, each with a white or yellow eye, from April to June.

The chief use of forget-me-nots is for bedding, but they also make long-lasting cut flowers, and it is generally only when sprigs are taken indoors that the neatness and delicate colouring of the diminutive flowers is appreciated to the full.

Forget-me-nots are also useful plants for the mixed border, wild garden and shrub border. In the mixed border they provide fine companions for early paeonies and oriental poppies (*Papaver*).

It is a good idea in bedding schemes to use an edging of a compact dwarf cultivar, such as 'Blue Ball' (a hybrid originating from *Myosotis alpestris*), and to merge this into a taller sort, say 'Blue Bird', to form a gradual lead-up to the higher level of other bedding plants, like wallflowers (*Cheiranthus*) or tulips.

Following this scheme, you could make an association in which large drifts of 'Blue Ball' and 'Blue Bird' give way to the gold dust *Alyssum saxatile* 'Citrinum', a 12 in. high perennial which bears its bright lemon flowers at the same time as the forget-me-nots bloom. The plants together could form a carpet for yellow tulips – 15 in. high 'Sulphur Triumph' and 18 in. high 'Purissima', which flower in April and May. Such an exquisite combination of fresh blue and yellow would capture the very essence of spring.

HOW TO GROW
Myosotis sylvatica: for best results, raise these plants as biennials, sowing seeds during summer in trays in a cold frame; transplant in autumn, 6 in. apart. In cold gardens and in poorly drained soil, overwinter in a cold frame or under cloches and plant out in spring. Best in fertile, moisture-retentive soil and in partial shade. Myosotis seeds freely.
Alyssum saxatile: see p. 197.
Tulipa: see p. 169.

Forget-me-nots, tulips and wallflowers massed together informally make a vivid colour mixture in a border.

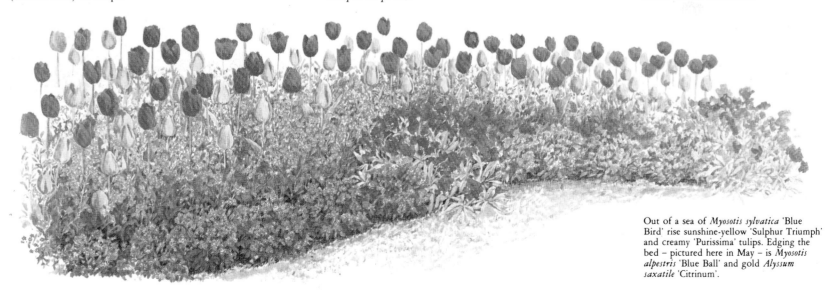

Out of a sea of *Myosotis sylvatica* 'Blue Bird' rise sunshine-yellow 'Sulphur Triumph' and creamy 'Purissima' tulips. Edging the bed – pictured here in May – is *Myosotis alpestris* 'Blue Ball' and gold *Alyssum saxatile* 'Citrinum'.

Mimulus × hybridus (MONKEY FLOWER)

Some of these hybrids – which all flower freely from July to October – are among the most brilliant of all garden plants. 'Queen's Prize', for example, has vividly blotched wide-mouthed flowers in varying purples, reds, yellows and creams. The new 'Royal Velvet' is almost as striking: each flower is a shade of mahogany-red and has a large yellow, red-speckled throat. Both are about 12 in. high.

Uniformly coloured cultivars – such as 'Firedragon' (6-8 in.), orange-red, and 'Mandarin' (12 in.), bright orange – are less striking but still handsome with their discreetly mottled throats that give emphasis to the flowers.

HOW TO GROW
Sow under glass in early spring, harden off and transplant, 6-9 in. apart, in May. Mimulus thrive in moisture-retentive garden soil and do not object to a partially shady site. Also suitable for pot cultivation.

Mimulus × 'Queen's Prize' is a large-flowered dwarf strain with variously coloured blotches marking the petals.

Mimulus guttatus flourishes in a waterside position.

Nemesia strumosa

With its solid masses of funnel-shaped blooms in so many vivid colours, this bushy annual symbolises summer. In very fertile and moist soils, it puts on a splendid show all summer long. But in other conditions it soon flowers itself to death, and a long floral display can be achieved only by successive sowings at six-week intervals from early March.

Fine garden cultivars include 'Carnival Mixed', 9 in. high, and 'Tapestry', 10 in., both available in a wide range of colours. 'Blue Gem', 8 in. high, is a delicate lavender-blue. It is overpowered by mixed cultivars and needs to be grown by itself for its quiet charm to be fully appreciated.

HOW TO GROW
Sow successive batches under glass in spring; harden off before planting out, 6 in. apart, from late May onwards. Nemesias grow best in full sun, in fertile soil that is moist but well drained. Nemesia strumosa is suitable for planting in containers and for window-box cultivation.

The sky-blue flowers of *Nemesia strumosa* 'Blue Gem' are slightly smaller than those of the other cultivars.

'Sutton's Mixed' comes in a range of bright colours.

Nemophila menziesii (BABY BLUE EYES)

The common name of this easily grown hardy annual was suggested by the innocent gaze of its rounded, white-centred pale blue flowers. The foliage of the plant, which forms a trailing mound 6-9 in. high, is also charming – a feathery, fresh, pale green. If successive sowings are made in autumn and early spring, the flowering season will extend through most of summer and autumn.

Nemophila menziesii (syn. *N. insignis*) associates well with the equally enchanting, yellow-and-white poached egg flower (*Limnanthes douglasii*), which is similar in habit and flowers from June to August.

HOW TO GROW
Sow in the flowering site, in autumn or spring, making several sowings at three to four-week intervals; thin seedlings to stand 6 in. apart. Nemophilas will grow in any ordinary garden soil but will flourish in fertile, moist soils (especially sandy loams enriched with compost) in sun or light shade.

Clumps of *Nemophila menziesii* planted with yellow-and-white *Limnanthes douglasii* create a fresh, cheerful effect.

A good edging plant, *Nemophila menziesii* can also be grown in pots.

Nicotiana alata (TOBACCO PLANT)

Like so many tobacco plants, *Nicotiana alata* (syn. *N. affinis*) opens its flowers only in the evening, when it sends out waves of heady fragrance. A half-hardy perennial usually grown as an annual, it produces a strong basal rosette of pale green leaves from which rise elegant, but strong, branching stems to a height of 2-3 ft. The many flowers are starry and long-tubed and appear in clusters during late summer and autumn – though when the plant survives the winter in a very mild situation, it will flower earlier during the following summer.

The species and several varieties have white flowers, and these are the most beautiful, showing up well as they perfume the dusk. However, the soft pink, lavender-pink and deep red hybrid cultivars are also extremely attractive. For the garden where space is at a premium, some of these are now available in dwarf forms. A recent addition to the colour range is 'Lime Green', much appreciated by flower arrangers but also delightful in the garden.

Tobacco plants mix well with many other flowers but are especially useful among bearded irises, to conceal the leaves after the flowers are over. Try mingling tobacco plants and the irises and edging the group with pale blue lobelias and clumps of *Nerine bowdenii*.

HOW TO GROW
Nicotiana alata: sow under glass in late winter/early spring; harden off and plant out in May, 12 in. apart (8-9 in. for dwarf types). Best in fertile, well-drained soil, and equally good in sun or light shade, thriving in a north-facing border.
Iris, bearded hybrids: see p. 97.
Lobelia erinus: see p. 40.
Nerine bowdenii: see p. 166.

Some modern cultivars of *N. alata* open their flowers in the daytime.

Nicotiana alata 'Lime Green' seen in September with clumps of pink *Nerine bowdenii* and *Miscanthus sinensis* 'Zebrinus' – a grass with yellow cross-banding on its leaves. Blue *Lobelia erinus* edges the border.

The tall *Nicotiana sylvestris* bears white flowers which close in full sun. Behind is *Clematis recta* in seed.

Newer forms of *Nigella damascena* include a greater variety of colours, including red, pink, purple and mauve.

Papaver nudicaule is the only poppy suitable for cutting. The colours of 'Champagne Bubbles' are enticingly beautiful.

Nicotiana sylvestris (TOBACCO PLANT)

This stately tobacco plant from Argentina is not listed by many seedsmen, but it is well worth searching for and growing. It carries its large, handsome leaves at an angle to the ground in a bold rosette at least 2 ft across. From this, flowering stems rise to a height of 5 ft, bearing at the top, in August, a cluster of long, white trumpet flowers, both elegant and fragrant.

The plants can be used in loose drifts among shrubs, where their silhouettes can be seen to full advantage, or planted to give height to a border of annuals.

HOW TO GROW

Cultivation as for Nicotiana alata; sow at a temperature of 64°F (18°C) and grow the seedlings on at 55-60°F (13-16°C). Plant out, 2 ft apart, when all danger of frost is past; the plants, perennial by nature, often survive the winter in very mild gardens.

Nigella damascena

(LOVE-IN-A-MIST, DEVIL-IN-A-BUSH)

The blue or white flowers of this enchanting 2 ft tall hardy annual bloom all summer long in a haze of feathery, soft green foliage – love-in-a-mist. As the flowers fade, each seed pod of the bushy plant swells and ripens into a pale brown, red-barred, spiky globe – the devil-in-a-bush. Invaluable for the border, the plant also provides superb cut flowers. 'Miss Jekyll Blue', with semi-double blue flowers, is one of the finest of the cultivars. The more recent 'Persian Jewels Mixed' contains semi-double flowers in shades of blue, mauve, purple and rose-pink.

HOW TO GROW

Sow in the flowering site during spring, in successive batches (and, in mild areas, during autumn for early flowering). Thin seedlings to 8 in. apart. Grow in any well-drained soil, in full sun. Dead-head unless you want seed heads, which can be dried for winter decoration, or self-sown seedlings.

Papaver nudicaule (ICELAND POPPY)

This biennial from the sub-Arctic is one of the most elegant of all poppies. The flowers, borne in early summer on wiry, leafless stems, 1½-2 ft tall, have delicate, tissue-thin petals; and the soft green leaves, which form a flat basal rosette, are pale, slender and deeply lobed.

Mixed varieties, such as 'Champagne Bubbles', provide a wide colour range – white, yellow, apricot, pink, salmon, orange and scarlet – and these are best if the plant is being grown chiefly for cut flowers. Slightly taller – 2½ ft in height – is another cultivar, 'San Remo', which produces a long-stemmed mixture in pastel shades.

HOW TO GROW

Sow in early summer, ideally in the flowering site, as poppies resent transplanting; thin the seedlings progressively to 12 in. spacings, and in cold, wet gardens give cloche protection during winter. Poppies need a sunny position. Any garden soil is suitable, provided that it is well drained.

Caption (top left photo): Pink and white poppies *Papaver rhoeas* flutter in an annual border.

Caption (top middle illustration): Scarlet field poppies and a common box (*Buxus sempervirens*) can transform part of the garden that has been left to run wild.

Papaver rhoeas (FIELD POPPY)

Our native poppy of the cornfields, which hoists its bold scarlet flags atop slender 2 ft high rigging from June to August, is such a graceful plant that it is surprising not to find it in seed catalogues. However, it can be introduced successfully as a pinch of seed from the wild into the long grass of an orchard or on to a bank beneath a hedge.

Quite different in colour but even more elegant are the colour forms sold under the names 'Shirley Single Mixed' and 'Shirley Double Mixed', in white, pink, rose, salmon and crimson, often edged with a deeper colour. These are, like the wild poppy, splendid for naturalising.

HOW TO GROW
Sow in early autumn or in spring where the plants are to flower (or broadcast seeds in semi-wild sites), thinning seedlings to 12 in. apart. Any well-drained soil, in a sunny open site, is suitable.

Pelargonium peltatum (IVY-LEAVED GERANIUM)

With its abundant flowers, from May to October, its polished, pale green leaves and its graceful, 3 ft long, trailing stems, the ivy-leaved geranium is a favourite plant for hanging baskets or for trailing down the face of a wall. It can also be used for ground-cover or for training up a support to form either a pyramid or a slender weeping standard. Plants grown upwards, however, are not so profuse in their flowering.

Among the lovely named sorts are: 'Galilee', deep pink; 'Eulalia', deep mauve; 'L'Elegante', white, with cream-edged leaves that are flushed purple, particularly in autumn; 'La France', double mauve flowers flecked with maroon above; 'Madame Crousse', double, bright pink; and 'Mexican Beauty', vigorous, with single crimson flowers.

HOW TO GROW
Set out as bedding and container plants in late May, when all danger of frost is over, in ordinary, well-drained garden soil or in potting compost. Site in full sun. Lift the plants before autumn frosts; cut them back by a half, pot up and overwinter without watering in a frost-free place. Propagation as for Pelargonium zonale.

Caption (bottom left photo): When planted at a height, the ivy-leaved geranium will cascade gracefully down the sides of its container.

Caption (bottom right photo): A flourishing window-box containing *Pelargonium peltatum* and *P. zonale*.

Pelargonium zonale

Hybrid pelargoniums – generally but incorrectly known as geraniums and cherished in a million pots and window-boxes – are far from limited to the familiar scarlet-flowered forms. The group also contains exuberantly coloured cultivars, ranging in height from 6 in. to 6 ft. These bedding and pot plants should not be confused with the hardy herbaceous perennials of the genus *Geranium*.

Of the old sorts those grown mainly for their flowers include: 'Maxim Kovaleski', orange; 'Gustav Emich', vermilion; 'King of Denmark', pink; 'Hermione', white; 'A. M. Mayne', magenta; and 'Paul Crampel', scarlet. Among those notable for their foliage are: 'Chelsea Gem' and 'Caroline Schmidt', both with pale green leaves edged with white; 'Golden Harry Hieover', pale gold leaves with brown zones; and 'Henry Cox', mid-green leaves with red and cream splashes and zones.

Good modern cultivars include 'Grenadier', which has particularly fine scarlet blooms, and the seed strain 'Sprinter', which provides a mixture of flower colours.

In the garden, zonal pelargoniums are generally grown as bedding plants, but they can also be successfully used in mixed borders. You could, for example, choose 'Mrs Parker' – white-variegated leaves topped by pale pink flowers – as a centrepiece, and edge it with the bellflower *Campanula portenschlagiana*, a dwarf perennial that is a mass of open, bell-shaped blue-purple flowers from July until autumn; and with the 2 ft high silver-leaved perennial *Pyrethrum ptarmaciflorum*.

These plants make a long-lasting grouping that follows the traditional pelargonium bedding scheme of red, white and blue – only in a softer, more subtle manner.

HOW TO GROW
Pelargonium zonale: cultivation as for P. peltatum. Propagate old varieties from tip cuttings in late summer or, in spring, from stem cuttings taken from overwintered plants started into growth. Rooted cuttings need careful watering as they are prone to black leg disease, which causes them to collapse and die. Modern varieties may also be raised from cuttings, or from seeds sown under glass in late winter, pricked out and hardened off before planting out in June.
Campanula portenschlagiana: see p. 200.
Pyrethrum ptarmaciflorum: see p. 52.

Pink *P. z.* 'Mrs Parker', silver *Pyrethrum ptarmaciflorum* and blue-purple *Campanula portenschlagiana* pictured in August.

Pelargonium zonale 'Mrs. Henry Cox' has pink flowers and tricolour leaves.

A lavish display with *Pelargonium zonale* 'Paul Crampel' in the background, ivy-leaved *P. peltatum* and *Lobelia erinus*.

Petunia × hybrida

Since the first species was introduced to Europe about 1830, the petunia has grown in favour until it is now one of the most popular of half-hardy annuals.

The large funnel-shaped flowers of the Multiflora group, especially the heavy double blooms, are susceptible to rain damage, but the new F¹ hybrid types, with many smaller flowers on compact plants, are much more weather-resistant. The larger Grandiflora hybrids, which have a more trailing habit, put out large double flowers that can sometimes be too showy. Except in the most sheltered places, they are best grown in pots.

Petunias come in a wide range of colours. Pink, lavender, purple and red varieties blend beautifully and create a delightful mixture, either by themselves or with roses of similar colouring and grey foliage plants. White can also be mixed with them to lighten the effect. Pale yellow varieties, which are usually less vigorous, look extremely attractive grown by themselves or with white or pale lavender varieties. Petunias are 12-18 in. tall, according to variety, and all flower over a very long season, from June to the first severe autumn frosts.

A combination of the yellow Multiflora petunia 'Summer Sun', the upright, deep blue *Salvia farinacea* and the frothily silver-leaved *Pyrethrum ptarmaciflorum* would provide beauty from early summer to autumn.

HOW TO GROW
Petunia × hybrida: sow under glass in spring, pricking the seedlings out into pots and hardening off before planting out in late May, 10-12 in. apart (6-8 in. for dwarfs). All thrive in good, well-drained soil, in a sunny site sheltered from strong winds, or can be grown in hanging baskets, pots or window-boxes.
Pyrethrum ptarmaciflorum: see p. 52.
Salvia farinacea: see p. 54.

Petunias add a deep purple to an attractive pot containing *Helichrysum petiolatum*. Below the pot is a pink-flowered polygonum.

In this August bed the stunning effect of an uninterrupted mass of the yellow Multiflora petunia 'Summer Sun' is enhanced by a contrasting clump of blue *Salvia farinacea* and the delicate tracery of *Pyrethrum ptarmaciflorum*.

Penstemon × gloxinioides

With their long spikes of tubular red, pink, purple and white flowers, these hybrid penstemons are an attractive halfway house between foxgloves and snapdragons. The plants, 1½-2½ ft tall, robust and flowering from July to autumn, make fine border annuals and provide handsome flowers for cutting.

The large-flowered mixtures such as 'Bouquet' and 'Skyline' are extremely colourful, but look overdone compared with some of the older, smaller-bloomed kinds.

HOW TO GROW
Sow under glass in February and March. Set out young plants in late spring, 12 in. apart, in ordinary, well-drained soil, and in full sun. In all but the coldest areas penstemons may be grown as perennials, the plants being cut back to ground level in autumn and given cloche protection. Propagate named strains from sideshoot cuttings in late summer.

The charming, bell-like blooms of *Penstemon × gloxinioides* are ideal for a border or as cut flowers.

Smaller-flowered forms harmonise well with silver-leaved senecios.

Phlox drummondii

In their general appearance the dwarf cultivars of this half-hardy annual resemble *Nemesia*. In both plants, sturdy 9 in. stems are topped by round heads of small flowers in a range of colours. However, the reds, mauves, pinks and whites of the phlox are softer in tone, and each flower has a contrasting zone of colour around its eye. In the cultivars 'Twinkles' and 'Twinkling Stars' the petal tips are drawn out into slender points, creating a star-shaped flower. Both have a wide colour range and are compact plants only 6-8 in. tall.

All these dwarf phlox bloom from July to September, provided they have not been crowded in the seed tray.

HOW TO GROW
Sow under glass in spring; harden off and transplant in late May, 6-8 in. apart, as edgings to borders and summer beds. Grow in any good, well-drained soil, in full sun. Dead-heading, though time consuming, extends the season.

Splashes of brilliant colour in a bed of mixed annuals, including *Phlox drummondii*, *Tagetes*, *Lobelia* and *Callistephus*.

Phlox drummondii makes an informal edging to a garden path.

Portulaca grandiflora (SUN PLANT)

A swathe of sun plants makes a gloriously bright display, especially so when the flowers are allowed to tumble down a bank. The elegant, cylindrical, succulent leaves of each plant form dense mats, 6-9 in. high and at least 12 in. across, that throughout the summer are smothered by a mass of purple, red or yellow, single or double flowers with tissue-delicate petals. However, these need sunshine before they will open fully; all except the new variety 'Cloudbeater', which is less particular about weather.

For a garden sunset effect, try growing sun plants with *Eschscholzia* varieties in the same colour range.

HOW TO GROW
Sow in the flowering site in late spring (or earlier under glass); thin seedlings to 6 in. apart. Easy to grow, these plants revel in hot and dry soils, in full sun, and need little attention. Under good conditions, self-sown seedlings are common.

In a hot, dry part of the garden, a carpet of *Portulaca grandiflora* will produce flowers in profusion from June to September.

Portulaca grandiflora scattered around a *Kochia scoparia* 'Childsii'.

Standing tall in the centre of this spring bed are 'Beauty of Apeldoorn' tulips. Shorter 'General de Wet' tulips, 'Barnhaven' polyanthus and *Alyssum saxatile* 'Dudley Neville' complete the fiery effect.

Primula Polyanthus group

The polyanthus, or bunch-flowered primrose, has been a popular plant since its introduction in the 19th century. But it is only since the development of the large-flowered hybrids – such as the 'Pacific Giant' strain – that it has become widely used as a bedding plant and, even more recently, as a pot plant.

The large-flowered hybrids produce blooms in compact, long-lasting clusters on tall, sturdy stems 9-12 in. high. The flowers appear from March to early May in a wide spectrum of colours that embrace red, pink, white, yellow, orange and blue, and they usually have a distinct yellow eye. The 'Barnhaven' cultivars are an outstandingly rich-coloured range that includes apricot, burnt orange, warm brown and deep crimson. 'Gold-laced' sorts, which have a clear gold rim to each deep red bloom, and double-flowered kinds, are both best appreciated grown singly rather than in groups.

Flower size decreases after the first year and the plants become more leafy, but particularly good colour forms can be divided and replanted after flowering, year after year. These older plants can be used to provide a rich carpet of colour beneath spring-flowering trees.

A general mixture of polyanthus is cheerful, but they are much more effective when grown in a limited colour range. Tulips blend well with polyanthus; apricot-orange cultivars, such as the scented 'General de Wet' and the taller 'Beauty of Apeldoorn', both burst into flame in April. The planting could be softened with an edging of biscuit-yellow *Alyssum saxatile* 'Dudley Neville'.

HOW TO GROW
Primula: most seed strains are of mixed colours; sow in a cold greenhouse or frame from spring until midsummer for planting out in autumn or for potting up for indoor culture. In bedding schemes and as edgings, space polyanthus 12 in. apart; they need fertile, moist soil and do best in light shade. Protect polyanthus from birds with netting or black cotton.
Alyssum saxatile: see p. 197.
Tulipa: see pp. 169-171.

Pyrethrum ptarmaciflorum

Sometimes wrongly listed in catalogues as *Pyrethrum ptarmicaefolium*, this lacy, silvery-grey pyrethrum has an almost metallic sheen. The plant, a tender shrub usually grown as a half-hardy annual, forms a compact mound 15 in. high and is similar to a more refined version of the whiter-leaved *Senecio maritimus*.

The finely fretted leaves of the pyrethrum are excellent as a foil for the vivid blue or purple blooms of heliotropes, for breaking up and introducing lightness to the solidity of massed fibrous begonias, or as edging for groups of fuchsias.

HOW TO GROW
Sow under glass in spring. Harden off and plant out in late May, 12 in. apart, as dot plants in summer bedding schemes and in borders. Pinch out young plants to induce side branching. Any well-drained soil is suitable. The plants need a sunny site.

Pyrethrum ptarmaciflorum is the perfect foil for brightly coloured fuchsias such as the scarlet and purple 'Mrs Popple'.

'Silver Feather' intensifies the violet of *Salvia farinacea* 'Victoria'.

Reseda odorata (MIGNONETTE)

The Victorians and the Edwardians adored mignonette because of its unforgettable fragrance, which fills the air for yards around. To look at, the 1-2½ ft high plant has only a modest charm. The leaves resemble those of spinach, and the flower spikes, produced from June to October, consist of minute, yellow-green blooms with tufted brown stamens.

'Machet', a variety with red-tinged flowers, is particularly fragrant and is attractive to bees. It is suitable for the border and can also be used for cutting, or as a pot plant. 'Goliath' produces large spikes of red flowers.

HOW TO GROW
Make successive sowings in the flowering site during spring, thinning the seedlings to 10 in. The plants thrive in ordinary fertile, well-drained soil, in sun or dappled shade. Also good for window-boxes. Pinch out the growing tips of young plants to encourage branching.

Delicate crimson touches on the small flowers of *Reseda odorata* 'Machet' enrich the gentle charm of this hardy annual.

In every typical cottage garden, mignonette is grown for its sweet scent.

Ricinus communis (CASTOR OIL PLANT)

This tropical plant, whose seeds are used to make castor oil, is a particularly striking half-hardy annual. Robust and shrubby, it will grow 5 ft high, and nearly as wide, in the course of the year. The leaves, up to 12 in. across, are shaped rather like the human hand; in the species, these are mid-green, but there are several coloured cultivars, including: 'Gibsonii', bronze; 'Impala', bronze-carmine, and 'Zanzibarensis', green with conspicuous pale midribs. Castor oil plants make eye-catching additions to a bedding scheme, whether grown with other foliage plants or among groups of tall, vivid-flowered annuals or perennials.

HOW TO GROW
Soak the seeds before sowing them individually in pots under glass. Pot on as necessary and plant out in late May, 2-3 ft apart for background plantings and quick screens or singly as specimen and dot plants. Fertile, well-drained soil, full sun, staking and ample watering are essential.

With its handsome leaves and elegant shape, *Ricinus communis* is well able to stand on its own in the middle of a bed.

R. communis combined in a formal scheme with dwarf snapdragons.

Salpiglossis sinuata

The velvety, funnel-shaped blooms of this Chilean half-hardy annual create a dramatic effect in the mixed border, with their kaleidoscope of purples, reds, pinks, oranges and yellows. The display lasts from July to September and can be made the more vivid with an edging of the grey-leaved *Pyrethrum ptarmaciflorum*.

Salpiglossis sinuata, which is 2 ft tall, has long been prized as a cool greenhouse or conservatory plant; this and the plant's slender, frail appearance have led to its being neglected as a garden annual. It is, in fact, tougher than it looks. This is especially true of the new, shorter, hybrids such as 'Bolero', 1½-2 ft.

HOW TO GROW
Sow under glass in spring, transplanting (after hardening off) 12 in. apart in late May. Best in fertile, well-drained but moisture-retentive soil, in full sun sheltered from strong winds Provide twiggy supports.

Delicate veining in deeper tones often appears in the multi-coloured, trumpet-shaped blooms of *Salpiglossis sinuata*.

A rich mix of colours makes a striking effect in conservatory or bed.

Purplish-blue *Salvia farinacea* in front of *Cleome*, *Nicotiana* and *Zinnia*.

Salvia farinacea

When considering salvias, many gardeners never look beyond the scarlet *Salvia splendens*, completely closing their minds to the delights of *S. farinacea*. This 2½-3 ft tall tender perennial can be grown as a half-hardy annual and is excellent for borders, bedding or cutting.

Its name is derived from the farina, or waxy dusting, that covers the stems and foliage and gives them a soft, grey-green appearance.

The faintly purple-flushed, blue flowers are carried high above the slender leaves, in narrow, dense spikes that bloom from July to autumn. The deep purple-blue cultivar 'Victoria' is only half the height of the species.

HOW TO GROW
Sow in early spring under glass, at 64°F (18°C); harden off and plant out, 12 in. apart, when danger of frost is past, in borders and summer beds. All salvias need fertile, well-drained garden soil, preferably in full sun.

Salvia farinacea 'Victoria', a shorter form, makes a pleasing contrast of colour with the silvery leaves of *Senecio maritimus*.

Salvia splendens

The genus *Salvia*, which occurs in many widely separated parts of the world, includes sage, *Salvia officinalis*, the culinary and medicinal herb of Europe. But to flower gardeners, the first salvia to spring to mind is *S. splendens*, the scarlet plant from Brazil which has been a feature of bedding displays for many decades now. The brilliant spikes and bracts (petal-like leaves) rise to 15 in. high from a compact base of rich green foliage, and flaunt their tropical colouring from July to autumn.

Modern scarlet-flowered cultivars, such as 'Blaze of Fire' and 'Carabiniere', differ from older ones in being earlier to flower, more compact (8-12 in. high) and an even brighter red over darker green leaves. Recent cultivars now include pink, purple and white, giving the plants a place in the subtler bedding schemes – with purplish-blue penstemons, for example, and with blue-toned roses and grey foliage.

Scarlet salvias are so bright that they must be used with great care. The traditional red, white and blue of salvias, alyssum and lobelias is rather crude, but a softer variation is possible with silver-leaved *Senecio maritimus* in place of alyssum, and the little-used pale blue lobelias instead of deep blue ones. Among the best of the light blue cultivars is 'Cambridge Blue'.

On the other hand, you could make the whole association fiery by planting *Salvia* 'Carabiniere' with the 12 in. high ember-red French marigold *Tagetes patula* 'Fiesta', which flowers from June until the first frosts, and a coleus with dark red or bronze-red foliage.

HOW TO GROW
Salvia: cultivation as for S. farinacea, with similar planting distances. On both species, pinch out the growing points when seedlings are 6 in. high, to encourage branching. While S. farinacea is excellent as a cut flower, S. splendens, and in particular the scarlet forms, quickly lose their colours in water.
Coleus blumei: see p. 23.
Lobelia erinus: see p. 40.
Senecio maritimus: see p. 56.
Tagetes patula: see p. 56.

The careful use of white *Senecio maritimus* foliage provides a dramatic effect derived from brilliant contrasts.

A clump of scarlet *Salvia splendens*, orange *Tagetes patula* and dark red *Coleus blumei* blaze brilliantly in the sun.

A blaze of colour, provided by *Salvia splendens* and mixed antirrhinums.

Scabiosa atropurpurea (SWEET SCABIOUS)

The sweet scabious is an airy, graceful plant. Its close-packed, fragrant, crimson globes of flowers, which appear from July to September, are carried on slender stems 3 ft tall, and its foliage is elegantly divided. The plant is ideal both for cutting and for the border, though here it may need discreet staking with brushwood, especially in exposed gardens.

There are mixed cultivars, such as 'Double Large-flowered', in maroon, purple, pink, lavender and white, colours that blend most beautifully together. 'Dwarf Double Mixed' is half the height of the species, lacks some of its ancestor's grace, but it is still admirable, and extremely useful for combining with a tall sort.

HOW TO GROW
Sow under glass in spring, or in the flowering site in early autumn or mid-spring. Space plants 8-9 in. apart, in fertile, well-drained soil and in full sun. Tall sorts need twiggy supports on windy sites.

The glossy green leaves of *Choisya ternata* show off sweet scabious.

A fragrant display of multi-coloured rosettes is made by *Scabiosa atropurpurea* 'Sutton's Large Double'.

Schizanthus pinnatus (BUTTERFLY FLOWER)

When this Chilean annual is in bloom, it is as though a host of butterflies has taken up summer-long residence in the garden; and, indeed, the common name for *Schizanthus* is butterfly flower. The blooms are produced in shades of pink, red and purple, each with a pale throat veined with a darker colour; the display is given a perfect setting by the exquisite, pale green, deeply divided foliage, which is almost fern-like in appearance.

The species and taller cultivars, up to 4 ft high, can be grown outside as annuals but do best in cool conservatories. Better as summer annuals are the newer, more sturdy dwarf sorts, 12-18 in. tall. These include 'Dwarf Bouquet', 'Hit Parade' and 'Butterfly Mixture' – all in a wide colour range. Outdoors, the flowering period commences in June and may be extended well into the autumn.

HOW TO GROW
Sow in spring under glass, transplanting in late May, 12 in. apart. The short flowering season can be extended by successive outdoor sowings, at two-week intervals. Grow in fertile, moisture-retentive soil, in a sunny or very lightly shaded site sheltered from strong winds. Twiggy supports are required, especially for the taller varieties.

S. pinnatus and pink *Cistus × purpureus* both need shelter.

The speckled, orchid-like blooms grow in bushy masses.

'Diamond' produces a mass of off-white, deeply divided leaves.

A flourishing clump of *Senecio maritimus* – grown for its foliage rather than for its insignificant yellow flowers.

Senecio maritimus

Arching sprays of intricately dissected, white-felted leaves make this 2 ft high half-hardy shrub, grown as an annual, a superb foliage plant. It is also known as *Senecio cineraria.* 'Diamond' is a particularly bold cultivar with a loose, fountain-like spray of foliage, ideal for use with begonias, marigolds, salvias and other compact, colourful plants. 'Silver Dust' and 'Dwarf Silver', both 18 in. high, make excellent edging plants for soft-coloured annuals, such as *Ageratum houstonianum.*

S. leucostachys (syn. *S. vira-vira*) has leaves almost identical to those of *S. maritimus* and can be used for the same purposes.

HOW TO GROW
Sow under glass in late winter, and harden off before planting out in late May. Use as dot plants or space 12 in. apart (dwarf forms 8 in.). Any kind of garden soil, well drained to dry, is suitable, in full sun. Plants usually survive mild winters.

Tagetes patula (FRENCH MARIGOLD)

If they thought about the matter at all, most gardeners would probably think of the French marigold – actually a native of Mexico – as a modern bedding plant; but in fact it has been grown in Europe for more than 400 years. The vast number of cultivars, however, is a development of recent decades. The plant is a bushy but compact half-hardy annual, 12 in. high, which has deep green, attractively dissected foliage. The flowers are freely produced from June to autumn. In the species, they are single and either yellow or mahogany-red.

Some of the cultivars, too, are single, others have domed double flowers with broad tubular petals or globular double flowers with quilled petals. The colour range is limited to yellow, orange and deep red, but these are in many different combinations.

The French marigold is such a lovely plant, both in the species and in its older forms, that the new sorts, with their larger and brighter flowers on lower and tighter plants, have the appearance of straining for effect. They do, however, have the advantage of being much more weather-resistant, standing up well to wind and rain. 'Honeycomb', 9 in. high, is a new kind with mahogany-red and gold double flowers. 'Goldfinch' is also 9 in. high and has double, deep orange-crested flowers.

The loveliest effects are achieved with the clear yellow or orange marigolds, *Tagetes patula* 'Yellow Boy' or 'Orange Boy', grown with an edging of pale blue lobelia and interspersed with spires of dark purple-blue *Salvia farinacea* 'Victoria'.

HOW TO GROW
Tagetes patula: raise French – and African – marigolds under glass during spring and plant out when danger of frost is past. Space French marigolds 12 in. apart, dwarf types for edging and window-boxes 6 in. apart. They flourish in fertile, well-drained soil, and in full sun, but do well anywhere.
Lobelia erinus: see p. 40.
Salvia farinacea: see p. 54.

A group of French marigolds adds brilliant colour to the front of a border of zinnias, gaillardias and salvias.

Tagetes erecta (AFRICAN MARIGOLD)

From July to autumn the African marigold (whose native ground, in fact, is Mexico) puts on a glowing display of large lemon-yellow pompon flowers above its aromatic, finely divided, deep green foliage. The plant is vigorous and bushy and grows to a height of 2-3 ft. The many cultivars extend the colour range to golden-yellow and to shades of orange. These include: 'Doubloon', 2½ ft high with fully double globular flowers, and 'Superjack', 2 ft high, with frilled and ruffled rich orange flowers.

The rich, clear colours of African marigolds lend themselves to fine groupings in the mixed border or in the formal bed. One good association is to grow them with the bronze-leaved foliage plant *Ricinus communis* 'Gibsonii', with an edging of deep-blue lobelias.

HOW TO GROW
Tagetes erecta: cultivation as for Tagetes patula, with 12 in. distances between compact types, 18 in. between tall cultivars. Dead-head regularly. There is some evidence that growing marigolds rids soil of parasitic eelworms.
Lobelia erinus: see p. 40.
Ricinus communis: see p. 53.

A border of orange-yellow *Tagetes erecta*, lighter yellow *Tagetes patula* and kochias illuminates an ivy-covered wall.

Tropaeolum majus (NASTURTIUM)

The spurred, lightly perfumed orange and yellow flowers, trailing stems and round, smooth, green leaves of this hardy annual are one of the most familiar of summer sights in gardens – and along suburban fences, too. The plant trails or climbs 6-8 ft and blooms from June to September. It is excellent for training up an unsightly wall or for covering a bank. Its drawback is that blackflies find its leaves irresistible, and can destroy the plant if they are not controlled.

The modern cultivars have wide-petalled, often upward-facing, flowers and are extremely free-flowering. Among them are the Gleam strains, which grow to 15 in. in height. They are vigorous, trailing plants with semi-double flowers in yellow, scarlet and orange shades. 'Jewel Mixed' (height 12 in.) is an early flowering cultivar with semi-double flowers of yellow, salmon, scarlet or crimson.

The Tom Thumb strains are dwarf and compact, growing to only 10 in. They have single flowers that are available in many colours. 'Empress of India' combines scarlet blooms with purple-flushed foliage; 'Alaska' has variegated leaves and variously coloured flowers. 'Red Roulette' has large orange-scarlet semi-double and upfacing flowers; and 'Whirlybird' produces single, non-spurred blooms in a wide range of colours.

Nasturtiums can also be grown as summer-flowering pot plants. Alternatively, they provide a fine show when allowed to trail from hanging baskets.

HOW TO GROW
Sow in the flowering site in mid-spring, thinning the seedlings to 6 in. for compact dwarf types, 12 in. for Gleam strains and 'Red Roulette', both of which are also suitable for hanging baskets. All do best in poor, light and well-drained soil, in full sun. Use twiggy sticks to support the young growths. Spray against aphids with malathion or dimethoate.

Trailing gracefully over a wall, the nasturtium *Tropaeolum majus* is seen in its full glory, next to *Cotoneaster horizontalis*.

A pot of *Thunbergia alata*, amply repaying its owner's loving care.

Thunbergia alata (BLACK-EYED SUSAN)

The charming common name of this South African climbing annual was inspired by the dark brown centre of each of its clear orange, five-petalled flowers. These are borne singly where the pale green leaves join the stems.

Black-eyed Susan flowers through most of the summer, but only in very sunny, sheltered corners in mild southern and western areas. A little more hardy is the new cultivar 'Susie', which produces yellow and white as well as orange flowers, and also bears more blooms.

HOW TO GROW

Sow under glass in spring; germination is slow and seedlings make little growth in the early stages. Harden off and delay transplanting to the open until night temperatures remain around 50°F (10°C). Fertile, moist soil, full sun and shelter are essential even in southern gardens. Support with canes or string, or grow in hanging baskets.

Thunbergia alata can be trained against strings or wires. In a sunny, sheltered spot it will flower from July to September.

'Sunstar' is a richly coloured form with flowers nearly 2 in. across.

Ursinia anethoides

This South African daisy-like annual is a particularly bright and graceful plant. The pale green, finely dissected foliage forms a misty-green mass, above which, at a height of 18 in., are borne brilliant orange-yellow, purple-centred flowers. The floral display extends from June to September. When each flower fades, the protective sepals around it become papery white, and so the plant provides a second crop of 'flowers'.

'Sunstar' is an especially attractive cultivar which has deep orange flowers with a dark red central zone. Mixed kinds are available, with flowers ranging from pale yellow to deep orange.

HOW TO GROW

Sow under glass in spring; harden off and plant out in late May, 10-12 in. apart. Best in light soil of average-to-poor fertility, and in an open, sunny site. Also suitable for growing in containers.

Ursinia anethoides, the most popular species, adorns the flower bed with a mass of blazing orange all summer long.

A fiery wall of colour, provided by vivid *Verbena* and *Tagetes* varieties.

Verbena × hybrida

The many cultivars of *Verbena × hybrida* are beautiful plants that, throughout summer, produce tight clusters of small, pale-eyed, primrose-like flowers in scarlet, crimson, purple, lavender, pink and white. Providing a foil for these gay colours are attractively toothed, slender, dark green leaves.

The plants are 6-12 in. high, and most are bushy. An exception is the cultivar 'Showtime Mixed', which has a trailing habit and creates a splendid effect if allowed to wander informally among taller neighbours.

HOW TO GROW

Sow under glass in late winter and transplant in May, after hardening off. Space compact types ('Blaze') for edging and window-boxes 8-10 in. apart; sprawling forms ('Showtime Mixed') 15 in. apart; and tall, large-flowered types 12 in. apart. All flourish in fertile, well-drained but moist soil and in full sun.

A bushy plant of *Verbena × hybrida* gives the flower arranger several ready-made posies of deep pink flowers.

Viola × wittrockiana (GARDEN PANSIES)

Pansies, giant-flowered, whiskery-faced or velvety, are all descended from *Viola tricolor*; hence the plants' alternative names of *V. tricolor hortensis* and *V. t. maxima*. Among the best loved of all garden plants, pansies are wonderfully versatile – equally good for pots, spring bedding and summer use, though in a hot summer they tend to go to seed very quickly.

Given a lightly shaded position and a moist soil, each plant will quickly form a well-spread tuft of colour 6-9 in. high and 12 in. across.

It is quite possible to have pansies in the garden most of the year through. From May to September there are summer-flowering cultivars such as the velvety-red 'Ruby Queen'; the cool blue 'Premier Azure Blue'; the velvety, masked-faced 'Roggli Giants'; and the clear-coloured, unpatterned 'Clear Crystals'. Then there are winter-flowering cultivars, such as 'Floral Dance', that start to bloom in autumn and, in mild winters, will continue to flower until the following spring.

Pansies make enchanting ground-cover or informal edging for roses and other shrubs, and can also be used to provide splashes of colour in spaces among border perennials. The smaller-flowered cultivars are not out of place on the rock garden, where they combine well with *Dianthus deltoides*, *Primula auricula* and *Geranium dalmaticum*.

HOW TO GROW
Viola × wittrockiana: pansies and violas give of their best when raised as biennials, though they will flower the same year from seeds sown under glass in spring. For winter, spring and summer-flowering biennials, sow in an outdoor nursery bed during summer; thin seedlings to 4 in. and transplant to flowering sites in autumn, 10 in. apart. All need fertile, moist but well-drained soil, and sun or very light shade. Deadhead regularly or the plants seed themselves to death.
Dianthus deltoides: see p. 204.
Geranium dalmaticum: see p. 207.
Primula auricula: see p. 213.

'Jackanapes' edges a rock garden planted with yellow primulas, deep pink *Dianthus deltoides*, and *Geranium dalmaticum*.

Viola × wittrockiana 'Ruby Queen'.

Ilex aquifolium in a tub, with yellow pansies placed effectively beneath.

Zinnia elegans

The specific name *elegans* has become increasingly inappropriate for this Mexican half-hardy annual since variety breeders started producing ever-larger flowers on ever-smaller plants. However, in compensation, there is now a wide range of flower colours: white, cream, yellow, orange, scarlet, crimson, purple and even green. The flowers of almost all the varieties are fully double and are rather like more solid, drier-petalled ball dahlias. They bloom from July to September on plants that range from 6 to 30 in. in height.

HOW TO GROW
Sow under glass in spring at 70°F (21°C), spacing the seeds singly in 3 in. pots, as zinnias dislike root disturbance. Plant out when danger of frost has passed, 12 in. apart for giant-flowered, tall types, to 6 in. for dwarf, compact edging types, which are the more weather-resistant. Grow in fertile, well-drained soil, in full sun.

Resembling a brilliant, mop-headed daisy, *Zinnia elegans* is a perfect flower for borders, bedding and cutting.

A bed of bright zinnias, showing a few of the many colours available.

The History of the British Garden

From the baroque splendour of Blenheim to the simplicity of Sissinghurst

The earliest gardens in Britain were designed by the Romans during their occupation of the country from the 1st century to the 4th century AD. Painstaking archaeological research and pollen analysis has provided clues to what they might have looked like. For example, the Roman palace at Fishbourne in West Sussex probably contained a formal garden of hedge-lined paths and lawns with ornamental fountains, as well as informal terraces planted with trees and shrubs.

It was not until the Renaissance came to Tudor England, bringing with it a new appreciation of design and art, that gardening and garden design took on a new importance. The knot-garden style – beds laid out and planted in intricate patterns – characterised many Elizabethan gardens. An interesting example can be seen at the Tudor House Museum in Southampton. The garden is planned around a central knot, the pattern of which reflects the carved design on the doors of the house.

In the late 17th century, garden design was influenced by Italian, French and Dutch ideas: extended vistas, parterres (ornamental arrangements of flower beds), fountains and cascades. The National Trust is restoring the garden of Ham House, in Richmond, Surrey, according to the original plans, so that the design of the parterres and formal wilderness will be the same as that which impressed the diarist John Evelyn when he visited the house in 1678.

The influence of the French landscape gardener André Le Nôtre (1613-1700) – an exponent of the dramatic, ornate style known as the baroque – brought a new grandeur to English garden design. The formal garden, with its parterres, statuary and fountains, was extended by geometric groves and vast avenues. The reconstructed water parterre at Blenheim Palace in Oxfordshire is perhaps the best example of baroque splendour in a British garden, but something of the Le Nôtre style can also be seen at Melbourne Hall, in Derbyshire.

The 18th century, however, saw an English reaction against taming and regimenting nature. English garden design began to liberate nature, in the form of the landscape garden – rolling grassland, naturally grouped trees and irregular stretches of water, simulating nature and seeming to merge with the surrounding landscape. One of the earliest landscape gardens still intact is at Rousham House in Oxfordshire, designed by the man who started the movement, William Kent (1685-1748).

The greatest exponent of landscape gardening was Lancelot 'Capability' Brown (1716-83), so named because after he set up as a professional gardener he found what he called capabilities in every property he visited – among them Blenheim, and Chatsworth in Derbyshire.

Eventually there came a reaction to Brown's ideas. People decided that they no longer wanted to live in mock Classical rusticity with cows on their doorstep. Humphry Repton (1752-1818), who became the fashionable landscape gardener after Brown's death, therefore abandoned the pastoral setting for an ornamental area extending away from the house.

The 19th and 20th centuries

The Victorians, in gardening as in everything else, were prepared to take advantage of anything on offer. Their gardens contained every type of bed, cast-iron ornaments, rockwork, shrubberies and ferneries. Flowers, which had been relegated to the kitchen garden in the great 18th-century houses, made a spectacular return. Ground carpet-bedding floral displays – of the kind seen now only in municipal parks – were common.

In the late 19th century a controversy arose as to who was best fitted to design a garden – the architect who could plan the formal layout the garden needed, or the gardener, with his intimate knowledge of garden materials. At the same time, William Robinson (1838-1935), author of *The Wild Garden*, was arguing for informality of planting.

The present century saw the design argument resolved in a brilliant partnership between the architect Sir Edwin Lutyens (1869-1944) and the gardener Gertrude Jekyll (1843-1932). Lutyens built the formal brick and stone basis of the design and Jekyll softened it with cottage-garden-style plantings. One of the few good remaining examples of their collaboration is the painstakingly restored garden at Hestercombe in Somerset.

Gertrude Jekyll was an artist who excelled in harmoniously coloured herbaceous borders. Though most of her gardens have disappeared in their original form, her memory lives on in some of the great gardens that were inspired by her: Hidcote Manor in Gloucestershire; Sissinghurst in Kent; and Great Dixter in Sussex.

The baroque style in English gardens reached a peak at Blenheim Palace, Oxfordshire. Above is one of the elaborate parterres.

Stourhead in Wiltshire, among the most complete and best preserved 18th-century gardens landscaped in the Classical style, was mostly created by two amateurs – Henry Hoare (1705-85) and his grandson Richard Hoare (1758-1838).

Perennials

The mainstay of most gardens, perennials provide colourful support in many ways

◆

LAMB'S TONGUE AND LUPIN, columbine and bellflower, monkshood and lady's mantle – all are common names that create a picture in the mind's eye of the cottage garden of long ago. For these are the classic perennials which were once grown as a happy miscellany among the soft-fruit bushes and the vegetables, with an intermingling of spring bulbs to fill the early gaps.

Perennials are herbaceous, or non-woody plants which live for an indefinite period, dying back in autumn to some simple resting rootstock, and then reappearing in spring. For this reason, the well-tried cottage-garden classics were among those chosen by the gardener-writers William Robinson and Gertrude Jekyll towards the end of the 19th century in their successful efforts to move away from the monotonous formality of Victorian garden bedding schemes.

At the simplest level, perennials can be used in an almost unplanned fashion to provide an effective, traditional cottage-garden medley: a tumble of growth is more attractive than widely spaced annuals in a formal scheme. The next level is the mixed border, which is planted in the cottage-garden style but with flowering and fruiting shrubs replacing the soft-fruit bushes of the cottage garden. In this sort of scheme, either the shrubs are considered as background or winter interest in a mainly herbaceous perennial planting or the perennials take on a ground-cover, shade-accepting role amongst the shrubs.

It is also possible to produce a border of perennials alone, where the plants are chosen for their length and period of flowering, and ease of cultivation. With careful selection, the plants can be brought together to form a series of 'garden pictures' as the associations on the following pages show.

Blue and mauve delphiniums stand imposingly in this perennial border, where *Clematis heracleifolia* and *Rosa* 'Iceberg' stand over achilleas, flax, dianthus and potentillas.

Acanthus spinosus (BEAR'S BREECHES)

Acanthus, those handsome perennials, have been favourites for a very long time. The Romans and Greeks wove them into garlands that they draped about their houses, their furniture and themselves; and they immortalised their fondness for the plant by carving acanthus foliage upon the capitals of the Corinthian columns that supported so many of their public buildings.

The leaves of *Acanthus spinosus* are large – often at least 2 ft long – dark green, hairy and deeply cut. The splendid flower spikes, 4-5 ft tall, are crowded with mauve-and-white hooded flowers in late summer. Both the tips of the leaves and the calyces (outer protective parts) of the flowers are spiny, and can scratch the unwary. Even so, this species is usually preferred to others less spiky, because of its splendid flowers.

The plant can spread exuberantly and needs plenty of space, so it is not ideal for the mixed border. It looks positively statuesque in a bed of its own, but it can also be grown in the company of a good tough shrub that can stand up to the competition – *Rosa glauca* (syn. *R. rubrifolia*) for example, a 7 ft species that bears small, pink flowers in June. The rose puts out its blue-green, red-backed foliage in early May, just as the acanthus leaves are unfolding, and from then through to October the leaves of the two plants marry in a pleasant harmony of shape and colour.

HOW TO GROW
Acanthus spinosus: plant between autumn and spring, in fertile, well-drained soil. The plant is drought-resistant and does best in full sun. In early autumn, or during spring in cold areas, cut all stems back to ground level. Propagate in winter by root cuttings or in spring by seeds.
Rosa glauca: see p. 244.

The small, dark grey-purple leaves of *Rosa glauca* make a fitting background to the handsome foliage and magnificent flowers of *Acanthus spinosus*. The group here is pictured in late August.

The variety 'Gold Plate' backed by the rich foliage of *Sambucus racemosus*.

Achillea filipendulina (YARROW)

Achillea supposedly springs from the blood of Achilles, killed by Paris at the siege of Troy. This species, which was introduced to Britain in 1803, is one of the most dependable of tall perennials for dry soil. It forms a clump of feathery green leaves that, like those of many other achilleas, are pleasantly aromatic. Strong, 4 ft high stems emerge from the foliage, carrying mushroom-like flower heads. Each head consists of tiny, bright yellow flowers that last through from June until September. The flowering stems make a fine nucleus for dried-flower arrangements and will retain their colour all winter long.

HOW TO GROW
Plant from autumn to spring, in any type of soil that is well drained. Set in groups of three or five, spacing the plants 2 ft apart, in full sun. Staking is seldom necessary. Cut down to ground level in autumn. Propagate in the same way as Achillea taygetea 'Moonshine'.

In front of a beech hedge, the brilliant yellow flower heads of *Achillea filipendulina* crown stems of ferny foliage.

Achillea taygetea 'Moonshine'

The feathery foliage of this achillea is a gentle grey-green – a perfect foil for the pale sulphur-yellow flower heads, which are borne on 2 ft high stems in June and July. They are flat, and consist of a myriad little flowers. When examined closely, each tiny flower looks like the heart of a daisy.

Unlike most herbaceous plants, 'Moonshine' retains a hummock of attractive leaves throughout the winter. It looks best grown in a mass that could be splendidly set off by an association with the purple-leaved *Berberis thunbergii* 'Atropurpurea'.

HOW TO GROW
Cultivate in the same way as Achillea filipendulina, with 15 in. spacings between plants. Propagate both achilleas by division in spring, ideally every two or three years. A. filipendulina can also be raised from seeds in spring, but will not flower until the following year.

The yellow flowers of *Achillea taygetea* 'Moonshine' harmonise with the blooms of *Geranium sanguineum lancastrense*.

The achillea is well worth growing for its plume-like foliage alone.

Aconitum napellus (MONKSHOOD)

One of the common names for the genus *Aconitum* is monkshood – in recognition of the cowl or helmet-like upper petal that occurs in each bloom. The blue flowers of *Aconitum napellus* are borne in July and August on 5 ft tall spikes, and somewhat resemble those of a delphinium. The hybrid variety 'Bressingham Spire' has violet-blue flowers.

The tuberous roots of all species are highly poisonous. Old-time herbalists, however, used to make an ointment from them for the relief of rheumatism and allied disorders. *A. napellus* is a tough plant that will look after itself from generation to generation. It needs little care.

HOW TO GROW
Plant 15-18 in. apart, between autumn and spring, in rich, deep, cool and moist soil, and in light shade. Mulch annually in late spring, and cut back to soil level in autumn. Propagate by division in autumn, or by seeds when ripe or in spring.

A robust clump of *Aconitum napellus* can be obtained in summer by cutting back the flowering stems to soil level in October.

'Bressingham Spire' harmonises with the copper of *Cotinus coggygria*.

Ajuga reptans (BUGLE)

Bugle, a woodland plant, bears its 9 in. tall spikes of blue flowers above spreading evergreen leaves. In the half light of tree shade, flowers and foliage assume a bronze, metallic lustre from which the common name is derived; in 'Burgundy Glow' and 'Atropurpurea' *syn.* 'Purpurea', two purple-leaved forms, the sheen is particularly pronounced.

Bugle roots itself by runners, and makes admirable low ground-cover for shady spots, though the colours of forms with variegated foliage will be seen much better if there is a light dappling of sun. An especial advantage is that, unlike many ground-cover plants, its spread is easily controlled and it does not become rampant.

HOW TO GROW
Plant in spring, 8-12 in. apart, in any fertile, moist soil and in dappled shade or sun. Propagation, if necessary, is by division at any time between autumn and spring. Alternatively, remove and replant rooted runners.

Ajuga reptans 'Burgundy Glow' grows in the levels between log steps, alongside a clump of *Hosta sieboldiana*.

Bugle provides splendid ground-cover that can easily be kept in check.

Alchemilla mollis (LADY'S MANTLE)

Lady's mantle was alleged to have played a part in alchemy, the art of turning base metals into gold; hence its botanical name. It is a beautiful plant that forms a 12 in. high clump of pleated, downy, grey-green leaves, in which dewdrops are caught and gleam in the early morning sun like beads of mercury. Above the foliage, dense sprays of tiny, cool green-yellow flowers are produced from early June to August. They make gentle harmonies with other plants, and are excellent in cut-flower arrangements.

When lady's mantle is well established, its knack of sowing seeds all around itself can become too much of a good thing. The practical solution to this problem is to cut off the dead flower sprays before the plant has a chance to produce seeds and distribute them.

HOW TO GROW
Plant in autumn or spring, 18 in. apart, in ordinary garden soil, and in sun or light shade. Dead-head before the seeds form, except in semi-woodland situations. Easily propagated by seeds in spring (it self sows freely), or by division during the dormant season – October to March.

Lady's mantle spills over paving, at the foot of a mixed planting of roses and *Centranthus ruber* 'Albus'.

Anchusa azurea 'Loddon Royalist'

This anchusa, sometimes called *Anchusa italica*, is a spectacular plant. Growing to a height of 3-5 ft, it carries clusters of flowers of a deep, pure blue without a hint of mauve. They are rather like large forget-me-nots and bloom all through July. As in most members of the borage family, the foliage is coarse and hairy; and the leaves at the base look gross unless partly covered. Care is needed; the plant will topple over unless supported. It is also best to replace it every three or four years.

The fine blue of 'Loddon Royalist' is shown to best effect by a foil of pale yellow, which might be provided by a tall backing of the golden privet *Ligustrum ovalifolium* 'Aureum'. This shrub also lends sunshine to the garden in winter.

A second associate, making a bold clash against the quiet pastel shades, could be a group of mixed sweet williams (*Dianthus barbatus*), with their deep reds, pinks and whites. They will also help to hide some of the lower foliage of the anchusa.

Finally, a grey-leaved plant is needed to set off the whole association, and nothing could be better for this than lady's mantle, *Alchemilla mollis*. This should skirt the group, with a few plants infiltrating among the sweet williams, so that its froth of green-yellow flowers can echo the bold yellow of the golden privet.

HOW TO GROW
Anchusa azurea: plant from autumn to spring, in fertile, well-drained soil – heavy clays need the addition of sand, leaf-mould or peat. Plant 1½-2 ft apart, in full sun or very light shade. Support stems with strong twiggy sticks. Cut stems back by half after flowering, and to the ground in autumn.
Propagate by root cuttings in late winter.
Alchemilla mollis: see p. 66.
Dianthus barbatus: see p. 26.
Ligustrum ovalifolium: see p. 292.

In July, a mass of golden privet *Ligustrum ovalifolium* 'Aureum' adds substance to a pairing of the clear blue *Anchusa azurea* 'Loddon Royalist' with bright *Dianthus barbatus*. In the foreground blooms a froth of *Alchemilla mollis*.

Anaphalis cinnamomea

Like all *Anaphalis* species, this native of the Himalayan foothills is remembered for its everlasting blooms, which are admirable both as cut flowers and in dried-flower arrangements. Papery white, each with a yellow eye, they are carried in heads at the top of 2 ft tall stems from July to autumn.

The grey-green leaves of *Anaphalis cinnamomea* (syn. *A. yedoensis*) have a white, felted underside until autumn, when they turn a soft straw colour. *A. triplinervis* is similar but half the height.

HOW TO GROW
Plant between autumn and spring, 12 in. apart, in any kind of well-drained soil. The plant does best in full sun or light shade. Remove dead leaves and stems in late autumn. Propagate by division during autumn or spring.

Anaphalis triplinervis grows to a height of only 12 in. In front, *Colchicum speciosum* adds a splash of bold colour.

Dividing *Anaphalis cinnamomea* quickly builds up an extensive display.

Anemone × hybrida

The white to deep rose flowers of this group of anemone hybrids would make a perfect accompaniment to, say, a stand of Michaelmas daisies. They are the result of crossing two oriental anemones, the Japanese *Anemone hupehensis japonica* and the Nepalese *A. vitifolium*, and it is from this second parent that the hybrids derive their handsome, dark green, vine-like leaves.

The oldest named selections – fine 4-5 ft high plants that carry a succession of wide, saucer-shaped flowers from August to October – include the lovely white-flowered 'Honorine Jobert' and the rose-pink 'Mont Rose'. More recent introductions are smaller.

HOW TO GROW
Plant between October and March in any fertile, well-drained, but moisture-retentive soil, ideally in partial shade. Cut to ground level after flowering. Propagate by division between October and March, but leave newly planted specimens undisturbed for the first few years.

Anemone × hybrida 'September Charm' has delicately flushed blooms.

A swathe of the beautiful old form 'Honorine Jobert' fills a bed in a classically styled garden.

Anthemis cupaniana

This daisy-like perennial from Italy is one of the loveliest and most useful plants to use at the front of the border. It forms a wide mat of bright, silvery foliage, the leaves cut as delicately as those of parsley. Then, from late April onwards, for several weeks, there appears a splendid display of pure white flowers, raised on stems 6-12 in. high. A few blooms continue to emerge at odd intervals through summer.

This anthemis is a perfect companion for sun roses (*Cistus*) and lavenders – Mediterranean herbs that are its natural neighbours at home – and also looks splendid in front of irises.

It is wise to take a few cuttings of the plant in early summer as a precaution against a harsh winter.

HOW TO GROW
Plant in spring, 10-12 in. apart for edging, in any well-drained garden soil, and in full sun. Propagate by seeds sown in April, or by cuttings of young growths in summer or early autumn, overwintered in a cold frame.

The sparkling white of *Anthemis cupaniana* tumbles down a dry wall.

Anthemis cupaniana fronts the rosy blooms of *Cistus × purpureus* and the purple spikes of *Lavandula angustifolia* 'Hidcote'.

Aquilegia vulgaris
(GRANNY'S BONNET, COLUMBINE)

Like all columbines, granny's bonnet has flowers with a spur on each petal. These appear in late May and June on the strong 2 ft tall stems that have arisen from the delicately dissected and lobed foliage. The nodding flowers vary in colour – white, pink or blue – from plant to plant, all with short spurs. Unless they are removed as soon as they are dead, they shed a prodigious amount of seeds.

There are many fine hybrids created by crossing *Aquilegia vulgaris* with other species. Some of these have wide flowers with long, slender, elegantly flared spurs; the 'McKana Hybrids' are among the best. These have flowers ranging from cream through pink and crimson to blue.

HOW TO GROW
Plant from autumn to spring, 12-15 in. apart, in good, loamy soil, moist but well drained, and in sun or light shade. Dead-head after flowering to prevent seeding, since these plants rarely come true to type. Propagate by division in the dormant season, or by purchased seeds in early summer or spring.

A mass of mixed *Aquilegia vulgaris* hybrids with their long spurs growing in front of a bush of *Hydrangea petiolaris*.

The species, *Aquilegia vulgaris*, has shorter spurs than the hybrids.

Artemisia absinthium 'Lambrook Silver'

This is one of a number of exceptional garden plants selected by plantswoman Mrs Margery Fish, and named after her garden at East Lambrook Manor, Somerset. The plant is a good bushy form of our tall native herb, wormwood, which is listed in old herbals as a cure for all sorts of ailments.

'Lambrook Silver' has silky, grey, much-divided leaves and 2½ ft high branching stems which, in July and August, are aglow with very small, round, yellow flowers, looking a little like mimosa. It makes a charming foil for plants of stronger colours, especially those that are purple or bronze; and its leaves exude a pleasantly sharp aroma when crushed. Unlike other artemisias, this one does not run underground to turn up in the midst of neighbouring plants.

The plant is sometimes listed as an evergreen, but in fact it looks miserable in winter and is best cut back. Even so, the foliage remains attractive for seven or eight months of the year.

A well-planned association might place a large group of the artemisia against a 7 ft high background of the rose species *Rosa glauca*, which has blue-green, red-backed leaves that grow darker as summer advances. To give foreground scale, try the 2 ft high *Sedum maximum* 'Atropurpureum', which, with its broad, toothed, purple leaves, provides a contrast of form and colour in foliage.

This would make a quiet planting, but gardeners who wanted a splash of colour in midsummer could make the clump of artemisia smaller and add a bush of the crimson-and-white rose 'Versicolor'.

HOW TO GROW
Artemisia absinthium: plant in autumn or spring, in any type of well-drained garden soil, preferably in sun. Set plants 12-18 in. apart and cut back to near ground level in autumn or spring. Propagate in late summer by heel cuttings under glass or division in spring.
Rosa 'Versicolor': see p. 240.
Rosa glauca: see p. 244.
Sedum maximum: see p. 121.

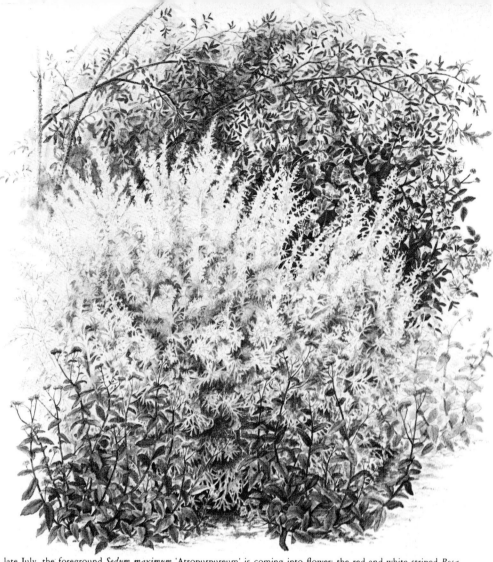

In late July, the foreground *Sedum maximum* 'Atropurpureum' is coming into flower; the red-and-white striped *Rosa gallica* 'Versicolor' is already in glorious bloom, forming the focal point of the association; the *Rosa glauca* is just forming pale hips. In the centre is a shimmering mass of *Artemisia absinthium* 'Lambrook Silver'.

Arum italicum 'Pictum'

(LORDS-AND-LADIES)

One of the joys of the English garden is that, even in the dead of the year, some plant or other always seems to be stirring. For example, this lovely form of lords-and-ladies thrusts up its 12 in. tall spears of glossy green, cream-and-grey marbled leaves in late November. Through the succeeding months they increase in beauty and make an exquisite foil for one of the dark purple forms of *Helleborus orientalis*, snowdrops and other early flowering plants, both in the garden and when added to a posy for indoors.

The flowers, in April or May, are pale yellow-green and hooded. In August, after the leaves have died down, glowing (and poisonous) red berries appear.

HOW TO GROW
Plant in autumn, in ordinary, moist soil and in dappled shade. Suitable for naturalising in grass. Propagate in early autumn by division and separating offsets.

Arum flowers consist not of petals but of a modified leaf, called a spathe, surrounding a spike, known as a spadix.

Arum italicum 'Pictum', snowdrops and *Helleborus orientalis*.

Aster × frikartii

In September, when apples are ripening and leaves beginning to turn yellow or bronze, a pastel mauve and pink group of Michaelmas daisies, anemones and nerines makes the garden look young again.

The showpiece of the group is a large planting of *Aster × frikartii*, which has the virtues denied to so many other Michaelmas daisies: despite being 3 ft tall, it does not need staking; it rarely needs dividing to prevent overcrowding; and it never suffers from powdery mildew. It is a lovely plant, its branching stalks starry with lavender-coloured, yellow-centred flowers from August to October. The best form is 'Mönch'.

The pink saucer-shaped flowers of *Anemone × hybrida*, which bloom at the same time as the Michaelmas daisies, provide a charming backcloth for them. Good named varieties include the clear pink 'September Charm' and the white 'Honorine Jobert'.

At the front of the group, you could place clumps of the 18 in. tall South African bulb *Nerine bowdenii*, which puts out clusters of pink flowers from September until late autumn. 'Fenwick's Variety', with carmine-pink blooms, is a more robust form.

The group would look even more splendid if planted in front of a bush of *Hydrangea villosa*, whose flowers turn from mauve to dusty pink.

HOW TO GROW
Aster × frikartii: plant all asters between autumn and spring, in fertile, moisture-retentive but well-drained soil, and in full sun. Space A. × frikartii 12-15 in. apart and cut flowered stems back to ground level in autumn. Propagate in the same way as A. novae-angliae.
Anemone × hybrida: see p. 67.
Hydrangea villosa: see p. 287.
Nerine bowdenii: see p. 166.

The soft pastel hues of *Aster × frikartii*, anemones, nerines and a hydrangea bring a touch of youth to mature autumn.

Aster novae-angliae (MICHAELMAS DAISY)

The very name Michaelmas daisy conjures up the early morning mists, dews and mellowness of autumn, and no garden is complete at that season without a display of the daisy's soft and varied colours.

This species, brought here from New England at the beginning of the 18th century, has 5 ft high stems so woody that, if cut and stripped of foliage in late autumn, they make good substitutes for bamboo canes as plant supports. The broad heads of pale mauve, yellow-centred flowers start in August and in a good year last for several months. A fine variety, shorter than the species, is 'Harrington's Pink'.

HOW TO GROW
Plant in the same way as Aster × frikartii. Soil should be kept moist at flowering time. Staking of tall cultivars, planted 2-2½ ft apart, is advisable. Propagate this and other asters by division in spring or autumn.

The pale mauve flowers of *Aster novae-angliae*.

Fiery autumnal colour – *Aster novi-belgii*.

Aster novi-belgii (MICHAELMAS DAISY)

This plant is now represented only by its varieties, which provide a wealth of autumn colour from September to November. The colour of their yellow-centred flowers ranges from white and pink to wine-red, purple and several shades of blue.

Old named varieties, such as the lovely tall blue 'Climax', are long-lasting plants that need no special attention. But most of the newer cultivars, such as the light blue 'Marie Ballard' and the semi-double pink 'Orlando', must be divided annually – or at least every other year – if they are to maintain their quality.

HOW TO GROW
Plant in the same way as Aster × frikartii; space tall cultivars 2 ft apart, dwarf types, 1-1½ ft. All forms of this species should ideally be divided annually or every two years, so as to retain vigour. Watering the soil in spring and summer and mulching will discourage powdery mildew.

Astilbe × arendsii

This hybrid astilbe, a descendant of several wild oriental species, has attractive, ferny foliage, from which spires of tiny, graceful, long-lasting flowers push up in late June. Like all the other members of the genus, this plant needs a permanently moist soil.

As might be expected of a plant with such a mixed origin, it is extremely variable. The leaves range from mid to very deep green and in some cases are bronze-tinted, especially when young. Some cultivars are compact and under 2 ft high; others are looser and more than 3 ft. The floral plumes may be dense or spreading.

A wide selection of cultivars is available, with colours ranging from white, through pinks to deepest crimson. Among the best are 'Bressingham Beauty', 2½-3 ft, which has rich pink flowers; 'Deutschland', 2 ft, white; 'Fanal', 2 ft, dark red; 'Federsee', 2½ ft, rose-red; 'Fire', 2 ft, intense salmon-red; 'Hyacinth', 2½-3 ft rose-pink; 'Red Sentinel', 2½ ft, brick-red; 'Rhineland', 2½ ft, pink; and 'Snowdrift', 2 ft, pure white.

The flower spikes are attractive even after the blooms have faded, turning russet and on winter mornings sparkling with dew or frost.

HOW TO GROW

Plant in autumn or spring, in fertile, moist soil. Astilbes do best in light shade and are particularly suitable for the sides of pools and streams. Elsewhere, water freely during hot dry summers and mulch well with decayed manure. Set 12-15 in. apart; divide and replant every three years in autumn, to maintain healthy, plentifully flowering plants.

Warm plumes of colour rise above a mass of *Astilbe × arendsii*.   *A. × arendsii* mingles with a yellow hemerocallis.

Astrantia major

The beautiful masterwort from Central and Eastern Europe has been grown in this country since at least the late 16th century. Sturdy 2-3 ft tall stems rise above clumps of coarsely dissected leaves, bearing exquisite miniature rosettes of flowers.

Each rosette is composed of a posy of tiny, white, pink-stalked flowers surrounded by green-and-white bracts (petal-like leaves). The charming floral display lasts through June and July and, if the flowers are removed as they fade, will continue into autumn.

Astrantia major, most widely grown of the ten known species, has given rise to some highly distinctive cultivars. Well worth growing purely for its foliage is 'Sunningdale Variegated', which has deeply lobed leaves splashed and striped with yellow. 'Shaggy' has longer white floral bracts that are less neatly – but not shaggily – disposed. Richest-coloured of all is the naturally occurring *A. m. rubra*, with plum-red bracts.

HOW TO GROW

Plant between autumn and spring, in ordinary garden soil, setting the plants 15-18 in. apart. Dappled, and even full shade suits these plants best. Propagate by division between October and March. Alternatively, sow seeds in September in trays and place in a cold frame. Prick out seedlings in the following spring then plant out in a nursery bed in June or July and grow on. Plant out the following spring.

A mass of starry *Astrantia major* crowds the border, with goat's beard (*Aruncus dioicus*) in the background.

Bergenia cordifolia

Few plants are so valuable for ground-cover as bergenias, because their slow-spreading, thick, paddle-shaped leaves are, unlike the foliage of most herbaceous plants, truly evergreen.

Bergenia cordifolia is a popular species, and deservedly so. The thick flower stems start to elongate in the dead of winter. In a mild season they often reach their full height of about 12 in. by March, when they put forth sprays of pale pink, bell-shaped blooms – a display that becomes more striking with each passing week. And if this whets your appetite for bergenias, you might try *B.* × 'Silberlicht', with its pink-white bells and broad heart-shaped leaves that sometimes turn red-bronze in autumn. Alternatively, there is 'Abendglut', 9 in. high, which has red-purple bell-shaped flowers. Another hybrid form, *B. purpurascens* × 'Admiral', has larger flowers which are fuchsia-red.

HOW TO GROW
Plant between autumn and spring, in ordinary soil, in light shade or sun, 12 in. apart. Bergenias do not object to dry soil, although growth is slower than in moist conditions. Remove faded flower stems, but otherwise leave plants undisturbed until crowding encourages division in autumn or spring.

Bergenia cordifolia and ferns edge a flight of steps in spring.

A scattering of silvery-pink spires of *Bergenia* × 'Silberlicht' rise above fleshy, heart-shaped evergreen leaves.

Campanula persicifolia
(PEACH-LEAVED BELLFLOWER)

This old-fashioned cottage-garden plant has been with us since the 16th century at least. It forms wide clumps of interlocking rosettes of narrow, leathery, evergreen leaves, from which flowering stems push up to a slender 3-4 ft. Between June and August, these are hung with clear blue, cup-shaped, nodding blooms. Cut down faded spikes to encourage fresh flowers.

HOW TO GROW
Plant in the same way as Campanula lactiflora. Propagate named cultivars by division. The species itself can also be increased by seeds sown in spring. Dead-head regularly to encourage more flowers. Rust may develop on these campanulas, and the spores overwinter on the leaves of C. persicifolia. Burn affected leaves, and spray with thiram or zineb at fortnightly intervals during the growing season.

Campanula persicifolia 'Alba' (right foreground) forms part of a white border, with paeonies, convolvulus and pinks.

The shape of its blooms gives the campanula its common name, bellflower.

Campanula lactiflora 'Pritchard's Variety'

The midsummer border can easily become too hot in colour, especially if the gardener has planted an excess of yellow and copper-coloured flowers, such as *Helenium*, *Rudbeckia* and *Heliopsis*. What is needed is a grouping such as that described here: blue, apricot and white flowers and green foliage plants which together make a welcome cloud of soft colour.

The focal plant of the association is a group of *Campanula lactiflora* 'Pritchard's Variety', a perennial that grows up to 5 ft high, with large branching heads of lavender-blue, bell-shaped flowers from June to September and light green, oval, toothed leaves. The stems are strong, and, despite their height, this campanula rarely needs staking.

The 6 ft high hybrid musk rose 'Buff Beauty', which from June bears a long succession of pale apricot, double flowers, is chosen as a background for the grouping. It is tea-scented, prolific and remarkably immune to rose diseases. Alongside the campanulas is a group of Chinese lilies, *Lilium regale*, 4-6 ft tall. In July these flaunt beautiful trumpet flowers, streaked inside with yellow and outside with wine-purple.

The campanulas and lilies are erect plants, and clumps of foliage plants at their feet will give the association variety of shape as well as cool greenery. Chosen here are lemon-scented thyme (*Thymus × citriodorus*), and the crane's-bill, *Geranium endressii*, whose old flowering stems should be clipped back to encourage new growth.

HOW TO GROW
Campanula lactiflora: plant in early autumn or late spring, in any good, well-drained soil, in full sun or light shade. Space 18 in. apart, and dead-head after flowering. Propagate by division in autumn or spring.
Geranium endressii: see p. 89.
Lilium regale: see p. 162.
Rosa 'Buff Beauty': see p. 234.
Thymus × citriodorus: see p. 219.

Campanula lactiflora 'Pritchard's Variety' bloom alongside a striking group of *Lilium regale*, with a fringe of *Thymus × citriodorus* and *Geranium endressii*. Forming a graceful background is *Rosa* 'Buff Beauty'. The time of year for this setting is July.

A bed of *Catananche caerulea* (upper right), artemisias and gaillardias.

Catananche caerulea (CUPID'S DART)

The charming Mediterranean Cupid's dart has blooms of pale purplish-blue, darkening towards the centre. Borne from June until late summer, they are at their best at the beginning of the season. But in a dull year or in shade they may hardly open at all. The flowers are carried at the top of 2 ft high, leafless, wiry stems, which rise from a basal clump of grassy, grey-green foliage.

The flowers are superb in both fresh and dried-flower arrangements; sadly, the plant lives for only three or four years, but replacements are easily raised from seeds or from root cuttings.

HOW TO GROW
Plant in autumn or spring, in any kind of soil provided it is well drained, especially in winter. Full sun is essential. Space plants 10 in. apart and cut them down to ground level in autumn. Propagate by root cuttings in late winter or by seeds in spring; named forms rarely come true.

A mixture of the cornflower-like Cupid's dart with the shorter, bright yellow *Layia elegans* will last all summer.

Centaurea dealbata 'John Coutts'

This delightful cornflower forms a broad, gradually spreading clump of grey-backed, green, dissected leaves, above which clear, rose-pink, yellow-centred flowers rise upon 18 in. high stems. The main flush of blooms appears in June; it is followed by a succession of flowers throughout summer and into autumn.

If it is used in a grouping, an excellent backdrop would be the colourful bushy shrub *Fuchsia magellanica* 'Versicolor', which in June makes a 4 ft high dome of grey, green and pink foliage to frame the rosy blooms of the centaurea. In front of the fuchsia you could place the dark green leaves of *Colchicum autumnale* and the strap-shaped foliage of *Nerine bowdenii*.

In such an association, the main display of flowers comes in September and October: the centaurea is still in flower, the fuchsia drips with purple and pink, while down below, the colchicums, whose foliage has now died away, push up their lilac cups from the bare soil. These are accompanied and succeeded by the silvery-pink, strap-petalled flowers of the nerines, on leafless stems.

Some silvery-grey bushes of the 3 ft tall wormwood *Artemisia absinthium* 'Lambrook Silver' could be planted round about to provide a cool setting for the group.

HOW TO GROW
Centaurea dealbata: plant between autumn and spring, in good, well-drained soil and in full sun. Set out at 15-18 in. intervals. The plants are vigorous growers and benefit if they are divided in the dormant season, every three years. Remove faded blooms to extend the flowering season.
Artemisia absinthium: see p. 69.
Colchicum autumnale: see p. 147.
Fuchsia magellanica: see p. 281.
Nerine bowdenii: see p. 166.

By mid-September the group is at its most colourful. The centaurea is still strongly flowering at the front, and the fuchsia, nerines and colchicums are in bloom. Artemisia adds a quieter touch of silver.

Centranthus ruber (VALERIAN)

The fierce red flowers of this valerian brighten ancient walls and cliff faces all over the south of England, from June right through summer. The plant is 2-3 ft tall and has somewhat fleshy, bright to grey-green leaves. It is easy to grow – in the wild it flourishes on what appears to be naked chalk.

Its seedlings shoot up all over the place, though usually not in sufficient numbers to be a nuisance. Some, indeed, may turn out to be attractive natural variants. Named varieties include the white 'Albus' which, with its paler green leaves, is a good plant for an early summer association.

HOW TO GROW
Plant 12-15 in. apart, in spring, in any well-drained soil – for preference, chalky soil – and in sun. Cut back to ground level in late autumn. Propagate in spring by seeds and by division of named colour forms.

A common wild plant in Britain, valerian grows happily in paving cracks.

Fiery red valerians lie smouldering between golden kniphofias and cool, lilac delphiniums.

Chrysanthemum coccineum

The cottage-garden air of this fine chrysanthemum – also known as *Pyrethrum roseum* – makes it an admirable border perennial for early summer. The species has been superseded by named varieties, all about 3 ft tall, with bright green, ferny leaves and flowers that range from white through pinks to reds.

To glorify autumn there is *Chrysanthemum rubellum*, which makes a 2 ft high dome of branches, covered in September and October with wide, open, daisy-like flowers of warm coppery-pink. Fine cultivars include the crimson 'Bressingham Red', the purple 'Royal Command' and the salmon-pink 'Evenglow'.

HOW TO GROW
Plant, about 15 in. apart, in spring. Well-drained but moisture-retentive soil is essential. It should also be nourished with plenty of organic matter dug in before planting. Support the plants with thin canes or twiggy sticks; cut them back to ground level after flowering. Propagate by cuttings of basal shoots in spring, rooted under glass, or by division of established clumps.

'Bressingham Red' is one of the hybrid varieties of *C. coccineum*. It is a single, but there are also doubles.

The single, pink flowers of *C. rubellum* have a pleasing fragrance.

Chrysanthemum maximum (SHASTA DAISY)

The Shasta daisy, *Chrysanthemum maximum*, which came to Britain from the Pyrenees in the early 19th century, is like a giant form of the ox-eye daisy that dots our meadows and lawns. It is about 3 ft tall and has dark green, toothed, lance-shaped leaves. It is happiest, and perhaps looks at its natural best, in the thin grass of orchards – but its bold white, yellow-eyed blooms will make a splendid show anywhere.

Of the many named varieties for the border, 'Wirral Supreme' is probably the best – though the old and popular 'Esther Read' is still well worth growing, especially for cut flowers. Both have double white blooms. The flowering period, starting in June, can last for about eight weeks, especially if faded blooms are removed immediately.

'Wirral Supreme' is an excellent plant for an all-white border, but it is also splendid as the cool, central foil in a range of warm yellows. In front of the chrysanthemum you might plant the 2 ft tall, bushy perennial *Coreopsis verticillata*, whose ferny, bright green foliage is smothered with brilliant yellow flowers from June to September, and white *Lamium maculatum* 'Album'.

An ideal framing for these herbaceous plants would be two or three shrubby tree lupins (*Lupinus arboreus*). These should be grown from seeds – when they will flower in their second year – to provide yellow, white and pale mauve spires that harmonise from June to August with the other flowers in the association.

As an alternative, the chrysanthemums could be used to brighten the front of a dark evergreen shrub such as holly or yew. In the foreground some mignonette (*Reseda odorata*) would both hide the bare base of the chrysanthemums and lend fragrance to the grouping.

HOW TO GROW
Chrysanthemum maximum: plant in the same way as C. coccineum (see previous page), with copious watering in prolonged dry spells in summer. Propagate by division in spring, every third year.
Coreopsis verticillata: see p. 77.
Lamium maculatum 'Album': *see p. 98.*
Lupinus arboreus: see p. 293.
Reseda odorata: see p. 53.

A mass of *Chrysanthemum maximum* smothered in single white flowers.

Yellow, green and white makes a refreshing change from the hot colours seen in August. Plant *Chrysanthemum maximum* 'Wirral Pride' and *Coreopsis verticillata*, with tree lupins behind and *Lamium maculatum* 'Album' in front.

Coreopsis verticillata

This easily grown plant, superb for the front of the border, is one of the many daisy-like perennials from the eastern United States that, in the last two centuries, have made so welcome a contribution to the English summer garden. It has vivacious yellow flowers that are carried from late June right through into autumn, above a dense, twiggy bush of wiry stems and tiny, bright green, fern-like leaves.

The coreopsis spreads enough for the gardener to give the occasional clump to a friend; but it will not take over. It looks well with white and cream-flowered plants, to cool its brilliance.

HOW TO GROW
Plant from autumn to spring, 12 in. apart, in any soil with good drainage, and in full sun. In windy sites, low twiggy supports may be necessary; cut flowered stems back to base to encourage more blooms. Propagate by division in spring; self-sown seedlings rarely appear.

Coreopsis verticillata blooms profusely even in polluted areas.

Well-established clumps of the coreopsis light up a mixed border, with roses and a sambucus behind.

Corydalis lutea

Spikes of tubular, spurred, yellow flowers and grey-green leaves as delicate as those of maidenhair fern are the outstanding feature of this perennial. Planted in the garden, it will soon colonise any available space – paving cracks, old walls, even roofs – and many of its seedlings will need to be pulled up to keep it in check.

Corydalis lutea is particularly valuable for those dank, shady sites that see hardly any direct sunlight; occasionally it can even be seen clinging to the brickwork of disused wells, dwelling among ferns.

However, though it looks charming in such spots, it needs somewhere more congenial to look at its best. What it really likes is a site which is dappled with the shade of a deciduous tree – preferably an old apple or cherry – and whose soil is fertile, well drained but never dry.

On almost every day from April to November some plants will be in flower. If, after a dry period, any plant looks limp or faded, clip it over and water it well, and soon it will spring up as fresh as ever.

HOW TO GROW
Plant in spring, 10 in. apart, in any good soil. Good drainage is vital, and light shade preferable. Clip the plants over after flowering to keep them compact and to prevent self-seeding. Propagate by seeds in spring.

The explosive pods of *Corydalis lutea* scatter seeds liberally: it crops up on old walls and other out-of-the-way sites.

Clipping last year, after flowering, has kept this plant compact.

Crambe cordifolia (GIANT SEA-KALE)

The giant sea-kale is a Caucasian relative of our native sea-kale, *Crambe maritima*. It makes a huge clump – 6 ft or more tall and wide – of dark green divided leaves from which strong flower stems push up in early summer. The tiny white flowers make a charming display.

In the herbaceous border this sea-kale needs companions approaching its own size if it is not to overcrowd them; and it is unsuitable for most small gardens because of the gap it leaves after it has died down. But in larger plots it is useful for masking any spring-flowering shrub that looks dreary in summer.

HOW TO GROW
Plant in spring, 3-4 ft apart, ideally in groups of three or five, in fertile, well-drained soil, and in sun or light shade. Plant in autumn or early spring and mulch the root area annually in late spring. Cut back to ground level in autumn. Propagate by division in spring.

The handsome deep green foliage of the giant sea-kale supports a cloud of minute white flowers in June.

Cynoglossum nervosum (HOUND'S TONGUE)

Probably the plant's common name comes from the shape and soft texture of the leaves; but by association, perhaps, it was believed to have the ability to cure the bite of a mad dog, while for a person to stand on three or four of the leaves was a sure way to prevent a dog from barking. *Cynoglossum nervosum* comes originally from the Himalayas, and is a most spectacular plant consisting of a 2 ft high dome of narrow, hairy leaves that in June and July is covered with vivid blue blooms.

To prevent heavy early summer showers breaking up the plant's compact growth, support it with twiggy sticks.

HOW TO GROW
Plant between autumn and spring, 10-12 in. apart, in ordinary to rich well-drained soil, and in full sun. Support the stems with low, twiggy sticks and cut them back to ground level in autumn. Propagate by division in early autumn, or by seeds in spring.

Hound's tongue and *Crocosmia × crocosmiiflora* make a bright display.

The intense blue flowers of hound's tongue, borne in June and July, are rather like those of a forget-me-not.

Belladonna delphiniums are elegant plants with loose spikes of flowers.

Delphinium Belladonna varieties

These delphiniums do not have the magnificence of the Large-flowered varieties, but then neither do they have their unwieldiness and their unfortunate susceptibility to wind damage. Seedlings of all shades of blue can be obtained from a single packet of seeds, and selections made from them can then be planted in the herbaceous border for permanent flowering. The plants attain a height of 3½-4½ ft. A word of warning: they are attractive to slugs and snails, so sprinkle slug pellets around the emerging shoots.

HOW TO GROW
Plant in autumn or early spring, 18 in. apart, in well-drained but moisture-retentive soil enriched with organic matter. Best in full sun and in a site sheltered from strong winds, otherwise staking with thin canes may be necessary. Propagate in the same way as Large-flowered hybrid delphiniums.

Against a background of dark greenery, a Belladonna delphinium raises aloft its delicate blue blooms in June and July.

Delphinium Large-flowered hybrids

Few plants resemble their wild ancestors so little as the Large-flowered hybrid delphiniums. Theatrical in stature, colour and sheer wealth of flower on the stalk, they are the stars of the herbaceous border in June and July. Descended partly from *Delphinium elatum*, the hybrids have large, flat flowers, often with a contrastingly coloured eye. They are available in an ever-widening colour range that extends from the old white and blues to yellow, pink, purple and even red, both single and double.

In association, they should be exploited for the maximum dramatic effect, and for this you could do no better than to plant Pacific Hybrid 'Blue Jay'. It is a 5 ft high plant whose mid-blue blooms have a large blue-and-white eye, and crowd like butterflies on the stems. Its foliage is deeply cut and elegant.

The delphiniums – which need to be staked with canes up to the base of the flower spike – can easily out-top their neighbours, which should all be traditional border plants: the 4 ft tall, white-flowered madonna lily (*Lilium candidum*), perhaps, that flowers in June and July; the meadow-rue (*Thalictrum speciosissimum*) 5-6 ft high, with fluffy yellow flowers in July and August and deeply divided, almost blue leaves; and the lavender-blue bellflower, *Campanula lactiflora*, 3-5 ft tall and in bloom during June and July.

In the foreground you might place groups of the tobacco plant *Nicotiana alata*, whose white or lime-green flowers preserve the freshness of the border in August and September and also scent the evening air.

HOW TO GROW
Delphinium: plant in the same way as the Belladonna varieties, staking where necessary. All delphiniums are fairly short-lived and should ideally be replaced every third year by young plants raised from basal cuttings or by division in spring. Discourage slugs with pellets.
Campanula lactiflora: see p. 73.
Lilium candidum: see p. 161.
Nicotiana alata: see p. 46.
Thalictrum speciosissimum: see p. 123.

The cool, towering spikes of *Delphinium* Large-flowered hybrids,

A Large-flowered delphinium hybrid rises above a background of yellow *Thalictrum speciosissimum*. Beneath are blue *Campanula lactiflora*, white *Lilium candidum* and acid yellow *Nicotiana alata* 'Lime Green'. The time of year is July.

A straggling row of modern pinks forms a lovely edging to a border filled with roses and irises.

Dianthus Modern pinks

These superb plants, ideal for the front of a border or bed, are all descended from the hybrid *Dianthus × allwoodii*. They are 10-15 in. tall, have grassy, grey-green leaves and bear a profusion of flowers in June and July and usually again during the autumn.

Fine cultivars include: 'Cherry Ripe', which is double and has cherry-pink flowers; 'Daphne', a single variety, with pale pink, crimson-eyed blooms; and 'Doris', which is double with pale salmon-pink flowers.

HOW TO GROW
Plant in autumn or spring, 10-12 in. apart, setting them shallowly in limy to neutral soil with sharp drainage. Avoid mulches and remove dead leaves round the stems where moisture might collect. Position the plants in full sun, and water them only in excessively dry spells. Propagate in the same way as old-fashioned pinks.

Dianthus Old-fashioned pinks

Few garden plants are more delightful than old-fashioned pinks, which on hot days have about them the drowsy air associated with cottage gardens of tradition. Their flowers, which rise from a hummock of grassy, grey-green leaves, are richly scented, bursting with petals and come in a range of pure, bright colours, ranging from white through pinks to deep red.

These pinks have many uses – to decorate the front of the herbaceous border, to provide edging for beds and to add variety to the rock garden. A grand association for the border might be based on a group of 'Mrs Sinkins' or 'Whiteladies' – whichever is available. Both plants have double white blooms, flower in June and are 10-15 in. high. Behind them you could plant a 3 ft tall bush of the scarlet *Rosa gallica* 'Versicolor' (syn. 'Rosa Mundi'), which also flowers in June and whose blooms are prominently streaked with white.

Then, to complete the cottage-garden picture, you could add three plants of the deep purple-blue old English lavender, *Lavandula angustifolia* 'Hidcote', each 1-2 ft high and spreading some 1½-2 ft.

If the garden is open to cold spring winds, the lavender should be on the side where it can protect the pinks. These might be balanced on the other side with the wormwood *Artemisia absinthium* 'Lambrook Silver', a 3 ft high shrub with silvery leaves.

Fill any gaps in the association with night-scented stock (*Matthiola bicornis*), a 12 in. tall annual whose dull mauve blooms fill the air with a heady fragrance on July and August evenings.

HOW TO GROW
Dianthus: plant in the same way as modern pinks. All pinks lose their vigour after a couple of growing seasons: named forms are easily increased from cuttings from non-flowering sideshoots in late summer. Root in sand.
Artemisia absinthium: see p. 69.
Lavandula angustifolia: see p. 291.
Matthiola bicornis: see p. 43.
Rosa 'Versicolor': see p. 240.

The eye-catching white *Dianthus* 'Mrs Sinkins' is a perfect balance to the handsomely striped showpiece *Rosa* 'Versicolor' in this June group. *Lavandula angustifolia* 'Hidcote' adds a toning purple, and *Artemisia absinthium* a muted silver. Between the pinks are dotted night-scented stock *Matthiola bicornis*.

Dicentra formosa

Bleeding heart (*Dicentra spectabilis*) is one of the most beautiful of spring-flowering plants, but it is sometimes short-lived and *D. formosa*, a true perennial and almost as lovely, is the better garden plant. With its deeply cut, bright green leaves, it makes attractive fern-like ground-cover. Above this foliage the 12-18 in. high flower stems bend over in May and June with the weight of dangling, deep rose-pink, heart-shaped blooms. The fine named varieties include the crimson 'Luxuriant'; the white 'Alba', which is smaller and bears pale green leaves; and 'Bountiful', whose flowers are dusky reddish-purple.

HOW TO GROW
Plant between autumn and early spring, in ordinary soil, ideally enriched with organic matter. Space 18 in. apart, in light shade and with shelter from strong winds. Divide well-established clumps every three or four years.

As well as lending charm to the border in late spring, *D. formosa* makes a decorative plant for the top of an old wall.

One of the finest varieties is the crimson-flowered 'Luxuriant'.

Dictamnus albus (BURNING BUSH)

On hot summer evenings the volatilised oil of this plant can sometimes be lit, and a brief flash of flame surrounds it. Pyrotechnics, however, are not the main reason for growing *Dictamnus albus* (also called *D. fraxinella*), for the perennial is attractive, strong, upright and long-lived. The 3 ft high stems carry lustrous, dark green, divided leaves and in June and July spikes of wide-open long-stamened white flowers. The plant has a pungent aroma reminiscent of rue; *D. a. purpureus* is an excellent form with pink, red-veined flowers.

HOW TO GROW
Plant from autumn to spring, 2 ft apart, in any kind of well-drained soil, preferably limy, and in full sun. Once they are growing strongly the plants require no attention, apart from cutting the stems back to ground level in autumn. Propagate by seeds in spring or late summer. It will be three or four years before the plants flower.

Burning bush is a strongly aromatic plant, whose volatilised oil can sometimes be ignited. It bears fragrant white flowers.

Dictamnus albus purpureus, blue crane's-bills and gold-leaved sage.

Digitalis grandiflora (FOXGLOVE)

Originally, *Digitalis* came from *digitale*, meaning a 'thimble' or 'finger-stall', a reference to the size and shape of the foxglove's flowers. *D. grandiflora* (syn. *D. ambigua*), which is closely related to the common foxglove, *D. purpurea*, is a superb foxglove that forms a clump of soft, hairy, toothed leaves. In July and August, this foliage is topped by long spikes of clear, creamy-yellow flowers that stretch to a height of 3 ft. Though happy in full sun, it looks better in shade. Try it there with a few Welsh poppies (*Meconopsis cambrica*) for company.

HOW TO GROW
Plant between autumn and spring, 18 in. apart, in any soil, including limy, that is well drained yet moist. After flowering, cut the stem back to the lowest leaves to encourage sideshoots, and take these out at ground level in autumn. Short-lived, the species needs replacing every second or third year by seed-raised plants.

Digitalis grandiflora blends its long creamy-yellow bells with the deeper yellow of an expanse of eriogonums.

Orange Welsh poppies complement a bed of foxgloves.

Doronicum plantagineum
(GREEN LEOPARD'S BANE)

The bright yellow daisies of this perennial, which begins blooming in April, bring much-needed colour to the herbaceous border at a time when it consists mainly of foliage. The plant has become naturalised in some open woodland areas of Britain.

Above its bright green, heart-shaped leaves rise 2 ft stems, each carrying three or four of the large daisy-like flowers, which last until June. Two fine old varieties are 'Excelsum' (syn. 'Harpur Crewe'), which has larger flowers, and 'Miss Mason', which is shorter and more clumpy.

HOW TO GROW
Plant from autumn to spring, 12 in. apart, in ordinary soil and in sun or light shade. Apply a spring mulch over the shallow roots. Tidy plants by removing dead foliage in the autumn. Propagate by division in the dormant season.

A splash of spring gold, *Doronicum plantagineum* 'Miss Mason' intermingles with white Lily-flowered tulips.

The cones of *Echinacea purpurea* are as decorative as its petals.

Echinacea purpurea (PURPLE CONE FLOWER)

Although this splendid perennial came to us from North America as long ago as 1799, it has never been really popular – probably because it produces few flowers for its 3-4 ft of height. However, this deficiency is offset by the fact that the blooms appear from July until September and are large, long-lasting and impressive.

Each flower consists of a hard orange-brown central cone surrounded by a ring of long, drooping petals of a lovely and unusual dusky pink. The lance-shaped leaves are rough and toothed. 'Robert Bloom' has larger, brighter pink flowers.

HOW TO GROW
Plant between autumn and spring, 18 in. apart, in ordinary fertile soil and in full sun. Reasonably moist soil is important during the growing season, but prolonged winter wetness at the roots can be fatal. Propagate by division or root cuttings in early spring.

'Robert Bloom' is a vivacious variety, with spreading purple-pink petals and more free-flowering than the parent species.

Epimedium × rubrum

The epimediums are among the most delightful of all ground-cover plants. Their foliage is ornamental and the spring flowers appear to hover above it.

Epimedium × rubrum, a hybrid 12 in. tall, starts into growth in March with tiny flower buds. These open into red, white-spurred blooms in May, when the new foliage is developing on its wiry stems. Each stem carries a spray of heart-shaped leaflets, at first deep bronze-pink, then pale green – invaluable for use in arrangements of small cut flowers. Deep green in summer, the leaves turn orange and yellow in autumn.

HOW TO GROW
Plant in autumn, 12 in. apart, in ordinary soil, ideally enriched with organic matter, and in light shade. Tidy plants, removing dead foliage, in early spring and mulch the soil with peat in late spring. Propagate by division in autumn or early spring.

Epimedium × rubrum stands out against a bronze-leaved maple behind.

In late spring the heart-shaped leaflets of the epimedium become pale green and suffused with dusky red.

Echinops ritro (GLOBE THISTLE)

This is a perfect plant to grow in front of shrub roses towards the back of a mixed border. Its generic name derives from *echinos*, the Greek for 'hedgehog' – a reference, like the British common name, to the spiky appearance of the flowers.

The large, round blooms are steely blue in bud but burst open in July and August to reveal a deep mauve. The narrow, jagged leaves, that grow all the way up the 4 ft tall stalks, are green above, grey and downy beneath. Both this plant and the white-flowered form 'Albus' will, if cut before the flowers are fully open, make a fine addition to dried-flower arrangements.

In the garden, however, a large group of three mature *Echinops ritro* – measuring altogether about 6 ft across – might be planted to good effect in front of two intermingling bushes of the hybrid musk rose 'Penelope'; the roses are 6 ft high and, together, 12 ft across. 'Penelope' produces clusters of large, double, heavily scented pink to white flowers, from mid-July to the end of summer.

A strong colour contrast to both the pink and the blue might be provided by a group of the magenta-flowered campion *Lychnis coronaria* (syn. *Agrostemma coronaria*) at the front of the border. The flat, single flowers are carried from July to September on 2 ft high branching stems, above woolly, silvery-grey foliage.

HOW TO GROW
Echinops ritro: plant from autumn to spring, 2 ft apart, in any kind of deep, well-drained soil and in sun; the plant is drought-resistant. Cut the woody stems back to ground level in autumn. Propagate by division or root cuttings in the dormant season.
Lychnis coronaria: see p. 103.
Rosa 'Penelope': see p. 237.

In the planting above, *Echinops ritro* 'Veitch's Blue' contrasts with pale *Campanula lactiflora*. In the August group pictured on the left, the hybrid musk rose 'Penelope' is past its first magnificent display of blooms but still shows a mass of flowers. The colour of *Echinops ritro* is splendid against the pinkish rose, and *Lychnis coronaria* adds a splash of vivid magenta to the association.

In a summer garden the lilac, golden-centred daisies of *Erigeron speciosus* are backed by roses and *Senecio maritimus*.

Erigeron speciosus (FLEABANE)

From June to August this fleabane from the western United States fully lives up to its name *speciosus*, which means 'showy'. Its neat, 2 ft high dome of leafy stems is covered with a splendid, warm summer mass of pale lilac, yellow-centred, daisy-like flowers.

There are several good cultivars in different colours, just as easy to grow as the species but needing a little support with brushwood or canes to prevent them falling apart after heavy rain. 'Charity', clear pink, and 'Darkest of All', purple are both fine garden plants. So, too, are the deep pink 'Foerster's Liebling' and the lighter 'Unity'.

HOW TO GROW
Plant in spring, in ordinary, fertile soil in full sun. Space plants 12 in. apart; dead-head regularly and cut stems down to ground level in autumn. Propagate by division in spring every three years.

Eryngium × *oliverianum*

Unusual metallic-looking flowers and an acceptance of the poorest soil are the outstanding features of this hybrid perennial, as with its relative the wild sea holly, *Eryngium maritimum*. The 2 ft high stems, which are themselves an extraordinary steely blue, emerge from spiny, blue-green foliage to carry the heads of large, glinting, deep blue flowers from July to September. Each flower consists of a central cone surrounded by narrow, prickly bracts (leaf-like petals). Even in autumn, when the flowers are brown and dry, the eryngium remains interesting. An excellent foil for it, at all seasons, is a grey-leaved plant, such as the evergreen shrub *Senecio* 'Sunshine'.

HOW TO GROW
Plant between autumn and spring, 18 in. apart, in ordinary well-drained soil. Best in full sun. Staking is rarely necessary, but cut flowered stems down to ground level in late winter. Propagate in the same way as Eryngium variifolium.

The bold, jagged flower heads and stout stems of *Eryngium* × *oliverianum* give it a striking sculptural appearance.

Metallic eryngium forges a silver link here with *Senecio* 'Sunshine'.

Eryngium variifolium

This Moroccan sea holly is markedly different from *Eryngium* × *oliverianum*. It is an evergreen that develops an attractive 12 in. wide rosette of lustrous, dark green, spiny leaves with conspicuous white veins. From this rosette – which builds up into a hummock as the season progresses – rise stiff, wind-proof, 2 ft high stems that in July and August carry heads of metallic-blue flowers, each of which is surrounded by spiny white bracts (petal-like leaves). These spiky flowers can be dried for winter decoration. *E. variifolium* is best used in the border as a companion for dwarf bulbs and Mediterranean plants, both of which, like itself, need full sun and a dry soil.

HOW TO GROW
Plant in the same way as Eryngium × oliverianum, and space 12-15 in. apart. Propagate both species by root cuttings in late winter or by seeds in spring. Both are tightly clump-forming and division is seldom required; though possible in spring.

By late summer Moroccan sea holly has built up into a profusion of spiky, metallic-looking flowers.

Eupatorium purpureum

This North American hemp agrimony is one of the largest of herbaceous plants – 6-7 ft high and 3-4 ft across – and, except in the biggest gardens, it is best omitted from the border and grown with shrubs.

The purplish stems, which carry whorls of slender, pointed leaves, attain their full height in August, when the heads of buds at the tips open into small pink-purple flowers that last into October. The plant is most effective in a position where a low autumn sun will set its blooms aglow.

HOW TO GROW
Plant from autumn to spring, 3 ft apart, in any good garden soil that is well drained but moisture-retentive. The shallow-rooted plants benefit from a peat mulch to conserve summer moisture. In late autumn, cut back to near ground level. Divide every third year between October and March.

The flowering stems of *E. purpureum* reach head-high in summer and need plenty of space in which to develop.

E. purpureum and a blue *Hydrangea macrophylla* make a fine pair.

Euphorbia griffithii 'Fireglow'

Euphorbias are supposedly named after Euphorbus, court physician in the 1st century AD to Juba II, the Romanised king of the North African kingdom of Mauretania. There are a great many of them – about 2,000 species – with an enormous diversity of form, ranging from annual and perennial herbaceous plants to shrubs, trees and succulents. They are found growing wild in most of the temperate to subtropical regions of the world. All, when cut or damaged, exude a milky latex that can irritate the skin and eyes.

The Himalayan *Euphorbia griffithii* 'Fireglow' comes into its own in British gardens in late May, when it puts forth round heads of brilliant orange bracts (petal-like leaves) on 2½ ft high stems.

A very pleasant grouping would be to grow three or four of the plants behind an equal number of the shorter and bushier *E. polychroma*, which has yellow bracts and greyish-green foliage. It starts to flower before 'Fireglow', and a little later will combine with it to create a most unusual oranges-and-lemons effect.

At the foot of the euphorbias, and giving a dash of cool colour, could be a ribbon of poached-egg flower (*Limnanthes douglasii*), a 6 in. high hardy annual whose common name does it less than justice. It has lovely, fragrant, primrose-like flowers of white-bordered deep yellow, and its leaves, deeply cut and of a lustrous fresh green, are almost as decorative. It blooms from June to August in the first year, a month earlier in subsequent years if it is allowed to self-seed.

HOW TO GROW
Euphorbia griffithii 'Fireglow': *plant between autumn and spring, setting the plants 18 in. apart each way, in ordinary garden soil and in full sun or light shade. Propagate in the same way as* E. polychroma.
Euphorbia polychroma: see p. 86.
Limnanthes douglasii: see p. 38.

Two euphorbias combine to make a brilliant glow in the spring border. *Euphorbia griffithii* 'Fireglow' flaunts its fiery orange bracts, which are petal-like leaves; beneath it *E. polychroma* has burst into bright yellow. Lending a coolness to the association is *Limnanthes douglasii*.

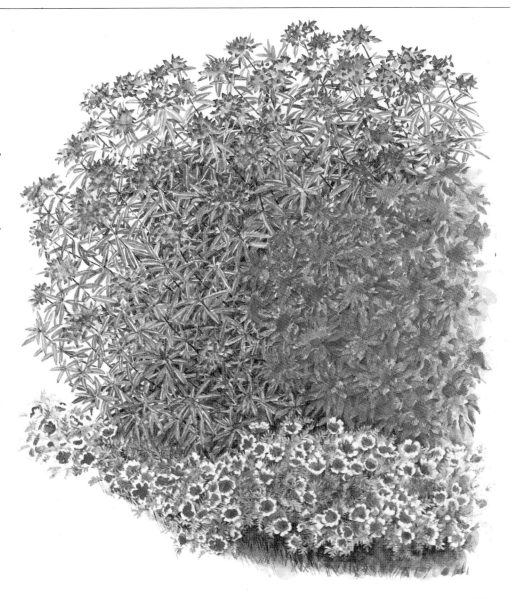

Euphorbia characias

In spring the usually arid Mediterranean hillsides come to life in places with the greenish-yellow flowers and grey-blue leaves of various shrubby species of *Euphorbia*.

The evergreen *Euphorbia characias* forms a clump of leafy shoots 4 ft high. In March the flowering stems produce long heads of tiny, brown-eyed yellow blooms which last until July. When the stems have died, cut them out to allow new leafy growth to develop. A companion, or an alternative, might be *E.c.wulfenii* (syn. *E. veneta*) 'Lambrook Gold', whose flowering spikes are a deeper, clearer yellow and lack the brown eyes.

HOW TO GROW
Plant in autumn or spring, 2½-3 ft apart, in ordinary, well-drained soil, including thin, chalky ones, and in full sun. Both species may prove half-hardy in cold areas and need the shelter of a wall or fence. Cut flowered shoots out at the base. Propagate in the same way as Euphorbia polychroma.

The great club-like yellow panicles of *Euphorbia characias wulfenii* 'Lambrook Gold' have an almost primeval look.

Euphorbia polychroma is free-flowering, long-lived and very reliable.

Euphorbia polychroma

This small, round, bushy perennial, also known as *Euphorbia epithymoides*, was introduced to Britain from Eastern Europe in 1805. It makes a regular 18 in. high hummock of narrow, pale green leaves, topped between March and May with heads of bright yellow bracts (petal-like leaves) tinged with green.

E. polychroma – like our own woodspurge, *E. amygdaloides*, also a fine garden plant – is happy in sun or shade, but more compact in the former, where the foliage often takes on colourful autumn tints.

HOW TO GROW
Plant in the same way as Euphorbia characias, spacing the plants 1½-2 ft apart. Most euphorbias are best propagated by seeds sown in spring, under glass, and set out later as young pot-grown plants as they resent root disturbance. Propagate also by cuttings of basal shoots in spring.

With each passing year the euphorbia produces more and more of its 3 in. wide heads of brightly coloured bracts.

The foaming white flower heads of *Filipendula ulmaria*.

Filipendula vulgaris 'Flore Pleno'
(DROPWORT)

Filipendula vulgaris (syn. *F. hexapetala*), a charming wild flower of chalky grassland and limestone hills, is represented in gardens by the double-flowered variety 'Flore Pleno', which blooms more freely and for a longer period – from mid to late summer. The flowers, a lovely creamy-white froth, are borne at the top of stems 2-2½ ft high.

This filipendula looks well grown with various other plants that share its liking for lime: *Cistus*, *Helianthemum*, and dwarf spring bulbs. Similar but larger is *F. ulmaria*, the meadow sweet. This is a moisture-lover, which makes a fine addition to a poolside planting scheme.

HOW TO GROW
Plant between autumn and spring, 12-18 in. apart, in limy soil that is well drained but moisture-retentive and in full sun or very light shade. Support with twiggy sticks and cut down in autumn. Propagate by division in spring.

'Flore Pleno's' delightful double blooms make an attractive foil for small, bright flowers such as those of *Cistus crispus*.

Foeniculum vulgare 'Purpureum'
(COMMON FENNEL)

Common fennel is the most decorative of all the culinary herbs, as much at home in the flower border as in the herb garden. It makes a feathery, 4-6 ft high bush of shiny, branching stems and green, threadlike, aromatic foliage (bronze in the form 'Purpureum'). The heads of tiny yellow flowers borne in July and August look like umbrellas blown inside out.

The seeds are used in pickling gherkins and in bread and cakes, while the stalks, the most intensely flavoured part, give savour to all kinds of fish dishes and can be shredded raw into salads.

The plant seeds itself freely. If the seedlings are wanted, either for other parts of the garden or to replace ageing parent plants, they must be transplanted when small, before their tap-roots have gone deep.

In a border association, 'Purpureum' would make a superb background for the 3 ft tall Hybrid tea rose 'Madame Butterfly', with perhaps a group of the 2½ ft high hardy annual mallow *Lavatera trimestris* 'Mont Blanc' added. The rose gleams palely with delicate pink-and-white blooms from August until the first frosts, and the mallow, a bushy plant, is covered with white, widely funnel-shaped flowers from July until the rose withers.

To melt into the mallow, you might add a pool of annual bedding dahlias, *Dahlia variabilis*, of the 'Redskin' strain, 15 in. high, with scarlet semi-double blooms and deep bronze leaves – a rich swirl of colour for the front of the border.

HOW TO GROW
Foeniculum vulgare: plant in spring or autumn, 18 in. apart, in ordinary, well-drained soil and in full sun. Remove flower heads unless seedlings – or seeds for culinary use – are wanted. Cut all stems back in autumn or winter. Propagate by division in spring, or by seeds, under glass or outdoors in spring.
Dahlia variabilis 'Redskin': see p. 25.
Lavatera trimestris: see p. 38.
Rosa 'Madame Butterfly': see p. 228.

Foeniculum vulgare 'Purpureum' at the back, with *Lavatera trimestris* 'Mont Blanc', *Dahlia variabilis* 'Redskin' and *Rosa* 'Madame Butterfly' as seen in August.

Gaillardia aristata (BLANKET FLOWER)

Fiery-brilliant flower colour is the glory of the genus *Gaillardia*. In *Gaillardia aristata* (syn. *G. grandiflora*) the 3 in. wide daisy-like blooms are bright yellow and purple-red and heavy enough to make the 2 ft tall, almost leafless stems bow beneath their weight. The base is an attractive cushion of soft, grey-green foliage.

This gaillardia is a parent of many vividly hued cultivars with names such as 'Dazzler' (orange-yellow and maroon) and the dwarf 'Goblin' (14 in. tall) (deep red and gold). These make superb cut flowers. Provided specific colour is of no concern, plants can be renewed regularly from seeds.

HOW TO GROW
Plant in spring, 12 in. apart, in ordinary, well-drained soil; not recommended for heavy, wet clay. Needs full sun and low twiggy supports. Propagate named cultivars by division or root cuttings in spring; otherwise sow seeds under glass in early spring. Seedlings will usually flower the same year.

Few perennials are more dramatic than *Gaillardia aristata* hybrids, with their heavy blooms of gold with deep red hearts.

Large flowers and straight stems make gaillardias excellent for cutting.

Geranium psilostemon (CRANE'S-BILL)

Magnificently showy, *Geranium psilostemon* is one of the largest of the crane's-bills. By June it has built up a great dome of foliage, over 2½ ft high and as much across. The leaves are deeply and elegantly lobed, and in autumn, before they die down, they often turn red.

From mid-June to late July, *G. psilostemon* (also known as *G. armenum*) is a mass of flat, round flowers of brilliant magenta with a jet-black eye. Magenta is a rare and lovely colour, but one that can so easily clash with other garden hues, so great care is needed in selecting companions for it. Among the most suitable flowering partners would be Welsh poppies (*Meconopsis cambrica*). From June to September these 18 in. tall perennials put forth simple flowers of soft yellow or orange that harmonise perfectly with the magenta of the geranium.

To provide earlier colour – in February and March – it would be a good idea to plant clumps of snowdrops (*Galanthus*) and the yellow-tipped snowflakes *Leucojum vernum*; both of them will be out of sight by June. The grouping would be particularly effective beneath the 10 ft high deciduous shrub *Corylopsis willmottiae*.

In March this dangles primrose-yellow, catkin-like flowers above the snowdrops and snowflakes, and when it unfolds its bright green leaves later in spring they provide light shade for the summer flowers. Finally, in autumn, when the leaves turn yellow, they blend beautifully with the bright geranium foliage beneath.

A simpler association would be to surround the geranium with cool whites and greys, choosing plants whose flower shape and leaf form contrast with those of the geranium. Try *Anaphalis cinnamomea* and *Anthemis cupaniana*, both grey leaved and white flowered.

HOW TO GROW
Geranium psilostemon: plant in the same way as G. endressii, but with 2 ft intervals between plants. Twiggy supports may be necessary in windy sites. Propagate by division in the dormant season. Plants can also be raised from seeds sown in spring.
Anaphalis cinnamomea: see p. 67.
Anthemis cupaniana: see p. 68.
Corylopsis willmottiae: see p. 268.
Galanthus: see p. 155.
Leucojum vernum: see p. 160.
Meconopsis cambrica: see p. 104.

The yellow and orange of Welsh poppies form a warm, bright colour harmony with the magenta of *Geranium psilostemon*.

The vivid blooms of *Geranium psilostemon* are separated from the softer purplish-blue of *G. 'Johnson's Blue'* by the bold foliage of *Hosta sieboldiana*.

Geranium endressii (CRANE'S-BILL)

The name of the genus comes from the Greek *geranos*, meaning 'crane', since its seed pod is thought to resemble the beaked head of that bird; hence, too, the plant's common name of crane's-bill. *Geranium endressii*, 12-18 in. high, is a vigorous, weed-smothering plant from the Pyrenees that creates a dense layer of daintily edged pale green foliage. Above this the plant hoists pink flowers all summer, and often through autumn, too. 'Claridge Druce' is a larger, spreading hybrid, up to 18 in. tall, with darker green foliage and large magenta-pink flowers. It makes excellent all-year-round ground-cover.

HOW TO GROW
Plant from autumn to spring, 18 in. apart, in any well-drained garden soil, in sun or light shade. Remove faded flower stems, but leave clumps to spread undisturbed. Propagate in the same way as Geranium psilostemon.

Geranium endressii is valuable for its long flowering season, which lasts from May to October or November.

The geranium is also useful for providing ground-cover in dry conditions.

Sweeping stems of vivid blue flowers make the gentian a lovely plant.

Willow gentian is so named because its leaves resemble those of willows. The flowers are 1-1½ in. long.

Gentiana asclepiadea (WILLOW GENTIAN)

The blue flowers of many species of gentian have an intensity of colouring not found in other plants. The trumpet blooms of the willow gentian, in July and August, are of a particularly ravishing blue, which is sometimes heightened by a white throat.

When growing in ideal conditions, the plant makes a graceful fountain of arching stems up to 3 ft tall. The pairs of narrow leaves remain horizontal whatever the angle of the stem. Seedlings produce flowers that vary considerably in colour from the parents' blue, and some never quite match it.

HOW TO GROW
Plant between autumn and spring, 12-15 in. apart in ordinary, moist, loamy and acid soil and in full or partial shade. Propagate by seeds in autumn or spring, in a cold frame. Plants can also be increased by division in early spring, or from basal cuttings later.

Gunnera manicata has the largest leaves of any plant hardy in Britain.

In May, when the gunnera's young leaves are only just unfolding, the unusual flower cones, later hidden, can be seen clearly.

Gunnera manicata

Looking like enormous rhubarb, *Gunnera manicata*, which grows to a height of 5-8 ft, makes a dramatic focal point in any garden spacious enough to take it. In April, great corrugated, dark green leaves, the size of golf umbrellas, push up on thick, prickly stems from furry crowns. The tiny spring flowers, which turn from green to brown, are massed in large cones. However, they hide beneath the foliage and add nothing to the plant's visual effect.

G. manicata is often grown by the side of water: it likes the moisture, and its effect is heightened by reflection. In cold areas, protect the leaf crowns in winter with the gunnera's own dead foliage.

HOW TO GROW
Plant in late spring, in rich, moist soil. Site in sun or partial shade, with shelter against prevailing winds. In autumn, cover the crowns with a protective winter mulch. Propagate by division in spring or by seeds sown under glass when ripe.

The background plant in this summer group is *Helleborus foetidus*, which continues to provide a mass of attractive foliage behind the brilliant orange *Geum × borisii* and the glowing yellow *Oenothera missouriensis* when its own flowers are over.

Geum × borisii (AVENS)

The saucer-shaped blooms of this perennial, which flowers off and on from June to September, are a pure bright orange. Some gardeners are wary of this colour and do not use it at all. Others use it only with cool white alongside, while some make use of it quite indiscriminately – for example, growing harsh orange marigolds as an edging for beds of pink roses.

A superb judge of colour in plant associations was Gertrude Jekyll (1843-1932), whose 200 ft long herbaceous border in her garden at Munstead Wood, Surrey, became celebrated among plant lovers. The centrepiece of that border was a blaze of orange lilies, red hot pokers and other fiery plants. These were approached from both ends of the border by flowers that became increasingly warmer and stronger in colour towards the middle – a sort of pyramid of brilliant hues.

Geum × borisii, which creates useful ground-cover with its rosettes of beautiful, crinkly, evergreen leaves, is not a large plant – only 12 in. high and with flowers 1 in. across – but the intensity of its colour is such that it needs placing with care. Perhaps it is best to follow Miss Jekyll's example by siting a group of it alongside a planting of the bright yellow, dwarf evening primroses *Oenothera missouriensis*, which bloom from June to August.

In the background you could place a group of stinking hellebore (*Helleborus foetidus*), a 2 ft tall evergreen perennial whose greenish-yellow flowers are finished by June. It is grown here for its dark green, deeply cut, elegant foliage, which sets off the orange and yellow to perfection.

HOW TO GROW
Geum × borisii: plant between autumn and spring, 12 in. apart, in ordinary fertile soil, either in sun or in dappled shade. Remove faded flower stems. Propagate by division in spring; it is, at any rate, a good thing to lift and divide plants every second or third year to ensure that they maintain vigorous growth.
Helleborus foetidus: see p. 92.
Oenothera missouriensis: see p. 107.

Gypsophila paniculata

No other plant creates such an airy cloud of bloom as *Gypsophila paniculata*. It forms a bushy mass of grey-green leaves about 3 ft high and more across, which is covered with tiny white flowers from June to August. It combines well with pinks (*Dianthus*) and also helps to hide their declining foliage. When the flowers are over, the plant turns a soft brown, later to take on a new and icy beauty with the first hoar frosts.

The variety 'Bristol Fairy' has double flowers and seems to be a brighter white. 'Flamingo' and 'Rosy Veil' have double pink blooms.

HOW TO GROW
Plant in spring or autumn, 2 ft apart, in well-drained, preferably limy soil, and in full sun. Cut down to ground level in autumn (in late spring in cold areas). Propagate by basal cuttings in late spring, by stem cuttings in summer or by seeds in spring.

The vigorous, reliable, free-flowering 'Flamingo' is the finest of the double pink cultivars of *Gypsophila paniculata*.

A bush of *G. paniculata* resembles the Milky Way fallen to Earth.

Helenium autumnale

This robust, bold-flowered, 5 ft high perennial can look rather coarse when grown in isolation, but with the right companions it makes a striking border plant. From August to October, above its mass of lance-shaped leaves, it carries branching heads of daisy-like flowers. These are yellow with prominent, satiny-brown centres. It looks best when grown with white flowers and variegated foliage.

Among the finest of the hybrid cultivars are: 'Butterpat', rich yellow; 'Bruno', cinnamon; 'July Sun', golden-orange; and 'Wyndley', brownish-red and gold. All these varieties are 2-3 ft high.

HOW TO GROW
Plant between autumn and spring, 18 in. apart, in ordinary, fertile garden soil in full sun or light shade. Provide twiggy supports on windy sites. Cut to ground level in late autumn. Propagate by division while dormant.

Helenium autumnale makes a splash of gold in a mixed border.

A glowing, bronze-red cultivar of *Helenium autumnale* is overhung by yellow *Heliopsis* and flanked by *Crocosmia*.

Helianthus × multiflorus (SUNFLOWER)

Perennial sunflowers such as this do not produce the dramatic cartwheel blooms of the giant annual species, but their flowers are of an equally brilliant yellow. Those of *Helianthus × multiflorus* crown its 5 ft high bush of broad, sharply toothed leaves from late July to September. This sunflower is too bright to consort with more delicately coloured herbaceous plants; probably it looks best grown against the greenery of shrubs that have finished flowering, especially those with white-variegated foliage. In such company, no staking is required. If stems do flop, they still send up vertical, flowering shoots.

HOW TO GROW
Plant between autumn and spring, 1½ - 2 ft apart, in any well-drained garden soil and in full sun. On windy sites, staking is useful for keeping plants tidy. Cut down in autumn. The plants can spread rapidly and should be divided every two or three years when dormant.

The brilliant semi-double, golden-yellow flowers of *Helianthus × multiflorus* 'Loddon Gold' blaze out in late summer.

Some forms of *Helianthus × multiflorus* have more petals than others.

Helleborus foetidus (STINKING HELLEBORE)

The stinking hellebore, whose close-up smell is actually no more than mildly unpleasant, is well worth growing both for its handsome evergreen foliage and for its early spring flowers. It is one of the more unusual of our native plants. It looks just like a shrub, though in fact it is a hardy herbaceous perennial with a growth habit the same as *Helleborus lividus corsicus*.

The plant, which is 2 ft tall, bears rich, dark green leaves that are so deeply cut as to appear finger-like. The flowers, appearing from March to May, form sprays of wide-open bells, pale greenish-yellow and tipped with purple. The plant produces a host of self-sown seedlings.

HOW TO GROW
Plant in the same way as Helleborus lividus corsicus. Both species increase from self-sown seedlings. Transplant these to permanent quarters while still small.

The green flowers of *H. foetidus* are actually sepals, not petals.

Stinking hellebore and the lungwort *Pulmonaria saccharata* join together to make a fine spring association.

Helleborus lividus corsicus

(CORSICAN HELLEBORE)

The evergreen perennial Corsican hellebore, known as *Helleborus argutifolius* and before that simply as *H. corsicus*, is one of the gems of the border.

The habit of the plant is distinctive. In spring, stout stems arise from its centre, carrying dark, greyish-green, leathery leaves, each divided into three saw-edged leaflets. By the end of the year the stems have each developed a great pointed bud. From this emerges a spreading head of flowers, which open in succession in March and April – but sometimes, in mild winters, as early as December and as late as May. Each flower is like a large, lime-green buttercup, composed of sepals that remain while the flowers are developing their seed pods in spring.

Here is a rare chance for a winter association of evergreen plants. Make hellebore the centrepiece, and frame it with the 9 ft high shrub *Mahonia japonica*, which produces fragrant lemon flowers from October or November to March, and flank it with clumps of the 2 ft tall, pale purple-flowered stinking iris (*Iris foetidissima*), whose glossy swords of foliage contrast effectively with that of the hellebore.

In front of this grouping the small-leaved variegated ivy *Hedera helix* 'Glacier' would make attractive ground-cover and a fine launching pad for snowdrops (*Galanthus nivalis*) and *Iris reticulata*.

HOW TO GROW
Helleborus lividus corsicus: plant in autumn, 2 ft apart, in ordinary, fertile garden soil. Partial shade is best. Disturb established plants as little as possible, but cut off faded flower stems and old leaves in summer. Propagation: see H. foetidus.
Galanthus nivalis: see p. 155.
Hedera helix: see p. 183.
Iris foetidissima: see p. 96.
Iris reticulata: see p. 158.
Mahonia japonica: see p. 295.

A winter association of evergreens is centred on *H. l. corsicus* with *Mahonia japonica* behind. In leaf in front are *Iris foetidissima* and *Hedera helix* 'Glacier', with snowdrops and *Iris reticulata* in flower.

Helleborus orientalis (LENTEN ROSE)

The first flowers of the lovely winter-blooming lenten rose open in February and the display continues until late March: wide, nodding cups of cream, but sometimes of white, dusky pink or plum-purple, and each darkly speckled inside. All are of hybrid origin between several species, but go under the main parents' name for convenience.

Swathes of this 18 in. high plant are the best possible underplanting for deciduous shrubs. They flower when the shrubs are still bare, and their dark green, leathery leaves suppress weeds better than any hoe.

HOW TO GROW
Plant in the same way as Helleborus lividus corsicus, with plants spaced 18 in. apart. Established clumps can be divided in autumn, but new plants are better raised from seeds sown in a cold frame when ripe or in early autumn; they usually flower after two or three years.

One of the dark purple forms of the lenten rose shows to perfection the delicate petals and exquisite beauty of this perennial.

A group of *Helleborus orientalis* with pink primroses planted in front.

Yellow *Hemerocallis flava* rises above *Geranium* 'Johnson's Blue', with bearded irises in the background.

Hemerocallis flava (DAY LILY)

The flowers of day lilies – as the genus *Hemerocallis* is popularly known – each last for only one day. But the shortness of their life is compensated for by the freshness of each new daily crop.

Hemerocallis flava is a robust, spreading day lily, 1½-2 ft high, that bears clear yellow, richly scented blooms on bare stems from late May to early July. Another fine day lily is *H. fulva*, whose 3 ft high clumps are crowned with orange-brown flowers in June and July.

HOW TO GROW
Plant between autumn and spring, 18 in. apart, more for large-growing cultivars, less for miniatures. All thrive in ordinary garden soil, ideally with plenty of organic matter added at planting time, and sun or light shade. After flowering, remove faded stems. Leave established clumps undisturbed until they become overcrowded. Then divide during dormancy.

Heuchera sanguinea (CORAL FLOWER)

This coral flower from Mexico and Arizona forms dense hummocks of toothed, somewhat rounded, dark evergreen leaves that make excellent ground-cover, and its brilliant crimson candles of tiny flowers decorate the plant from June right through to September.

Crossed with the more robust but even smaller-flowered *Heuchera micrantha*, and perhaps *H. americana*, the coral flower has produced a host of lovely cultivars with equally attractive names. Examples are 'Pearl Drops', almost white; 'Firebird', deep red; and 'Scintillation', with bright pink, coral-tipped bells.

HOW TO GROW
Plant between autumn and spring, 12 in. apart, in ordinary garden soil, ideally enriched with organic matter, and in full sun or dappled shade. Remove flowering stems as they fade or in autumn. Propagate by division in the dormant season or by seeds in spring.

In most forms of *Heuchera sanguinea*, pale marbling on the foliage adds interest and makes a cool foil for the flowers.

Coral flowers and *Rosa* 'Buff Beauty' make a splendid association.

Hosta crispula (PLANTAIN LILY)

For sheer luxuriance of foliage, it is hard to beat plantain lilies, as hostas are often known. Their leaves are magnificent not only in the garden but also in flower arrangements.

Hosta crispula, from Japan, is one of the finest species, forming a dense mass of elongated, heart-shaped, boldly ribbed leaves, dark green and with a broad, wavy margin of white. From this foliage rise 2 ft high flower stems, topped in late summer with spikes of nodding, trumpet-shaped blooms of pale mauve.

The wavy nature of the pointed leaves gives them an elegance and lightness that is missing from the more massive and flatter leaves of *H. fortunei* and *H. sieboldiana*. Nevertheless, the density of foliage is such that it makes an equally effective ground-cover plant. For this reason it is invaluable for mixing with the broader-leaved species when a massed planting is undertaken. It will add a sprightly note to a more solid group.

Occasionally, nurserymen and garden centres confuse this plant with its close relative, *H. albomarginata*. However, that species has larger leaves bearing a narrower white border which lacks a wavy edge.

HOW TO GROW
Plant from autumn to spring, 1½-2 ft apart, in any good garden soil. All hostas need plenty of moisture in the soil and do best in light shade. Set groups of three or five, as waterside plantings or as a fronting to shrub and herbaceous borders. Propagate in the same way as Hosta fortunei.

Hosta crispula, on the left, flanks *Centaurea montana*, in the foreground, with *Polygonatum × hybridum* above.

Hosta plantaginea (PLANTAIN LILY)

With its long-stemmed, glossy, bright green leaves and its snowy-white, trumpet-like flowers, this Chinese plantain lily is a distinctive and beautiful plant. It blooms in August and September, the flowers crowning the top of stems that rise from a dense mass of foliage to a height of 1½-2 ft.

Unlike other plantain lilies, which do well in semi-shade, this one needs a sunny spot. But often it is planted in the wrong place, does not flower and so fails to win the high regard it deserves. In the South of France it is commonly grown in a container, and in this country it should be tried more often as a tub plant, to enliven an unheated conservatory or terrace.

However, it could also be the centrepiece of an association whose background might be provided by the smoke tree *Cotinus coggygria* 'Royal Purple', an 8 ft high shrub with deep purple leaves. It would supply a magnificent dark contrast for the snowy-white blooms of *Hosta plantaginea*, and also for an earlier display of Jacob's ladder *(Polemonium caeruleum)*, a 2 ft tall perennial that puts out spikes of blue or white flowers from May to July.

HOW TO GROW
Hosta plantaginea: plant in the same way as H. crispula, and in sun and shelter, with copious watering during dry spells in summer and early autumn. Propagate in the same way as H. fortunei.
Cotinus coggygria: see p. 268.
Polemonium caeruleum: see p. 112.

Cotinus coggygria 'Royal Purple' perfectly sets off the heart-shaped leaves and white blooms of *Hosta plantaginea*.

Hosta sieboldiana (PLANTAIN LILY)

If *Hosta crispula* is among the most brightly decorative members of its genus, *H. sieboldiana* is unquestionably the most imposing. It is certainly the largest hosta, and well-established clumps present a massive appearance. But though large, it is by no means gross. It is, in fact, one of that small select band of hardy perennials that can be used, like a shrub or tree, as an eye-catching feature on its own.

H. sieboldiana forms rounded clumps of leaves up to 2 ft tall. Each leaf blade is 10-15 in. long, boldly veined and blue-green; in *H. s. elegans* the colouring is more intense. The pale lilac flowers are a little disappointing, being partly hidden by the leaves.

A single large clump of *H. sieboldiana* provides a striking focal point. Alternatively, a group of plants can fill a small bed in a shaded lawn. Where space allows, this hosta can be kept to scale by associating it with other massive perennials. For example, it combines most effectively with the larger sorts of *Inula*, *Filipendula*, *Rodgersia* and *Phormium*. A particularly happy partnership can be achieved with the taller bulbous plants, notably *Lilium tigrinum*. For an earlier display, the blue species of *Camassia leichtlinii* look lovely with the unfurling leaves of the hosta.

HOW TO GROW
Plant in the same way as Hosta crispula, spacing plants 2½ - 3 ft apart. It is tolerant of sun if the soil is kept moist. However, moist soil almost invariably attracts slugs which, in extreme cases, can reduce the leaves to skeletons. Slug deterrents are a must.

Hosta sieboldiana provides foreground interest beneath shrub roses, while acting as ground-cover to smother weeds.

Hosta fortunei 'Albopicta' (PLANTAIN LILY)

This plantain lily is lovely to behold from the moment it starts into growth in spring, when at ground level its lavender-sheathed shoots push forth tightly furled leaves. By May these have opened out and become clear yellow with a pale green edge. A few weeks later the yellow pales and the green darkens, until each leaf is charmingly patterned in two shades of green that take on golden tones with the first autumn frost. Above this foliage, slender spikes of lilac, bell-shaped flowers are borne aloft in July, the tops of the strong, erect stems reaching to a height of 1½-2 ft.

Like other plantain lilies, this one looks superb in front of shrubs and also makes a splendid adornment for a courtyard or half-shaded terrace.

Bulbous plants will fill the gap after the leaves fade in autumn, but they must be planted with care. Small species, such as snowdrops and crocuses, look delightful, but must be kept far enough away from each clump to avoid excessive shade later. It is better to use the taller bulbs, such as daffodils, which hold their own against the advancing hosta leaves.

HOW TO GROW
Plant in the same way as Hosta crispula, with 2 ft between plants. The variegated foliage of 'Albopicta' shows up best in a shady site. Established clumps can be left undisturbed for many years. Propagate by dividing and replanting in early spring.

By midsummer the leaves of *Hosta fortunei* 'Albopicta' have lost most of their yellow and acquired two tones of green.

The exotic-bloomed *Incarvillea delavayi* is fully hardy in Britain.

Incarvillea delavayi

The exotic beauty of this Tibetan perennial makes it one of the glories of the early summer garden. The flowers, which appear from May to July in groups of up to half a dozen at the top of fleshy, 2 ft tall stems, are large, tubular and deep pink, like expanded foxgloves.

The plant is much too grand for the border, and is best grown in a low raised bed with other choice plants – late winter bulbs to precede its flowers, irises to accompany them, and autumn crocuses to follow them.

HOW TO GROW
Plant in spring, about ·18 in. apart, in rich and well-drained soil and in full sun. Renewed growth starts in late spring and to prevent damage from cultivation in the border, mark established plants with sticks when the dead foliage is removed in autumn. Cut faded stems back to ground level in autumn. Propagate by seeds under glass.

The fleshy, many-leafleted, handsome foliage of the incarvillea develops fully only after the flowers have started to bloom.

Iris foetidissima is unique among irises in producing brilliant seeds.

Iris foetidissima

(STINKING IRIS, GLADDON OR GLADWYN IRIS)

Any plant that is evergreen and thrives in complete shade is worth most gardeners' attention. Such a one is our native stinking iris, *Iris foetidissima* – whose smell, to be fair, is only really noticeable if it is severely bruised. The plant makes a 20 in. high fan of rich, dark green foliage that reflects every gleam of light. The small, pale purple flowers that appear in June are pretty but hardly noticeable, and the iris's most spectacular moment comes in late autumn, when it hangs out its seeds of glowing, brilliant orange.

'Variegata' is a decorative white-striped form. 'Citrina' has longer, soft foliage and yellow flowers.

HOW TO GROW
Plant in autumn, 16 in. apart, in ordinary garden soil. While the species thrives in deep shade, variegated forms do better in dappled shade. Propagate by division in early autumn or spring.

Iris foetidissima's glowing green leaves are a welcome sight in winter, especially when interspersed with clumps of snowdrops.

The flowers of *Iris pallida dalmatica* are pale blue and sweetly scented.

Iris pallida dalmatica

The flowers of this bearded iris are of enchanting simplicity. Both the falls (the drooping outer petals) and the standards (erect petals) are of a pale, satiny blue, the falls being embellished with bright yellow beards. To these visual delights the blooms add the benison of an orange-blossom fragrance. Then, when the 2½ ft high stems are cut down after the May-June flowering period is over, the vertical, soft grey leaf fans grace the garden right through into autumn.

'Argenteo-variegata' has white-striped foliage and 'Aureo-variegata' is yellow striped.

HOW TO GROW
Plant in the same way as bearded irises (see opposite page), spacing the rhizomes 18 in. apart. Propagate by division of the rhizomes – replanting only the younger, outer sections – immediately after flowering, and preferably every three years in order to maintain flowering vigour.

Iris pallida dalmatica 'Argenteo-variegata' makes a dramatic fan of broad, tightly folded, white-striped leaves.

Iris Bearded hybrids

One of the great joys of the June garden is the bearded iris, and where a whole enclosed garden or large section of a garden can be devoted to the plant the effect is stupendous. All colours from white to near-black are there, creams shading through every subtlety of yellow to near-brown, pinks (just) and, of course, all the blues the spectrum offers. The brilliant, exquisitely scented flowers are carried, like medieval banners, on strong stems above the spears of foliage.

But few of us can devote a whole garden, even a whole bed, to three early summer weeks alone. Therefore, in selecting bearded irises for a plot to be shared with other plants, not only colour must be taken into account but also ease of cultivation. For general garden use, it is best to stick to the old, well-tried, favourite cultivars, such as the white-etched, blue-purple 'Dancer's Veil'; 'Party Dress', soft pink and ruffled; 'Jane Phillips', pale blue; and the bright yellow and chestnut-red 'Staten Island'. They have sturdier, shorter stems than the newest varieties (bearded irises in the border should never need staking). In addition, their flowers are slightly smaller and have drooping falls – or outer petals – so that, unlike show variety blooms, which have horizontal falls, they are less likely to snap off in the wind.

HOW TO GROW
Plant between midsummer and early autumn, setting the top of the rhizomes level with the soil surface and spacing intermediate types 12 in. apart, tall types 18 in. apart. Before planting, reduce the leaf fans by half and cut them right back in late autumn. All bearded irises thrive in ordinary soil, even in thin, chalky ones, and full sun. Propagate in the same way as Iris pallida dalmatica.

A rich blend of colour is produced by an apricot-and-cream variety of bearded iris, a pink peony and climbing roses.

Bearded irises grow beside a pond, with true water irises beyond

Kniphofia 'Maid of Orleans' (RED HOT POKER)

In recent years, nurseries have produced a range of *Kniphofia* hybrids very different from the robust red and orange red hot pokers of traditional country gardens. This breeding programme has concentrated on raising small forms in a wider colour range.

'Maid of Orleans', introduced in 1950, is one of the best of the modern hybrids. Its dense spikes of tubular flowers are of a creamy-white, to rest eyes that are wearied by the hot colours of high summer. The spikes, blooming from July to September, crown slim, 2½ ft tall stems that rise from a tuft of grassy foliage.

If you have room, it is a good idea to establish a good-sized clump of the plants and to match them with an equal number of *Sedum maximum* 'Atropurpureum', about the same height and producing purple-pink flowers at about the same time. Complete the picture with a surrounding of the lady's mantle *Alchemilla mollis*, producing 12-18 in. high clouds of yellow-green flowering heads that open from June to August.

HOW TO GROW
Kniphofia 'Maid of Orleans': *plant in autumn or spring, setting the plants 2 ft apart in deep, well-drained holes in ordinary garden soil and preferably in full sun. In cold areas, and especially for the first year or two, cover the crowns with a cloche to protect them against heavy frost and rain. Cut off faded flower stems in autumn. Propagate in the same way as* K. caulescens.
Alchemilla mollis: see p. 66.
Sedum maximum 'Atropurpureum': *see p. 121.*

Soft ivory-cream flower spikes are still appearing on *Kniphofia* 'Maid of Orleans' in September. A flourishing mass of *Sedum maximum* 'Atropurpureum' adds its warm tones of purple and pink, and *Alchemilla mollis* makes a frothy edging of pale yellow to the group.

'Beacon Silver' as ground-cover below peonies, a phormium, arum, and hostas.

Though flowering fairly briefly, in May, the plant's silver-striped leaves remain attractive right through the growing season.

Lamium maculatum (DEAD NETTLE)

Creeping between broken flagstones, infiltrating between border plants, spreading beneath shrubs, this little dead nettle is a traditional carpeting plant in old-fashioned English gardens. The soft, heart-shaped, silver-centred green leaves that corner the invasive stems make a charming display. In the variety 'Beacon Silver' the foliage is entirely silver; in 'Aureum', entirely gold. All three plants are 9 in. high.

The tubular, hooded flowers that appear in May vary in colour from plant to plant – they may be purple, white or pink. *Lamium maculatum* is useful for forming an attractive mat through which larger spring bulbs can grow, and for giving ground-cover to a neglected corner that might otherwise be taken over by weeds.

HOW TO GROW
Plant between autumn and spring, 18 in. apart, in any type of soil, reasonably well drained, and in sun or shade. After flowering, clip over the plants with hedging shears to maintain a dense covering of leaves. Propagate, if necessary, by division in autumn or spring.

Kniphofia caulescens (RED HOT POKER)

This red hot poker is as valuable for its bold all-year-round foliage as for its decorative spikes of bloom. The leaves – long, broad-based and grey – spring in tufts from the top of the very thick stems. At first the stems grow vertically, but as the kniphofia ages they lean and then fall outwards, root where they touch the soil and send up further stems. Thus a wide clump of permanent foliage is slowly built up around the original plant.

The stems are even more of a feature of this plant once they have lengthened and become prostrate. If the old leaves are pulled off carefully as they wither, a smooth, attractive surface, strongly stained the colour of amethyst, is revealed.

The flower buds, which appear in early autumn, are a soft coral-red that gradually cools to cream as the flowers mature. The plant, which grows to a height of 2 ft, makes a fine background for nerines in autumn.

Not infrequently, this species is wrongly listed by nurserymen and seedsmen as *Kniphofia northiae*. The latter is a superior foliage plant, having great grey-green leaves, 4-6 ft long and 6 in. wide at the base. They are arranged in large, imposing rosettes, though on windy sites they can get rather untidy by the end of the year. The flowers are similar to those of *K. caulescens*, but are rather less brightly coloured.

HOW TO GROW
Plant in the same way as Kniphofia 'Maid of Orleans'. All red hot pokers can be increased by division of clumps in spring, though they resent root disturbance. Seedlings take two or three years to flower and though they are unlikely to come true provide some interesting and colourful results.

The red-tipped blooms, like hot metal drawn from a furnace, reflect the plant's exotic South African origins.

Liatris spicata (BLAZING STAR)

With its thick, erect, 2 ft high stems topped with long dense spikes of flowers, this blazing star of the American prairies somewhat resembles the red hot poker (*Kniphofia*). It is admirable for lending height to the front of a border, yet does not overshade plants growing behind.

The flowers, borne in August and September, are a reddish-purple, a colour that marries well with the grey foliage of either modern or old-fashioned pinks (*Dianthus*) or with the silvery filigree leaves of artemisias.

Alternatively, being a plant with slim, vertical lines, it contrasts splendidly with broad-leaved species. It looks especially effective thrusting up behind a bold clump of *Bergenia* 'Silberlicht'. It can be grown in front of a bold-leaved evergreen shrub, such as *Mahonia aquifolium* or *Prunus lusitanica*.

Take care in winter; the plants die down completely and it is easy to damage them when cultivating.

HOW TO GROW
Plant in autumn or spring, 12 in. apart, in ordinary, well-drained soil and in full sun. Water during dry spells in summer and, as the plants disappear below ground in winter, mark their sites with a cane to avoid forking them out or damaging them during cultivation. Propagate by division in spring, at least every three or four years.

Backed here by *Artemisia absin. hium*, the brilliant blooms of *Liatris* bring a welcome warmth to the late-summer border.

Unlike other species, this liatris will thrive in damp, even boggy, soil.

Ligularia dentata 'Desdemona'

Great orange-red, dark-eyed, daisy-like flowers, 3-4 in. across, are the first things about 'Desdemona' to catch the eye. But even if they did not appear at all, the lustrous deep green leaves and stems, backed or suffused with bright purple, would by themselves be spectacular. Each plant makes a leafy dome of foliage 3-4 ft high and as much across, over which the flowers burn brightly in July and August.

The plant (also listed as *Ligularia* and *Senecio clivorum*) needs plenty of moisture as well as space, and is ideally suited to a position beside a river or pond. In such a waterside site it should be grown with plants that echo its boldness without challenging it.

One possible companion is the skunk cabbage, *Lysichiton americanus*, which in March bears highly unusual flowers, followed by striking leaves.

The royal fern (*Osmunda regalis*), whose broad, bright green fronds rise to 4 ft or more, would also provide distinctive foliage in this grouping. A second blaze of colour could be given by a mass of purple loosestrife (*Lythrum salicaria*), a perennial 2-5 ft high that is crowded from June to September with flowering steeples of bright purple-red.

HOW TO GROW
Ligularia dentata: plant between autumn and spring, 3 ft apart, in ordinary, moist to wet soil, ideally in boggy conditions or in damp woodland. Best in dappled shade, though sun is acceptable if the soil is kept moist. Cut back to near ground level in late autumn. Contain the spread, and obtain new stock, by division every three years in spring.
Lysichiton americanus: see p. 368.
Lythrum salicaria: see p. 369.
Osmunda regalis: see p. 131.

The deep orange flowers and purple-backed leaves of *Ligularia dentata* 'Desdemona' spread themselves beside a pond in summer. Beside them rises the great leaf-green foliage of the skunk cabbage, *Lysichiton americanus*. Beyond extends purple loosestrife, *Lythrum salicaria*, and in the background are tall clumps of royal fern, *Osmunda regalis*.

Limonium latifolium

(SEA LAVENDER, STATICE)

This sea lavender from southern Russia is a larger version of its familiar salt-marsh cousin *Limonium vulgare* and, like it, bears flowers that can be dried for everlasting displays. In the garden it is seen at its best in a raised bed.

L. latifolium, which is 2 ft tall, produces a rosette of dark, leathery leaves, which are maintained throughout the winter, and in August carries clouds of tiny funnel-shaped blooms of lavender-blue. If these are wanted as everlasting flowers they should be picked just before they open. Left on the plant, they make, in their sere brown state, charming additions to dried winter arrangements.

HOW TO GROW
Plant in spring, 18 in. apart, in ordinary garden soil, in full sun. Cut any remaining flower stems back to the ground in autumn. The plants resent root disturbance, and the best propagation method is by seeds sown under glass in spring.

Statice, as this plant is often called, thrives in seaside gardens.

In August *Limonium latifolium* becomes a lavender-blue cloud of bloom. Here it is accompanied by *Malva moschata* 'Alba'.

Linum narbonense (FLAX)

To see common flax (*Linum usitatissimum*) covering a field with its lovely haze of pale blue is a sadly rare sight now that its cultivation as a source of linen and linseed oil has declined. But the gardener can make his own contribution to nostalgia by growing a patch of another flax, *L. narbonense*, whose rich blue rivals even that of gentians. It makes a twiggy bush, 1-2 ft high, of narrow grey-green leaves, over which the massed silky flowers spread their deep blue glory from early June almost to the end of summer. *Linum perenne* is a lighter shade of blue.

The flax associates well with the two grey shrubs *Cistus crispus* and *Senecio maritimus*.

HOW TO GROW
Plant in autumn or spring, in any well-drained garden soil, and in full sun. Space plants 12 in. apart and trim back in late autumn. Linums are short-lived, but are easily propagated by basal cuttings or by seeds in spring, under glass.

The linum's brilliant blue flowers can be set off to perfection by a grey-leaved foliage plant, such as this *Senecio maritimus*.

Linum perenne helps to soften the edges of paths and steps.

Liriope muscari (LILY TURF)

Good ground-cover plants are always in demand, especially if, like *Liriope muscari*, they offer in addition attractive flowers. Throughout the year this plant provides 12 in. high fountains of grassy, dark, shining green foliage that gives weeds no chance to develop. Stiff, 18 in. tall stems push up from the leaves, and in September and October their top halves are tightly packed with violet bead-like flowers resembling those of grape hyacinths (*Muscari*).

The plant makes a fine association with pink nerines (*Nerine bowdenii*) and pink autumn crocuses (*Colchicum autumnale*) in front.

HOW TO GROW
Plant in spring, 12 in. apart, in ordinary garden soil and in full sun or light shade. After flowering, remove faded stems at ground level, leaving the evergreen foliage intact. Propagate by division in spring.

With flowers like a grape hyacinth and grassy foliage, this member of the lily family is also known as lily turf.

Lobelia fulgens

To any gardener who knows lobelias only as annual bedding plants with tussocks of blue flowers, it comes as a surprise that this stately, brilliant perennial (also known as *Lobelia splendens*) belongs to the same genus. In spring, rosettes of narrow, toothed leaves build up. From these rise slender 4 ft tall flowering stems whose tops develop into spikes of the most vivid red flowers imaginable. Similar to, and often confused with, *L. fulgens* is the more robust *L. cardinalis*, which may however rot during mild, wet winters.

HOW TO GROW
Plant in late spring, 12-15 in. apart, in rich, moisture-retentive soil, in a sheltered site and in sun or light shade. In autumn, cut plants back, lift the root balls carefully and plant in a well-ventilated cold frame or greenhouse for the winter. Propagate by division as new growth begins in spring, or by basal cuttings or seeds.

Scarlet *Lobelia cardinalis* 'Queen Victoria' against the leaves of *Spiraea arguta* sets the border aflame in July and August.

The glossy green leaves of *Fatsia japonica* overlook *L. cardinalis* in flower.

Lupinus (RUSSELL STRAIN)

Lupins seem as inseparable from traditional cottage gardens as old ladies in poke bonnets; yet these flamboyant popular hybrids are actually of fairly recent origin. The pioneer breeding work, crossing *Lupinus polyphyllus* with *L. arboreus*, was carried out at the end of the last century by the nurseryman James Kelway. The resultant hybrids were in their turn crossed early this century by G. R. Downer and John Harkness to bring about lupins much as we know them today. Finally, in the 1930s, George Russell raised many of these lupins from seeds and by painstaking selection from them created the superb Russell strain.

Russell lupins thrust up great, densely packed spires of bloom to an average height of 3 ft. These colourful steeples, many bicoloured, rise in May from a base of soft green, hand-shaped leaves, each consisting of many lance-shaped leaflets, and last until July.

For an association, it might be better to choose a few fine-flowering soft-hued cultivars such as the pink 'Mrs Noel Terry'; 'George Russell', which is pink paling to cream; 'Blue Jacket', deep lavender-blue and white; and 'Susan of York', whose flowers are primrose-yellow.

For contrast of shape, alongside the lupins, you could grow *Iris pallida dalmatica*, with lavender-blue blooms and grey-green sword leaves. The foreground might be occupied by the silver-blotched green foliage of the lungwort, *Pulmonaria saccharata*.

This dramatic grouping could be given a backdrop of the 6-8 ft high plume poppy *Macleaya cordata*, which carries long soft sprays of white flowers all summer, and has grey leaves with a white underside.

HOW TO GROW

Lupinus: plant between autumn and spring, in sun or dappled shade, 18 in. apart, in ordinary garden soil, ideally neutral to slightly acid. Remove flower spikes as soon as they fade, to prevent self-seeding and to encourage a second show. Propagate by seeds in spring, but for true colours take basal cuttings.
Iris pallida dalmatica: see p. 96.
Macleaya cordata: see p. 104.
Pulmonaria saccharata: see p. 116.

Russell lupins – the very spirit of sunny, lazy days in early summer.

A blend of blues and purples and an interesting variety of leaf and flower shapes are here provided by *Lupinus* Russell hybrids with *Macleaya microcarpa* behind, *Iris pallida dalmatica* to the left, and *Pulmonaria saccharata* in the foreground. This association is pictured in June.

Lychnis chalcedonica
(MALTESE CROSS, CAMPION)

This is surely the finest of all the truly perennial campions and deserves to be grown more often. It forms sturdy clumps, each year sending up a sheaf of knotted, 3-4 ft tall stems. These are clad with rough-textured, bright green leaves and topped by scarlet flowers.

The arrangement of the flowers and their colour creates a plant of distinction. Individual blooms are comparatively small, but worth examining in detail. Each petal tip is boldly notched and, although there are five instead of four, the overall effect is that of a Jerusalem or Maltese cross.

HOW TO GROW
Plant from autumn to spring, 10-12 in. apart, in ordinary, fertile garden soil, in sun. Dead-head unless seeds are required and cut plants back to ground level in late autumn. This species is easily raised from seeds sown under glass in spring or by division at the same time.

The scarlet blooms of Maltese cross form bold splashes of colour above a mass of rough-textured, bright green leaves.

A snow-white mock orange lends added brilliance to the vivid flowers.

Lychnis coronaria (CAMPION)

The flower of this campion from southern Europe (it is also known as *Agrostemma coronaria*) is of a bright purplish-red, a difficult colour with which to harmonise. Yet, with perfect good taste and colour sense, the plant sports this brightness in a setting of suede-soft, silvery-grey leaves and stems. Good associates for the campion, when it flowers from June to September, are *Rosmarinus officinalis* and old-fashioned pinks (*Dianthus*).

A white-flowered form, 'Alba', is, with its white-felted leaves, the palest of plants.

HOW TO GROW
Plant and propagate by seeds in the same way as Lychnis chalcedonica. Self-sown seedlings frequently appear in the border; these can be replanted if desired. Dead-head unless seeds are required. The plants are short-lived and do not divide easily.

Eye-catching in a quiet sort of way, this lychnis tends, unfortunately, to be a rather short-lived plant.

Lysimachia punctata (YELLOW LOOSESTRIFE)

This yellow loosestrife, a native of Asia Minor, has escaped from gardens to grow wild in several places in Britain. Resembling our native purple loosestrife (*Lythrum*), it makes great clumps of growth, and is especially vigorous by the waterside or in a bog garden. From June to August the 3 ft high stems carry spikes of cup-shaped, bright yellow flowers that look like those of the allied *Lysimachia nummularia* (creeping jenny).

In a wild garden, yellow loosestrife combines well with *Hosta sieboldiana*. If this grouping is backed by dogwoods, such as *Cornus alba* 'Spaethii', an attractive area can be created that requires hardly any attention.

HOW TO GROW
Plant between autumn and spring, 1½-2 ft apart, in any soil, even heavy clay, that is permanently moist. Suitable for marshy and waterside conditions, in sun or shade. Cut stems down in autumn. Plants can be divided in the dormant season.

Free-flowering and fully hardy, lysimachias present only one problem: they may sometimes prove invasive.

Lysimachias growing with *Hosta sieboldiana* and *Cornus alba* 'Spaethii'.

The pale buff-pink flower plumes and magnificent foliage of *Macleaya microcarpa* tower above pink *Phlox paniculata*.

Macleaya microcarpa (PLUME POPPY)

A giant of a perennial, this poppy shoots up to anything between 6 and 8 ft high, carrying throughout summer 3 ft plumes of tiny pale buff-pink flowers. It is often confused with *Macleaya cordata*, a similar plant with white flowers.

Planted in the border, most plants of this height would require a lower-growing front screen to conceal their duller, lower extremities. But the plume poppy has splendid deeply lobed leaves, grey-green above and milky white beneath, that clothe the stems right up to the flowers. *M. microcarpa* (syn. *Bocconia microcarpa*) produces a beautiful effect grown with creamy-orange roses, such as 'Buff Beauty'.

HOW TO GROW
Plant between autumn and spring, 3-4 ft apart, in ordinary, fertile, reasonably moist soil, and in a sunny spot sheltered from the wind. Best at the back of a border, or in an isolated site, since the underground runners of plume poppies are fairly invasive. Remove the flower heads after blooming and cut down the stems to just above ground level in autumn. Divide and replant every three or four years in the dormant season. Alternatively, replant rooted runners in April.

Malva moschata (MUSK MALLOW)

Not only is the musk mallow one of our most beautiful wild flowers, it is a champion in the border too – not least because it is just as happy there as it is by the roadside and field edge. It forms a 3 ft high bush of finely cut, light green foliage, above which silky, open flowers of clear rose-pink nod all summer through. 'Alba' is a lovely pure white form. *Malva moschata* is ideal for planting behind modern pinks, or combined with silver *Santolina chamaecyparissus*.

HOW TO GROW
Plant in autumn or spring, 12-15 in. apart, in any ordinary, well-drained to dry soil. Drought-resistant and suitable for full sun or light shade. Cut back to near ground level in autumn. Propagate by basal cuttings or by seeds in spring.

The masses of pink flowers make a fine show of colour in a sunny garden. The leaves give off a musky scent when crushed

Malva moschata 'Alba' is the white form of the musk mallow.

Meconopsis cambrica (WELSH POPPY)

The Welsh poppy loves damp, rocky places, and in the garden it will soon colonise cracks in old walls or paving. It is an endearing little plant, only 12 in. high, with fresh green leaves and elegant flowers of soft yellow or orange, single or double, that bloom throughout summer.

The plant harmonises particularly well with purple flowers – in swathes under rhododendrons, for instance. Alternatively, the yellow form nicely complements the species rose *Rosa xanthina* 'Canary Bird'.

HOW TO GROW
Plant in spring, 12 in. apart, in ordinary garden soil, moist or dry, and in sun or shade. Cut back to near ground level in autumn. Propagate by seeds sown in spring or when ripe; the double forms can also be increased by division in spring, as they produce very little seed. This usually comes true to type.

The Welsh poppy, with its clear yellow blooms, readily seeds itself over a wide area

Meconopsis betonicifolia
(HIMALAYAN BLUE POPPY)

For perfection of colour and form, the Himalayan blue poppy, found naturally in Tibet, Yunnan and Upper Burma, is nearly unrivalled in the British garden. A clump of dark green, hairy, oblong leaves is followed by 3-4 ft high stems carrying more leaves. Magnificent clear blue flowers, 3 in. across, open at the tops of the stems during June and July. At first they are shallow cups, but as they mature the petals extend to display the large cluster of golden stamens at their centres. During the following weeks, each stem may produce a dozen blooms. The effect is breathtaking.

Introduced from the Himalayas in 1924, *Meconopsis betonicifolia* (syn. *M. baileyi*) is naturally more at home in the hilly parts of Scotland and Wales. There, it revels in the cool air, moist, acid soil and light mid-day shade that brings out the flowers in their purest blue.

Given reasonable conditions, you might plant the Himalayan blue poppy in the corner of a walled garden, together with the plantain lily *Hosta fortunei* 'Albopicta'. This is a 2 ft high perennial that has yellow foliage and bears lilac flowers in July. As a background you could establish the honeysuckle *Lonicera × tellmanniana*, which revels in shade and can twine over a wall at least 15 ft high. It produces a wealth of soft orange flowers in June and July.

HOW TO GROW
Meconopsis betonicifolia: plant in autumn or spring, 1½ - 2 ft apart, in ordinary, preferably humus-enriched soil, and in light shade in an open position. Propagate by seed sown under glass when ripe, or in spring.
Hosta fortunei 'Albopicta': see p. 95.
Lonicera × tellmanniana: see p. 187.

A group of *Meconopsis betonicifolia*, seen here in July planted in front of *Lonicera × tellmanniana* with a foreground of *Hosta fortunei* 'Albopicta'. This association makes an interesting contrast in both colour and leaf texture.

Mimulus luteus (MONKEY MUSK)

The monkey musk – so called because each flower bears some resemblance to a monkey's open mouth – was introduced to Britain from North America during the 19th century. Since then it has colonised the banks of streams throughout the country. From May to August, in the north and west especially, it forms great waterside drifts of vivid yellow that make perfect foils for the slowly colouring heather of late summer.

The monkey musk is also splendid when grown as a single plant in the garden, where it can form a clump 2 ft tall and wide. There are many differently coloured hybrids.

HOW TO GROW
Plant in spring, 8-9 in. apart, in ordinary soil that is, ideally, permanently moist, and in sun or light shade. Remove stems as the flowers fade to encourage a further display and prevent self-seeding. Propagate by division or by seeds in spring.

Mimulus luteus provides a patch of brilliant colour with its yellow flowers and shining green leaves.

The plant thrives by water, and is ideally sited at the edge of a pond.

An infusion of the dried leaves makes a refreshing drink. For drying, the leaves should be picked before the flowers open.

Monarda didyma 'Croftway Pink' (right) with the dahlia 'Edinburgh'.

A cloud of lavender catmint bloom softens the edge of a path at the front of a mixed shrub and perennial border.

Monarda didyma 'Cambridge Scarlet'

(OSWEGO TEA, SWEET BERGAMOT, BEE BALM)

Oswego tea, sweet bergamot, bee balm or *Monarda didyma* – whichever name you prefer, this is one of the finest herbs for the border, exciting in colour and form and highly aromatic. The flowers are rich in nectar, so they are usually buzzing with bees, and the leaves can be dried and infused to make a herb tea.

The most brilliant variety is 'Cambridge Scarlet', whose 3 ft tall stalks, bearing bright green, oval, hairy leaves all the way up, are crowned with large clusters of small, tubular, bright scarlet flowers from June to September. As each cluster develops, another inch or two of stem grows from the middle of it topped with a second, smaller whorl.

HOW TO GROW
Plant between autumn and spring, 15-18 in. apart, in fertile, moist soil, and in full sun or light shade. Cut stems down in late winter. Divide in the dormant season.

Nepeta × faassenii (CATMINT)

No garden with aspirations towards the traditional can afford to be without catmint, with its aromatic grey-green leaves. In May, sprays of little lavender-coloured flowers begin to appear, reaching to a height of 12-18 in. Throughout June they cover the plant entirely.

A group of catmint is perfect as a billowing foreground for old Gallica roses, such as *Rosa* 'Versicolor'. Many of these flower during June only, but the catmint, if clipped over as soon as its main flush of bloom declines, will flower on and off until October. The variety 'Six Hills Giant', twice the size of normal catmint, is well worth trying if a bolder effect is desired.

HOW TO GROW
Plant from autumn to spring, 12-15 in. apart, in ordinary garden soil, ideally in full sun. After the first flowering, trim back to the leaf mounds with hedging shears. Propagate by division or by stem cuttings in spring.

Catmint is flanked by *Heuchera sanguinea* and backed by an artemisia.

Oenothera missouriensis

(EVENING PRIMROSE)

Unlike some species of *Oenothera*, this evening primrose, from the southern United States, blooms not only in the evening but also during the day. Its lovely, satiny, pale yellow flowers, which are borne above a spreading mat of dark, lance-shaped leaves, are 3 in. wide – amazingly large considering that the plant is only 4-6 in. high. The plant blooms from June to August.

Oenothera missouriensis is best grown in a site that allows its prostrate habit to be fully appreciated – the front of a border or the edge of a raised bed. *Eryngium variifolium* or Belladonna varieties of *Delphinium* make fine companions.

HOW TO GROW

Plant between autumn and spring, 15-18 in. apart, in ordinary garden soil and in full sun. Good drainage is important in winter, in damp soil the roots may rot. Propagate by division or by seeds in spring.

The delicate yellow flowers of the evening primrose *Oenothera missouriensis* combine beautifully with *Eryngium variifolium*.

Oenothera missouriensis gleams above ferns and a yellow lysimachia.

Paeonia lactiflora (PEONY)

This peony (also called *Paeonia albiflora*) has been used to produce many of the beautiful Chinese hybrids, and is itself as lovely as any. It has elegant bronze, coarsely dissected foliage that opens very early in spring – dangerously early if the site is a frosty hollow. In May or June, flowers the size of breakfast cups appear. These are of an unsurpassed satiny whiteness enhanced by bright golden stamens at the centre. There is also a wide range of other colours and forms, including 'White Wings' and the pink 'Country Girl'.

The flowering season is short, but the 3 ft high plant maintains its attractive foliage until well into autumn, when it often takes on gentle orange tints. The long life of this and other species of peony makes them ideal for planting between shrubs to provide a long-lasting display that needs little attention.

HOW TO GROW

Plant between autumn and spring, 3-4 ft apart. Most peonies take a couple of years to settle, but once established they will flourish in the same site for up to 50 years. They do best in fairly heavy, well-drained soil, acid or alkaline, enriched with organic matter before planting. Set the crowns 1 in. below soil level, 2 in. on light soil, in sun or light shade, ideally in a site where morning sun after a spring frost cannot damage developing buds. See also Paeonia mlokosewitschii on page 108.

Paeonia lactiflora 'White Wings' blooms beside *Ajuga reptans* 'Variegata'.

The exquisite blooms of two varieties of *Paeonia lactiflora* crown their rich green foliage. Bordering them is white sage.

Paeonia mlokosewitschii (PEONY)

This most exquisite of all peonies, a native of the Caucasus usually known as 'Mlok', also has the most fleeting flowers – but there are compensations. In early spring, for several weeks before the flowers appear, there is beauty both in the bright red shoots that emerge from the cold soil and in the elegant blue-green leaves that develop on them. The flowers appear singly, crowning the 2 ft tall stems in April. Their great lemon-yellow cups, 4-5 in. across and crowded with golden stamens in the centre, create an enchanting display for up to two weeks.

In autumn the large seed pods split open to reveal a double row of shiny seeds, the fully developed ones blue-black, the sterile ones scarlet. This helps to compensate for the brevity of its flowering period.

'Mlok' does not usually flower until four years after seeds are sown and, since its life is short, it might be better to buy plants from nurseries. The peony needs little in the way of companion plants until midsummer, when the leaves are losing their freshness – a time when plantain lilies and bellflowers are at their best. You might, therefore, add the 2 ft tall plantain lily *Hosta fortunei* 'Albopicta', which is grown mainly for its heart-shaped green-and-yellow leaves. In July, it also puts out clusters of lilac flowers.

With the lily you might grow the 2-3 ft high bellflower *Campanula persicifolia* 'Snowdrift', whose pure white, bowl-like blooms open from June to August.

HOW TO GROW
Paeonia mlokosewitschii: cultivation as P. lactiflora (see previous page). Failure to flower is usually caused by peonies being planted too deeply. They also resent disturbance and lifting, and for this reason their permanent sites should be carefully chosen. In autumn, cut the dead foliage back to ground level and top-dress the root area with well-rotted manure or bonemeal. Propagate in the same way as P. officinalis.
Campanula persicifolia: see p. 72.
Hosta fortunei: see p. 95.

Paeonia officinalis
(APOTHECARIES' PEONY)

The great blood-red globes of this old plant are one of the pleasures of May – a sign that the soft shades of spring are being left behind and the strong colours of summer are on their way. The wild single-flowered species was brought here from southern Europe in the 16th century, and within 100 years double forms were in cultivation.

The plant became known as the 'Apothecaries' Peony' – and, as late as the beginning of this century, Sussex children wore peony-root necklaces to ward off toothache. Both single and double forms make 2 ft high, tough hummocks of deeply divided leaves.

HOW TO GROW
Plant in the same way as Paeonia lactiflora and P. mlokosewitschii. Propagation is by division, preferably by cutting through and removing rooted portions from the outer edges of established clumps. Seed propagation, in spring, should produce flowering plants after four or five years.

A bed of lemon-yellow *Paeonia mlokosewitschii* bursts into full flower in a spring display that lasts a fortnight.

This form, *Paeonia officinalis* 'Rubra-plena', has deep crimson blooms. It is edged here with *Stachys lanata*.

Papaver orientale (ORIENTAL POPPY)

Few hardy perennials have such magnificent flowers as the oriental poppy. In early June the buds split to reveal crumpled petals that unfurl into great bowls of brilliant vermilion, often marked by a black 'thumbprint' at the base of each petal. The flowers rise to a height of 2-3 ft above spreading clumps of bristly foliage.

In the centre of each flower is an urn-shaped seed capsule which, if cut soon after the petals drop, dries well for winter decoration. Different-coloured varieties are available, including the salmon-pink 'Mrs Perry' and 'Perry's White'.

HOW TO GROW
Plant in autumn, 1½-2 ft apart, in any ordinary garden soil and in full sun. Remove faded petals and flower stems unless the seed pods are wanted. Tidy away the leaves at crown level as they yellow and shrivel. Propagate by root cuttings in late winter.

The 'thumbprints' clearly show on these pink and white poppies.

Several varieties of *Papaver orientale* mix cheerfully together to produce a colourful display during June

Peltiphyllum peltatum (UMBRELLA PLANT)

Great, long-stalked bright green discs of leaves, 12 in. across, make this a handsome foliage plant, and in autumn its appeal is heightened when the leaves turn a delightful bronze-pink. The heads of pink flowers that appear in early spring are unexceptional in themselves but, opening on top of bare stems that have pushed up from empty ground before other herbaceous plants have started into growth, they create an odd effect.

The plant, which builds up to a height of 2-3 ft and needs plenty of space, associates well with its compatriot, the skunk cabbage (*Lysichiton americanus*), which is the same height and has large leaves and yellow spring flowers between March and early May.

HOW TO GROW
Plant in autumn, 3 ft apart, in moisture-retentive soil, ideally enriched with humus. Not recommended for small gardens, but ideal for pool and stream sides, in sun or light shade. Propagate by division of the rhizomes in the dormant season.

Peltiphyllum peltatum thrives in moist conditions. The thick, bare stems support rounded heads of small, rose-pink flowers.

A crowd of 'umbrellas' are seen here in their autumn colours.

Penstemon campanulatus

The vivid, foxglove-like flowers and evergreen foliage of *Penstemon* look splendid in the mixed border. *Penstemon campanulatus*, a plant 1-2 ft high, has flower sprays ranging from pink to purple from plant to plant. A fine flush of bloom appears in mid-June, and if flowers are removed as soon as they have faded the display will continue until the end of September.

The striking hybrids *P.* × *gloxinioides* have *P. campanulatus* as one of their parents. Recommended are 'Firebird', scarlet; 'King George', salmon-red with a white throat; and 'White Bedder', pure white.

HOW TO GROW
Plant in spring, 12 in. apart, in ordinary garden soil, ideally humus-enriched, and in full sun or partial shade. Cut back to ground level in autumn and in cold areas protect the crowns with cloches. Except in the mildest areas, overwinter late summer stem cuttings under glass. Propagate by seeds.

The 'White Bedder' form will set off other more colourful penstemon flowers to perfection in a mixed bed.

Different varieties of *Penstemon campanulatus* make a bright display.

Phlox paniculata

The violet, wine-red, salmon-pink and other richly coloured varieties of *Phlox paniculata* are truly beautiful plants, but it is the pastel-coloured cultivars, with their freshness rivalled only by sweet peas, that give such pleasure in August when earlier summer flowers look tired and dusty.

With such a wide number of shades, you can make almost any summer association you choose. For example, you might begin with 'Franz Schubert', a lilac phlox with a yellow eye, grown as a group of five plants; and beside it, as a contrast and in a group of three, the claret-red 'Vintage Wine'. Both cultivars carry dense, wide clusters of flowers on top of 3 ft high stems clothed with pointed leaves. An alternative to 'Vintage Wine' would be the crimson 'Starfire'.

Behind the phlox could be put the dense *rugosa* shrub rose 'Roseraie de l'Hay', 6 ft high and wide. This bears crimson-purple, fragrant double flowers from June to autumn and has attractive, crinkled leaves.

In the foreground, to hide the rather uninteresting stalks of the phlox, it would be a good idea to plant clumps of the cotton lavender *Santolina chamaecyparissus*, each dwarf shrub an 18 in. high mound of soft, silver foliage. In June the shrublets carry small lemon-yellow flowers that should be sheared off to produce denser foliage.

Two outstanding alternatives to 'Franz Schubert' are the warm pink 'Pastorale' and the pure white 'White Admiral'. But there are so many splendid cultivars of all colours to choose from that gardeners planning to grow phlox should try to see the plants for themselves at an August flower show.

HOW TO GROW
Phlox paniculata: plant in the same way as P. maculata. Propagate all phlox by division in autumn or spring, or by root cuttings in the dormant season. Stem cuttings may perpetuate stem eelworms, which are difficult to eradicate as there are no safe chemical-control methods.
Rosa rugosa 'Roseraie de l'Hay': *see p. 239.*
Santolina chamaecyparissus: *see p. 314.*

An August mass of *Phlox paniculata* 'Pastorale' (pink) and 'Vintage Wine' (claret), above a carpet of the silver-leaved *Santolina chamaecyparissus* and overhung by the delightful crimson *Rosa rugosa* 'Roseraie de l'Hay'.

Phlox maculata

This phlox does particularly well in the cooler parts of the country. Great swathes of it, together with other late perennials, form a magnificent floral sea in the Gardens of the National Trust for Scotland at Threave, in Dumfries and Galloway. In humbler plots, too, from July to September, the long tapering clusters of flat, purple blooms rise to a height of 2-3 ft above a compact mass of lance-shaped leaves. Good cultivars include 'Alpha', which is pink; 'Alba', white; and 'Omega', white with a pink eye.

HOW TO GROW
Plant in autumn or spring, 18 in. apart, in humus-rich soil, in sun or light shade. Water frequently during dry spells. Cut down to soil level in autumn. Propagate in the same way as Phlox paniculata.

Phlox maculata 'Alba' is a white variety with a yellow eye. All the *maculata* cultivars of *Phlox* have maroon-spotted stems.

A group of pink *Phlox maculata* planted alongside a garden path.

Phygelius capensis

Few South African shrubs can withstand the outdoor chill of British winters. An exception, however, is the gaily flowered *Phygelius capensis*, which, though cut back to ground level by winter cold, springs up vigorously each spring. It behaves just like a herbaceous perennial, which is how it is generally grown in this country.

From a base of deep green, oval leaves, the flowering stems rise to a height of 3-4 ft, bearing open sprays of warm red, foxglove-like blooms with a yellow throat from July to October. It looks particularly effective with a backing of the climber *Lonicera japonica* 'Halliana' – one of the Japanese honeysuckles.

HOW TO GROW
Plant in spring, 2 ft apart, in ordinary garden soil, in full sun and, ideally, with wall or fence shelter. In late spring, cut back all stems to ground level. Propagate by division in spring.

This species grows excellently as a border plant, but with the shelter and support of a wall may reach 6 ft or more in height.

Phygelius capensis flourishes in front of a *Lonicera japonica* 'Halliana'.

Physostegia virginiana (OBEDIENT PLANT)

This is a plant with a difference. The flowers – which are like particularly bright, small snapdragons – have hinged stalks so that when they are pushed to a new position they stay there.

Flower arrangers would wish that more plants were so accommodating.

But the obedient plant deserves to be grown not just for its oddity but for its value as a late summer perennial, flowering as it does during July and August. Best for the border are the garden cultivars, which flower more freely than the wild species. 'Vivid', only 12 in. tall, is a fine sort, making a dense clump of stems that prolong summer brightness into September with flower spikes of deep pink. 'Summer Snow' has flowers of pure white and 'Rose Bouquet' is lilac-pink.

HOW TO GROW
Plant in autumn or spring, 12 in. apart, in any moisture-retentive soil, and in sun or light shade. Apply a mulch and water freely in dry spells. Cut down in late autumn. Propagate by division in autumn or spring.

A gift to flower arrangers, obedient plant is also a delight in the garden, where colour and shape can be equally well used.

A pink physostegia adds a delicate touch to the herbaceous border.

Blue-flowered platycodon blends sweetly with a grey-blue *Picea pungens*.

Platycodon grandiflorum (BALLOON FLOWER)

Children should be discouraged from bursting the balloon flower's buds, for the shallow bells in various shades of blue that the plant produces throughout the summer can be one of the minor glories of the border. The variety *Platycodon grandiflorum mariesii* is more commonly available than the species. It is smaller, 9-12 in. high, and ideal as a foreground plant.

The balloon flower was introduced to Britain in the 18th century from China, where it was valued for the supposed tonic qualities of its roots.

HOW TO GROW
Plant in autumn or spring, 12 in. apart, in any good, well-drained soil and in full sun or very light shade. Mark the sites to avoid damage during spring cultivation. Remove stems after flowering and avoid disturbance of the roots. Propagate by seeds in spring; from seed to flowering usually takes two years.

The flowers of *Platycodon grandiflorum*, in bloom from June to August, vary in shade from pale to deep blue.

Feathery leaves form an attractive foil to the clusters of blue flowers.

Polemonium caeruleum (JACOB'S LADDER)

The leaflets of this plant are arranged in pairs on each long midrib – hence its common name. At any time between April and July it will produce a crowd of flowers of the most delicious misty blue. If these are cut back immediately after they have faded, you should have a second, smaller crop later in the season. The variety *Polemonium caeruleum cashmirianum* has larger flowers of a clearer blue. Sadly, the plants are not long-lived, especially on drier soils, but they compensate for this with an abundance of seedlings, which may even produce flowers in their first year.

HOW TO GROW
Plant between autumn and spring, 15-18 in. apart in ordinary soil, preferably enriched with humus, in sun or light shade. After flowering, remove stems at the base. Propagate by division in the dormant season or by lifting and replanting self-sown seedlings.

Paler shades of blue and white are also found within the same species. The flowers are bowl or saucer-shaped.

Polygonum affine bears spikes of tiny, bell-shaped, pinkish-red blooms.

Polygonum affine (KNOTWEED)

The little mat-forming species of *Polygonum*, such as this 9 in. high plant, give a low, unexpected flash of colour at the front of the border. *Polygonum affine*, a native of Nepal, makes a wide clump of creeping stems with narrow, dark green leaves, and in late summer and autumn produces spikes of flowers, rather like a pink or rosy-red lavender. Soft-hued Michaelmas daisies make a fine background for this compact perennial.

Another low-growing species from the Himalayas is *P. vacciniifolium*. This is only 6 in. tall, and bears smaller, paler red flowers from August to October.

HOW TO GROW
Plant between autumn and spring, 18 in. apart (for ground-cover), in ordinary, fertile soil and in sun or light shade. Remove faded flower stems in late autumn, and in spring trim the leaf mats hard back. Propagate in the same way as Polygonum campanulatum (see p. 114).

Michaelmas daisies, *Aster novae-angliae*, stand above a dense carpet formed by the leaves and flowers of *Polygonum affine*.

Polygonatum × hybridum (SOLOMON'S SEAL)

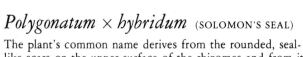

The plant's common name derives from the rounded, seal-like scars on the upper surface of the rhizomes and from its supposed ability to seal wounds. Whatever the case, it is one of the most elegant of garden perennials: its slender, arching stems, rising to a height of 2-4 ft, carry pairs of graceful upward-curving leaves along their length and are decorated in June with rows of small, hanging bellflowers. These are creamy-white, tipped with green, and are not unlike narrow snowdrops.

An excellent backdrop to the Solomon's seal would be a bush of the evergreen *Rhododendron* 'Goldsworth Yellow', which makes a dome 8 ft high, and more across. In late May and early June its pink buds open out into balled trusses of soft yellow.

In the foreground you might establish the gold-and-green foliage of the plantain lily *Hosta crispula*, 1½-2 ft high. As summer advances, the leaves mature into different shades of green that give way in autumn to soft yellow.

If you have the space, you could surmount the entire grouping with violet willow, *Salix daphnoides*, a deciduous tree that eventually grows to 30 ft or more but that is easily kept shorter by regular pruning. In winter its young stems bear a blue-white waxy patina, in spring they carry garlands of pussy-willow catkins, and in summer they are clothed with lance-shaped leaves, dark above, blue-white beneath.

HOW TO GROW
Polygonatum × hybridum: plant between autumn and spring, 18 in. apart, in ordinary, fertile soil, and in light shade. On light soils, mulch in spring to conserve moisture. Cut back to ground level in autumn. Propagate by division in autumn or spring.
Hosta crispula: see p. 94.
Rhododendron 'Goldsworth Yellow': *see p. 307.*
Salix daphnoides: see p. 354.

In early June, both the *Polygonatum × hybridum* and the *Rhododendron* 'Goldsworth Yellow' are in full bloom. A luxurious carpet of *Hosta crispula* in front of the polygonatum stems completes the group, its lilac-purple flowers appearing in August.

Low, bushy foliage is well placed alongside a garden path.

Polygonum campanulatum (KNOTWEED)

Thriving in a wide range of soil types, including acid and alkaline, this plant will reward you with lush, fast-spreading clumps of soft, grey-green foliage. From these, slender, branched stems rise to a height of 2½-3½ ft; they are massed with sprays of soft pink flowers, like heather bells, from June to September.

Polygonum campanulatum is perfect for lending colour to the edge of a water garden, between late summer and autumn, after Primula and Meconopsis have faded. It will do well, too, in the drier soil of a border, where it can be combined with blue monkshood (Aconitum napellus).

HOW TO GROW
Plant in the same way as Polygonum affine (see p. 112), setting the plants 2 ft apart. P. campanulatum is invasive, and most suitable for waterside planting in large gardens or between shrubs. Propagate by division in autumn or spring.

Polygonum campanulatum's 2-3 in. wide heads of shell-pink flower clusters bloom profusely from June to September.

'Miss Willmott' is a tall hybrid (about 2 ft) with cherry-pink flowers.

Potentilla atrosanguinea (CINQUEFOIL)

The green, strawberry-like leaves of this potentilla are framed with silvery hairs, and this foliage makes a perfect foil for the sprays of flowers that appear throughout the summer. Each bloom, the size of a 10p piece, is of a velvety, deep, intense red. Three brilliant garden hybrids, developed partly from this potentilla, are 'Gibson's Scarlet', 'Yellow Queen' and the semi-double, deep reddish-orange 'William Rollison'.

Very much like Potentilla atrosanguinea is the other parent of these hybrids, P. nepalensis, which bears rose-red flowers. Amongst its offspring is 'Miss Willmott'.

HOW TO GROW
Plant between autumn and spring, 18 in. apart, in ordinary, fertile soil, and in full sun. Top-dress in spring with garden compost or peat, and water copiously during long, dry spells. Propagate in spring by basal cuttings under glass or by division.

Potentilla atrosanguinea 'William Rollison' is a shorter form (about 18 in.) with rich flame-orange blooms.

While yellow primroses remain the favourites, the pink forms are attractive and add a welcome splash of extra colour.

Primula vulgaris (PRIMROSE)

Primroses – the 'first roses' – are a lovely guarantee of the unfailing advent of spring each year, and, whether in the hedgerow or the garden, there are few sights more cheering than the plants' soft, yellow flowers and distinctive rosettes of corrugated leaves. They normally bloom in March and April, but in mild winters in the south their pale gold often appears much earlier. Although yellow is the most familiar colour, primroses also come in shades of red, purple, pink and white.

Establish primroses almost anywhere; especially, mingle them with violets to make a delicate ground-cover in the shade of a woodland garden or in thin grass beneath a large tree on the lawn.

HOW TO GROW
Plant in the same way as Primula denticulata. Sow seeds in late spring or summer in a cold frame, or divide after flowering.

The familiar common primrose heralds a warmer spell after winter cold.

Primula denticulata (DRUMSTICK PRIMROSE)

The drumstick primrose, which came to Britain from the Himalayas in 1840, has the doll's-house neatness that the Victorians loved. From its rosettes of light green, toothed leaves there rise, guardsman-straight, 12 in. high stems topped from March to May by a single globe, measuring 2-3 in. across, of tightly packed misty-mauve, yellow-eyed flowers. The plant is also available in white, pink, purple and crimson varieties.

Long ago, in the spring garden at Sissinghurst Castle, Kent, it was planted with a mixture of early spring flowers, and this planting could be followed in spirit. Ideal would be to make a centrepiece of the sycamore *Acer pseudoplatanus* 'Brilliantissimum' and to cut an 8 ft circle out of the turf around it. Eventually, this tree will grow to 15-20 ft, so you should strip its lower branches to form an umbrella over the bed beneath.

The bed would be crowded with spring flowers: a few small groups of the drumstick primrose in mauve and purple, *Anemone blanda*, *Muscari armeniacum*, *Narcissus pseudonarcissus*, *Fritillaria meleagris*, *Primula vulgaris* and *Pulmonaria saccharata*. In April, it looks as though some goddess had passed, scattering flowers.

The glory does not end with the fading of the flowers, for then the whitebeam unfurls its silver leaves above the bed of foliage, most handsomely set off by the enlarging, white-splashed leaves of the pulmonarias.

HOW TO GROW
Primula denticulata: plant from autumn to spring, 12 in. apart, in ordinary garden soil, in sun or light shade. Water well during dry spells in spring and summer. Propagate by division and immediate replanting once flowering is over.
Acer pseudoplatanus: see p. 331.
Anemone blanda: see p. 143.
Fritillaria meleagris: see p. 153.
Muscari armeniacum: see p. 163.
Narcissus pseudonarcissus: see p. 165.
Primula vulgaris: see p. 114.
Pulmonaria saccharata: see p. 116.

A glorious profusion of spring colour beneath a sycamore centres around the upstanding spherical heads of drumstick primroses. With them are daffodils, purple-chequered *Fritillaria meleagris*, *Pulmonaria saccharata*, with its white-spotted leaves, and blue grape hyacinths. Intermingled are starry-flowered *Anemone blanda* and jaunty yellow primroses.

Prunella grandiflora (SELF-HEAL)

Like all prunellas, this is a most obliging plant. It is as happy in a shaded city backyard as it is providing colour in front of shrubs whose flowers are finished; or creating ground-cover for a damp soil. Its tight mass of dark leaves grows flat to the ground, and from it rise square-sectioned stems to a height of 12 in. The top half of each stem carries whorls of leaves, which from late spring to autumn are adorned with 2-3 in. long terminal spikes of bright purple tubular flowers.

Varieties in different colours include 'Loveliness', pale violet; 'Alba', white; and the pink 'Rosea'.

HOW TO GROW
Plant in spring, 15-18 in. apart, in ordinary garden soil, and in sun or partial shade. Dead-head regularly, and cut back to ground level in autumn after flowering has finished in October. Prunellas can be invasive. Propagate by division in autumn or spring, or by seeds in spring.

Purple flowers, with spreading lobes, are borne on densely packed spikes. They can look very effective in a rock garden.

Prunella grandiflora seeds itself and quickly spreads over a large area.

Ornamental foliage: *Pulmonaria saccharata* and (right) *P. s.* 'Argentea'.

Pulmonaria saccharata (LUNGWORT)

The name is derived from the Latin *pulmo*, meaning 'lung', probably because the spotted leaves resembled the lungs.

A highly ornamental early flowering perennial, *Pulmonaria saccharata* is useful as ground-cover in semi-shade. The long, hairy, oval leaves are green splashed with silver. *P. s.* 'Argentea' is a rich form in which the silver spots fuse together, so creating a wholly silvered leaf. In March and April, heads of flowers appear at the top of 12 in. stems; they begin as bright pink, then mature to blue. The foliage develops fully only after the flowers have faded.

HOW TO GROW
Plant from early autumn to early spring, 10 in. apart, in, ideally, moist garden soil and in semi-shade. The plants will be all the better if, in late spring, a mulch of peat or rotted manure is spread beneath the leaf mounds. Propagate by division in autumn or spring.

Although lungworts are grown primarily for their silver-spotted foliage, their colourful spring flowers are highly decorative.

Ranunculus aconitifolius 'Flore-pleno'
(FAIR MAIDS OF FRANCE)

Known as Fair Maids of France (or, by some, Fair Maids of Kent), *Ranunculus aconitifolius* is a charming member of the buttercup family that enlivens April with its 2 ft high branching sprays of pure single white flowers carried above dark green leaves. However, much better for the border is the exquisite, double-flowered cultivar, 'Flore-pleno', that blooms a little later, in May and June.

The flowers, each consisting of a flat, crowded button of petals, last considerably longer than the single flowers of the species. To get the best out of the plant, grow it in full sun; this will flatter its dazzling, snowy whiteness.

HOW TO GROW
Plant from early autumn to early spring, 15 in. apart, in ordinary garden soil that, ideally, has been enriched with humus. Best in dappled shade, or in sun in the moister soils. Propagate by division in autumn.

The ranunculus combines well with mauve-flowered *Lamium maculatum*.

Ranunculus aconitifolius 'Flore-pleno' is a lovely plant in late spring, when it puts forth its dazzling white buttons of bloom.

Rheum palmatum (ORNAMENTAL RHUBARB)

If rhubarb were not confined to the kitchen garden, its foliage might be as highly praised as that of its close relative *Rheum palmatum*. This plant first pushes up a great knob of furled leaves, like the heart of a giant red Chinese cabbage; they then unfold into leaves like jagged-edged, red-flushed umbrellas 2-3 ft across. These turn to green after the plant has flowered.

In June, the 6 ft high flowering stem bears a cluster of crimson fluffy bloom, followed by attractive brown seed capsules. All this productivity requires a lot of moisture, and the plant does best by the pond side.

HOW TO GROW
Plant between autumn and spring in ordinary soils, ideally enriched with humus, in full sun or partial shade. Water frequently in dry spells. Cut faded flower stems back to their base. Propagate by division in the dormant season or by seeds in spring.

In June *Rheum palmatum* 'Atrosanguineum' bears aloft soft red flowers.

Clearly showing its relationship to rhubarb, a young plant of *Rheum palmatum* thrusts up its deeply divided, red-tinged leaves.

Romneya coulteri (TREE POPPY)

The Royal Horticultural Society awarded a first-class certificate to this lovely Californian plant only 12 years after it was introduced here in 1876 – a measure of the warmth with which it was welcomed. It is a glorious plant. On a bushy specimen, 4-5 ft high, appear great scented flowers with crinkled, pure white taffeta petals and a prominent golden centre. Framing them is a mass of lush, grey-green, deeply lobed leaves.

The plant has a woody rootstock, but its common name of tree poppy is a misnomer and it is best treated as herbaceous. It is capricious in establishing itself: some gardeners always fail with it, others succeed.

Another species, *Romneya trichocalyx*, or hybrids between it and *R. coulteri*, are sometimes offered at nurseries. They are virtually identical to *R. coulteri*, though if anything the hybrids are the best of all.

The tree poppy would make a fine nucleus for an association to be grown in a warm border backed by a south or west-facing wall; such a site is essential in all but very sheltered parts if the tree poppy is to succeed. The wall would also suit the passion flower, *Passiflora caerulea*, which can easily climb 20-30 ft. Its large white-and-blue flowers, that open from June to September, would make a splendid backing to the group.

The blue in the passion flower could be echoed by clumps of the African lilies *Agapanthus* 'Headbourne Hybrids', grown in front of the poppy; the lilies, 2-3 ft or more high, bloom in July and August. To one side of them you might plant *Crinum* × *powellii* 'Album', 2 ft tall, a bulbous plant whose shiny, strap-shaped leaves support heads of fragrant white flowers.

HOW TO GROW
Romneya coulteri: plant in spring, in ordinary soil. It thrives in the better-drained types of clay. In late autumn, cut the woody stems back to near ground level and in very cold areas cover the crown and root area with a winter mulch. Romneyas can be difficult to establish; they resent root disturbance and are best propagated by replanting rooted suckers in spring or by root cuttings.
Agapanthus 'Headbourne Hybrids'*: see p. 140.*
Crinum × *powellii* 'Album'*: see p. 147.*
Passiflora caerulea: see p. 188.

In the shelter of a wall in August, a spread of the lovely white-and-gold tree poppy *Romneya coulteri* backs the blue African lilies *Agapanthus* 'Headbourne Hybrids' and the scented white *Crinum* × *powellii* 'Album'. Climbing the wall is the beautiful passion flower *Passiflora caerulea*.

A healthy, very free-flowering clump of *Romneya coulteri*.

A well established and highly decorative group of *Rodgersia aesculifolia*.

Rodgersia aesculifolia

One of the many joys of this perennial is that its leaf pattern consists of a fan of leaflets, rather like the foliage of a horse chestnut. Each of these groupings, about 12 in. across, is carried on a 2 ft high hairy stalk that emerges from the rootstock. In July clusters of white flowers appear above the leaves in 12-18 in. long plumes. *R. pinnata* 'Superba' has similar charms but pink flowers.

This is one of those rare plants that are as attractive in adolescence as in maturity. Rodgersias associate well with deciduous azaleas, rhododendrons or almost any other moisture-loving woodland plants.

HOW TO GROW
Plant in spring, singly or as a group of three spaced 2½ ft apart each way. Rodgersias thrive in rich, moist soil, full sun and shelter from strong winds. Set the rhizomes just below soil level; water in dry spells. Propagate by division in spring.

The plant is cultivated as much for its ornamental foliage as for its flowers. The leaves often have a tinge of bronze.

Rudbeckia laciniata (CONE-FLOWER)

These flowers are as exuberant as North America, the land that gave them birth – strong plants of open, elegant growth that on good soil reach at least 6 ft in height. Their bright yellow, green-centred blooms appear in August and September, and deeply cut leaves are produced the full length of the stems.

The yellow blooms of the plant go well with white flowers – for example, those of the Shasta daisy (*Chrysanthemum maximum*).

Another, shorter but very similar species is *Rudbeckia nitida*, which has an exceptionally attractive double-flowered cultivar in 'Goldquelle'.

HOW TO GROW
Plant in autumn or spring, 3 ft apart in ordinary, fertile and well-drained soil, in full sun or very light shade. Cut back to ground level in late autumn. Propagate by division during the dormant season, every third year.

Rudbeckia nitida 'Goldquelle' flowers brightly in late August.

The cone-shaped centre is a distinctive feature of rudbeckias. *R. laciniata* has a green cone and a single yellow flower.

Salvia × superba

This is a plant that would be wasted anywhere other than in pride of place at the front of the border. From July to September it puts forth deep delphinium-purple blooms, and when the petals fall the mauve, crimson-tinged outer parts of the flowers remain to prolong the display still further. Three to five plants together make a great dome of growth, 3 ft high and across. The plant is sometimes listed as *Salvia virgata nemorosa*.

'Lubeca', a dwarf form half the size of the species, and 'East Friesland', somewhere between the two in height, are valuable for the smaller garden. They both bear purple flowers that contrast admirably with *Achillea filipendulina* in a summer display.

HOW TO GROW
Plant in the same way as Salvia haematodes, spacing plants 2 ft apart (dwarf forms 15 in.). Propagate by division in autumn or spring.

A rich display of purple *Salvia × superba* makes a splendid foreground to yellow achilleas and blue delphiniums.

Salvia haematodes

One of the most hackneyed of gardening clichés is the combination of the scarlet *Salvia splendens* with white *Alyssum* and blue *Lobelia* in a formal, patriotic bedding scheme. Alternatively, the common name for *Salvia* – sage – simply conjures up an aromatic herb used for stuffing. But the plant is much more versatile than this; in fact, it encompasses a vast genus of 500 annuals, perennials and shrubs from all over the world. Many are marvellous garden plants, and *S. haematodes*, from Greece, is one of the finest.

The plant forms flat rosettes of dark green leaves, from which flower stems shoot up to a height of 3-4 ft. From June to September, these are topped by a cloud of lavender-blue flowers.

This salvia is attractive seen both at close quarters and in a mass from some distance away. In an association it looks very well behind the lady's mantle, *Alchemilla mollis*, a 15 in. high plant whose froth of lime-green flowers coincides with the display of the salvia. Behind this again you could plant the purple-leaved fennel (*Foeniculum vulgare* 'Purpureum'), 3-5 ft high, to frame the salvia in a thundercloud of developing foliage.

Alongside the fennel you could try the 3 ft high sub-shrub *Phygelius capensis*.

HOW TO GROW
Salvia haematodes: plant between autumn and spring, 15-18 in. apart, in ordinary garden soil with good drainage and in full sun. Remove faded flower stems unless seeds are wanted; cut others back in autumn. This short-lived plant should be propagated regularly by seeds in late spring.
Alchemilla mollis: see p. 66.
Foeniculum vulgare 'Purpureum'*: see p. 87.*
Phygelius capensis: see p. 111.

Along a garden path, plant a generous border of *Salvia haematodes* to give a profusion of light purple blooms all summer long. Behind it, *Foeniculum vulgare* 'Purpureum' makes a perfect companion providing both colour and shape; and in front, *Alchemilla mollis* adds a fluffy green-and-yellow fringe to the group.

Saponaria ocymoides

This low, trailing plant, only 6-9 in. high when in bloom, makes a cushion of pale green leaves that are almost hidden in June beneath a mass of bright, rose-pink flowers. It is closely related to pinks and carnations (*Dianthus*), for both of which it provides an admirable base. This combination with pinks and carnations is effectively used in the National Trust garden at Mottisfont Abbey, Hampshire, to give ground-level interest to a collection of Old roses. Another, and glorious, way to use the plant is to allow it to trail over rocks, the retaining walls of a raised bed or the edge of a border.

HOW TO GROW
Plant from autumn to spring, 15 in. apart, in ordinary garden soil, and in sun or dappled shade. Unless grown for ground-cover, check the plant's invasive habit by shearing back after flowering. Propagate, if necessary, by cuttings in summer or early autumn or by seeds in spring.

The distinctive strong pink of *Saponaria ocymoides* 'Splendens', here seen trailing luxuriously over a garden wall.

The paler *Saponaria ocymoides*, growing at its best in a rock garden.

Almost leafless stems support the frilly flowers of *Scabiosa caucasica*.

Scabiosa caucasica (SCABIOUS)

Though the flowers are sometimes as big as saucers, this scabious has the same fresh charm as its wild relatives of the chalk and limestone grassland. The blooms of *Scabiosa caucasica* are clear blue and appear on the 2 ft high stems from June to September. There are several good cultivars, including 'Bressingham White', the lavender-blue 'Clive Greaves', the darker 'Moerheim Blue', and 'Penhill Blue', which is shaded mauve.

Worth growing for cut flowers alone, this is also a fine plant for backing old-fashioned pinks (*Dianthus*) in the border. Together they provide a softly coloured display all summer through.

HOW TO GROW
Plant in spring, 18 in. apart, in ordinary garden soil, preferably limy, and in full sun. Dead-head regularly and cut stems back to ground level in autumn. Propagate by division in spring, every three or four years, or by basal cuttings under glass. Seeds may be sown in spring but may not come totally true to type.

Scabiosa caucasica and *Dianthus* 'Inchmery' form a charming association of delicate colours and graceful, curving lines.

Sedum × 'Autumn Joy' (STONECROP)

This splendid great stonecrop, which makes a clump of fleshy stems and leaves, is a hybrid between our native *Sedum telephium* and the Chinese *S. spectabile*. From its Chinese parent, 'Autumn Joy' has inherited smooth, waxy, pale green leaves and an attraction for late summer butterflies.

In late August, after the foliage is fully developed to a height of 1½-2 ft, every stem is topped with flat heads of starry flowers, deep pink at first, then, as summer turns to autumn, deepening to bronze-red – a hue that continues until the first frosts.

Because the plant is beautiful for so long, a number of different associations can be built up around it, according to the time of year. Here, for example, is a grouping for the end of summer, either in the herbaceous border or in front of shrubs that have flowered in spring; it combines striking foliage with a burst of late bloom.

In such an association, the sedum would be accompanied by *Miscanthus sinensis* 'Silver Feather', a silvery-flowered grass 3-5 ft high; *Ceratostigma willmottianum*, a 3 ft tall shrub, which has dark foliage that sometimes turns red in autumn; and the very distinctive golden rod, *Solidago* × 'Crown of Rays', a clump-forming plant.

Complete the picture with *Liriope muscari*, an 18 in. high perennial with deep green, grassy leaves and mauve, autumn-blooming, bell-shaped flowers.

HOW TO GROW
Sedum × 'Autumn Joy': *plant between autumn and spring, 18 in. apart, in ordinary soil, and in sun or light shade. Remove dead flower stems in winter or early spring. Easily propagated by division in the dormant season, or by stem cuttings in spring.*
Ceratostigma willmottianum: see p. 261.
Liriope muscari: see p. 101.
Miscanthus sinensis 'Silver Feather': *see p. 133.*
Solidago × 'Crown of Rays': *see S.* × 'Goldenmosa', *p. 123.*

A September bed of *Sedum* × 'Autumn Joy' is backed by handsome, silver-flowered *Miscanthus*, the blue of *Ceratostigma willmottianum* and stately golden rod. Mauve *Liriope muscari* edges the border.

Sedum maximum 'Atropurpureum'

(STONECROP)

As its name suggests, this stonecrop is a large plant: 2½ ft high and almost as much across. The fleshy leaves, typical of the genus, are often borne along the thick stems in groups of three. 'Atropurpureum' is a lovely form in which the leaves are of a deep purple-red overlaid by a grape-like bloom. This purple colouring extends into the flat heads of yellow-white flowers, carried in August and September.

The flower heads maintain their shape and texture after the blooms have faded, and the leaves are succulent throughout the growing season.

HOW TO GROW
Plant and propagate in the same way as Sedum × 'Autumn Joy'. This species thrives best of all in soils that are well drained but do not dry out in summer, and needs a position in full sun.

Fleshy, grey-green leaves and generous flower heads are tinged throughout with a deep, rich purple.

Sedum maximum 'Atropurpureum', *Acanthus spinosus* and *Aster × frikartii*.

Sidalcea malviflora

Rather like a more delicate kind of hollyhock, this Californian perennial pushes up spikes of satiny flowers to a height of 2½-4½ ft above clumps of shallowly lobed leaves. The flowers are of a variable pink and add elegance to the garden from June to September. 'Sussex Beauty' (4 ft tall) is the loftiest cultivar and carries the clearest pink flowers. 'William Smith' (3 ft) is a charming shade of salmon-pink. 'Rose Queen' and 'Oberon' (both about 2½ ft) are two smaller varieties.

The pink of the sidalcea looks exquisite with silvery plants, such as *Senecio maritimus*, or behind the metallic-blue flowers of *Eryngium × oliverianum*.

HOW TO GROW
Plant in autumn or spring, 18 in. apart, in ordinary, well-drained soil, and in a sunny and sheltered position. Dead-head after flowering, and cut stems back to base in autumn. Propagate by division in spring.

Sidalcea malviflora 'Loveliness', which grows to a height of about 2½ ft, set off by the blue flowers of *Eryngium × oliverianum*.

The cup-shaped blooms of the 'Rose Queen' form are a clear, pale pink.

Smilacina racemosa (FALSE SPIKENARD)

Introduced to Britain from North America in 1632, only a dozen years after the Pilgrim Fathers landed in the New World, the false spikenard is a plant of unusual elegance and poise. Gracefully arching stems spread outwards from dense clumps, carrying closely set, faintly glossy, pale green leaves along their 3 ft length. Each stem is tipped with a plume of fragrant flowers. These start off as green, then mature in May and June to a rich cream.

The flowers are short-lived, but the foliage remains striking until well after the first autumn frosts, which turn it a clear gold.

HOW TO GROW
Plant between autumn and spring, 18 in. apart, in ordinary garden soil, ideally enriched with humus, and in partial to full shade. Ideal for woodland conditions. Cut down in late autumn. Propagate established clumps only, by division of the rhizomes in autumn.

A bed of mixed shapes and colours, with *Smilacina racemosa's* fluffy cream flowers in the foreground.

Introduce a continental mood to a sunny corner of the garden by surrounding an edging of silvery lamb's tongue with Mediterranean plants such as purple-blue flowered, purple-leaved sage, blue-leaved rue and *Allium karataviense* (left and right). The pale mauve flowers of *Rosmarinus officinalis* 'Jessop's Upright' make a fine backing. The scene here is set in July.

Stachys olympica (LAMB'S TONGUE)

Lamb's tongue is one of the most handsome and useful of ground-cover plants. Also known as *S. lanata* and *S. byzantina*, it comes from S.W. Asia and European Turkey, and so it can take all the sun it is likely to get in this country. Its mat of silvery, fleecy-looking evergreen leaves, which develops by the rooting of horizontal stems, spreads extensively. From this foliage rise 18 in. high spires that are white and woolly, and in June and July small purple flowers peer through like the eyes of an Old English sheepdog.

Lamb's tongue associates beautifully with a wide range of plants, including pinks, Old roses, irises and most blue flowers. But to enliven what is often rather a dull collection of plants, it might be a good idea to grow it with herbs – preferably Mediterranean ones, which are lamb's tongue's natural companions.

Behind the silvery *Stachys olympica*, you could establish a purple-leaved sage (*Salvia officinalis* 'Purpurascens'), 12-18 in. high, with purple-blue flowers in late summer. Forming an azure haze beside the sage there could be the tighter, rather taller growth of the blue-leaved rue, *Ruta graveolens* 'Jackman's Blue'. To this grouping there could be no better backing than the 6 ft spires of the erect rosemary (*Rosmarinus officinalis* 'Jessop's Upright'), which puts out pale mauve flowers on and off from early spring to the end of summer. Finally, as an outer fringe, you could put in a few of the summer bulbs *Allium karataviense*, 12 in. tall, with large, handsome, blue-green foliage and greenish-purple flowers in spheres, that remain decorative even after they have gone to seed.

HOW TO GROW
Stachys olympica: plant in autumn or spring, 12-15 in. apart, in ordinary garden soil, and in full sun. On flowering forms, remove dead stems in late autumn. Propagate by division, in autumn or spring.
Allium karataviense: see p. 141.
Rosmarinus officinalis: see p. 310.
Ruta graveolens: see p. 312.
Salvia officinalis: see p. 313.

The silver-white foliage and tall, fleecy spikes of *Stachys olympica* adorn the front of this summer border.

Solidago × 'Goldenmosa' (GOLDEN ROD)

In late summer, great swathes of golden rod (*Solidago*) can be seen brightening many suburban railway embankments. But in the small garden, one of the modern dwarf hybrids might be more suitable than these tall species, which can soon become rampant clumps.

'Goldenmosa' is one of the best of such hybrids. It makes a regular clump of yellow-green foliage 2½-3 ft high, which in late August is decorated with sprays of fluffy yellow flowers. These are like mimosa in colour and texture. A member of the same hybrid group is 'Crown of Rays', with broad, bright yellow flower clusters.

HOW TO GROW
Plant from autumn to spring, 2 ft apart – the shorter ones 18 in. – in ordinary, fertile soil, in sun or light shade. Staking is necessary only on windy sites. Cut to ground level in autumn. Propagate by division in autumn.

Solidago × 'Goldenmosa', so called because it resembles mimosa, makes a fine show with *Physostegia virginiana* 'Summer Snow'.

Solidago 'Crown of Rays' adds a vivid patch of yellow to the garden.

Stokesia laevis (STOKES' ASTER)

The delightful cornflower-like Stokes' aster – also known as *Stokesia cyanea* – has been with us since the 1760s but, strangely, has never been particularly well known. The blooms are large for the size of the plant – 2½-4 in. across, on top of stalks only 12-18 in. high. Their usual colour is blue, but a batch of seedlings may well produce a colour range from white to pink and purple. Creamy-yellow is not unknown.

The low clump of lance-shaped, evergreen leaves dislikes being shaded, especially in winter, so, although the plant is suitable for the front of a border, it will probably do best of all in a raised or terrace bed.

HOW TO GROW
Plant in spring, 12-15 in. apart, in ordinary soil and in an open, sunny site. Remove dead flower stems in late autumn. Propagate in spring by division, or by seeds. Seedlings, however, may vary in colour.

Butterflies flutter over a clump of bright pink *Stokesia laevis* on a warm summer afternoon.

Thalictrum speciosissimum
(MEADOW-RUE)

This meadow-rue well earns its Latin superlative of *speciosissimum*, meaning 'the most showy'. Purple-tinged stems reach up to 6 ft and carry sprays of beautiful leaves that resemble the fronds of a blue-grey maidenhair fern – until autumn frosts turn them an equally delightful yellow. In July and August the stems are crowned by fluffy heads of lemon-yellow flowers.

It associates well with blue flowers: delphiniums (large-flowered ones behind or Belladonna sorts in front) and, to accompany the foliage in autumn, Michaelmas daisies.

HOW TO GROW
Plant in spring, 2½-3 ft apart, in ordinary fertile soil, ideally enriched with humus. Best in light shade, though the plants can take full sun if the soil is moist. Cut down in late autumn. Propagate by seeds in summer; it takes two years for seedlings to flower.

A handful of dancing yellow powder-puffs decorates the top of each tall, branching stem of *Thalictrum speciosissimum*.

Autumn leaf sprays of thalictrum combine with Michaelmas daisies.

Thermopsis montana

Despite its invasive tendencies, this attractive perennial
from the Rocky Mountains is well worth consideration. In
May and June it looks like a yellow-flowered lupin when it
opens up its spikes of bloom above a mass of trifoliate
grey-green foliage, making a compact bush 2-3 ft high and
wide. *Thermopsis caroliniana* is a little taller, and more
stately in habit.

Because the plants are rather aggressive in their territorial
demands, they are more suitable for growing with flowering
shrubs than in the herbaceous border. *T. caroliniana*
harmonises particularly well with the white blooms of the
mock orange *Philadelphus* × 'Beauclerk'. Hummocks of blue
Veronica teucrium in the foreground give added interest.

HOW TO GROW
*Plant between autumn and spring, 2 ft apart, in ordinary
fertile soil, and in full sun or in very light shade. Cut flowered
spikes off as soon as they fade; remove dead stems in winter.
Propagate by seeds in spring or division in autumn.*

The towering golden spires of *Thermopsis
caroliniana* elegantly belie its rampant,
spreading root system.

Thermopsis montana, white philadelphus and blue *Veronica teucrium*.

Tradescantia × andersoniana (SPIDERWORT)

The main parent of this garden hybrid, *Tradescantia
virginiana*, was introduced here from Virginia in the early
17th century by the younger of the two royal gardeners
whose name it bears: John Tradescant, father and son. This
2 ft high hybrid is a border plant that is extremely easy to
grow and most interesting in form. The spear-shaped leaves
first develop vertically, then surround the flower heads in a
starry halo.

The blue-purple flowers, which appear from June to
September, are three-petalled and have hairy stamens within
(hence spiderwort). Cultivars range from white through blue
and pink to purple. 'Isis' is a splendid rich purple; 'Iris
Pritchard' is white, stained azure.

HOW TO GROW
*Plant between autumn and spring, 15-18 in. apart, in
ordinary garden soil, and in sun or very light shade. Support
with twiggy sticks in windy areas. Propagate named forms by
division in spring; seed-raised plants may vary considerably,
both in colour and performance.*

The purple flowers of *T. × andersoniana* measure 1-1½ in. across.

Tradescantia × andersoniana planted in front of a massive group of *Campanula lactiflora* 'Pritchard's Variety'.

Trillium grandiflorum (WAKE ROBIN)

Trilliums are exquisite plants that have all their parts in groups of three; the leaves, high up on the stem, look like a ship's propeller. Wake robin, one of the loveliest species, and also one of the easiest to grow, makes a 12-15 in. high clump of dark green foliage, above which nodding white flowers appear from April to June.

A good site for wake robin is a woodland garden, in which shafts of sun piercing the tree canopy will sporadically light up the flowers with dazzling gleams. However, so pretty is the plant that you may prefer instead a place where it can be kept in constant view. In this case, a semi-shaded courtyard bed would provide an ideal setting.

HOW TO GROW
Plant in late summer, early autumn or spring, 12 in. apart, in humus-rich and moist but well-drained soil, and in dappled shade. Propagate by division of the rhizomes during the dormant season; set the divisions 3-4 in. deep.

Best known of its genus, *Trillium grandiflorum* is also the largest.

Splashes of pure white against the deep green leaves of *T. grandiflorum* create a fine effect under a variegated weigela.

Trollius × hybridus (GLOBE FLOWER)

These hybrid globe flowers have lost none of the charm of their wild parent, *Trollius europaeus*. This once grew in damp meadows in central and northern Britain – William Wordsworth found it in abundance near his Lake District cottage in 1800 – but it is now rare.

The hybrids resemble large, luscious buttercups, with semi-double flowers in yellow or orange, and bright green, deeply cut leaves. They look good in a border, but even better naturalised beside a pool or stream with other moisture-loving plants. Flowering is in May and early June, before the big rush of summer perennials starts.

You might, for example, try two groups of *T. × hybridus* 'Commander-in-Chief' or 'Fireglobe' in a planting beside a pool. Both cultivars are 2½ ft tall and bear deep orange flowers 2-3 in. across. Only a few plants are required, put in 18 in. apart, then allowed to develop slowly but steadily into a dense clump.

The brightness of the globe flowers could then be set off in the background by the dogwood *Cornus alba* 'Spaethii', a shrub 6-8 ft high. Often this is cut back hard each spring to encourage the growth of winter-red stems, but here it is allowed to grow naturally so that in May and June it provides a fine display of small white flowers and pale green leaves bordered with yellow.

Completing such an association might be a third plant that starts to flower in June and continues into July – the deep blue *Iris xiphioides*.

Two other good *T. × hybridus* cultivars that could be planted instead of 'Goldquelle' are the lemon-yellow 'Canary Bird' and the deep orange 'Salamander'.

HOW TO GROW
Trollius × hybridus: plant in autumn or spring, 12-18 in. apart, in fertile, moist-to-wet soil, and in full sun or very light shade. Cut out faded flower stems at the base. Propagate named forms by division in autumn or spring.
Cornus alba 'Spaethii': *see p. 266.*
Iris xiphioides: see p. 159.

The golden globe flowers *Trollius × hybridus* glorify any pool edge. Here they are backed by *Cornus alba* 'Spaethii' and the blue *Iris xiphioides*.

Canary-yellow flower spikes crowd together in a long-lasting display.

Verbascum × *hybridum* 'Gainsborough'

(MULLEIN)

The majestic quality of mulleins (*Verbascum*) makes them superb plants for the back of a border. Some of them reach heights of over 6 ft.

Verbascum × *hybridum* are the offspring of a purple-flowered species from southern Europe, *V. phoeniceum*. They all bear long spikes of almost flat blooms from June to August, in colours which range from white through yellow, terracotta and amber to rose-purple.

One very good cultivar for the rear of a border association is 'Gainsborough', 3-4 ft tall, with lemon-yellow flowers and handsome grey leaves.

HOW TO GROW
Plant in autumn or spring, 12-15 in. apart, in ordinary garden soil and in full sun. Cut out flower stems as they fade, to encourage a second blooming. Verbascums are short-lived plants and are best propagated by root cuttings in early spring.

The tall spears of 'Gainsborough' make a sharp contrast behind shorter, rounded flower heads such as those of a phlox.

Viola cornuta (VIOLET)

The best violets for garden decoration are the large, robust species. One of the most striking is *Viola cornuta*, a lusty Pyrenean which can reach 12 in. in height and whose oval, toothed evergreen leaves spread considerably more. The main display of purple, 1 in. wide flowers is from May to July, with a lesser display into the autumn. Varieties include 'Jersey Gem', a deeper, blue-purple, and 'Alba' (white).

HOW TO GROW
Plant in autumn or spring, 12 in. apart, in ordinary garden soil in sun or partial shade. If possible, dead-head regularly to extend flowering. Propagate by seeds, in spring in a cold frame, or by division in spring.

A vigorous mass of *Viola cornuta* beneath a group of cool regale lilies.

Purple and white *V. cornuta*, fronting geraniums and other plants, overshadowed by pink *Rosa* 'Fantin Latour'.

Veronica incana (SPEEDWELL)

All speedwells (*Veronica*) are beautiful – even those that we curse as weeds in the lawn. The Russian *Veronica incana* (syn. *V. spicata incana*), 12-15 in. high, is one of the finest of the species that carry their flowers in spikes. It forms a dense carpet of narrow, silvery-grey leaves that remains lovely throughout the year, and from June to August raises up spires of clear blue flowers to marry with the silver in a pattern of heraldic splendour.

This speedwell makes a perfect foreground plant in a blue and silver association, which might, for example, include *Dryas octopetala*; its white saucer-shaped flowers appear in June and July.

HOW TO GROW
Plant between autumn and spring, 10 in. apart, in ordinary garden soil and in full sun. Cut down to ground level in late autumn. Propagate by division or basal cuttings in spring, ideally every three or four years.

The graceful, fluffy, silvery seed heads of *Dryas octopetala* beside the last flowers of *Veronica incana* at the end of August.

The slim blue spires make an elegant group against any background.

Zantedeschia aethiopica 'Crowborough'

(ARUM LILY)

The arum lily, *Zantedeschia aethiopica*, is no longer raised only in greenhouses; in mild areas it has become well established by the sides of ponds, lakes and rivers, where it can keep its roots well away from frost. And recently a form that is hardier and more tolerant of dry conditions has become available: 'Crowborough', 1½-2½ ft high.

Like the wild species, 'Crowborough' has glossy, arrow-shaped, deep green leaves and large flowers that each consist of a white spathe (a modified leaf) surrounding a golden spadix (central spike). These appear from June onwards. The plant is suitable for many positions, including shady gardens.

HOW TO GROW
Plant in spring, 1½-2 ft apart, in good but not over-rich, preferably moist to wet, soil, or as a waterside plant in mild areas. Protect the fleshy crowns with a winter mulch, or lift and store them, potted, in a frost-free frame or greenhouse until the following spring. Propagate by division in spring.

Dazzlingly white arum lilies – traditionally carried by the June bride.

Zantedeschia aethiopica adds a stately touch behind pale yellow *Primula florindae* and the feathery spikes of astilbes.

Set around a garden pond, ferns luxuriate in their watery habitat.

FERNS

Long before the first flower appeared, much of the Earth's plant life consisted of ferns. The shadows of their elegant, intricately divided fronds can still be seen, stamped on to coal, and looking little different from the 10,000 or so species of fern that still grow upon the planet.

The reproductive process of ferns depends not upon flowers but upon minute spores, which are carried in dense groups on the underside of the fronds and eventually drift to the ground. The spores grow into tiny, leaf-like bodies called prothalli, on which both male and female cells are borne. The male swims to the female cell – ferns can reproduce only in moist conditions – and, upon their fusion, a new fern plant begins to develop. A fascinating method of propagating ferns is to leave a mature frond in a white envelope; after a few days, it will dry off and deposit the powdery spores on to the white paper. Sprinkle the spores on to a tray of compost that has been previously sterilised by soaking in boiling water, and place the tray in a plastic bag. Keep it out of direct sunlight, and when the prothalli are well developed, spray them lightly with tepid water every few days. When fronds appear and the tiny plants are large enough to handle, treat them in the same way as seedlings.

Asplenium scolopendrium

(HART'S-TONGUE FERN)

The heavier growth of the trees, the darker green of the meadows and the deep fern-hung banks are the tell-tale signs to every West-country-bound traveller that his destination is almost reached.

One of the most distinctive of the native ferns is *Asplenium scolopendrium*, hart's-tongue, formerly known and still listed as *Phyllitis scolopendrium*. It makes, when seen as a single plant (which, except in cultivation, is most unlikely), a shuttlecock of long, bright, deep green blades with waved edges; in quantity on a bank, a positively undersea effect is produced, especially in the dark quietness of a wood. *A. s.* 'Undulatum' has more deeply waved leaf margins.

In the garden, hart's-tongue has so many uses that it is surprising that it is seen so seldom. It is able to take full shade – though gleams of sunshine light up the fronds wonderfully – and any sort of soil, even pure chalk, so long as it does not dry out. Exposure to cold, drying winds as the new foliage develops is lethal and drought, either at the root or in the air, causes miserable and untypically mean growth. It can, if all the conditions are right, grow to 2 ft.

For an association, the first image to come to mind is one of hart's-tongue as evergreen ground-cover in woodland with Solomon's seal, perhaps, and bluebells. In the shady corners of paved areas it can be used as a permanent link plant, always in leaf, with *Arum italicum* 'Pictum' and, behind, some Turk's cap lilies (*Lilium martagon*). Wood anemones (*Anemone nemorosa*) in the foreground would give a lift to early spring.

HOW TO GROW
Asplenium scolopendrium: plant in shade during April in ordinary, preferably humus-rich, soil. Propagate by spores in April, or by division in March.
Anemone nemorosa: see p. 144.
Arum italicum: see p. 69.
Lilium martagon: see p. 163.

Both *Asplenium scolopendrium* and *A. s.* 'Undulatum' are used to edge this flight of garden steps; also in the scheme are *Lilium martagon* and *Arum italicum* 'Pictum'. The group is illustrated in July.

Adiantum pedatum

The fronds of maidenhair fern (*Adiantum capillus-veneris*), like showers of green raindrops and once prized possessions in many a cottage, are sadly not for the open garden in Britain. But a couple of other species of *Adiantum* are both possible and highly desirable.

A. *pedatum* has been with us since the 1600s, with reintroductions and newly discovered forms added over the years. Throughout its season of growth it provides continual pleasure, from the moment the tiny and exquisitely delicate fronds begin to unfurl in spring until their autumn demise. Fully grown, the plant appears as an airy cloud of foliage over 12-15 in. high and as much across.

Moisture and spring and summer shade are essential for good growth.

HOW TO GROW
Adiantum pedatum: plant during April in semi-shade in soil enriched with leaf-mould or peat and with a thoroughly mixed handful or two of bonemeal. Propagate by division or spores in March.

Flanked by yellow mimulus, this fine clump of *Adiantum pedatum* guards a small rock-garden pool.

Dryopteris filix-mas (MALE FERN)

There are several fine *Dryopteris* species native to Britain, and all make good garden plants. *Dryopteris filix-mas* is the male fern (still employed in medicine); *D. dilatata* is the broad buckler fern; and the less common *D. pseudomas* (syn. *D. borreri*) is the golden-scaled male fern.

D. *filix-mas* likes a lot of moisture and can be used to lighten the often heavy leaf patterns of the bog garden; it also makes a splendid background for exhibition dahlias. Like other dryopteris, though enjoying a leafy woodland soil, it will take even dry shade and still look well. But, as with many other foliage plants, good living brings out its true potential.

HOW TO GROW
Plant dryopteris in March or April in shade and in ordinary garden soil, preferably enriched with humus. Propagation by division in spring.

Dryopteris filix-mas will grow to a height and spread of 2-4 ft.

Dryopteris filix-mas planted at the foot of a wall below a fine specimen of the pale purple shrub *Hydrangea villosa*.

Athyrium filix-femina (LADY FERN)

Unlike hart's-tongue, with its year-round evergreen interest, the lady fern is at its most attractive while the fronds are still developing. During this time, and while they retain their early freshness, the plant justifies its name by the delicacy of its much-divided fronds and the fresh, bright green of the young growth.

The craze for ferns in the last century caused every possible variant to be collected and propagated; sadly, with later change of taste, most collections were dispersed, leading to the loss of some remarkable specimens of *Athyrium filix-femina*. A few, occasionally available today, have crested fronds or even further division of the pinnae (as lobes of the fronds are called). None of them likes cold winds.

HOW TO GROW

Plant during April or September in light shade and in a humus-rich soil. Enrich this annually with a top-dressing of compost mingled with a little bonemeal. Propagate by division in spring.

Lady fern and lady's mantle (*Alchemilla*) combine delightfully by water.

The delicate and fresh young fronds of lady fern awash in a sea of fragrant blue forget-me-nots (*Myosotis sylvatica*).

Matteuccia struthiopteris

(OSTRICH-PLUME FERN, SHUTTLECOCK FERN)

Named in honour of the Italian physicist Carlo Matteucci (1811-68), this graceful, moisture-loving fern adds considerable charm to a woodland garden.

While the thick rhizomes of *Dryopteris* grow along the ground with only the ends appearing much above it, those of *Matteuccia*, the ostrich-plume fern, develop vertically, so that an old plant grows its fronds from the top of a short, thick 'trunk'. This trunk is unlikely to exceed 12 in. in height, but, even so, the plant is both beautiful and distinct. It does, however, spread widely by slender underground rhizomes.

The spring growth is a circle of perfectly matched fronds making a regular shuttlecock of clear, pale green. From the centre there emerge half a dozen or so fertile fronds that eventually turn to a dark suede, both in colour and texture; it is these fronds that suggested the ostrich-plume name. They are particularly distinctive in winter, when the leafy fronds have died down.

Matteuccia dislikes dryness, but is remarkably tolerant even in this respect. It looks well beside water and prefers light shade during the hottest part of the day. The plant appears on some lists as *Onoclea germanica*.

Of all the commonly grown larger ferns, *Matteuccia struthiopteris* has the most sculptural appearance. It combines well with other large waterside perennials, especially *Rodgersia aesculifolia*, *Peltiphyllum peltatum* and *Primula florindae*.

The fern may grow to between 3 ft and 5 ft in height, and has a spread of about 3 ft, so it is wise to select bold plants in any association.

HOW TO GROW

Plant from October to April in partial shade and at least 4 ft apart to give plenty of room for root growth. They will do well in any ordinary, moisture-retentive soil. Propagate by removing offsets and replanting them in April.

Matteuccia struthiopteris, a hardy, moisture-loving fern of elegant, arching habit enjoys dappled shade beneath trees.

Osmunda regalis (ROYAL FERN)

The royal fern is well named. It is the biggest and most noble fern that can be grown in normal circumstances outdoors in Britain. (The gardens at Logan, in south-west Scotland, and at Tresco Abbey in the Scillies, with their 15 ft high tree ferns, can hardly be classed as 'normal'.) *Osmunda*, moreover, is not only grown here, but is, in fact, a native.

Eventually, in the water's-edge position that it loves, it builds up an enormous fibrous clump of black roots, often a foot or so above ground, and from this the crowns put up their elegant fronds each spring. They unfurl crosier-fashion, buff-pink in colour with cream streaks of soft down. Like the velvet on a stag's antlers, this soon rubs off the mature fronds, which eventually stand up to 6 ft in height – smooth and perfect, clear green until the autumn cold turns them a warm brown.

The fertile parts of *Osmunda* are utterly unlike those of other hardy ferns. The tops of some of the fronds, instead of continuing leafy, become plumes of spore-bearing leaflets standing high above the rest. The pattern is indeed a lovely one.

Thus, in association, the *Osmunda* must quite clearly be the dominant member. It should be planted at the edge of water to ensure full growth. A suitable companion to one side might be *Peltiphyllum peltatum*, whose pink flower heads are up and finished almost before the fern has woken from winter. Later, its pram-wheel leaves make a perfect contrast. At the royal fern's foot you could plant a group of *Primula florindae*; they will flower among the young fronds and will come to no harm when, in late summer, they are shaded over by the spreading adult fern. Finally, the foliage of all the plants will take on autumn tints together.

HOW TO GROW
Osmunda regalis: plant in semi or partial shade, in any waterside humus-rich soil, during March or April; the crowns should be at soil level to start with. Propagate by dividing widely separated multiple crowns in spring; closely set crowns are unlikely to survive unless treated with care.
Peltiphyllum peltatum: see p. 109.
Primula florindae: see p. 372.

A waterside group in its autumn colours: *Osmunda regalis* stands guard over the broad pram-wheel foliage of *Peltiphyllum peltatum* and the arrow-head leaves of *Primula florindae*.

Bright green *Osmunda regalis* makes a fine summer specimen plant.

Feathery *Cortaderia selloana* with *Miscanthus sinensis* just below.

GRASSES

Since most people would be hard put to identify even a dozen different grasses, it comes as something of a surprise to learn that there are some 700 genera and about 10,000 species. Most of them closely resemble the kinds that grow on the lawn and are very difficult to distinguish one from the other, especially when not in flower; no one would think of making them a feature in a bed in any event.

Recently, however, quite a number of gardeners have re-awoken to the possibilities of ornamental grasses – the soaring, spectacular pampas grass *Cortaderia selloana*, for example, or the strikingly variegated gardener's garters, *Phalaris arundinacea* 'Picta'. Only a few of the ornamental grasses now available are described in the following pages, and species new or reintroduced to this country are appearing in the nurseries each year. All make splendidly exotic patches in the garden, are fairly easy to grow and are well worth looking for at the garden centre.

HOW TO GROW
Plant in ordinary garden soil. Some perennial species are a little slow to become established. Planting should take place in spring. Annuals may be sown in their permanent site at the same time, or earlier under glass. Propagate perennials by dividing and replanting in spring.

Cortaderia selloana (PAMPAS GRASS)

There is no other ornamental grass that grows to such a size, nor one so able to dominate the scene – so it needs siting with care – by water, perhaps, with a background of dark-leaved shrubs that have finished summer flowering.

Pampas grass makes a wide, 3 ft high clump of long arching leaves, sharp-edged enough to slice ungloved fingers. In August, thick flower stems start to push up from the clump until in September, like a fountain in incredibly slow motion, the top bursts out in a great plume of smoky feathers, glistening creamy-white in some forms with a tinge of sunset pink.

Height varies according to the form chosen. Best for small gardens is the compact 'Pumila', which is only about 5-6 ft high, but if your garden can take it, you might plant the majestic 7-8 ft 'Sunningdale Silver'.

HOW TO GROW
See above.

The silky, silvery plumes of pampas grass, up to 18 in. long, contrast perfectly with a background of tall, dark evergreens.

Festuca glauca

Festuca glauca beside a clump of yellow-flowered *Allium moly* in summer.

Sheep's-fescue (*Festuca ovina*) is a fragment of the upland downs transported, a tussock-forming little grass with leaves as fine as hair and that show silver then dark as they toss in the wind. The closely allied *F. glauca*, which forms tufts of blue-grey leaves, is a valuable garden plant for a number of positions. Planted in broad swathes it looks equally well at the front of an association of grey-leaved plants or in a 'white garden'. As it maintains its pattern and colour throughout winter, it provides useful in-scale background to the earliest of spring bulbs; *Iris histrioides*, which flowers without foliage, is helped immeasurably by it. Later, the smaller ornamental onions such as *Allium moly* make good associates.

Only soil that remains soggy throughout winter is resented; otherwise it is an easy plant to satisfy. It can be propagated from seeds or by division.

HOW TO GROW
See above.

The dense tufts of blue-grey leaves and flower spikelets, up to 9 in. high, add interest to the edge of a border.

Miscanthus sinensis

In full summer growth, this lovely grass might easily be mistaken for a light-weight bamboo. With its willowy wands clothed with long, arching leaves reaching up to 6 ft, the whole effect is graceful in the extreme. The type species seems not to flower, but two superlative forms, 'Silver Feather' and 'Zebrinus', can both be depended upon to produce heads like a silky reed-grass in autumn. 'Zebrinus' develops transverse bars of gold across the blades, while 'Variegatus', has leaves with longitudinal white stripes.

Though this is a typical herbaceous plant with top growth that dies in autumn, it is of sufficient strength to remain as a pleasing winter shape.

Such lightness of form, married with height, means that these grasses can be joined with shrubs and herbaceous plants and brought forward in the border. Try making *Miscanthus sinensis* the backdrop to a grouping that repeats shades of pink from March to September.

In the foreground, falling over a paved edge, is *Bergenia cordifolia*, whose flower heads take colour in late winter. The strong, leathery leaves then give weight to a clump of *Paeonia lactiflora* 'Globe of Light'. As these fade in June, the miscanthus reaches upwards and outwards to frame some pink August phloxes, such as *Phlox maculata* 'Mother of Pearl'. The final, delicate display in this grouping will be that of autumn-tinted peony foliage in contrast with dark, evergreen *Bergenia*.

HOW TO GROW

Miscanthus sinensis: see p. 132. Cut dead stems down to ground level in March. The foliage may be cut in fine weather in August and hung up to dry for flower arrangements.
Bergenia cordifolia: see p. 72.
Paeonia lactiflora: see p. 107.
Phlox maculata: see p. 111.

A handsome clump of *Miscanthus sinensis* 'Zebrinus', next to flowering *Phlox maculata*, with the fading leaves of *Paeonia lactiflora* behind and a carpet of *Bergenia cordifolia*.

Pennisetum villosum

The beauty of this charming grass is enhanced by its 4 in. cylindrical flower spikes, whose long white hairs give them the appearance of some strange sea creature that has taken to the land. These spikes are held on 18 in. stems, around which are grouped grassy leaves.

Pennisetum villosum (syn. *P. longistylum*) comes from north-east Africa, and is therefore not entirely happy in the climate of northern Europe. Fortunately, it flowers well if grown as a half-hardy annual, and it might be a good idea to try a number of plants in different situations to see how it behaves. It is certainly worth the trouble – not least for its plumes, which if cut and hung up to dry, add splendour to any winter arrangement.

HOW TO GROW

See p. 132. Even in southern areas, this plant requires a sheltered site. In chillier regions it might be worthwhile lifting in autumn, placing in pots and overwintering in a frost-free greenhouse.

About 18 in. high, *Pennisetum villosum* is a useful and decorative addition to a sunny corner in the garden.

Phalaris arundinacea 'Picta'
(GARDENER'S GARTERS)

Gardener's garters, a variant of fenland reed-grass, has been recognised as one of the most handsome of garden grasses since the 16th century at least. It is a plant of moist, rich soils and in such situations will overwhelm any ground it can seize upon and grow to a height of 5 ft. On dry, thin soils, however, it will reach only about half that height and is perfectly manageable. The mass of white-striped leaves makes a striking pattern from the moment the first shoots spear the ground in spring until autumn frosts turn them yellow and sere. Throughout the winter they keep their shape and texture, and therefore should not be cut down until spring. Wherever it grows, phalaris is a vigorous grass and soon builds up into picturesque clumps.

Its exuberant habits might be considered a virtue or a vice, but either way it is a lovely plant for a white and green association, cool as Regency-striped chintz on the hottest day.

You might try blending it with a foreground group of white bearded irises. To one side, following a few white hyacinths, is *Nicotiana alata* 'Lime Green' for summer effect. Behind is the blue sheen of *Eryngium × oliverianum*, while at the back the presiding genius with flowers from June to October is *Rosa* 'Iceberg'.

An alternative association blends the cool colours of *Papaver orientale* 'Mrs Perry' and the yellow *Santolina chamaecyparissus* with the stripes of 'Picta'.

HOW TO GROW
Phalaris arundinacea: see p. 132. Restrict the creeping rhizomes by replanting every two or three years or inserting vertical slates around the clumps.
Bearded irises: see p. 97.
Eryngium × oliverianum: see p. 84.
Nicotiana alata: see p. 46.
Rosa 'Iceberg': see p. 230.

An association of delicate colours: *Phalaris arundinacea, Papaver orientale* 'Mrs Perry' and *Santolina chamaecyparissus.*

Spartina pectinata 'Aureo-marginata'
(PRAIRIE CORD GRASS)

Our own native cord-grass is *Spartina × townsendii*, an interesting natural hybrid between two species, which appeared on the edges of Southampton Water around the middle of the last century; every visitor to muddy shores recognises its sharp-tipped leaves and one-sided flower spikes, half drowned at high tide.

Though invaluable as a binder of mud-flats, it is no garden plant. But a North American relation, bigger and less demanding of salty water (though still able to take a brackish situation), can be useful, especially at the edges of ponds. This is the Prairie cord-grass, *S. pectinata*, which can reach 6 ft in height, though it is usually less. Leaves are a couple of feet in length, arching and elegant, and in the variegated form 'Aureo-marginata' are extremely ornamental, especially when the tall green flower spikes are hung with purple anthers. The plant can become somewhat invasive in the moist positions it enjoys.

HOW TO GROW
See p. 132.

A flourishing clump of *Spartina pectinata*, with *Crocosmia × crocosmiiflora* 'Solfatare' in the foreground.

Stipa gigantea (FEATHER GRASS)

There is always a place in the garden for a plant which has height without heaviness and so can be brought forward in the herbaceous border. Such a plant is also useful for standing in front of shrubs without shading them, yet giving interest to a group whose main display is over.

Stipa gigantea is a fine example of these eye-catching plants. It makes a grassy clump of thin leaves 2-3 ft long, which is in itself a pleasant contrast to the heavy leaves of, say, *Bergenia cordifolia* or *Pulmonaria saccharata*, which might well front it.

From this clump in July, enormous yet airy spikes spring up to a height of quite 6 ft, each established plant carrying at least a dozen stems.

When the heads are young they are a delicate purple, but they soon take on the colour of ripe corn and this is maintained for many weeks.

HOW TO GROW
See p. 132. For dried-flower arrangements, cut the inflorescences when they are fully developed in July.

Stipa gigantea surrounded by the foliage of *Pulmonaria saccharata*.

The handsome, feathery plumes of *Stipa gigantea* tower above the other inhabitants of the herbaceous border.

Stipa pennata (FEATHER GRASS)

The aptly named feather grass is a close relation of esparto, whose tough leaf fibres are such a valuable constituent of paper and cordage. The highly ornamental *Stipa pennata*, a native of eastern Europe and Siberia, has been in cultivation here since the late 17th century. Surprisingly, considering its origins, it is apt not to survive British winters, resenting perhaps their erratic blow-cold, blow-mild pattern.

But if even in a well-drained, sunny spot it fails to behave like the perennial it is, feather grass can easily be raised annually from seeds. A mature plant makes a strong grassy clump a couple of feet high and the same across. From this, arching flower stems emerge, their top 9 in. airy and glistening white.

In the garden, the feather grass associates most effectively with the bold flowers of Californian poppy (*Eschscholzia californica*) or Shirley poppy (*Papaver rhoeas*). For a more subtle blend of colours it can be ringed around with the prostrate shrublet *Hebe* 'Pagei'.

HOW TO GROW
See p. 132.

The silvery-buff 'feathers' of *Stipa pennata* bloom from June to August. They are particularly suitable for drying.

Plumes of *Stipa pennata* wave gently above bright Californian poppies.

The Cottage Garden

Where flowers and foliage blend to create a picture of simplicity and charm

The cottage-garden style that evolved in the 19th century was a practical yet decorative blending of the formal garden and the small-scale, mixed plantings of the rural cottager.

The true cottage garden had paths edged with low hedges, usually of dwarf box (*Buxus sempervirens* 'Suffruticosa') but occasionally of lavender or trained fruit bushes. Within the hedges, flowers, fruit and vegetables were planted together, often with the most useful herbs near the door, while fragrant roses, honeysuckles and lilies were set near the windows.

A generously planted cottage plot would contain clumps of goat's rue (*Galega*), lupins, meadow-rue (*Thalictrum*) and peonies, all underplanted with clove-scented pinks (*Dianthus*). Its paths might be lined with London pride (*Saxifraga × urbium*) and mossy saxifrage (*S. moschata*), while violas and sedums would seed themselves in cracks between

paving or bricks. Alchemillas, campanulas, delphiniums and irises would flourish alongside the columbines (*Aquilegia*), and in the shade of the hedges there would gleam primroses (*Primula*), foxgloves (*Digitalis*), artemisias and Jerusalem sage (*Phlomis fruticosa*).

Towards the end of the 19th century the influential gardener-writers William Robinson and Gertrude Jekyll recognised the aesthetic appeal of hardy cottage-garden plants and their ready adaptability to a new form of gardening in large gardens. In different compartments of these gardens, attractive seasonal displays were created with mixed plantings of shrubs, perennials and bulbs, while other areas might be devoted to particular colour schemes or to one genus only. The emphasis was on moderation of colour and form, for heavy-headed, vivid show blooms were considered to be against the true spirit of the cottage garden.

Few of Gertrude Jekyll's own exquisite gardens survive, but others modelled on her principles can still be seen. Two of the finest are Hidcote in Gloucestershire, designed by Major Lawrence Johnstone, and Sissinghurst in Kent, the creation of the writers Victoria Sackville-West and Sir Harold Nicolson. Both are large, and each hedged or walled-in compartment is a garden in itself.

A much smaller garden at Tintinhull, in Somerset, has ornamental plantings in strict colour schemes and a kitchen garden in which rows of espalier pears and catmint break up the mixed planting of vegetables, Shrub roses, perennials and bulbs.

A superb cottage garden was created at East Lambrook Manor in Somerset by another gardener-writer Margery Fish (1893-1969). In each separate area plants with similar needs were encouraged to spread and seed haphazardly in natural conditions. Moisture-loving plants and bulbs covered the steep

In the idealised picture of the cottage garden, flowers and vegetables blend naturally with fruit trees and bushes in an informal setting.

Victoria Sackville-West (1892-1962) and her husband Sir Harold Nicolson restored Sissinghurst Castle and redesigned its gardens, which they modelled on the principles of Gertrude Jekyll.

Gertrude Jekyll (1843-1932) devoted the later years of her life to the garden of her home at Munstead Wood; the garden was designed by Sir Edwin Lutyens and embellished by her.

banks of an old stream bed, dappled with the light shade of apple trees. Elsewhere, in full sun, silver and grey-leaved plants mingled in well-drained soil. Rather than seeking effects from splashes of flower colour, Margery Fish preferred a tapestry of green, grey, gold and variegated foliage. Long-forgotten species were grown in their wild form, without the 'improvement' of hybridising, many of them having been gathered from neglected rustic gardens.

Designing a cottage garden

If you are about to cultivate a cottage garden, remember that though plantings ought to give an impression of natural, random luxuriance, the lines of the hedges and paths that contain them must be straight and functional, since without this firm framework the garden will simply look as if it has been allowed to run wild. Ideally, the outer hedges round the garden should be of solid holly, yew or beech, with the inner hedges of some low, fragrant foliage plant such as lavender, rosemary, box or santolina, and the paths of local stone or brick, with their joints left free of cement so that chance-sown seeds can germinate in them.

Apple, pear or mulberry trees add to the rustic effect, especially mulberry, with its gnarled wood and shaggy crown. Old fruit trees look even more lovely smothered by a climbing rose, together with a small-flowered clematis to extend the flowering season. Beneath the trees, bulbs, hellebores and Solomon's seal (*Polygonatum*) will thrive in the rough grass and light shade.

Evergreen bay (*Laurus*), myrtle (*Myrtus*), winter-flowering laurustinus (*Viburnum tinus*) and glossy-leaved bear's breeches (*Acanthus*) are old favourites for decorating sheltered corners or framing an archway or door. More recent introductions, such as ceanothus, escallonia and osmanthus, also look well in such roles.

Senecio 'Sunshine' and *Artemisia* 'Lambrook Silver' make soft, silvery, cascading bushes that blend with every flower colour. The sculptural form of another silver-leaved plant, the globe artichoke (*Cynara scolymus*), lends some solidity to a looser planting of the herbaceous perennials such as sweet rocket (*Hesperis matronalis*), euphorbia and eryngium. Perennials can also be interspersed with deciduous shrubs planned to give a succession of flowers throughout summer: ceratostigmas and *Sedum spectabile* mix well with butterfly-attracting buddleias, old scented Shrub roses and caryopteris.

Chaenomeles and both winter and summer-flowering jasmines are other fine cottage-garden shrubs, especially when underplanted with crown imperials (*Fritillaria imperialis*), madonna lilies (*Lilium candidum*), amaryllis and nerines.

A modern evocation of the cottage-garden style adopted by Gertrude Jekyll, where a profusion of traditional perennials and shrubs make a harmonious blend.

Bulbs, corms and tubers

Once established, bulbs give a succession of colour from bright spring to bleakest winter

FOR MOST GARDENERS, the joy of returning spring is heralded by the appearance of early flowering bulbs in all their amazing variety. Gentle nodding snowdrops, sun-catching crocuses, golden daffodils and stately tulips take us from January to May in a seasonal succession of extraordinary beauty.

Bulbs (and corms, tubers and rhizomes – all of which are included in this section) are perennial plants in which part of the plant has evolved into a subterranean storage chamber where food created from one year's work is held to nourish the plant in the next. These are fully equipped 'packaged products'. With their growth and development programmed by nature, they require only the most basic help from the gardener to fulfil the promise of the nurseryman's catalogue.

Bulbs, corms and tubers are valuable components of a complete garden. Because they vanish from sight at certain times of the year – the pattern varies according to the plant and to its original home – they can be overlaid by other plants or they can be used to underplant in a variety of situations. Naturalised snowdrops and aconites in a woodland setting, daffodils in orchard grass or crocuses beneath shrubs – all provide ground-level interest before overshadowing foliage takes over.

But the succession does not end in spring. Lilies, alliums, colchicums and cyclamens provide continuity through summer to autumn – in fact, *Nerine bowdenii* can be picked in late November, no more than a few weeks before the first snowdrops appear above the ground to start the cycle once again.

Set against a high sheltering wall, the white flowers and tall, spiky stems of madonna lilies stand out dramatically against the foliage of the strawberry tree, *Arbutus unedo*.

Agapanthus × 'Headbourne Hybrids'
(AFRICAN LILY)

African lilies, as perennials of the genus *Agapanthus* are known, provide a striking late-summer display of bloom. Among the best are the hardy *Agapanthus* × 'Headbourne Hybrids', which are free-flowering in any ordinary garden soil. Given an open, sunny site, each plant will form a clump of flowering stems about 2 ft high. As few as three specimens grown together, and planted about 18 in. apart, will provide a fine splash of colour, carrying heads of mid-blue, trumpet-shaped flowers from July to September.

The bold spikes of the red hot poker *Kniphofia* 'Maid of Orleans' would make a striking contrast with the loose habit of the African lily, and their greenish-yellow flowers harmonise well with the clusters of blue.

Both colours would be enhanced by a foreground planting of the silver-leaved *Stachys olympica*. For a more immediate association, try *Achillea filipendulina* 'Coronation Gold', whose flat, brilliant yellow flower heads look as well in a dried flower arrangement as they do in the border. Couple it, perhaps, with the woolly, silver-grey foliage and white flowers of *Lychnis coronaria* 'Alba', or with the red blooms of the Californian fuchsia *Zauschneria californica*.

HOW TO GROW
Agapanthus × 'Headbourne Hybrids': *plant in mid-spring, in any good, well-drained soil and a sunny sheltered site. The plants tolerate lime. Set the crowns 2 in. deep and 15 in. apart; in cold areas cover them with a winter mulch. Cut the plants back to ground level in autumn. Avoid unnecessary root disturbance; propagate by division in spring.*
Achillea filipendulina: see p. 64.
Kniphofia 'Maid of Orleans': *see p. 98.*
Lychnis coronaria 'Alba': *see p. 103.*
Stachys olympica: see p. 122.
Zauschneria californica: see p. 221.

Allium albopilosum

Only a few of the vast array of onion-type plants are of ornamental value, but among them are some that look very good indeed. The hardy, 18 in. high Asiatic *Allium albopilosum* is one of these, being admired in June for its large spherical heads of starry, metallic-pink flowers and in autumn and winter for its attractive seed heads. It is best grown among plants that will hide its untidy leaves but not cast too much shade.

Try planting a group of at least five alliums – spacing them 4-5 in. apart – with clumps of the blue-grey grass *Festuca glauca* and the dwarf shrub *Genista lydia*, whose slender, arching stems bear bright yellow flowers in May and June.

HOW TO GROW
Plant in autumn, in any – even poor – soil, provided it is well drained, and in an open, sunny situation. The plants are most effective in clumps of five or more, set in holes three times the depth of the bulbs, and spaced 9 in. apart. They can be left undisturbed for years, but should be given a spring dressing of fertiliser. Prevent slug damage as for Allium siculum.
Propagate as for A. moly.

Here the blue trumpets of the agapanthus hybrids form part of a late-summer association with *Achillea filipendulina* 'Coronation Gold' and *Lychnis coronaria* 'Alba'.

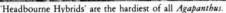
'Headbourne Hybrids' are the hardiest of all *Agapanthus*.

Allium albopilosum, which brightens the garden in June with its pink flower heads, flourishes in hot dry conditions.

Allium karataviense

Striking foliage is the main attraction of this bulbous Asiatic plant. The broad leaves are dark green suffused with purple. Like the greenish-white, purple-flushed flowers that appear in spherical heads during May and June, the leaves are nearly stemless – so, to be seen properly, the plant needs to be grown near the front of a border.

The subtle colouring of *Allium karataviense* combines well with greyish-leaved plants, especially if they have a contrasting form of growth. Spiky clumps of irises are ideal for the purpose. Soft blue *Iris pallida dalmatica*, planted behind the alliums, will give height to the grouping.

HOW TO GROW

Cultivate as for Allium albopilosum, with bulbs set 8 in. apart. Prevent slug damage as for A. siculum. Propagate as for A. moly. This and other alliums which have been growing in the same site for years benefit from a dressing of general fertiliser in spring.

The pale globes of bloom borne by *Allium karataviense* in late spring are carried at the top of 6-9 in. high stems.

Iris pallida dalmatica makes a perfect accompaniment for *A. karataviense.*

Allium moly (GOLDEN GARLIC)

A native of rocky, semi-shaded places in Spain, this 12 in. high hardy allium is valuable for providing an early summer display in rock gardens. Here, its sunny splashes of yellow flowers and grey leaves are shown to fine advantage by a background of sandy-coloured rock.

However, it will also succeed in a border. In such a setting, an attractive gold-and-silver combination can be obtained by growing it with the silvery-leaved perennial *Lamium maculatum* 'Beacon Silver', which rapidly makes wide carpets of foliage.

HOW TO GROW

Cultivate as for Allium albopilosum; space bulbs 3-4 in. apart. Propagate this and other species by division of overgrown clumps in autumn or spring; replant immediately. Ripe seeds can be sown under glass, but seedlings take up to four years to reach flowering size. Prevent slug damage as for A. siculum. Apply general fertiliser in spring.

Golden garlic, which produces its 2 in. wide clusters of flowers in June and July, will colonise a border rapidly.

This allium's starry flowers bring a sparkle of colour to a dull corner.

Allium siculum

This hardy bulbous plant, growing up to 4 ft high, is equally becoming whether flowering in the garden in May and June or dried as a winter decoration. Its hanging, bell-shaped flowers are a greenish-white tinged with muted red-purple. Plants which associate well with a group of these alliums are: *Anchusa azurea*, which bears tiny blue flowers from June to August; *Helleborus orientalis*, which carries crimson-freckled cream flowers in February and March; and any of the pulmonarias.

HOW TO GROW

Cultivate as for Allium albopilosum. Set bulbs 9 in. apart, and provide cane supports on windy sites. All alliums grow from leafy clumps close to the ground and are liable to slug damage, so scatter slug pellets over the soil or water with a metaldehyde solution. Apply a general fertiliser in spring. Propagate as for A. moly.

The seed heads of *A. siculum*, which can be dried for indoor use, look splendid when set against dark copper beech leaves.

Allium siculum blooms above the bowl-shaped leaves of *Hosta sieboldiana.*

Alstroemeria Ligtu hybrids (PERUVIAN LILY)

These bizarre but beautiful flowers, which have been raised from a Chilean species, provide glorious colour not only in the herbaceous border but also in the home, as long-lasting cut flowers. The funnel-shaped blooms are borne from July to September in clusters of up to 20 at the top of each flowering stem. On every flower, two of the upper petals are soft yellow, streaked and splashed with deep red; the remaining, broader petals, which form the tubular shape, are all pink or apricot or yellow-orange. The sunset hues are delicately offset by the plant's slender, twisted, silvery leaves.

For the most eye-catching effect, these 2-3 ft high alstroemerias should be grown in a group of three or more. They are hardy but need a warm, sunny border, a position which also suits the grey-leaved plants that make their best companions. Try planting the hybrids between several bushes of rue (*Ruta graveolens*). In the foreground, the saucer-shaped flowers of *Helianthemum nummularium*, the

familiar rock rose, would be at their best during the first few weeks of the alstroemerias more extended flowering period. The effect of the grouping would be enhanced by setting the plants against a subdued background – for example, a mellowed brick wall or a shrub with dull green leaves, such as bay (*Laurus nobilis*).

A grey-leaved companion – rue – blends well with the Ligtu hybrids. The familiar rock rose adds sparkle to the foreground.

HOW TO GROW
Alstroemeria Ligtu hybrids: *plant pot-grown specimens in spring, setting them 6 in. deep and 12 in. apart, handling the brittle roots as little as possible. Alstroemerias need fertile to rich, well-drained soil, in sun and shelter. They may take a year or two to become established. Dead-head them regularly, cut them back to the ground in late autumn and give them a winter mulch. Propagate as for A. aurantiaca.*
Helianthemum nummularium: see p. 208.
Laurus nobilis: see p. 290.
Ruta graveolens: see p. 312.

A multicoloured mass of *Alstroemeria* Ligtu hybrids, intermingled with a few blue spikes of tall delphiniums, is fronted by yellow *Lysimachia punctata*, or yellow loosestrife as it is commonly known.

Alstroemeria aurantiaca (PERUVIAN LILY)

This is the most flamboyant and strongly growing of the alstroemerias in cultivation – as well as the hardiest. From July to September its fiery orange, trumpet-shaped flowers, splashed with maroon on the upper petals, make a brilliant display.

The 3 ft high plant is at its most dramatic against a dark background, such as the deep purple foliage of the deciduous shrub *Cotinus coggygria* 'Royal Purple'. The leaves at the base of the alstroemerias' stems die. To hide these, grow in the foreground a drift of the purple-leaved *Salvia officinalis* 'Purpurascens'.

HOW TO GROW
Cultivate as for Alstroemeria Ligtu hybrids; the species is hardier and strong-growing but may need twiggy support on windy sites. Propagate alstroemerias by division in spring – but only when clumps become obviously overgrown – or sow seeds singly in small pots under glass in spring.

Alstroemerias between a purple cotinus and a drift of sage.

Alstroemeria aurantiaca is ablaze throughout summer.

Amaryllis belladonna

Saving its floral display until autumn, this superb bulbous plant from South Africa then flaunts satiny-pink, sweet-smelling, trumpet-shaped flowers as much as 4-5 in. across. It is also known as *Hippeastrum equestre*.

Because the plant's 2-2½ ft purple stems are leafless at flowering time, a large group presents a bare area unless other plants are grown to break it up. Clumps of *Caryopteris × clandonensis* make good companions. In late summer and early autumn they bear neat clusters of tiny, bright blue tubular flowers.

HOW TO GROW
Plant in summer, 6-8 in. deep and 12 in. apart. Best in well-drained, sandy loam enriched with organic matter and sited at the foot of a sunny wall. Remove flower stems as they fade. Root disturbance is resented; lift only for propagation, in summer, when the foliage turns yellow; divide up the bulb clumps and replant at once.

The superb lily-like *Amaryllis belladonna* needs a sunny position in the shelter of a south or west wall.

Anemone blanda (WINDFLOWER)

The Grecian spring is personified in this lovely anemone, which from February to April carpets the Peloponnesian hills with sky blue. It is particularly delightful in a natural setting and left undisturbed to form extensive colonies. A wide variety of forms is available in white and tints of blue, mauve and pink.

Anemone blanda, a hardy plant that grows to about 6 in. high, does best in dappled shade. If possible, plant a batch of the tubers beneath a tree with attractive young foliage – a birch or a witch hazel, for example.

HOW TO GROW
Plant in autumn, 2 in. deep and 4-6 in. apart, in fertile, well-drained soil, neutral to alkaline, and in light shade or naturalised in grass and woodland settings. Propagate by division in late summer, or by ripe seeds under glass; seedlings usually flower after one or two years.

Anemone blanda spreads to form an enchanting floral carpet.

The anemone is ideal for naturalising in woodland.

'De Caen' seedlings charm with their unpredictable colour.

Anemone coronaria 'De Caen' (WINDFLOWER)

This is the anemone whose stained-glass reds, purples and blues – and white, too – make such a vivid appeal in florists' shops. The wild species, of which this anemone is a strain, grows on sunny Mediterranean hillsides, and not unnaturally 'De Caen' itself flowers best in summer, in a warm, sheltered position.

Since this anemone is less than 12 in. high, it should be grown at the front of a border. Try planting it in patches between muted foliage plants, such as clumps of the grey grass *Festuca glauca*.

HOW TO GROW
Soak the rhizomes for several hours before planting, 1½ - 2 in. deep and 4 in. apart. Plant in succession from late November until late April for a continuous display from spring onwards. Propagate by division as the foliage dies down; seedlings do not come true, but are usually worthwhile.

Given warmth and shelter, each plant produces at least a score of 1½-2 in. wide flowers in pure, vivid hues.

Anemone nemorosa (WINDFLOWER)

Being a native plant of English woods, *Anemone nemorosa* looks at its very best when in a semi-natural woodland setting. Large clusters of graceful fern-like leaves are crowned with cool, starry flowers that sway on their slender stems in the slightest breeze. They form exquisite ground-cover, either to harmonise with the early spring floral displays of such shrubs as *Forsythia* and *Corylopsis* – both yellow flowered – or to make a light contrast with the rich white, purple-stained blooms of a *Magnolia × soulangiana* tree.

If the anemone is to be grown in the more confined space of a rock or peat garden, one of its varieties will need to be chosen, since these are less vigorous than the species. The most beautiful variety is the large-flowered, lavender-

hued 'Robinsoniana'. Two admirable companions for 'Robinsoniana' would be the taller spring woodland plants wake robin (*Trillium grandiflorum*), which has wide, white flowers, and *Erythronium tuolumnense*, which bears nodding yellow flowers.

HOW TO GROW
Anemone nemorosa: plant in early autumn, 1½ in. deep and 6 in. apart. This lime-tolerant native species does best in moist soil in a shady and cool site; it is ideal for ground-cover in woodland conditions. Propagate, if necessary, by division as the foliage dies away.
Erythronium tuolumnense: see p. 152.
Trillium grandiflorum: see p. 125.

The pink form, *Anemone nemorosa rosea*.

Anemone nemorosa 'Robinsoniana', seen here in April, flanked by yellow *Erythronium tuolumnense* and white *Trillium grandiflorum*.

The graceful 1½ in. wide blooms of the hardy St Bernard's lily open on wand-like stems in late spring.

Anthericum liliago looks well with the pink-bloomed *Armeria maritima*.

The double-flowered cream form of *Camassia leichtlinii*

'Atrocoerulea' is a blue-purple form of *Camassia leichtlinii*. Left to itself, the plant forms vigorous clumps.

Dropping its seeds freely, *Chionodoxa luciliae* soon creates a carpet of dazzling blue. It is extremely easy to grow.

Anthericum liliago (ST BERNARD'S LILY)

This hardy herbaceous perennial produces in May and June starry white flowers on top of 1½-2 ft tall, slender stems. They are ideal for flower arrangements. The leaves are grass-like and grow in tufts. To create a good display, a group of at least five should be planted.

Surrounding plants should be chosen to show up the white flowers of the anthericum. Ideal would be orange-bloomed Siberian wallflowers (*Cheiranthus* × *allionii*) or the pink-flowered thrift *Armeria maritima*.

HOW TO GROW
Plant in autumn or spring, 4 in. deep and 12 in. apart, in well-drained but moisture-retentive soil and in sun or light shade. Leave the plants undisturbed, but dress in spring with an organic mulch. Propagate crowded plants by careful division in spring or after flowering. Seeds often germinate erratically.

Camassia leichtlinii (QUAMASH)

North American Indians are said to have eaten the bulbs of a related species, *Camassia quamash*, long before the garden value of either plant was appreciated in Europe.

A semi-wild grassy area or a spot beside a garden pool are ideal sites for clumps of the plant, which thrives in damp conditions. In June and July the 3 ft tall stems are crowned with spikes of flowers ranging from purple-blue to white. These associate well with the broad, deep green, paddle-like leaves and white flowers of another perennial, *Bergenia* × 'Silberlicht', which blooms in spring.

HOW TO GROW
Plant in autumn, 6 in. deep and 8 in. apart, in any ordinary to moist or even very wet soil, and in full sun or light shade. Remove faded flower stems, but otherwise leave the plants undisturbed until crowding makes division, in early autumn, necessary. Ripe seeds take up to five years to produce flowering plants.

Chionodoxa luciliae (GLORY OF THE SNOW)

Casting swathes of brilliant sky-blue flowers on 6 in. stems over the ground in March and April, here is a plant for brightening up dull days with its taste of spring – an effect that can be heightened by planting it in a drift beneath the yellow blooms of a *Forsythia* shrub.

For a rock garden, too, there is no bulb more suitable, for it is hardy, drops plenty of seeds and has very little foliage to crowd neighbouring plants. On an upper level its white centre and cone of creamy stamens can best be appreciated. A good rock-garden companion is gold dust (*Alyssum saxatile*), a shrubby perennial that is a mass of yellow flowers from April to June.

HOW TO GROW
Plant in early autumn, 2-3 in. deep and apart, in large groups. Any well-drained soil, in sun, is suitable. Little maintenance is necessary. The plants can be propagated by division after flowering, but they seed themselves freely.

Colchicum speciosum (AUTUMN CROCUS)

Large, glowing, rosy-purple goblet-like flowers make this one of the most handsome of autumn crocuses. It is also one of the most robust: the 6 in. tall leafless tube (an extension of the petals) that in autumn crocuses takes the place of a stem in supporting the flowers is much stronger in *Colchicum speciosum* than in most other species. For this reason there is little likelihood of the flowers, which are produced from September to November, being knocked over by autumn winds and rain. And this means that the plant does not have to be grown only where there is support from grass or other vegetation – it can be placed in a border by itself.

In spring the plant develops particularly large, handsomely glossy leaves – up to 16 in. high. These can smother small neighbouring plants, so its site must be chosen with some care. It is best planted as a group of at least ten bulbs in the dappled shade of a shrub or small tree. A shrubby rose species would be perfect, since there are few more cheerful sights in the autumn garden than a drift of glowing *C. speciosum* overhung by bright red rose hips. Rose species which produce a mass of fine hips include *Rosa moyesii* and *R. glauca (rubrifolia)*, which has the extra attraction of delicate blue-grey, purple-tinted leaves.

A nearby tree or shrub whose leaves will colour and fall in autumn among the colchicum flowers would add further to the enchantment of the scene. Suitable would be the smaller-leaved forms of Japanese maple (*Acer palmatum*), such as 'Senkaki'.

HOW TO GROW
Colchicum speciosum: cultivate as for C. agrippinum. Set the large bulbs at least 4 in. deep and 8 in. apart in large groups to the front of shrub borders. Propagate as for C. autumnale; seedlings, which take up to six years to reach flowering size, may not breed true.
Acer palmatum: see p. 332.
Rosa glauca: see p. 244.
Rosa moyesii: see p. 245.

Naturalised *Colchicum speciosum* bulbs produce a sea of autumn colour around a bed planted with red-hipped *Rosa moyesii*.

Colchicum agrippinum (AUTUMN CROCUS)

The 3-4 in. high rosy-lilac flowers of this hardy crocus-like plant last from September to November, and so can help to brighten up the dullness of a garden in mid-autumn. As with most other autumnal colchicums, the plant's leaves have withered by flowering time, and large groups of flowers may look rather naked unless some foliage plants are grown between them.

The colchicum's rosy colour combines beautifully with grey foliage. Try old-fashioned pinks (*Dianthus*) or the blue-flowered *Nepeta × faassenii*.

HOW TO GROW
Plant in July or August, 3-4 in. deep and 6 in. apart. Colchicums will grow in any, even poor, soil that is well drained, but they thrive and colonise in one that is fertile, in sun or dappled shade, and beneath shrubs. Remove the foliage as it dies down in early summer. Propagate as for Colchicum autumnale.

Each bulb of *Colchicum agrippinum* produces many crocus-like flowers.

The grey-green leaves and lavender-blue flowers of *Nepeta × faassenii* provide a muted setting for the soft rose of *C. agrippinum*.

Colchicum autumnale (AUTUMN CROCUS)

In the wild, *Colchicum autumnale* grows in moist
pastureland, sometimes staining whole meadows in
September and October with its 6 in. high, lilac-pink
goblet-shaped flowers. In the garden, too, these flowers,
fragile-stemmed and leafless at flowering, should be grown
in long grass to support them and to make up for their
lack of autumn foliage. What is needed is an area of lawn
or orchard that can be left uncut in autumn and also in
spring, when the coarse leaves develop. The double-
flowered variety *C. autumnale* 'Roseum-plenum' is a strong
rose-pink and is easily grown.

Plant some of the white form 'Album' to break up the
lilac-pink of the species. Other meadow-dwelling bulbs that
could be planted in the same turf include the graceful
daffodil *Narcissus cyclamineus*, which flowers in February
and March, and the summer snowflake (*Leucojum aestivum*),
whose white bells appear in April and May.

HOW TO GROW
*Cultivate as for Colchicum agrippinum, spacing the bulbs 8 in.
apart. The plant is suitable for naturalising in moist grass.
Propagate all colchicums by division, in summer as the leaves
die down; separate and replant the small bulbils in the
flowering site, or grow them on for a year or two in a spare
piece of ground.*

Autumn sunshine lights up an area of uncut lawn planted with clumps of *Colchicum autumnale*.

Convallaria majalis (LILY OF THE VALLEY)

It is hard to credit that the heady fragrance of lily of the
valley emanates from tiny flowers only ¼ in. long. Waxy
white and bell shaped, they are borne in loose spikes in
April and May. Clear green, broad leaves growing up
among the delicate blooms set off their fragile snowy
charm to perfection.

The genus contains only one species and this well-known
plant grows from a branched, creeping, horizontal rhizome.
It will spread quickly under suitable conditions.

Lily of the valley has been cultivated for more than 500
years, but it can also be found growing in the wild where it
forms patches of pure white on the woodland floor. It is
excellent for planting in wild gardens or in massed clumps
in a cool shady corner.

Since lily of the valley spreads over a wide area, it is a
shame to waste it in confined spaces. A good site for it is a
corner of the garden in dappled shade – in that provided by
deciduous shrubs, for example. Absolutely ideal would be
Viburnum × bodnantense, since its white flowers, which
appear on bare wood from December to February, are also
sweetly scented, and this corner of the garden would then
be fragrant for most of winter and spring.

HOW TO GROW
*Plant in early autumn, with the crowns set shallowly –
pointed ends uppermost and just below the surface of the soil –
and 4-6 in. apart. Alternatively, plant small clumps of
crowns, 6-8 in. apart. Grow in a shady site, in any moist soil
– though it does best in acid loam. After the leaves have died
down in summer, top-dress with peat or leaf-mould. Propagate
by division of the rhizomes in autumn. Replant and give a
top-dressing of compost or leaf-mould, and water well.*

Lily of the valley bears waxy white bells.

Crinum × powellii has trumpet-shaped blooms.

Crinum × powellii

Most of the *Crinum* species are not very hardy, but a group
of hybrids derived from two South African species and
known as *Crinum × powellii* will thrive in all but the coldest
gardens. In August and September, the 3 ft tall stems carry
clusters of up to ten elegantly arched, trumpet-shaped
flowers, which open in succession. Named forms are
available that range in colour from pure white ('Album') to
deep pink ('Krelagei').

The plants are best grown in clumps in a sunny position
protected from north and east winds. The shelter of a wall
or conifer hedge is ideal for this purpose. The white variety
of crinum, 'Album', will show up beautifully against a misty
backing of one of the blue-grey varieties of Lawson cypress
(*Chamaecyparis lawsoniana*) such as 'Pembury Blue' or
'Grayswood Pillar'.

In another association, try setting clumps of the blue-
flowered perennial *Agapanthus* 'Headbourne Hybrids' in the
foreground or front of the bed. They will flower at about
the same time as crinums and will harmonise charmingly
with pink varieties.

HOW TO GROW
*Plant in late spring, 10-12 in. deep and apart, in a sunny,
sheltered site, such as the foot of a south-facing wall. Not
recommended for cold gardens, but elsewhere the plants thrive
in rich, moisture-retentive but well-drained soil; cover with a
winter mulch. Water freely during the summer. Leave
undisturbed if possible. Propagate by removing offsets in
March. These take about three years to grow into flowering
plants. Alternatively, sow the large ripe seeds singly in 4 in.
pots; pot on the seedlings as necessary. Plants grown from seed
take four or five years to flower.*

Crocosmia × crocosmiiflora (MONTBRETIA)

This popular bulbous plant was raised over 100 years ago as a cross between two less striking South African species, *Crocosmia aurea* and *C. pottsii*. It is vigorous and has become naturalised in many parts of Britain, particularly the south and west, where it can be seen growing on banks, in hedges and on rough ground.

The funnel-shaped flowers, which flare out widely at the mouth into a star shape, are borne from July to September on wind-proof 2 ft high stems, amid fans of sword-like green leaves. The plant is hardy in all but the harshest winters, and in the garden it can be grown in any position.

The slightly less rampant named forms – of which the yellow 'Solfatare', with bronzed leaves, is one of the most attractive – are best grown in a sunny herbaceous border. Other garden cultivars include 'Bressingham Blaze', which is orange-red; 'Emberglow', also orange-red but with very large flowers; 'Jackanapes', which produces a mixture of yellow and orange blooms; a fiery orange form called 'Spitfire', and the aptly named 'Vulcan', also orange-red.

HOW TO GROW
Plant in early spring, 2 in. deep and 4 in. apart, in light, well-drained soil, in full sun and shelter. Water copiously in summer. Cover the root area with a winter mulch; in cold gardens lift the corms, dry them off and store them in a frost-free place. Propagate from cormlets in spring, or from seeds.

Crocosmia × crocosmiiflora – popularly known as montbretia – spreads quickly and needs to be divided every three years.

Crocus aureus 'Dutch Yellow'

In early spring there are few more cheerful sights in the garden than a colony of *Crocus aureus* (syn. *C. luteus*) 'Dutch Yellow'. After the spiky leaves have appeared, in February or early March, they are soon followed by goblet-shaped buds that open out into bowls of deep yellow. This hardy and reliable form is more compact than the species. They look particularly fine set amid rough, uncut grass on a sunny bank. But almost any open site will suit them, and they are equally at home in the rock garden or in a border beneath deciduous shrubs.

If the crocuses are planted in grass, this must not be cut until the plants' leaves have withered in late spring – but this is a small price to pay for a golden spring display that will be repeated for years and years.

For a completely different colour scheme, plant *C. aureus lacteus*, which produces superb milk-white flowers. It will make an elegant spring association with a shorter-stemmed, early flowering bulb – for example, the rich golden *Narcissus cyclamineus*, with its long, pendant, trumpet-shaped flowers. Another hardy species with rich yellow flowers is *C. ancyrensis* – often listed as 'Golden Bunch'. The 2-2½ in. tall flowers appear in February and March. Each corm will produce as many as 20 flowers.

HOW TO GROW
Plant winter and spring-flowering crocuses as soon as available in autumn. Set the corms 2-3 in. deep and 4 in. apart, in any reasonably fertile, well-drained soil and in sun or light shade. All are ideal for rock gardens and edgings, for naturalising in grass and for planting beneath deciduous trees and shrubs. For propagation see Crocus tomasinianus.

Crocus aureus 'Dutch Yellow' intermingles with *C. vernus*.

The crocus brings golden splendour to rough grass.

Crocus speciosus

Of all the autumn crocuses, this delightful plant is perhaps the best to grow. Others may be more beautiful, but they are not nearly so free-flowering, nor do they multiply so readily. In October the elegant, 4-5 in. tall, pointed flower buds of *Crocus speciosus* open into deep cups of violet-veined, lilac-blue petals with a frilly orange centre. There are several fine cultivars, including the pure white 'Albus' and the violet-blue 'Oxonian'.

An excellent place for growing them is in a heather garden. There, the long leafless tubes that serve as stalks are protected by the stems of the heather, and the heather's uniformity is relieved by the crocuses. Another good site is an area of rough grass beneath trees.

HOW TO GROW
Cultivate as for Crocus aureus, but plant this autumn-flowering species in July or August, setting the corms on a sprinkling of coarse sand if the soil is heavy and slow draining. Avoid mowing the grass until the leaves have died down naturally. For propagation see C. tomasinianus.

C. *speciosus* has delicately patterned cups.

C. *vernus* gleams in a semi-shaded spot.

Crocus vernus (CULTIVARS)

These are the 'large Dutch' spring crocuses, the ones with the great goblet-shaped flowers. They come in shades of white or lilac or purple, with striking purple veining on the outside. The wild species *Crocus vernus* from which they were raised – and which they have now generally supplanted in cultivation – is a plant of Alpine meadows, and its progeny are likewise best planted in grass. This should not be cut until the crocus leaves have died away.

Grown with clumps of bright yellow *Narcissus* 'February Gold', the crocuses, which flower in March, will create a display guaranteed to gladden eyes wearied of winter.

Among numerous cultivars, 'Purpureus Grandiflorus' is one of the best, with large, shining purple-blue flowers. It makes an excellent foil to 'Queen of the Blues', which is lavender-blue.

HOW TO GROW
Cultivate as for Crocus aureus. The Dutch hybrids are perhaps the loveliest for naturalising in grass, in large drifts of mixed colours. For propagation see C. tomasinianus.

Crocus tomasinianus

This wild crocus, originally from Yugoslavia, is now happily established in British gardens. The slender buds emerge from the ground as early as January or February, and only a few sunny days are needed for them to surge up into bloom. At the top of each white tube that serves as a stalk there opens a starry 3 in. high lilac flower with golden stamens. It grows in almost any situation, seeding itself freely in any crevice or crack in path or pavement.

Variations from the lilac colour are often found. Some flowers have three paler outer petals, others darker, and some with paler tips to all the petals. Varieties range from deep purple to pure white.

The crocus is ideal for bringing extra colour to a corner of the garden devoted to winter or early spring flowers. It would be particularly delightful as a bright carpet in front of or around a deciduous shrub such as *Chimonanthus praecox*, which carries yellow and maroon flowers, heavily scented, throughout the winter, or an evergreen shrub like *Mahonia japonica*, whose fragrant lemon-yellow blooms appear from January to March.

Clumps of dwarf spring bulbs look well scattered among the crocuses: the yellow winter aconite (*Eranthis hyemalis*), which peeps above the ground in February, and *Cyclamen coum*, whose pink, crimson or white flowers appear from December to March.

HOW TO GROW
Crocus tomasinianus: cultivate as for C. aureus. All crocuses are propagated from the small corms they produce. These can be lifted when the leaves are dying down, graded to size and replanted in new flowering sites. However, propagation of C. tomasinianus is usually unnecessary: under good conditions it multiplies naturally from cormlets· and self-sown seedlings.
Chimonanthus praecox: see p. 262.
Cyclamen coum: see p. 150.
Eranthis hyemalis: see p. 153.
Mahonia japonica: see p. 295.

Spring bulbs brighten early March: lilac *Crocus tomasinianus* surrounds *Cyclamen coum*, with yellow *Eranthis hyemalis* beyond. Above them blooms *Chimonanthus praecox*.

Cyclamen coum

A lovely 3 in. high winter-flowering plant, *Cyclamen coum*, a native of the woods and mountains of Asia Minor, is often in full bloom at Christmas. It varies in colour from pure white to pink or crimson. The rounded, deep green and silver leaves are dark red beneath.

To make a cheering winter scene, plant a mixture of predominantly pink-flowered *C. coum* alongside the white heather *Erica carnea* 'Springwood' or put white cyclamens near the pink *E. carnea* 'Winter Beauty'. Ideally, the planting should be in full view of a window.

Forms of the variable *C. coum* are known to some nurserymen as *C. ibericum*, *C. orbiculatum* and *C. vernum*.

HOW TO GROW
Plant from July onwards, setting the corms an inch or two beneath the soil surface and about 6 in. apart. Natural woodland plants, cyclamens thrive in humus-rich, well-drained soil, preferably limy. Choose a shaded site sheltered from cold winds, where the plants can remain undisturbed. For propagation see Cyclamen hederifolium.

Cyclamen coum, which does best under trees, forms a mat of sweetly coloured flowers and silver-marbled leaves.

Cyclamen hederifolium (neapolitanum)

Though its ancestral home is dry Mediterranean woods and hillsides, this cyclamen is surprisingly hardy in our chillier, damper plots. It is a delightful, autumn-flowering plant for rock gardens, or beneath shrubs where the soil is little disturbed, for it does best when its tubers are left to grow without interruption.

From August to October delicate pink or white flowers are carried on slender 4 in. stalks just above the decorative silver-and-green variegated leaves. This foliage remains attractive through winter until the following May, when it dies down. A drift of the cyclamen can be planted with great effect intermingled with snowdrops (*Galanthus*) beneath a deciduous tree such as *Prunus subhirtella* 'Autumnalis', which allows enough winter light to fall on the plant.

HOW TO GROW
Cultivate as for Cyclamen coum. Plant 1-2 in. deep; the corms tend to push themselves out of the soil and should be given an annual top-dressing of leaf-mould in late summer. Cyclamens are propagated only by seeds sown when ripe or in autumn. Seedlings usually flower within two years.

Growing among ferns and saxifrages, *Cyclamen hederifolium* displays its clusters of delicate pink blooms.

'Album' is a pure white form of *Cyclamen hederifolium*.

Dierama pulcherrimum (WAND FLOWER, ANGEL'S FISHING ROD)

The common name for bulbous perennials of the genus *Dierama* are wand flower and angel's fishing rod – both a reference to the plant's slender, gracefully curving and pendulous stems. This species' tufts of long, narrow, grass-like leaves are overtopped in summer by 4-6 ft stalks that carry drooping, funnel-shaped, purple-red flowers.

The plants, hardy in all but the coldest districts, look superb when grown in gaps in the paving around a garden pool, in a situation where their elegant growth is reflected in the water. Other plants about them should be of lower habit to accentuate the dieramas' willowy stature. Suitable crevice-loving evergreen companions would be varieties of wild thyme (*Thymus drucei*) and of rock rose (*Helianthemum*), together with gold dust (*Alyssum saxatile*). All of these would provide attractive foliage throughout the winter, when the dieramas are dormant.

A less dramatic but equally satisfying association can be created by planting dieramas with other moisture-loving plants – for example, the ferny foliage and airy floral plumes of *Astilbe × arendsii* cultivars. For spring interest, you could plant groups of drumstick primrose (*Primula denticulata*).

HOW TO GROW
Dierama pulcherrimum: plant in autumn or spring, 4-6 in. deep and 2 ft apart. It does best in well-drained, organically rich soil, and in full sun with some shelter. In cold gardens give winter protection or lift and store the corms in a frost-free place until spring. Propagate from offsets separated from established clumps at planting time.
Alyssum saxatile: see p. 197.
Astilbe × arendsii: see p. 71.
Helianthemum: see p. 208.
Primula denticulata: see p. 115.
Thymus drucei: see p. 219.

The slender grace of angel's fishing rod, mirrored in a pool in August, is stressed by its combination with smaller plants like alyssum, wild thyme and a rock rose.

Endymion hispanicus (SPANISH BLUEBELL)

The Spanish bluebell is a fine, robust plant, bigger and broader than the English bluebell. Its glossy green leaves are wide and strap-like, a fine foil for the blue bells that appear in 12 in. spikes from April to June. There are a number of attractive named hybrid forms, in pure white and in shades of blue and pink.

The bluebell is a plant that likes semi-shade, and is consequently ideal for growing beneath trees or shrubs. *Endymion hispanicus* 'Myosotis' is lovely planted in quantity underneath an established spring-flowering shrub, such as *Magnolia × soulangiana*. A scattering among the bluebells of the white *Narcissus* 'Actaea' is especially charming.

E. hispanicus is also known as *E. campanulatus, Scilla campanulata* and *S. hispanica*.

HOW TO GROW
Plant bulbs in autumn, as soon as available; otherwise they will quickly dry out. Set them 3 in. deep and 4-6 in. apart in ordinary, preferably limy, soil that is moist but well drained. Self-sown seedlings are not uncommon; propagate also by offsets removed during the dormant season.

The blue-belled *Endymion hispanicus* 'Myosotis' is here planted with *Narcissus* 'Actaea' beneath *Magnolia × soulangiana*.

An *Endymion hispanicus* hybrid contrasts boldly with red polyanthus.

Erythronium revolutum

(AMERICAN TROUT LILY)

No spring bulbous plants are more graceful than erythroniums. *Erythronium revolutum* has two beautifully brown-and-white mottled leaves, from which arise slender, 12 in. high stems carrying one or two flowers with prominent stamens. In the wild species, from the western states of North America, the flowers are pink, but in the free-flowering garden form 'White Beauty', the blooms are cream with a yellow centre.

A delightful companion for 'White Beauty' is the soft-blue wood anemone *Anemone nemorosa* 'Allenii'.

HOW TO GROW

Plant in September or earlier, setting the corms 3-4 in. deep and 4-6 in. apart in moist soil and in a shady site. Top-dress annually in late summer with peat or leaf-mould, but disturb the plants as little as possible. Propagate as for Erythronium tuolumnense.

Erythronium revolutum 'White Beauty' does best in a moist, shady spot. Beneath deciduous trees it spreads rapidly.

Erythronium tuolumnense

This hardy, bulbous plant is named after California's Tuolumne River, on whose banks it grows. It has taken readily to cultivation, and in the garden will quickly form clumps of long white tubers. In April and May, each plant puts out a pair of pale green leaves and bright yellow, drooping flowers with gracefully curved petals, on 9-12 in. stems.

This erythronium is admirable for lighting up a space between small-leaved rhododendrons, such as 'Blue Tit', that do not cast too much shade upon it. Plants similar in size to the erythronium and that associate well with it include wake robin (*Trillium grandiflorum*), which bears white flowers, flushed with pink as they age, and the yellow-flowered *Corydalis lutea*.

HOW TO GROW

Cultivate as for Erythronium revolutum. Left undisturbed, Erythronium species sometimes seed themselves. However, named cultivars produce variable seedlings and must be increased from offsets removed in early autumn and replanted at once, for flowering in two or more years.

The orchid-like blooms of *Erythronium tuolumnense* make good cut flowers.

The bright yellow *Erythronium tuolumnense* 'Pagoda' and starry white *Magnolia stellata* make a splash of fresh spring colour.

Eranthis hyemalis (WINTER ACONITE)

Being a diminutive, tuberous-rooted hardy perennial, winter aconite is a perfect winter carpeting for shady patches beneath trees or shrubs. The plant's stems peep only a few inches above ground before the yellow buttercup-like flowers open, surrounded by a collar of deeply lobed green leaves.

The winter aconite flowers early, often in January or February. It is at its best when planted in quantity, mixed with snowdrops (*Galanthus nivalis*) and grown beneath trees or shrubs – especially those with attractive bark or stems.

HOW TO GROW
Plant in late summer or early autumn. Set in large groups, 2 in. deep and 3 in. apart, in full sun or beneath deciduous shrubs and trees. Any soil, including clay, is suitable so long as it is moist during the growing season. Propagate by division as the leaves die down; replant immediately.

Eranthis hyemalis does well planted beneath deciduous trees. Here it pushes up sunnily through the debris of dead leaves.

Winter aconites surround the snowdrop *Galanthus nivalis* 'Flore-plena'.

Fritillaria meleagris (SNAKE'S HEAD)

It is thought that the name *Fritillaria* is derived from the Latin *fritillus* (dice box), though somehow or other, in England, it seemed to mean a chessboard, too. At any rate, the name refers, apparently, not to the flowers' cup shape but to their chequered pattern. Appearing in April and May, they are large drooping bells whose squared markings are in deep purple. The tall stems and the few, narrow grey-green leaves give the whole plant a delicate, graceful appearance. Various forms are available – including white ones with green or pink chequering – and a mixed planting is the most effective.

Snake's head, which in the wild inhabits moist meadows, looks beautiful in uncut grass, but it is equally at home in an undisturbed border or a peat garden. It looks particularly fine when allowed to spring up informally from the seeds it scatters.

In a border, try planting a drift of snake's head with a soft combination of forget-me-not (*Myosotis*) hybrids in pink, white and blue. Choose a position which will be undisturbed so that the forget-me-nots can spread freely. Some clumps of white, cream, pink or purple lenten roses (*Helleborus orientalis*) can be used to begin the display before the snake's head starts to flower.

A particularly effective site in the garden is by a pool, where the snake's head can be seen reflected in the water. Here it can be used to fill in gaps between late-flowering primulas and other waterside plants, providing beauty and interest before they get going.

HOW TO GROW
Fritillaria meleagris: plant in late summer or autumn, 4 in. deep and 6 in. apart, in ordinary fertile, moist soil, and in sun or light shade. Fritillarias are suitable for naturalising in short grass. Propagate by seeds as for F. imperialis (p. 154), or by bulbils from lifted plants. Grow them on for several years to reach flowering size.
Helleborus orientalis: see p. 93.
Myosotis: see p. 44.
Primula: see p. 372.

A shaded informal setting for snake's head, beneath a birch tree; here, lenten roses form the background, and forget-me-nots frame this April composition.

Fritillaria imperialis (CROWN IMPERIAL)

The glorious crown imperial is the most spectacular and stately of all fritillarias and, despite its tropical appearance, has been happily settled in Britain and northern Europe since the 16th century at least.

The 2 ft tall, stout stems are leafy at the base, then bare up to the flowers. In April they carry a cluster of large hanging bellflowers, which contain drops of glistening nectar. Legend has it that the plant remained upright in the Garden of Gethsemane when all the others bowed their heads as they witnessed the agony of Christ. Now it blushes and hangs its own head for shame, and weeps tears of repentance.

In the sunbaked mountains of Iran and Afghanistan, where the plant originates, the flowers are brick-red, but modern garden forms come in a range of lovely yellows, oranges and scarlets. Above each cluster of flowers is a crowning tuft of leaves that completes the faultless beauty of the plant.

The crown imperial comes into bloom at a time when there are many other flowers from which to choose its companions. A group of about five lemon-yellow *Fritillaria imperialis* 'Lutea' would stand out beautifully against a grey stone wall.

To accentuate the stature of crown imperials, you could grow in front of them much smaller plants. A delightful foreground could be produced by planting *Viola labradorica* 'Purpurea', with mauve flowers and purple-tinged leaves, and a small drift of the miniature tulip *Tulipa tarda*, which has white flowers with a yellow centre.

HOW TO GROW
Fritillaria imperialis: plant during summer and autumn, 8 in. deep and 9-15 in. apart. Fertile, well-drained soil is essential, and waterlogging can be fatal. Choose a sunny or lightly shaded site where the plants can remain undisturbed. Propagate by fresh seeds under glass in summer, or by offsets removed during the dormant season.
Tulipa tarda: see p. 171.
Viola labradorica: see p. 221.

Backed by the cool grey of an old stone wall, *Fritillaria imperialis* makes an impressive sight. Its stately image is further accentuated by growing small plants in front – mauve-flowered violas and white and yellow miniature tulips. This association is pictured in April.

Crown imperial hangs its blushing heads.

The golden form 'Lutea' rears behind white narcissi and erythroniums

Grown here with warm-coloured gladioli, the tall spires of *Galtonia candicans* make a crisp white display in late summer.

Cheering February, the common snowdrop *Galanthus nivalis* blooms beneath the ivy *Hedera colchica* 'Paddy's Pride'.

The red flowers of *Gladiolus byzantinus* mingle here with irises.

The rich red blooms of the gladiolus, which appear in profusion at the height of the summer, make superb cut flowers.

Galtonia candicans (SUMMER HYACINTH)

Pendulous bell-shaped flowers of pure white, faintly tinged green at the base, make this a crisply beautiful summer plant. The flowers are borne from July to September in a cluster of 10-25 at the top of a single, leafless stem; this rises about 4 ft from a nest of arching, strap-like grey-green leaves.

Galtonia candicans (syn. *Hyacinthus candicans*) would make a suitable background in a sunny border for a group of lower plants with similar needs, *Hosta crispula*.

HOW TO GROW
Plant in spring, 6 in. deep and 12-15 in. apart in deep, fertile soil, moisture-retentive but well drained. Leave undisturbed. Full sun is best, with copious watering during dry spells. Cut faded stems back to ground level in late autumn. Propagate from offsets when dormant or from seeds under glass in spring.

Galanthus nivalis (SNOWDROP)

Known for centuries under such beautiful names as 'Fair Maids of February' and 'Candlemas Bells', snowdrops must surely be the best-loved harbingers of spring. The common wild species, *Galanthus nivalis*, together with its double-flowered form, never looks better than when planted in drifts beneath deciduous trees to flower in early spring amid the fallen brown leaves.

Another species, *G. elwesii*, has broad grey leaves and large flowers on long stems. To make a corner of the garden sing in the very depths of winter, plant this with blue and purple varieties of *Iris reticulata*.

HOW TO GROW
Plant in September, 2-3 in. deep and apart. Snowdrops do best in good, well-drained loam, in a shady site with a northerly aspect. Propagate by division after flowering, before the leaves die down, and replant immediately. Once established, snowdrops also seed themselves.

Gladiolus byzantinus (SWORD LILY)

Up to 20 wine-red flowers are borne in June and July on the 2 ft high, stout stem of this handsome gladiolus. The lower three petals of each bloom are marked with pale spear shapes outlined in dark crimson, so the plant is excellent for a sunny spot where intense colour is needed. A few corms will soon produce good-sized clumps of plants, and since the corms are hardy they do not need to be lifted each winter for storage.

Gladiolus byzantinus looks particularly fine behind a group of *Iris pallida dalmatica* 'Argenteo-variegata', which has lavender flowers and white-striped leaves.

HOW TO GROW
Plant in autumn or spring, 4 in. deep and 6 in. apart, in well-drained, fertile, organically rich soil, in a sunny border or bed. Cut off flower stems as they fade, and yellowed foliage at ground level. Propagate by cormlets in autumn or spring or by seeds under glass in spring.

Gladiolus (LARGE-FLOWERED)

The familiar large-flowered gladioli, which are often grown as formal bedding plants or as cut flowers for decoration or exhibition, are hybrids between several South African species. In this country they are tender and their corms must be lifted each winter – but this does not mean they are suitable only for summer bedding schemes. With the right companions, they can blend beautifully into a herbaceous border.

The deep salmon-orange flowers of the variety 'Albert Schweitzer' are carried in 3-4 ft high, dense spikes between July and September. This colour combines well with the silvery-grey filigree foliage of the robust, 4 ft high *Artemisia absinthium* 'Lambrook Silver'.

There are numerous other varieties providing a range of colours to satisfy a host of associations. Among them are 'Tiger Flame' (orange-scarlet, fringed petals), 'Snow Princess' (creamy white), 'Peter Pears' (apricot-salmon with chestnut-red markings), 'Green Woodpecker' (lime-yellow and purple), 'Blue Isle' (bright bluish-violet), 'Friendship' (creamy-pink, frilled), 'Flower Song' (golden-yellow, crimped petal margins), 'Venice' (mandarin-red), and 'Forgotten Dreams' (primrose, with yellow falls edged in carmine).

HOW TO GROW
Plant corms of large-flowered gladioli at ten-day intervals from mid-March to mid-April. Set them 4 in. deep on heavy soils, 6 in. on light soils, and 4-6 in. apart. A well-drained fertile soil, previously enriched with organic matter, gives the best results; sandy loam is ideal. The plants need full sun. In autumn, lift the plants, cut off their stems and leaves, dry the corms rapidly in warmth and place in a frost-proof store. Propagate as for small-flowered gladioli.

Gladiolus (SMALL-FLOWERED)

Some types of hybrid gladiolus – primulinus, butterfly and miniature hybrids – tend to have smaller blooms and sometimes shorter stems than the large-flowered varieties. They can look very effective planted in groups in a formal bedding scheme where the large-flowered gladioli might be too dominant. The brilliant display is heightened if broken up with silver-white foliage plants such as *Senecio maritimus*. These hybrids are also suitable for providing a splash of colour in July and August in a mixed border of shrubs and herbaceous perennials. Keep foreground plants soft in colour so that they do not compete with the main scheme.

One of the most attractive of the butterfly hybrids – which have a characteristic blotch of contrasting colour at the throat – is 'Melodie'. It has deep salmon-pink flowers patterned with orange-scarlet at the throat. These colours harmonise with the creamy flowers of *Kniphofia* 'Maid of Orleans', grown in clumps flanking the gladioli.

HOW TO GROW
Cultivation is as for large-flowered gladioli. Propagate from the cormlets which form around the new corms. When lifting the plants in autumn, grade the cormlets to size and plant in an outdoor nursery bed the following spring. Grow the young plants on like their parents, lifting and replanting annually until they reach flowering size, usually after one or two years.

Large-flowered gladiolus hybrids make a splendid focal point among *Eucalyptus gunnii*, *Lythrum salicaria* and heleniums.

The *Gladiolus* butterfly hybrid 'Melodie' is here accompanied by the red hot poker *Kniphofia* 'Maid of Orleans' and purple-leaved sage.

The blooms of *Gladiolus* butterfly hybrids, thickly clustered on the stems, as here on 'Little Lady', look just like butterflies.

Hyacinthus orientalis hybrids
(DUTCH HYACINTHS)

In the garden the large-flowered Dutch hyacinths have almost completely displaced the wild species – the common hyacinth, *Hyacinthus orientalis* – from which they are descended. Because of their deliciously scented spikes of flowers they are popular for window-sills in winter and early spring, or for bedding schemes or sunny borders in April. Plant them in separate groups of one colour. Blue cultivars, such as the pale azure 'Queen of the Blues', look delightful among the creamy-veined leaves of *Arum italicum* 'Pictum' and yellow cottage tulips, such as 'Golden Harvest'.

HOW TO GROW
Plant in autumn, 4-6 in. deep and 10-12 in. apart, in any kind of light and well-drained soil and in full sun. Dead-head after flowering. Propagate by seeds – though named cultivars do not breed true.

Large-flowered Dutch hyacinths, here grown with pansies, will flower for years in a sunny bed if left undisturbed.

Plantings of Dutch hyacinths look best if restricted to a single colour.

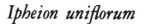

Ipheion uniflorum

This native of Argentina is one of the few really hardy bulbous plants to have come to Britain from South America. Its narrow, pale green leaves are produced from autumn onwards, and the lilac-blue flowers come in spring.

A delightful association can be formed by planting as many bulbs as possible beneath deciduous azaleas, such as *Azalea pontica*, or in front of a border of mixed shrubs. However, the bulbs spread rapidly and should be planted only where there is plenty of space.

Ipheion uniflorum has a number of synonyms: *Brodiaea uniflora*, *Milla uniflora* and *Triteleia uniflora*.

HOW TO GROW
Plant in late summer or early autumn, 2 in. deep and 5 in. apart, in any kind of soil, acid or alkaline, so long as it has good drainage. It tolerates full sun or light shade, and grows well by the sea. Propagate by division and replanting in autumn.

The 1½-2 in. wide flowers of *I. uniflorum* are fragrant as well as attractive. The variety shown is 'Violaceum'.

Ipheions clump up quickly to create a galaxy of spring stars.

Iris bucharica

There are few sunnier sights in late April and early May than this lovely and unusual iris from Turkestan, with, on each stem, up to six flowers of bright yellow and creamy-white. The flowers are not typical of the iris, in that the creamy standards (the upright parts of the flower) are scarcely more than bristles.

The iris should not be grown in a mass, but be used to provide a point of interest in the spring garden. For this, only three bulbs are necessary. The plant associates well with the purple blooms and fern-like leaves of the pasque flower *Pulsatilla vulgaris*.

HOW TO GROW
Plant in September, 3 in. deep and 6 in. apart, taking care not to break the thick roots below the bulbs. They need a fertile, limy, well-drained soil, in sun and with shelter from shrubs to keep the bulbs dry. Propagate by division after the foliage dies down.

The golden-bloomed *Iris bucharica* needs its bulbs kept dry and does best in sheltered parts of the garden or in deep pots.

Iris bucharica used as a focal point in spring with *Pulsatilla vulgaris*.

Iris histrioides

The Reticulata group of irises provides some of the most attractive of all dwarf early spring-flowering bulbous plants, and *Iris histrioides* rates as one of the best of the group. The name *histrioides* means to be 'showy or gaudy in the manner of an actor or clown', presumably a reference to the lively, violet-blue mottling and yellow central ridge on the flowers' falls (lower, drooping petals). The standards (erect petals) are blue, the depth of colour varying with the different forms. All are beautiful.

The pointed flower buds spear through the ground ahead of the leaves, in late winter. This is the time that snowdrops (*Galanthus*) appear, and the two plants make fine companions, creating a pattern of bright blue and white. The leaves of this iris, and all others in the Reticulata group, are almost square in cross-section. The plant will not tolerate much shade, but accepts dappled shadow. It is very hardy, and the blooms remain unscathed through even the hardest frosts.

Try a massed planting of iris and snowdrop bulbs in a warm border backed by a wall or fence covered with yellow winter-flowering jasmine (*Jasminum nudiflorum*). In this grouping, two other bulbous plants, the golden *Crocus aureus* and the carmine-pink *Cyclamen coum*, will intermingle beautifully.

When planting this group of bulbs, make no attempt at formality or the charming effect of a rainbow of colours will be lost – just scatter the entire mixture of bulbs and plant them where they fall.

HOW TO GROW
Iris histrioides: plant in early autumn, 2 in. deep and apart. Like all bulbous irises, Reticulatas do best in chalky or limy soil, fertile and well drained. Plant in a sunny, sheltered site, where the bulbs can remain as dry as possible while they ripen. For propagation, see I. reticulata.
Crocus aureus: see p. 148.
Cyclamen coum: see p. 150.
Galanthus: see p. 155.
Jasminum nudiflorum: see p. 185.

Beneath a golden cascade of winter-flowering jasmine, the splendidly showy *Iris histrioides* sparkles among a mixture of other early flowering bulbs – golden crocuses, carmine-pink cyclamens and snowdrops.

Wild thyme protects the tiny *Iris reticulata* from soil splashes in rain.

Easy to grow and only 6 in. high, *Iris reticulata* is ideal for planting in pockets in the rock garden.

Iris reticulata

This is the best known of the small bulbous irises, easily grown and flowering as early as February or March. The flowers are a deep violet-blue with a gold spot in the centre of each fall (lower, drooping petal).

Because *Iris reticulata* is so small (only 6 in. high) and sun-loving, it is ideal for planting at the front of a border – if possible, near the house where its beauty makes a welcome sight at the beginning of the year. Try planting a few groups of the iris between tufts of the ferny, grey-leaved *Achillea clavenae*, or with a ground-cover of the greyish-leaved wild thyme (*Thymus drucei*).

HOW TO GROW
Cultivate as for Iris histrioides. This species is suitable for edging, rock gardens and paving pockets where the plants can be left undisturbed. Propagate by division in summer or early autumn, replanting larger bulbs in their flowering sites, smaller ones in a nursery bed.

Iris xiphioides hybrids (ENGLISH IRISES)

The name 'English iris' originated in the 16th century, when the Dutch botanist Carolus Clusius, having seen some *Iris xiphioides* being grown near Bristol, mistakenly believed them to be English; they are actually native to the Pyrenees. Over the centuries, the hybrids have been raised in shades of blue, violet and purple, all with a central gold stripe on the falls (the lower, drooping petals). They usually flower in July.

English irises look charming in groups near plants with silver or gold foliage, such as *Senecio maritimus* or *Thymus × citriodorus* 'Aureus', which will mark the site when the leaves of the irises have died back.

HOW TO GROW
Plant in early autumn, 4-6 in. deep and 6 in. apart, in ordinary, moisture-retentive soil, and in sun or dappled shade. Propagate by division after the foliage has withered, replanting at once.

A grouping of Dutch irises is best in association with a plant that will mark the site, such as silvery Senecio maritimus.

Dutch irises flaunt their bright banners atop 1-2 ft tall stems

Iris xiphium (SPANISH IRISES)

These slender irises are characterised by the clean-cut lines of their flowers, which appear in late June or July in a wide range of colours: deep blue, bright cornflower blue, white, yellow, bronze or bicoloured.

You might like to make a mixed planting of yellow and bronze Spanish irises in front of the rock rose *Cistus × corbariensis*, a splendid shrub which carries a mass of white, yellow-centred blooms in May or June. Plant mostly yellow irises, with just a few bronze, group them informally and allow plenty of space for the rock rose to develop – it can spread as much as 8-10 ft.

The popular Dutch iris is a hybrid from this species, and resembles it closely except for a wider colour range.

HOW TO GROW
Plant in autumn, 4-6 in. deep and 4 in. apart, in fertile, well-drained soil. Full sun is essential, as is some winter protection in cold gardens. Propagation is by division of established clumps while dormant.

English irises and the spreading daisy-like *Anthemis cupaniana* make a lovely association at the height of summer.

Leucojum aestivum (SUMMER SNOWFLAKE)

At 2 ft high, this is the tallest of the snowflakes, which are near relatives of snowdrops. It is ideal for a moist site, especially one by the edge of a garden pool. Between March and May nodding, white, bell-like flowers appear in clusters at the top of the plant's erect stems, each petal tipped with bright green.

Good garden associates include the golden double kingcup *Caltha palustris* 'Flore Pleno' and the young yellow-striped leaves of *Iris pseudacorus* 'Variegata', which will later put out yellow flowers.

HOW TO GROW
Plant in late summer or early autumn, 4 in. deep and 6-8 in. apart, in any good, moist soil, and in sun or light shade. Divide as for Leucojum vernum (p. 160) when clumps are crowded and more leaves than blooms are produced.

The crisp white bells and spiky fresh green leaves of summer snowflakes enhance the coolness of a garden pond.

Leucojum vernum (SNOWFLAKE)

Too often overlooked, this relative of the snowdrop is a splendid plant for the garden – attractive, easy to grow and early flowering. In February or March it produces bright green leaves and large, bell-like, white flowers, whose petals are tipped with green or yellow in the variety *Leucojum vernum* 'Carpathicum'.

The 8 in. high plant is ideal for naturalising in damp, grassy places, and its dwarf stature also makes it suitable for a rock garden that needs brightening in late winter. A good companion for it in the rock garden is the blue-flowered anemone-like *Hepatica nobilis*.

HOW TO GROW
Cultivate as for Leucojum aestivum (p. 159). The plant is good for naturalising. Propagate every few years by division, replanting the bulbs at once in fresh sites, 4 in. deep. Seedlings take three to four years to reach flowering size.

Leucojum vernum, when used in the rock garden, has an early flowering companion in the blue *Hepatica nobilis*.

'Enchantment', an Asiatic hybrid lily, bears up to 16 flowers on each stem.

Lilium 'Bright Star' Trumpet hybrids

Of a more delicate appearance than the better known large trumpet lilies, this delightful Asiatic hybrid has 6 ft tall stems bearing white, almost silvery flowers with backward-arching petals, a light orange star in the centre, and protruding, rust-coloured anthers.

If a shorter hybrid is desired, try planting one of the Mid-Century ones, such as 'Enchantment'. It grows 3-4 ft high and carries magnificent upright orange flowers.

A small group of the lilies planted amid deciduous azaleas will bring colour in July to an area that seems drab after the spring display. With the lilies you might plant the blue-flowered willow gentian (*Gentiana asclepiadea*).

HOW TO GROW
Plant between autumn and spring, 6 in. deep and 8-10 in. apart, in ordinary, loamy, well-drained soil, and in dappled shade. Mulch with organic matter in spring, and water freely during growth. Propagate as for Lilium Aurelian hybrids.

The truly outstanding Trumpet hybrid lily 'Bright Star' bears 5 in. wide blooms that are long-lasting when cut for indoor display.

Lilium 'Shuksan' Bellingham hybrids

Dramatic-looking and 7 ft high, this American lily is ideal for a moist, semi-shady corner of the garden, or part of a woodland garden, that needs some colour in July. It is one of the Bellingham hybrids, a sub-division of the American hybrid group, raised in the United States in the 1920s. Their drooping flowers are carried on long, slender stalks that stand out horizontally from the stems.

The flowers of 'Shuksan' are light orange, turning to red at the tips, with deep crimson-brown spots near the centre. Ideal companions for 'Shuksan' are primulas such as pale yellow *Primula florindae* which flowers in June and July.

HOW TO GROW
Plant in autumn, 5 in. deep and 8-10 in. apart, in lime-free fertile soil, well drained but moisture-retentive. The plants do best in light shade and are suitable for woodland conditions. Top-dress annually with peat or leaf-mould. Propagate by division in autumn or winter.

One of the finest of the Bellingham hybrid lilies, the beautiful 'Shuksan' is tall, vigorous and easy to grow.

Lilium Aurelian hybrids

This lovely group of Chinese trumpet lilies is called after the Roman name for the city of Orleans – for it was there that the original hybrid, *Lilium × aurelianense*, first flowered in 1928. Aurelian lilies now include many different strains in varying colours, but the factors common to them all are that they are easy to grow, hardy and disease-resistant – and they add a truly splendid note to any garden.

It is hard to make a distinction, but ranking high among the well-established favourites is 'Limelight', whose trumpets are of a soft lime-green, and 'Green Dragon', a delicate shade of chartreuse. But most striking of all, perhaps, is 'Golden Clarion', whose strains range from clear lemon-yellow, through straw and buttercup, to deepest gold; they hold their handsome heads horizontally, or in a slightly drooping position, so that the brown anthers within are clearly visible. They are stately plants, 5-6 ft high, and bear fine heads of flowers, making a planting of half a dozen or so bulbs quite sufficient for a display.

The paler-yellow strains have a particularly soft, cool appearance – an effect that might be built upon with, say, the variegated leaves of *Hosta fortunei* 'Albopicta'. If a wall is in the background, you could plant a variegated ivy – one of the *Hedera helix* cultivars – to enhance the cool dignity of the scene.

HOW TO GROW
Lilium Aurelian hybrids: cultivate as for L. 'Bright Star'. Propagate by division and replanting of congested clumps in autumn. Small bulblets are often produced on the stems, just below ground level; remove them in autumn and grow on for up to three years.
Hedera helix: see p. 183.
Hosta fortunei: see p. 95.

'Golden Clarion', the most glorious of Aurelian hybrid lilies, blends perfectly with *Hosta fortunei* 'Albopicta'. The cool elegance of this July-August picture is enhanced by the ivy on the wall behind.

Madonna lilies, the longest cultivated and best known of their genus, thrive by a warm, sunny wall.

Lilium candidum (MADONNA LILY)

The popularity of this plant dates from at least about 3500 BC, when it was depicted on a bronze Minoan dagger; and, because it has long been a symbol of purity, many artists have incorporated it in religious paintings.

In June, a 4-5 ft tall stem arises from the lily's rosette of overwintered leaves and is crowned with fragrant, funnel-shaped flowers of purest white, with a golden centre. The lily is set off perfectly by grey-leaved herbs, such as rosemary (*Rosmarinus officinalis*) and the purple sage *Salvia officinalis* 'Purpurascens'.

HOW TO GROW
Plant in August, setting the bulbs only 2 in. deep and 9-10 in. apart, in ordinary to alkaline, fertile, well-drained soil. The lily does best in full sun, with shelter. Propagate by division of the rootstock in early autumn. The plant is often subject to botrytis disease; spray frequently with a copper fungicide or benomyl (Benlate) from spring onwards.

Lilium regale

For beauty and ease of culture *Lilium regale* is unrivalled among the large white trumpet lilies. In bud its clusters of wonderfully fragrant flowers are wine-red, but, on opening in July, the petals show pure white inside, arching back to reveal a pale yellow throat and golden stamens. Grace is added to beauty by the narrow, dark green leaves carried on the plant's wiry stems.

The lily enjoys a warm border, backed by a wall or other protection. In such a sheltered position it is an ideal companion for the African lilies *Agapanthus* 'Headbourne Hybrids', which bear large rounded flower heads of varying shades of blue. For the best effect, a patch of at least six *L. regale* bulbs should be planted, and about three clumps of African lilies, which will take a year or two to settle down and flower well.

To create a truly spectacular association, also plant the evergreen shrub *Senecio* 'Sunshine', which will provide not only brilliant-yellow daisy-like flowers, but also fine silvery foliage for the drab winter months when the bulbs are resting.

HOW TO GROW
Lilium regale: plant between autumn and spring, 6-8 in. deep and 12 in. apart. Ordinary fertile and well-drained soil, mulched in spring, is suitable, with a sheltered site in full sun. Propagate as for L. Aurelian hybrids (p. 161), or, since the bulbs increase rapidly, by autumn division. Seedlings take only two years to attain flowering size.
Agapanthus 'Headbourne Hybrids': see p. 140.
Senecio 'Sunshine': see p. 315.

The beautiful trumpet lily *Lilium regale*.

Growing in the shelter of a warm wall, a group of *Lilium regale* rises gloriously above the blue African lilies *Agapanthus* 'Headbourne Hybrids'. At their foot is the evergreen shrub *Senecio* 'Sunshine', covered in bright yellow daisy-like flowers. The time of year pictured is July.

Lilium martagon (TURK'S CAP LILY)

This European mountain lily is a tough, vigorous plant. Two extremely handsome variants are 'Album', a pure white, waxy-petalled form, and 'Cattaniae', which has wine-dark purple flowers.

Lilium martagon stands 3-5 ft tall. The petals roll right back on themselves into the turban-like form that gives the plant its common name.

These woodland lilies are perfect for growing between evergreens in dappled shade. Mingle them with ferns such as *Athyrium filix-femina* and *Dryopteris filix-mas*, and incorporate them in groups among rhododendrons.

HOW TO GROW

Plant in early autumn, 4 in. deep and 8 in. apart, in moisture-retentive, fertile soil in partial shade. These lilies are generally lime-tolerant. The species can seed itself; propagate forms and cultivars by autumn division of the bulbs.

Lilium martagon, the Turk's cap lily, so called because its flowers are turban shaped. Each one is about 1¼-1½ in. long.

Harmony in pink and white: *Lilium martagon* and *L. m.* 'Album' intermingle.

Lilium tigrinum (TIGER LILY)

Ever since the extravagantly hued, easily grown tiger lily was introduced to Britain from the East in 1804, it has been a wild success with gardeners. Its large, bright orange, summer blooms are spotted with purplish-black, a colour repeated in the 3½ ft stems, especially so in the variety 'Splendens'.

The tiger lily reaches its peak in late August. It is best to plant it against a pale-leaved shrub such as the gold-and-green *Cornus alba* 'Spaethii'. This would also brighten up the winter with its bare red stems.

HOW TO GROW

Plant between autumn and spring, 6 in. deep and 10 in. apart. This lily needs a rich, lime-free, well-drained soil, in full sun. Staking may be necessary for the late, tall flower stems. Propagate with the small bulbils that are produced in the leaf axils along the stems; remove in autumn and grow on to flowering size, after about two years.

The fiery blooms of *Lilium tigrinum* are perfectly set off by the golden variegated foliage of *Cornus alba* 'Spaethii'.

Lilium tigrinum 'Splendens' has spotted stems as well as flowers.

Muscari armeniacum (GRAPE HYACINTH)

The common grape hyacinth *Muscari racemosum* spreads so extensively that it can be a nuisance in the garden. More suitable for cultivation is *M. armeniacum*, which, though it also increases rapidly, tends to stay in clumps. In April it bears on the 8 in. high stems, densely packed, rich blue flowers with white rims.

In a rock garden the brilliant blue of *M. armeniacum* contrasts strikingly with the yellow flowers of *Alyssum saxatile* 'Citrinum' or 'Dudley Neville'. Grape hyacinths planted beneath an early flowering ornamental cherry, such as *Prunus* 'Accolade', form a lovely expanse of blue beneath a canopy of pink or white blossom.

HOW TO GROW

Plant in late summer or early autumn, 3 in. deep and apart, in any well-drained soil, preferably in full sun. Propagate by division in summer. Lifting and replanting is usually necessary every three years, after the foliage has withered.

Together with forms of *Primula vulgaris*, blue *Muscari armeniacum* brightens a garden in spring.

Narcissus cyclamineus 'February Gold'

Only in a very mild winter indeed would this narcissus actually manage to produce its bright yellow flowers in February – but it seldom blooms later than mid-March. The petals of the flower curve sharply back on themselves, like those of a cyclamen, and leave the trumpet projecting prominently.

The plant is one of a group of beautiful garden narcissi descended from the wild species *Narcissus cyclamineus*. This dwarf plant from Spain and Portugal is well suited to the rock garden. The narcissi hybrids to which it has given rise have larger flowers and are more vigorous, like their other parent, the trumpet daffodil.

N. cyclamineus and its progeny prefer moist, grassy places in full sun or dappled shade, and 'February Gold' is ideal for naturalising with other plants that like the same conditions: mixed white and purple *Crocus vernus* and yellow *C. aureus* (syn. *C. luteus*), for example.

In the rhododendron garden the narcissus could also be used with great effect beneath or alongside the very early rose-purple flowers of *Rhododendron mucronulatum*. For a subtle contrast of colours, you might plant irregular patches of 'February Gold' interwoven with the light blue glory of the snow (*Chionodoxa luciliae*), crowding about the foot of the rhododendron.

HOW TO GROW
Narcissus cyclamineus 'February Gold': plant all narcissi bulbs as soon as they are available, from late summer on, at a depth three times the size of the bulbs. They thrive in fertile, humus-rich soil supplemented at planting time with bonemeal or a general fertiliser. Moderate drainage is essential – but dry soil from spring to summer inhibits next year's blooms.
Propagate as for N. pseudonarcissus.
Chionodoxa luciliae: see p. 145.
Crocus aureus: see p. 148.
C. vernus: see p. 149.
Rhododendron mucronulatum: see p. 305.

The species *Narcissus cyclamineus* lights up the garden as early as February.

A spring rhapsody: the brilliant yellow trumpet blooms of *Narcissus cyclamineus* 'February Gold' mingle with blue *Chionodoxa luciliae* beneath the rosy-purple flowers of *Rhododendron mucronulatum*.

Narcissus poeticus 'Recurvus' (POET'S NARCISSUS)

Ovid was the first poet to tell the story of Narcissus, the Grecian lad who died of love for his own reflection and was transformed into a flower. Hence the poet's narcissus (*Narcissus poeticus*) and its many varieties that emerge in May. These are some of the most attractive and fragrant of all narcissi, and are easily grown. The variety 'Recurvus', which flowers in late April or May, is particularly fine, with its spreading white petals and small yellow crimson-edged cup.

'Actaea' blends well with the honesty *Lunaria annua*, which is covered with soft-purple flowers at the time when the narcissus blooms.

HOW TO GROW
Cultivate as for Narcissus cyclamineus. This plant is better for borders and beds but can be naturalised. Plant the bulbs 4-6 in. apart and leave them undisturbed until clumps become congested. Propagate as for N. pseudonarcissus.

A drift of the graceful, fragrant *Narcissus poeticus* 'Recurvus' brings charm to a patch of semi-wild garden in spring.

Narcissus pseudonarcissus 'Golden Harvest'

(WILD DAFFODIL, LENT LILY)

This yellow trumpet daffodil sings the praises of early spring from almost any position. In March and April it brings cheer on the dullest of days, because its flowers never close up, no matter how bad the weather.

The 15 in. high daffodil is at its best grown in drifts in long grass beneath trees or, as Wordsworth noted, beside the water. Another companion worth considering is the shrub *Spiraea japonica* 'Goldflame', whose young foliage is bronze-red and provides crimson flowers in late summer.

HOW TO GROW
Cultivate as for Narcissus cyclamineus. Propagate all narcissi by lifting them as the leaves die down and removing the smaller bulbs round the parent. Grade the bulbs to size, plant in early autumn in a nursery bed and grow on to flowering size, after a year or two.

The trumpet daffodil *Narcissus pseudonarcissus* 'Golden Harvest' does best naturalised in grass beneath trees.

Narcissus triandrus 'Thalia'

The species *Narcissus triandrus* comes from the mountains of northern Spain. It is easily recognised by its small nodding flowers, several to every stem and each with a cup-shaped centre and backward-arching petals.

'Thalia' is taller and more robust than the species – 10-15 in. high – and has larger flowers; two to four lovely creamy-white blooms on each stem. It blooms in April, when cultivars of the heather *Erica carnea* are still in full flower. A small group of the narcissus bulbs planted alongside a drift of the pink-flowered *E. carnea* 'Winter Beauty' would make a delightful combination.

HOW TO GROW
Plant 6 in. apart. Cultivate as for Narcissus cyclamineus. Propagate as for N. pseudonarcissus. Failure to flower may be due to narcissus flies, or to various virus diseases. There is no chemical remedy, and affected plants should be dug up and burned.

The lovely all-white 'Thalia' is a hybrid of *Narcissus triandrus*, whose drooping head and backswept petals it inherits.

The narcissus is suitable for naturalising in a border among small plants.

Nerine bowdenii

From mid-September to November, when most other plants are finishing their display, this beautiful South African bulbous plant produces large heads of up to eight flowers. Each has six elegant, narrow, backward-arching petals of bright glowing pink – deep pink in the case of 'Mark Fenwick' ('Fenwick's Variety') – and a waxy, orchid-like texture.

The 2 ft high leafless stems rise from tufts of uninspiring, strap-shaped leaves just starting to fade, so it is best to fill the foreground with plants. They should be low growing so that they do not shade the sun-loving bulbs. The grey-green leaved sub-shrub *Helianthemum nummularium* is ideal for the purpose.

HOW TO GROW
Plant in late spring, 4-6 in. deep and 6-8 in. apart, in any well-drained soil, in full sun and ideally protected by a wall. Propagate by division in late spring; nerines flower best when crowded. Do not disturb for four or five years.

The blushing *Nerine bowdenii* brings a warm glow to autumn, but to succeed it needs full sun and the shelter of a wall.

Purple grape hyacinths accentuate the green and white *Ornithogalum nutans*.

Ornithogalum umbellatum
(STAR OF BETHLEHEM)

This dwarf plant, about 12 in. high, with its glistening white stars of flowers that only open on sunny days, makes a fine show in late April and May when the last of the tulips are in flower. A charming association may be created by planting stars of Bethlehem and forget-me-nots (*Myosotis*) beneath a group of pale creamy-yellow *Tulipa* 'Niphetos'.

More subtle in effect is *Ornithogalum nutans*, also known as drooping star of Bethlehem. This has 15 in. high spikes of nodding flowers with silvery-white and green petals. These are charming close to, but have no impact at a distance.

HOW TO GROW
Plant bulbs of both species in autumn, 3 in. deep and 4-6 in. apart, in any fertile, well-drained soil and in sun or light shade. Propagate by bulblets and offsets or division of clumps in late summer.

Planted in a mass, *Ornithogalum umbellatum* looks dazzling when the sun persuades it to open its starry blooms.

Puschkinia scilloides (STRIPED SQUILL)

This fine spring-flowering bulb (also known as *Puschkinia libanotica*) is not seen as often as it deserves to be. Its clusters of bell-shaped, hyacinth-like flowers are a strikingly unusual pale icy blue, with a white centre and a darker blue stripe on the inside of each petal.

The smallness of the striped squill – it is only 4 in. high – makes it best suited to the front of a border. There, from March to May, it harmonises well with the deep purplish foliage and mauve flowers of the pansy *Viola labradorica* 'Purpurea'; this may need to be kept in check, for it spreads rapidly.

HOW TO GROW
Plant in autumn, 3 in. deep and apart, in well-drained, loamy soil and in an open position in sun or light shade. Leave undisturbed for several years. Propagate by division as the foliage dies down in summer.

Striped squill – so called because of the blue line on each petal – is a small plant ideal for the front of a sunny border.

Hyacinth-like striped squill blends well with a mauve *Viola labradorica*.

Schizostylis coccinea (KAFFIR LILY)

Although this splendid autumn-flowering member of the iris family is a native of South Africa, it is hardy in Britain, except in the very coldest areas of the north and east. The flower spikes, which overtop the erect sword-like leaves, each bear up to ten bright scarlet flowers, somewhat crocus-shaped at first but later opening out in bright weather to stars 1½ in. across. The plant is a valuable one for the herbaceous border, since it blooms at a time – September to November – when most other herbaceous plants are coming to the end of their display. It also makes an excellent, long-lasting cut flower.

The kaffir lily associates well with Michaelmas daisies (*Aster novi-belgii*), in particular the powder-blue ones, such as 'Marie Ballard', and the clear white 'White Ladies'. Try growing all these plants together with *Santolina chamaecyparissus*, a lovely dwarf evergreen shrub that has silvery, finely dissected leaves.

Several named varieties of the kaffir lily have been raised, most notably 'Mrs Hegarty', which has charming soft pink flowers that stand out beautifully against a background of silver foliage. The Sawara cypress *Chamaecyparis pisifera* 'Boulevard' is ideal for this purpose.

HOW TO GROW
Schizostylis coccinea: plant in spring, 2 in. deep and 9 in. apart. Ordinary moist, fertile soil is suitable, and a sunny, sheltered position. Water copiously and keep the soil cool and moist with a deep peat mulch. Propagate by division every other year in spring.
Aster novi-belgii: see p. 70.
Chamaecyparis pisifera: see p. 201.
Santolina chamaecyparissus: see p. 314.

The pink kaffir lily 'Mrs Hegarty' punctuates a border of silver *Santolina chamaecyparissus*. The Michaelmas daisies 'Marie Ballard' (blue) and 'White Ladies' (white) make a gentle contrast, while the background Sawara cypress 'Boulevard' continues the silver theme. This delightful association is pictured in October.

Scilla sibirica 'Spring Beauty'

The blue of this plant is of an intensity unexcelled by any other early-blooming bulbs. Its small, drooping bells appear on the 6 in. flowering stems in March and, since each bulb produces several stems, only a few plants are needed to make a vivid splash of colour which will overwhelm any other blue in the vicinity.

The scilla makes a splendid underplanting for the purple blooms of the lovely spring-flowering shrub *Daphne mezereum*, or the massed white of *D. m.* 'Alba'.

HOW TO GROW
Plant as soon as the scillas are available, from late summer. Set 2-3 in. deep and 3-4 in. apart, in fertile to rich, moist but well-drained soil, preferably alkaline, and in sun or light shade. The plants are suitable for naturalising in short grass and beneath deciduous shrubs. Propagate as for Scilla tubergeniana (p. 168).

On a crisp March day *Scilla sibirica* 'Spring Beauty' and *Daphne mezereum* 'Alba' reflect the fleecy-clouded blue sky above.

Primulas sparkle alongside the brilliant blue of 'Spring Beauty'.

Scilla tubergeniana here combines beautifully with *Crocus aureus*.

Another lovely spring association: the silvery-blue scilla and yellow *Eranthis hyemalis* flower beneath nodding snowdrops.

Scilla tubergeniana

Silver-blue striped with a darker blue is the arresting coloration of this bright Iranian plant that appears in late February or early March. The first flowers, opening as the 4 in. stems emerge from the soil, are bell-like to begin with, before flattening out in the sun; they are set among glossy, bright green leaves.

Scilla tubergeniana does well in semi-shade, where the bright yellow winter aconite (*Eranthis hyemalis*) and snowdrops (*Galanthus nivalis*) make good companions. These would all mingle well beneath the rosy-white blooms of the winter-flowering shrub *Viburnum* × *bodnantense*.

HOW TO GROW
Cultivate as for Scilla sibirica (p. 167). Both species increase slowly and should be left undisturbed. Propagate by lifting well-established clumps in summer, dividing, removing offsets and replanting them at once. Seeds, sown under glass in summer, take at least three years to reach flowering size.

The clear yellow flowers of *Sternbergia lutea* make beautiful companions for a euphorbia (right), with sombre blue-grey foliage, and a lavender bush (left), with spiky silver-grey branches and foliage, though its flowers have finished. The time of year is October.

Sternbergia lutea

Although this plant is crocus-like in appearance, it is more closely related to the narcissus. There are few other autumn-flowering bulbs of such splendour. The goblet-shaped flowers, each upon an individual stem, are a brilliant, waxy yellow; in sunshine, each bloom responds by opening up to about 2 in. across. The blooms, which appear from August to October, are perfectly set off by the deep green strap-like leaves. These are shorter than the flowers, and do not reach their full length until the following spring.

In summer, when sternbergia bulbs are dormant, they still require the sun's warmth. This rather dictates their planting position, and their accompaniment, too. In the wild, where *Sternbergia lutea* grows in sunny rock crevices and scorched scrubland, its companions are often herbs and silvery-leaved shrubs. In the garden, it is a good idea to imitate nature and plant the same kind of associates.

Try growing at least a dozen *S. lutea* in a sunny border – preferably at the foot of a south-facing wall or fence – in front of either the silver-grey-leaved rock rose *Cistus crispus* or the blue-grey-leaved *Euphorbia characias wulfenii*. A lavender bush (*Lavandula*) might also be incorporated into the scheme. This might still have a few flowers in autumn, its soft lilac-blue harmonising beautifully with the clear yellow of the sternbergia.

Another fine combination may be achieved by planting *S. lutea* behind the sprawling blue-grey-leaved perennial *Sedum cauticolum*, which bears rosy flower heads in late summer and early autumn.

HOW TO GROW
Sternbergia lutea: plant in late summer, 3-4 in. deep and apart, in a sunny and sheltered site. Any well-drained – or even dry – soil is suitable. Leave undisturbed for as long as possible; lift only to propagate, by division, in late summer.
Cistus crispus: see p. 264.
Euphorbia characias wulfenii: see p. 86.
Lavandula: see p. 291.
Sedum cauticolum: see p. 217.

Tulipa clusiana (LADY TULIP)

Some of the wild tulips have a grace which the large-flowered, more colourful hybrids do not possess; the lady tulip is one of the loveliest. In April, its pointed flower buds open out to white stars flushed pink on the outside of the petals, framing hearts of an intense crimson-purple. The narrow, greyish leaves, standing 9-12 in. high, are often edged with red. Grow companion plants that echo the grey of the foliage, such as purple-leaved sage *Salvia officinalis* 'Purpurascens'.

HOW TO GROW
Plant in November, 4 in. deep and 3-4 in. apart, in light, well-drained soil, ideally in a south-facing, sheltered position. On heavy soils incorporate plenty of grit; dress others with bonemeal. Tulips grown as perennials need deep soil cultivation before planting. Also, they do not need lifting; apply a general fertiliser each spring, dead-head regularly, and remove stems and leaves as they fade. Propagate as for Tulipa greigii.

Pointed-petalled flowers and tall, slender stems make *Tulipa clusiana* one of the most elegant of all tulips.

'Chrysantha' has more brilliant colouring than the parent species.

Tulipa Darwin group

The Darwin tulips are notable for their rich colours, rather cylindrical flower shape and robustness. They are used mainly for bedding displays, but can be planted in groups in a mixed border, combined with herbaceous plants and shrubs. 'William Pitt' is a 2 ft tall, bright red cultivar and 'Niphetos' a yellow one that look effective planted in informal groups of 15-20 bulbs.

The similar Darwin hybrids make an even greater impact in the garden with their larger, broader blooms. A fine example is red-tipped, sulphur-yellow 'Jewel of Spring'.

All the cultivars described here look particularly fine against a background of evergreen shrubs, particularly *Prunus lusitanicus.*

HOW TO GROW
Cultivate as for Tulipa clusiana, but space Darwin tulips 6-8 in. apart. Propagate as for T. greigii.

The vivacious Darwin tulips 'William Pitt' rise magnificently above an underplanting of white pansies.

Tulipa greigii hybrids

The wild species *Tulipa greigii* is a magnificent, scarlet-flowered dwarf tulip, no more than 18 in. tall, with broad grey leaves strikingly mottled and streaked with purple-brown. It has passed its low stature and attractive foliage on to its offspring.

The hybrids' flowers, borne in April, are large for the size of the plants. Triangular in bud, they open out to wide cups, the tips of whose petals curve sharply back on themselves in sunshine. Flower colours range from scarlet through orange and yellow to bronze-green, in some cases with the petals outlined in bright yellow.

HOW TO GROW
Cultivate as for Tulipa clusiana. Space bulbs 6 in. apart. Propagate all perennial tulips from offsets which form round the bulbs and the base of the flower stems. Lift plants when the foliage turns yellow, remove offsets and grow them on to flowering size, after one or two years.

With their richly coloured, unusually shaped, long-lasting flowers, *Tulipa greigii* hybrids are outstanding.

The hybrids associate well with grape hyacinths and *Alyssum saxatile.*

Tulipa kaufmanniana hybrids
(WATER-LILY TULIP)

The early spring-flowering *Tulipa kaufmanniana* is 6-10 in. high with large, wide, star-shaped flowers of creamy-white, flushed with red. Its hybrids come in a wide range of hues. For example, 'The First' is close to the species in colour, 'Stresa' is a particularly gay yellow with a broad red band on the outside and a red centre, and 'Fritz Kreisler' is salmon-pink. The leaves of the hybrids with *T. greigii* in their ancestry are purple striped as in 'Heart's Delight'.

The compactness of the tulips makes them good plants for rock gardens, where they can be grown in small groups among later-flowering alpine plants.

HOW TO GROW
Cultivate as for Tulipa clusiana (p. 169), with 6 in. between the bulbs. Propagate as for T. greigii (p. 169) – though T. kaufmanniana, one of the most reliable and long-lived of tulips, increases naturally from offsets below ground.

'The First' planted in a rock garden with *Potentilla tabernaemontani*.

Tulipa kaufmanniana, opening out flat in full sun, is also known as the water-lily tulip. This hybrid is 'Heart's Delight'.

Tulipa Lily-flowered group

Waisted flowers and long, pointed petals that arch gracefully outwards at the tips make the Lily-flowered group of tulips highly distinctive. In addition, the greyish leaves are bold and the stems robust and weather-resistant.

'China Pink' has beautiful deep pink flowers, which are an exquisite rose-pink within. A group of the tulips would be given additional distinction if they were grown in front of a blue-grey-leaved bush of *Euphorbia characias wulfenii*, with a foreground of silvery foliage. An alternative to 'China Pink' is 'Mariette' which has long-lasting, satiny, deep pink flowers, or the golden-yellow 'West Point'.

Other good varieties include 'White Triumphator' (white); 'Lilac Time' (violet-purple); and 'Dyanito' (red).

HOW TO GROW
Cultivate as for Tulipa clusiana (p. 169), setting bulbs 6 in. apart. Propagate as for T. greigii (p. 169).

A large group of 'China Pink' brings a warm glow to the April garden.

The Lily-flowered tulip 'West Point' looks spectacular when interplanted with grape hyacinths over the full length of a border.

Tulipa tarda

Known by some nurserymen as *Tulipa dasystemon*, this delightful little 4-6 in. high plant from central Asia is one of the smallest of all tulips and, as such, is perfect for growing at the edge of a sunny border or on a rock garden. Narrow, slightly grey-green leaves form a rosette around a tight bunch of up to five starry, pointed-petalled white flowers with brilliant yellow centres. In the spring sunshine, several flowers on each plant open together, so a group of about ten bulbs is all that is necessary to present a most marvellous display.

T. *tarda* associates well with the purple pasque flower (*Pulsatilla vulgaris*). The two plants can be grown to great effect on the sunny side of a grey-leaved bush of rosemary (*Rosmarinus officinalis*).

HOW TO GROW
Cultivate as for Tulipa clusiana (p. 169), setting bulbs 3 in. apart. Propagate as for T. greigii (p. 169).

A mass of *Tulipa tarda*, several flowers opening on each plant, blooms in March beside the purple *Aubrieta deltoidea*.

An effective grouping of T. *tarda*, purple pasque flower and rosemary.

Tulipa Cottage group

A charming cottage-garden effect can be achieved by a plant association that centres on Cottage tulips. This tulip group, related to the Darwins and containing some of the very latest hybrids, bears egg-shaped flowers, opening wide to about 5 in. across. Although up to 3 ft tall, their stiff, erect stems are strong enough to resist all but the harshest spring weather. The Cottage tulips range in colour from fiery reds and oranges to the misty hues of 'Artist', which has petals in delicate shades of sea green, salmon pink and purple.

'Halcro' is a magnificent hybrid, crimson on the outside, turning to orange-red at the tips of the petals, and flaring on the inside to a bright orange-scarlet. For a fine but informal display you might try a mingling of 'Halcro' with soft blue forget-me-nots (*Myosotis*) and orange-red wallflowers (*Cheiranthus cheiri*), which repeat the warm colours of the tulips.

As a pleasant afterthought, you might add *Tulipa* 'Dillenburg', a rich salmon-orange member of the Cottage group. This is one of the latest-flowering of all tulips, a plant that will prolong the colourful show even further. Such an association would make a delightful gathering under old apple trees – provided they do not cast too much shade.

On the other hand, you could use the same plants to create a more formal arrangement: a border or island bed of mingled tulips and forget-me-nots, with the wallflowers used as an edging. For this association, the lemon-yellow 'Golden Harvest' would make a fine addition.

Among other recommended hybrids in the Cottage group are 'Aster Nielsen' (cream-yellow); 'Bacchus' (dark violet-blue); and 'Chappaqua' (deep violet-rose).

HOW TO GROW
Tulipa Cottage group: cultivate as for T. clusiana (p. 169), with 6-8 in. between bulbs, and propagate as for T. greigii (p. 169).
Cheiranthus cheiri: see p. 20.
Myosotis: see p. 44.

Scarlet and yellow Cottage tulips and wallflowers rise from a blue sea of forget-me-nots and grape hyacinths.

'Artist' is a subtle blend of colours.

Cottage tulips – the subtle gradations of colour that can be achieved.

Plants for Town Gardens

Be it box, tub or yard, there are plants to brighten any spot

Overall, the great benefit of a sensibly planned town garden is its ability to soften an angular world of walls, windows and roofs. In a sense, the plants also become the soft furnishings of what often tends – in summer, at any rate – to assume the role of an additional outdoor room.

Brick walls and high chimneys may be far removed from the natural environment of most plants, but they do provide uniquely sheltered conditions. As a consequence, there are climbers and other plants that will prosper in inner London that are, at the least, unreliable in many other parts of Britain. Examples are the trumpet creeper (*Campsis*) and mimosa (*Acacia dealbata*).

The main drawback of such sheltered gardens is that they can become excessively dry in summer. The soil is often thin and exhausted, incapable of retaining moisture, while the base of surrounding walls tends to soak up whatever water there is. Daily watering is essential from late spring until autumn, when each established plant needs the equivalent of a bucket a day.

Another problem is that of uneven daylight, for while one side of a town garden may bask in full sun, the other is likely to lie in the perpetual shade of buildings.

How many plants you use will depend on the size of the garden; but, as a general rule, avoid dotting small plants about the place, choosing one of this and one of that. The effect will be unrestful, and generally out of scale with the surrounding buildings. Be bold – if anything make your permanent planting rather prominent to ensure an eye-catching effect.

Selecting the right trees

The background, which should consist of shrubs, might include a tree or two as well. Choose from the smaller, decorative trees. Spring-flowering cherry is a long-established favourite, but you could be a little more adventurous and instead have one that flowers in winter – *Prunus subhirtella* 'Autumnalis' – adding to it *Catalpa bignonioides* 'Aurea', whose gold foliage brightens the winter months. Around it you might create a golden garden, especially if your walls are yellow or corn-coloured.

With their delicate, pale foliage, gleditschia and robinia are both fine trees for a town garden. Some sorbus have even more attractive leaves, with fruits and autumn colour as added attractions. Foliage trees also offer other rewards – the way they look

when viewed from indoors, for example, whether from ground level or from upstairs, and their ability to enhance the light in a garden.

Take care, when choosing trees and the plants that you grow beneath them, to keep to a mood or style. Silver birches, for example, tend to be out of character in a town, looking much more at home in light woodland, as do many conifers. But, oddly enough, our indigenous box, yew and juniper appear perfectly happy.

Shrubs and climbers

The main bones of the planting should be shrubs, together with climbers. These will create that essential, year-round green mass. On the whole, bold foliage is probably more important than flower colour, though it is pleasant to combine the two. Autumn-flowering fatsia does very well in shady city gardens, while the sweet-scented Mexican orange blossom, *Choisya ternata*, likes warmth and shelter. Any kind of cistus will flourish on the sunny side of the garden, and may be mixed with shrubby herbs such as rosemary and the coloured sages. Then you might choose a hebe for form and flower colour, and a brilliant phormium for contrasting foliage. With them you could mingle tree paeonies and olearias, the daisy bushes from New Zealand.

Remember to give yourself some winter joys, too – early flowering, sweetly scented species that bring a touch of optimism to the dreary end of January. Early daphnes will do just this, together with *Lonicera fragrantissima* and winter jasmine set against the green catkins of *Garrya elliptica*.

Once you have established the shrub grouping, smother the surrounding walls with climbers or wall shrubs – or both. Roses are excellent for town gardens, but so too are rampant, free flowering *Clematis montana* and pale wisteria. For heady, evening scents, you might try the lemon-scented verbena (*Lippia citriodora*), summer jasmine, honeysuckles or myrtle.

The spaces between shrubs and climbers are the obvious spots for favourite herbaceous perennials – large-leaved hostas, perhaps, for light shade; rheums where there is enough moisture; pretty alchemillas and late-flowering white anemones beneath. The foreground is for bulbs, corms and rhizomes. Those well-suited to towns include Solomon's seal (*Polygonatum × hybridum*), lily-of-the-valley (*Convallaria majalis*) and lily-flowered tulips. For continuing colour, you might add alliums, large and small, late-summer hyacinths (*Galtonia candicans*),

Chaenomeles speciosa and *Kerria japonica* climb a sheltered south-facing wall behind tulips, wallflowers and rock plants.

lilies and, in shade, the little *Cyclamen hederifolium*.

Tubs and containers are the very essence of city gardens, and are best used to hold the movable feast of your spring and summer colour – points of brilliant emphasis which, when their flowering has finished, can quickly be renewed. Window-boxes should be equally dramatic – overflowing with colour, and preferably composed of the same flower species throughout.

In the smallest of town gardens, on the roof or balcony, the choice of plants is governed very much by the time you can give to looking after them, for the sun and wind will dry them out much more quickly than in gardens at ground level. Where wind is a problem, establish a background of tough, naturally wind-resistant plants such as low junipers, gorse or shrubby willow, and front them with plants that do not mind drought – yuccas, mesembryanthemums and geraniums, for example. Often, a check upon a plant's native habitat or country of origin will suggest the kind of climate and weather conditions it can withstand.

A word of warning. Earth-filled containers weigh far more wet than dry, so consult an architect or structural engineer before beginning extensive gardening on a balcony or flat-topped roof, even if you are using lightweight containers.

A begonia and a fuchsia displayed in an ornamental container.

A small town garden, where cement predominates, can be turned into a green paradise by using climbers and plants in tubs and pots.

Climbing plants

*Using climbers, the ugliest fence can vanish under
a cascade of flowers or foliage*

AN ENORMOUS NUMBER of fine plants, especially shrubs, can be considered climbers because they are trained against walls and fences to give them protection. But in the race for light in the wild woodland of their origins, true climbers have renounced the development of self-supporting woody tissue and exchanged it for speed of growth. These plants must have some kind of support – it can be a sophisticated trellis, wires on a wall, or a tree – but they repay this consideration by doing more than most plants to add 'maturity' to a new garden.

Used with care, climbing plants take on many roles. In open positions *Clematis montana* will rush up into a tree, tumble over an ugly shed, or fill every gap in a chain-link fence. If a building is elegant in design or a wall is made of beautiful material, climbers chosen with restraint will complement existing virtues, not hide them. Though the prospect of a north wall may daunt new gardeners, it presents few problems. Many climbers – for example, *Hydrangea petiolaris* – thrive in this situation.

Remember that a climber must be in proportion to its support. A 50 ft spread is nothing to a wisteria and the necessary twice-a-year pruning to encourage development of flowering wood can be a mammoth operation. However, there are many other climbers, such as *Jasminum nudiflorum*, which can easily be controlled.

No wall need be without its furnishing. The analogy is with rooms in the house; every window needs its curtains, but taste and choice will determine their colour, size and pattern.

Providing a superb June picture, a honeysuckle sprawls over an old brick wall and frames the garden beyond containing clipped box and silver-grey *Anaphalis*.

A. kolomikta with *Eccremocarpus scaber* and *Lonicera japonica* 'Halliana'.

Trained on wires, a kolomikta vine clothes a wall with its variegated leaves. Fully hardy, it flourishes best in full sun.

Actinidia kolomikta (KOLOMIKTA VINE)

One of the vigorous climbing relatives of this plant is *Actinidia chinensis*, whose hairy, egg-shaped fruits are sold under the name of Chinese gooseberries, or Kiwi fruit. *A. kolomikta* itself is a smaller climber, growing to 12 ft or so high, and suitable for a low wall. Its heart-shaped green leaves are splashed pink and white at the ends, creating a vivacious, warm pattern that lasts throughout the season until autumn leaf-fall.

HOW TO GROW
Plant between autumn and spring, in any fertile and, ideally, humus-rich soil that is well drained but moist. A position in full sun, such as a south-facing wall or fence, will encourage more pronounced leaf variegation. The plant needs training when young on strong wall supports. Propagate by cuttings under glass in summer, or by seeds in autumn. Prune to shape in early spring.

The energetic climber *Akebia quinata* is ideal for training over a pergola.

Plants carry both female and male flowers (the latter are smaller); cross-pollination is usually needed to obtain fruits.

Akebia quinata

Hardy, vigorous and easily grown, akebias are not showy climbers but are well worth growing for the spreading, rich green tapestry that they so quickly weave.

Of the two species readily available (the other is *Akebia trifoliata*), *A. quinata*, about 15 ft high, is the more accommodating. The foliage which clothes its slender twining stems generally persists through all but the coldest winters. Then, in spring, it is joined by purple-flushed young leaves and small strings of flower buds that open into three-petalled, fragrant purple blooms in April.

HOW TO GROW
Plant in autumn – or in spring in cold gardens – in ordinary well-drained soil. The position should be sunny or lightly shaded. Akebias will climb through trees; on walls they need support. Propagate by cuttings under glass in late summer. After flowering, prune out weak shoots and, where space is restricted, cut others hard back.

Campsis grandiflora (TRUMPET VINE)

There are so few self-supporting climbers that the best possible use should be made of those that are available. One such is this vine from China, which, given a south wall in a mild part of the country, climbs 20 ft, clinging to the surface by means of aerial roots, rather like those of ivy.

The vine has elegant foliage, with leaves somewhat resembling those of the ash. In late summer, the ends of non-climbing shoots carry clusters of brilliant orange, trumpet-shaped flowers.

HOW TO GROW
Plant in autumn or spring, in rich soil that is moist but well drained and contains plenty of humus. A sheltered wall in full sun is essential. Tie in shoots as necessary. Propagate in summer by cuttings under glass, or in spring by layering. Prune in early spring, cutting young climbers back to 6 in. (to encourage basal growth). Young plants may also need root protection during winter until they become established.

Campsis grandiflora blooms in September.

Fruits of *Celastrus orbiculatus* in October.

Celastrus orbiculatus (STAFF VINE)

One of the most spectacular of fruiting shrubs, the staff vine is completely hardy and full of vigour. Given good soil and a suitable tree support, it can climb to 40 ft, its rounded leaves hanging in great curtains that turn clear yellow in autumn. This is when the yellowish-brown husks of the fruits split, each revealing a golden lining in which is set a lustrous scarlet berry.

It is vital to obtain a hermaphrodite plant – one that will bear both male and female flowers – otherwise, the glory of the vine, its fruits, will not appear.

HOW TO GROW
Plant between autumn and spring, in ordinary, well-manured soil that is well drained but moist, and in sun or light shade. The strong twining shoots are best suited to climbing through trees. Propagate in autumn by cuttings under glass or by layering. Prune wall climbers in early spring, thinning out weak shoots and shortening others.

CLEMATIS

Mention climbing plants, and the name that springs to most people's minds is clematis, an extremely varied genus numbering about 150 species of almost world-wide distribution. Most of the species are climbers, some being high fliers that will scale quite tall trees, others low scramblers. There are also herbaceous perennial clematis that make free-standing border plants. Some species are deciduous, others evergreen.

Although clematis is commonly associated with large, flat, circular flowers, as in the ever-popular 'Nellie Moser', some species in fact have quite small blooms that are shaped like urns, bells or stars. The colour range runs through shades of blue, purple, red, yellow and white.

Clematis scale their supports in an intriguing way. Whereas most climbers either twine or have tendrils or special sucker roots, the clematis hangs on by its foliage. Each leaf is composed of several leaflets, the long stalks of which rapidly encircle any likely support and thus act as tendrils. After the leaflets fall, the stalks thicken and become woody. Clematis will climb almost anything, but look especially fine in trees or tall shrubs.

HOW TO GROW

Plant all clematis between autumn and late spring. Although lime is not essential, they thrive in neutral to alkaline soil of average fertility and with good drainage. Clematis resent root disturbance and should be planted out as pot-grown specimens. Put them in a position where stems and flowers are in sun but the roots are cool, moist and shaded. To help achieve this, the root area can be covered with stones or planted with low ground-cover.

Support is needed for all climbing clematis, and the young shoots must be trained by tying them in. Propagate in spring by layering, or in summer by stem cuttings under glass. The species can also be increased from seeds in autumn.

Pruning is governed by three factors: plant vigour, flowering season, and available space. If necessary, strong growers, such as Clematis macropetala and its forms, and C. montana, which blooms on shoots made the previous year, should be pruned immediately after their single flowering period, in late spring or early summer. Where space is unlimited, the only pruning needed is to thin out tangled shoots occasionally. If space is restricted, take out old and weak stems, and shorten other flowering shoots by up to two-thirds.

The thin, less vigorous growth of early summer-flowering clematis (such as the large-flowered hybrids 'Lasurstern' and 'Nellie Moser', which also flower on the previous year's stems) should be encouraged to branch from low down on the plant. Prune young plants back to 8-9 in. from ground level in early spring. In subsequent years, thin out weak shoots and tie in replacement stems. After the second show of flowers in late summer, the shoots may be shortened by up to one-third if they are outgrowing the space available.

Summer-to-autumn-flowering clematis (which include C. viticella, C. × jackmanii and its forms, and large-flowered hybrids such as 'Ernest Markham', 'Huldine' and 'Perle d'Azur') flower on shoots of the current season. If they are left to scramble at will, the only pruning needed is to remove weak and old stems in spring; wall-trained plants should also be pruned in spring, by cutting shoots of the previous season back to a pair of strong buds.

'Nellie Moser' climbs a wall, attaching itself by its leaves. Beneath it is *Zantedeschia aethiopica* 'Crowborough'.

Clematis armandii

The great plant collector Ernest Wilson (1876-1930) brought this lovely evergreen clematis to Britain from Western China in 1900. In the wild, like most other clematis, it scrambles through trees, but in this country, where it requires a sunny wall to ensure its success, a good wire or net support must be provided in advance. This is because no established clematis can be retrained; indeed, *Clematis armandii* may cut off the flow of sap to any of its shoots that have been interfered with.

Young growth must be tied to the support as soon as it appears. Once a framework is built up, curtains of dark green gleaming foliage will develop, a perfect backcloth for the clusters of large, saucer-shaped, creamy flowers in April and May. In the variety 'Apple Blossom', the flowers are flushed with pink; in 'Snow Drift' they are pure white.

HOW TO GROW
See p. 177.

Clematis armandii, one of the few evergreen clematis, needs a sunny, sheltered wall to guarantee its success.

The gleaming flowers of 'Snow Drift' are larger than those of the species.

Clematis (LARGE-FLOWERED HYBRIDS)

For magnificent effects in a wide range of colours, the large-flowered clematis hybrids are difficult to beat. Large-flowered is no misnomer. Most produce great starry blooms, 6 in. and more across; and most, too, in an off and on way, flower for several months on end. Each individual bloom has a long life due to its unusual structure of tough, coloured sepals – not tender petals.

There are a large number of hybrids from which to choose, of which the bicoloured are among the most striking. Typical and ever-popular is 'Nellie Moser', with pale pink, carmine-striped flowers that are at their best on a north-facing wall. Then there is 'Lasurstern', deep blue with lavender overtones, and – to take random and widely differing examples from among the splendid single-coloured plants – the pale blue 'Mrs Cholmondeley', 'Perle d'Azur', and the velvety-red 'Ernest Markham'.

HOW TO GROW
See p. 177.

The clematis hybrid 'Lasurstern', covered in lavender-blue flowers, rambles over a low wall in glorious abandon.

Clematis 'Ernest Markham' glows alongside *Hedera helix* 'Goldheart'

Clematis × 'Jackmanii Superba'

This is the best known and most popular of all hybrid clematis, and justly so. The velvety, dark purple, white-centred flowers are enormous – up to 6 in. across – and plentiful. If the plant is pruned almost to the ground in early spring it will climb to 10-12 ft by midsummer. It is on this new growth that the flowers appear, most abundantly in July but continuing into October if there is the odd shower to bring the plant refreshment during relatively dry periods.

Large-bloomed clematis such as this have a stately quality, and should not be allowed to scramble through trees and shrubs as their small-flowered cousins do. 'Jackmanii Superba' is a clematis for a pillar, pergola or porch where air circulates freely; without this, the plant may suffer from mildew. If mildew does occur, spray the plant with benomyl solution. Clematis wilt is another problem, but one that occurs most often on wall-trained plants; whole shoots wilt and die rapidly, though plants are rarely killed outright. Wilted shoots should be cut out. Healthy new stems to replace them usually develop from ground level. Like other hybrids, 'Jackmanii Superba' is deciduous.

Clematis and roses make a partnership as mutually flattering as buttercups and daisies, and the deep hue of this clematis harmonises equally well with pink, creamy-white, or yellow roses. You might, for example, train it up a dark brown trellis on one side of a stone porch, with the climbing rose 'The New Dawn' growing up the other side, so that the two meet and intertwine in a riot of colour at the top.

The soft, silvery-pink, double flowers of the rose bloom, like the clematis, throughout the summer, and add their sweet fragrance to what is a particularly charming association.

At its foot you could include a clump of the pink-flowered rock rose *Helianthemum nummularium* 'Wisley Bridesmaid', only 4-6 in. high but with a spread of around 2 ft. This flowers profusely in June and July above a mass of grey foliage, useful for shading the roots of the clematis.

HOW TO GROW
Clematis × 'Jackmanii Superba': *see p. 177.*
Helianthemum nummularium: see p. 208.
Rosa 'The New Dawn': *see p. 243.*

The magnificent purple-bloomed 'Jackmanii Superba', grown on a trellis, climbs one side of a porch to intertwine with the pale pink-bloomed climbing rose 'The New Dawn' on the other side. At the base of the clematis is a clump of the rock rose *Helianthemum nummularium* 'Wisley Bridesmaid'. The association is shown in July, when all three plants are in full bloom.

Clematis montana

Few climbers yield a more magnificent display of flowers or more glorious mass of foliage than this splendid Himalayan clematis. The wide, white flowers are carried in May in such quantities as almost to hide the leaves. 'Rubens' is a splendid cultivar that has bronze foliage and puts out rose-pink flowers in May and June.

The plant will take happily to a wall of any aspect, even one facing north. But such is its vigour – it can climb to 40 ft – that it tends to produce a tangle of growth. The best course is to encourage it up a tree trunk or a pergola. When the main shoots reach a horizontal support some way up, they should be trained carefully along it. They will then let fall a cascade of foliage and flowers.

HOW TO GROW
See p. 177.

The rose-tinged 'Rubens' is one of the finest forms of *Clematis montana*.

The vigorous 'Grandiflora' is best confined to a pergola or archway. The plant seen growing here is about five years old.

Clematis macropetala

It is difficult to believe that this delicate little clematis, with its apparently double blue flowers borne in May and June, actually grows wild in Siberia and in the bleak and rugged uplands of Northern China. The double effect is produced by a mass of broad staminodes (rudimentary petal-like stamens) in the centre of each flower. Blue at first, the staminodes pale to white. The bell-shaped flowers are 2-3 in. across.

The plant is one of the best of all climbers for growing in the small garden.

The slender growth of dark green leaves can reach a height of 12 ft, but is quite happy trailing over a much lower support than this – the front railing of a town garden, for example, or an already established wall shrub through which it can clamber.

It can also be planted in a large container, from which it can burgeon and flow over the sides. There are a number of named cultivars, including the deep blue 'Maidwell Hall' and the lovely 'Markhamii', which has flowers with a colour like crushed strawberries. This cultivar also goes under the name 'Markham's Pink'. After *Clematis macropetala* has finished flowering, its beauty continues with a show of silky, fluffy seed heads.

HOW TO GROW
See p. 177.

An excellent way of growing the slender climber *Clematis macropetala* is in a large container, over which it can cascade.

Clematis viticella

Nothing sounds easier than training a clematis up a shrub –
often to cast an attractive mantle over the supporting plant
when it has finished blooming for the year. But, in fact, it
is a task that needs considerable care. After the clematis has
been pruned in spring, every new shoot must be tied to the
support until the plant has established its own climbing
habit. However, the result is usually so delightful that the
trouble is well worth while.

Clematis viticella is a vigorous deciduous plant, partly
woody, climbing 9-12 ft, with small, nodding purple flowers
borne in abundance from July to September and graceful,
dark green leaves divided into leaflets. An excellent
companion and support would be a large bush of
Viburnum × bodnantense, 9-12 ft high, planted some years
previously.

The viburnum is a joy in winter, with its rosy-white
blooms on bare stems, but it looks gawky and drab in
summer, when all it has to show is sombre green foliage.
Wherever the clematis emerges into the light, its rich
flowers and leaves look all the more regal for their subdued
background.

At the foot of the viburnum you could place a group of
summer bulbs – the 18 in. high *Allium albopilosum*, which
produces starry pink flowers in June. Accompany them,
perhaps, with *Campanula persicifolia*, an evergreen border
perennial 1-3 ft high, which glows with white or blue
flowers throughout the summer.

Any of the fine *C. viticella* cultivars can be grown instead
of the species itself. They include 'Abundance' (soft purple);
'Alba Luxurians' (white, tinted with mauve); 'Kermesina'
(crimson); and 'Minuet' (creamy-white with purple).

HOW TO GROW
Clematis viticella: see p. 177.
Allium albopilosum: see p. 140.
Campanula persicifolia: see p. 72.
Viburnum × bodnantense: see p. 322.

Supporting the *Clematis viticella* 'Royal Velours' is a *Viburnum × bodnantense*, its dark foliage providing a perfect
background to the rich red blooms. In front are *Campanula persicifolia* and *Allium albopilosum*.

Clematis tangutica

China has provided British gardens with several lovely
yellow-flowered clematis. This species is one of the best,
with its elegant, grey-green, divided leaves and profusion of
lantern-shaped flowers, which are about 1½-2 in. across and
are carried singly on stems some 6 in. long. These blooms,
which appear from August to October, soon turn into silky,
fuzzy seed heads, so that throughout the flowering season
there is always a fascinating combination of the two. The
seed heads are particularly beautiful when sparkling with
dew in the early morning sun.

Clematis tangutica will grow on a wall of any aspect –
climbing to 20 ft or more – or is just as happy wending its
way through a large shrub, tumbling down a bank or
growing up a tall tree stump. An interesting association
might be to grow the clematis beside a stag's horn sumach,
Rhus typhina, so that the climber's flowers combine with
the tree's brilliant autumn leaves.

HOW TO GROW
See p. 177.

In September *Clematis tangutica* is decorated with an assortment of flowers in bud, fully open blooms and seed heads.

Cobaea scandens

(CUP AND SAUCER PLANT, CATHEDRAL BELL)

It may take several years for perennial climbers to clothe a bare wall, whereas the cup and saucer plant, which is usually grown here as an annual, provides quick cover. Soon after a young plant is put into the ground at the end of May, growth speeds up, tendrils at the ends of the leaves develop, and by the end of the season the plant should have reached 12 ft or more.

In early August, green calyces (the outer protective parts of the flowers) split open at the ends of long stalks to reveal green blooms that change to purple. The display continues until the first hard frost. The lovely white form 'Alba' is even more vigorous and has larger flowers.

HOW TO GROW
Raise plants from seeds sown under glass in spring. Harden off and plant out, 2 ft apart, in late May when night frost is no longer a danger. Cobaea thrives in well-drained but moisture-retentive ordinary soil. Site against a warm, sheltered wall, with wire or trellis support. Pinch out growing points to encourage side-branching.

The cup and saucer plant, *Cobaea scandens.*

A yellow form of *Eccremocarpus scaber.*

Eccremocarpus scaber (CHILEAN GLORY FLOWER)

In its native South America, this plant is a perennial, woody-stemmed evergreen, but in Britain, except on light soil in sheltered spots, it will probably be a casualty to the first severe frost. Even so, after planting it rapidly climbs to a height of 10 ft, and so it is admirable for covering a bare wall quickly. Throughout the summer it puts on a bright display of tubular orange flowers that flame against the dark, airy foliage.

The plant is excellent for growing at the base of a climber whose flowering season ends as that of the eccremocarpus begins – for example, *Rosa* 'Mme Grégoire Staechelin', which is over in July. In most years, the Chilean glory flower produces a large number of intriguingly warty seed pods and a mass of viable seeds.

HOW TO GROW
Sow seeds under glass in spring, several to a pot and thinning to one seedling later. Harden off and plant out the seedlings in late spring or early summer. The plants grow in ordinary soil, moist but well drained, and need a sheltered, sunny wall. Support them with pea sticks, wires or trellis.

Hydrangea petiolaris

(JAPANESE CLIMBING HYDRANGEA)

This hardy, handsome deciduous climber requires no support and as little attention from the gardener as ivy does. Considering these benefits, it is remarkable that it is not more widely grown. Also to its advantage is the fact that it will flourish happily in gardens situated near industrial areas, as it stands up well to atmospheric pollution.

The pale brown shoots have ivy-like aerial roots, and broad leaves that are deep green above and downy, pale green beneath. Creamy-white flower clusters like those of a well-spaced Lacecap hydrangea are carried in June. A mature plant makes a fine sight, especially when covering a wall up to the eaves. It will also climb into trees, but then its stately appearance is rather obscured. Botanists now call this plant *H. anomala* var. *petiolaris.*

The Japanese climbing hydrangea, which will thrive on a north or north-east wall, can also be used as a screening plant but will need a strong supporting structure to carry its vigorous growth. An evergreen cousin, *H. integerrima*, has similar flowers but needs a sheltered position to perform its best.

Hydrangea petiolaris associates well with other climbers, especially those that will bloom after its own flowering season has finished. Among such plants are Chilean glory flower, *Eccremocarpus scaber*, and the annual climbing nasturtium *Tropaeolum majus.*

HOW TO GROW
Plant in autumn or spring, in any kind of soil enriched with plenty of humus, well drained but moist, especially in the early years. Once established, it tolerates drier soil. It is suitable for walls of any aspect except constant deep shade. It may require initial support until its aerial roots become active. Propagate in summer by cuttings under glass. If necessary, prune in spring to maintain shape and size.

Crowned with white blooms in June, *Hydrangea petiolaris* is a vigorous climber that will reach a great height on a wall.

Hedera helix 'Goldheart' (IVY)

For brightening up a wall, few plants can rival this variety of our native ivy, an evergreen climber that in 1970 gained the Royal Horticultural Society's Award of Merit. It has small, bright green leaves splashed in the middle with sunny yellow – colours that remain true all the year round. Also, they gleam even more readily in a shady place than in full sun – where they may become scorched.

Like all ivies, *Hedera helix* 'Goldheart' (also known as 'Jubilee') needs no special support, and it will clamber up a wall to a height of 5 ft or more. The young growth, which has pink leaf stalks, is the most decorative and carries the brightest, neatest leaves, whereas the old branches end in bushy growth. This old growth can, if required, be cut back in spring.

Because 'Goldheart' takes to shade so well and occupies no ground space, it is a perfect ivy for the wall of a small, paved garden, where in front you could place pots and a trough containing a variety of spring bulbs. In summer, you could allow the tobacco plant (*Nicotiana alata*), petunias, heliotropes and ivy-leaved geraniums (*Pelargonium peltatum*) to trail over the edges of the containers. The pots and trough should be replanted each spring and autumn, because in such a small garden dying foliage cannot be concealed beneath other growth.

Where space is limited, you could grow instead a smaller variegated ivy, such as *H. helix* 'Glacier', or a plain green one – for example, the fine *H. h.* 'Deltoides', known as the shield ivy from the shape of its leaves.

HOW TO GROW
Hedera helix 'Goldheart': *see p. 183.*
Heliotropium × *hybridum: see p. 34.*
Nicotiana alata: see p. 46.
Pelargonium peltatum: see p. 48.
Petunia × *hybrida: see p. 50.*

The ivy *Hedera helix* 'Goldheart' and the scarlet-flowered *Tropaeolum speciosum* make a glorious combination on a wall.

Hedera colchica 'Dentata Variegata'

(PERSIAN IVY)

Persian ivy (*Hedera colchica*), from the forests of the Russian Caucasus, is the largest-leaved of all ivies and a truly eye-catching climber. The great luxuriant leaves sometimes reach a length of 12 in., and left to its own devices on a wall the plant can swarm to a height of 20-30 ft.

The most commonly grown form is *H. c.* 'Dentata', which carries broadly oval, toothed leaves of a dark green that is for some tastes a little sombre. *H. c.* 'Dentata Variegata', on the other hand, really sparkles. Each leaf has a central green area that merges, through grey-green, into a broad pale yellow edge, and the whole glints with reflected light.

HOW TO GROW
Plant between autumn and spring, in any good, well-drained soil. A sunny position produces better-coloured variegation. In the first spring after planting, cut the young climbers back to 6 in. to induce branching growth. Occasionally spray established climbers with a foliar feed. Propagate in summer or autumn by stem cuttings. If necessary, prune in spring and/or summer by thinning out old and woody stems and by reducing long new shoots.

The large, lustrous, yellow-edged leaves of *Hedera colchica* 'Dentata Variegata' make it perhaps the most striking of all ivies.

'Dentata Variegata' will rapidly form a frame for a door or window.

Ipomoea tricolor (MORNING GLORY)

The flower colour of this beautiful annual morning glory is often described as a heavenly blue and, indeed, the wide trumpet-shaped blooms shade imperceptibly from azure to white, just like a perfect sky on a summer's day.

The plant, which climbs to at least 8 ft, should either be grown on a wall or allowed to twine through an earlier-flowering wall shrub. It is essential to grow it where it can be enjoyed in the morning, for in the brightest sites the flowers will fade by early afternoon. This plant is named *Ipomoea rubro-caerulea* or *I. violacea* by some nurseries.

HOW TO GROW
Sow seeds under glass in spring, having first soaked them to speed up germination. Harden off the seedlings and plant them out in early June, 2 ft apart, against sheltered walls, fences or other supports, in full sun. Morning glories thrive in ordinary, well-drained soil. They are also suitable for hanging baskets.

The heart-shaped leaves of *Ipomoea tricolor* accentuate its delicate flowers. With it grows *Clematis montana* 'Rubens'.

Jasminum officinale (COMMON WHITE JASMINE)

The rich, heavy scent of white jasmine is the very breath of the warm eastern countries from whence it came. Yet it has been sweetening the evening air in British gardens since the 16th century – not only that about the great houses but the humbler atmosphere surrounding labourers' cottages too. In his *Essay on the Picturesque*, written in 1794, Sir Uvedale Price proposed that every cottage should have a porch so that jasmine could wreathe the door.

It is a vigorous, twining climber with a beauty to match its fragrance; clusters of small, white, primrose-like flowers are borne from June to October in a setting of elegant leaves, each consisting of several pairs of leaflets. A golden-variegated form is also available.

Perhaps it would be a good idea to adapt Sir Uvedale's advice and grow the jasmine upon an arbour – a curved-over rustic trellis with a seat inside – so creating a fragrant resting-place from which to contemplate the garden on summer evenings. The jasmine would climb up and over the arbour, then tumble down the other side where it could mingle with another deciduous climber, *Clematis macropetala*.

Another old-fashioned touch would be to add a clipped mound of the lavender *Lavandula angustifolia* 'Hidcote' to both sides of the arbour's entrance. The lavender, only 1-2 ft tall, produces spikes of purple-blue flowers.

HOW TO GROW
Jasminum officinale: plant between autumn and spring, in any fertile, well-drained soil, in sun or partial shade. In cold northern gardens protect young plants in winter. Tie the shoots to supports. Propagate in late summer or early autumn by cuttings under glass or by layering. Prune after flowering, by thinning out tangled shoots.
Clematis macropetala: see p. 177.
Lavandula angustifolia: see p. 291.

Common white jasmine scales one side of an arched trellis in high summer. At the top it meets *Clematis macropetala*, once adorned with blue bell-flowers but since the end of June decorated with fluffy seed heads. Beneath each is a clump of *Lavandula angustifolia* 'Hidcote'.

Jasminum nudiflorum
(WINTER-FLOWERING JASMINE)

The British plant collector Robert Fortune (1812-80) introduced several fine plants to this country, but we owe him a special debt of gratitude for winter-flowering jasmine, which he brought here from China in 1844. Almost every day from November to March it carries sprays of golden starry flowers on bare twigs, perfect for picking. Although a frost will spoil the open blooms, it does not affect the bronze-tinted buds lined up waiting to replace them.

This jasmine is not strictly a climber, but a shrub whose slender, wand-like branches can be allowed to tumble down a bank. On the other hand, they can be trained loosely against a wall, where the plant will reach a height of 10 ft, tied back against a trellis, or guided up and over a stone post or pillar.

HOW TO GROW
Cultivate as for Jasminum officinale. The plant is best trained on trellis against any but an east-facing wall or fence. Prune in spring by cutting flowered shoots back to near their base, taking out weak and old stems at ground level and tying in replacement shoots.

With its glorious mass of yellow blooms, *Jasminum nudiflorum* adds its own brightness to the pale sunshine of winter.

Lathyrus odoratus (SWEET PEA)

So popular are sweet peas as plants grown solely for cut flowers that they tend to be forgotten as climbers. Yet they are splendid for covering a wall or fence with great speed: in well-manured soil they soon reach a height of 7 ft or more, with the first flowers opening in June. Provided all dead blooms are rapidly removed, the display will continue through summer. Other good ways of growing sweet peas as climbers are to allow them to scramble up established shrubs, or to set half a dozen or so swarming up a wigwam of pea sticks in the border.

There are many new cultivars, but the old-fashioned ones still take a lot of beating. Their flowers, which last well into autumn, come in a wide bicoloured range and are abundant and richly scented.

HOW TO GROW
For best results, sow soaked seeds individually in peat pots under glass in early autumn or spring. Harden off the seedlings and plant out in late spring, 6-10 in. apart, against supports. Sweet peas thrive best in deep, well-manured soil.

Full-sized sweet peas at the height of their summer glory.

Behind blue echiums, orange marigolds and white dimorpothecas, red and pink Knee-hi sweet peas grow on supports.

Lonicera japonica 'Halliana'
(JAPANESE HONEYSUCKLE)

The only place on earth where a gift of this lovely Japanese honeysuckle would be unwelcome would be in the southern United States, where they already have so much of it that it has become a major, if local, pest. In this country, though it is splendidly vigorous, the climate is not warm and moist enough for it to outgrow its welcome. Even so, it still makes a tangle of twining shoots that can reach 20 ft in height. From June to October, and often until Christmas, the young stems are decorated with small clusters of tubular, scented flowers, opening white and turning yellow as they age. This honeysuckle is evergreen, but in cold areas becomes deciduous in winter. In a severe winter it can be cut back to ground level.

HOW TO GROW
Plant in spring, in any kind of well-manured, well-drained soil; this should be moisture-retentive – though older plants do tolerate drought. Honeysuckles thrive equally well in full sun or light shade. Propagate as for Lonicera periclymenum; prune as for L. × tellmanniana.

The most commonly grown form of Japanese honeysuckle, 'Aureoreticulata', is used here to hide an ugly feature.

Lonicera japonica 'Halliana' has an unforgettable fragrance.

Lonicera × *americana* can climb to a height of 30 ft.

Lonicera periclymenum
(HONEYSUCKLE, WOODBINE)

In midsummer, our native honeysuckle – the ancient symbol of fidelity and true love – beautifies the hedgerows with its heads of pale yellow, purple-tinged blooms and sends out heady waves of fragrance.

It is not surprising that the plant has been a cottage-garden favourite for centuries, nor that cultivars have been raised during that time. Two lovely examples of these are the early and late Dutch honeysuckles 'Belgica' and 'Serotina', both with a flower tube of a darker yellow than in the species and flushed with purple-red. 'Belgica' starts to flower in May, 'Serotina' in June, both remaining in bloom, off and on, until October. L. × *americana* creates a similar effect. All grow to 15-20 ft or more.

HOW TO GROW
Cultivate as for Lonicera japonica, planting between autumn and spring. Propagate by cuttings in summer or autumn, by layering or by seeds. The common honeysuckle is prone to aphid attacks; spray with malathion before infestation becomes severe. Prune as for L. × tellmanniana.

L. × *americana*, often confused with *L.p.* 'Belgica' and 'Serotina'.

Lonicera × tellmanniana (HONEYSUCKLE)

The fact that this hybrid deciduous honeysuckle has no
scent is a minor drawback, since to look at it is perfection:
a strong, climbing plant with dark green leaves, set at the
top with glorious clusters of coppery-yellow flowers in
June and July.

The honeysuckle will grow in full shade and will happily
climb through shrubs or up a tree. It can be made the star
of a wild garden, but can also be a major feature in a
large, formal plot if trained up a west wall, where it will
grow to a height of 15 ft. In that position it might be
flanked by two other climbers – a clematis, say, grown for
its flowers, and a grape vine, for its foliage.

A fine clematis for this purpose would be 'Mrs
Cholmondeley', which has large flowers of a gentle blue
that open from May to September, so providing colour
when the honeysuckle is over. A suitable vine might be
Vitis coignetiae, whose large, lustrous leaves change to red
and yellow in autumn.

At the foot of the honeysuckle you could plant a
winter-flowering jasmine (*Jasminum nudiflorum*), which is
trained against a support for the first few feet, then
allowed to fall forwards. This will most handsomely
display the sprays of starry, bright yellow flowers which
open on bare wood from November to April.

HOW TO GROW

*Lonicera × tellmanniana: cultivate as for L. japonica – but
this honeysuckle is also suitable for heavy shade. Propagate as
for L. periclymenum. Prune after flowering, cutting back long
shoots to maintain shape and size and removing old and bare
stems.*
Clematis 'Mrs Cholmondeley': see p. 177.
Jasminum nudiflorum: see p. 185.
Vitis coignetiae: see p. 190.

Trained up a wall, *Lonicera × tellmanniana* displays its rich yellow flowers
in June. Intertwining with it are the blue-flowered clematis 'Mrs
Cholmondeley' and the finest of all ornamental vines, *Vitis coignetiae*.

The vigorous Chinese Virginia creeper can cover a wall rapidly.

Parthenocissus henryana

(CHINESE VIRGINIA CREEPER)

True Virginia creeper, *Parthenocissus quinquefolia*, which
turns walls to flame in autumn, is well known. Much less
common is its Chinese relative. This has fingered leaves of
a velvety dark green, with the midrib and veins of each
finger silver and pink. This variegation is most pronounced
on a shady wall. In autumn the foliage turns a bright red;
sometimes there are bunches of dark blue fruits.

On a wall, the creeper can climb to 25-30 ft by means of
tiny sucker pads on its tendrils. It therefore requires no
support, making it a splendid plant for a walled garden.

HOW TO GROW

*Plant pot-grown specimens between autumn and spring, in
humus-rich well-drained but moist soil, at the base of shaded
walls sheltered from strong winds. Provide initial support for
the young stems, and pinch out growing tips to induce
branching. Propagate in late summer by stem cuttings. Prune
only to maintain or restrict growth, in autumn.*

The pale midribs and veins on the leaves of
P. henryana become much more distinct in
autumn, when the foliage turns red.

Passiflora caerulea (COMMON PASSION FLOWER)

When Spanish priests first saw this plant growing in the forests of Brazil, they regarded it as a token that the Indians would one day be converted to Christianity. For there in the flowers were what they took to be the symbols of Christ's Passion. Each bloom opens flat to reveal an outer circle of ten white petals (the Disciples, minus Judas and Peter); within these, a ring of fine purple-blue filaments (the crown of thorns); and in the centre, conspicuous anthers and stigmas (the nails); while the wounds are represented by five yellowish stains.

The flowers, carried in profusion from June to September, are 3 in. across and somewhat fragrant, and in good years they are followed by orange, egg-shaped fruits. The plant climbs rapidly by its tendrils to 20-30 ft and has evergreen leaves like open hands. Even to unbelievers, the passion flower is a dramatic and most unusual plant.

To plant the passion flower with another climber can only be detrimental to its companion. So provide it instead with a thick mixed planting of low shrubs and early flowering bulbs. The shrubs might be the 3 ft high evergreen *Daphne odora* 'Aureomarginata', which bears pale purple flowers from January to April, and the 3 ft tall shrubby cinquefoil, *Potentilla* × 'Elizabeth', which puts on a show of canary-yellow flowers from May to autumn.

These shrubs will provide a backing for a late summer display of the elegant, white-belled summer hyacinth, *Galtonia candicans*, and perhaps one of the small-flowered Butterfly gladioli, such as the orange-red 'Chinatown' or the crimson-maroon 'Mokha'.

HOW TO GROW

Passiflora caerulea: only mild gardens are suitable. Plant during late spring in any type of well-drained soil, in sun or light shade, against a sheltered wall with trellis or wire supports. Protect young plants with a winter mulch. Propagate in summer by stem cuttings under glass. Prune hard in spring, cutting out dead stems at ground level and shortening sideshoots to 6 in. from their base.

Daphne odora 'Aureomarginata': see p. 274.
Galtonia candicans: see p. 155.
Gladiolus: see p. 156
Potentilla × 'Elizabeth': see p. 302.

Flowers of *Passiflora caerulea*.   Fruits of *Passiflora caerulea*.

A late July display in which *Passiflora caerulea*, carrying a glorious mass of flowers, climbs above a mixed planting which includes the Butterfly gladioli 'Chinatown' (orange-red) and 'Mokha' (crimson-maroon). The canary-yellow *Potentilla* × 'Elizabeth' will continue to flower until autumn, but the evergreen *Daphne odora* 'Aureomarginata' with its cream-white margined leaves will not flower until January.

Polygonum baldschuanicum (RUSSIAN VINE)

Russian vine is an ideal plant for gardeners with little time to spare. Immensely vigorous, it will tumble over anything in its path, making further gardening in that area not only unnecessary but impossible; it is not unusual for the vine to throw out 10 ft of growth a year and 60 ft altogether. For this reason it should not be planted without some thought as to how it might spread over the years, even though an 'instant' screen or cladding may be needed.

From July to September it is a most beautiful plant, its massed, bright, pale green foliage foaming with long flower sprays of pale pink on the current year's growth. It can be encouraged to climb up wires, trellis or an old tree, instead of being allowed to sprawl. It is perfect for screening an unsightly shed or other garden eyesore, but its ultimate size should not be forgotten.

It is often confused with *Polygonum aubertii*, which has white or greenish-white flowers.

HOW TO GROW
Plant in spring, in any type of soil that is well drained to dry. Either sun or light shade is suitable. Protect young plants in winter. Propagate, if necessary, by heel cuttings in summer. Pinch out the growing points to induce branching, and thin out the plant in spring. Pruning, in the selective sense, is impossible. Remove old tangled growth entirely so that new stems have light and air to develop.

Putting on about 10 ft of growth a year, *Polygonum baldschuanicum* soon screens an unattractive view.

Solanum crispum (CHILEAN POTATO-TREE)

When this splendid climber is in full bloom, it is hard to credit that it belongs to the same genus as the potato. From June to September the dark green foliage is hung with great clusters of purple starry flowers with prominent yellow stamens, and the plant is truly one of the finest of all summer climbing shrubs. As with its more widely known relation, the blooms are mildly fragrant, while the leaves smell faintly rank when bruised.

The plant, which is loose, bushy and scrambling, needs tying to a support and can then be allowed to climb to 15-20 ft and spread as much across. It is particularly suitable for training on wires on a wall, and looks equally effective when allowed to scramble over small fences, sheds and similar structures.

'Glasnevin Variety', also known as 'Autumnale', which flowers well into autumn, is the only cultivated form. Its beauty has been recognised by a Royal Horticultural Society's Award of Merit.

Less hardy than *Solanum crispum* is its cousin *S. jasminoides*, which is semi-evergreen and has pale slate-blue flowers with conspicuous golden anthers.

HOW TO GROW
Plant in spring, in any type of well-drained soil, though this climber does best in a chalky soil. Select a spot in full sun and against a sheltered south or west-facing wall. Tie in the growing shoots to trellis or wire supports; it will need tying in position at intervals throughout the summer as the shoots increase in length. Propagate in summer by cuttings under glass. Prune in spring, removing untidy shoots and shortening side branches to 6 in. from their base.

Solanum crispum 'Glasnevin Variety' bears its large clusters of blooms more freely and for longer than in the parent species.

The Chilean potato-tree should be grown against a sunny, sheltered wall.

Tropaeolum speciosum (FLAME CREEPER)

Flame creeper is a Chilean plant with an air that is positively theatrical in the right setting. If it is allowed to weave its way through a dark green tree or shrub, its scarlet flowers emerge from the sombre foliage with the brilliance of jewels. The flowers, five-petalled, flat and with inch-long spurs behind them, are abundant from July to September. Even before they appear, the creeper is an attractive plant, with its six-lobed leaves borne on slender, probing stems. In most years the flowers are followed by a show of metallic-blue fruits.

Flame creeper is a deciduous perennial, 10-15 ft high, that dies down in autumn. It is not a plant for every garden, since it is happiest in cool air with acid, peaty soil and with plenty of rain. Therefore, it does particularly well on the west coast of Scotland.

Many trees and shrubs make a suitable host for the creeper – rhododendron, holly, yew, even a climbing hydrangea on a north wall. But nothing sets off the plant so well as a tallish old ivy-covered tree stump or an ancient fruit tree.

So striking a climber needs no more companionship in summer than the plant that supports it. However, since it has nothing to show for itself during the rest of the year, you might care to plant some surrounding ground-cover. Ideal would be *Bergenia* × 'Silberlicht', which combines bold evergreen leaves with a spring crop of rose-tinted white flowers. For a late summer contrast, add a few clumps of *Gentiana asclepiadea*, the deep-blue flowered willow gentian.

HOW TO GROW

Plant in autumn or spring, in peaty, acid, moist soil, with shade over the roots. In all but cool, western gardens mulch the root area thickly with peat, keep this moist and water the plant freely during summer. Propagate by division of the rhizomes in spring.

Flame creeper covers a stump in late July. Beneath are the fleshy leaves of *Bergenia* × 'Silberlicht' and the blue-flowered *Gentiana asclepiadea*.

Vitis coignetiae mingles with *Euonymus fortunei* above a garden seat.

Vitis coignetiae (JAPANESE CRIMSON GLORY VINE)

When it comes to sheer magnificence of foliage, no other hardy climber can excel this vast vine. Clinging by its tendrils, it can swarm 30-40 ft before putting out a great drape of rounded, bold leaves, each of which is up to 12 in. across. Through the summer these are smooth green above, rust-felted beneath; then from September or October they begin to flame into yellow, orange, scarlet and crimson. The effect is breathtaking.

HOW TO GROW

Plant between autumn and spring, ideally in a humus-rich soil that is well drained but moisture-retentive. This climber does best in full sun but tolerates light shade. To cover a large wall, space plants 8 ft apart. Propagate in autumn by layering. If it is grown on a wall, pinch off some of the shoot tips in spring and summer to encourage bushy growth. Soon after leaf-fall, prune back the whole plant to the supporting framework.

In its full autumn colours, *Vitis coignetiae* makes a wall of flame to match the most spectacular of sunsets.

The great flower clusters of *Wisteria floribunda* 'Macrobotrys' tumble down a wall like a cascade of water.

Wisteria sinensis (CHINESE WISTERIA)

Only those who possess a flourishing wisteria realise what an amazingly vigorous climber it is. Capable of reaching a height of 70 ft in a tree, it is obviously not a plant for small gardens unless it is drastically pruned. Over most of the country the wisteria must be grown on a firm support against a sunny wall. In sheltered parts of the south it can be grown up a tree.

The flowers that appear in May are one of the joys of the gardener's year. As the many-leafleted foliage unfolds, foot-long streamers of pale mauve blooms hang from every twig. To combine them with the soft yellow flowers of *Rosa banksiae* is to form one of the most delightful of all spring associations.

Just as lively and joyful as the species is the double variety *Wisteria sinensis* 'Plena' – while, for those whose gardens already have enough colour, there is white 'Alba'.

If *W. sinensis* is the most popular of wisterias, the Japanese *W. floribunda* is a close runner-up. It boasts more leaflets to each leaf, but the floral chains tend to be a little shorter. *W. floribunda* is justly famous for its cultivar 'Macrobotrys', which has lilac-blue flowers in chains up to 3 ft long.

HOW TO GROW
Wisteria sinensis: set out container-grown plants between autumn and spring in humus-rich soil, moist but well drained, and in full sun. Mulch and water during the growing season. Propagate in spring by layering. Encourage flowering, which is often delayed for several years, by summer pruning of long shoots back to four or five leaves. In late winter, prune sideshoots back to three or four buds from their base.
Rosa banksiae: see p. 244.

Wisteria sinensis, the most popular of all wisterias, needs a sunny wall if it is to produce a good crop of flowers.

Wisteria sinensis 'Alba' shows to best effect against a dark background.

The Herb Garden

Creating a place where ornamental appeal combines with practical use

Herbs are truly undemanding plants, asking only for soil of a reasonable quality and some sunshine – though nearly all the richly aromatic ones from the Mediterranean, such as lavender (*Lavandula*), rosemary (*Rosmarinus*), rue (*Ruta*), lemon-scented verbena (*Aloysia triphylla*) and sage (*Salvia officinalis*), appreciate a protected site.

The traditional herb garden is a formal arrangement of small rectangular beds, with only one kind of plant in each bed. The modern, more decorative version of this style is a chessboard pattern, the dark squares being beds planted with low-growing herbs and the light squares paved areas of brick or stone. A colourful garden planted in this way would even be suitable at the front of a house. You could use such ornamental herbs as the golden-leaved marjoram, *Origanum onites* 'Aureum'; the blue-leaved rue, *Ruta graveolens* 'Jackman's Blue'; the cream-flowered chamomile, *Anthemis nobilis*; rosy-pink bloomed chives, *Allium schoenoprasum*; and blue-flowered borage, *Borago officinalis*.

More usual today is a formal herb garden based on a simple design with a central focal point – for example, a sundial, bird bath or statue. To make the design clear and crisp, each bed needs to be outlined by a border of only one kind of plant. Glossy dark green box (*Buxus sempervirens*) has been used for this purpose since Roman times. It needs regular clipping, as does another suitable edging, cotton lavender (*Santolina*) – a good dwarf form is silver-leaved *S. chamaecyparissus* 'Nana'. An alternative that has the advantage of not needing to be trimmed is the pink-flowered germander (*Teucrium chamaedrys*).

Each bed can be filled with a variety of herbs, or it can be devoted to plants grown for one particular purpose. Thus you could have a physic bed, containing herbs grown for medicinal use; a kitchen bed, to provide flavourings and garnishes; and a nosegay bed, to yield sweet-smelling plants for a posy or a pot-pourri. The following are suggestions, from the many plants available, for each bed.

The physic bed

Comfrey (*Symphytum officinale*) has a reputation for healing broken bones – hence the plant's old names of boneset and knitbone. Herbalists also believe that it can mend sprained joints and relieve rheumatism and bruises. The leaves and roots emit a sticky fluid that forms a quick-setting paste, and this is used to make a poultice to apply to the skin.

Tea made from the leaves of the peppermint plant (*Mentha × piperita*) is credited with relieving headaches and indigestion, while an infusion of the leaves of meadow sweet (*Filipendula ulmaria*), once used to flavour mead and wine, was believed to help people recover from fever, influenza, gout and peptic ulcers. Hyssop (*Hyssopus officinalis*) is an age-old treatment for coughs, catarrh, asthma and other throat and chest disorders. It is taken in the form of a tea made from the flowers and sweetened with honey.

The kitchen bed

Because of its slightly bitter flavour, bay (*Laurus nobilis*) is one of the few herbs not used fresh in cooking. Instead the leaves are used dried and sparingly to add pungency to pâté, pickles, casseroles and cooked meats. The leaves, which can be harvested at any time of the year, should be kept in a dark, dry place, when they will last for years.

The dainty, faintly sweet-tasting foliage of chervil (*Anthriscus cerefolium*) is widely used in French cooking to lend a subtle flavour to egg dishes and sauces. To safeguard its elusive flavour, add it only at the end of cooking, or use it as a garnish.

Garlic (*Allium sativum*) must be one of the most widely used flavouring plants in cookery and is certainly the strongest flavoured. Chopped or crushed, it heightens the flavour of meat, fish and vegetable dishes and cold cooked meats.

The luscious green leaves and young stalks of lovage (*Levisticum officinale*) have a slightly nutty taste and make a good pot herb. The roots are also edible: stripped of their bitter skin, they add flavour to casseroles. The ripe seeds can be harvested in late summer and sprinkled on pastries, bread or boiled potatoes to give them an aromatic savour.

The nosegay bed

Lavender (*Lavandula angustifolia*) has been grown since ancient times for its unique, refreshing perfume. As with all aromatic plants, rich in essential oils, it is at its best just as the flowers mature. The dried foliage and flowers can be used to make a scented sachet.

The tobacco plant, *Nicotiana*, is usually most fragrant at twilight. 'Sensation Mixed', a variety of *N. affinis*, produces flowers in white, cream, yellow, red and pink; *N. sylvestris* – which is only for warm gardens in southern England – is pure white. Both should be picked and dried when fairly young.

The aroma of burning rosemary (*Rosmarinus officinalis*) was once used to purify the air of hospitals and sick-rooms. Its all-year-round fragrance is so powerful that only a sprig is needed for a pot-pourri – otherwise it will overwhelm the rest of the mixture.

If you have only a small space available for growing herbs, you should forget edging plants and aim for complete informality. Select for the front of the plot low-growing herbs, such as common thyme (*Thymus vulgaris*) and mint (*Mentha*); plant taller herbs – for example, lavender and dill (*Peucedanum graveolens*) – towards the centre; and fill the back with the tallest, such as lovage and angelica.

In addition to growing herbs in beds and as edging plants, try planting them in cracks in paving, where they will emit delightful wafts of fragrance when trodden upon. Try chamomile, which gives off an apple scent; pennyroyal (*Mentha pulegium*); and common and lemon-scented thyme. And if space is limited, you can grow herbs in almost any container except hanging baskets.

East Lambrook Manor, Somerset – a corner of the garden where herbs intermingle informally with other plants.

Herbs grow quickly – this traditional-style garden is a year old.

A formal herb garden in which hedges of box – radiating from a central feature – surround the various beds.

Where space is limited, herbs like parsley and chives, variegated sage, thyme, mint and rosemary (above) can be pot grown.

Rock garden plants

Small, colourful rock plants bring a sparkle to nooks and crannies all over the garden

———————◆———————

THE FIRST ROCK GARDEN in Britain was built in the 1770s in Chelsea Physic Garden by Sir Joseph Banks, the explorer and natural historian. It consisted of a brooding heap of black basaltic lava from the Tower of London. Though unattractive, it was nevertheless important as an attempt to grow plants in a way which reproduced their natural habitat.

However, the vast Victorian models of the Matterhorn, whitened on top to suggest snow, show how easy it is to get carried away by this approach. Modern gardeners now appreciate that reproduction of habitat is concerned basically with soil type, drainage or availability of moisture, and aspect.

Rock plant is a collective name for an enormous range of plants, characterised by their generally small stature and brilliant flowers, rather than their mountain origins. Many of them make such a show as to completely hide their leaves behind a cascade of colour. Some of the most popular, such as alyssum and aubrieta, have no need of rock-garden conditions or care – good drainage and an open position are all they require. At the other end of the scale are the high alpines – rare gentians, androsaces and primulas. Exquisite in detail, their successful cultivation is often a considerable test of skill.

Between the two extremes is a host of lovely plants for rock gardens proper, cracks and crannies in walls, sinks and troughs or a single block of tufa rock which, nestling in moist sand, can provide a home for some of the most beautiful plants anyone can grow.

A cleverly balanced rock garden, with water as an added attraction, has campanulas, thrift, potentillas, primulas, saxifrages, polygonums and ferns leading up to a juniper.

The tiny daisy-like flowers of *A. × argentea* form loosely massed heads.

Achillea × argentea

Among the various dwarf achillea species and hybrids, one of the best is *Achillea × argentea*, which has slender, silvered leaves and forms 6 in. high clumps, whose flowering heads, in early summer, put on a show of immaculate white. Near by you could plant *A. tomentosa*, a species which makes a wide carpet, some 2-3 in. high, of grey-green filigree leaves and which from May onwards bears flat heads of bright yellow flowers on 6 in. stems. The hybrid 'King Edward' combines the characters of the two species and bears charming pale yellow flowers.

HOW TO GROW
Plant in spring, spacing Achillea clavenae 8 in. apart, Achillea tomentosa slightly further. Both thrive in ordinary, well-drained soil, in full sun. Propagate by division after flowering, or in spring by taking young, basal cuttings and rooting them under glass.

A. tomentosa grows quickly to make a dense mat, spreading to 12 in., covered with tightly packed clusters of flowers.

Aethionema × 'Warley Rose'

Aethionemas thrive in dry, sunny positions where many other plants would fail, and they also survive all but the fiercest winters. *Aethionema × 'Warley Rose'* is a 6 in. high hybrid that carries deep pink flowers on short spikes in early May and has the delightful habit of producing a further scattering of blooms throughout its 12 in. spread at any time during the summer. However, if you have room for a taller plant, try *A. grandiflorum* whose dense covering of paler pink, 12-15 in. high flowering spikes appears in May and June. When the spikes die back, there remains a handsome, globular-shaped mound of grey, needle-like leaves that will last until the next flowering season.

HOW TO GROW
Plant from autumn to spring in any well-drained soil. Full sun is essential. Propagate Aethionema × 'Warley Rose' by cuttings in summer, rooted in a cold frame. Grow A. grandiflorum from seeds sown under glass in spring.

After flowering, 'Warley Rose' will provide a cover of grey-blue leaves.

Above a twiggy body of grey-green leaves, *A. grandiflorum* produces a bustling mass of dome-shaped bunches of flowers.

Androsace carnea (ROCK JASMINE)

The small size of *Androsace carnea*, which grows to 3 in. high and about twice that across, makes it ideal for a trough garden in a sunny spot. It forms close-packed rosettes of narrow leaves, with clusters of up to a dozen rounded, pink or off-white blooms in May and June. There are various forms of this alpine plant, of which the finest is the deep pink, golden-eyed *A. c.* 'Laggeri'.

    A. sarmentosa is a larger species for a sunny scree bed. It makes a pad of 1½-2 in. wide rosettes of hairy leaves that carry rose-pink blooms in May and June.

HOW TO GROW
Plant in autumn or spring, setting Androsace carnea 6 in. apart and A. sarmentosa 12 in. apart. Both need well-drained soil, preferably mixed with limestone grit, and full sun. Cover their immediate surroundings with stone chippings. Propagate in autumn or spring by division, or by detaching and rooting small rosettes under glass in summer.

The flowers of *Androsace carnea* form small clusters on 2-3 in. stems.

The foliage of *Androsace sarmentosa* is predominantly mid-green in summer. The flowers are set in closely packed heads.

Alyssum saxatile (GOLD DUST)

Alyssum, it used to be said, possessed the ability to allay anger and, indeed, there can be few more soothing sights in April than a bank or wall clothed with the brilliant yellow flowers of this lovely plant. It proclaims that dreary winter is past and gives bright promise of the colourful months to come. *Alyssum saxatile*, growing up to 12 in. high and 18 in. across, is one of the easiest grown and most adaptable of plants, demanding only an open, sunny position. Varieties include 'Citrinum', with pale sulphur-yellow flowers, and 'Dudley Neville', whose blooms are of a subtle biscuit hue. *Aubrieta deltoidea*, with its pink, red, purple and lavender varieties, is a usual and appropriate companion.

To keep the show going for months on end, you might add *Cerastium tomentosum* (snow-in-summer) and *Armeria maritima* (thrift), which start to bloom just as the alyssum and aubrieta reach their peak. For a time they will make a brilliant quartet, then the thrift and snow-in-summer will go on together, often into early autumn. Lady fern, *Athyrium filix-femina*, will supply some necessary shade and a touch of elegance; male fern, *Dryopteris filix-mas*, is almost as good.

HOW TO GROW
Alyssum saxatile: plant between autumn and spring in any well-drained soil and in full sun; set plants not less than 12 in. apart. After flowering, cut the woody stems hard back to encourage new growth. Propagate by stem cuttings under glass in summer.
Armeria maritima: see p. 198.
Athyrium filix-femina: see p. 130.
Aubrieta deltoidea: see p. 199.
Cerastium tomentosum: see p. 200.
Dryopteris filix-mas: see Dryopteris dilatata, p. 129.

A summertime wall is a canvas for a showy palate of colour. *Alyssum saxatile* pours out of cracks like a torrent of molten gold. Beside it are the glowing carmine flowers of *Aubrieta deltoidea*. *Armeria maritima* perches on top of the wall and tumbling through the alyssum is fresh white *Cerastium tomentosum*.

Delicate flowers – deep blue *A. bertolonii* and softer blue *A. flabellata* – flutter like fairies at the bottom of the garden.

Aquilegia bertolonii (COLUMBINE)

Columbines come in a wide range of colours, but the dwarf ones best suited to the rock or trough garden are mostly blue. *Aquilegia bertolonii*, which comes from the Italian Alps, is one of the most irresistible of these small gems. Its foliage, no more than 4 in. wide or high, is of a uniform grey; above it, in May and June, float single blooms of the clearest deep sapphire. Should you require a rather different colour scheme in the same situations, there is *A. flabellata*, whose blooms are of a white-tinted violet hue; there are also variations on this theme, such as the bicoloured violet-and-white *A. f.* 'Pumila', and the pure white *A. f.* 'Nana Alba'.

HOW TO GROW
Plant in autumn or spring, 6 in. apart, in well-drained but moisture-retentive soil, and in sun or light shade. Alpine aquilegias usually self-seed and can be left to increase as far as you please.

Spring bulbs and foliage of 'Variegata' sparkle below a dwarf juniper.

Arabis ferdinandi-coburgii 'Variegata'

Invaluable for the rock garden is any miniature, evergreen carpeting plant that is not dense enough to prevent upright plants, such as dwarf irises and crocuses, growing through it. *Arabis ferdinandi-coburgii* 'Variegata' is such a plant. Its white, cross-shaped flowers are insignificant, but its foliage is superb all the year round. In almost any soil or situation the dark green leaves, splashed with silver, will form a 1 in. thick, absolutely flat carpet. Individual plants have a spread of up to 12 in. 'Variegata' makes perfect ground-cover beneath the enchanting little Noah's Ark juniper (*Juniperus communis* 'Compressa').

HOW TO GROW
Plant in autumn or spring, spacing plants intended for ground-cover 9 in. apart. They grow in any well-drained soil, in sun or light shade. After flowering, remove spent flower stems. Propagate by stem cuttings in late summer, or by division in autumn.

'Variegata' roots as it spreads and is a useful filler between rocks. The small flowers appear between February and June.

Armeria maritima 'Merlin' is a rich pink form with grey-green leaves.

Armeria maritima (THRIFT, SEA PINK)

The thrift *Armeria maritima* forms 6-9 in. wide hummocks which in early summer it smothers with flowers of bright pink. Use it to fill a 12 in. wide pocket in the rock garden or to make an edging for borders or beds. The various fine forms include 'Bloodstone', a glowing crimson; 'Merlin', a warm pink; and 'Alba', pure white.

A more compact species, *A. caespitosa*, from the mountains of Spain, makes rounded domes of close-packed leaves. These are hidden in May and June beneath short-stemmed heads of pink blossom. Because the plant spreads so little, it is ideal for the miniature world of the trough garden.

HOW TO GROW
Plant in spring, in ordinary, well-drained – or even dry and gritty – soil, and in full sun. For edging, space Armeria maritima 12 in. apart. Dead-head the plants after flowering. Propagate by cuttings in spring.

Planted in a sunny spot in a rock garden, *Armeria maritima* 'Bloodstone' forms a radiant crimson carpet.

Purple-flowered *Aster alpinus* growing below *Helianthemum nummularium*.

Aster alpinus

The very spirit of the steep upland meadows of the Alps, *Aster alpinus* scatters its jewels over the turf far and wide in July. Above a spread of grey-green, spoon-shaped leaves, it bears daisy-like flowers, 2 in. wide, in purple to lavender-blue, with a central orange disc.

There are various named forms, all worth growing, each about 6 in. high and with a spread of 8-10 in. 'Beechwood' has clear blue flowers; 'Albus' is snow white with a yellow centre. Unfortunately, slugs have a particular liking for alpine asters, and to keep them away it is wise to scatter slug pellets among the plants.

HOW TO GROW
Plant between autumn and spring, in deep, loamy, well-drained soil, and in a sunny spot. Space 8 in. apart and dead-head after flowering. Propagate by division in autumn or by cuttings in spring.

A good albino form, but less vigorous than the species, is 'Albus'. Its pure white flowers help to set off a mixed bed.

Aubrieta deltoidea

The true ancestry of our garden aubrietas is a puzzle. That they are named after the 17th-century botanical artist Claude Aubriet is not much help. However, *Aubrieta deltoidea*, which comes from the mountainous areas of the eastern Mediterranean, is usually credited with being the main parent, but any of the dozen or so other wild species may also have been involved.

Aubrietas, which flower between March and June, are among the most colourful, popular and easily grown of all rock-garden plants. They are, however, most often used as a covering for banks and terrace walls, often accompanied by such plants as *Alyssum saxatile*, *Phlox subulata* and *Phlox douglasii*. In fact, they are highly versatile and can be used to splendid effect in, for example, the mixed or herbaceous border, where, planted as an edging, they provide the first clear, colourful note of spring. A good background companion in the border is the golden-flowered *Doronicum plantagineum* 'Miss Mason', which flowers around about the same time – between April and June.

Aubrietas also make good plants for the cracks in paving. Here, in March and April, they form low cushions in all shades of red, pink, purple and mauve, and act as a curtain raiser for the later-flowering *Dryas octopetala* and *Helianthemum*.

Double-flowered varieties of *A. deltoidea* tend to last longer in bloom than the single-flowered ones; and the cultivars with variegated leaves – 'Aurea', which is gold-edged, and 'Variegata', white-rimmed – prolong the interest of the plants after flowering.

HOW TO GROW

Aubrieta deltoidea: plant in autumn or spring, in ordinary well-drained soil and in full sun; for edgings, space plants at least 12 in. apart. After flowering, clip the plants hard back to near ground level, to control size and encourage compact growth. Propagate by seeds in spring, named cultivars by division in early autumn.
Alyssum saxatile: see p. 197.
Doronicum plantagineum: see p. 82.
Dryas octopetala: see p. 205.
Helianthemum: see p. 208.
Phlox douglasii and P. subulata: see p. 212.

Contrasting the extravagant pinks and purples of *A. deltoidea* with the gold of *Doronicum plantagineum* creates an eye-catching effect.

Aubrieta deltoidea is ideal for softening the lines of stonework.

Cascading down a stone wall, *A. deltoidea* makes a warm backing to the fresh green of newly opened spring leaves.

C. cochleariifolia produces tufts of glossy, shallowly toothed leaves.

Campanula cochleariifolia (BELLFLOWER)

This charming little plant, some 3-4 in. high, is a nomad whose thread-like roots infiltrate deep into the territory of neighbouring plants. It will not bother strong-growing companions, but is best kept at a safe distance from others less robust. It is particularly happy in paving, where it will run along the cracks between slabs to form a living mortar of tiny glossy leaves, decorated in July with nodding bells of sky blue.

Two of the best named forms are 'Alba', with its pure white flowers, and 'Miranda', which carries shorter bells of an unusual milky blue.

HOW TO GROW
Plant in autumn or spring, in any well-drained soil. Best in full sun. For ground-cover, space plants 10-12 in. apart. Plants with more than a single crown can be propagated by division in autumn or spring.

'Alba', the white form of *C. cochleariifolia*, bears ½ in. long bell-shaped flowers and sometimes blooms until September.

A clump of C. portenschlagiana cascades among valerians and ferns.

Campanula portenschlagiana
(BELLFLOWER)

This lovely bellflower, and its slightly less boisterous relative, *Campanula garganica*, are outstanding among the larger, vigorous but not too rampant campanulas. *C. portenschlagiana* (syn. *C. muralis*) makes a 6 in. high, domed mass of small, glossy leaves that from July cascades with violet-blue, bell-shaped flowers. With luck, they may be produced off and on until autumn.

C. garganica has radiating stems strung with blue, star-shaped flowers. It thrives almost anywhere, but looks at its best clinging to a wall, its stems in the crevices. Both plants produce occasional seedlings that flourish in the most unlikely crannies.

HOW TO GROW
Plant out in spring or autumn, in any soil and in either light shade or sun. Propagate by division.

C. portenschlagiana will happily invade lightly shaded rock crevices to produce a thick blanket of ¾ in. long flowers.

Colonising readily, C. tomentosum quickly produces a deep, snowy carpet.

Cerastium tomentosum (SNOW-IN-SUMMER)

Mats of bright grey leaves and a profusion of neat white flowers comprise the charms of snow-in-summer. There is a drawback, however. In most garden soils it spreads outrageously, infiltrating its neighbours. The ideal site for it is a soil-filled hollow wall where it can roam without harming slower-growing companions. Another good situation is a dry bank, where it can be grown alone or with grasses; it can even be mown after flowering in May and June.

If you are still a little nervous at the thought of the plant's escape into surrounding soil, then one of the best ways of displaying snow-in-summer is to show it tumbling from a stone urn set on a patio or terrace.

HOW TO GROW
Plant in spring or autumn in gritty, well-drained to dry and poor soil. Set in a sunny position, though some shade is tolerated. Propagate snow-in-summer by division, and replant in spring.

The May to June flowering of *Cerastium tomentosum* is replaced during the winter months by a blanket of silver-grey leaves.

Chamaecyparis Dwarf forms (FALSE CYPRESS)

No rock garden or alpine bed is really complete without one or two dwarf, or semi-dwarf, conifers, for if carefully chosen for colour, form and proportion, they can contribute great charm, even in the depths of winter. But with the bewildering array of conifers now being offered, the decision as to which are the most suitable for a particular garden is by no means simple. It is only too easy to yield to the temptation of a pot-grown nursery plant without taking into account that in ten years it may be far too big for its surroundings. So, before selecting a plant, talk the matter over with a knowledgeable person.

Chamaecyparis lawsoniana 'Pygmaea Argentea' makes a dense, softly conical tree with blue-green foliage tipped with silvery-white; this produces a decorative effect that is particularly welcome in winter. 'Minima Aurea', which is rather more sharply conical, has small golden-leaved branches that are as bright as a flame and hold their colour throughout the year. Extremely slow growing, 'Minima Glauca' forms a dense barrel of sea-green foliage that eventually reaches about 2 ft in height. Similar, but only half the size, is 'Pygmy', a grey-green globe that looks charming in a sink garden.

C. obtusa 'Nana' is one of the most beautiful of all semi-dwarf conifers, with small, dark green fans of leaves that build up slowly into an irregular pyramid, usually broader than it is high. *C. o.* 'Nana Aurea' is slightly taller, with golden-yellow foliage.

The spectacular feathery, silver-blue foliage of *C. pisifera* 'Boulevard' has made it one of the most popular of all semi-dwarf conifers. However, with an eventual height of about 15 ft, it needs plenty of room around it.

HOW TO GROW
Plant in spring or autumn, in soil that retains moisture but is well drained. The plants do best in sun and sheltered from drying winds. Propagate by heel cuttings in late summer or early autumn, under glass. Pruning is unnecessary.

Chamaecyparis pisifera 'Boulevard' produces fern-like sprays of silvered foliage which becomes purple-tinged in winter.

The semi-dwarf *C. obtusa* 'Nana Gracilis' forms a dark green conical bush.

C. lawsoniana 'Minima Glauca' may reach 2 ft in 20 years.

'Pygmaea Argentea' has a silvery sheen.

The slow-growing 'Elegans Nana' backed by spikes of *Polygonum affine*.

Cryptomeria japonica (JAPANESE CEDAR)

Only one species of *Cryptomeria* is known – *C. japonica*, which is an important source of timber in Japan. Even so, there are many dwarf, compact forms good for the rock garden. These have feathery, needle-sharp, green leaves that turn bronze in winter.

A decorative form is *C. japonica* 'Globosa Nana', which makes a tight, globular bush 3 ft high and broad. Another form, *C. j.* 'Elegans Nana', has very dense, crowded twigs and forms a compact, rounded bush. Its blue-green leaves turn bronze in winter.

HOW TO GROW
Set out container-grown plants in autumn or spring, in ordinary soil and preferably in sun, in a south or west-facing site. Water young plants freely during the first growing season. Propagate in late summer by cuttings under glass. Pruning is not required.

Arching branches of 'Globosa Nana' spread in maturity to make a slightly flattened bush that turns bronze-green in winter.

The ½ in. long flowers of *Cytisus × kewensis* often appear in clusters.

Cytisus × kewensis (BROOM)

This broom is the exuberant offspring of a marriage that took place 100 years ago at Kew between *Cytisus ardoinii* and *C. albus*. It is a lusty, sprawling shrub, 2 ft high and more than 4 ft across. In May, as it cascades over a wall or decorates a large rock garden, its green leaves almost disappear beneath creamy blooms. For smaller sites, it is better to use its half-brother, *C. × beanii*, which is more restrained in its habits and is about 12 in. shorter all round. It does not flower quite so freely as *C. × kewensis*, but the golden-yellow clusters and single blooms it bears during May are marvellous for lighting up some austere corner of the garden.

HOW TO GROW
Plant young container-grown specimens in autumn or spring, in ordinary, deep and well-drained soil, and in full sun. Propagate by heel cuttings in late summer. No pruning is required.

The grey-blue foliage of *Hebe pinguifolia* 'Pagei' provides a subtle background to the bright flowers of *Cytisus × kewensis*.

D. blagayana brings a welcome sparkle to shady parts of the garden.

Daphne blagayana

There are some 70 species of this lovely flowering shrub, many of them excellent for the rock garden. *Daphne blagayana* is no more than 6 in. high, yet, in the shade it needs, spreads out to 3 ft or more in a loose tangle that looks most attractive when set among rocks. It flowers in April and May, in dense heads of 20 or more creamy-white blooms which appear above the mats of mid-green leaves that crowd the ends of the shoots.

A good contrast for colour and height, but requiring a sunny position, is *D. collina*, which grows up to 2 ft and produces red-purple flower clusters, each 1½ in. across, in May and June. Both species are fragrant.

HOW TO GROW
Plant in September or March in ordinary, well-drained soil – Daphne collina in sun, D. blagayana in partial shade. Propagation is by late summer cuttings, but not easy. Pruning is unnecessary, but straggly growths may be removed in March.

Clothed in blunt-tipped, deep green leaves, *D. collina* carries its 1½ in. flowers in terminal clusters of six to ten or so.

Daphne cneorum (GARLAND FLOWER)

Every rock garden deserves at least one specimen of this glorious dwarf evergreen shrub. Success is by no means guaranteed, for it is a temperamental shrub; but once it does get under way you should have no trouble. In any case, so great are the rewards for success that the plant is worth any number of trials. One important point is that it resents root disturbance, so it is best to start with a small, young, potted plant rather than with a large one that has been dug up. *Daphne cneorum* has wiry stems which bear narrow, deep green leaves and make a low, spreading growth some 6 in. high and 2-3 ft wide. In May and June, once the plant is established, each shoot carries at its end a tightly clustered head of rich pink blooms with a heady fragrance. The plant's eventual spread may be several square feet, and its scent will carry through the garden. The form 'Eximia' is larger than the species in every way, while its flowers are a deeper, richer pink in bud.

Try growing next to *D. cneorum* the silver-leaved dwarf shrub *Euryops acraeus*. This can withstand the daphne's rather overbearing ways and its foliage makes a striking contrast. The daphne is also of the right height and habit to be planted among heaths (*Erica carnea* and *E. vagans*).

Certain bulbs, too, can be allowed to grow up through or near the edge of the daphne – for example, the St Bernard's lily, *Anthericum liliago*, which has beautiful trumpet-shaped white flowers on 2 ft stems.

HOW TO GROW

Daphne cneorum: plant in spring, from young container-grown specimens, in ordinary, well-drained soil. D. cneorum tolerates lime. It does best in full sun and some shelter, with the roots kept cool. Propagate by layering in autumn. It can be pruned lightly to shape after flowering.
Anthericum liliago: see p. 145.
Euryops acraeus: see p. 206.
Erica: see p. 277.

A rose-pink swathe of *Daphne cneorum* is enhanced by the silver leaves of *Euryops acraeus* and the white blooms of St Bernard's lily, *Anthericum liliago*.

Daphne cneorum 'Eximia'.

Dianthus alpinus (ALPINE PINK)

Dianthus means 'divine flower', and this little species from high in the Austrian Alps goes far to justify the name. Unusually for a dianthus, its leaves are a glossy green; the plants form dense, 2 in. high hummocks which in June are completely hidden by single, serrated-edged flowers up to 1½ in. across. The flower colour is usually a strikingly rich rose-pink, but can vary from blood red to white. Each bloom has a distinct central zone speckled with deepest red. There are several named forms.

The plant is of perfect size and habit for growing in a trough garden, or for filling a corner in a rock garden or raised bed.

HOW TO GROW

For cultivation see Dianthus deltoides, p. 204. The alpine pink is a variable species, best raised initially from seeds in late spring. Good colour forms can be propagated in summer by cuttings under glass.

The overlapping petals of *Dianthus alpinus* form a delicate carpet of colour, which may continue from June into August.

Some forms of *Dianthus alpinus* produce deeply coloured flowers.

A good coloniser, *Dianthus deltoides* thrives even between paving slabs.

Dianthus deltoides (MAIDEN PINK)

The cultivated varieties of maiden pink will grace any rock garden with their vividly coloured flowers and leaves, and they are also valuable for the ready way they colonise any sunny position. The following varieties all stand 6-9 in. high and flower from early June for several weeks. 'Wisley Variety' has deep crimson blooms and dark bronze-red foliage. 'Flashing Light' is named from its near-fluorescent crimson flowers; its leaves are a purple-flushed dark green. Then there is 'Albus', an attractive combination of pure white blooms and pale green leaves. 'Brighteyes', another colourful variety, has red-centred white flowers.

HOW TO GROW
Plant in spring, or early autumn, about 9 in. apart, in light, well-drained and preferably limy soil. All thrive in full sun. Propagate by seeds sown in spring in a cold frame or in gentle heat.

'Albus' – a pure white form – will, like other cultivars, come true from its seeds if kept clear of neighbouring dianthus.

If cut back after flowering, a new flush of blooms will appear.

Diascia × 'Ruby Field'

It is only a few years since this beautiful and unusual plant was introduced, but already its unique colour and long flowering period have made it an established favourite with gardeners. It is said to be derived from crossing the South African species, *Diascia barberae* and *D. cordata*, and, due to its ancestry, there is nothing it likes better than the base of a south-facing wall or large rock.

The plant forms a mat of small, toothed leaves and puts out slender flowering stems up to 12 in. high, which from May and throughout the summer are strung with flat blooms of a warm glowing pink. Behind each bloom is a pair of curved horns – it is from these that the name diascia derives, meaning 'two spurs'.

HOW TO GROW
Plant in spring, 12-14 in. apart, in ordinary, well-drained soil. Full sun is best, but light shade is tolerated. Propagate by basal cuttings rooted under glass.

The plant may lose vigour rather quickly. To maintain strong growth, dress with fertiliser or divide and replant in spring.

The cross-shaped flowers of *Draba bryoides* are carried on 2 in. stems.

Draba bryoides (WHITLOW GRASS)

Ideal for the trough or sink garden, *Draba bryoides* (syn. *D. rigida bryoides*) slowly builds up nearly solid, domed rosettes of tiny pointed leaves, some 2 in. high and 3 in. across. In March the new leaves flare a vivid emerald-green and are highlighted by many small golden flowers carried on wiry stems.

Another fine draba for the same sites is *D. aizoides*. This has larger, looser, bristly haired rosettes of foliage that produce small bunched heads of lemon-yellow flowers in March and April. It has the valuable habit of placing its seedlings in odd yet suitable corners.

HOW TO GROW
Plant drabas in spring, in light soil with good drainage. Both are suitable for sink gardens and should be sited in full sun. Draba bryoides is perfect for growing in a hole bored in tufa or some other soft rock. Propagate D. aizoides by seeds in spring, D. bryoides by late summer cuttings.

Draba aizoides will grow 4 in. high and spread up to 9 in. The bunched heads of tiny flowers are carried on 2-4 in. stems.

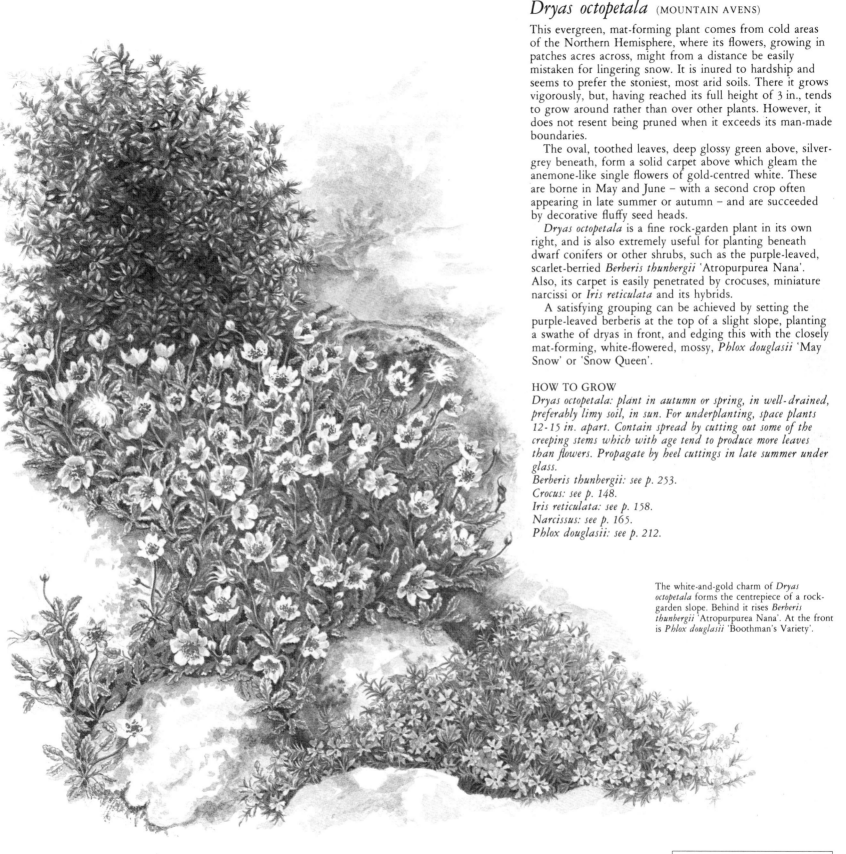

Dryas octopetala (MOUNTAIN AVENS)

This evergreen, mat-forming plant comes from cold areas
of the Northern Hemisphere, where its flowers, growing in
patches acres across, might from a distance be easily
mistaken for lingering snow. It is inured to hardship and
seems to prefer the stoniest, most arid soils. There it grows
vigorously, but, having reached its full height of 3 in., tends
to grow around rather than over other plants. However, it
does not resent being pruned when it exceeds its man-made
boundaries.

The oval, toothed leaves, deep glossy green above, silver-
grey beneath, form a solid carpet above which gleam the
anemone-like single flowers of gold-centred white. These
are borne in May and June – with a second crop often
appearing in late summer or autumn – and are succeeded
by decorative fluffy seed heads.

Dryas octopetala is a fine rock-garden plant in its own
right, and is also extremely useful for planting beneath
dwarf conifers or other shrubs, such as the purple-leaved,
scarlet-berried *Berberis thunbergii* 'Atropurpurea Nana'.
Also, its carpet is easily penetrated by crocuses, miniature
narcissi or *Iris reticulata* and its hybrids.

A satisfying grouping can be achieved by setting the
purple-leaved berberis at the top of a slight slope, planting
a swathe of dryas in front, and edging this with the closely
mat-forming, white-flowered, mossy, *Phlox douglasii* 'May
Snow' or 'Snow Queen'.

HOW TO GROW
*Dryas octopetala: plant in autumn or spring, in well-drained,
preferably limy soil, in sun. For underplanting, space plants
12-15 in. apart. Contain spread by cutting out some of the
creeping stems which with age tend to produce more leaves
than flowers. Propagate by heel cuttings in late summer under
glass.
Berberis thunbergii: see p. 253.
Crocus: see p. 148.
Iris reticulata: see p. 158.
Narcissus: see p. 165.
Phlox douglasii: see p. 212.*

The white-and-gold charm of *Dryas
octopetala* forms the centrepiece of a rock-
garden slope. Behind it rises *Berberis
thunbergii* 'Atropurpurea Nana'. At the front
is *Phlox douglasii* 'Boothman's Variety'.

The glowing 'Mrs Charles Boyle' warms even the coldest grey stone.

Erinus alpinus (FAIRY FOXGLOVE)

If you are just starting a rock garden, then you could do a great deal worse than begin with *Erinus alpinus*. It possesses just about everything that a rock plant should have: neatness, compactness, bright colours, undemanding habits and the ability to colonise pockets of soil between rocks or even between bricks.

The plant forms small tufts of dark green rosettes of leaves, about 3 in. high and 6 in. across, that in May are covered with small flowers. In the wild these are in shades of lavender. For the garden, brighter forms are available: 'Mrs Charles Boyle', which is glowing pink; 'Dr Hanele', carmine; or 'Albus', pure white.

HOW TO GROW

Plant in autumn or spring, in dry walls, troughs or rock gardens, spacing them 6 in. apart. Any ordinary soil is suitable. Site in full sun. The plant self-seeds freely, and named cultivars come more or less true to type.

'Albus' produces pure white flowers and, like other varieties of *E. alpinus*, has distinctive deeply toothed leaves.

Euryops acraeus provides a crock of gold in the early-summer rockery.

Euryops acraeus

When this bright-leaved miniature shrub was first introduced from South Africa's Drakensberg Mountains, some gardeners suspected that it might be too tender for Britain's glum winters. In fact, it seems to survive perfectly happily in every part of the country.

The plant, also incorrectly called *Euryops evansii*, makes a rounded dome of woody stems, densely clothed in narrow leaves that look as though they have been fashioned from beaten silver. In early summer this glistening orb is embossed with golden, daisy-like flowers. The plant is evergreen, which makes it a year-round joy. After a few years it may spread to about 2 ft across, but it seldom grows higher than 12 in.

HOW TO GROW

Plant in autumn or spring, in ordinary soil and in a sunny site. Good drainage is essential – excessive moisture at the roots invites fungal diseases. Propagate by soft cuttings under glass in summer.

The woody stems of evergreen *Euryops acraeus*, dressed in silver leaves, bring a sparkle to any sombre winter garden.

The blue of *G. septemfida*, which may be tinged with mauve as here, shimmers among the white flowers of a gypsophila.

Gentiana septemfida (GENTIAN)

This is surely the most obliging of all the gentians, for, unlike many of its cousins, it will flower exuberantly in almost any soil and in most conditions.

The plant passes the winter as no more than a cluster of ground-level buds. By July these have produced, above tufts of lance-shaped leaves, a wealth of prostrate stems carrying packed heads of up to 20 blue, trumpet-like flowers, the blue varying from a clear, light hue to a darker shade tinged with mauve. The flowers are speckled green in the throat and have a 'beard' of thread-like growths between the petals.

HOW TO GROW

Plant in spring, in ordinary to rich, moisture-retentive soil in light shade or sun. Space plants 12 in. apart. Propagate in spring by seeds or basal cuttings, both under glass.

Reliable and practical, *G. septemfida* will grow in almost any sunny spot.

Gentiana acaulis (TRUMPET GENTIAN)

According to the old herbalist Robert Turner, gentians steeped in wine are very good for those 'lamed in their joynts by cold or bad lodgings', and even modern travellers in the Alps are cheered by the brilliant blue patches, like slabs of sky fallen to earth, that these gentians make in the high meadows. Often, too, they are accompanied by spring gentians, *Gentiana verna*, in a glorious combination that can, with care, be repeated in the rock garden.

The trumpet gentian, once established, will remain happy for many years. It grows into 18 in. wide and 3 in. deep pads of prostrate foliage that in May puts forth great trumpets of vivid blue, freckled green in the throat. In cultivation, however, the more compact spring gentian averages only three or four years of flowering life – but what a rewarding life it is, in early spring particularly, when each plant blazes with 20 or 30 blooms of intense sapphire blue.

To complete a truly Alpine corner, you might surround the gentians with a planting of *Saxifraga* × 'Valerie Finnis'. Though barely 2 in. high, it forms dense, flat cushions of grey leaves.

HOW TO GROW
Gentiana: plant both species in autumn or spring in good garden loam, slightly gritty if possible, and in full sun. Propagate in spring by division or by cuttings.
Saxifraga × 'Valerie Finnis': see Saxifraga (Kabschia group) p. 216.

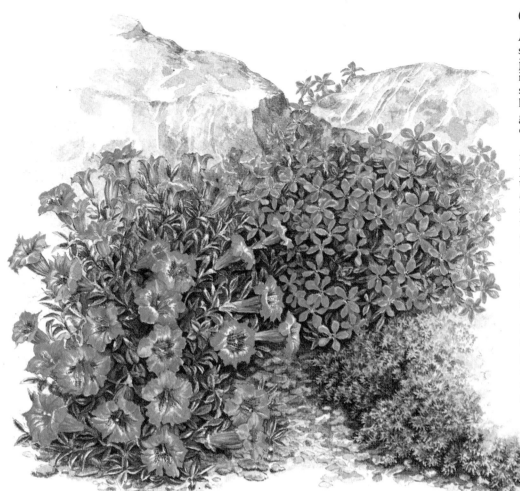

The clump of *Gentiana acaulis* with its trumpet-like flowers, on the left, blends almost imperceptibly into the more intense blue of *Gentiana verna*. The alpine flavour is rounded off by the addition of the grey-leaved *Saxifraga* 'Valerie Finnis'.

Geranium dalmaticum (CRANE'S-BILL)

True geraniums – as opposed to pelargoniums – do very well in a rockery, and *Geranium dalmaticum* can spread to form a solid patch of foliage a yard wide, yet no more than 4 in. high. In June the whole plant is smothered in blooms of clear rose-pink, about 1 in. across. The leaves, which make low, dense cushions, are round, thumbnail-sized and crinkled, and between flowering and late October some of them are attractively tinted with red and orange.

The plant quickly fills any soil pocket in the rock garden. It is particularly at home on a terrace wall or in a raised bed, over whose edges it will erupt in a brilliant extravaganza of colour.

HOW TO GROW
Plant in autumn or spring, in any – even poor – soil which is light and well drained; in rich soil the plants spread too rapidly. Best in full sun, but light shade is tolerated. Space at 12 in. intervals. Dead-head after flowering unless self-seeding is desired. Propagate by division and replanting of rooted underground rhizomes.

An easily grown plant for the rock garden, *G. dalmaticum* carries its clear rose-pink flowers on 4-5 in. stems.

The summer flowers of *G. dalmaticum* form a frothy mound of colour.

Gypsophila repens 'Dorothy Teacher'

Both in the wild and in the rock garden, *Gypsophila repens* (syn. *G. prostrata*) is a plant that sprawls for 2 ft and more. So if space is limited it might be better to plant the more restrained, compact variety 'Dorothy Teacher', whose stems are covered throughout the year with lance-shaped leaves of soft grey-green and from June to August with small, starry, clear pink flowers. *G. r. fratensis* has deeper pink blooms. All these plants are happy trailing over a rock garden or trough garden. If any shoots start to wander, they can be cut back without harming the plant.

HOW TO GROW

Plant in spring or autumn, in ordinary soil if necessary, kept open and well drained by the addition of grit. Suitable for chalky soils and happy on lime, the plant needs full sun. Clip lightly after flowering, to contain spread and encourage flowers. Propagate in spring or late summer by cuttings under glass.

Another compact version of *Gypsophila repens* is *G. r. fratensis*, which grows 3-4 in. high and spreads about 18 in.

'Dorothy Teacher' shows best when trailing over walls or down rocks.

Helianthemum nummularium

(ROCK ROSE)

This is the well-known rock rose, which few plants can equal as a quick covering for sunny areas; after a year's growth, a single specimen may well have spread 2 ft. The plant makes a 4-6 in. high carpet of evergreen foliage, massed in June and July with bright flowers. Named forms range in colour from white, cream and yellow through orange, scarlet and bronze to crimson and pink. Foliage varies from deep glossy green to soft silver-grey. Two good cultivars are 'Wisley Pink' and 'Wisley Primrose'. All forms are excellent for clothing walls or paving.

HOW TO GROW

Set out young container-grown plants in spring, 18 in. apart. Plant in well-drained to dry, ordinary, poor or sandy soil, and in full sun. Prune after the first flush of flowers, cutting hard back by at least one-third. Propagate in late summer by heel cuttings under glass.

The variety 'Wisley Primrose' carries light grey-green foliage and primrose-yellow flowers with deeper-toned centres.

'Fire Dragon', like other forms, should be neatly trimmed after flowering.

Hepatica nobilis

Early in the New Year the plump little ground-level buds of this anemone (previously known as *Hepatica triloba*) can be seen stirring into life. During the first mild spell in February, a bloom or two will unfold its petals, soon to be followed by many more, spreading out into a 12 in. mat. The colour of the flowers is variable; most commonly lavender-blue, it may also be white, red or dark blue, against which the white centre stands out strikingly. *H. n. rosea* is a charming pink form. A near relative is *H. transsilvanica*, which has larger, mauve-blue flowers.

HOW TO GROW

Plant in spring or autumn, 8-10 in. apart, in moist, loamy soil enriched with peat; it thrives in limy soil. Best in light shade, but slow to become established. Root disturbance should be avoided; propagate by division immediately after flowering or by sowing seeds when they are ripe but still green.

Hepatica transsilvanica has delicate pale mauve-blue flowers, 1 in. across. The stems are usually about 4 in. high.

Hepatica nobilis grows well in a lightly shaded woodland setting.

Hypericum olympicum (ST JOHN'S WORT)

Hypericum is St John's Wort, which supposedly flowers on August 29, the anniversary of John the Baptist's martyrdom. And, indeed, in July and August *Hypericum olympicum* does put forth a mass of golden, bowl-shaped blooms nearly 2 in. across, their centres a haze of pale gold stamens. Throughout the year the plant's 12 in. stems are clothed with small, grey-green leaves, making it suitable for rock gardens, walls or paving.

Another, rather more delicate species, which may suffer in harsh British winters, is *H. coris*. This is much smaller, has greener, heath-like foliage and bears star-shaped flowers of pale gold in July.

HOW TO GROW
Plant in spring, in any good, well-drained soil, spacing both species 12 in. apart. Full sun is essential, and Hypericum coris requires a sheltered spot. Propagate in spring or late summer by cuttings under glass.

Excellent for wall tops and crevices, *Hypericum olympicum* bears numerous flowers at the tips of its shoots.

Juniperus communis 'Compressa'

(NOAH'S ARK JUNIPER)

As one of the smallest of all conifers, the charmingly named Noah's Ark juniper has prickly, grey-green leaves, and is the perfect dwarf conifer for growing with alpine plants. With its very slow growth and slim, upright branches compressed into a tightly columnar form, it never looks out of place, whether it is grown in the rock garden, raised alpine bed or trough garden. In addition, it makes a splendid pot specimen for the unheated alpine house.

Since this conifer is likely to live a long time, its initial placing is important. Do not plant it at the top or bottom of a rock garden; its 1-2 ft stature looks more telling somewhere in between, particularly on a gentle slope where it will not look out of proportion.

In a trough garden, the tree looks best placed towards the edge and away from any rocks. In a spacious rock or trough garden, a group of three or four trees creates a fine effect. In groups, the trees should be planted 12-18 in. apart to allow for spread.

Even if the Noah's Ark juniper is grown in a group, it should be kept well away from larger plants or rocks, which could easily dominate it. You might try growing beneath it low, creeping alpine plants to create a miniature alpine meadow. Good for this purpose would be wild thyme (*Thymus drucei*) varieties, *Arabis ferdinandi-coburgii* 'Variegata' and *Potentilla tabernaemontani* 'Nana', and all will intermingle quite happily. Break up the ground-cover with a few upright dwarf plants, such as *Aquilegia bertolonii*, for example.

Blue *Aquilegia bertolonii*, golden *Potentilla tabernaemontani* and fresh green and white *Arabis ferdinandi-coburgii* 'Variegata' surround the eye-catching vertical line of the Noah's Ark juniper. *Thymus drucei* will burst into a carpet of pink later in the year.

HOW TO GROW
Juniperus communis 'Compressa': *plant in spring, in ordinary soil, acid or alkaline, preferably in sun. No pruning is necessary. Propagate in September and October by 2-4 in. long heel cuttings under glass.*
Aquilegia bertolonii: see p. 197.
Arabis ferdinandi-coburgii: see p. 198.
Potentilla tabernaemontani: see p. 212.
Thymus drucei: see p. 219.

A starry mass of edelweiss blooms at the edge of an alpine bed.

Leontopodium alpinum (EDELWEISS)

This charming flower, which can achieve a height and spread of 8-9 in., looks in June and July like a group of ten-pointed stars cut out of well-washed flannel. As stamp collectors and lovers of musicals are aware, it grows in the Tyrol, and it – or one of its close relatives – is also found in most of the other great mountain ranges of the Northern Hemisphere as well.

Despite this fondness for high altitudes, it will do perfectly well in the less rarefied air of the rockery, provided it is planted on the sunny side of the mound.

HOW TO GROW
Plant in spring, 6 in. apart, in ordinary garden soil. Good drainage is essential to avoid root rot, and heavy soils should be lightened with gravel or grit. Use cloches to protect plants from winter rain. Edelweiss is easily propagated from seeds sown in spring in gentle heat.

With its off-white, cloth-like petals and grey leaves, edelweiss is one of the most curious yet charming of rock plants.

Lewisia cotyledon hybrids

In May and June *Lewisia cotyledon* and its hybrids put out a 12 in. high, many-branched display of gorgeous crimson, pink or white flowers. But as natives of California – their name honours the 18th-century American explorer Meriwether Lewis – they are not too keen on British winter damp, so it is best to plant them in a sloping or vertical crevice, where moisture will quickly drain away. They also make splendid pot plants in the alpine house or cold frame.

HOW TO GROW
Plant in spring, 6-8 in. apart, setting the crowns 1 in. above soil level or, preferably, on a slope between rocks or in a retaining dry wall. The crowns are susceptible to rot: protect them against excessive moisture with a collar of stone chippings, and in winter with cloches or raised glass panes. They need rich soil, with added gravel for good drainage, and full sun. Propagate in summer by rooting detached rosettes under glass, or in spring from seeds.

In a rock crevice a *Lewisia cotyledon* hybrid displays its satiny flowers.

Lewisia cotyledon hybrids are fleshy-leaved semi-succulents that put out a profusion of warm-hued flowers in late spring.

Linum flavum (YELLOW FLAX)

A flax from eastern Europe, *Linum flavum* produces its golden-yellow, funnel-shaped flowers from mid to late summer, when colour in the rock garden is scarce. The stems that bear the grey-green leaves become almost woody, like those of a shrub, but even so they die back during winter. At flowering time a well-grown plant can be 12-18 in. high and about 18 in. across.

Another attractive flax is *L. salsoloides*. In midsummer, this lovely plant, which makes a dense 6-8 in. high spread of slender twiggy stems clad with needle-like grey-green leaves, produces pearly-white flowers as graceful as a flight of butterflies.

HOW TO GROW
Plant in autumn or spring, 18 in. apart. Any well-drained garden soil is suitable, in full sun. Propagate by seeds in spring; named forms may not come true and are better increased from basal cuttings under glass in spring.

Snowy *Linum salsoloides* cascades over the edge of a rock garden.

From June to August, when the rock garden is short of bright colours, the flax *Linum flavum* produces a mass of yellow blooms.

Lithodora diffusa

When all the battles over nomenclature are done, it is probably easier to remember this much-loved plant (also listed as *Lithospermum prostratum*) by the names of its two cultivars, 'Grace Ward' and 'Heavenly Blue'. Both put out a 2 ft wide sprawl of dark green leaves that from June to early autumn are well-nigh hidden by a mass of flowers of the deepest, most intense, truest blue. The blooms on 'Grace Ward' are a little larger and perhaps a little brighter than those of 'Heavenly Blue', but both produce a riot of colour that will illuminate an entire corner of the garden.

Curiously, for a plant whose native habitats include some of the limestone uplands of southern Europe, it is usually described as a lime-hater. In the garden, certainly, it seems to do better in a lime-free soil. However, if the lime content of your ground is not too high, it might still be worth giving it a trial.

In general, it prefers an open, sunny position with plenty of room to spread into wide mats. It associates very well with heathers, bridging the floral gap between the winter-flowering *Erica carnea* and the summer-blooming *Calluna*. It will also grow very happily on the edge of a retaining wall, eventually pouring a flood of colour down the face, in combination with such plants as *Helianthemum*, *Campanula portenschlagiana* and *Genista lydia*.

HOW TO GROW
Lithodora diffusa: plant in spring, in full sun and in neutral to lime-free, well-drained, sandy soil enriched with peat or leaf-mould. For ground-cover, space the plants 18 in. apart. Propagate by heel cuttings of woody sideshoots in summer, under glass.
Calluna: see p. 256.
Campanula portenschlagiana: see p. 200.
Erica carnea: see p. 277.
Genista lydia: see p. 283.
Helianthemum: see p. 208.

Lithodora diffusa 'Heavenly Blue' tumbles down a rock to mingle with the blue-purple *Campanula portenschlagiana*. Beside the lithodora is an orange-yellow *Helianthemum*. On the rock behind is *Genista lydia*.

In a sunny position *Penstemon roezlii* produces a mass of bright blooms.

Penstemon roezlii

It is well worth including a few penstemons in the rock garden. One of the best is *Penstemon roezlii*, which forms a low, spreading evergreen plant no more than 6 in. high that, in late May, is covered with tubular flowers of bright cherry-crimson. The plant is best grown on a rocky ledge or on the rim of a large trough garden.

Another fine penstemon, suitable for anywhere in the rock garden, is *P. scouleri*, which is taller. It makes an upright bush crowned in June and July with cool lavender-blue flowers. 'Alba' is a smaller, white form.

HOW TO GROW
Plant all penstemons in autumn or spring, in well-drained soil, and in full sun. They need a position where they can sprawl or trail freely. After flowering, clip the plants to prevent seeds forming. Propagate in summer by cuttings under glass, or in spring by seeds.

Penstemon scouleri flowers freely for many years, particularly if its seed pods are removed immediately after flowering.

Phlox subulata 'G. F. Wilson' is one of the finest of rock-garden phloxes.

Phlox douglasii

If you have a well-drained sunny patch in the alpine garden, it could be most pleasantly filled with *Phlox douglasii* cultivars and *P. subulata* hybrids. Both form bright green mats and from mid-May onwards flower in a variety of colours, from white to crimson.

The *P. subulata* hybrids, growing to about 4 in. high, make a spectacular follow-on to aubrietas and alyssum in rock-garden walls and paving, while the slightly smaller *P. douglasii* forms might be allowed to tumble over the side of a trough garden or down the face of a rock. Both groups have a spread of about 18 in.

HOW TO GROW
Plant in spring or autumn, 12-18 in. apart for ground-cover. They thrive in any good, well-drained garden soil, and in full sun. In troughs and paving pockets, clip the plants after flowering to keep them compact. Propagate named forms in late summer by cuttings under glass.

'Rosea', like other cultivars of *Phlox douglasii*, makes a tight compact mat of foliage covered with tiny flowers.

The miniature form of the spring cinquefoil, *Potentilla tabernaemontani* 'Nana', has evergreen foliage and bright yellow flowers.

Potentilla tabernaemontani 'Nana'

(SPRING CINQUEFOIL)

When he saw it growing on its native limestone hills in Yorkshire, rock gardener Reginald Farrer hailed *Potentilla tabernaemontani* (syn. *P. verna*) as 'our own golden alpine'. But sadly, when brought into the garden, it all too often develops into a rather straggly, undistinguished plant. Far better is its dwarf form 'Nana', which is only 1 in. high and whose vivid foliage grows in compact, 10 in. wide mats.

From midsummer until late autumn, 'Nana' puts on a non-stop display of stemless golden blooms. It is an ideal plant for brightening a corner of the trough garden; grow it there with other plants of the same stature.

HOW TO GROW
Plant in autumn or spring – 8 in. apart for a carpeting effect – in ordinary, well-drained soil or paving pockets, in full sun. Propagate in spring by division or by basal cuttings under glass.

Potentilla tabernaemontani 'Nana' is long-flowering and long-lived.

Primula auricula hybrids

There are more than 500 wild species of *Primula* and thousands of garden hybrids in an immense variety of shapes, sizes and colours, so that you could plant your spring beds with different groupings each year for a lifetime and never repeat the pattern once.

Among the most varied, adaptable and useful, however, are the *Primula auricula* hybrids, which include the show auriculas, adored by some, loathed by others. They are staging a spectacular return to the popularity they enjoyed a century ago. Most are grown in an unheated greenhouse to protect their delicate beauty from bad weather, but many are robust enough for the rock garden, where they seem to prefer level ground and some shade. Their primrose-shaped flowers, borne from March to May, come in a wide range of yellows, lavenders, purples and crimsons. One of the most endearing is 'Blairside Yellow', no more than 2 in. high and very free-flowering.

The *P. × pubescens* hybrids – derived from *P. auricula* and *P. rubra* – also provide a wonderful and diverse adornment for the rock garden in spring. They are usually more compact than the auriculas and have rather more funnel-shaped flowers, often produced in dense heads. The blooms range in colour from white through pink and lavender to purple. The crimson 'Faldonside' or the purple 'Mrs J. Wilson' look splendid as a carpet of colour on a sloping rock-garden wall facing north or east. A compact form, 'Argus', produces purple flowers with white centres.

Plants that enjoy the same growing conditions as the primulas and associate well with them include *Hepatica nobilis* and *Cyclamen neapolitanum*.

HOW TO GROW
Primula: plant in autumn or spring, 6-8 in. apart, in well-drained fertile soil enriched with humus. They thrive in light shade, but do not object to sun. Excessive soil moisture may lead to crown rot. Propagate in summer by cuttings, or seeds under glass in spring.
Cyclamen neapolitanum: see p. 150.
Hepatica nobilis: see p. 208.

The green and silver leaves of *Cyclamen neapolitanum* complement a spring mix of primulas and *Hepatica nobilis*.

Primula frondosa

Early in the year the ground-level buds of this primula unfurl into rosettes of leaves dusted in a waxy, golden powder. This is washed away after a few heavy showers, and in April the flowers appear, rosy-lilac and golden-eyed, borne on 4 in. high stems. A fine companion would be the Japanese primrose, *Primula sieboldii*, which enjoys the same conditions. It wanders underground, sending up tufts of long-stalked leaves, above which, in April and May, flutter clusters of primroses – purple, pink or white according to cultivar. The flowers may be cup-shaped or have deeply fringed petals.

HOW TO GROW
Plant in spring or after flowering in a spot shaded from full sun, in gritty soil that contains plenty of humus, well drained but moist round the roots. Space 6 in. apart. Propagate by division after flowering – every two or three years to prevent overcrowding – or by seeds sown when ripe.

Cultivars of the Japanese primrose, *Primula sieboldii*, provide a range of flower colour from white, through pink, to purple.

Each flower stem of *Primula frondosa* bears 10-30 golden-eyed blooms.

Primula marginata

Even if this primula produced no flowers at all, it would be still worth growing for the beauty of its foliage. Each spring it puts out a fresh growth of tooth-edged leaves, spreading some 6-9 in. across and covered with a silvery, waxy powder known as farina. Though most of this is washed off by rain, enough remains to give the leaves a permanent, glistening border.

The flowers – there may be as many as 20 separate blooms – arrive in April and continue into May, when each plant vies with the next upon a delicate theme of lavender-blue. The finest of the many named forms is 'Linda Pope', which has broader leaves than the species and larger flowers of a soft lavender-blue.

HOW TO GROW
Outdoor cultivation as for Primula auricula (see p. 213), but in full sun. In the alpine house, grow the plants in 4-5 in. pots of a proprietary compost.

Toothed leaves and lavender-blue flowers – *Primula marginata* makes a fine display in a rock crevice.

Pulsatilla vulgaris (PASQUE FLOWER)

The pasque flower, as its name implies, is a flower of Easter; its petals yield a rich, green dye that at one time was used to stain Easter eggs. It is a lovely plant, with purple, golden-centred, goblet-like flowers, which are followed in May by charming fluffy seed heads. The foliage is finely dissected, like that of parsley.

Pulsatilla grows wild on the chalky downlands of southern England, so it will settle quite happily into an open part of the rock garden. There are several named varieties, in shades of purple, lavender, red, pink and white, all of which grow to about 8-12 in. high and achieve a spread of some 15-18 in.

HOW TO GROW
Plant in autumn, 8-10 in. apart, in well-drained and, preferably, slightly limy soil. Best in full sun. Pulsatillas have deep roots and do not transplant easily; they are best propagated by seeds sown when ripe, and planted out from pots the following autumn.

Well-established pasque flowers improve their display with every year.

Forms may be larger flowered and more robust than the type species.

One of the most attractive varieties of *P. vulgaris* is 'Alba', with pure white petals surrounding golden stamens.

As though its beautiful spring display of bloom were not enough, the pasque flower offers a bonus of decorative seed heads.

Salix reticulata (NET-LEAVED WILLOW)

One of the most beautiful of dwarf willows for the rock garden, *Salix reticulata* seldom grows more than 3 in. high. It is essentially a foliage plant with glossy, rich green, beautifully veined leaves that are woolly when young. Slim, reddish catkins appear with the leaves in early spring to add to its decorative quality.

To enhance the lilliputian image, grow it in company with *S. myrsinites*, a taller, mat-forming willow with bright green leaves and charming little pink catkins. The best form is *S. m. jacquiniana* (syn. *S. alpina*), which is flatter in growth and has toothless leaves.

HOW TO GROW
Plant from autumn to spring in ordinary garden soil, preferably moist, and in sun or partial shade. Propagate in autumn by hardwood cuttings in a cold frame. Pruning is rarely necessary, but straggly shoots may be cut back to shape in spring.

With its unusual lustrous foliage, *Salix reticulata*, a rare dwarf willow of British mountains, is an outstanding rock plant.

Female plants of *Salix myrsinites* bear decorative red seed pods.

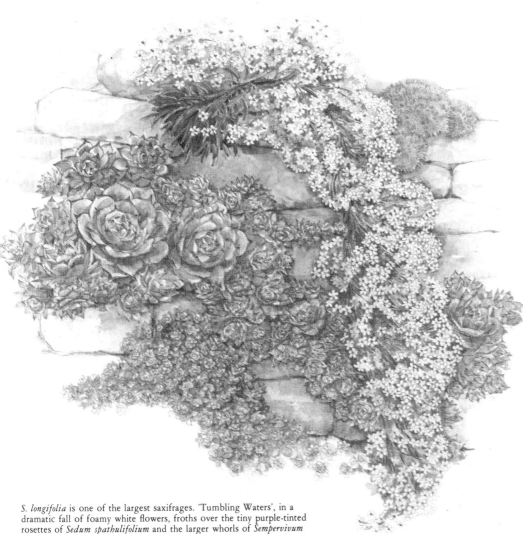

S. *longifolia* is one of the largest saxifrages. 'Tumbling Waters', in a dramatic fall of foamy white flowers, froths over the tiny purple-tinted rosettes of *Sedum spathulifolium* and the larger whorls of *Sempervivum tectorum*.

Saxifraga longifolia

The genus *Saxifraga* contains 370 species of so many different shapes and sizes that it has been divided into 16 quite distinct sections. Together they comprise one of the most beautiful and varied groups of plants for the rock garden, raised bed, trough garden and alpine house.

You might do well to begin your collection with *Euaizoonia*, the 'silvers', if for nothing other than their close-packed, frosted-silver rosettes of leaves. These rosettes gradually join up to form dense hummocks that, towards the end of May, produce loose sprays of anything from eight to 100 flowers, mostly white but occasionally faint pink or yellow. The 'silvers' are easy-to-grow plants, ideal for filling narrow crevices between rocks or covering a wall.

The odd man out in the section is *Saxifraga longifolia*, a native of the Pyrenees. This forms a single elegant rosette of narrow, brilliantly silver leaves, which takes at least three, and sometimes considerably more, years to bloom. When it does so it flaunts an 18 in. arching plume of snow-white flowers. After flowering, however, the plant dies – but not before producing a mass of seeds to perpetuate itself. The hybrid 'Tumbling Waters', almost as fine as the species, produces a few separate side rosettes that can be used as cuttings.

The 'silvers' are best treated as loners: they do not mix happily with other plants – except perhaps *Sempervivum tectorum*, *Draba aizoides* or one of the smaller species of sedum, such as *Sedum spathulifolium*.

HOW TO GROW
Saxifraga: plant silver saxifrages in autumn or spring, singly, in vertical sunny crevices. They thrive in any gritty, well-drained soil, and although lime is not essential it improves the encrustation on the leaves. All except S. longifolia can be propagated by detaching and rooting single side rosettes under glass in summer. Propagate S. longifolia by seeds sown in spring under glass.
Draba aizoides: see Draba bryoides, p. 204.
Sedum spathulifolium: see Sedum, p. 217.
Sempervivum tectorum: see p. 218.

Saxifraga 'Elizabeth' lights up the rock garden.

Saxifraga × 'Jenkinsae' blooms in a scree bed.

Saxifraga (KABSCHIA GROUP)

Ideal plants for the trough garden, the Kabschia saxifrages produce small, tight, 6-7 in. wide domes of close-packed grey-green rosettes with white, yellow or pink flowers. Most of them, such as the pale yellow *Saxifraga* × 'Valerie Finnis' and the pale, clear pink *S.* × 'Jenkinsae', flower in March, but a few unfold their first blooms in January or February. Some of the more vigorous, such as the rich yellow-flowered *S.* × *haagii* and the softer yellow *S.* × *apiculata*, will accept full exposure to the weather, but most need a more protected site in light shade. All members of the group have a height of some 2-3 in.

HOW TO GROW
Plant in autumn or spring, in gritty, well-drained soil, preferably chalky or with lime added. These saxifrages should not be exposed to midday sun. Propagate by detaching single, non-flowering, side rosettes in summer and rooting them under glass.

Saxifraga (MOSSY GROUP)

The 'mossies', which form 1-2 ft wide hummocks of a handsome emerald green, are mostly vigorous plants, whose solid evergreen carpet quickly fills the outskirts of a rock garden. In early summer they present 6-8 in. high displays of small, saucer-shaped flowers in colours ranging from white to blood red.
   Saxifraga 'Edie Campbell' has rich green foliage and a profusion of large pink flowers. *S.* 'Peter Pan' makes smaller cushions thickly set with crimson flowers.

HOW TO GROW
Plant in autumn or spring, in ordinary, well-drained but moisture-retentive soil. For edging and carpeting, space mossy saxifrages 12-15 in. apart, the more compact 'Peter Pan' 6 in. apart. Most do best in light shade. Propagate as for other saxifrages, or by cuttings in spring or autumn.

'Edie Campbell' is among the most shade-tolerant of all saxifrages.

Mossy saxifrages make ideal ground-cover for lightly shaded sites. Here one forms a carpet around an unfolding hosta.

Saxifraga umbrosa (PYRENEAN SAXIFRAGE)

This tough saxifrage will live quite happily in the least hospitable parts of the rockery. It loves shade, and in this situation will produce 12-18 in. wide rosettes of thick, fleshy, dark green leaves that in May are overhung by masses of star-shaped pink flowers. There is a dwarf form, *Saxifraga umbrosa primuloides*, that also produces pink flowers; but 'Elliott's Variety' is even more compact, and puts forth deep rose flowers in clusters 4-7 in. high.

The famous London pride, *S. × urbium*, an 18th-century cross between *S. umbrosa* and *S. spathularis*, is an attractive plant, much like *S. umbrosa* but more vigorous and with larger, darker rosettes, taller stems and paler flowers.

HOW TO GROW
Plant these saxifrages in autumn or spring, in any well-drained soil. All thrive in shade, but will also grow in sunny sites. Propagate by detaching non-flowering side rosettes in late summer and treating them as cuttings.

Saxifraga × urbium makes a colourful edging, as in this extensive planting along a drive. It can be trimmed after flowering.

Flourishing in shade, London pride is an excellent plant for town gardens.

Sedum (STONECROPS)

Sedums – some of which will 'sit' on rocks and walls – constitute an extremely large genus, and among them is probably one of the ten best alpine plants available – *Sedum cauticolum*. If possible, this should be grown in a raised position or on the edge of a trough, where you can appreciate its dove-grey leaves throughout the summer and its heads of rich pink blooms in August and September.

Another popular sedum is *S. spathulifolium*, which lights up with bright yellow flowers in May and June and forms 3 in. high compact clumps of fleshy, evergreen leaf rosettes. These are dusted with a powder of silvery-white in the form 'Cape Blanco' (commonly miscalled 'Cappa Blanca'), and of rich plum-red in 'Purpureum'.

Equally adaptable is *S. spurium*, an evergreen that forms mats about 12 in. across. This has two lovely forms: 'Atropurpureum', with bronze leaves and pink flowers; and 'Schorbusserblut', with blooms of brilliant crimson that are adored by butterflies. Both flower in July. Another striking plant is *S.* 'Vera Jameson', a beautiful chance hybrid that a few years ago was given two awards by the Royal Horticultural Society. As much a delight as the burgundy leaves are the dusky-pink blooms.

All these stonecrops will associate together, providing a succession of colour from early summer until autumn. They can be grown very effectively as single specimen plants in a trough or sink, both united and contrasted by the rich green of *Lithodora diffusa*. The latter will also look splendid in early summer, with its deep sky-blue flowers, against the yellow blooms of *S. spathulifolium*.

HOW TO GROW
Sedums: plant in autumn or spring, in any kind of well-drained soil and in sun or light shade. Sedums thrive even in poor, thin soils and are suitable for rock gardens, troughs, walls and paving cracks. They require the minimum of attention. Space at 10-12 in. intervals. Propagate by division during the dormant season, or by stem cuttings during the growing periods.
Lithodora diffusa: see p. 211.

In August the glowing leaves and blooms of *Sedum* 'Vera Jameson' and the rosy blush of *S. cauticolum* suffuse this trough with pink, but in early summer it is a mass of sky blue (*Lithodora diffusa*) and sunshine yellow (*S. spathulifolium* 'Cape Blanco').

A red form of *Sempervivum tectorum*, backed on the right by *S. montanum*.

Sempervivum tectorum (HOUSELEEK)

Houseleeks used to be planted on rooftops to ward off lightning and witchcraft; so effective were they held to be that Charlemagne ordered that every roof in his kingdom should be decorated in this way.

In this more prosaic age, the houseleek is generally planted in rock gardens, where it will flourish in the narrowest of cracks and in the most sun-baked, least-nourishing soil, expanding into a 12 in. wide dome of fleshy-leaved rosettes standing some 3 in. high. This foliage is usually bright green, tipped with maroon, but is variable. Reddish to pinkish-purple star-shaped blooms appear in July at the top of stout stems.

HOW TO GROW
Plant from autumn to spring, 12 in. apart, in any kind of soil, however thin or poor, provided that it is well drained and in full sun. Propagate by detaching and replanting offsets in autumn or spring.

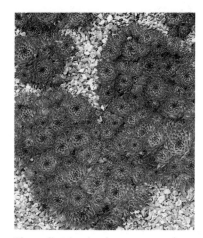
The small, rich red and grey rosettes of *Sempervivum tectorum calcareum* 'Mrs Giuseppi' build up into compact hummocks.

A pink drift of *Silene schafta* mingles with *Campanula portenschlagiana*.

Silene schafta

Not an outstanding beauty, this plant has nevertheless earned its place in the rockery by its adaptability to most conditions and by its long flowering period, from July to October. In spring it is freshly decked out in apple-green leaves, which are later accompanied by a spread of magenta-pink blooms, standing some 6 in. high.

Silene schafta grows with equal zest in sun or light shade, in sand or clay. It associates well with some of the more showy bellflowers such as *Campanula portenschlagiana*, which flowers at the same time.

HOW TO GROW
Plant from autumn to spring, 12 in. apart, in ordinary well-drained soil – preferably one that is deep and moisture-retentive. The plants spread slowly, and the far-ranging, fleshy roots resent disturbance. Propagation is therefore best from seeds sown in spring, or in summer from young stem cuttings grown under glass.

Silene schafta, a very long-lived rock plant, admirably fills a pocket in a rock garden with its bright blooms.

Regular shearing in spring stops the wall germander from sprawling.

Teucrium chamaedrys (WALL GERMANDER)

The modest wall germander has won its way into rock-gardeners' hearts by its quiet charm and reliability. A 6-9 in. high evergreen sub-shrub that enjoys all the sun it can get – but that will also tolerate some shade – it will eventually achieve a spread of some 15 in. It has dark green, slightly crinkled leaves and is decorated from July to September with spikes of lavender-pink, hooded flowers, the lower lips of which are sometimes spotted with red and white. There is a white-flowered form, and one with leaves gaily – though variably – splashed with gold.

HOW TO GROW
Plant from autumn to spring, in well-drained soil and in sun or partial shade. In cold gardens, the shrubs benefit from wall shelter. Propagate in late spring from cuttings grown under glass. Prune off frosted shoot tips in spring, at the same time reducing vigorous shoots by up to half.

If the mass of evergreen young foliage on *Teucrium chamaedrys* is clipped in spring it will produce robust growth ideal for edging.

Thymus × citriodorus (LEMON-SCENTED THYME)

Believed to be a hybrid of the culinary thyme (*Thymus vulgaris*), lemon-scented thyme is a rather more delicate plant which bears pink flowers from June to August.

There are a number of decorative varieties, 3-8 in. high and spreading to 15 in. across, which have aromatic leaves that can be used in cooking. The best is 'E. B. Anderson', whose foliage forms a spreading carpet of sunshine gold. 'Silver Queen' bears leaves of variegated green and silver, and 'Aureus' has suffused yellow foliage that ages to yellow-green.

HOW TO GROW
Plant thymes from autumn to spring in sandy, well-drained soil and in full sun. For ground-cover, space plants 12 in. apart. The plant also does well on walls and in paving crevices. Propagate in late summer by cuttings under glass. Prune hard – by up to half – in spring, to keep the plants compact.

Above the strongly aromatic, lemon-scented leaves of *Thymus × citriodorus* appear clusters of tiny flowers, barely ⅛ in. across.

Thymus × citriodorus 'Aureus' is a fine year-round golden foliage plant.

Thymus drucei (WILD THYME)

All attempts to re-create the short, flower-studded turf of the alpine meadow in this country have failed. In Britain's gardens the grasses grow lush and tall, and soon smother the small flowers planted among them. However, a very passable imitation of an alpine lawn can be achieved by planting the rock garden with varieties of wild thyme. Set about 8 in. apart, they will knit together in a year to form a 3 in. thick flowery carpet from June to August, and grey-green cover for the rest of the year.

Good cultivars of *Thymus drucei* (syns *T. praecox arcticus* and *T. serpyllum*) include 'Coccineus', with crimson flowers and deep green leaves; 'Annie Hall', pink flowers with pale green foliage; 'Lanuginosa', which has mauve flowers and grey, hairy leaves; and 'Albus', a white-flowered form with light green leaves.

The thymes' foliage can be varied by intermingling a few low, spreading foliage plants such as *Geranium dalmaticum*, whose leaves become ruddy in autumn. Into this groundwork can be introduced some of the lovely flowers that grow in high alpine turf – for example, the deep blue, trumpet gentian (*Gentiana acaulis*), the lavender-blue *Viola cornuta* (best in its dwarf form, 'Minor') and the purple-blue, orange-centred *Aster alpinus*. These beautiful little blooms also make an addition to the flowering season covered by the thymes, giving an extra month of colour at each end of the period.

Just a few taller plants, grown in isolation, will break up the horizontal habit of this miniature lawn. Try the April-blooming purple pasque flower (*Pulsatilla vulgaris*) with a group or two of dwarf bulbs, such as narcissi or crocuses, to provide colour in early spring.

HOW TO GROW
Thymus drucei: see T. × citriodorus.
Aster alpinus: see p. 198.
Gentiana acaulis: see p. 207.
Geranium dalmaticum: see p. 207.
Pulsatilla vulgaris: see p. 214.
Viola cornuta: see p. 126.

Three varieties of *Thymus drucei* – pale pink 'Annie Hall' in the foreground, white 'Albus' in the centre and lilac 'Lanuginosa' at the back – form a fragrant midsummer carpet broken by purple *Aster alpinus* and *Viola cornuta*, with pink *Geranium dalmaticum*. *Pulsatilla vulgaris* – only seed heads remain – and *Gentiana acaulis* provided colour earlier.

Veronica (SPEEDWELL)

Speedwells produce an abundance of charming flower spikes in early summer and are easy-going, thriving in most soils and situations.

Veronica prostrata, which soon fills an open pocket in the rock garden or makes an informal edging to a border, puts on a massed display of deep blue flowers from May to July. It looks particularly effective when planted together with one of its pink varieties – either 'Rosea' or the deeper-hued 'Mrs Holt'.

The similar but shorter *V. teucrium* and its varieties can be grown in the rock garden and also in an alpine lawn, where they will contrast pleasingly with the lawn's creeping foundation plants – varieties of wild thyme (*Thymus drucei*) – and add their shades of blue to the thymes' crimsons and pinks. Two outstanding *V. teucrium* varieties are 'Crater Lake Blue', which is a rich blue, and 'Trehane', pale blue, with golden foliage.

Other pleasing colour combinations result from planting *V. teucrium* or any of its cultivars near the yellow of such vigorous, adaptable plants as *Hypericum olympicum* (especially the lemon-yellow form 'Citrinum') or *Linum flavum*. Flowering periods will not coincide exactly in some cases, but will always at least overlap.

HOW TO GROW
Veronica: plant between autumn and spring, in any ordinary well-drained soil, and in full sun. For edging, space V. prostrata and its forms 10-12 in. apart; in an alpine meadow, V. teucrium can be set at 8 in. intervals. Propagate all veronicas by division in spring.
Hypericum olympicum: see p. 209.
Linum flavum: see p. 210.
Thymus drucei: see p. 219.

Veronica prostrata sprawls beneath a bush of yellow-flowered *Hypericum olympicum*, with the flax *Linum flavum* to the left.

V. prostrata 'Mrs Holt' fills a border, edged with *Bellis perennis* 'Pomponette'. *Veronica teucrium* makes a vivid splash of colour in front of the woolly, greyish young stems of *Lychnis coronaria*.

Tiarella cordifolia (FOAM FLOWER)

For the dark, arid places beneath the overhangs in a rockery or beneath a tree canopy, where little else will grow, it would be a good idea to obtain a few plants of *Tiarella cordifolia*, which makes splendidly vigorous ground-cover. Its strawberry-like runners will carry it into the most unpromising situations, where its heart-shaped, dark-veined leaves give year-round cover.

From April to July it puts out the 10 in. high clusters of white, starry flowers that give the plant its English name. It is important to remember that it is a woodland plant and therefore the more closely you can reproduce its natural habitat the better it will respond.

HOW TO GROW
Plant in autumn or spring, in a cool, shady site, and in ordinary moist soil to which peat has been added. The plant spreads widely of its own accord, but, if necessary, propagate by division in autumn or spring.

In full bloom *Tiarella cordifolia* more closely resembles sparkler fireworks than the foam of its common name.

Viola biflora (YELLOW WOOD VIOLET)

After lying dormant all winter, this charming little plant puts forth handsome, vivid green, kidney-shaped leaves in early spring. The foliage is soon followed in April and May by small, bright yellow violets.

Viola biflora occurs naturally throughout the Northern Hemisphere, towards the northern limit of the tree line. With its rich colours, the plant makes a fine addition to the alpine lawn, where competing roots below ground, and growth above, will prevent it from becoming too dominant.

HOW TO GROW
Plant in spring or autumn, about 10 in. apart, in rich, well-drained but moisture-retentive soil. Although preferring cool shade, violas will grow in sun given moist soil. The plants spread naturally from the slowly creeping rootstock; in addition to division in autumn they may also be propagated by seeds sown in spring or when ripe.

The diminutively flowered *Viola biflora* blooms in a spring woodland garden with the common primrose, *Primula vulgaris*.

Flowers and leaves of *Viola biflora* have a vivid freshness of colouring.

Viola labradorica 'Purpurea' (VIOLET)

A wanderer by nature, this self-propagating violet can be let loose on the shady outer reaches of the rock garden or among mixed shrubs. In either site, it – and its descendants – will form an attractive low ground-cover of rich plum-purple foliage.

The lilac-mauve flowers that appear in April and May contrast deliciously with the dark evergreen leaves. The plant looks particularly effective grown near the silver foliage of the ornamental grass *Festuca glauca* or the golden leaves of the lemon-scented thyme *Thymus × citriodorus* 'E. B. Anderson'.

HOW TO GROW
Cultivation and propagation as for Viola biflora. The plant does best in shade, but is satisfactory in the sun needed for festuca and thyme.
Festuca glauca: see p. 132.
Thymus × citriodorus: see p. 219.

Viola labradorica 'Purpurea'.

Zauschneria californica.

Zauschneria californica
(CALIFORNIAN FUCHSIA)

By coincidence, the last plants in this section also sound the last notes in the symphony of the rock-gardener's year. *Zauschneria californica* makes a particularly triumphant entry; in September and October it bursts into life with 1½ in. long, scarlet tubular flowers that flame above grey-green foliage. Spreading to 2 ft, it is a vigorous plant, and if the rock garden is small it is probably better grown on a wall or bank in a sheltered part of the garden. A relative, *Z. cana*, is similar but has softer blooms of tangerine and narrower, ash-grey leaves.

HOW TO GROW
Plant in late spring, in any good, well-drained soil, in full sun and shelter. Not recommended for cold and exposed gardens, and elsewhere it is advisable to cover the crowns with a protective mulch in winter. Propagate in early summer by basal cuttings, rooted and overwintered under glass.

The Flower Arranger's Garden

A selection of the best flowers and foliage for indoor decoration

Even a comparatively small garden can be of tremendous value to the flower arranger if the plants are carefully selected to provide flowers and foliage all year round. There is no need to devote your entire garden to flowers for cutting. It should be sufficient to maintain a border – or part of one – devoted to plants that yield an unfailing variety of foliage.

All flower arrangers have their own particular favourites. Nevertheless, it is still possible to nominate an arranger's basic collection. It would include: *Alchemilla mollis, Arum italicum pictum, Bergenia, Elaeagnus, Euonymus, Euphorbia, Hedera* (ivy), *Helleborus, Hosta,* and *Sedum* × 'Autumn Joy'.

Alchemilla mollis has feathery, lime-green flowers that enhance any arrangement. The beautiful arrow-shaped, white-veined leaves of *Arum italicum pictum* grow larger month by month. They come up in November or earlier and may well be usable in arrangements as late as June.

The glossy green leather-like foliage of *Bergenia* helps to create splendid effects for the flower arranger all year round. The leaves of *B. crassifolia*

are spoon-shaped, those of *B. cordifolia* rounded. In addition, both species produce clusters of enchanting, bell-shaped pink flowers in spring.

For bringing a touch of sunlight to a dark corner of the house in winter, few foliage plants can match the evergreen leaves of *Elaeagnus pungens* 'Maculata', splashed with gold, or *E. p.* 'Variegata', edged with cream-yellow. Marrying them with winter-flowering heathers adds to the radiance.

Euonymus is a hardy, small-leaved evergreen shrub whose popularity has steadily increased over the past few years. Some forms have variegated foliage that will light up any winter arrangement. Among the best are *E. fortunei* 'Silver Queen', whose leaves have broad white edges, and *E. japonicus* 'Macrophyllus Albus', with silver-splashed leaves.

Euphorbias are attractive plants that remain fresh-looking long after cutting. A long-time favourite is *E. wulfenii*, which puts out spikes of lime-green flowers from March to May. *E. griffithii* 'Fireglow' blazes with flame-orange flowers in early spring and mingles magnificently with azaleas. More early spring colour is provided by *E. polychroma*, whose

bright yellow combines beautifully with the golden foliage of *Philadelphus coronarius* 'Aureus'. From early spring to summer there is *E. robbiae*, refreshing as late as June and July with its faded but still firm yellow-green floral bracts and rosettes of dark evergreen leaves.

Hedera (ivy) is an essential stand-by for the flower arranger. Its hardy evergreen foliage is always available. Perhaps the most useful form is the rather delicate green-and-white *H. canariensis* 'Variegata'. But also well worth growing is *H. colchica* 'Dentata Variegata', which has large green leaves beautifully edged with cream.

Hellebores and hostas

Flower arrangers have a special affection for *Helleborus*, another genus which combines beauty and longevity when cut. *H. lividus corsicus* (syn. *H. argutifolius*) bears large heads of open cup-shaped green flowers, and the thickly clustered drooping bells of *H. foetidus*, the stinking hellebore, are also green. Both bloom from late winter to late spring. *H. orientalis*, the lenten rose, brightens up the end of winter with its range of purples, crimsons, pinks and white. But loveliest of all perhaps is the pure white, golden-centred *H. niger*, the Christmas rose, which in an arrangement with yellow jasmine can bring springtime indoors in midwinter.

Among the many hostas, the forms with grey-green leaves are especially good for cutting in midsummer. They include *H. fortunei* 'Aureomarginata', which has gold-edged leaves, and *H. f.* 'Albopicta', whose young spring foliage is a striking lime-green and buff-yellow.

In early spring an oriental touch can be brought to the home by single sprays – no more – of flowering cherries (*Prunus*). If you live in an area where azaleas and rhododendrons grow well, spring would also be the time for an extravaganza indoors. If not, then you can seize your moment in early summer with cuttings from philadelphus, or in autumn with a display incorporating the brilliant berries of cotoneaster or the equally decorative fruits of pyracanthus.

Hellebores predominate in this cool March arrangement – *H. foetidus, H. orientalis* and *H. lividus corsicus* – to which zest is added by the flowers of *Erica carnea, Daphne odora,* forced *Jasminum polyanthum,* and the variegated leaves of *Euonymus fortunei.*

Tulips and polyanthus – among the many heralds of spring – make a warm apricot and pink glow in this April bouquet. Yellow forsythia and white cherry blossom also feature strongly. Other flowers include pink flowering currant (*Ribes sanguineum*), green *Helleborus foetidus* and white *Pieris floribunda.* Amongst the foliage visible is variegated ivy, mahonia and bergenia.

Roses

*Rich colours, heady scents and diversity of form put
the rose high among garden favourites*

———◆———

IN MEDIEVAL TIMES the rose was named 'Flos Florum', the flower
of flowers. Adopted as the special flower of the Virgin, it was
the symbol of both earthly and heavenly perfection. In modern
times, the rose continues to reign supreme, both as a symbol of
purity and as a joy for the gardener.

It is, though, hardly possible to conceive of 'the rose' as a
singular object; garden roses have attained a diversity which
would have seemed impossible two centuries ago. There are
roses for every garden and almost every garden position.
Although today they are seen in every country of the world, they
are in fact plants that originated in the Northern Hemisphere.
Many of the 100 or so wild species, grown in their original form,
are valuable garden shrubs.

A single, short flowering period was the expected norm with
virtually all roses until the beginning of the last century. This is
still to be expected of most 'old-fashioned' roses. And such is
the beauty and scent of the old Musks and Albas, the Centifolias
and Damasks that it would be unreasonable to expect more.
These are the shrubs to associate with the herbaceous plants that
celebrate the pleasures of early summer – backed by foxgloves
and hollyhocks, with a tumble of paeonies and pinks at their
foot, they make an unforgettable picture.

Modern roses, however, flower from late June until the frosts
of autumn. As a result of hybridisation programmes these roses
appear now in almost every colour – only true blue is missing.

Each gardener has to decide what his needs are. If it is for
perfection of individual bloom, a row of Hybrid teas in the
kitchen garden will suffice. But if it is for all-round garden
ornament the associations which follow provide a broader view
of these marvellous flowers.

A glorious spread of 'Plena', a sweetly scented, double-flowered variety of the species
Rosa californica. Like other species roses, it stands up well against pests and diseases.

HYBRID TEA (LARGE-FLOWERED BUSH) ROSES

The forbears of these plants were known as Tea-scented roses, from a fancied resemblance between their delicate fragrance and that of tea. And though the scent has changed considerably since Hybrid perpetuals were first crossed with Teas in the 1870s, the name has stuck.

Quite probably, Hybrid teas represent the ultimate in rose-breeding skills. Certainly, the group embraces plants that produce the largest and most perfectly formed roses, and in a colour range that seems to except only true blue. From *Rosa chinensis* in the group's ancestry comes its ability to flower from June to November – so-called perpetual blooming – while many other classic species have contributed beauty of foliage and form.

Opinions vary about the place of Hybrid teas in the garden. Some people fervently believe that they should be grown only in large, important masses, with no more accompaniment than finely mown turf, while others feel that their beauty is given greater prominence if the plants are grown in groups of single varieties, or as the centrepiece a group. All courses are worth trying.

HOW TO GROW
Plant in October or November, or in March, in any good, well-drained soil, which should be enriched with well-rotted manure or compost and with bonemeal. Hybrid teas that are planted in March may be pruned back to two or three buds before planting; established plants should also be pruned at this time. Propagate by budding in summer or by hardwood cuttings in autumn.

A harmony in gold is created by 'Spek's Yellow' backed by a laburnum.

Golden-crowned stems of 'Spek's Yellow' rise from an underplanting of purple-leaved sage, which hides the rose's spindly base.

'Spek's Yellow'

'Spek's Yellow' was bred in Holland and introduced to this country in 1948. It is one of the brightest of roses; a brilliant gold that positively glows, even from a distance. The flower shape, too, is very distinctive: as the classically pointed bud opens, many of the petals roll back along their length, giving the open flowers a somewhat spiky appearance.

'Spek's Yellow' grows into a rather gawky bush with sparse, thin foliage. It is therefore best, perhaps, for a grouping in the shrub border with other plants in front. It could, for example, be planted to emerge from clumps of lavender or purple-leaved sage (*Salvia officinalis* 'Purpurascens'), when its straggly base would be hidden. This is an association that will harmonise ever more closely.

HOW TO GROW
See above.

'Josephine Bruce' has a velvety texture that seems to glow in half-light.

The variety is very vigorous and needs to be pruned back to inward-growing buds to control its sprawling habit.

'Josephine Bruce'

A deep, dark dusky red, with a perfume to match, is everyone's idea of a rose. That such a colour and scent are difficult to produce is made apparent by the fact that 'Josephine Bruce' has held this particular niche in the rose world for over 30 years, without any real challenger.

One of 'Josephine Bruce's' parents is the famous 'Crimson Glory', which for years from its introduction in the mid-1930s was the most favoured red rose of all. Though not as dark as its daughter, it is clearly the source of much of 'Josephine Bruce's' scent. A disadvantage with the older variety is its rather weak 'neck' – the stem behind the flower – which causes the bloom to fall forward. However, this failure becomes a virtue in a tall plant such as 'Climbing Crimson Glory', which from high on a wall, is able to gaze down on its admirers.

HOW TO GROW
See above.

'Pascali'

Raised in Belgium in 1963 from a marriage between 'Queen Elizabeth' and 'White Butterfly', 'Pascali' is one of the most successful pale Hybrid teas we have. It is very nearly white, with only a hint of cream at the centre.

White petals, whether they belong to camellias, lilies or roses, are highly susceptible to the vagaries of the weather, but 'Pascali', with its slim, tight buds, resists wind damage better than most. Although the open flower may become bruised with pink spots in heavy rain, it is still probably the most robust of all white Hybrid teas.

Virtually scentless, 'Pascali' is nevertheless extremely attractive with its snowy blooms gleaming against a rich, dark green foliage. It is a tall, elegant, upright grower and averages about 3½ ft in height. The plentiful flowers are usually produced one to each long stem, making them ideal for cutting.

To cover the bare stems of 'Pascali', underplant it with *Tiarella cordifolia* (foam flower), which will provide a carpet of handsome leaves and, in May and June, 6 in. spikes of creamy-white flowers.

HOW TO GROW
See p. 226.

'Pascali' grown as a standard rose is used here to punctuate bushes of the same variety and lend form to the group.

'Grandpa Dickson'

A. Dickson & Sons, the Ulster firm of rose breeders, first produced this hybrid in 1966. With an ancestry that includes 'Kordes' Perfecta', 'Governador Braga da Cruz' and 'Piccadilly', 'Grandpa Dickson' is a credit to them all.

A straight, sturdy, vigorous plant, some 3 ft tall, it produces masses of glossy, dark green leaves and, in summer and autumn, great trusses of shapely flowers. These are generally a clear, pale yellow when they open, but this colour matures to a creamy-yellow tinged with green and with the faintest touch of pink at the edges; they have a light, sweet fragrance. It is a tough rose, which will take wet weather and drought alike with equanimity.

It is a good plant for many different situations, but as an idea for an association for a small garden you might try a grouping of five 'Grandpa Dicksons' in front of a *Berberis thunbergii* 'Atropurpurea', which will provide a royal-purple background for the yellow flowers. The roses, planted a couple of feet apart, would leave room for a few clumps of narcissi. To continue the yellow motif, you could plant any yellow strain of polyanthus – *Primula × polyantha (thomasinii)* – which, when they have finished flowering in mid-May, could be split up into a nursery bed to await replanting in November.

During the summer, the polyanthus could be replaced by *Nicotiana alata* 'Lime Green', a tobacco plant whose acidic yellow-green flowers set off 'Grandpa Dickson' to perfection and add a delicious scent to the evening air.

HOW TO GROW
'Grandpa Dickson': *see p. 226.*
Berberis thunbergii: see p. 253.
Narcissus: see p. 165.
Nicotiana alata: see p. 46.
Primula (Polyanthus group): see p. 52.

A late August group of 'Grandpa Dickson' against a background of *Berberis thunbergii*, with *Nicotiana alata* 'Lime Green'.

'Madame Butterfly'

'Madame Butterfly' is a sport of the old, but well-loved, blush-white rose 'Ophelia', introduced by William Paul in 1912 and still often held to be the model of a Hybrid tea. It stands about 2½ ft tall, while its flowers are of moderate size, graceful and elegant in comparison with some of the monster roses bred after the Second World War.

'Madame Butterfly' has flowers of the same classic, pointed, Hybrid tea shape, but it is shell-pink slightly flushed with yellow, and has deeper tones at the bud stage. It is scented, generous in flowers and vigorous, and is one of the few Hybrid teas that will succeed on chalk, provided the soil is well cultivated and the plant well fed. It is, however, attractive to some destructive insects.

Whether Hybrid teas look better formally planted or thrust into the hurly-burly of the shrub bed or mixed border is an argument that will probably persist for ever. The formal school insists that they require symmetry, and associate best with neat, prim plants, especially box and clipped herbs. Edgings of clipped lavender (*Lavandula*) or rue (*Ruta*) give beds of Hybrid teas a neat finish, and if other flowers are wanted among the roses then they should be well-behaved bedding plants.

Following this discipline into a town garden, you might create there a small, slightly raised bed 10 ft square and plant in it five bushes of 'Madame Butterfly'. Edge the bed with a low hedge of 'Jackman's Blue' rue, the steel-blue foliage blending beautifully with the soft pink roses. Then, planted symmetrically between the roses, you could set clumps of blue or white pansies (*Viola × wittrockiana*).

HOW TO GROW
'Madame Butterfly': *see p. 226.*
Lavandula angustifolia: see p. 291.
Ruta graveolens: see p. 312.
Viola × wittrockiana: see p. 59.

Clipped clumps of blue-green rue *Ruta graveolens* 'Jackman's Blue' make a tidy edge to two circular beds of the delicate pink 'Madame Butterfly'. Masses of sky-blue pansies *Viola × wittrockiana* fill the space between, and complete the July colour scheme.

'Whisky Mac'

There is a particular delight about apricot roses – so long as they are kept well clear of the fiercer pinks and reds – that makes them difficult to resist. 'Whisky Mac' is among the most popular. Brilliant orange-yellow with a fine bud shape and delicious perfume, it stands out strikingly from the bronze young foliage.

Sadly, it declines noticeably after the first few years and needs, more than most Hybrid teas, to be treated as a 'bedding rose' – that is, replaced often.

A similar colour, though softer, occurs in 'Lady Hillingdon', an old rose with narrow, pointed buds, slim, graceful leaves and an open habit. It has an art nouveau elegance and is remarkably long-lived. Grown as a single bush, as the tallest specimen in a bed of rather special plants, it produces occasional flowers over many weeks.

HOW TO GROW
See p. 226.

The rich tangerine-and-gold blooms of 'Whisky Mac' gleam against the deep holly green of mature foliage.

FLORIBUNDA (CLUSTER-FLOWERED BUSH) ROSES

Next to Hybrid teas, Floribundas are the most popular of the rose groups. In fact, in abundance of blossom and variety of colour, they may even better the Hybrid teas, their only drawback being that their flowers lack the rich perfume of the more modern Hybrid teas. Their branches are armed with hooked thorns.

Floribundas evolved through a crossing of the now seldom-grown Dwarf Polyantha roses with a number of Hybrid teas. The Polyanthas – descended from the wild climbing species *Rosa multiflora* – supplied the large, clustering flower heads, and the Hybrid teas passed on their size, colour variation and form. All Floribundas flower during June and July, and again, usually, in September and October.

Most Floribundas are seen to their best advantage when grown in a roses-only bed in the middle of a lawn. However, well placed single specimens can also present a good appearance in a mingling of smaller, unrelated plants.

HOW TO GROW
Plant Floribundas in the same way as for Hybrid teas. Pruning, however, need not be so severe, and should consist of shortening the strongest shoots back to six or seven buds from the base and the removal of weaker or damaged stems. Propagate by cuttings or by budding.

'Chinatown'

It is a glorious feature of most wild roses that they carry not just two or three flowers at the ends of their flowering stalks, but a whole mass that, from a distance, conveys the impression of one enormous bloom. Obviously, if this habit could be married to a variety of colours, it would be of great value in the garden, and some plant breeders have spent their lives creating such unions.

'Chinatown' is a recent Danish introduction, a vigorous bush of bright green foliage, covered for months with heads of yellow, fragrant flowers touched with pink on the outer petals. Lightly pruned, it behaves more like a shrub than a colourful plant for the rose bed, and can be used to make a fine hedge, 5-6 ft high.

'Allgold', similar to 'Chinatown' though only half its size, is one of the best yellow roses ever raised.

HOW TO GROW
See above.

At the edge of a rose bed a row of golden 'Chinatown' is bordered by grey *Stachys lanata* 'Silver Carpet' and purple *Nepeta*.

'Allgold' mingles beautifully with *Clematis* 'Countess of Lovelace'.

'Frensham'

'Frensham' was introduced in 1946, an opportune time for a new rose, when, after years of wartime austerity, people wanted beauty again. And, despite its fierce thorns and susceptibility to mildew, its popularity has never waned.

Being a Floribunda it can be grown, hard-pruned, as a normal bedding rose. The lovely, semi-double, blood-red flowers eventually open sufficiently to show a heraldic boss of golden stamens – a show that is maintained from early July until autumn. But such is its vigour, even on thin, acid soils, that it is better treated as a shrub; a single bush will reach 6-8 ft in height, making a mound of bright green foliage that starts to flower early in the season. Used with spring-flowering shrubs and good ground-cover, 'Frensham' is a fine garden plant; it also makes an admirable hedge. There is also a climbing form of 'Frensham'.

HOW TO GROW
See above.

'Frensham' has been popular since it was raised nearly 40 years ago as a seedling of the celebrated dark red 'Crimson Glory'.

A climbing form of 'Frensham' provides vivid, vigorous wall cover.

'Iceberg'

The charming conceit of a whole garden or border devoted to both white flowers and white foliage has become fairly widespread. Vita Sackville-West did not invent the notion, but her exquisite white garden at Sissinghurst, visited by many thousands of people each year, has certainly done a great deal to advance it, and to encourage more gardeners to attempt similar ventures themselves.

If you include Species roses as well as hybrids (Sissinghurst has the huge *Rosa longicuspis* over the white garden's central pergola), there are plenty of white roses to choose from; but the Species flower just once a year, and few white hybrids make much of a display.

An honourable and invaluable exception is the lovely 'Iceberg'. It actually does better if treated as a flowering shrub, without hard pruning and without the company of its relations to pass on the dread black spot disease. In this way it makes an open shrub with delicate, slightly greyish leaves and great sprays of pure white flowers. The buds make perfect small buttonholes.

For a white border (or even just a white corner) the main backing plant could well be *Hoheria lyallii*, whose branches are weighed down with milk-white flowers in July or August. It could act as a frame to three 'Icebergs' planted 2 ft apart, so that eventually they will mingle into one bush. White hyacinths in between will give a spring bonus. As a final touch at the very front of the association, there could be white old-fashioned pinks (*Dianthus*) and *Stachys olympica* tumbling forward on to the path.

HOW TO GROW
'Iceberg': *see p. 229.*
Dianthus, old-fashioned pinks: see p. 80.
Hoheria lyallii: see p. 286.
Hyacinthus orientalis: see p. 157.
Stachys olympica: see p. 122.

In the rose garden at Polesden Lacey, Surrey, one of the finest white Floribundas, 'Iceberg', displays its snowy blooms.

'Lilac Charm' needs a little shade to stop its delicate tints fading.

'Blue Moon', a descendant of 'Sterling Silver', the first so-called blue rose, makes a superb long-lasting cut flower.

'Lilac Charm'

With roses, no gene for blueness exists – it was difficult enough to bring yellow into the garden rose spectrum, even though there were plenty of wild yellow species available as potential parents.

Yet hope continues to burn brightly in the breeders' breasts: if a mutant gene could produce pelargonidin, the pigment that enabled day-glow varieties like 'Super Star' to be created, then perhaps the truly blue rose is possible after all. The commercial rewards for introducing one would be very great indeed.

Meanwhile, grey, or lavender, or purplish roses have to be called blue: many, in an extraordinary way are most attractive. 'Blue Moon' is a silvery-lilac Hybrid tea of perfect form which is lovely as a cut flower, and beautifully fragrant. 'Lilac Charm' lives up to its name as one of the best 'blue' Floribundas. It looks well with the billowing grey foliage of *Artemisia* 'Lambrook Silver' and *Eucalyptus gunnii* that has been 'stooled' – cut down to ground level each spring.

HOW TO GROW
See p. 229.

'Queen Elizabeth'

One of the most famous of modern roses is 'Queen Elizabeth', first raised in California in 1954. It is a rose with many fine qualities. It is perhaps the best of all Floribundas for cutting, with its full, long-stemmed flowers of Hybrid tea shape and quality. Its colour is a perfect rose-pink, its scent is sweet, and it flowers almost continuously from midsummer to autumn. It is a strong rose, not prone to disease nor choosy as to soil.

Yet, it can fail if it is badly sited. It is stiff and tall, growing to 6 ft or more, and most of the flowers appear on the crown. This makes it an awkward plant in the rose garden, dwarfing most other varieties, and still worse as a rose hedge, for which it is often recommended. Its lower limbs should be shrouded; the ideal way to grow it perhaps, is as a shrub in a mixed border backed by a yew hedge, with low foliage shrubs in front to hide its gawky stems.

Try, for example, a group of three 'Queen Elizabeth' roses, planted in a triangle in a long, wide, mixed border which has a yew hedge behind, making a perfect backdrop for the fresh, pink flowers. In front of the roses you could plant two bushes of *Rosmarinus officinalis* 'Severn Sea' – about 3 ft high – and in front of these again, groups of 'Hidcote' lavender. To translate the idea to a smaller garden, one rose bush and one rosemary, again with lavender, would look just as well.

Encircled by dark green and grey plants, there is no danger of the pink roses clashing with the summer perennials, however bright they may be. Clumps of blue plants might come next in the border, then white and pale yellow flowers, then more low evergreens.

HOW TO GROW
'Queen Elizabeth': *see p. 229.*
Lavandula angustifolia 'Hidcote': *see p. 291.*
Rosmarinus officinalis: see p. 310.

'Queen Elizabeth', with *Rosmarinus officinalis* and *Lavandula angustifolia* 'Hidcote' in front, is backed by a yew hedge.

'Rosemary Rose'

The spiky habit of many hybrid roses is accentuated by drastic pruning methods designed to produce quality, rather than a quantity of flowers. This is a perfectly laudable course if you wish to make a mark at flower shows. But if you want a garden display that will last throughout the season, then you should impose a lighter pruning regime upon those favourite varieties that combine beauty of flower with good foliage.

Such roses, too, can be used in association with other plants to ensure that their particular part of the garden is not bare for half the year.

'Rosemary Rose' is a good plant to use in this way. It makes a wide-spreading bush whose new foliage is an attractive plum-purple before turning to green. Regular dead-heading ensures a continuous supply of young leaves, and of flowers, too. These open flatly to a dark carmine-pink, a colour that looks extremely well above the leaves. Clumps of the Corsican *Helleborus lividus-corsicus* make an interesting association.

HOW TO GROW
See p. 229.

The rosette-shaped blooms of 'Rosemary Rose', unusual in a Floribunda, are produced in large clusters.

MINIATURE ROSES

True to their name, Miniature roses, 10-16 in. high, look for all the world like tiny Floribundas, with miniature leaves and flowers in perfect proportion. Their origins lie in a diminutive mutant of the China rose, *Rosa chinensis minima* (syn. *R. rouletii*), crossed with some of the old Polyantha and some of the newer Floribunda cultivars. In the garden, they can be used to create miniature rose beds or to lend unusual interest to the rock garden; they also look splendid in the window-box or in any other small, decorative container – even a 5 in. earthenware pot.

Although Miniatures are the latest of the rose groups and contain relatively few cultivars, they show a wide range of colours – from scarlet through pink and buff-orange to yellow. Like their larger relatives, Miniature roses flower in June and July, and usually put on a second performance in autumn. The stems are almost thornless and the leaves are each composed of five or seven toothed leaflets.

The tiny 'Red Imp' (also called 'Maid Marion' or 'Mon Tresor') reaches a height of only 8-10 in., and is perfectly suited to rock gardens.

HOW TO GROW
Plant Miniatures in the same conditions as required for Hybrid teas, and prune in the same way as for Floribundas. Propagate by cuttings only, taking strong, non-flowering lateral shoots with heels in August or September. Those Miniatures grown from budded rootstocks soon lose their dwarf character.

'Baby Masquerade'

When massed, the kaleidoscope of colour presented by full-sized 'Masquerade' can be overwhelming, and sometimes a little difficult to fit into the garden scheme. 'Baby Masquerade', however, though just as richly hued, grows to no more than 15 in., and therefore does not impinge upon its neighbours.

It is a particularly lovely little rose for miniature cut-flower arrangements. The thimble-sized buds are pale orange with long sepals; as they open they are at first yellow and cup-shaped, but then, shading through pink to crimson, the petals roll back to make a final shape that looks for all the world like a tiny cactus dahlia.

For those who prefer less exuberant colours, the canary-yellow 'Gold Coin' would be ideal. Another advantage is that it is even more truly a Miniature than 'Baby Masquerade', since it seldom attains a height of more than 6 in. This is one of the best yellow Miniatures.

HOW TO GROW
See above.

The top of a wall makes an excellent site for tiny 'Baby Masquerade'.

'Gold Coin' is a bushy, compact dwarf; its small double flowers are among the finest of the yellow Miniatures.

'Perla de Monserrat'

'Small is beautiful' is a sentiment that appeals powerfully to that large number of rose breeders who, over the last half century, have been devoting considerable time and effort to producing miniature replicas of many of the classic rose cultivars.

'Perla de Monserrat', which looks like a tiny version of the Hybrid tea 'Lady Sylvia', first came on to the scene in 1945. And after almost 40 years, it is still one of the finest of the Miniature roses.

Never more than 12 in. high, it has beautifully shaped buds and flowers of a true, glowing rose-pink. It makes a splendid feature in the rock garden and looks especially enchanting if surrounded by a pool of sky-blue *Campanula cochleariifolia*.

HOW TO GROW
See above.

'Perla de Monserrat' emerges from a carpet of *Campanula cochleariifolia*.

Unusually for a double rose, 'Perla de Monserrat', one of the most beautiful Miniatures, has prominent yellow stamens.

SHRUB ROSES

As a rough definition, Shrub roses are hybrid species that are grown as shrubs – that is, they are given little or no pruning. Rose specialists divide the category up into several lesser groupings, but for practical purposes, these may be summed up as Old and Modern shrub roses. Old shrub roses have an ancestry that includes *Rosa × alba*, the White Rose of York, *R. × centifolia*, the cabbage or Provence rose, and *R. damascena*, the Damask rose.

Most Modern shrub roses are hybrids between wild species and members of such groups as Hybrid tea and Floribunda. All but a few flower intermittently from early summer to late autumn; some have single flowers, others semi-double or fully double, in a wide range of colours.

As might be expected, Shrub roses are extremely varied in habit, leaf shape and floral form. They have a lot of character and look equally well whether grown as specimens or as dominant members of an association.

HOW TO GROW
Plant Shrub roses in the same way as for Hybrid teas. Pruning should be limited to removing weak or damaged wood and any laterals that have borne flowers the previous year; cut soft tips back to firm wood on main growths. Propagate by cuttings or budding.

'Fantin-Latour'

Marcel Proust said of the rose paintings of his contemporary, Henri Fantin-Latour, 'The painter looks, and at the same time seems to see deep inside himself and inside the bouquet of flowers.' It seems only just, therefore, that a rose should be named after him; yet, surprisingly, the origin of this exquisite old-fashioned rose is unknown.

It appreciates good living – decent garden soil, preferably limy and in full sun. In these conditions it will make a bush 5 ft high and wide. The broad, smooth foliage frames the wide flowers that are carried in bunches. Only one or two open at a time so that, though it has only one season of flower, it is a relatively long one – through the latter half of June. The colour is the softest of rose-pinks, darkening towards the centre.

HOW TO GROW
See above.

'Fantin-Latour' flanks a pathway bordered by ground-cover plants that give greenery and colour when the roses are not in bloom.

The cool foliage of a hosta skirts a robust bush of 'Fantin-Latour'.

'Königin von Dänemark'

Like all forms of *Rosa × alba*, 'Queen of Denmark' is free from the rose scourges of black spot and mildew and will settle happily in most soils and conditions – substantial advantages for the busy gardener.

It has the deepest colour of all the *× alba* forms – a fine, clear pink. The double flowers seem to open rather slowly – an advantage in a plant that has but one flowering season. Flowers opening in succession, all accompanying one another at different stages of development, help to prolong the period of display. In the right kind of weather, their heavy scent will permeate the garden. The plant quickly builds into a large shrub, 6-8 ft in height and as much across.

It associates well with other roses – as a backing for smaller modern hybrids for example – but is equally splendid by itself, or as a companion to other shrubs that flower at the same time.

HOW TO GROW
See above.

'Königin von Dänemark' has the dense, gathered, semi-quartered petal formation that is typical of Old shrub roses.

A mature specimen of the rose blooms against the grey leaves of a *Pyrus*.

'Buff Beauty'

In the early years of this century the Rev. Joseph Pemberton, who lived, rather suitably, at Havering-atte-Bower, in Essex, raised a group of roses which he called Hybrid musks. Hybrid they certainly are, with a complicated family tree: but musk hardly at all, for the historic *Rosa moschata* plays only the smallest part in their ancestry. However, the Hybrid musks have inherited one of its attributes – the ability to cast their scent upon the air. On moist, warm evenings in late June and early July this fragrance is carried for a considerable distance.

'Buff Beauty' is a very lovely rose with fine heads of creamy flowers darkening to apricot in the centre. In habit it is rather like an enormous, lax Floribunda: pruned hard back, it can indeed be treated as one. But it is better either to support its natural fountain-like shape with an inverted pyramid of four stakes held by top rails, or to tie it loosely to a stout stake or pillar.

In spring, the ground at the foot of the pillar could be illuminated with Darwin tulips, scarlet and white, purple and white, or a glorious mixture. But when 'Buff Beauty' is in bloom, soft, uncompetitive perennials will show it to best advantage: a blue group of *Nepeta* × *faassenii* could melt into white oriental poppies – *Papaver orientale* 'Perry's White' – for example. This small herbaceous lake could be pierced with tall, gold and red-brown bearded irises to give muscle to an otherwise soft arrangement.

HOW TO GROW
'Buff Beauty': *see p. 233.*
Iris, bearded hybrids: see p. 97.
Nepeta × *faassenii: see p. 106.*
Papaver orientale: see p. 109.
Tulipa, Darwin: see p. 169.

In late June, a mass of 'Buff Beauty' stands surrounded by the tall bearded iris 'Staten Island', black-eyed *Papaver orientale* 'Perry's White' and delicate blue *Nepeta* × *faassenii*.

'Cecile Brunner'

The beauty of 'Cecile Brunner' lasts the season through. It is difficult to overpraise the slim buds, only an inch in length, which unfurl to display the softest conch-shell pink, gently tinted with a warm flush of dawn-yellow at the base of the petals.

It makes a bush 2 ft or so high; flowers, leaves and habit are all in proportion. The blooms are much in demand for miniature flower arrangements, and if this is one of your objects in growing it, it is wise to plant as well a sport from 'Cecile Brunner', called 'Bloomfield Abundance'. Individually, the flowers are almost identical, but are carried on a bigger, more lax bush in huge sprays that offer a magnificent show for many months.

The small size of bush is repeated in another highly desirable little rose, 'Perle d'Or'. Like a darker, more golden 'Cecile Brunner', it makes an admirable companion for it. The flowers are slightly larger, and open from pointed, tightly rolled buff-apricot buds to form pale apricot – almost white – clusters of blooms.

HOW TO GROW
See p. 233.

As well as a shrub form, 'Cecile Brunner' also exists as a climbing sport, seen here growing in glorious profusion up a wall.

'Cecile Brunner' combines exquisite flowers with robust growth.

'Constance Spry'

While most rose breeders have been concentrating upon bigger and better Hybrid teas and Floribundas, David Austin, of Wolverhampton, has been bringing the scent and shape of old-fashioned roses to new varieties.

'Constance Spry', introduced in 1961, is one of his great successes. Grown either as a soaring wall plant or as an enormous bush, its early summer display is stupendous. Huge, flat, double flowers, like those of the old Centifolias, almost hide the dark foliage. Their colour is a strong, clear pink and their scent sweetly aromatic.

The parents of 'Constance Spry' are now known to be the Floribunda 'Dainty Maid' and the old Gallica 'Belle Isis'. Growing all three together would make an attractive display of three different habits and shades of pink.

HOW TO GROW
See p. 233.

The large, densely petalled blooms of 'Constance Spry' are 4 in. across.

Unlike many Modern shrub roses, 'Constance Spry' flowers only once a year, but its superb display is fine compensation.

'Mme Hardy'

This is an old Damask rose, first raised in the Jardin de Luxembourg, Paris, in 1832. Probably a hybrid of *Rosa centifolia*, it has full white flowers, each a perfect circular cup with crowded, folded petals and a green eye; its scent is the true rich Damask fragrance used for centuries in the manufacture of the perfume, attar of roses. Tradition has it that Damasks were originally brought to Britain from Damascus by the Crusaders.

Whatever its origins, 'Mme Hardy' makes a strong, beautiful shrub of 5-6 ft in height and spread, with plenty of flowers in midsummer and fresh green leaves.

Every collector of Old shrub roses has his or her own way of growing them. At Charleston Manor, in East Sussex, for example, you can see a celebrated rose garden in a fold of the Downs, where round beds were carved out of lawns that slope down to a pool. Groups of roses were trained in each bed and, where necessary, supported upon wooden tripods. In other gardens, they are grown in mixed borders. But, wherever they are planted, one thing is certain: since the Old roses will not flower again after the midsummer flush, they need herbaceous and foliage plants near by to give colour for the rest of the year.

'Mme Hardy', for example, would look well in a flower bed about 15 ft square, with other Old roses and an underplanting of other old-fashioned flowers. The whole bed might be edged with 'Mrs Sinkins' pinks, which have evergreen foliage, while between the rose bushes you could plant clumps of hardy *Geranium endressii*, *Viola × wittrockiana* and some mignonette, *Reseda odorata*.

HOW TO GROW
'Mme Hardy': *see p. 233.*
Dianthus 'Mrs Sinkins': *see Modern pinks, p. 80.*
Geranium endressii: see p. 89.
Reseda odorata: see p. 53.
Viola × wittrockiana: see p. 59.

Bushes of 'Mme Hardy' rise from a bed of pink *Geranium endressii* edged with 'Inchmery' pinks and *Viola × wittrockiana*.

The second, autumn flowering of 'Mme Isaac Pereire' is often the finer.

'Mme Isaac Pereire'

Bourbon roses have nothing directly to do with the royal house of France. The origin of the name was a chance seedling grown on the Île de Bourbon (now called Réunion), in the Indian Ocean – a cross between a China and a Damask rose. This began a strain of roses that leads through the 19th century to our modern roses.

The flower of 'Mme Isaac Pereire' is the quintessence of what is regarded as an old-fashioned rose – a huge, full flower with a petal arrangement that seems to divide the bloom into four. The colour is a deep pink with purple undertones, and it is one of the most deliciously scented roses in the world. All this magnificence is borne on a huge, lax bush 6 ft or more in height which generally needs some support. With this in mind, the plant can even be used as a wall shrub.

'Mme Isaac Pereire' would be superb in a garden with room for a group that would combine the roses with double peonies, tulips, lilies and lilacs.

HOW TO GROW
See p. 233.

A full-grown bush of the richly coloured 'Mme Isaac Pereire' is surrounded by clumps of *Paeonia lactiflora* hybrids.

'Maigold'

There is a whole range of lovely little roses that are based upon *Rosa spinosissima*. One of these, from the Altai Mountains of Siberia, is *R. s. altaica*, a fine, vigorous and very early flowerer. It has been used a good deal by the German rose-breeding firm of Kordes to produce wide, single or semi-double roses on strong open bushes, whose names often start with 'Frühlings', meaning 'Spring' in German.

'Frühlingstag' is a parent of 'Maigold', which is splendid either as a pillar or for covering a low wall, growing as it does to about 12 ft in height. However, it can be grown as a loose, open shrub about 8 ft high. Among the glossy foliage, the bronze-yellow flowers stand out, cup-shaped, as if to hold the intense fragrance for which 'Maigold' is famed. Its other parent is a pink Floribunda that provides the gene for 'Maigold's' continuity of flowering which the 'Frühlings' are apt to lack. However, its double flowers are only recurrent if they are quickly dead-headed, when a second crop will be produced in autumn.

HOW TO GROW
See p. 233.

After 'Maigold' has flowered in early summer, it should be dead-headed immediately to ensure further blooms.

'Penelope'

Like the rest of its race, 'Penelope' can be treated as a very robust Floribunda, but should be allowed to get big – 6-8 ft high and as much across. Like this, it makes a splendid backing for herbaceous plants.

The first flowering is of incredible profusion. The buds begin dark pink, then open very pale, and end as creamy-white. All three colours occur on enormous broadly domed clusters, often a foot across, and throw out a fragrance that will float through the garden.

'Penelope's' only disadvantage is that petals, in some conditions, wither on the plant before falling. This makes early dead-heading essential; it is in any case desirable, since it encourages a good second crop of flowers, which if left on the bush will produce autumn hips.

HOW TO GROW
See p. 233.

'Penelope' is noted for the reliability of its flowering and colour.

One of the most popular of all Hybrid musk roses, 'Penelope' makes a splendid specimen flowering shrub.

'Nevada'

This lovely shrub was bred in Spain and introduced to Britain by its raiser, Pedro Dot, in 1927. One of its parents was a Hybrid tea; the other is recorded as *Rosa moyesii*, that marvellous blood-red Himalayan, but doubts have been raised about this.

Questions of origin apart, this is a noble and extraordinary plant that sends a fountain of almost entirely thornless stems shooting 8 ft into the air. In June and July, these and their pale foliage disappear behind a foaming bounty of blossom. Each flower is single, unfurling cream and ageing to white, around 3 in. across and with a central boss of yellow stamens. Further flowers appear as the summer weeks go on, but nothing subsequently approaches that first wild generosity of bloom.

It is this, therefore, that should be celebrated by the chosen association. If 'Nevada' were backed by dark evergreens the effect would be even more impressive, but in most gardens an 8 ft shrub is itself likely to be in the back row.

In front and to one side, therefore, you might plant large-flowered delphinium hybrids, whose blue spires attain two-thirds the height of the rose. Flowering times will coincide and, as with the rose, some desultory later flowering could be expected. On the other side, and running to the front of the border, you could put in *Campanula persicifolia* whose 2½ ft spikes are covered with blue or white bells for weeks on end. Contrast in texture might be provided by *Tradescantia* × *andersoniana*, whose spiky leaf pattern – vertical at first, then arching – is topped by pale blue, three-petalled flowers. Each is short-lived, but the display is of summer-long duration. The fresh blue and white colouring of this association could be maintained into autumn by a bush of *Caryopteris* × *clandonensis*, which would also hide the bases of the delphiniums.

HOW TO GROW
'Nevada': *see p. 233.*
Campanula persicifolia: see p. 72.
Caryopteris × *clandonensis: see p. 259.*
Delphiniums, large-flowered: see p. 79.
Tradescantia × *andersoniana: see p. 124.*

A magnificent display of 'Nevada' stands like a foaming cascade with *Delphinium* hybrids, *Tradescantia* × *andersoniana* in the foreground, the pale blue bells of *Campanula persicifolia* and, to the left, the narrow, grey-green leaves of *Caryopteris* × *clandonensis*.

'Nevada' bears larger blooms than other perpetual-flowering Shrub roses.

'Roseraie de l'Hay'

Having given the world 'Blanc Double de Coubert', the same firm of Cochet-Cochet in France introduced 'Roseraie de l'Hay', one of the best of all roses to grow either as an individual specimen or as a 6 ft high impenetrable hedge. Probably a sport from *Rosa rugosa rubra*, it can, like the species, take even coastal exposure.

After the first fine flush of flower it continues to delight eye and nose – its perfume is positively intoxicating – until autumn. Even then, the leaves turn brilliantly yellow, to make a final eye-catching display.

But in mixed plantings considerable care is required if its combination of vivid purple flowers and glossy green leaves is not to jar on sensitive observers. The grey foliage of lavenders, sages and other Mediterranean 'herb-shrubs' helps to soften its brilliance.

HOW TO GROW
See p. 233.

If 'Roseraie de l'Hay' is planted at 1½-2 ft intervals, it will form, as here, a thick hedge in three or four years.

'Souvenir du Docteur Jamain'

The deep, velvety smoothness of the Hybrid tea rose 'Josephine Bruce' seems to be as dark as a rose can be. But several shades deeper still is 'Docteur Jamain', which in some lights appears to be perfectly black. As with all so-called Hybrid perpetuals, it is actually occasional not perpetual in its flowering – but even when the first June flush is over, flowers continue to appear in abundance.

'Docteur Jamain' is not a strong grower: at the National Trust's collection of old and historic roses at Mottisfont Abbey, in Hampshire, it is given the protection of a wall. It is a plant to associate with other period flowers such as Darwin or cottage tulips, old-fashioned pinks and, for the beginning of autumn, *Colchicum speciosum*, so providing interest throughout the entire season.

HOW TO GROW
See p. 233.

'Souvenir du Docteur Jamain' is possibly the most fragrant and the deepest-coloured of all roses.

This historic Old rose associates perfectly with old-fashioned pinks.

'Tuscany Superb'

In John Gerard's *Herball*, first published in 1597, he describes a number of roses that were in cultivation in his day. One of them is what he calls the 'Velvet Rose'; rose names change with the centuries, and it is very likely that Gerard's 'Velvet Rose' is our 'Tuscany'.

Actually, there are two 'Tuscanies', both an unusual maroon. The original has semi-double flowers with yellow anthers, while the other is more fully double and is therefore known as 'Tuscany Superb'.

The 'Tuscanies' make 4-5 ft upright bushes and produce fewer suckers than most gallicas. However, like most old-fashioned roses, they have but one flowering period. For this reason, later flowering herbaceous plants should be grown at their feet; or the stems can act as supports for a morning glory, or late-sown sweet peas.

HOW TO GROW
See p. 233.

Grown up the stems of 'Tuscany Superb', *Ipomoea tricolor* provides interest when the rose has finished its one flowering spell.

Velvet-petalled, golden-stamened, 'Tuscany Superb' lives up to its name.

'Versicolor'

For centuries this cultivar of *Rosa gallica* was known as *R. mundi*. 'Versicolor' began, probably in the early 17th century, as a sport of the Apothecary's Rose (*R. g.* 'Officinalis') and from time to time it produces stems that revert back to its ancestor. Anyone growing 'Versicolor', therefore, may well end up with an Apothecary's Rose as well. Both are lovely little shrubs, 3-4 ft in height, that make small thickets with their suckering stems.

The Apothecary's Rose has flowers of a strong, clear red, which are heavily fragrant: they are flat and semi-double, making a fine show in June and, further north, well into July. 'Versicolor' has similar attributes, except that the flowers are striped red and pink like a fairground awning or Blackpool rock.

The small size and historical connections of these roses make them admirable associates for a herb garden. All have the added virtue of aromatic, and often decorative, foliage that maintains interest when the plants are not in flower.

HOW TO GROW
See p. 233.

Pruned hard, 'Versicolor' makes a splendid low, thick hedge. Here it divides a vegetable garden from a flower garden

The Apothecary's Rose is also known as the Red Rose of Lancaster.

'Sarah van Fleet'

Where a substantial hedge is needed to divide one part of the garden from another, no rose is more effective than 'Sarah van Fleet', which gained the Royal Horticultural Society's Award of Merit in 1962. This fine Rugosa rose makes a bushy 6 ft shrub which blooms perpetually from June to autumn, with large, semi-double, scented flowers of an unusual mallow-pink with a hint of blue. The wrinkled leaves are shiny and of a fresh, bright green; they unfold before the flowers, making a hedge that is beautiful for many months. However, the plant is so prickly that it may be too fierce for a boundary hedge – at least in a place where children might fall into it.

Therefore, it might be better to plant 'Sarah van Fleet' as a divider within the garden – say, as a rose hedge of eight bushes planted 4 ft apart to separate the flower garden from the kitchen garden beyond. There could be a narrow bed on the flower-garden side and paving on the other.

HOW TO GROW
See p. 233.

'Sarah van Fleet' has a rich fragrance.

'William Lobb' changes colour as it ages.

'William Lobb'

Probably the first Moss rose in Britain was *Rosa centifolia muscosa*, grown at the Chelsea Physic Garden in 1727. It created quite a stir, and subsequent sports of different form and colour were in great demand. *R. c. muscosa* is still well worth growing for its lovely, scented, shell-pink flowers. The moss referred to in the name is a green fuzziness on flower stalks and buds that is heavily aromatic and sticky to the touch.

'William Lobb' was introduced in France in 1855. It is a fine, deep purple-magenta that pales with age; moss is conspicuous on the buds, but vanishes as the flowers open.

All Moss roses are lax in growth, flopping about in a rather ungainly manner unless given some sort of support. When the flowering season is over, the bushes look rather shabby and undistinguished; however, in a mixed border this disadvantage can be concealed by a selection of later-flowering herbaceous plants.

HOW TO GROW
See p. 233.

CLIMBERS AND RAMBLERS

Some rose specialists regard Climbers and Ramblers as two distinct groups, but since both climb and produce cultivars with common characteristics, it is reasonable to join them under the same heading. Ramblers produce several strong new stems from their bases each year. These carry the best and most prolific flowers the following year in the plants' single display, which takes place during June and July. Ramblers are, in fact, climbing plants of limited agility, and as such make perfect pillar roses.

Climbers, on the other hand, can make strong stems from any part of the plant. Their height potential is far greater than that of Ramblers, and they are useful for fanning out upon walls or for scrambling up trees to produce a burst of colour among the high branches. Some Climbers flower just once a year, but others bloom at intervals from June until autumn.

HOW TO GROW
Plant Climber and Rambler roses in the same conditions as Hybrid teas, but close to the wall or support over or upon which they are intended to grow. Prune Climbers in spring by cutting back the lateral flowering shoots to two or three buds, and prune Ramblers by cutting flower-bearing stems back to ground level immediately after flowering; tie new, developing stems in to replace them in the following year. Propagate by cuttings or budding.

'Bobbie James' (RAMBLER)

The charming idea of putting climbing roses up superannuated fruit trees has spread from large gardens which have plenty of space to small ones. The effect is truly delightful.

The idea of naturally rambling Ramblers is full of potential if the right rose is chosen. 'Bobbie James' is a controllable giant descended from a chance seedling that appeared at the Sunningdale Nurseries in 1960.

About 20 ft is its ultimate height, with great showers of semi-double flowers, cream coloured in the petals and with a golden, central stamen boss. It is deliciously fragrant, with a scent that carries in the air across the garden. At Chilland, in Hampshire, a yew tree is kept as a vertical green pillar up and through which 'Bobbie James' grows; its effect against the dark yew foliage is remarkable.

HOW TO GROW
See above.

'Bobbie James' is a magnificent rambling rose, producing an extravagance of creamy, headily scented blooms in June and July.

'Bobbie James' covers a pergola flanked by catmint and pelargoniums.

'Aloha' (CLIMBER)

Over the years many Hybrid tea roses have produced climbing sports. The great virtue of these is that, unlike the Rambler roses and most other Climbers, they flower throughout the summer once a good framework of growth has been established. And if they are grown on a warm wall, their first flowers appear at least a month before those on their bush-rose relatives.

'Aloha', however, is not so much a sport as a Hybrid tea climber in its own right: 'The New Dawn' is one of its parents. Because it is not very big, 'Aloha' is an ideal rose for garden walls and fences: too often, climbing roses rush to the top of the wall to decorate next door's garden rather than one's own. But 'Aloha's' attractive, very full flowers of dark pink, paling towards the centre, will alone colour your plot from early June until October.

HOW TO GROW
See above.

Climbing up a south-facing fence, 'Aloha' will give you an abundance of glorious pink blooms for fully four months.

The open, erect habit of an 'Aloha' gives support to a Dutch honeysuckle.

'Guinée' (CLIMBER)

Much darker than 'Crimson Glory', with sombre, nearly black, velvety blooms rivalling the old 'Souvenir du Docteur Jamain', this is the darkest red rose to make a good climber.

The colour is not ideal for making a great visual splash from a distance. 'Guinée' is best suited to a house wall above a terrace or patio where people sit. There, its beauty can be admired in close-up and its perfume enjoyed. Flowering continues throughout June and recurrently into late summer.

'Guinée's' foliage is not exciting, but, since most recurrently flowering climbing roses get bare at the base, they can be used as support for other, thin-growing climbers, such as *Clematis viticella* or honeysuckle.

HOW TO GROW
See p. 241.

'Guinée' stands out best by a pale wall.

'Mermaid' produces large, yellow blooms.

'Mermaid' (CLIMBER)

This great Climber, viciously armed with a multiplicity of scimitar-sharp thorns, must be one of the most splendid roses ever raised. It was bred by William Paul in 1918. From the lovely *Rosa bracteata*, its seed parent, it inherits not only the thorns but its glossy, near-evergreen foliage. From this same parent, too, 'Mermaid' has also inherited a certain tenderness to frost.

The thick, leafy shoots produce a continuing display of huge, single flowers up to 5 in. across. They are a clear, pale yellow with a central boss of gold stamens and open flowers that in a sheltered spot will continue blooming until Christmas. It is not for small areas, nor for growing near a path; but wherever it is planted it is essential to tie in the sappy new shoots before they can catch unwary feet.

HOW TO GROW
See p. 241.

'Mme Grégoire Staechelin' (CLIMBER)

This most attractive and useful rose flowers but once in the season, which is probably why it is so often neglected. Yet it has all kinds of advantages.

Every aspect suits it; on a warm wall the first flowers – loosely double blossoms, dark pink on the outside, paler within and with a fine scent – open in May. On a north-facing wall they blossom just as spectacularly in June.

'Mme Grégoire' needs only the gentlest of pruning; just tie the stems in as they appear, to prevent them being blown out. Even dead-heading is unnecessary; no further flowers will be produced anyway. Besides, leaving the dead heads on the plant permits the development of the large hips which in the height of summer will hang down like unseasonable Christmas decorations.

HOW TO GROW
See p. 241.

One of the loveliest climbing roses, the vigorous 'Mme Grégoire Staechelin' can grow 20 ft each way in three or four years.

Do not dead-head; when the hips ripen, they turn a rich apricot colour.

'The New Dawn' (CLIMBER)

One of the finest specimens in Britain of this incomparable climbing rose is planted in a pocket of soil in the dark basement area of a London house. From there it climbs to smother the front of the house with flowers, overtopping the first-floor windows to attract the admiring glances of passers-by. This is typical of the vigorous nature of 'The New Dawn' which grows equally strongly on a wall, up a tree, or trained on a trellis. It is a sport of the Wichuraiana hybrid rambler 'Dr van Fleet', which it closely resembles, except that it is not once-flowering but perpetual. It produces its clusters of shell-pink, heavily scented, semi-double flowers continuously from early July to the end of September.

Another good quality is its foliage; the leaves are small, glossy, nearly evergreen and resistant to disease. Yet another is the way in which it sheds its petals when they are faded.

In an ideal situation, 'The New Dawn' would be trained on a rustic trellis in a narrow bed edging a lawn in full view from the house; there, its beauty and scent could be enjoyed for many weeks. Perhaps it could be underplanted with small spring bulbs, including snowdrops (*Galanthus nivalis*) and *Crocus tomasinianus*, and with groups of *Hosta sieboldiana*, whose huge blue-green, deeply veined leaves would harmonise well with the soft pink of the rose. A splendid notion, too, would be to present *Clematis* 'Perle d'Azur', as a companion to 'The New Dawn'; it could be trained up through the lower branches of the rose, and bring forth its azure-blue flowers at the same time.

HOW TO GROW

'The New Dawn': *see p. 241.*
Clematis: see p. 177.
Crocus tomasinianus: see p. 149.
Galanthus nivalis: see p. 155.
Hosta sieboldiana: see p. 95.

'The New Dawn' makes an ideal support plant for another climber, such as *Clematis* 'Perle d'Azur' (above), which intermingles its azure blue with the soft pink of the rose. 'The New Dawn' was raised in the USA in 1930 but has become so widely established in this country that it is generally thought of as British. Extremely vigorous, hardy and reliable, it is suitable for growing up house walls or over pergolas.

SPECIES ROSES

In the category Species roses should be grouped all the roses that are grown in their original wild form – but, in fact, climbing species are sometimes hived off and attached to the Climber group instead. Most Species roses are, in fact, shrubs and have much the same uses as the Shrub rose group in the garden, though their colour range is not so extensive. However, among all the rose groups, they are particularly resistant to pests and diseases.

Their flowers are invariably single and fine-petalled, and they appear only once in the year. To make up for this, however, many species have showy, berry-like hips, which may be black, red or orange. Some species – *Rosa moyesii*, for example – produce hips so big and vividly red that it would be worth growing the shrub for the fruit alone. Others, such as *R. glauca* (syn. *R. rubrifolia*), with grey-purple leaves, and the bright green *R. xanthina*, are admired as much for their foliage as for their flowers.

HOW TO GROW
Plant Species roses in the same manner as Hybrid teas; they require little pruning apart from the removal of soft tips and straggly growths. Propagate by cuttings (see Miniature roses) or by seeds obtained from the hips and sown when ripe in a cold frame.

R. glauca on the left mingles with a white philadelphus and a kolkwitzia.

Rosa banksiae lutea spreads itself in golden profusion on a trellis.

Rosa glauca

The old name of this plant is *Rosa rubrifolia*, which is considerably less accurate than the new one. For the exquisite foliage of this shrub from the mountains of Southern Europe is not red, but glaucous indeed.

It makes an open, 6 ft high bush of smooth purple-red stems; grown in sun, the foliage is near purple with a grape-bloom overlay; in shade, the colour pales to greenish-grey – glaucous – with purple leaf stalks and midribs. The dog-rose flowers in June are clear pink, not large, but perfectly in accord with the lightness of the plant. The end of summer sees a good crop of scarlet hips, which remain after the leaves are over.

R. glauca is easy to grow and propagate; self-sown seedlings often appear, which can be moved to where they are required for further associations.

HOW TO GROW
See above.

In summer, the blushing dog-rose flowers and grey-green leaves of *R. glauca* are joined by hips that later turn bright red.

Rosa banksiae lutea

Lady Banks's Rose deserves the tallest and warmest wall available; the south front of a three-storey house is ideal – anything smaller will do less than justice to the fountains of long, olive-green thornless wands and the near-evergreen foliage.

In spite of its size, Lady Banks's Rose, which was brought from China early in the 19th century, is extremely elegant. Any attempt to prune it conventionally leads to lots of growth but no flowers.

Instead, the main vertical shoots should be pinned back to make a wall-covering framework from which secondary shoots can cascade forwards. In their third year, in late April or May, they carry bunches of little double yellow flowers, each rather like a double primrose.

Only after flowering is some thinning needed, and even this should not be too drastic.

HOW TO GROW
See above.

The small, butter-yellow flowers are delicately scented. *Wisteria sinensis* is a handsome companion to this rose.

Rosa × 'Canary Bird'

Over the years, the Orient has given us several very beautiful yellow rose species to brighten our gardens. All flower in May and June – early, by rose standards – and amongst them, one of the very best is 'Canary Bird'. Both its parents, *Rosa xanthina* and *R. hugonis*, are lovely plants, too, so it starts from a good genetic base.

'Canary Bird' seems to like the well-drained limy soil of our drier south-eastern counties and, when happy, can exceed 6 ft in height with a spread of about the same. It makes a fountain of warm, brown stems covered with bright green, ferny leaves and so, even out of flower, makes an elegant plant for a mixed shrub border. In late May, it is studded with clear yellow dog-roses, whose effect is enhanced because, as they are carried on forward-showering twigs, they look their admirers full in the face. In good years, the little black hips provide something of a show in late summer.

HOW TO GROW
See p. 244.

One of the earliest roses to appear, May-flowering 'Canary Bird' blooms generously each summer in all but dry soils.

On good moist soil, 'Canary Bird' can attain large shrub size.

Rosa moyesii

In all respects, *Rosa moyesii* is a marvellous monster of a rose. When happy (and it usually is, given reasonable soil and good drainage) it builds up a great fountain of prickly shoots 10 or even 15 ft in height. The foliage is that of an elegant dog-rose and the flower shapes show a similar influence. But the colour has nothing of the dog-rose pink and white; rather it is a glowing red, accentuated by the golden centre. The buds open over several weeks from late June, and are followed by fine, flask-shaped fruits that flare into orange-red from the middle of August onwards.

R. moyesii is superb in a large crowded shrub border where it can push shoots up erratically through other things, so that first the flowers and then the hips are seen against different foliage; blue-green Lawson cypress looks especially well with it. Where there is less space, it is best to choose a Wisley cultivar of *R. moyesii* called 'Geranium'. Dating from the 1930s, it is noticeably more bushy than the species but is just as good in flower and fruit. Pink flowers and forms exist both in the wild and in cultivation, but they lack the originality of the type.

Any association built around *R. moyesii* would be concerned with foliage and shape as much as with flower colour. A single specimen of *Chamaecyparis lawsoniana* 'Pembury Blue', for example, provides a vertical element and some support to the rose. In front of the rose, a flat-topped lace-cap *Hydrangea macrophylla* 'Lanarth White' would provide unusual interest and, at the same time, help to conceal the gaunt base of the rose.

HOW TO GROW
Rosa moyesii: see p. 244.
Chamaecyparis lawsoniana: see p. 335.
Hydrangea macrophylla: see p. 286.

Planted in front of a blue-green Lawson cypress, *Rosa moyesii* – shown here in hip in early·September – is ideally placed. 'Lanarth White' hydrangeas complement the group.

Wild Gardening

Making your garden a natural home for woodland and meadow plants

The whole of gardening being, in reality, an artificial assemblage of materials, 'wild gardening' is really a contradiction in terms. But you will not be doing too badly if your efforts at least appear natural and spontaneous.

Leaving out what might be done, for instance, just behind the seashore line or on a rocky mountain, wild gardening can be divided into two broad areas: sites under trees, where woodland plants will thrive, and open grassland, where the most striking effects are achieved by flowering grasses and other plants that grow naturally in turf.

You have only to take a springtime walk in open woodland composed mainly of broad-leaved trees to appreciate how just a few flowers, when seen massed, can create a captivating world of their own. Bluebells and wood anemones grow in drifts, while primroses form clumpy groups. In parts of Britain – close to the Yorkshire moors, for example – you will come across sheets of lent lilies (our native trumpet daffodil), while along the becks great clumps of vivid yellow kingcups shine in the spring sunlight. A little later, in drier places, a display of lilies-of-the-valley takes over.

By the time the trees are in full leaf, the woodland floor will have darkened and the display will largely have finished for the season. But in clearings there may still be seen avens, butterfly orchids, ragged robin, herb paris – not to mention wild woodbine (our native honeysuckle) – taking flowering well past midsummer.

Few people have woods, or even copses, in their gardens, but much can be achieved under a few trees or even under a single large specimen. Taking the year from its start, you could enjoy the yellow cups of winter aconites in January and February. These look marvellous with clumps of snowdrops and with a drift of the self-seeding, lilac-mauve *Crocus tomasinianus*. Even the dense shade of a beech will support these early flowers, which can make their annual growth while there is still plenty of light reaching them and moisture from winter rains.

There is a whole range of anemones that can be brought in, including forms of our own *Anemone nemorosa* and such species as *A. blanda*. Then there are the daffodils – *Narcissus cyclamineus* and the hoop petticoat, *N. bulbocodium* – and dog's tooth violets, with their marbled leaves and Turk's-cap flowers.

In summer, it is better not to struggle to keep interest in the wild woodland garden. Turn your attention to other areas, then at their peak. But in autumn you can have the delightful *Cyclamen hederifolium* (syn. *C. neapolitanum*) whose pink or white flowers are soon followed by beautifully marked leaves that remain right through the winter.

The richest tapestry of meadow flora occurs in open sites and under rather starved conditions. As soon as manure or fertiliser is applied, a few strongly growing (and usually boring) species will take over from the rest. In fact, if the turf is already over-fertile and rank, it may be necessary to reduce its vigour by close and frequent mowing for a few years, removing the mowings so that they are not returned to nourish the soil.

Once a turf of fine grasses is established, it need not be cut from November until late July or early August. Then cut it tightly, and again a few weeks later before autumn bulbs start flowering. When they have finished, give a last tight cut in late November. The turf will then be short enough to make a background for winter crocuses, snowdrops and the great tide of flowers that follows, including celandines, wood anemones (which grow well in grass), cuckoo flower, goldilocks (the earliest buttercup) and snake's head fritillary.

Flowering grasses

Many of the meadow grasses are exquisite in flower. From the time that sweet vernal grass and meadow foxtail are blooming in April until the rosy haze from common bent (which is also a fine lawn grass) in July, their flowering season is a long one.

Major contributions are also made by several species of buttercups and by red and white clover. Some of the clovers used nowadays in grassland are over-invasive, but the truly wild strains are a delight. Another showy member of this family of legumes is the tufted vetch, which makes swathes of blue in July. It will hitch itself to any nearby support, such as a hedge or a fence.

Ox-eyed daisies are especially successful on moist soils – you can buy the seeds if you have none to start with. Their flowering season starts in May and continues until September; with them you can grow meadow crane's-bill *(Geranium pratense)* which flowers from July to September. To complete the year in the meadow garden, colchicums and winter-flowering crocus bring a final sparkle in October.

The wild garden in open woodland provides a splendid sight in spring – daffodils, celandines and primroses sparkle in the sunlight before the overshadowing trees come into leaf.

In a sun-dappled clearing, a Species rose scrambles through an ornamental cherry. Below, foxgloves bloom in the grass.

A mass of *Cyclamen hederifolium* spreads its autumn carpet of pink and white flowers beneath a tree. Later, the beautifully patterned leaves remain to provide winter interest.

Shrubs

As supporting cast or leading player, shrubs always have a role in the garden scene

———————◆———————

A GARDEN WITHOUT SHRUBS is like a stage without the star performers – all the props are there, as well as the supporting cast, but the main actors who give weight and substance to the play have not appeared.

Though shrubs are usually chosen for their floral display, this often covers a relatively short period. Of much longer duration is the show of foliage – with some deciduous species the spring unfolding and the autumnal fall provide spectacular pictures in their own right. But apart from these special periods, there are leaves throughout the year in every shade of green.

Evergreens, on the other hand, do not go through such amazing colour changes. However, their diversity of leaf form is extraordinary, ranging from the wide, fan-like leaves of fatsias and the great whorls of *Mahonia japonica* to the delicate sprays of box and berberis.

Even more exciting possibilities are introduced by variegated leaves – for example, *Eleagnus pungens* 'Maculata', whose mottled gold provides a year-round display as bright as forsythia in all its spring glory. Purple foliage, too, adds another dimension to the garden – *Berberis thunbergii* and the smoke bush *Cotinus coggygria* are among the best. Then there are the felted-leaf shrubs – lavenders, sages and santolinas – which present the gardener with a choice of grey foliage.

But in the final choice, flower colour is likely to be among the main reasons for selecting one shrub rather than another. Fortunately, such is the range of shrubs that it is possible to find some to flower in every month of the year: from winter sweet (*Chimonanthus praecox*) and Chinese witch hazel (*Hamamelis mollis*) in January, right round to a burst of blossom from winter viburnum (*Viburnum* × *bodnantense*) to welcome Christmas Day.

A striking shrub, the dark-leaved *Cotinus coggygria* 'Royal Purple' makes a splendid centrepiece in this wild garden, pictured here in June. Roses stand in the background.

Abutilon vitifolium

Plants that grow wild in Chile include species suited to gardens in the milder parts of Britain. Among them is *Abutilon vitifolium*, which can even tolerate some frost. It may reach 15 ft or more when loosely trained against a high, sheltered wall, but displays its elegant shape to better advantage as a free-standing shrub. Its leaves are vine-like; their soft grey-greenness perfectly complements the wide-open, mallow-like flowers of palest lavender-blue. The white forms 'Album' and 'Tennant's White', and the darker blue 'Veronica Tennant', provide variety in gardens large enough for more than one abutilon.

Although normally evergreen, abutilons often lose much of their foliage in a hard winter. Flowering in June, when competition from other plants is intense, the abutilon remains quietly distinctive.

It would be a mistake to make such a gentle plant compete with fierce colours. Suitable companions are the Californian tree lupins, *Lupinus arboreus*, especially the paler yellow and lavender forms. Though hardly 'trees', they do reach 3-4 ft. At their base, flag irises in similar colours are perfect. *Iris pallida dalmatica* with blue-grey foliage spears, is best of all.

HOW TO GROW

Abutilon vitifolium: plant around mid-spring in good, well-drained soil, preferably in full sun. Shelter is essential, and it is as well to cover the roots in winter. Propagate from cuttings in late summer or from seeds under glass in spring. Prune to remove dead shoots only.
Iris pallida dalmatica: see p. 96.
Lupinus arboreus: see p. 293.

Abutilon vitifolium 'Tennant's White'.

In spite of its delicate colouring, this lovely abutilon draws the eye irresistibly when placed as a background to the soft shades of the June-flowering tree lupins and the gentle blue of stately flag irises. For a complete symphony in tones of blue, the yellow form of *Lupinus arboreus* can be replaced by a lavender one. Alternatively, the foreground can be brought into stronger contrast by planting yellow-flowering irises.

Abelia × grandiflora

As August gives way to September, many plants of high summer begin to look a little ragged. This is the time when an early autumn shrub, such as *Abelia × grandiflora*, set boldly in a prominent position beneath a window, comes into its own.

This abelia makes a twiggy mound, about 5 ft high and 4 ft across, of shining, near-evergreen leaves. By late August the tip of every branchlet holds sprays of white flowers, each one backed by a reddish-purple calyx. The show goes on for weeks, quietly and undramatically yet with infinite charm. The branchlets also make a fine basis for a table decoration.

HOW TO GROW
Plant during early autumn or spring in any ordinary soil and in full sun, preferably against a south-facing wall. Propagate in summer by cuttings under glass. No pruning, except for thinning out old wood after flowering.

Abelia × grandiflora's white and purple flowers are long-lasting and scented. Usually, they start to open in July.

Aesculus parviflora (BOTTLEBRUSH BUCKEYE)

A native of the United States, this deciduous shrub is known there as the bottlebrush buckeye – a reference to its long stamens. Although the white flowers are individually smaller than those of related species, the upstanding spikes that they form, often 12 in. tall, provide one of the best of high-summer displays.

In Britain, the bottlebrush buckeye makes a suckering bush, rising to 8 ft and spreading more widely, with typical horse-chestnut leaves that turn clear yellow in autumn. It fits perfectly in the corner of a lawn, and may be underplanted with spring bulbs for an early show.

HOW TO GROW
Plant between autumn and spring. Easily grown in any good soil, in sun or light shade. Readily increased from suckers in autumn or winter. Keep growth in check by cutting out old shoots during late winter.

The Latin name *parviflora* – 'small-flowered' – is misleading. The foot-long spikes make a striking display in July and August.

A plant spreads until deliberately checked. This one is 30 years old.

Amelanchier lamarckii (SNOWY MESPILUS)

A springtime display of pure white flowers on upright spikes justifies this deciduous shrub's evocative name. It comes from Canada, like its close relatives *Amelanchier canadensis* and *A. laevis*, with which it is often confused. *A. lamarckii* grows to 10 ft and carries its fine show of large, though short-lived, flowers in April.

The fleeting blooms are not the only attraction of the snowy mespilus, however. In autumn its leaves turn bright orange and yellow, and in late summer it bears red fruit, turning purple or black. These are edible and may be used in desserts. Like all amelanchiers, this one is extremely hardy and thrives in the coldest gardens.

HOW TO GROW
Plant during the dormant season, in any ordinary garden soil that is moist but well drained, and in sun or light shade. Increase by layering or suckers in autumn. No regular pruning is needed.

Golden narcissi accentuate the beauty of an amelanchier in full flower, together providing a spectacular show.

There is more colour to follow in autumn, this time from tinted leaves.

'Aureovariegata' is a distinctive form with yellow-splashed leaves.

Non-variegated forms, such as *A.j.* 'Salicifolia', do best in shade.

Aralia elata (JAPANESE ANGELICA TREE)

Gawky in winter, its 10 ft high stems resembling nothing so much as a cluster of bean poles, *Aralia elata* earns its place in the garden with a fast-changing display of leaves and flowers in spring and summer. In spring, the terminal buds – and sometimes a couple lower down as well – begin to unfold great rosettes of attractive leaflets. It is as though the herb angelica – itself no dwarf – has been transformed into a small tree.

In late summer the picture changes again, as wide branching heads of tiny white flowers appear. Unlike ivies, to which they are related, aralias lose flowers and leaves with the first fierce frost.

HOW TO GROW
Plant during autumn or spring, in fertile, moist but well-drained soil. Light shade is preferable, together with shelter from winds. Propagate from rooted suckers. No pruning; cut out some shoots at ground level to prevent excessive spread.

Showing its true colour in spring, 'Variegata' has leaves that are irregularly margined in creamy-white blotches.

Aucuba japonica (SPOTTED LAUREL)

Its decorative leaves and handsome scarlet berries made the spotted laurel so popular among Victorian gardeners that a good plant in fruit could cost a huge sum. Today, this evergreen is more often relegated to the back of the shrubbery – but it deserves better.

Many forms are cultivated, including the females 'Salicifolia' and 'Longifolia' which have narrow, vivid green, willow-like leaves on a domed bush 6 ft high. They produce fine crops of berries provided that a male plant is at hand; the bright, gold-splashed 'Crotonifolia' is ideal, and one male plant is sufficient for three females. The berries last until Easter.

HOW TO GROW
Plant during autumn or spring, in any soil and situation. Excellent for shady town gardens, but variegated forms are best in an open position. Propagate by heel cuttings under glass in late summer. No pruning.

The berries borne by *A.j.* 'Longifolia' and other female plants are at their brightest between Christmas and Easter.

Berberis darwinii (BARBERRY)

One of the less noted achievements of Charles Darwin was to introduce to Britain plants that gave new shapes and colours to the garden scene. One of the finest of these, the Chilean barberry, was named in Darwin's honour.

This barberry, one of the hardiest of Chilean shrubs, makes a rather upright bush about 8 ft high. In winter its dark, shining evergreen leaves make it look like a miniature holly, but in spring (April and May) these are almost hidden behind a shower of brilliant orange-yellow blossom. In some years Darwin's barberry offers, too, a late summer spectacle of grape-bloomed, blue-black fruit.

HOW TO GROW
Plant during autumn or spring, in any well-drained soil, including shallow chalk. It grows well in sun or light shade. Propagate by heel cuttings under glass, in late summer, by seeds when ripe, or by rooted suckers. No pruning is needed.

A well-grown specimen of *Berberis darwinii*, some 15-20 years old

As though spring flowers were not enough, festoons of purple fruits burden the branches at summer's end.

Berberis × rubrostilla (BARBERRY)

Like all the barberries this is a formidably armed plant, having a trio of cactus-sharp spines behind every leaf to repel animal or human intruders. A hybrid between two low, deciduous shrubs from the Himalayas, *Berberis wilsoniae* and *B. aggregata*, it is slightly taller than its parents – about 4 ft high, and rather more in spread. And it is even more brilliant in autumn.

The flowers that appear on the arching branches in May are mid-yellow and not very distinctive. It is in autumn that the shrub really comes into its own. Starting in October, and often lasting until Christmas, the bush presents a continuous pageant of colour as the large egg-shaped berries change from green to pink to coral-red.

HOW TO GROW

Plant between autumn and spring in any soil. Best in full sun for autumn colours and fruit. Propagate by cuttings or seeds, though seedlings seldom come true to type.

Brilliant, ruby-tinted foliage and innumerable coral-red berries give this barberry a fiery image in autumn.

The egg-shaped fruits are one of the shrub's chief attractions.

Berberis thunbergii 'Atropurpurea'

(BARBERRY)

Late July and early August are dog days in the shrub garden; there is too often a dull interval between the fresh-looking blossoms of June and the fiery leaves of autumn. One way of bridging this gap is to grow shrubs in purple and silver, which hold their leaves all summer long. They are effective used as a low, dense, colourful bank on both sides of a shallow flight of stone steps.

The jewel in each planting could be a single specimen of *Berberis thunbergii* 'Atropurpurea', a dense shrub 4 ft high with a spread of 6 ft. Though deciduous, its dark purple leaves appear quite early in spring. It has the drawback of vicious thorns, so it is advisable to plant a buffer shrub between the berberis and the steps. Try the evergreen *Senecio* 'Sunshine', an almost hardy plant from New Zealand about 3 ft high and 4 ft across. It has silver leaves that make a fine foil for the purple berberis. Senecio carries a mass of yellow, daisy-like flowers in July.

An 8 ft tall bush of the summer-flowering horse chestnut, *Aesculus parviflora*, provides an eye-catcher behind the lower shrubs. Its white candles, with long red-tipped stamens, bring the display to a climax in late July and August.

HOW TO GROW

Berberis thunbergii 'Atropurpurea': *plant between autumn and spring, in any soil. Colours show best in full sun. Propagate by heel cuttings in August or September. Little pruning is necessary; straggling branches can be shortened or removed entirely in late winter.*
Aesculus parviflora: see p. 251.
Senecio 'Sunshine': *see p. 315.*

A paired grouping beside steps in July includes *Aesculus parviflora*, purple-leaved *Berberis thunbergii* and clumps of silver *Senecio* 'Sunshine'.

Allowed to grow almost unpruned, this specimen is about ten years old.

Berberis × stenophylla (BARBERRY)

Most of the 450 different barberry species come from the Northern Hemisphere. There is, however, a small southerly population in temperate South America, which includes one of the finest of all – *Berberis darwinii* (see p. 252). On the mountain screes above its home grows the almost prostrate, needle-leaved *B. empetrifolia*.

The garden 'marriage' of these two has resulted in *B. × stenophylla*, perhaps the finest hybrid barberry known. More vigorous than either parent, it produces long, arching stems and eventually grows to a height of 8 ft or more. In leaf it resembles *B. empetrifolia*; in flower, *B. darwinii*, though the blooms have a pronounced yellow tint. They are borne profusely in spring, often with another scattering of flowers in autumn. The dwarf cultivar *B. × s.* 'Irwinii' has coral-red flower buds.

HOW TO GROW
See *Berberis × rubrostilla*, p. 253.

The yellow flowers of *B. × stenophylla* appear in April. Later they are replaced by a scattering of small purple berries.

Buddleia fallowiana 'Lochinch'

Beauty emerged triumphant from evil when bomb sites in London became covered – almost overnight, as it seemed – with purple buddleia. The butterfly bush (*Buddleia davidii*) is now grown widely, in a range of colours. All are irresistible to butterflies and other insects. Remember, though, that flowers feed only the adults, and a patch of nettles is essential for breeding the caterpillars.

B. davidii, however, has the disadvantage of strong, rampant growth, with uninteresting foliage. The less common (and less hardy) deciduous *B. fallowiana* maintains a weeping habit, about 6 ft high and rather less across, with handsome woolly grey foliage. It flowers from July to September. The somewhat taller, deliciously scented 'Lochinch' hybrid is a clear soft lavender, each tiny flower having a tangerine eye. The grey-green and lavender composition is perfectly complemented by the vertical shoots of *Lavatera olbia*, rising to as much as 6-7 ft beside the buddleia, like elegant pale pink hollyhocks.

Growing happily in front is one of the grandest of late-summer bulbs, *Crinum × powellii*, whose fountain of pale green leaves supports tall spikes of clear pink, trumpet flowers.

HOW TO GROW
Buddleia fallowiana 'Lochinch': *plant in autumn or spring, in rich, well-drained soil. A sheltered site is best, in full sun. Propagate by heel cuttings only. Prune in March to maintain height and shape; cut the lavatera hard back at the same time.*
Crinum × powellii: see p. 147.
Lavatera olbia: see p. 291.

The hint of orange in the eye of each tiny, delicate lavender flower of *Buddleia fallowiana* 'Lochinch' gives a warm touch to the whole shrub. The grey-green of its soft foliage and of the tall *Lavatera olbia* on the left is given an added dimension by the long, pale green leaves and bold trumpet-shaped flowers of *Crinum × powellii* in front. The time of year is late August.

Buddleia alternifolia

One disadvantage of the common butterfly bush (*Buddleia davidii*) is that it does not appear at its best until July. This relation, brought from north-west China in 1914 by the English botanist Reginald Farrer, has the distinct advantage of flowering a good month earlier.

Farrer's own description of the plant in the wild is equally accurate for a well-grown specimen in Britain. It resembles, he said, 'a gracious small-leaved weeping willow when it is not in flower, and a sheer waterfall of soft purple when it is'. This deciduous buddleia may be grown as a standard, or simply be allowed to build up a 10 ft high dome of cascading branches.

HOW TO GROW
Plant during autumn or spring, in good garden soil and in full sun. The shrub is lime-tolerant. Propagate by heel cuttings under glass in late summer. Flowers on previous year's wood, so any pruning must be done immediately after flowering.

Each of the sweetly scented flower clusters, borne on arching, year-old stems, measures about an inch across.

Farrer's sheer waterfall of soft purple is a spectacular sight in June.

Bupleurum fruticosum

Carrots, fennel and parsley sound unlikely relatives for this evergreen garden shrub – yet, like them, *Bupleurum fruticosum* is a member of the *Umbelliferae* family, and one of the few woody species. Only as it flowers, between July and September, can its relationship be guessed, as the flattened, rounded flower heads, greatly prized by flower arrangers, change colour from fennel yellow to angelica green.

The shrub's narrow sea-green leaves build up into a low dome 6 ft high and wide. Resistant to salt spray, but needing warmth, the plant is admirable for an exposed seaside garden in a mild area.

HOW TO GROW
Plant during early autumn or late spring in any well-drained soil, including chalk. Propagate by cuttings under glass, in late summer. No pruning is needed, but cut out frost-damaged shoots in spring.

The fennel-like blooms of *B. fruticosum* can be used to provide a delicate contrast in flower arrangements.

In late summer, massed flowers almost hide the evergreen foliage.

Buxus sempervirens (COMMON BOX)

One of Britain's few native broad-leaved evergreens, box in its dwarf form has been part of the English garden for centuries. It was grown as a surround for medieval herb plots, and formed the basic pattern of the Elizabethan knot garden. The full-sized box is, with yew, the commonest and most suitable shrub for topiary work.

Left alone and allowed to mature, box makes an elegant tree, rising to 10 ft, spreading to 4-6 ft, and flourishing even in shade. *Buxus sempervirens* 'Aureovariegata' has gold-variegated leaves. The slow-growing 'Elegantissima' is the best silver box.

HOW TO GROW
Plant in autumn or spring, in any type of soil and in sun or shade. For hedging, space plants 12 in. apart. Propagate from cuttings under glass, in late summer. No pruning of specimen plants; trim topiary and hedges to shape in June.

'Elegantissima' has silver-edged leaves.

'Suffruticosa' is a dwarf form.

Calluna vulgaris (HEATHER, LING)

Vast tracts of acid moorland, heath and bog are covered in August and September with the purple flower spikes of our best-loved native undershrub. Though sometimes called Scottish heather, it is found wild all over Britain. A white form, the 'lucky white heather' once hawked by gypsies, occurs rarely.

Calluna is a genus of only one evergreen species, but there are hundreds of cultivars showing a wide range of colours in both flower and leaf. The flowers may be purple, pink, red or white. The leaves are green, gold or bronze, though sometimes changing colour with the season. Those with coloured foliage are especially worth growing, for they remain attractive right through the year.

It has become something of a cliché to grow heathers in a flat mass punctuated by dwarf upright conifers – like exclamation marks – but nothing looks more unnatural. It is more restful to the eye if heathers of contrasting colours are planted to form a tapestry, and if the shrubs are grouped, either in the heather bed itself or as a background.

Gardeners who do not have space to do this should treat heathers as individual dwarf shrubs. They can also use them to create effective mini-associations. Try, for example, planting the dark, grassy tufts of *Liriope muscari* alongside the double rose-pink heather 'H. E. Beale', and surrounding them with a silvery-grey mat of *Hebe pinguifolia* 'Pagei'.

Three varieties of ling which combine well to make a carpet of colour all the year round are 'Orange Queen', with lavender flowers and yellow spring foliage deepening to orange in summer; the single white 'Alba'; and 'H. E. Beale', an old pink favourite which is 2 ft tall and flowers late, from September to November.

HOW TO GROW

Calluna vulgaris: plant in autumn or spring in any acid soil and in a sunny position. Propagate by layering in spring, or by cuttings under glass in late summer. If necessary, clip the stems to half their length in early spring.
Hebe pinguifolia: see p. 285.
Liriope muscari: see p. 101.

For the smaller garden, heathers should be treated as dwarf shrubs. Here the rose-pink flowers of the variety 'H. E. Beale' blend attractively with the dark foliage and mauve-lilac blooms of *Liriope muscari*. Frame this early September group with the silver-grey of *Hebe pinguifolia* 'Pagei'.

Calluna vulgaris 'Alba Plena' growing behind *Erica carnea* 'Aurea'.

'Robert Chapman' has spectacular foliage.

CAMELLIA

Camellias began their European existence as pampered denizens of heated orangeries and glasshouses. Such is the extraordinary luxury of their flowers that it is hardly surprising they were not considered suitable for the rigours of an English winter. It is only in the last 20 or 30 years that these magnificent evergreens from China and Japan have found their way into almost every British garden that can grow them.

The appeal of camellias lies in their rich green, usually lustrous foliage and their cup-shaped or bowl-shaped flowers ranging from white through all shades of pink to reds of varying intensity. These blooms, which may be single or double, are invaluable for bringing beauty to the garden in late winter and early spring.

The commonest garden species is *Camellia japonica*, the first to be introduced in 1739 when specimens flowered for Lord Petre at Thorndon Hall, Essex. These were the single, wild Japanese types, a red and a white. Further introductions from the Far East, as well as mutant forms originating in Europe and deliberately produced hybrids, soon gave rise to a huge number of named forms, and today there are thousands.

One camellia, *C. sinensis*, is the commercial tea plant, its leaves more important than its flowers. Many ornamental camellias were brought to Britain in the 19th century by clipper ship, and in 1820 the clipper master Captain Rawes brought home the first specimen of one of the most beautiful of all camellias, *C. reticulata*. A further species, *C. saluenensis*, introduced from western China in 1924, has strongly influenced the camellias grown in British gardens. With *C. japonica* it has produced a number of exquisitely beautiful hybrids known as *C. × williamsii*. 'November Pink' flowers as early as its name suggests, while silver-pink 'Donation' continues into May. This group is by far the best for general use.

One other species deserving a space in the garden is *C. sasanqua*. This needs a warmer and milder location in which to ripen its wood and open its slightly fragrant flowers.

HOW TO GROW

Camellias are generally hardy in Britain, though in cold northern regions they succeed better in cool greenhouses and conservatories. Like rhododendrons, they are lime-haters, but camellias will tolerate neutral soil, and thrive in light to deep shade. Correct siting is of the utmost importance – the shelter and shade of light woodland is ideal, but in the average garden a site near a west, south, or even north-facing wall is quite suitable.

Camellias are admirable for town gardens, objecting to neither air pollution nor lack of sun. Eastern exposures should be avoided, especially for early flowering types, as morning sun after night frosts scorches and kills the developing buds. Drying winds have the same effect, and during the growing season the soil must be kept moist, preferably under a peat or leaf-mould mulch over the shallow roots.

Propagate by leaf-bud or semi-hardwood cuttings under glass in summer. Pruning is unnecessary, though straggling shoots may be shortened in late spring. Dead-head all camellias after flowering, except for C. × williamsii types, which shed their faded blooms naturally.

The hybrid *C. × williamsii* has the carefree charm of a wild rose but flowers from November to April.

C. reticulata bears superb single flowers.

'Rubescens Major' is a large double cultivar of *C. japonica*.

'Narumi-gata' is perhaps the hardiest of the *C. sasanqua* cultivars.

The free-flowering *C. saluenensis*.

Camellia japonica 'Adolphe Audusson'

The camellia's fragile flowers and handsome glossy leaves belie the hardiness of the plant itself. In lime-free soil and a sheltered site, the exotic blooms create a magnificent display, year after year.

One of the oldest – and still one of the finest – of scores of *Camellia japonica* cultivars is 'Adolphe Audusson', which builds up a narrow, 12 ft pyramid at the rate of a foot a year. The semi-double flowers begin to open in the first week of February, their clear red petals set off by the central yellow stamens. Since each plant has buds at different stages of development, the flowering season may last into May, and any frost-damaged flowers are soon replaced by fresh blooms.

However big the garden, a camellia never looks right – nor does it thrive – in an exposed position. Where there is space, it can be backed by deciduous trees or conifers. In a small yard it can stand in a corner, preferably facing west. In either case, *Leucothoe fontanesiana*, broad and spreading, gives good foliage contrast at the camellia's foot. Its white bells can give way in June to spikes of white and purple Turk's-cap lilies (*Lilium martagon*) planted in between. In autumn the leucothoe carries bronze-purple leaves and the camellia is covered with fat buds to give, even so early, a promise of spring.

HOW TO GROW
Camellia japonica 'Adolphe Audusson': *see p. 257. Birds may damage the opening flowers, but given good growing conditions few diseases affect camellias. Bud-drop is often caused by lack of soil moisture while the buds are building up.*
Leucothoe fontanesiana: see p. 291.
Lilium martagon: see p. 163.

With a wall for protection, and the ground-covering *Leucothoe fontanesiana* at its foot, this five-year-old 'Adolphe Audusson' gives an outstanding spring display.

Camellia × williamsii 'J. C. Williams'

An elegant camellia, ideally suited to the smaller garden, *Camellia × williamsii* has glossy leaves and is free-flowering. The hybrid group was raised by that distinguished gardener John Charles Williams, at Caerhays Castle, Cornwall. The spring-flowering cultivar which bears his name marries the grace of a June dog rose to the constancy of an evergreen.

The single flowers of softest pink have a central boss of yellow stamens, remarkably like the wild rose of our hedgerows, and are carried with the same abandon. There the similarity ends, however, for the camellia flowers for up to three months.

HOW TO GROW
See p. 257. The camellias in this group are particularly free-flowering – even the young plants. Curiously, red-flowered cultivars appear to be less prone to frost damage than white.

'J. C. Williams' has single blush-pink flowers.

C. × williamsii is noted for its prolonged flowering.

Carpenteria californica

Many Californian plants, not surprisingly, are vulnerable to frost. Even if they can withstand the cold of a British winter, the lack of southern sun may prevent them from ripening sufficiently to form effective flower buds. This is true of the lovely *Carpenteria californica*, but it can succeed if given the right conditions and loving care.

In its best forms, such as 'Ladham's Variety', the shrub makes an 8 ft bush – higher against a wall – spreading to 6-8 ft, with narrow, evergreen glossy leaves, pale on their undersides. In June and July each shoot produces a cluster of half a dozen pure white, fragrant flowers with yellow stamens, each bloom like a giant mock-orange.

HOW TO GROW
Plant in late spring, in fertile, well-drained soil. The shrub is lime-tolerant. It needs full sun and protection from strong, cold winds; best on a south-facing wall. Propagate by cuttings under glass in summer, or from seeds in spring. Prune to shape after flowering.

The glistening white blooms of *C. californica* are sweetly scented.

A seven-year-old *Carpenteria*, a genus with only one species, growing where it is happiest – against a south-facing wall.

Caryopteris × clandonensis

One of the very best blue-flowering shrubs of any season, *Caryopteris × clandonensis* is a perfect precursor in September to the blues and purples of Michaelmas daisies in autumn. The deciduous bush makes an aromatic grey-leaved mound about 2 ft high and the same in spread.

Its scent and the colour of its leaves alone make caryopteris an effective addition to the herb garden, notably in August when its appearance changes as the grey foliage is hidden by a profusion of clear blue flowers. Good deeper blue forms include 'Kew Blue'.

HOW TO GROW
Plant during autumn or spring, in any well-drained soil; excellent on chalk. Full sun and a sheltered site are best. Protect during winter in cold areas. Propagate in late summer by cuttings under glass. Prune back to just above ground level in spring.

The flowers of this scented shrub appear in late summer.

'Kew Blue' in front of *Cortaderia selloana* 'Gold Band'.

It is worth waiting ten years for this 'Delight' to mature.

Ceanothus × 'Delight'

Most ceanothus are natives of California, where they are known as blue blossom, or Californian lilacs. No other race of shrubs more perfectly embodies the sun-drenched character of its home landscape. Most have dense, glossy foliage and an abundance of small blue to purple-blue flowers which seem to glow with a light of their own.

So many ceanothus have a deserved reputation for tenderness, but happily there are some exceptions. The garden-bred *Ceanothus* × 'Delight' is one of these. Attaining 10 ft in time, it has small, dark leaves and abundantly borne rich blue flowers in late spring. Although hardy, it still benefits from a warm south or west-facing wall.

HOW TO GROW
Plant in late spring, in good, well-drained, preferably neutral soil. It is best in full sun and, ideally, should be grown against a sheltered wall. Propagate by cuttings under glass in summer. Prune after flowering, shortening young shoots to 3 in.

Each panicle of brilliant blue flowers, appearing in May, is some 2-3 in. long. The foliage of this shrub is evergreen.

Judicious pruning will preserve the compact form of this ceanothus.

Ceanothus × 'Gloire de Versailles'

Without ceanothus, Britain would have virtually no large blue-flowered shrubs. Many of the lovely species collected from North America – ranging in size from mat-forming plants, such as *Ceanothus prostratus*, to small trees – are not reliably hardy in Northern Europe. In 1830 a breeding programme was set up in France to establish hardier hybrids, and the deciduous 'Gloire de Versailles' has been one of its happiest products.

Panicles of gentle blue flowers, rather like those of a delicate buddleia, begin to appear in early July and continue until autumn. The plant's soft colouring makes it an ideal companion for many herbaceous-border plants. Although it can reach 8 ft or more in height and spread, annual pruning back to a framework keeps it compact.

HOW TO GROW
See *Ceanothus* × 'Delight'; *but prune in early spring.*

Large, rich green leaves, and flower panicles fully 7-8 in. long, have made this the most popular deciduous ceanothus.

C. thyrsiflorus combines beautifully with a wisteria growing above it.

Ceanothus thyrsiflorus 'Repens'

Although California, with its gentle climate, is the homeland of most species of ceanothus, good drainage and protection from cold winds will enable even the less hardy evergreen species to be grown in Britain. *Ceanothus thyrsiflorus* is one of the most reliable of these, and 'Repens' is a more compact form of it.

After ten years the shrub makes a regular dome 3-4 ft high and rather more across, ideal for a large rock garden or as ground-cover for a sunny bank. Flowering begins while the plant is still young and is remarkable in its persistence. The climax is a mound of mid-blue in May, but there is a lesser display, resembling distant puffs of blue smoke, which continues well into late autumn.

HOW TO GROW
Plant and propagate as advised for Ceanothus × 'Delight', though it will grow in limy soil. Pruning is unnecessary, but untidy shoots may be shortened as necessary in late spring.

The Cambridge-blue flowers are first carried when the shrub is only two years old, earlier than most species.

Ceratostigma willmottianum

Two plants raised at Warley Place, in Essex, early this century were the forerunners of every specimen of *Ceratostigma willmottianum* to be found in gardens today. Ellen Willmott raised the plants from seeds brought back from China in 1908 by Ernest Wilson.

In mild winters this deciduous shrub maintains its 3-4 ft dome of twiggy growth, though hard frost damages the upper branches. The first sign of new growth comes when tiny coral-red buds open into tidy, narrow leaves along the pink stems. By early July the first flowers show in rather bristly heads; the petals are clear blue, above pink corolla tubes, and flowering continues over a long period.

HOW TO GROW
Plant during late spring, in good, well-drained soil. Needs full sun and a sheltered site. Propagate from heel cuttings, in late summer. No pruning, but remove any frost-damaged shoots in spring. Can be cut back hard annually.

The rich blue flowers of *C. willmottianum* are carried in spreading clusters above the dark green stalkless leaves.

The lovely July-autumn display is often followed by tinted leaves.

Chaenomeles speciosa (JAPANESE QUINCE)

A limy soil that rules out the rich reds and scarlets of rhododendrons and camellias often restricts gardens to more muted spring colours. To some extent, however, the deciduous 'japonicas', or Japanese quinces, can take over the camellias' role.

The fiery scarlet flowers of *Chaenomeles speciosa*, notably in *C. s.* 'Cardinalis', provide the sort of brilliance associated with some of the deciduous azaleas, and make a striking centre for a group whose surrounding plants play an almost heraldic role by their display of strong yellows, both in flower and foliage.

The quince makes a twiggy bush 6 ft or more tall, with a spread of 5-7 ft. Sometimes a flower or two opens in midwinter, and often it is well in bloom by March. But suddenly, in April and May, the fire takes full hold. This is the moment to add fuel to the flames with companion plants.

Doronicums provide the comforting simplicity of their daisy-like flowers early in the year; *Doronicum plantagineum* 'Miss Mason' is one of the best forms. *Euphorbia polychroma* repeats the japonica shape in a smooth dome of brilliant yellow-green, gradually paling as the season progresses but catching light again before it dies down in autumn. The gracefully arching leaves of *Spartina pectinata* 'Aureomarginata' maintain their golden edges throughout the summer and autumn. The same shape on a broader scale is echoed by *Hemerocallis fulva*, with its near-upright foliage.

HOW TO GROW
Chaenomeles speciosa: plant between autumn and spring, in any type of moisture-retentive soil, if possible in full sun. Propagate by cuttings in late summer, or by layering in autumn. Prune to maintain shape only, immediately after flowering.
Doronicum plantagineum: see p. 82.
Euphorbia polychroma: see p. 86.
Hemerocallis fulva: see H. flava, p. 93.
Spartina pectinata: see p. 134.

In full flower during late spring, the fiery quince is complemented by the yellow-green bracts of the euphorbia and flanked by golden-yellow doronicums. The planting is about five years old. Day lilies and ornamental grasses will take over as the spring display fades.

Chimonanthus praecox (WINTER SWEET)

Winter sweet is either a joy or a disaster. Experienced gardeners plant the shrub knowing that they must not expect it to produce flowers for seven years – and that even then they may be lost in a single violent frost. Yet in a good year the blossoms that earn this deciduous shrub its common name are so unusual in shape and so exquisitely scented that they are worth the hazards. Appearing around Christmas, the claw-shaped flowers are waxy in texture and pale lime-yellow stained with purple in the centre. A few flowering twigs will scent a whole room.

Winter sweet, which attains a height of 10 ft and a spread almost as great, can be underplanted with winter-flowering bulbs and herbaceous plants. Early flowering snowdrops such as *Galanthus nivalis* 'Atkinsii' usually flower in January, at which time *Helleborus foetidus* is green in bud and leaf, a rich covering for the shrub's skimpy lower stems.

The problem of the dreary appearance of winter sweet in summer – all twigs and uninteresting leaves – is solved by interlacing it with a scrambling clematis. *Clematis viticella* 'Rubra', pruned hard to about 2 ft from the ground in March, uses the shrub as a helpful host and produces quantities of wine-red flowers in July and August.

HOW TO GROW

Chimonanthus praecox: plant between autumn and spring, in any kind of soil; it grows well on chalk. A sunny, sheltered site is best. Propagate by layering in early autumn or by seeds in spring under glass. After flowering, remove crowded branches on free-standing shrubs; cut flowered stems back by half on fully established wall shrubs.
Clematis viticella: see p. 181.
Galanthus nivalis: see p. 155.
Helleborus foetidus: see p. 92.

Slow to mature and vulnerable to frost, winter sweet earns its place in the garden by flowering in midwinter. To complete the garden display (right) are small clumps of snowdrops, together with a few hellebores to take the eye from the shrub's gawky lower branches.

Choisya ternata (MEXICAN ORANGE)

For a shrub from Mexico, *Choisya ternata* is remarkably hardy. Though appreciating protection from searing late-winter north-easters, it happily builds up its dome of glossy, divided leaves, 6 ft or more high and wide, in almost any area. Even if it never flowered, it would be a valuable evergreen, so adaptable is it.

The blossoms are a bonus: fine heads of sweet-scented white flowers that give the plant its common name. *C. ternata* is indeed related to the citrus family, and the leaves when crushed are pungently aromatic. The main display comes in April and May, but there are occasionally flurries of white later, especially in a mild autumn.

HOW TO GROW
Plant during late spring in any good soil. The shrub does best in sun, though light shade is tolerated on sheltered sites. Propagate by cuttings under glass in late summer. No regular pruning, but in spring cut out frosted shoots at the base. Trim to shape after flowering.

The flat-topped clusters of flowers grow from the leaf axils at the ends of the shoots. The display lasts for months.

The shrub attains its full height of 6 ft or so in about six years.

CISTUS (ROCK ROSE, SUN ROSE)

Cistuses are true plants of the Mediterranean, familiar to all who have clambered among the dry mountains of Spain or Crete or have pushed through the scratchy *maquis* of Corsica – and even to those who, less adventurously, have motored through the hinterland of the Côte d'Azur. To smell their aromatic leaves even in winter is to be transported from an English garden to a sun-baked hillside a thousand miles to the south.

These so-called 'sun roses' – they are not related to true roses – may, as John Gerard said in his *Herball* of 1597, be 'impatient of our cold climate'. However, they do well in the south, given conditions as near as possible to those of their native lands, and if a harsh winter does knock them out they are easily and quickly replaced.

Some 20 distinct species are available, as well as a number of wild and garden hybrids which often seem more robust and hardy. All are evergreen, and provide a daily succession of exquisite flowers from late May until early July.

Cistus × cyprius reaches 6 ft in height and has leathery leaves and 4 in. wide flowers, white with dark red central blotches; those of 'Pat' are even bigger. *C. × corbariensis* makes a bush 2 ft high and 4 ft wide covered with small white 'roses' opening from pink calyces. The exceptionally hardy 'Silver Pink' is a little taller, but carries its exquisite flowers in upright spikes.

HOW TO GROW
Plant all sun roses in late spring, using young, container-grown specimens to minimise root disturbance. Any well-drained to dry soil will do, including shallow chalk. The plants are resistant to wind but not severe frost, and are ideal for milder seaside gardens. Full sun is essential, with shelter from north and east gales. Propagate species from seeds in spring, hybrids and species from heel cuttings in late summer, both under glass. After flowering, shoot tips may be trimmed to maintain shape, but any severe pruning, apart from removal of frosted shoots, can cause die-back.

'Pat', a beautiful, hardy hybrid, has blooms fully 5 in. wide.

Cistus × cyprius is a particularly vigorous hybrid, with crimson-blotched flowers, which may grow 6 ft high.

'Silver Pink', with its long flower clusters, is noted for its hardiness.

The slightly crinkled flowers tend to crowd together in clusters.

Cistus crispus

One of the most distinctive, as well as one of the most frost-resistant, of the rock roses, *Cistus crispus* makes a low, wide, evergreen tuffet, 2 ft high at the most in summer but doubling that in width. As its name suggests, the plant has a rather crimped appearance, with wavy and deeply veined grey-white leaves.

The flowers appear in the latter half of July – later than those of any other cistus in cultivation. The flower heads, held tight among leafy bracts, open one by one their purple-red blooms, about the size of an old penny and deepening in colour towards the yellow centre.

Its late flowering season and light, low growth make *C. crispus* an ideal companion for other plants from its Mediterranean home.

HOW TO GROW
See p. 263. Most rock roses tend to grow scruffy with age and should, ideally, be replaced after seven or eight years; rooted cuttings will begin to flower quite early.

Compact tuffets of grey-white foliage, about 2 ft high, emblazoned with flowers over an inch across in late July, look well in paving.

Cistus × purpureus

In an English garden, cistus look best in clumps with other dwarf shrubs and bulbs of the Mediterranean which share their taste for a hard, dry life in well-drained soil. Cistus, lavender and *Allium siculum* can make a harmonious group some 12 ft wide and rather less in depth.

The hybrid *Cistus × purpureus*, with a height and spread of about 4 ft, is one of the most spectacular of the whole cistus family, having large crimson-magenta flowers crinkled like tissue paper and splashed purple-brown in the centre. It flowers in the morning and sheds its petals at midday, but next day the bush is covered with new flowers and the display continues for several weeks from late May through June and July. To one side of the bush a clump of the 4 ft tall Sicilian garlic (*Allium siculum*), with its large heads of green, purple and creamy bell-shaped flowers, picks up all the colours of the cistus.

The cistus has a lax manner of growth, while the allium stems are tall and ungainly and need some cover. A semicircle of three plants of *Lavandula angustifolia* 'Hidcote' on each side pulls the group together. The lavender, clipped hard in early April, provides tight grey foliage, with spikes of mauve flowers in July; these can be left to flower or be cut in the bud for drying.

HOW TO GROW
Cistus × purpureus: see p. 263. While one of the finest rock roses in flower, C. × purpureus is, unfortunately, rather tender and needs a well-sheltered position in full sun.
Allium siculum: see p. 141.
Lavandula angustifolia: see p. 291.

The delicate spires of 'old-English' lavender, the bell-shaped flowers of the allium and the mottled blooms of the cistus complement each other's colouring, while the semicircle of lavender brings cohesion to the grouping. Mediterranean plants all, the three grow best in full sun. It would take about three years to achieve the effect illustrated. The time of year is June.

Clerodendrum trichotomum

Beautiful both in flower and in fruit, *Clerodendrum trichotomum* is one of the best late-summer shrubs, though one that is sadly under-used. Its heads of white flowers develop in August and September, above the heart-shaped leaves. Each bloom is like that of a jasmine, and just as fragrant, held in a dark red starry calyx. The flowers are replaced by brilliant blue pea-sized fruit, still held in their calyces like sapphires in crimson cases.

This clerodendrum is deciduous, but the berries continue to provide a show even after the leaves have fallen; the leaves are the plant's only disadvantage, for when bruised they have a curious almost unpleasant odour. The shrub commonly grows to 8-10 ft high and wide, and can be twice that size, but it is easily restricted.

HOW TO GROW
Plant in autumn or spring, in ordinary fertile soil and full sun. Shelter is advisable. To propagate, remove rooted suckers in autumn and replant. Do any hard pruning in April.

The calyces, or outer parts of the flowers, become crimson settings for the turquoise berries which develop in late summer.

It takes about ten years for the shrub to grow to its mature size.

Clethra alnifolia (SWEET PEPPER BUSH)

With the arrival of new plants from North America in the 18th century, the so-called 'American garden' became fashionable in Britain and the sweet pepper bush was one of its most popular adornments. It remains a valuable August-flowering deciduous shrub for an acid soil.

The best form, 'Paniculata', with its masses of long spikes of white, scented flowers, is ideal for extending the season in a garden whose main emphasis is upon early flowering rhododendrons. It grows to 6-8 ft high and wide, and clumps of summer-flowering heaths make a good shelter for its roots, which need constant moisture. 'Rosea' bears pale pink flowers, but in smaller spikes.

HOW TO GROW
Plant in autumn or spring, in moist to wet acid soil. Sun or light shade. Propagate in late summer by cuttings under glass, or by layering in spring. Prune, if necessary, in early spring.

Calluna vulgaris 'Robert Chapman' shades the roots of *Clethra alnifolia* and provides a delightful colour contrast.

In damp, lime-free soil, clethras attain full size in up to 20 years.

Colutea arborescens (BLADDER SENNA)

A display of yellow, pea-like flowers that begins in June and continues without a break until early autumn is only one of the attractions of this deciduous shrub. Its great joy comes with the appearance of the pods, which follow the flowers and give the plant its common name. They are 3 in. long inflated purses, flushed with red.

Colutea is a native of Mediterranean hillsides, though it has been known in Britain since the 16th century. It makes an open, wide-spreading bush 8-10 ft high, and it would be worth growing for its grey-green ferny foliage alone.

HOW TO GROW
Plant between autumn and spring, in ordinary, well-drained sandy, even poor, soil, and in full sun. The shrub is fast-growing and useful for screens. Propagate by heel cuttings under glass in late summer, or from seeds in spring. Tolerant of hard pruning in early spring.

Although grown mainly for its autumn seed pods, the bladder senna's yellow flowers are a delight throughout summer.

In spite of their exotic-looking pods, coluteas are easy shrubs to grow.

Variegated 'Spaethii' contrasts vividly with red *Lobelia cardinalis*.

Cornus alba 'Spaethii' (GOLD-VARIEGATED DOGWOOD)

The deciduous *Cornus alba*, which is often called red-barked dogwood, makes a warm red mass of suckering leafless stems, 6 ft high and wide, which glow in any fleeting gleam of winter sun. For the double bonus of coloured bark in winter and variegated foliage in summer try 'Spaethii', whose yellow leaves are splashed with green in the centre, or *C. a.* 'Sibirica', which has shiny, bright coral-red stems. Unlike some variegated shrubs, 'Spaethii' does not bleach in full sun, yet keeps its bicoloured effect in light shade.

HOW TO GROW
Plant in autumn or spring, in any kind of moist soil and in sun or light shade. Outstanding at the edge of a pool as a specimen group of three plants; prune one to the ground each spring to encourage the growth of new, bright red winter stems.

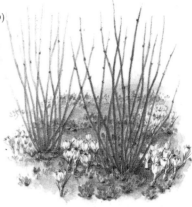

The stark brilliance of the winter stems of 'Sibirica' is relieved by the clumps of delicately coloured *Crocus vernus*.

Cornus kousa chinensis (DOGWOOD)

The best of the dogwoods grown for their flowers is the Chinese *Cornus kousa chinensis*, much more dependable in its flowering than American species. What appears to be a single bloom is in fact a mothball-sized knob of insignificant flowers held above a quartet of petal-like bracts, rather like John the Baptist's head on its charger. The 'charger' starts lime-green in June, pales to white, then turns a rich cream colour.

A good plant, 15 ft high and 10 ft wide, may carry hundreds of 'flowers' along the top of its horizontal tiers of branches, giving a dramatic effect. As the blossom fades, some of the glossy, oval, pointed leaves begin to turn purple, as a herald of the brilliant red and bronze autumn colour that is yet to come. Production of the strawberry-like fruits is rather erratic.

HOW TO GROW
Plant in autumn, in moist, acid to neutral soil. The shrub will grow in sun or partial shade and needs shelter from strong winds. Propagate by heel cuttings under glass in late summer. Avoid pruning, as cuts are slow to heal.

It takes at least 25 years for the Chinese strawberry tree, as *Cornus kousa* is sometimes called, to attain its full glory.

'Flaviramea's' brilliant stems – a cheering sight on a winter's day.

Cornus stolonifera 'Flaviramea' (DOGWOOD)

A dramatic winter display is provided by this dogwood's vivid yellow-green shoots, the colour of a green woodpecker's breast. The bush needs plenty of room, however, for it makes a thicket of 8 ft high suckering stems which, in damp soils, are extremely invasive.

John Tradescant collected *Cornus stolonifera* in North America and brought it back to his garden in Lambeth as early as the 1640s. It therefore found a home in Britain more than a century before the Asiatic red-barked *C. alba*, which has similar leaves and flowers. The bright red-stemmed *C. a.* 'Sibirica' can be planted with 'Flaviramea' to create a brilliant winter show.

HOW TO GROW
Plant and prune as for Cornus alba. Propagation of both species is by hardwood cuttings or rooted suckers, in autumn.

The yellow-white flowers of *Cornus stolonifera* 'Flaviramea' are borne in June. The shrub flourishes in damp situations.

Coronilla glauca

Elegant fronds of grey-blue foliage – rather like rue, but without rue's too-pungent perfume – decorate this Mediterranean evergreen shrub throughout the year. The coronillas, or small crowns, of golden, pea-like flowers make their bravest show in March and April, but in a mild year a few will appear throughout the winter.

Coronilla glauca (syn. C. valentina glauca) is less hardy than its larger, later-flowering cousin C. emerus, but has even greater charm. In a warm, sheltered position it grows about 6 ft high and slightly less wide.

HOW TO GROW
Plant in mid-spring in any ordinary well-drained soil. The shrub is lime-tolerant and does best against a warm, sheltered wall in full sun. Propagate by seeds (spring) or cuttings (summer) under glass. Prune to shape in spring.

The main flowering display is in spring, but a scattering of golden blooms may appear at any time during the year.

Full height and flowering potential are reached in three or four years

Corylus avellana 'Contorta' (CORKSCREW HAZEL)

In his garden at Myddleton House, near Enfield, the late E. A. Bowles, noted plantsman and breeder, cultivated a collection of what he called 'lunatic plants'. Many of them can now be seen at 'Bowles Corner', at Wisley, and several have a strong claim to be seen more often in normal gardens. One such is the corkscrew hazel, or 'Harry Lauder's Walking Stick'.

This hazel was first found in 1863 in a Gloucestershire hedgerow, where a mutant plant was seen to have spirally twisted stems and oddly crumpled leaves. Even its lamb's-tail catkins had kinks in them. Brought into cultivation, usually grafted on to the wild hazel, it slowly makes a deciduous bush 6-10 ft high and as much wide, with an unpredictable branch pattern. Long wands shoot up from the base and bend back on themselves, or twist like sticks of old-fashioned barley sugar.

Hung with yellow catkins in January and February, the branches are ideal for indoor arrangements on the oriental pattern, with a winter iris or two at the base. In the garden, some strikingly leaved evergreen plants at the foot of the tree can give a similar effect; *Iris foetidissima* 'Variegata', with clumps of white-striped, dark evergreen foliage, is good. The display continues into autumn, as the hazel leaves turn clear yellow before they fall. In summer, a large specimen of the hazel can support a climber, one of the smaller forms of *Clematis viticella*, such as 'Royal Blue', being very effective.

To provide colour and interest in the dark days of late winter, plant some small drifts of the purple-blue *Iris histrioides* and the orange-yellow *Crocus* 'Golden Bunch'.

HOW TO GROW
Corylus avellana 'Contorta': *plant between autumn and spring, in any well-drained garden soil. Does best in full sun, with protection from east winds. Propagate by layering in autumn. Prune only to remove congested old wood near ground level, in autumn.*
Clematis viticella: see p. 181.
Crocus 'Golden Bunch': *see Crocus aureus, p. 148.*
Iris foetidissima: see p. 96.
Iris histrioides: see p. 158.

As the winter joy of the yellow catkins of 'Contorta' fades, an underplanting of daffodils signals spring's return.

Hazel nuts grow in clusters of two to four, enclosed in sheaf-like cups among the crinkled leaves. The nuts ripen in October.

Crocuses and irises brighten late winter under a catkin-clad 'Contorta'.

Expect to wait 20 years for *C. willmottiae* to reach full height.

Corylopsis willmottiae

The 19th-century gardener and plantswoman Ellen Willmott is immortalised by a wealth of plants bearing her name. *Corylopsis willmottiae* is one of several similar species of elegant spring-flowering shrubs whose generic name means, simply, 'like a corylus' – that is, hazel. The 10 ft wands of growth do indeed seem to bear soft yellow catkins; these are, however, true flowers, both male and female, and have an exquisite scent.

The leaves, which appear after the flowers, maintain the same elegance. They have a bloom when young, during summer they develop a soft, purplish tinge in full sun, and they turn clear yellow before falling.

HOW TO GROW
Plant between autumn and spring in good, moist soil that is acid to neutral. Sun or light shade. The shrub is hardy, but best in a sheltered site. Water in dry summers. Propagate by layering in autumn. No pruning.

The catkin-like flowers, which are carried so generously in March and April, have a scent similar to that of cowslips.

Cotinus coggygria 'Royal Purple' (SMOKE TREE)

The rich colour and bushy growth of this cotinus make it a prominent feature in the garden for many months in summer and autumn. It forms a regular dome, eventually reaching 10 ft high and wide, with smooth round leaves. In June and July these are half-hidden behind loose, feathery panicles of tiny purple flowers, which have earned the shrub its common name of 'smoke tree'.

In summer, when its leaves are deep plum-red, 'Royal Purple' makes a splendid backdrop for groups of madonna lilies (*Lilium candidum*), a favourite for centuries in cottage gardens, where they may be left undisturbed for a long period. After the lilies have flowered the cotinus plays host to a totally different plant, a well-established specimen of *Clematis viticella* 'Alba Luxurians' which will scramble through its branches.

HOW TO GROW
Cotinus coggygria 'Royal Purple': *plant between autumn and spring, in well-drained soil in a sunny position. The plant thrives in poor soil, which restrains its vigour. Propagate by cuttings under glass, or by layering, in autumn. Prune to shape only, in early spring.*
Clematis viticella: see p. 181.
Lilium candidum: see p. 161.

The plume-like sprays of flowers of July (above) eventually turn a smoky grey in late summer. The brooding depth of colour that characterises the smoke tree makes it a fine June background (right) for vivid white madonna lilies and, later, the entwined clematis.

Cotoneaster dammeri

There are cotoneasters for every position and every size of garden. *Cotoneaster frigidus* makes a full-sized tree, while at the other end of the height scale comes the lovely *C. dammeri* from the rocky uplands of Central China. This species keeps out of cold winds by growing flat.

It makes perfect ground-cover for almost any situation. On dry banks it makes a change from grass, which has to be mown. In light shade, beneath other shrubs, it smothers weeds. The creeping stems root as they go and carry small evergreen leaves. The flowers which appear in June, looking like white, ½ in. wide stars, are succeeded by brilliant red berries.

HOW TO GROW
Plant between autumn and spring, in any ordinary soil. Best in sun. Propagation is easiest by layering, in autumn, also by seeds and cuttings. If necessary, restrict spread by hard pruning in spring.

C. *dammeri* softens stone and brick edges.

This overhead view of C. *dammeri* shows its effectiveness as ground-cover.

Cotoneaster horizontalis

In shape and texture, in its seasonal changes in foliage and from flower to fruit, this cotoneaster, however familiar, is always beautiful. On flat ground it seldom grows to more than 2 ft high, but planted against a wall its fans of tiny leaves will climb much higher. It is seen at its best if planted at the top of a bank, where the serried sheaves of fishbone-patterned branches cascade outwards and downwards.

Although deciduous, the plant does not lack leaves for long. New, bright green growth starts early, and by May it is studded with tiny white and pink flowers, which are irresistible to queen wasps. The bright red berries are accompanied in late autumn by equally brilliant leaves.

HOW TO GROW
Plant between autumn and spring in ordinary well-drained soil and in full sun. Propagate by cuttings under glass – in summer or autumn, or by seeds when ripe. Prune lightly, if at all, in late spring.

In late summer, alongside a bed of white and pink petunias, a cascading *Cotoneaster horizontalis* is covered in immature berries.

Cotoneaster salicifolius floccosus

This cotoneaster is one of the finest of the genus. Introduced from China, it makes a splendid bush 10-12 ft high and, if allowed, as much through. It soon develops a pleasing, arching habit, with small, creamy-white flowers in flattish clusters.

The leathery evergreen leaves are white and woolly beneath. Bunches of green buds seem to cover the branches for a long time, but at last in June they open, immediately attracting a host of insects. The show for which the plant is renowned comes in autumn, when cascades of small red berries weigh down the branches.

HOW TO GROW
As for Cotoneaster dammeri. If used for hedging, space the plants 2-3 ft apart. If required, prune back to the nearest berry cluster after flowering.

This lovely evergreen, covered in clusters of flowers among willow-like leaves in June, has a particularly graceful habit.

Leaves usually accompany the berries, except in very harsh winters.

Cotoneaster × watereri

Many gardeners like to find a place for a tall, arching shrub that will form an umbrella for shade-loving plants beneath. If an underplanting that flowers in spring is followed by another in summer, and if the shrub itself is colourful in autumn and winter, pleasure is provided all the year round.

For this purpose the semi-evergreen *Cotoneaster × watereri* is ideal. It reaches a height of 15 ft, and its arching branches create a pool of shade at least the same distance across. Its glory, as with so many cotoneasters, lies in its heavy bunches of scarlet berries that appear in autumn. In a town garden these may well blaze through the winter, but in the country, unfortunately, birds usually make a feast of them. The leaves are dark glossy green above and pale green beneath, and in June the shrub is decorated with clusters of tiny cream flowers.

An ideal underplanting for late spring in the area of permanent deep shade is Solomon's seal (*Polygonatum × hybridum*), a beautiful May-flowering perennial, perfect for cutting. Pale green ribbed leaves clasp the arching 2 ft stems, and between them hang small, white, bell-shaped flowers tipped with green.

Outside the circle of Solomon's seal, where the shade is less deep, a few drifts of *Campanula persicifolia* can be planted. From June to August their sturdy 3 ft stems, which rise from rosettes of evergreen leaves, bear wide cup-shaped flowers of blue or white.

HOW TO GROW
Cotoneaster × watereri: as for C. horizontalis (see p. 269). In large gardens this cotoneaster may be grown as a hedge.
Campanula persicifolia: see p. 72.
Polygonatum × hybridum: see p. 113.

In autumn the heavy bunches of fruit on *Cotoneaster × watereri* 'Cornubia' (above) weigh down its branches. In spring and summer the shrub provides cover for shade-loving plants – the May-flowering Solomon's seal, which provides a green undercover in summer, and blue campanulas.

Crinodendron hookerianum (LANTERN TREE)

In September the lantern tree – a truly descriptive common name – puts out a mass of small, long-stalked buds. The following May the buds swell to become the lantern of the name. They hang in festoons from the dark, evergreen leaves – like masses of unopened fuchsia buds.

The plant collector William Lobb introduced the lantern tree to Britain from Chile in 1848, and since then it has become one of the most valued plants for mild, moist gardens in the western parts of these islands. It reaches an average height of 10-15 ft, with a similar spread, and flowers prolifically while still fairly young.

HOW TO GROW
Plant in late spring, in rich, moisture-retentive but well-drained soil. Light shade is needed and, except in mild areas, protection from a west wall. Propagate by heel cuttings under glass in late summer. No pruning.

In mild conditions the dense, bushy *Crinodendron hookerianum* can attain the height and spread of a small tree.

The brilliant crimson of its 'lanterns' gives the shrub a festive air.

Cytisus battandieri (MOROCCAN BROOM)

The Moroccan broom is a beautiful 10 ft high shrub that branches freely from the ground upwards. Its spreading habit should be encouraged by the occasional removal of old branches. The leaves, which are deciduous or semi-evergreen, of the same size and shape as laburnum, are silkily silver, flashing in the wind. The floral display is equally eye-catching, with upright spikes of gold lining the branches, like fir cones, in June and July. They are deliciously pineapple-scented.

HOW TO GROW
The shrub is remarkably hardy, though not in colder northern gardens. All cytisus resent root disturbance; plant pot-grown specimens in autumn or spring. Poor, dry and deep soil, neutral to acid, is best. The shrub is lime-tolerant, but is short-lived in alkaline soils. Cytisus battandieri is best trained loosely against a wall. For propagation and pruning, see C. scoparius 'Andreanus'; but cuttings are not easy.

At the height of summer, glowing yellow flower clusters up to 4 in. long light up the silvery foliage of Moroccan broom.

Growing 1-2 ft a year, the broom is a glorious plant for covering a wall.

Cytisus scoparius 'Andreanus' (COMMON BROOM)

Our native common broom, *Cytisus scoparius*, is so attractive that, if it were rare, gardeners would search avidly for it. As it is, the plant grows freely on heaths and roadsides, where its deep gold butterfly-like flowers brighten many a motorway journey in May and June.

Selected colour forms have long since superseded the common species. 'Andreanus', one of the first named cultivars, has flowers so deeply yellow as to be almost orange, with crimson-brown markings. The shrub grows to a height of 6-8 ft.

HOW TO GROW
Cultivation as for Cytisus battandieri, though it will also grow in the north. Propagate either by seeds under glass in spring, or by heel cuttings in late summer. The shrub flowers on shoots of the previous season, which may be cut back almost to base immediately after flowering. Do not cut into the old wood of the plant - it could prove fatal.

'Andreanus', an early French form of common broom, needs hardly any pruning to keep its growth to a manageable size.

All forms of the broom have a graceful arching habit and flower profusely.

Cytisus × praecox (WARMINSTER BROOM)

A trio of spring-flowering shrubs makes a predominantly golden group from March until May. First comes *Forsythia suspensa*, with dense clusters of bright yellow flowers on its bare, arching branches in March and April. It should not be squared off on top by clipping – the fate of so many forsythias – but pruned judiciously after flowering so that the new shoots are of variable heights and the shrub looks natural.

In front of the forsythia and beside the broom, a flowering currant, *Ribes sanguineum*, forms a little green thicket. The white-flowered form 'Album' is preferable to the rather harsh pinks and reds of other forms. The currant comes into flower in late March, while the forsythia still flaunts its bright gold.

The star of the show, the Warminster broom, an arching shrub 5-6 ft in height and spread, brings the group to its climax in late spring. It bears a cascade of creamy-yellow flowers in May, against the bright green background of the forsythia's unfurling leaves.

Ideally, this planting should be near enough to the house to be seen through the windows in bad weather, but not so near that the acrid smell of the broom will penetrate indoors. Both the forsythia and the currant are excellent for forcing into flower in a warm room. The forsythia can be cut as early as New Year's Day, the currant a little later in the month.

HOW TO GROW
Cytisus × praecox: cultivation, propagation and pruning as for C. battandieri and C. scoparius 'Andreanus' (see p. 271). At planting time, allow 5 ft between the broom and the currant, and the same distance to the forsythia in the background.
Forsythia suspensa: see p. 281.
Ribes sanguineum: see p. 310.

A breath of the warm south – the creamy flowers of the Warminster broom.

By May, the flowers of *Forsythia suspensa* and *Ribes sanguineum* 'Album' are almost over, though new leaves are appearing. *Cytisus × praecox*, in the foreground, is bearing lavish sprays of creamy-yellow blooms, but is not yet in leaf.

Daboecia cantabrica (ST DABEOC'S HEATH)

St Dabeoc, whose plant this is, was one of the numerous saints who flourished in Ireland's distant past. The shrub, a dwarf evergreen, also known as Connemara heath, is one of the loveliest members of the British flora. On a wide bush, 18 in. high, it carries from June to November long spikes of bright rose-purple urn-shaped flowers.

Daboecia cantabrica, also listed as D. polifolia, makes marvellous ground-cover and can look stunning at the base of the smaller rhododendrons, providing fine leaf contrast and continuing the floral display into autumn.

HOW TO GROW
Plant during autumn or spring, in fertile, acid and moisture-retentive soil. Full sun or light shade are equally suitable. Mulch the shallow roots in summer with moist peat. Propagate by layering or cuttings under glass, in autumn. Shear over lightly after flowering.

The flowers of *D. c.* 'Atropurpurea', seen behind *Calluna vulgaris* 'Hirsuta Typica', are a little darker than the species.

Among the several forms of *D. cantabrica* is the white-flowered 'Alba'.

Daphne × burkwoodii

This lovely hybrid – and the nearly identical clone, 'Somerset' – is one of the most dependable of daphnes, and one of the fastest-growing.

Produced in the 1930s as a deliberate attempt to create a good, easy garden plant, the hybrid is a semi-evergreen cross between the evergreen *Daphne cneorum* and the deciduous *D. caucasica*. It reaches a height and spread of 3-4 ft and carries small, leafy heads of fragrant, soft pink flowers in May and June, and again, more sparsely, during summer and autumn. A cluster of flowers in a rosette of leaves makes a perfect buttonhole.

HOW TO GROW
Plant during early autumn or spring, in ordinary, well-drained but moist soil; sun or light shade. Mulch in summer to keep roots cool. Propagate by heel cuttings under glass in summer. If necessary, prune to shape after flowering.

Each of these early summer flower clusters, emitting a distinctive, spicy scent, measures about 2 in. across.

Daphne × burkwoodii 'Somerset' stands over rose-pink *D. cneorum*.

Daphne mezereum (MEZEREON)

This is a rare, British native plant from southern woodlands, where it grows in moist, heavy, limy soil. It is, without doubt, the most common daphne in gardens. Unfortunately, it is not the easiest, though well worth an effort for its rewarding floral display and exquisite scent. From February to April, purple-pink flowers wreathe the previous year's leafless stems in dense clusters. In July and August, attractive, but highly poisonous, scarlet berries cover the branches. A well-established bush slowly makes a dome 3 ft tall and almost as wide.

'Alba' is a taller, narrower form that bears lovely white flowers and produces yellow berries. Both are more suited to simple rather than elaborate gardens.

HOW TO GROW
As for Daphne × burkwoodii. All daphnes, and in particular this species, are prone to a virus disease, transmitted by aphids, which causes leaf mottle and defoliation. Spray regularly against aphids to prevent infection.

Translucent, amber fruits follow the white flowers of the form 'Alba'. This species is particularly well suited to chalk soils.

Daphne mezereum's flowers greet the spring before the leaves have unfolded.

Daphne odora 'Aureomarginata'

To look its best, this lovely evergreen needs the help of discreet underplanting. Few gardeners would want to miss, in winter and early spring, the pleasure of its heavily scented rosettes of purplish-pink flowers, nestling in whorls of golden-edged leaves. But there is no denying its ungainly form, for its branches, reaching 4 or 5 ft in height and spread, flop awkwardly sideways. However, this defect may be overlooked if the eye is distracted downwards to a carpet of spring flowers.

For the underplanting, choose any colours except yellow. Clumps of *Viola labradorica* are not only decorative, but provide a living mulch for a shrub which dislikes bare, dry earth round its roots. To flower among the violets, plant such early spring bulbs as snowdrops, the pale blue grape hyacinth, *Muscari armeniacum* 'Cantab', and *Anemone blanda* in mixed colours. A burst of bluebells – *Endymion hispanicus*, in blue, pink and white – can follow to prolong this spring planting well into May.

The narrow glossy leaves of *Daphne odora*, a native of China and Japan, are to some tastes more charming when they are plain green, as in the species. However, the species is not fully hardy, whereas 'Aureomarginata' will thrive in cold gardens if sheltered from strong winds.

HOW TO GROW
Daphne odora 'Aureomarginata': *cultivation as for D. × burkwoodii (see p. 273). Initially slow to establish itself, this particular daphne is hardy in all but the severest winters and strong-growing. A sheltered site is best, to protect the early spring flowers.*
Anemone blanda: see p. 143.
Endymion hispanicus: see p. 151.
Muscari armeniacum: see p. 163.
Viola labradorica: see p. 221.

Enhance the appearance of *Daphne odora* 'Aureomarginata' by planting clumps of blue, pink and purple flowers beneath its branches. Try *Viola labradorica, Muscari armeniacum, Anemone blanda* and *Endymion hispanicus*.

Daphne odora 'Aureomarginata'.

When its buds open in May, *Daphne retusa's* scent rivals its looks.

Daphne retusa

Most of the popular and widely cultivated daphnes are natives of Europe, but the genus does extend along the Himalayas and into China. *Daphne retusa* is one of the finest of the dwarf Chinese species, and as long ago as 1946 was given an Award of Garden Merit by the Royal Horticultural Society. Dense and rounded of habit, it slowly builds up to about 2 ft in height. The leaves are leathery-textured and have a lustrous upper surface.

In late spring, the tip of every stem is crowned by a cluster of rose-purple buds which turn white as they expand and exhale the typical sweet daphne perfume. A similar but taller daphne is *D. tangutica*, which grows to 4 ft or more. The leaves are longer and the clusters of flowers, flushed purple on opening, are smaller. They appear earlier than those of *D. retusa*, in March or April.

HOW TO GROW
See *Daphne odora* 'Aureomarginata'.

The purple and white flowers of *D. retusa*, set among evergreen foliage, will be followed in autumn by bright red, oval berries.

Deutzia × hybrida 'Mont Rose'

Deutzias are an under-used group of beautiful June and July-flowering shrubs. They are reminiscent of the smaller philadelphuses, though lacking their scent. One of the finest is 'Mont Rose', which, before flowering, is an upright bush about 4-6 ft high. But in June its masses of pink, star-shaped flowers weigh the branches down and spread them elegantly outwards, presenting a splendid picture for almost a month.

The shrub is hardy, though in sheltered spots its long, narrow leaves are apt to appear too early and then to suffer from a late spring frost.

HOW TO GROW
Plant between autumn and spring, in any fertile, well-drained soil. Light shade or sun. Propagate by cuttings under glass in late summer. After flowering, prune flowered shoots back to old wood. Late spring frosts may damage flower buds.

The open, rich rose-purple blooms are delicately tinged with darker rose, and become gradually paler as they fade.

'Mont Rose' attains its full height of 4-6 ft in about as many years.

Elaeagnus angustifolia

(OLEASTER, JERUSALEM WILLOW)

Surprisingly, this splendid silver-leaved shrub, which is hardy in Britain and has been grown here for nearly 500 years, is rarely seen. The common name, oleaster, is derived from the Latin *oleum* (olive), and, indeed, the shrub is as silver as a breeze-blown olive on a Mediterranean hillside. The oleaster can reach a height of 15 ft, and as much across, so is best suited to quite large gardens. Its effect against a background of dark evergreens is dramatic. Small, scented, silver and yellow flowers generally appear in June (though some specimens do not flower every year) and are followed by silvery-orange edible berries.

HOW TO GROW
Plant during autumn or early winter, in any good garden soil; not recommended for shallow chalk. Full sun; wind-resistant. Propagate by cuttings under glass in early autumn, or by seeds. If necessary, prune to shape in spring.

The edible fruits of the willow-leaved oleaster are covered with tiny silvery scales and have a sweet, mealy taste.

Good cultivation will produce a tree-like plant within about ten years.

Elaeagnus × ebbingei

Grown as a hedge, this broad-leaved evergreen rapidly becomes impenetrable. Since it grows equally well in towns, in open country or by the sea, it is ideal for providing quick protection from traffic noise or strong winds. It is handsome, too: its foliage, green above, is silver on the reverse and flashes brilliantly in wind and sun. It is also a welcome late-flowering plant, bearing in October little flowers of silver-white, with a heavy scent of cloves. These are occasionally followed by a spring display of orange berries. *Elaeagnus × ebbingei* develops into a tall, wide shrub, 10 ft high and across, with stiff, backward-pointing side branches.

HOW TO GROW
Plant during early autumn in ordinary, well-drained soil. Excellent for windbreaks and shelter hedges, especially by the sea. Propagate and prune as for Elaeagnus angustifolia. Trim hedges once or twice in summer.

The evergreen foliage creates a dense hedge in practically any conditions, including both full sun or shade.

The foliage of 'Maculata' gleams in the winter sunshine.

Elaeagnus pungens 'Maculata'

Any dabbler in the garden can obtain plenty of colour in spring and summer. But when the dabbler starts taking his hobby seriously and widens his knowledge of plants, he will want to enjoy his garden all the year round. Winter colour then becomes essential.

One of the most brilliant of all winter shrubs is *Elaeagnus pungens* 'Maculata', a slow-growing evergreen with glossy oval leaves, splashed in the centre with buttercup yellow, and coloured cream beneath. The shrub is dense and grows 8-12 ft high, rather less in spread. Its growth is clumsy and it produces little effect at close range, but when viewed from several yards away it is glorious – a golden cumulus cloud if seen against a leaden sky.

HOW TO GROW
As for Elaeagnus × ebbingei (see p. 275). E. p. 'Maculata' is suitable for hedging and low shelter-belts. It tends to put out all-green shoots among the variegated foliage; cut these out at the base as soon as they are noticed.

The ovate, leathery leaves are a glossy dark green, splashed with gold. A red rose rambles over the branches.

In a mild area, *Escallonia × iveyi* grows vigorously into a rounded shrub.

Escallonia × iveyi

Although this shrub is not reliably hardy everywhere, it is so beautiful and distinctive that it should be tried wherever there is the least possibility of success.

It forms a glossy, dark evergreen bush, 10 ft or so high and spreading to 6-9 ft. From late July until well into autumn it is lit up by clusters of white flowers which are almost as large as those of hydrangeas. It makes an excellent courtyard shrub, for the sheltered conditions will help to ensure its survival.

HOW TO GROW
Plant during autumn or spring, in any kind of well-drained soil. It is lime-tolerant and resistant to drought, and needs full sun. It is best grown as a wall shrub, in all except southern gardens. Propagate by cuttings under glass, in early autumn. Remove flowering growths when finished.

Panicles of white flowers, 5-6 in. long, appear during the summer among the highly polished dark green leaves.

Given time and space, 'Alpina' will spread over a considerable area.

Erica arborea 'Alpina' (TREE HEATH)

The tree heath, *Erica arborea*, grows throughout the Mediterranean area and on mountains in East Africa but is too tender for many parts of Britain. Fortunately, however, the lovely form 'Alpina', introduced from Spain, is hardy in all but the coldest and most exposed districts.

It is grown principally for its feathery, pale, yet bright green leaves, which provide an overall effect not dissimilar to a juniper. The masses of tiny white flowers that appear in clusters in March and April are, in effect, a bonus. They have a honey-like scent which carries for some distance. The plant eventually makes a 10 ft high bush, and if left unpruned can achieve a greater spread.

HOW TO GROW
While an acid, sandy soil is ideal, this is one of the few ericas that will grow in moderately limy soil. It thrives in full sun. Propagate by cuttings under glass in summer or autumn. Trim after flowering, but only if necessary.

The little white, bell-shaped flowers of 'Alpina' bloom profusely throughout the spring and have a sweet scent.

Erica carnea (HEATH)

The completely hardy *Erica carnea* (syn. *E. herbacea*) is one of the joys of the winter garden, where it forms colourful ground-cover. Height is between 6 and 12 in., with an equivalent spread. The clusters of small flowers range in colour from white (as in 'Springwood White') through shades of pink ('Winter Beauty') to dark red ('Vivellii').

A careful selection from the many cultivars can provide flowering from November right through to April. Like other species of exposed uplands, they are best grown in groups and in close association with other plants.

HOW TO GROW
As for Erica arborea 'Alpina', but this heather is even more tolerant of lime. Light shade is acceptable, but it does best where winter sun catches the flowers. Propagate by cuttings or, more easily, by layering in spring. Clip with shears after flowering.

Two ericas are shown here in close-up as they appear in September: *E. vagans* 'St Keverne' in flower, with foliage of *E. carnea* 'Aurea'.

Erica vagans (CORNISH HEATH)

By choosing suitable species of heathers and their different forms, it is possible to have them in flower outdoors on every day of the year. Cornish heath provides a display from July to October, and often beyond. In this country the wild species is confined to the acid moors of the Lizard peninsula in Cornwall.

Cornish heath reaches up to 2 ft in height and spread. The flowers, which are borne in 6-9 in. long spikes at the ends of shoots, open in a succession lasting many weeks and are good for cutting. The named cultivars are more attractive than the purplish-pink species. They include the white 'Lyonesse' and the rose-pink 'St Keverne'.

HOW TO GROW
As for Erica arborea 'Alpina' – strictly in acid soil and full sun. Propagate by cuttings or by layering established plants. Prune in spring by cutting back any frost-damaged shoots and trimming off faded flower spikes.

About mid-September in the heather garden above, a band of *Erica carnea* behind the central *Juniperus chinensis* 'Pyramidalis' is not yet in flower. To the right and in front of the tree are the rose-pink flowers of *Erica vagans* 'St Keverne'. To left and right of the ericas in the foreground is a double-white variety of *Calluna vulgaris*.

Escallonia × 'Langleyensis'

Escallonias are pink, red or white-flowered shrubs from South America. Many are tender in this country, but those from Chile, in particular, have become valued garden plants. They accept salt spray with impunity, but in colder districts inland they need some shelter.

Escallonia × 'Langleyensis' is a hybrid with Chilean parents. A graceful evergreen, about 8 ft high, it has arching branches that are covered in June and July with short spikes of rose-pink tubular flowers. A few continue to open until well into autumn. The small, deep green leaves are glossy. If there is space, 'Langleyensis' – or one of its derivatives, the 'Donard' hybrids – can be planted to form a beautiful flowering hedge.

HOW TO GROW
Plant during autumn or spring, in any well-drained soil and in full sun. Suitable for hedging in seaside gardens, in which case plant 2 ft apart. Propagate as for Escallonia × iveyi (p. 276). Prune lightly after flowering.

In the summer, the arching boughs of *Escallonia* × 'Langleyensis' erupt into a pink, frothy mass of blooms.

'Langleyensis' harmonises beautifully with a mellow brick wall.

Eucryphia × nymansensis

There comes a time in the garden, not long after midsummer, when a fresh effect is needed. There is no better recipe for this than white or cream flowers, and few are more lovely than those of *Eucryphia* × *nymansensis*, whose dark evergreen foliage sets off to perfection the cream-coloured blooms. Borne in August, they have a delicate scent and are glossy and cup-shaped – rather like those of *Hypericum calycinum*, the Rose of Sharon.

The shrub, hardy throughout the south and west, except in the severest winters, reaches a height of 15 ft or more, and half that much across. It is named after the Sussex garden Nymans (now a National Trust property), where it arose in 1914. The form 'Nymansay' makes a tall, narrow tree which, except in exposed gardens, could well be chosen in place of the conventional columnar cupressus, since it grows much more rapidly.

E. × *nymansensis* appreciates shade at its roots, and this can be provided by a clump of blue lace-cap hydrangeas (*Hydrangea macrophylla*), which flower in late summer. The large, slightly flattened flowering heads of a variety such as 'Blue Wave' – like a soft frothy carpet – make a beautiful contrast with the more glossy flowers and vertical form of the eucryphia. The 4 ft spires of summer hyacinths, *Galtonia candicans*, will add a touch of glistening white to the picture. Plant among them Spanish bluebells, *Endymion hispanicus*, to give a splash of pink, blue and white during late spring.

HOW TO GROW
Eucryphia × *nymansensis: plant in autumn or spring, in ordinary fertile soil, preferably neutral to acid, although it will tolerate some lime. Choose a sheltered site, with a shaded root area. Protect young plants in winter. Propagate by heel cuttings under glass in late summer. Prune only to remove frost-damaged shoots in late spring.*
Endymion hispanicus: see p. 151.
Galtonia candicans: see p. 155.
Hydrangea macrophylla: see p. 286.

Flowers of *Eucryphia* × *nymansensis*.

This young *Eucryphia* × *nymansensis* is not yet fully grown and will become, in time, tall and column-like. In the foreground are blue hydrangeas 'Blue Wave' and summer hyacinths *Galtonia candicans*. The time of year for this setting is August.

Euonymus europaeus 'Red Cascade'

(COMMON SPINDLE TREE)

A major late autumn pleasure for any walker across our chalk and limestone hills is to find a wild specimen of *Euonymus europaeus* bedecked with brilliantly coloured fruits, like a Christmas decoration ahead of season. 'Red Cascade' is a beautiful cultivated form, with arching bright green stems up to 12 ft high. It has an open habit, so that plants which thrive in light shade can be planted beneath it. May sees the appearance of small green-white flowers, which give way to pink, long-stalked fruit capsules. But its true glory comes in September, when the leaves turn pink and the fruit capsules split open to reveal brilliant orange-red seeds.

HOW TO GROW

Plant between autumn and spring, in any well-drained soil. Excellent on chalk, in sun or light shade. Ideally, plant groups of several plants, 3-4 ft apart. Spray against black bean aphid in late spring with a systemic insecticide. For propagation and pruning, see Euonymus fortunei 'Silver Queen' below.

The graceful, arching branches of *Euonymus europaeus* 'Red Cascade' are wreathed with vivid colour in autumn.

The rosy leaves and brilliant berries create a cascade of flame

Euonymus fortunei 'Silver Queen'

Attractive, hardy and easy to grow, this evergreen is one of the most cheering of winter plants. The wild species, which is Japanese in origin, behaves rather like ivy: it trails along the ground or climbs by aerial roots. 'Silver Queen', however, forms a compact bush 3-4 ft high – somewhat taller when grown against a wall.

New leaves borne in spring are cream coloured, but by summer they have turned to deep green with a creamy-white edge. Well-established shrubs produce tiny green-white flowers in May and June, followed by orange seeds.

HOW TO GROW

Plant in a sheltered spot in autumn or spring, in any kind of soil. It thrives in sun or shade. Propagate by cuttings under glass, in late summer, or by layering. If necessary, prune to shape in early spring.

With its white-edged foliage, 'Silver Queen' scintillates against the shaded background in the summer garden

Euonymus japonicus 'Ovatus Aureus'

A mass of glossy leaves with dark green centres and pale creamy-yellow margins make this evergreen a handsome sight – a significant advance on the ordinary species which may easily be taken for a shiny-leaved privet. Left unchecked, it will eventually build up to a domed bush, 6 ft or so high and about half that across, but it is slow to do so and can easily be kept to any desired size. Pruned branchlets are splendid for flower arrangements.

Hardy in the south and west, the shrub tolerates salt spray and is ideal for growing by the sea. In some years it may bear pink seed capsules in the autumn.

HOW TO GROW

As for Euonymus fortunei 'Silver Queen'. It is tolerant of both town pollution and seaside conditions, and excellent for hedging. Set plants 2 ft apart. Prune to shape in late spring, and if necessary again in early autumn: remove whole shoots, rather than clip as for a formal hedge.

The richly yellow-suffused leathery leaves and compact growth of 'Ovatus Aureus' make it the most popular golden euonymus.

The plain green form 'Macrophyllus' has larger leaves than the species.

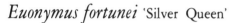

Festoons of fresh, snow-white flowers on pink-tinged shoots adorn the long, graceful branches of this unusual shrub.

Brief but beautiful – the free-flowering May display of *Exochorda giraldii*.

Exochorda giraldii

It is a pity that exochordas are so seldom seen outside specialist collections, because, even among the profusion of other May-flowering shrubs, a well-flowered specimen will always take the eye.

Exochorda giraldii is a hardy shrub some 12 ft high and wide. The young shoots are tinged with pink and often retain some of this colour in maturity. Against these shoots and the fresh green leaves, the sprays of starry white flowers stand out beautifully. The floral display, normally short, can be made to last a little longer by planting the shrub in half shade.

HOW TO GROW
Plant in autumn or spring in well-drained moisture-retentive soil. Avoid shallow, chalky soils. Sun or light shade is needed, with shelter from winds. Propagate by cuttings under glass, in summer, or by layering. No pruning, but remove weak shoots in late spring.

Fatsia japonica

Despite its exotic appearance, this Japanese relation of ivy is almost hardy and has been grown in Britain for 100 years. *Fatsia japonica* (syns. *Aralia japonica*, *A. sieboldii*) develops heavy stems, sometimes to 10 ft high, which carry glossy, evergreen, hand-shaped leaves often more than a foot across. In autumn, each stem bears at its tip a multiple head of creamy flowers, formed like those of ivy.

Because the plant looks so dramatic, it is possibly out of character in the average suburban garden. To show to full effect it really needs setting off against the wall of a gracious building, perhaps in a formal situation.

HOW TO GROW
Plant in autumn or spring, in any kind of well-drained soil. It is best in light shade and against a sheltered wall. Propagate by suckers or seeds under glass in spring. Prune only to restrict unruly shoots.

Massive and polished, fatsia's leaves gleam above *Hosta sieboldiana*. To the left lies variegated *Cornus alba* 'Spaethii'.

Globular flower heads are carried on the tip of each stem in October.

Forsythia suspensa

Magnificent though the large-flowered forsythias are, their effect is often too overwhelmingly bright, rather like that of a golden privet. *Forsythia suspensa* has a more delicate appearance, though it is fully hardy. The shrub has a rambling habit.

Its arching, interlacing branches make a bush 10 ft high and wide, though these measurements may be greater when it is grown against a wall. Long streamers of pale lemon-yellow flowers open in late March and generally continue well into April. When cut, they are admirable for indoor decoration.

HOW TO GROW
Plant between autumn and spring, in ordinary soil and in sun or light shade. Propagate by hardwood cuttings in autumn. Flowers are borne on wood from the previous year; prune after flowering, shortening young shoots by one-third. Remove a few old shoots from ground level annually.

Bell-shaped flowers, each 1 in. across, are carried in clusters along pendulous, year-old shoots during late March and well into April.

When grown against a wall, this lovely forsythia will spread widely.

Fuchsia magellanica gracilis 'Versicolor'

The ballerina skirts of typical large fuchsia flowers, petals contrasting in colour with the spreading sepals above, provide one of summer's most eagerly awaited displays. The most outstanding flowers are produced by the so-called florists' varieties of the plant, which really do best when grown under glass. It is left to the much hardier *Fuchsia magellanica gracilis*, from far down in South America, to bring something of the same delights to the open garden.

The best form is 'Versicolor', which grows up to 6 ft high and with a spread of 3-4 ft. Its leaves are a pleasure from the moment they unfold, beginning as pink, then gradually turning grey-green with a red midrib. The flowers start to open at the end of June and continue until autumn. As they sway on long stalks, in the slightest breeze, their long, spreading red sepals almost hide their purple mini-skirt petals below. Only the hardest of frost cuts 'Versicolor' to the ground – and, even when it does, a 3 ft high bush will build up by midsummer the following year.

Since the shrub prefers dappled shade, it would do well planted to the west of a large Moroccan broom, *Cytisus battandieri*. In June, this bears golden cones of flowers with a fruity scent.

As an accompaniment, you could try *Iris pallida dalmatica*, whose flowers are clear blue. The grey foliage of both plants makes a perfect framework for the fuchsia. A foliage contrast, in this case waved and white-banded and used as ground-cover, can be provided in front of the fuchsia by the large-leaved *Hosta crispula*, a handsome perennial that is now widely available.

HOW TO GROW
Fuchsia magellanica gracilis 'Versicolor': plant in spring or autumn, in any well-drained, humus-enriched soil. Light shade or sun. Protect roots in cold areas. Propagate by cuttings in spring or summer. Prune in spring, tipping plants lightly in mild regions but cutting back to ground level in colder areas.
Cytisus battandieri: see p. 271.
Hosta crispula: see p. 94.
Iris pallida dalmatica: see p. 96.

The delightful foliage of this hardy fuchsia would ensure it garden space even without its brilliant late-summer flowers. *Hosta crispula* and *Iris pallida* are worthy companions in this walled bed, adding interest with contrasting leaves and colour at different seasons.

Fothergilla major

This North American plant is a welcome shrub that has the same soil needs as rhododendrons and offers an interesting contrast with them. It is a slow-growing shrub that eventually reaches a height and spread of about 6 ft. Its name commemorates a Dr Fothergill who, in the 18th century, specialised in growing North American plants in his Essex garden.

In spring, bottlebrush-like spikes of white flowers appear before the glossy oval leaves unfold; these are dark green above, grey beneath. But the shrub is at its best in autumn when the leaves take on brilliant, unpredictable tints of red, orange and yellow.

HOW TO GROW
Plant in autumn or spring, in acid or neutral soil, moist and preferably with added peat. Autumn colours develop best in full sun. Propagate by layering in early autumn. Slow-growing; usually no pruning needed.

The shrub seen in its full finery of rich red-and-orange autumn colours.

Fothergilla major in its spring apparel of white flowers forms a sweetly scented mound of bottlebrush-like spikes.

Garrya elliptica

No other plant in cultivation has such splendid catkins as the male *Garrya elliptica*. Great festoons of silvery lime-green, up to 9 in. long, sway in the breeze from January to March. The female catkins are grey and smaller and are followed by strings of deep purple berries.

The shrub is generally hardy but resents searing winds, which often give its oval, leathery leaves an unsightly scorched margin. Protection by a wall, even a north-facing one, helps. The shrub can become massive – up to 15 ft high and almost as much across. But careful thinning of its shoots can make it suitable even for a small garden.

HOW TO GROW
Plant in late spring, using young, container-grown plants. Useful as a town shrub, in sun or dappled shade. Except in mild areas it is best grown against a wall or in a sheltered site. Propagate by heel cuttings under glass in late summer. If necessary, prune to shape in spring.

The rich green leaves of *Garrya* remain on the shrub all year round.

In the bleak months during the latter half of winter, the long catkins of *Garrya elliptica* give a festive air to the garden.

Genista aetnensis (MOUNT ETNA BROOM)

From July, this loose, twiggy shrub becomes transformed into a cloud of delicately scented, clear golden-yellow. Like most brooms, it is almost leafless.

When garden space is limited, the lightness of Mount Etna broom makes it an ideal shrub to train upwards on a single stem. But if space is no problem, it can happily be left to grow to 15 ft or so in height and spread. Flowering begins at an early age, and a three-year-old seedling only 3 ft high will put out an attractive display. The plant is hardy in all areas.

HOW TO GROW
General cultivation as for other brooms (see Cytisus battandieri, p. 271). Plant young container-grown plants between autumn and spring; best on poor, dry soil, acid to neutral, but also excellent on limy soil. Full sun. Propagate by seeds in spring. Thin out crowded shoots after flowering.

Golden-yellow flowers, about ½ in. long, adorn the branches in summer.

Genista lydia (BULGARIAN BROOM)

For much of the year this highly decorative dwarf shrub from south-east Europe forms wide, spreading hummocks of leafless stems that arch downwards at the tips, in the manner of a prostrate weeping willow. But in May and June, it is wreathed in small, yellow pea flowers, in such a prodigality of blossom that every twig is hidden and the plant is transformed into a dome of bright gold. At this time of year no other shrub in the garden can rival it for sheer glory of colour.

Considering its land of origin, *Genista lydia* is surprisingly hardy. It can provide a striking centrepiece for the larger rock garden, and is positively breathtaking as a cascade down a retaining wall.

HOW TO GROW
Plant in the same way as Genista aetnensis. This species is particularly suitable for informal planting on dry, sunny banks, where its spreading roots anchor the soil and prevent erosion. It will grow well on thin, chalky soils. No pruning is needed. Encourage bushy growth by pinching out the growing points on young plants after flowering has finished. Thin out the crowded shoots of mature bushes after flowering to keep the plants open.

Genista aetnensis, even when planted in poor soil, will repay you with a magnificent scented cloud of gold.

Genista lydia grows no more than 2 ft high, but will spread out – perhaps spilling over a wall – to cover an area 6 ft across.

Hamamelis mollis, Sarcococca confusa and Euonymus japonicus 'Duc d'Anjou'.

Hamamelis mollis 'Pallida'

(CHINESE WITCH HAZEL)

Perhaps the most striking of the Chinese witch hazels, *Hamamelis mollis* 'Pallida' is one of the classic winter-garden plants, and one of the few to provide a display when viewed from a distance. It arose earlier this century at Wisley. 'Pallida' grows into a fine deciduous bush 10 ft high and wide, its branches carrying bunches of furry buds which open early in the year into hydra-like flowers with wavy, pale yellow petals. These petals are broader and thicker than those of other witch hazels.

HOW TO GROW

Plant between autumn and spring in any humus-rich, moisture-retentive, but well-drained soil. Not suitable for limy soils. Best in sun. Propagate in autumn by layering. Prune lightly after flowering, if it is necessary to restrict growth.

'Pallida' has pale yellow flowers, faintly flushed with claret red at the centre and densely packed on the twigs.

Hibiscus syriacus makes a tropical focal point in the late summer garden.

Hibiscus syriacus

British gardens are not warm enough to grow the flamboyant hibiscus of Hawaii. But a close cousin, the hardy *Hibiscus syriacus* (syn. *Althaea frutex*) makes an attractive substitute. It forms a rather gaunt bush – perhaps 8 ft high and 5 ft wide – on which the downy, rich green leaves do not appear until late spring – and before then the pessimistic may think their plant has died. The wide flowers are borne from July or August until the first frosts. There are many named, variously coloured forms to choose from, all beautiful. A fine example is 'Hamabo' a faintly blushing white, crimson at the centre.

HOW TO GROW

Set out young container plants, between autumn and spring, in any humus-rich, well-drained soil. Full sun is ideal, preferably against a south-facing wall to make the most of autumn warmth. Propagate by heel cuttings under glass in summer. Remove frost-damaged tips in spring.

'Blue Bird', probably the best single blue hibiscus, has violet-blue flowers with a dark red centre, opening in succession.

The sea buckthorn's yellow flowers are barely noticeable in April, but they develop into thick clusters of orange berries.

Hippophae rhamnoides (SEA BUCKTHORN)

The sea buckthorn is one of Britain's most beautiful native shrubs, making great thickets in the shifting sands of the Norfolk coast and elsewhere. It is a remarkably accommodating plant that grows equally well inland.

Its scaly bark is covered not only with the sharp spines that give the plant its name, but also with elongated silver, willow-like leaves that glisten in the sun. But the sea buckthorn's true glory appears in autumn, when the leaves have fallen. Then it is wreathed with shining bright orange-gold berries, which can remain all winter, birds permitting. For female plants to produce berries, a male specimen is essential, ideally one to every three females.

HOW TO GROW

Plant between autumn and spring in any well-drained garden soil in a sunny spot. Ideal for hedges in coastal gardens. Space plants 2 ft apart. Propagate by seeds or rooted suckers in autumn. No pruning is needed, but plants may be trimmed to shape in summer.

The silvery shrub makes a good hedge on poor soil, growing 8-10 ft high.

Hebe pinguifolia (VERONICA)

The superb group of plants listed as hebe includes many that are loosely referred to as 'shrubby veronicas'. Indeed, the relationship between these two groups of plants becomes obvious when individual flowers are compared.

The dwarf species *Hebe pinguifolia*, and its more mat-forming hybrid 'Pagei', are accommodating and handsome evergreens hardy almost everywhere. Each spreads a couple of feet or so, joining up with its neighbours to form a permanent carpet of grey-blue leaves, enlivened, in May, by spikes of small white flowers.

HOW TO GROW
As for Hebe salicifolia but hardier and suitable for town gardens and light, dry shade. For ground-cover, space the plants 15-18 in. apart. Propagate by late summer cuttings or the removal and replanting of rooted shoots. No pruning.

A profusion of white flower spikes covers *Hebe pinguifolia* in May and June. A second flush may occur in late summer.

The crowded shoots form a grey-green mat in the crevices of a rock garden.

Hebe salicifolia (VERONICA)

This shrubby veronica from New Zealand is the hardiest of the large-leaved species. It forms a dense, rounded shrub that grows to 6 ft or more high, with bright green, willow-like leaves. In summer it produces tapered, arching spikes, up to 6 in. long, composed of small white flowers.

Although quite widely grown, this hebe is better known as a primary parent of many cultivars with coloured flowers. Among the best is 'Midsummer Beauty', with red-flushed leaves and lavender flowers. 'Pink Wand' is rather smaller, with clear pink flowers.

HOW TO GROW
Plant in spring, in any well-drained soil, including chalk, in full sun or partial shade. The shrub tolerates salt spray, and is excellent for mild coastal gardens; inland, shelter is advisable. Propagate by cuttings under glass in summer.

The flowers of *H. salicifolia* create a soft white haze all summer long.

Pink Wand' is one of the many attractive coloured hybrids bred from *Hebe salicifolia*. Its flowers are clear pink.

Hoherias are ideal plants for clothing walls facing south or south-west.

Hoheria lyallii

A native of New Zealand, *Hoheria lyallii* (often sold as *H. glabrata*) has an undeserved reputation for being tender and does in fact thrive in many parts of Britain. Any gardener who succeeds with the plant will be well rewarded, since it is one of the loveliest of white-flowered shrubs. The leaves are a distinctive downy grey-green that turns soft yellow in autumn. In July, the branches are weighed down by clusters of creamy-white flowers which have a faint ethereal fragrance.

The shrub reaches a height of about 10 ft, with a somewhat lesser spread. In favourable areas it can become a small tree.

HOW TO GROW
Plant in late spring, in fertile, well-drained soil. It grows in full sun or partial shade, preferably with shelter from the north and east. Propagate by cuttings in late summer or by layering in spring. Prune in spring, cutting out frost-damaged and overgrown shoots at the base.

The white, bowl-shaped flowers are borne in rich clusters in summer. In the autumn, the shrub sheds its leaves for winter.

The flowers can be left on Mopheads through winter to protect new buds.

Hydrangea macrophylla

The wild *Hydrangea macrophylla* (syns. *H. hortensis*, *H. opuloides*) comes from Japan. In its original state the blossom clusters are formed of two distinct components. In the centre of each flattened cluster are tiny fertile florets, and around the outside are others that are sterile and much longer. The overall effect is somewhat lacy, and cultivars have acquired the group name of Lacecap.

An increase in sterile florets at the expense of fertile ones has resulted in the popular hydrangea group known as Mopheads or, more technically, Hortensias. They are less elegant than the Lacecaps, but make a more striking display in the garden. Nevertheless, several Lacecap cultivars have found favour among gardeners and some have received awards. Particularly fine is 'Blue Wave', which is blue on acid soil and pink on alkaline soil.

For many gardeners a good display of mop-headed Hortensia hydrangeas at once evokes the memory of a West Country holiday. The plants certainly thrive in the moist atmosphere and relative freedom from hard frost of that area, making rounded, 5 ft high bushes covered in flower heads.

Except in the West Country and other very mild parts, it is vital to choose varieties selected for the open garden. Those bought for house decoration and then put outside may not flower or may barely survive. Most of them need the shelter of a wall. One fine variety that does not is 'Générale Vicomtesse de Vibraye'. From July onwards this bears large heads of flowers that are clear pink on alkaline soil, blue on acid soil. At summer's end they turn papery and become tinged with lime-green.

HOW TO GROW
Plant in spring in humus-rich, moist soil. On acid soil, blue flower colour persists, on alkaline soils it turns pink; but on the latter, alkalinity can be reduced with aluminium sulphate or proprietary blueing powder. Shelter and dappled shade provides ideal conditions. For propagation and pruning, see Hydrangea quercifolia.

As with other hydrangeas, the Lacecap's dead flowers can be removed in autumn to make the bush tidy for winter.

'Blue Wave' is an attractive and vigorously growing Lacecap hydrangea which has achieved great popularity.

Hydrangea quercifolia

The oak-like leaves of this hydrangea at once distinguish it from others of the genus. It comes from the south-east of the USA, whereas most of the familiar species come from Asia. The superb autumn tints of its large, deeply lobed leaves, white-downed beneath, are the plant's main attraction, though the colouring is often less pronounced in the humid west of Britain.

Hydrangea quercifolia makes a bush 5-6 ft high, with a spread of 4-6 ft, but by careful pruning (not clipping) it can be kept lower if desired. In July, a display of broad spikes of white flowers appears at the ends of the shoots. Often the outer florets of the flowers gradually become purple. The shrub makes a spectacular specimen plant in moist woodland conditions.

HOW TO GROW
As for Hydrangea macrophylla. Propagate by cuttings in a cold frame or greenhouse during summer. It flowers on wood of the previous year. Prune to shape after flowering.

The larger, sterile florets on the white flower spikes of *Hydrangea quercifolia* often turn purple as the flowers fade.

Staking the plant in spring can help to give it a well-formed shape.

Hydrangea villosa (aspera)

This hydrangea, a native of China, is among the most striking of late-flowering shrubs. The flat heads of flowers, which open out in August above fine velvety leaves, are of a blue-purple that is darker towards the centre and that varies markedly in tone with the light. It has a warm, glowing quality, which is particularly noticeable in the half-shady positions the plant prefers. The whole shrub – which is 6-8 ft high and as much across – gives an impression of downiness.

Planted here in the light shade of trees, though not too close to competing roots, the hydrangea is the centre-piece in a September group of purple and gold. Several St John's worts (*Hypericum*) provide the gold. *Hypericum* 'Hidcote' is the ideal choice in most situations. Its gently arching habit contrasts with the hydrangea's horizontal flower heads. To one side is *Prunus* × *cistena*, a dwarf ornamental plum with purple leaves and purple-black fruits. (When the plum puts out its white, faintly flushed blossom in the spring, it associates well with a few clumps of pale daffodils.)

Among these purple and gold shrubs a pink *Anemone* × *hybrida* (syn. *A. japonica*) 'Mont Rose' is allowed to wander, holding aloft its wide blooms above leaves that are as soft as those of the hydrangea.

HOW TO GROW
Hydrangea villosa: as for H. macrophylla, but best in half shade. This species appears to be indifferent to soil acidity and maintains its purple hues. Propagate and prune as for H. quercifolia.
Anemone × *hybrida: see p. 67.*
Hypericum 'Hidcote': see p. 289.*
Prunus × *cistena: see p. 302.*

The beauty of *Hydrangea villosa* is enhanced in this autumnal group by the dark purplish-red foliage of *Prunus* × *cistena*, a delicate pink *Anemone* × *hybrida* and a bright golden carpet of *Hypericum* 'Hidcote'.

Hypericum × inodorum 'Elstead'
(ST JOHN'S WORT)

One of the most striking of the linked gardens at Sissinghurst Castle in Kent is the Cottage Garden. In summer and autumn its shrubs and flowers blaze with the colours of a particularly brilliant sunset. On the perimeter are golden and orange-flowered hardy shrubs which put on their finest display in July and August. Conspicuous among these is *Hypericum × inodorum* (syn. *H. elatum*) 'Elstead', a semi-evergreen shrub that bears simultaneously a profusion of golden flowers and scarlet fruits in late summer. The shoots are crowded with 1 in. wide flowers, and the oval berries are carried in clusters.

The shrub, which can achieve 4 ft in height and rather more in spread, associates well with the taller golden privet (*Ligustrum ovalifolium* 'Aureum'), which grows in vigorous thickets up to 15 ft high. It has bright yellow leaves with a narrow green central stripe, and in all but the hardest winters it is evergreen.

Orange and yellow-flowered shrubby potentillas, blooming continuously from early summer into autumn, join this cheerful group. They include the small but striking orange *Potentilla fruticosa* 'Tangerine', 2 ft high and 4 ft wide; and the best of the yellow hybrids, *P.* × 'Elizabeth', which makes a dome-shaped bush up to 3 ft high and 4 ft wide, with flowers nearly 2 in. across.

HOW TO GROW
Hypericum × inodorum 'Elstead': *as for H. 'Hidcote'. In early spring, prune hard to maintain a bushy shape. Prone to rust disease: cut out and burn badly affected shoots and leaves and spray fortnightly during the growing season with a fungicide such as thiram or zineb.*
Ligustrum ovalifolium 'Aureum': *see p. 292.*
Potentilla fruticosa: see p. 302.

Left: In August the last flowers of *Hypericum × inodorum* 'Elstead' mingle with the first vivid clusters of berries. Below: Plant it, as here, surrounded by two potentillas – *P. fruticosa* 'Tangerine' and *P.* × 'Elizabeth' – against a *Ligustrum ovalifolium* 'Aureum', for a harmonious array of gold, orange and red in late summer.

Hypericum 'Hidcote' (ST JOHN'S WORT)

This is not only one of the most spectacular of late summer-flowering shrubs, but one of the easiest to grow. The plant builds up to a regularly shaped dome 5 ft high and across, its pinkish young stems furnished with regular pairs of oval, deep green leaves that in most years are at least half evergreen and in mild ones more so.

By the end of June, the first, saucer-shaped flowers open, their waxy golden petals enclosing a mass of golden stamens. In July and August there often appear to be more flowers than foliage on the plant, and with the coming of autumn it is usually only gradually that this display wanes.

HOW TO GROW
Plant between autumn and spring, in any fertile soil that is well drained but moisture-retentive; light shade is acceptable, but it flowers best in full sun. Propagate by cuttings in a cold frame, in late summer. No pruning, but long shoots may be cut back to near old wood in spring.

The glossy, golden flowers, up to 2 in. across, are larger than those of all the many other hardy hypericums.

A glorious bush of 'Hidcote' in high summer, smothered with blooms.

Kalmia latifolia (MOUNTAIN LAUREL, CALICO BUSH)

This hardy evergreen from the mountains of eastern North America is one of those plants with instant appeal to most gardeners. Out of flower, it looks like a glossy rhododendron with narrow leaves. In June each shoot is topped by a flower cluster, 3-4 in. wide, of the purest pink; each individual flower is crimped like calico – an effect which gives the plant one of its common names.

The shrub does best in the eastern counties of Britain, which provide the right growing conditions. In those areas it may reach a height of 10 ft, and more than that in spread, though this is exceptional.

HOW TO GROW
Plant in autumn or spring, in moist, acid soil; light shade preferred. Mulch annually with peat to keep the roots cool. Propagate in late summer by layering, or by cuttings in a cold frame. No pruning; remove faded flowers and seed capsules.

The lanceolate leaves are glossy, leathery, and a mid-to-dark green. The shrub usually grows to about 6-8 ft.

Each delicious icing-sugar-like flower has conspicuous deep pink stamens.

Kerria japonica (JEW'S MALLOW)

During April and May the shaggy, butter-yellow flowers of *Kerria japonica* are a familiar sight in gardens throughout the land. But most specimens are the double-flowered form 'Pleniflora', not the true, and more attractive, species.

Oddly enough, it was the double-flowered form, not the parent species, that was introduced from China in 1804; and it took another 30 years for the species to appear in Britain. Yet it is the latter, with its single, five-petalled potentilla-like flowers, that deserves first call on garden space. *K. japonica* makes an elegant arching shrub, with a height and spread of 4-6 ft, whose slender green stems are hidden by blooms throughout late spring.

HOW TO GROW
Plant from autumn to spring, in any soil, in shade or sun. Give wall protection in northern gardens. Propagate from rooted suckers or cuttings in autumn. If necessary, prune hard after flowering and remove annually some older stems.

In spring bright pompon flowers, 2 in. across, stud the gleaming foliage of *Kerria japonica* 'Pleniflora', known as bachelor's buttons.

The parent species, shown here, has slightly smaller, single blooms.

Kolkwitzia amabilis (BEAUTY BUSH)

The fragile appearance of porcelain is combined with a tough constitution in the hardy deciduous shrub *Kolkwitzia amabilis*. It makes a thicket up to 10 ft high, with a somewhat lesser spread, its branches arching over in June with the weight of its many clusters of pink, yellow-throated flowers. The shrub grows too close to the soil to be underplanted, but it will provide a splendid, shimmering pink background for the strong spikes of foxgloves.

Britain's native foxglove, *Digitalis purpurea* – with purple, pink or white flowers, mottled inside – goes superbly with kolkwitzias in a loosely planted shrubbery, but the larger-flowered 'Excelsior' hybrids might be preferred in a more formal border. Their flowers come in a wider colour range, including creamy-yellow, and are clustered more thickly round the stem.

Adding other summer plants to this association might spoil it, but planting autumn bulbs will bring fresh life in September when the foxgloves are long dead. Try the violet and white varieties of autumn crocuses. *Colchicum speciosum* would be ideal.

Gardeners who enjoy naturalised plantings should leave the spikes of *Digitalis purpurea* uncut until they have shed their seeds. This foxglove is a biennial, but if sown in two successive years there will be a show of self-sown flowers every summer.

HOW TO GROW
Kolkwitzia amabilis: plant during autumn or spring, in any kind of good garden soil and in full sun. Propagate by softwood cuttings in early summer, or by heel cuttings in late summer – both under glass. Prune after flowering, removing annually some of the older stems at ground level.
Colchicum speciosum: see p. 146.
Digitalis purpurea: see p. 27.

Outstandingly lovely with its matt dark green leaves, arching branches and delicate pink blooms, *Kolkwitzia amabilis* needs little help from other plants; but *Digitalis purpurea* adds a graceful foreground.

In spring the shrub is decorated with clusters of yellow-green flowers.

Laurus nobilis (SWEET BAY)

This beautiful shrub is the original laurel of the ancients, who used wreaths of its aromatic, dark evergreen leaves to crown the victors at games and festivals. It can attain tree size, but in Britain it usually grows to no more than a 10-15 ft high shrub or is planted in a tub.

Fine bushes of sweet bay grow at least as far north as Dundee, and the plant thrives by the sea. A very hard winter will cut it back, but it will invariably spring up again during the following year.

HOW TO GROW
Plant in spring, in any type of well-drained soil in a position in sun or partial shade and with shelter from cold winds. For tub plants, use a proprietary potting compost. Propagate by heel cuttings, under glass, in late summer. No pruning is needed for shrubs in the open, but trim others to shape in summer. This shrub is suitable for topiary.

Left unpruned, sweet bay forms an irregular pyramid-shaped bush of dense growth that will reach 15 ft in as many years.

Lavandula angustifolia (LAVENDER)

Lavender (also listed as *Lavandula spica*) has been grown and loved so long and so widely that there can be few who do not know the plant. Both flowers and leaves are aromatic, and the unique lavender scent is exuded as much in midwinter by the silver-grey foliage as in summer by the dense spikes of clear blue-purple blooms, borne from July to September.

The many cultivars range in colour from deepest purple ('Hidcote') to white ('Alba'), and in height and spread from 1 to 3 ft. All are hardy throughout Britain.

HOW TO GROW
Plant during autumn or spring in any well-drained soil, even a poor one. Choose a sunny position. For hedges, space plants 10-12 in. apart. Propagate by cuttings in late summer. For drying, pick flower spikes when these show colour. Trim the plants after flowering. Do any hard pruning in spring.

A brilliant blue-purple swathe of *Lavandula angustifolia* provides a rich carpet beneath a standard Floribunda rose.

'Hidcote', one of the most popular cultivars, is smaller than the species.

Lavatera olbia (MALLOW)

With their hollyhock-like flowers, mallows, as *Lavatera* species are commonly called, have a rather old-fashioned, cottage-garden appearance, and associate well with such plants as shrub roses, paeonies and pinks.

Although *Lavatera olbia* has been grown in Britain for 400 years, it is today greatly under-used. This is a pity, since it makes a valuable and attractive companion for herbaceous plants that flower from midsummer onwards. It forms a 6-8 ft high bush of pithy stems that from late May to November put out pink flowers and grey-green foliage.

HOW TO GROW
Plant in early autumn or in spring, in any ordinary, well-drained soil. The shrub needs full sun and shelter from cold winds, and is excellent for mild maritime gardens. Propagate by cuttings, under glass, in late summer. Prune shoots by half, to avoid wind damage, in autumn, and cut hard back in spring to maintain shape.

If mallows are to flourish throughout summer, in all their blushing beauty, they need full sunlight.

Leucothoe fontanesiana

Thriving on acid soils, this elegant shrub is valuable for the contrasting shapes and textures it can bring to gardens dominated by rhododendrons. From autumn onwards, its long, willow-like leaves develop bronze and purple tints to dispel winter gloom. The May floral display is equally distinctive, each stem massed with little white spikes of urn-shaped flowers. The plant is useful for ground-cover, developing a low, widespreading mass of gracefully arching stems. A mature specimen can grow about 4 ft high, with a spread of perhaps twice this.

HOW TO GROW
Plant during autumn or spring, in moist, peaty or loamy, acid soil. A position in light shade is best, and the shrub can provide extensive ground-cover or be planted in front of leggy, acid-loving shrubs and trees. Propagate by removing rooted suckers in autumn or early spring. Old stems may be pruned out at ground level in early spring.

The long, narrow leaves of *Leucothoe fontanesiana* are here shown in their autumn colours of deep purplish-red and bronze.

Pendent clusters of white flowers appear along the length of each stem.

Leycesteria formosa (HIMALAYAN HONEYSUCKLE)

A sort of unconscious garden snobbery is liable to downgrade those good-natured plants that prosper almost anywhere. At best they may be relegated to background positions; at worst neglected altogether.

Himalayan honeysuckle is just such a plant, for it will grow in almost any soil, and in full sun or shade. Yet it is highly distinctive, having arching 6 ft stems that bear spikes of white, tubular flowers during July and August. Each bloom is partially concealed by a purple, leaf-like bract. In autumn, the flowers are followed by shining, purple-black berries so that the spike – now even heavier – becomes entirely purple. As the year advances, colder nights turn the leaves a similar colour. Then, after leaf-fall, sea-green shoots are revealed.

Similar bright winter stems – of a clear glossy green – are provided by *Kerria japonica*. This low, twiggy bush covers itself with golden flowers in April.

Both these shrubs are for a moist, shady corner. A couple of strong-leaved perennials, equally shade-tolerant, may be placed at their feet to give 'weight' to the arrangement. What better for the purpose than *Helleborus lividus corsicus* which carries heads of lime-green flowers from January to May, and *Bergenia* 'Silberlicht'? The white flowers of the bergenia appear simultaneously with those of the kerria, while its massive flat leaves provide admirable, weed-smothering ground-cover.

HOW TO GROW

Leycesteria formosa: plant between autumn and spring, in ordinary, well-drained soil – preferably one with a good humus content – and in sun or light shade. Propagate by seeds in spring, or by rooting cuttings outdoors in autumn. Prune to remove frost-damaged shoot tips, and each year remove a few older stems in spring.
Bergenia 'Silberlicht': see B. cordifolia, p. 72.
Helleborus lividus corsicus: see p. 92.
Kerria japonica: see p. 289.

Ligustrum ovalifolium 'Aureum'
(GOLDEN PRIVET)

Grown singly, with branches thinned to provide an open bush, golden privet is a graceful and valuable plant – far removed from the all-too-familiar clipped hedge that has come to epitomise suburbia. Its clear, pale gold leaves, each with a mid-green centre, are borne on the shoots in long, elegant, arching sprays. Left to its own devices, the shrub grows about 12 ft high and wide.

Golden privet accepts any position, and retains its leaves in all but the hardest winters. Flower arrangers make extensive use of the shrub's glossy leaves, appreciating their all-the-year-round availability.

The creamy flowers, borne in July, have a heavy fragrance, that some find unpleasant.

HOW TO GROW

Plant between autumn and spring, in any kind of soil and in sun or shade. Propagate by hardwood cuttings outside in autumn. For specimen plants, restrict pruning to light tipping and the removal of any dead shoots in early spring.

At the front of the bed, plant a group of *Bergenia* 'Silberlicht' for its broad, heart-shaped leaves and white, bell-like flowers; behind put a mass of *Helleborus lividus corsicus* and a *Kerria japonica*. Then a *Leycesteria formosa* may be placed where its attractive blooms will hang gracefully over the group.

Hard pruning the first year creates sweeping branches from the base and a fine bushy habit.

Lippia citriodora (LEMON-SCENTED VERBENA)

The slightest brush against the leaves of lemon-scented verbena brings forth their delicious sharp smell: *Lippia citriodora* (syn. *Aloysia citriodora*) is a deciduous shrub that can grow 10 ft high, but winter cold generally restricts it to half that height and spread.

The plant is gawky in habit; its narrow leaves are willow-like and, appearing late, they shrivel at the first breath of autumn frost; and its clusters of tiny, pale mauve flowers are insignificant. But all these shortcomings are forgiven at the first waft of its lovely citrous fragrance.

HOW TO GROW
Plant in late spring, in ordinary, well-drained soil. Full sun is best; with the shelter of a south-facing wall. Propagate by cuttings under glass in summer. In late spring remove frost-damaged tips and prune main shoots back to 12 in. above ground and laterals to near their base.

The 3-4 in. long leaves of lemon-scented verbena are not only delightfully fragrant but also have a slender elegance.

In all but very mild areas the shrub must be grown against a warm wall.

Lonicera pileata (PRIVET HONEYSUCKLE)

This shrubby honeysuckle is one of the few of its kind really to earn its keep in the garden. It is an attractive evergreen (semi-evergreen in hard winters), valuable as ground-cover and uncommon in that it will happily accept dry shade under trees – yet it is strangely under-used.

The shrub, 2 ft high and about 4-5 ft across, has three seasons of quiet beauty: in spring when bright green leaves mingle with the last of the winter's dark foliage; in early summer, when honeysuckle fragrance is wafted from the clusters of tiny yellowish-white flowers hidden beneath the branches; and in early autumn, when some flower clusters produce shining purple berries.

HOW TO GROW
Plant between autumn and spring, in any ordinary, well-drained, but moisture-retentive soil. Choose a spot in light to deep shade. Propagate by cuttings under glass in summer, or in the open in late autumn. If necessary, prune lightly to shape, and remove dead wood in spring.

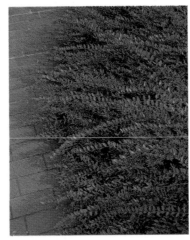

Small, narrow, elliptical leaves crowd the horizontal shoots. Bright at first, they gradually turn a lustrous dark green.

Privet honeysuckle burgeons richly in front of ivy-leaved geraniums in an urn.

Lupinus arboreus (TREE LUPIN)

Despite its name this lupin is little more than a shrub – and a pretty short-lived one at that. Nonetheless, it is an extremely attractive and useful plant. It grows rapidly, flowering in the second year from seeds and providing an almost 'instant' effect in new gardens. After three years it makes a 4 ft high bush, measuring at least as much across. On sandy banks it seeds itself on the soil around – as it has done on the Farnham (Surrey) bypass for years.

It is a typical lupin, bearing spires of scented pea-like flowers – mainly yellow, but sometimes mauve or even white – above elegant leaves from June to August.

HOW TO GROW
Plant between autumn and spring, in well-drained, light, not too limy soil. Grows best in full sun. Propagate by seeds in autumn or spring. After flowering, remove faded blooms and prune wayward shoots back to shape.

Throughout summer the tree lupin lights up with dense, 4-12 in. long clusters of bright, delicately fragrant blooms.

Seed is freely produced and is the best way of propagating the shrub.

Magnolia × loebneri

The magnolias most commonly seen in gardens are forms of *Magnolia × soulangiana*, which have large, usually pink or purple-flushed flowers. More elegant than these is *M. × loebneri*, which bears smaller, snowy flowers. At first, when they emerge from their furry buds in April, they have the typical magnolia upright-vase shape, but before long they open out into a mass of long, ribbon-like petals.

The plant flowers at an early age and increases in beauty year by year. It is a deciduous shrub that eventually reaches the size of a small tree, 15-20 ft high and with a spread of 6-12 ft. It should not be grown in a frost hollow – otherwise its blossoms may become browned.

HOW TO GROW
Plant in spring, in fertile, well-drained but moisture-retentive soil. The plant is excellent on chalk and is lime-tolerant, but needs a sunny position, with shelter from north and east winds. Propagate by layering in spring.

In good soil *Magnolia × loebneri* 'Leonard Messel' can reach the tree-like height of 20 ft after 15-20 years.

Magnolia sinensis

In late May, when the beauty of most magnolias has come to an end, the splendour of *Magnolia sinensis* is just beginning. It is a widespreading deciduous shrub, 8-10 ft high. When the first new leaves have matured, a pendulous white flower bud appears at the tip of each young shoot and soon opens into a wide cup-shaped bloom – one of the most exquisite flowers seen in British gardens.

The satin-like petals are of purest white, which is set off at their base by red stamens. The flowers send out waves of rich, soft aromatic scent. *M. s.* 'Highdownensis' is a particularly fine form or hybrid of this magnolia.

HOW TO GROW
Plant in spring, in fertile, lime-free soil. Mulch in late spring to conserve moisture. Choose a position in sun or light shade. Propagate as for Magnolia × loebneri, or by seeds in autumn. No pruning is needed.

Seen from a distance, the magnolia's flowers are masked by leaf sprays.

Close to, each bloom, 3-4 in. across, reveals its snowy brilliance, a beauty enhanced by a lemon-like fragrance.

Mahonia × 'Charity'

A hybrid between *Mahonia japonica* and *M. lomariifolia*, 'Charity' is a strong, hardy, statuesque shrub that eventually attains 10 ft in height and half as much across. The dark, 2 ft long evergreen leaves are each made up of paired spiny leaflets. Each spring the plant puts out new rosettes of leaves to join those that remain from past years, usually forming a dense mass of foliage.

In November, a great shuttlecock of brilliant golden-yellow flower spikes opens out at the end of each stem. Their scent is less pronounced than that of *M. japonica*, and the display is usually over soon after Christmas.

HOW TO GROW
Plant mahonias in autumn or spring, in any moisture-retentive but well-drained soil. It will grow in sun or shade, but flowers best in sun. Propagate by leaf cuttings, under glass, in autumn. No pruning is needed, but straggling shoots may be cut back to ground level in spring to regenerate them.

The upright, flame-like flowering spikes of *Mahonia × 'Charity'* brighten the end of the year with their sulphurous glow.

Mahonia aquifolium (OREGON GRAPE)

The Oregon grape is a splendid evergreen of North American woodlands which has adapted itself perfectly to British gardens since it was brought here in 1823. Like so many easily grown plants, it has tended to be undervalued. Yet, in the right site, and with well-chosen companions, it is one of the most attractive of small hardy shrubs.

The 8 in. long leaves are each made up of pairs of glossy, holly-like leaflets. They are carried in ruffs on the suckering stems, so that a tight mass of highly decorative foliage results. In sunny spots this often turns red in late autumn; the forms 'Atropurpurea' and 'Moseri' are preferable, since they turn bronze and reddish regardless of, respectively, sun or shade. The plant is one of the finest of foliage shrubs for flower arrangements.

In early spring the centre of each leaf whorl carries a dense cluster of bright yellow flower spikes 3-5 in. across. As these fade, plum-purple new leaves develop. This colour, deepened almost to black, reappears in autumn in the grape-like fruits which give the shrub its common name.

The plant association described here is one for shade, provided by open woodland or a building, and a fertile soil. Above the mahonia in March and April swing the soft yellow catkins of the hardy deciduous shrub *Corylopsis willmottiae*, which can eventually grow up to 10 ft high. Both shrubs stand in a pool of wild daffodils (Lent lilies), *Narcissus pseudonarcissus*, whose lemon trumpets and paler petals appear in April. A few *Cyclamen neapolitanum*, planted among the daffodils, provide a flare of mauve-pink blooms in early autumn.

HOW TO GROW
Mahonia aquifolium: as for M. × 'Charity'. Propagation is easiest by rooted suckers, but, except for named cultivars, can also be by seeds sown in late summer, under glass. Pruning, too, is as for M. × 'Charity'; if grown as ground-cover, height can be restricted by hard pruning in spring.
Corylopsis willmottiae: see p. 268.
Cyclamen neapolitanum: see p. 150.
Narcissus pseudonarcissus: see p. 165.

This spring association of yellow and green has *Mahonia aquifolium* as its centrepiece. Behind is a *Corylopsis willmottiae*; in the foreground are *Narcissus pseudonarcissus*, and *Cyclamen neapolitanum* for a change of colour in autumn.

Mahonia japonica

This hardy evergreen shrub is surely one of the most beautiful plants in cultivation. Dark, lustrous leaves, each made up of separate leaflets, form a superb, year-round display of great rosettes measuring fully 2 ft across. Sometimes a few take on autumn tints. In October, sprays of primrose-yellow flowers, with a lily-of-the-valley fragrance, develop from the centre of each leaf rosette.

The flowers open in succession until March or April. Only the hardest frost kills off open blooms, and there are always replacements soon to follow.

Mahonia japonica eventually reaches a height of 5 ft or so by as much or more across, but it can be kept smaller by occasionally cutting out whole stems.

HOW TO GROW
As for Mahonia × 'Charity', but it does best in semi-shade. In northern gardens, provide shelter from winds, which may dehydrate the foliage and kill the emerging flowers.

In spring pale-bloomed green berries appear among the rich foliage of *Mahonia japonica*. By early summer they have ripened to purple.

A mature shrub, about 15 years old, creates a glorious mass of greenery.

Myrtus communis (COMMON MYRTLE)

It seems likely that the original homeland of the common myrtle was Western Asia, but it has been grown so widely by man that it is now common in all Mediterranean countries. Accredited with a variety of medicinal properties, myrtle also has the qualities that make an attractive garden shrub. Its lance-shaped to oval leaves are dark green and lustrous, and pleasantly aromatic when bruised. In late summer, globular buds in the upper leaf axils open into white, fragrant flowers with a prominent boss of slender stamens. Purple-black berries sometimes follow.

One quality that the common myrtle does not possess is full hardiness. Even against a sheltered wall it seldom achieves more than 6-8 ft before being cut back by frost. If a greater degree of hardiness is required, *Myrtus communis tarentina* 'Jenny Reitenbach' should be chosen. This is quite distinctive, being a more compact shrub and having very much smaller leaves on downy stems.

This cultivar also produces its smaller flowers more freely, usually with a bonus of white berries to follow.

M. communis combines well with other evergreens, particularly those with grey or silver foliage. Companions should be chosen from among those plants that need the same sheltered, sunny site. A very satisfying association can be made by planting the dark green-leaved *Pittosporum tobira* alongside the myrtle and providing a foreground of the silvery-leaved *Senecio* 'Sunshine'.

HOW TO GROW

Myrtus communis: plant in spring, in any type of moisture-retentive but well-drained soil, in sun or partial shade. The shrub is excellent for western seaside gardens; inland it does best with shelter from a warm wall. Propagate by heel cuttings under glass in summer. Remove frost-damaged wood and, if necessary, prune lightly to shape in spring.
Pittosporum tobira: see p. 301.
Senecio 'Sunshine': *see p. 315.*

Long yellow stamens give a star-like radiance to the flowers of common myrtle. They are sometimes followed by purple-black berries.

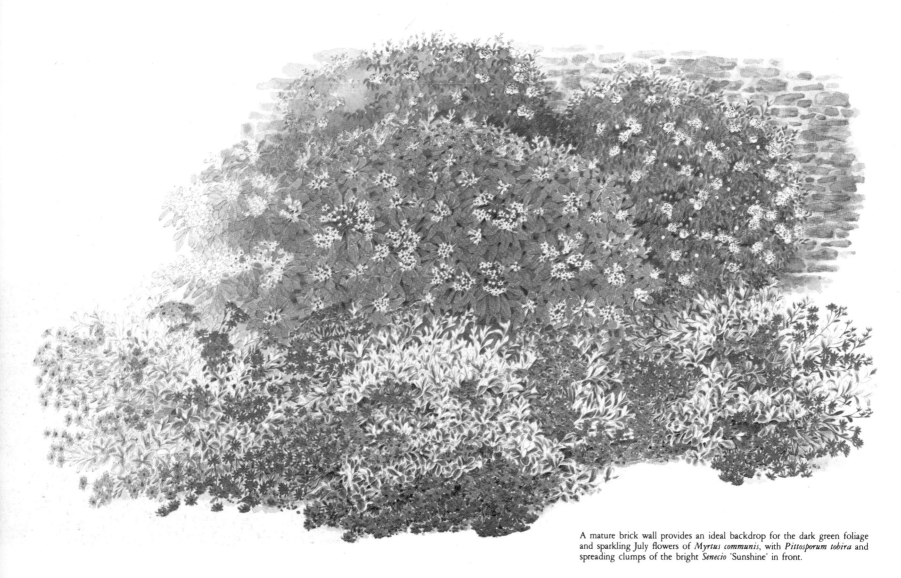

A mature brick wall provides an ideal backdrop for the dark green foliage and sparkling July flowers of *Myrtus communis*, with *Pittosporum tobira* and spreading clumps of the bright *Senecio* 'Sunshine' in front.

Olearia macrodonta (DAISY BUSH)

Whereas most daisy bushes are at their best when in flower, this semi-hardy New Zealand evergreen is equally notable for its foliage. The leaves, which are holly-like but not prickly, are deep glossy grey-green on top, with white felted undersides. In exposed gardens they scintillate in the wind. The wide heads of small white daisy-like flowers, carried in June and July, have a musky scent.

The plant makes a fine 8 ft high shrub, but if this is considered too large it can be kept down by hard cutting, preferably after flowering.

HOW TO GROW
Plant in spring, in any type of well-drained soil. It thrives on chalk and is tolerant of wind exposure and sea sprays, but full sun is essential for profuse flowering. Propagate by cuttings under glass in late summer. In late spring, remove any frost-damaged shoots. Olearias tolerate hard pruning, both as specimen and hedging plants.

The flowers of *Olearia macrodonta* form in clusters of up to 6 in. across. It stands up well to wind in exposed coastal gardens.

It would take eight to ten years for a daisy bush to reach this size.

Osmanthus heterophyllus

The quiet charms of this shrub (also listed as *Osmanthus aquifolius* and *O. ilicifolius*) owe something to the grace of its habit as well as to the attractions of its foliage. Growth is slow, for it takes perhaps 20 years to form a rounded, evergreen mass with a height and spread of up to 10 ft. With clipping, it will form a hedge, though in this case the shrub will bear few of the tiny white flowers that normally appear during September and October. The deep green leaves are variable in shape, some being prickly and holly-like, while others are virtually smooth.

HOW TO GROW
Plant between autumn and spring, in well-drained though moisture-retentive soil, and in light shade or sun. Propagate by layering in early autumn, or by cuttings under glass in late summer. If necessary, prune to shape after flowering, and trim hedges in late spring.

The leaves of the form 'Variegatus' are edged with creamy white. Yellow and silver variegated varieties are also available.

Like a ruby necklace, *Incarvillea delavayi* encircles an osmanthus.

× Osmarea burkwoodii

Only seldom does a plant sport an × at the start of its name, to signify that it is a cross between two unrelated groups of plants – a bigeneric hybrid. This hardy evergreen inherits most of its good looks from its Chinese parent, *Osmanthus delavayi*. It forms a tidy, domed shrub, 6 ft high and as much across, with lustrous, dark green leaves. Fragrant, tubular flowers cover it in April and May. With a single clipping after flowering, it can be grown as an attractive hedge.

The other parent is the Asian *Phillyrea decora*. Recently, this was reclassified as an osmanthus, so technically the bigeneric status is lost.

HOW TO GROW
Plant between autumn and spring, in any good, well-drained soil, including shallow chalk, and in sun or shade. Propagate by cuttings under glass in late summer. Specimen shrubs rarely need pruning; trim hedges after flowering.

The shrub is slow growing. After about ten years it forms a compact 6 ft high bush. The dark green leaves have serrated edges.

The ½ in. long white, tubular flowers appear in clusters along the stems.

Paeonia lutea ludlowii (TREE PEONY)

The spectacular shrubby peony that forms the centre of this group is a native of the Tibetan mountains. It is of such perfect all-round symmetry – up to 6 ft tall and broad – that, to be appreciated to the full, it should be planted at a distance from other tall-growing shrubs. Its flowering season, in May, is short but glorious, for it bears large, single, cup-shaped blooms of sulphur-yellow with a lily-like scent. Neither of the suggested companion plants blooms at the same time, for this deciduous shrub deserves a solo performance.

When its fleeting splendour is over, and the light green leaves are beginning to look tired, two groups of summer-flowering plants take the stage. The first to flower, in July, is *Phygelius capensis*, a South African evergreen plant that will reach its full height of 6 ft only when grown against a wall in the south and west. Here it is used as a 3 ft perennial, but it still bears its scarlet flowers into October.

Flowering in the same month as the phygelius are 2 ft high clumps of *Agapanthus* 'Headbourne Hybrids' which bear heads of violet to pale blue flowers.

Although the plants in the group are hardy, ideally they should be grown in a sheltered position out of the wind, but not against a wall. Shelter is particularly important to the peony, whose flowers are susceptible to frost.

HOW TO GROW
Paeonia lutea ludlowii: plant between autumn and spring, in any soil that is well drained and enriched with organic matter. Both sun and light shade are suitable, preferably in a position sheltered from spring frosts which will damage the early flowers and young shoots. Propagation and pruning as for P. suffruticosa, but it may also be raised from seeds.
Agapanthus 'Headbourne Hybrids': see p. 140.
Phygelius capensis: see p. 111.

When the peony's glorious yellow flowers have disappeared, the gardener will be cheered anew by the bright blooms of *Phygelius capensis* and *Agapanthus* 'Headbourne Hybrids'. The peony's foliage remains to give background substance to the group, pictured here in July.

'Rock's Variety' is one of the many cultivars. It may be single or double.

Paeonia suffruticosa (TREE PEONY)

The beauty of this deciduous shrubby peony's flowers has long inspired Chinese screen painters – and certainly no shrub that can be grown in Britain bears quite such exotic blooms. Opening in May, they are anything from 6 to 10 in. across and range in colour from white through yellow and near orange to deep pink. They are borne on bushes – not trees, as the common name suggests – which seldom exceed 5 ft in height and spread.

The shrub is fully hardy when dormant in autumn and winter, but new growth may be caught by late frosts. It should not therefore be exposed to east winds.

HOW TO GROW
Cultivation as for Paeonia lutea ludlowii. Plants are usually grafted, with the union 3-5 in. below the soil surface. Propagation is difficult, but layering can be tried in spring and hardwood cuttings outside in autumn. Usually no pruning is needed; but cut leggy shrubs hard back in early spring.

The semi-double *Paeonia suffruticosa* 'Duchess of Kent' produces clear bright pink flowers from early May to early June.

Pernettya mucronata

This Chilean shrub, some 2-3 ft high and wide, is as beautiful as it is hardy, and this beauty shows itself in two separate parts of the year. First, in June, the wiry stems and small evergreen leaves are whitened with tiny heather-like flowers. Then, through autumn and winter, bright marble-sized berries glow in a range of colour.

The various lovely forms include 'Bell's Seedling' (clear red fruits) and 'Alba' (pure white). The plants (except for 'Bell's Seedling') are unisexual, and both male and female specimens must be grown for fruits to be produced; most nurserymen stock free-flowering male plants.

HOW TO GROW
Plant between autumn and spring, in moist, but not wet, acid soil. Flowering and fruiting are most prolific in sun. Plant in groups of at least three, including one male. Propagate by cuttings under glass, in early autumn. Little pruning is needed except to cut back old, leggy plants in early spring.

Abundant small white flowers, only ⅛ in. long, are borne from the leaf axils in June. The leaves are a glossy dark green.

The bisexual 'Bell's Seedling' fruits satisfactorily if planted on its own.

Philadelphus × 'Beauclerk' (MOCK ORANGE)

The common name for the genus *Philadelphus* is mock orange, because the scent of its flowers is like that of orange blossom. In June and July the branches of this hardy, deciduous shrub are weighed down with sprays of fragrant 2-2½ in. wide flowers, which are white with a pale cerise blush at the base of each petal.

Philadelphus × 'Beauclerk' is one of the best of its kind for small gardens, attaining a height of about 4 ft and a somewhat wider spread. *P.* 'Bouquet Blanc' is smaller, with double flowers that are borne more profusely.

HOW TO GROW
Plant between autumn and spring. The shrub is easily grown in any type of well-drained soil, in sun or light shade. An occasional mulch of leaf-mould or rotted compost is beneficial. Propagate by cuttings under glass in summer, or in the open in autumn. Pruning as for Philadelphus coronarius 'Aureus'.

The flowers of 'Beauclerk' are single, broad-petalled and about 2-2½ in. across. They appear in June and July.

Bouquet Blanc's' clustered flowers are delicately orange scented.

Philadelphus coronarius 'Aureus'

(MOCK ORANGE)

Like *Philadelphus* × 'Beauclerk', this deciduous shrub is a particularly delightful mock orange, with flowers that smell intoxicatingly of orange blossom. Spring sees the unfolding of leaves of a clear soft gold that harmonises perfectly with the pale blues of irises and lupins. Then, at the end of June, sprays of white flowers open, the surrounding foliage seeming to warm their colour to cream.

Although the shrub, which is hardy, needs plenty of light for its wood to ripen, it must be kept out of full sun, which would soon cause unsightly bleaching of the foliage. Its mature height and spread are about 6-8 ft.

HOW TO GROW
Cultivation and propagation as Philadelphus × 'Beauclerk', though the plant does best in light shade. Prune all mock oranges immediately after flowering by thinning out the older, twiggy-flowered whippy growths at the base.

Though they are superb in the garden, it is usual to strip some of the rather dominant leaves when arranging cut stems indoors.

Golden 'Aureus' sparkles above a border of alyssum and spring bulbs.

Phlomis fruticosa (JERUSALEM SAGE)

In some plant associations, it is not so much the visual effect that holds the group together as some less tangible quality that the plants have in common. This group of summer-flowering shrubs, with *Phlomis fruticosa* as its focal point, comes directly from a sun-baked Mediterranean hillside – though an idealised one, since it is unlikely that such an arrangement would occur naturally.

The tallest plant, Jerusalem sage, is an evergreen shrub with a maximum height and spread of about 5 ft. Its soft foliage is grey and densely hairy, and provides a muted contrast to the brilliance of its whorls of hooded golden flowers borne in June and July. The foliage also offsets the strong rose-crimson blooms of *Cistus × purpureus*, another evergreen shrub, 3 ft tall and across; each of its flowers lasts only one day but they appear in a blazing succession over about three weeks.

In front of the two shrubs is a lavender bush (right), *Lavandula angustifolia* 'Hidcote'. Making a clump 2 ft high and wide, it displays its dark purple-blue spikes from July to September. The foreground (left) is occupied by the silver-haired foliage of lamb's tongue, *Stachys olympica* (*S. lanata*), a spreading shrub 12-18 in. high. Long spikes of pale pink flowers set it softly aglow in July.

The group needs the sunniest of spots, such as a south facing terrace to provide winter protection. They certainly do not relish a British north-easterly wind in March. In good conditions, the plants, with their aroma of the warm south, can banish distance and take you on an imaginary Mediterranean holiday.

HOW TO GROW
Phlomis fruticosa: plant in autumn or spring, in light, well-drained soil, and in full sun. Being drought-resistant, this shrub is ideal for dry, sunny banks. Propagate by cuttings, under glass, in late summer. Pruning is unnecessary, but dead-head after flowering.
Cistus × purpureus: see p. 264.
Lavandula angustifolia: see p. 291.
Stachys olympica: see p. 122.

In July, golden spires of Jerusalem sage tower over *Cistus × purpureus, Stachys olympica* and *Lavandula angustifolia*.

Foliage contrast – *Phormium tenax* 'Purpureum' and *Euphorbia wulfenii*.

Phormium tenax (NEW ZEALAND FLAX)

Because New Zealand flax is so dominant, it should be used with discretion – preferably in association with part of the house, a terrace, or other bold plants. It is hardy in all but the coldest districts, though its fine purple-leaved variety 'Purpureum' and the green-and-yellow striped 'Variegatum' are less resistant to frost. Protect the crowns with straw or bracken in winter.

In some years great 10 ft flower spikes shoot up in June. Their dull orange colour is not exciting, but their form is dramatic. Phormiums are evergreen perennials that play a shrub-like role. The near-vertical leaves are up to 8 ft long and build to a prominent clump several feet across.

HOW TO GROW
Plant in late spring, in any fertile soil in full sun or partial shade. The plant is resistant to winds, salt spray and town pollution. Propagate by division in spring. Cut frost-damaged leaves away at the base in spring.

The yellow-edged leaves of the variegated forms of New Zealand flax can be used very effectively in indoor flower arrangements.

The foliage of 'Forrestii' retains its brilliant colours for several weeks.

Pieris formosa 'Forrestii'

This remarkable evergreen, introduced to Britain from China, takes on three completely different aspects in as many months. Through the winter it is a mass of handsome, glossy, dark foliage. Then in April and May, grape-like clusters of white flowers cascade over it. Hardly have these begun to fade than brilliant new leaves unfold – scarlet, turning to pink and cream and, finally, green.

When mature, the shrub reaches a height and spread of 10 ft. In all but the mildest gardens – or sheltered shady courtyards, where it can be grown in a tub – the plant needs to face west and be sheltered by overhanging tree branches to protect the young growth from frost.

HOW TO GROW
Plant in autumn or spring, in a moist, acid soil. Mulch annually with moist peat to keep roots cool. Dappled shade provides the right conditions, ideally with a western aspect. Propagation and pruning as for Pieris japonica.

The vivid contrast in colour between leaves and flowers makes 'Forrestii' a major feature of the early summer garden.

'Variegata', a slow-growing form, has creamy-white edged leaves.

Pieris japonica

This lovely Japanese evergreen is safer to grow than its extravagantly beautiful relative *Pieris formosa* 'Forrestii', whose young growth is susceptible to frost. *P. japonica* (syn. *Andromeda japonica*) will do well in all except the most exposed and chilly spots. It builds up slowly – and attractively, in layers – in a dense bush of lustrous dark foliage 6 or 8 ft high, rather less across. October sees sprays of flower buds developing. By the New Year they have reached almost full size; then in March and April they unfold into urn-shaped flowers of pure white that form a beautiful cool cascade over the dark leaves.

HOW TO GROW
Cultivation as for Pieris formosa, but this species is hardier and more tolerant of sun if the soil is kept moist. Propagate by cuttings, under glass, in later summer. Dead-head after flowering, and prune wayward shoots back to shape.

The drooping sprays of white, waxy flowers, rather like lily of the valley in appearance, carry a slight fragrance.

The creamy flowers form clusters 2-3 in. across from April to July.

Pittosporum tobira

Sadly, this lovely shrub has never become as popular here as in southern Europe. Its countries of origin are China and Japan, whereas the pittosporum foliage sprays seen in florists' are from *Pittosporum tenuifolium*, a New Zealand species. *P. tobira* makes a domed bush some 6-8 ft high and rather less wide. It is at its most seductive in summer, when among its glistening dark green leaves clusters of white flowers send out waves of heady orange-blossom fragrance. Gradually the flowers turn cream, then a light butter-yellow before falling. Sometimes they are succeeded by berry-like seed capsules.

HOW TO GROW
Plant in late spring in any ordinary, well-drained soil. Choose a spot in full sun and, except in a mild maritime garden, sheltered by a warm wall. Propagate by cuttings under glass in summer, or by seeds under glass in spring. Prune to shape only, in spring.

This slow-growing species makes a fine wall shrub. Very drought-resistant, it is often used for hedging in southern Europe.

Potentilla × 'Elizabeth' (CINQUEFOIL)

Among the many different shrubby cinquefoils are plants that deserve a space in almost every garden. They will thrive in practically any soil, are neat and compact in habit, and flower for up to six months of each year. 'Elizabeth', 3-4 ft high, is one of the best examples. Its neat, close foliage and rich canary-yellow blooms are not unlike those of a small species rose. The flowers open in May, and after reaching a spectacular peak continue gently into late autumn. First raised in 1950, in 1969 the plant received the coveted RHS Award of Garden Merit.

HOW TO GROW
Plant between autumn and spring, in any type of garden soil. It does best in full sun, though light shade is tolerated. Propagate by heel cuttings under glass, in late summer. Little pruning is needed, except for occasional removal of old shoots at ground level.

The plant is suitable for sunny banks, and for mixed or shrub borders. The flowers grow on the stems in loose clusters.

The variety 'Vilmoriniana' has silvery leaves and cream-coloured flowers.

Potentilla fruticosa (CINQUEFOIL)

Little flowers like golden dog-roses cover this deciduous shrub in June and continue on and off until autumn. The plant makes a small, twiggy bush with deeply cut leaves, about 3 ft high and the same across.

There are many forms available, with flowers ranging in colour from white through cream and all shades of yellow to orange and red. The foliage varies too. Forms with grey leaves are particularly attractive.

'Tangerine' has pale, coppery-yellow flowers; those of 'Sunset' vary between deep orange and brick red; and 'Red Ace' has blooms of flaming vermilion.

HOW TO GROW
Plant between autumn and spring, in any type of garden soil. It does best in full sun, though pink, red and orange-flowered cultivars are better in light shade. Propagate by heel cuttings under glass, in late summer. Occasionally remove old shoots at ground level.

The vermilion flowers of 'Red Ace', which grows to a height of 20-30 in., are tinted pale yellow on the undersides.

A good show of flowers can be spoiled by birds, which may eat the buds.

Prunus × cistena (PURPLE-LEAF SAND CHERRY)

Purple-leaved shrubs like this small ornamental cherry provide a fine contrast to the predominant green of most other foliage. *Prunus × cistena*, which is usually less than 6 ft in height and spread, is equally beautiful grown as an individual shrub or as an informal hedge.

In April, the shrub's dark stems become studded with white flowers. As they fade, new shoots emerge, bright red at first, then deepening to a rich, warm purple which is maintained until leaf-fall. In some years there are enough sloe-black autumn fruits to make a striking show.

HOW TO GROW
Plant between autumn and spring, in ordinary, well-drained soil. It is especially good on chalk or slightly limy soil. An open, sunny position is needed. For hedging, set the plants 2 ft apart in a zigzag line. No regular pruning is required, but trim established hedges to shape after flowering. Propagate as for Prunus laurocerasus.

When the ½-¾ in. wide flowers break open in April, the stems are quite bare apart from a few red leaves at the tips.

Prunus laurocerasus

(CHERRY LAUREL, COMMON LAUREL)

Strictly speaking, the name laurel should be reserved for plants of the genus *Laurus*, such as bay laurel, but the name has spread to other plants. This fine shrub grows up to 15 ft high, with an equal or greater spread.

Introduced to Britain in the early 17th century, cherry laurel has been grown mainly as a tall, solid hedge – but where plenty of space is available it makes a magnificent specimen plant, its mass of dark, shining evergreen foliage decorated in April with white spikes of bloom.

HOW TO GROW
Cultivation as for Prunus × cistena. The species is not recommended for shallow chalk, but is suitable for shady sites and limy soil. Propagate by heel cuttings under glass, in late summer and autumn. Prune specimen and hedging plants with secateurs in spring, and hedges again in late summer.

The 3-5 in. long spikes of flowers are followed by small cherry-like fruits – red at first, but turning black when ripe.

Few hedges are denser or more easily grown than evergreen cherry laurel.

Prunus lusitanica (PORTUGAL LAUREL)

Portugal laurel is the centre-piece of this group, which forms a striking architectural pattern all the year round. The dominant shrub is a large, billowing evergreen that attains a height and spread of at least 15 ft. It is grown mainly for its dark, glistening foliage, but it does have other attractions. In June it is massed with long, slender bunches of small, creamy-white flowers that have a fragrance reminiscent of hawthorn. In autumn, these are followed by red fruits that turn to black-purple.

Against this dark background stands the erect, 8 ft high *Rosa moyesii*, a shrub rose from China which bears blood-red single flowers in June and has typical wild-rose leaves, each composed of leaflets. The scarlet hips that appear in autumn are carafe-shaped. The cultivar 'Geranium' has flowers of pillar-box red.

In the foreground of this association, and growing into one another, are three plants of *Cotoneaster horizontalis*. These are low, deciduous shrubs, only about 2 ft high, with horizontal branches spreading to at least 6 ft and crowded with tiny leaves. Little pink flowers, humming with bees, appear in June. Autumn sees the leaves colouring red and the branches thick with bright red berries. In winter, the bare sideshoots create an interesting fishbone pattern.

All three shrubs grow vigorously, and 5 ft of planting space should be allowed between the Portugal laurel and the nearest cotoneaster. However, the rose looks well growing up into the laurel.

HOW TO GROW
Prunus lusitanica: cultivation as for P. × cistena. It grows well on shallow, chalky soil. Propagation and pruning as for P. laurocerasus. If laurels suffer from leaf spot and powdery mildew diseases, spray with a fungicide containing copper, such as Bordeaux mixture.
Cotoneaster horizontalis: see p. 269.
Rosa moyesii: see p. 245.

Portugal laurel stands in its June array of white, candle-like flower clusters, with a glowing red *Rosa moyesii* clambering about its branches. At ground level spreads *Cotoneaster horizontalis*, its long horizontal boughs massed with minute leaves and small pink flowers.

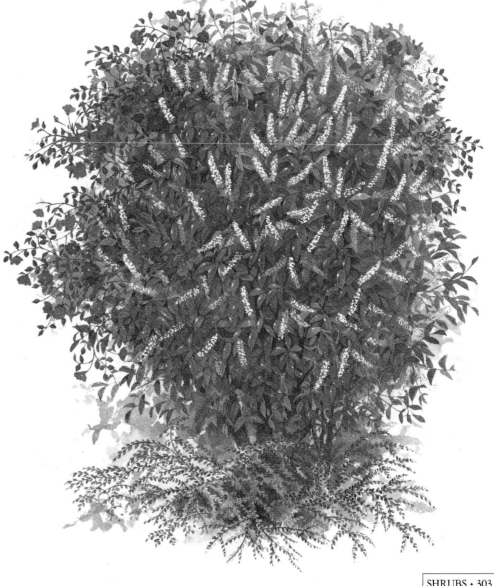

Pyracantha 'Orange Glow' (FIRETHORN)

Many plants chosen for their berries are struck down in their moment of glory. Either the birds steal the fruit or they are damaged by frost. But certain pyracanthas – or firethorns, as these hardy evergreen shrubs are commonly known – are less subject to such ravages.

'Orange Glow' is one of the finest, with masses of brilliant orange berries hanging from the thorny branches in heavy swags. The leaves are attractive, too, being glossy and of a particularly fresh bright green on the young shoots. In midsummer, white hawthorn-like flowers cluster thickly on the shrub.

This firethorn makes a fine, large specimen bush, some 10 ft high and wide, in open ground; it can be grown to a greater height – perhaps 15-18 ft – against a wall; or it can be trained as an espalier to mask a shed.

In this grouping, a bush of 'Orange Glow' grown in full sun provides a splendid green and white backdrop in summer for a group of perennials that needs similar soil and aspect. The yarrow, *Achillea filipendulina*, carries wide flat heads of deep yellow flowers from July to September. Although it is one of the tallest of the yarrows, it has strong stalks and does not need staking. In July and August its blooms melt into the yellow and white flower spikes of the mulleins *Verbascum × hybridum* 'Gainsborough' and 'Pink Domino', which begin flowering in June. 'Gainsborough' is a light lemon-yellow cultivar, 'Pink Domino' is deep rose-pink.

As the yarrow goes brown, the berries of the firethorn begin to change from green to their autumn brilliance.

HOW TO GROW

Pyracantha 'Orange Glow': *plant between autumn and spring, in any type of good, well-drained soil. It may be grown in sun or shade and is resistant to wind and pollution. Suitable for north and east walls. Propagate by cuttings, under glass, in late summer. Shorten lateral shoots of wall shrubs after flowering. No need to prune free-standing specimens.*
Achillea filipendulina: see p. 64.
Verbascum × hybridum: see p. 126.

The brilliant orange berries of 'Orange Glow' last well into winter.

Yellow, cream and green are the colours of this summer group; but in autumn, after the *Achillea filipendulina* and *Verbascum × hybridum* flowers have disappeared, the *Pyracantha* 'Orange Glow' is a flaming beacon of vivid orange.

RHODODENDRON

It is unfortunate that for many people the word
rhododendron conjures up one image only – a large,
purple-flowered shrub that dominates the June scene
wherever acid soil exists. This is a pity. For in fact
rhododendrons form one of the largest and most varied
genera in the world of garden plants. Some, such as
Rhododendron arboreum, make trees 60 ft high, while others,
such as *R. radicans*, are alpine shrublets seldom exceeding
6 in. Nowadays, the genus includes azaleas – formerly
classified separately.

There is a vast range of flower colours (white, cream,
yellow, orange, pink, scarlet, crimson, purple, violet,
lavender) and of flower shapes, textures and scents. In
addition, flowering is by no means limited to May and
June. The delicate *R. mucronulatum* will bravely, if unwisely,
bloom as early as January, while other species, such as
R. auriculatum, provide their display as late as August.

The beauty of rhododendrons is not restricted to their
flowers. The leaves of many species are an extra bounty:
for example, they are eucalyptus-blue in *R. concatenans*,
suede-felted in *R. fulvum* and brilliantly autumn-coloured in
many azaleas, including the glorious *Azalea pontica*. The
size of leaves varies widely, too. They may be little bigger
than those of heathers, whereas those of the great
R. sinograpode, which can grow nearly 2 ft long, are the
largest evergreen leaves of any outdoor flowering shrub
grown in Britain.

It is well to remember that many rhododendrons are
woodland plants, and that though they accept (with
sufficient moisture) the thin British sun, their growth habit
is more delicate in half shade. Shade also helps to tone
down the more brilliant colours, making possible many
combinations that would be less acceptable if they were
grown in the open.

HOW TO GROW

*Plant in autumn or spring. Rhododendron species and
hybrids, including azaleas, will not grow in soil containing
even small amounts of lime. They thrive in moist, acid soil,
which is rich in organic content. As they are surface-rooting,
they appreciate an annual mulch of moist peat or leaf-mould
over the root area. Most rhododendrons grow best in the light
shade and shelter provided by overhead trees, though dwarf
and small-leaved species, the generally hardy rhododendron
hybrids and the deciduous azaleas do not object to open, sunny
positions provided the roots are kept cool and moist.*

*All look best grown in harmonious groups rather than
singly – though the smaller kinds are suitable for tub culture
in lime-free potting compost. They associate well with
heathers, conifers, hydrangeas and sarcococcas.*

*Propagation from cuttings of young shoots during summer,
rooted under glass, is the usual method of increase for
rhododendron hybrids, dwarf species and evergreen azaleas.
These may also, like large-leaved species and deciduous
azaleas, be propagated by layering in spring. Seed propagation
is possible in the case of species, but the seedlings take at least
four or five years to reach flowering size.*

*Pruning is usually unnecessary, though old, leggy plants can
be cut hard back in spring. After flowering, all rhododendrons
should be dead-headed, unless seeds are wanted. Remove the
faded flowers by hand; secateurs may damage young buds.*

Rhododendrons are superb landscape plants, and when massed in a natural setting are unsurpassed for wealth of colour.

R. concatenans grows to 6 ft and flowers in April and May.

This young specimen of *R. sinograpode* may
eventually grow to 30 ft.

R. arboreum may flower as early as March.

'Blue Tit' needs space for its charm to be fully appreciated.

Rhododendron 'Blue Tit'

This lovely hybrid rhododendron, raised in 1933 at Caerhays Castle, Cornwall, has proved to be completely frost-resistant. Only 3 ft high and wide, it makes a compact, domed bush that is suitable, with heathers, for the front of a shrub border in a small garden, or for a rock garden.

In April, the tip of each branch carries a mass of little funnel-shaped flowers of a clear lavender-blue. As they age they darken nearer to true blue.

Such is the small scale of every part of this shrub that, unless placed with care, it runs the risk of being dwarfed by its neighbours. It does best in an exposed position – except in the south, where some shade in the middle of the day is desirable to prevent the flowers from bleaching.

HOW TO GROW
See p. 305.

The delicate flowers and small size of this rhododendron make it an ideal plant for the heather or rock garden.

Rhododendron calophytum

Growing to some 15 ft high, with a spread of 10 ft, this magnificent evergreen tree rhododendron is no plant for a confined space. It needs to be grown on the edge of a copse or in a large garden, where its majestic beauty can be appreciated to the full.

The glory of *Rhododendron calophytum* is its leaves; their unfolding is a miracle of movement. Above last year's foliage, each great leaf bud, emerging from an umbrella of the current season's mature leaves, sheds its brown scales and pushes out a new shoot.

At first pink bracts enclose this; then it develops into a silver shuttlecock of suede-soft true leaves, from which the bracts fall back like ribbons from a newly opened gift. Gradually the new leaves unfold, eventually reaching a length of 15 in.

R. calophytum is the hardiest of the big-leaved rhododendrons and is safe in all but the coldest gardens. When grown from seeds it takes about ten years to flower, producing then, in March and April, clusters of up to 30 white, bell-shaped blooms, which are purple-blotched and sometimes flushed with pink.

This rhododendron can easily overpower other plants, so those chosen to associate with it should have striking foliage of their own. Behind the tree would be a good place to plant the blue-leaved spruce, *Picea pungens glauca*, while around are herbaceous plants – *Peltiphyllum peltatum*, which has wheel-like leaves, *Rodgersia aesculifolia* and *Hosta sieboldiana* 'Elegans', whose foliage colour echoes that of the spruce.

At the very front of the suggested grouping is the ostrich-feather fern, *Matteuccia struthiopteris*, whose developing golden-green fronds repeat the shape of the rhododendron above.

HOW TO GROW
Rhododendron calophytum: see p. 305.
Hosta sieboldiana: see p. 95.
Matteuccia struthiopteris: see p. 130.
Peltiphyllum peltatum: see p. 109.
Picea pungens glauca: see p. 349.
Rodgersia aesculifolia: see p. 118.

Rhododendron calophytum's opening 'shuttle-cocks' are behind *Rodgersia aesculifolia*, *Matteuccia struthiopteris*, *Peltiphyllum peltatum* and *Hosta sieboldiana* 'Elegans'. At the back is a *Picea pungens glauca*. The time of year is July.

Rhododendron × cilpinense

It is foolish, but nonetheless tempting, to plant rhododendrons that will start to flower in March when there is still every likelihood of frosts. If you choose to do so, at least select a type small enough to be covered with a tablecloth on an evening when a clear sky threatens freezing temperatures. This hybrid displays the qualities of its exquisite Himalayan parents, *Rhododendron ciliatum* and *R. moupinense*. Forming a domed bush about 3 ft high, it has attractive netted, rather hairy leaves.

In some years, the fat flower buds start to cast off their protective scales as early as the end of February, and loose heads of pink and white trumpet-shaped flowers open within a couple of weeks.

HOW TO GROW
See p. 305.

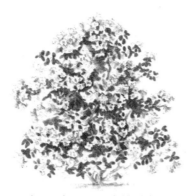

R. × cilpinense forms a rounded bush bearing a profusion of loose, white flowers, flushed and freckled with rose.

The blushing white blooms of the shrub bring sparkle to the end of winter.

Rhododendron 'Goldsworth Yellow'

Yellow-flowered rhododendrons always claim more attention than the common pink and purple kinds, but they do have disadvantages. Thus, *Rhododendron campylocarpum* is slow to flower and rather delicate and *R. caucasicum*, though more robust, is less attractive.

However, their offspring, 'Goldsworth Yellow', which was bred in about 1925, has neither of the parents' failings and is one of the most valuable of the hardy evergreen hybrids. Eventually making a wide-spreading bush, some 10 ft high, it is covered in early June with domed trusses of buds and funnel-shaped flowers, which produce an enchanting harmony of colour. The petals are apricot-pink in bud, but change as they open to a clear primrose-yellow. There is an area of brown spots inside each flower – a seductive path for bees.

HOW TO GROW
See p. 305.

The free-flowering, reliable 'Goldsworth Yellow' is one of the finest of all yellow-bloomed rhododendrons.

In June the rhododendron becomes a glorious mass of soft golden bells.

Rhododendron 'Homebush'

Even among the hundreds of named forms of azalea – a host which continues to grow year by year – there is something rather special about this beautiful plant. It is a member of the Knap Hill group of hybrids, a select band of deciduous azaleas that are named after the Surrey nursery where they were raised.

'Homebush' was one of the earliest, appearing in 1926, but it remains one of the most popular. It makes an open bush, some 6-8 ft high and wide, with fine, rounded heads of dusky-pink, semi-double flowers standing high above the foliage in May.

Midday shade helps the blooms, which are scentless, to last longer. As with most deciduous azaleas, attractive autumn leaf colour provides a bonus, though this varies from year to year depending on the prevailing weather conditions.

HOW TO GROW
See p. 305.

Rhododendron 'Homebush' puts forth its deep pink blooms from mid-May onwards, when the danger of frost damage is past.

'Homebush' is unusually open and airy for an azalea.

Rhododendron 'Hinomayo'

The Kurume group of hybrid azaleas, of which this is one, are evergreen shrubs with small, glossy leaves. Like all its tribe, 'Hinomayo' flowers from infancy, the branches and leaves disappearing in April and May under a cloud of clear soft pink.

In this association, perhaps in the entrance to a small courtyard, 'Hinomayo' is the centre of a group of plants which, when the azalea's display is over, provide interest for the rest of the year. Simple plants, they gain a certain glamour from the peacock in their midst.

One of them, the elegant deciduous shrub *Cotoneaster horizontalis*, produces broad fans of small leaves that are a perfect foil to the other plants during summer. Then, in winter, it provides its own splendour with scarlet fruit and leaves. The spindle tree, *Euonymus fortunei* 'Silver Queen', unfolds new leaves, soft and creamy-yellow, as the azalea flowers. Later these leaves become deep green, edged with white, and in autumn the plant puts forth orange berries in pink capsules.

Two other groups of predominantly foliage plants, the herbaceous plantain lilies (*Hosta fortunei* 'Albo-Picta') and *Ajuga reptans*, take the front line in this grouping. At the rear there rise the trunks of silver birches (*Betula pendula*).

The group is shown only four years after being planted at the foot of the silver birch, and it has already merged. In such a restricted grouping it is essential to keep the azalea dominant and the other plants balanced: entire branches of the cotoneaster will need to be taken out from time to time, to prevent it occupying too much space.

HOW TO GROW
Rhododendron 'Hinomayo': *see p. 305.*
Ajuga reptans: see p. 65.
Betula pendula: see p. 333.
Cotoneaster horizontalis: see p. 269.
Euonymus fortunei: see p. 279.
Hosta fortunei: see p. 95.

Rhododendron 'Hinomayo', fronted by cotoneasters, blooms among well-chosen companions beneath silver birches.

Rhododendron luteum

The honey from this azalea of the Pontic Alps, on the south shore of the Black Sea, is said to have stupefied an army of ancient Greeks – Xenophon's legendary 'Ten Thousand' – with its toxic substances. The commonest and easiest to grow of all the deciduous azaleas, the plant – which is also listed as *Azalea pontica* – is often used merely as a rootstock for the grafting of grander azalea hybrids – but it has a simple beauty of its own which the hybrids often lack and which makes it worth considering wherever space allows. It grows 6-8 ft high, with a spread of 4-6 ft.

The fat flower buds appear on the shrub's elegantly tiered branches the moment the leaves fall in a blaze of glory in October, and they remain all winter as a promise of the returning spring. At last, in May, they open into long-tubed flowers, clear yellow and intoxicatingly fragrant. If the shrub is grown in a natural setting, with bluebells beneath, there are few more charming sights.

HOW TO GROW
See p. 305.

Rhododendron luteum is a parent of many, varicoloured hybrids, which all flourish in shady spots.

Rhododendron 'Lady Chamberlain'

For rhododendron enthusiasts, and indeed for anyone who loves beautiful flowers, there are few greater pleasures than visiting the Rothschild rhododendron collection at Exbury, on the Solent coast of Hampshire. A particular delight is to stroll, in May or early June, down the woodland path lined with specimens of 'Lady Chamberlain'.

At flowering time these towers of small, blue-tinged, evergreen leaves, up to 10 ft high and 5 ft across, are aflame with long, waxy bells of sealing-wax red flowers tinged with orange.

But the shrub is variable, and some forms, while maintaining the shape, have flowers in a combination of pink, orange and yellow. The massed effect is glorious.

Variations of this hybrid are offered as separately named clones, such as 'Chelsea' (orange-pink), 'Ivy' (orange), 'Salmon Trout' (salmon-pink), 'Exbury' (yellow, overlaid with salmon-orange), 'Gleam' (orange-yellow, with crimson-tipped lobes) and 'Seville' (bright orange).

HOW TO GROW
See p. 305.

Though 'Lady Chamberlain' is an untidy shrub, this is forgotten in late spring when it blooms so prodigiously.

Rhododendron yakushimanum

Introduced in 1934 from the mountains of the Japanese island Yakushima, this striking evergreen rhododendron has in recent years been used as a parent of a number of hybrids. This is because of its compactness, and its hardiness in exposed positions.

The shrub, some 2 ft high and up to 3 ft wide, is shallowly domed. For so small a plant, its narrow leaves are fairly long – up to 5 in. They bear on their undersides a conspicuous pale buff felt. This also clothes the emergent shoots which, as they unfold, resemble some unusual magnolia flower. The trusses of bloom are, again, untypical of a dwarf rhododendron, being rounded and a definite pink in bud. They open to apple-blossom pink, then rapidly mature to white.

HOW TO GROW
See p. 305.

R. yakushimanum with yellow-flowered Fothergilla major behind and blue Endymion hispanicus in front.

Above leathery, lance-like leaves, the deep pink buds of R. yakushimanum open in May to blooms of snowy white.

Tulipa 'First Lady' fronts *Ribes sanguineum* to produce a harmony of reds.

Ribes sanguineum
(FLOWERING CURRANT)

One of the most popular of all flowering shrubs, the flowering currant is a deciduous, hardy bush, 6-8 ft high and almost as broad, with a pungent, curranty smell. The rose-red flowers appear in April in drooping racemes that elongate as they mature. The leaves are rounded and lobed, of a fresh green with a pale down on the underside. Blue-black fruits follow in early autumn.

The variety 'Albescens' is rather less vigorous, but carries fine racemes of white flowers tinged with pink. 'Album' has pure white flowers.

HOW TO GROW
Plant between autumn and spring. Easily grown in any well-drained soil, and in sun or light shade. The golden form does best in dappled shade. Propagate by hardwood cuttings in the open, in autumn. No pruning is needed, except for removal, at ground level, of old or congested shoots after flowering.

The rosy, drooping blossom of the flowering currant can be cut to provide warm spring colour in the home.

If allowed to spread freely, rose acacia will eventually cover a wall.

Robinia hispida (ROSE ACACIA)

This lovely pink-flowered shrub has no connection with the botanical *Acacia*, an entirely distinct genus of plants. Rose acacia, which makes a bush some 8-10 ft high and as much across, carries chubby, hanging racemes of deep rose-pink, pea-like flowers in May and June. Its deep green leaves each consist of several pairs of leaflets. It is hardy, but its brittle branches need protection from strong winds. For the same reason it is often given a sunny wall, with the back branches tied in for support.

HOW TO GROW
Plant between autumn and spring in any soil. Tolerant of drought and pollution. Does best in a sunny, sheltered spot. Grafted types look well as specimen shrubs; those on their own roots make good ground-cover on sloping sites. Propagate by cuttings in summer, or by rooted suckers. No pruning needed, but remove frost-damaged shoots and unwanted suckers.

Robinia hispida basks in the sunshine. The shrub is so attractive and unusual that it deserves to be grown much more than it is.

Plant rosemary by a path to get the full benefit of its scent.

Rosmarinus officinalis (ROSEMARY)

Rosemary, one of the classical Mediterranean herbs, has narrow, aromatic leaves that yield their oil freely. The shrub makes a 6 ft high evergreen, with a similar spread. 'Miss Jessop's Upright' is splendid for hedges, and there are lower-growing forms, such as 'Severn Sea'. Grey-blue flowers open from March, with the main display in May.

Although coming from hot, limestone hillsides, rosemary will nevertheless prosper in our colder, wetter climate, provided it has a sunny position. However, really severe winter cold will brown the leaves and even kill whole branches. The various forms are less hardy than the species and need protection even in the south.

HOW TO GROW
Plant in spring, in ordinary, well-drained to dry soil, and full sun. Wet clay soil is unsuitable. Propagate by hardwood cuttings in the open, in early autumn or spring. Stray branches may be cut to shape after flowering.

The shrub not only looks well in the border but also makes an excellent pot plant as above or an informal fragrant hedge.

Rubus × tridel 'Benenden'

Considered by many to be one of the finest shrubs in the garden, this fast-growing hybrid was raised by that doyen of plant collectors and hybridisers, Captain Collingwood Ingram. Known as 'Cherry' Ingram, because of his vast experience as a collector of flowering cherries in Japan, he died at the age of 100.

This association highlights one of Captain Ingram's best plants, which flowers more freely, and has larger, better-shaped flowers, than either of its parents. These are the Mexican *Rubus trilobus*, and R. *deliciosus* from the Rocky Mountains in Oregon. Since its introduction in 1950, R. × *tridel* has won several awards from the Royal Horticultural Society.

It is a deciduous shrub some 8-10 ft high, a little more in width, which in May bears white, saucer-shaped, yellow-centred flowers some 2 in. across. The flowers, of an exceptionally pure white, are well set off by bright green triple-lobed leaves.

This rubus can stand alone or can act as a background to tall, slender plants, such as a group of bearded irises. Here, the early flowering iris 'Jane Phillips' has been chosen for the fine, lavender-blue flowers that it carries on 3 ft stems in late May and early June.

At the foot of this planting, flowering with the irises, there is a wide band of *Saxifraga × urbium* (London pride). This beautiful saxifrage, with starry pink flowers growing from crowded rosettes of leaves, is sometimes despised because it is ubiquitous, but it is a charming plant with all the practical virtues – being adaptable, hardy, evergreen, and a steady spreader.

HOW TO GROW
Rubus × tridel 'Benenden': *plant between autumn and spring, in any well-drained soil, and in sun or light shade. Propagate by cuttings under glass, in late summer. Maintain shape by removing annually, at ground level, some of the older shoots after flowering.*
Iris 'Jane Phillips': *see bearded hybrids, p. 97.*
Saxifraga × urbium: see Saxifraga umbrosa, p. 217.

With its gracefully arching branches and attractive white blooms, *Rubus × tridel* 'Benenden' is a delightful centrepiece to this early summer association. Beneath its branches are purple irises and, in the foreground, pink London pride.

Ruscus aculeatus (BUTCHER'S BROOM)

Butcher's broom is one of those plants that hovers vaguely between being a shrub and a herbaceous plant. Certainly, its 2-3 ft high evergreen shoots do not die down in winter, but neither do they put on annual growth. In bud, the tiny cream flowers are little bigger than pinheads, and when they open in March and April are inconspicuous.

Small though the flowers may be, on female plants they are replaced by marble-sized berries of pillar-box red. This display is truly remarkable, especially when seen in a shady spot similar to the woodland and hedge bottoms where the shrub may occasionally occur growing wild.

HOW TO GROW
Plant autumn to spring, in any kind of soil, from heavy clay to shallow chalk. Exceptionally good in dense, dry shade, and spreads to form thickets. For fruit production, plant one male to three females. Propagate by division in spring. No pruning needed.

The 'leaves' of R. *aculeatus* are in fact cladodes, flattened stalks that function as leaves. On each a minute flower is borne.

In autumn, female butcher's brooms flaunt vivid cherry-like fruits.

Rue, with its neat, compact habit, is ideal for the edge of a border.

Ruta graveolens (RUE)

This hardy evergreen sub-shrub was once widely used as a medicinal and disinfectant herb, but is now chiefly grown for its decorative value, in particular for the filigree of blue-green foliage that clothes it to the ground. The plant grows to 2-3 ft high and about half as broad.

Above the leaves, heads of flowers are carried for at least two months, from June onwards. They are a distinctive sulphur yellow, with charmingly cupped, fringed petals. The seed capsules, which last through winter, have an interesting crown shape. The lovely, more compact form 'Jackman's Blue' has leaves of an almost metallic blue, but it seldom flowers.

HOW TO GROW
Plant in autumn or spring, in any type of well-drained soil and in full sun. Propagate by cuttings under glass, in late summer. It is prone to legginess, but plants can be pruned hard back to old wood in spring.

A harmony of blue-green and gold is created by a bush of rue surrounded by the young foliage of *Origanum vulgare aureum*.

In spring a mass of stout golden-yellow catkins bursts forth amid the grey-green foliage. Each is up to 2 in. long.

Salix lanata (WOOLLY WILLOW)

Willows are an extraordinarily diverse genus, varying from tiny creeping shrublets to fine forest trees. Many make admirable garden plants because of their foliage, flowers or coloured bark, and all are deciduous and hardy.

Salix lanata is often recommended for rock gardens, but with a height and spread of 3-4 ft it is really too big for such a setting and is better grown as a specimen shrub accompanied by choice plants. The shrub's main charm is its conspicuously grey-felted, rounded leaves, but the firm yellow catkins that burst out over the bush in April and May are also attractive. The woolly willow is a slow-growing plant, but even in youth it has an air of maturity.

HOW TO GROW
Plant between autumn and spring, in loamy, moisture-retentive soil and full sun. Propagated by cuttings in autumn under glass or outside in summer. Prune lightly to maintain shape, after the catkins have finished.

Woolly willow loves moist soil and thrives by the side of water.

Salix gracilistyla 'Melanostachys'

Black is a rare and not particularly inviting flower colour, and the idea of a 'black' pussy willow may seem positively bizarre. In reality, though, this Japanese willow is far more than a mere curiosity. In February, the smooth bud caps fall away to reveal oval, velvety catkins of jet-crimson. By early March the catkins are studded with red stamens. Finally, the stamens burst into a shower of golden pollen and the dark catkins are transformed.

Salix gracilistyla 'Melanostachys' forms a spreading bush, ultimately growing to 10 ft tall but, like most willows, it responds well to pruning. The Royal Horticultural Society conferred an Award of Merit on it in 1976.

HOW TO GROW
As for Salix lanata, but preferably in damp soil. Naturally bushy, the dwarf cultivar 'Gracilis' needs no pruning and makes a handsome low hedge if plants are set 1½ - 2 ft apart.

Catkins and daffodils provide an intriguing effect in early spring.

The catkins, which appear on bare branches before the leaves, start as black and gradually turn to gold.

Salvia officinalis (SAGE)

This aromatic evergreen sub-shrub provides the narrow, grey-green leaves that are so widely used in cooking. It has been grown in Britain since at least the 16th century.

Sage makes a low, wide, hardy plant, some 2 ft high and 18 in. wide, that in June and July provides a good show of purple, hooded flowers. It associates well not only with other herbs but also with pinks (*Dianthus*) and shrub roses. There are two excellent forms with coloured leaves: 'Icterina', which does not flower, has foliage of variegated green and gold; and 'Purpurascens', one of the best of all low foliage shrubs, has young leaves and stems of purple, and blue-purple flowers.

HOW TO GROW
Plant in spring, in ordinary, well-drained soil and in full sun. Propagate in late summer by cuttings of non-flowering shoots, rooted in a cold frame. Trim plants back by half in spring and replace with new stock every four or five years.

Sage flourishes in an open position. There it can receive the sun needed for its leaves to develop their full flavour.

'Icterina' makes a decorative foliage shrub, backed by *Lysimachia punctata*.

Sambucus canadensis 'Maxima'

(AMERICAN ELDER)

This association, centring on the American elder, is on the grand scale. The elder is a hardy, deciduous shrub that has been grown in Britain since the 18th century. The species generally is not so attractive as the British elder (*Sambucus nigra*) but a recently raised German variety *S. canadensis* 'Maxima' is splendid and is the form now usually grown in Britain and the one chosen for this grouping.

Pruned hard each spring to about 4 ft above ground, the shrub develops 8 ft long stems that bear vast leaves. The white flower heads of July are 12 in. across. They are followed by purple-black berries. If the plant is grown in isolation, the effect can be gross, but in the company of other plants of similar scale it looks magnificent.

In this grouping the elder is the only shrub. To one side of it a clump of the perennial *Gunnera manicata* displays the biggest leaves, up to 6 ft across, that can be grown in British gardens. Dark green, puckered and prickly, they resemble in shape those of some monstrous rhubarb. *Lysichiton americanus* has bright, shining, green paddle-shaped foliage that may attain a length of 3 ft.

The perennial *Ligularia dentata* 'Desdemona' matches the elder's purplish fruits with purple-flushed leaves and in summer blazes with heads of orange, daisy-like flowers.

HOW TO GROW
Sambucus canadensis 'Maxima': *plant between autumn and spring, in moisture-retentive soil enriched with plenty of organic matter; in sun or light shade. Propagate by cuttings, in summer in a cold frame, in autumn in the open. Prune hard each spring to encourage large leaves.*
Gunnera manicata: see p. 89.
Ligularia dentata: see p. 100.
Lysichiton americanus: see p. 368.

The group pictured in August, with the elder in full flower, includes the magnificent *Gunnera manicata* to the right, the glossy foliage of *Lysichiton americanus* to the left, and a foreground of *Ligularia dentata* 'Desdemona', which adds a touch of brilliant colour to the display.

'Plumosa Aurea' is a golden-leaved, slow-growing form of *S. racemosa*.

Sambucus racemosa (RED-BERRIED ELDER)

It is pleasant to record a shrub that actually succeeds better in the north of England than in the gentler south. *Sambucus racemosa* – a native of upland Europe, eastwards into Siberia – withstands all conditions except drought.

This elder develops into a shrub some 8 ft high and not quite as wide with pith-filled shoots and pinnate leaves typical of the genus. But it flowers early, in April, before the leaves fully unfold, producing panicles of flowers that are green at first but eventually turn to white. The shrub puts on another display in August, when the berries ripen to scarlet. Fruiting is generally less satisfactory in the south of England.

HOW TO GROW
Cultivation and propagation as for Sambucus canadensis: see p. 313. In semi-wild settings, pruning is unnecessary; elsewhere, prune to shape in early spring.

At summer's end 'Plumosa Aurea' becomes a glorious blaze of scarlet and gold as the heavy clusters of berries ripen.

Gold mingles with silver as *Santolina chamaecyparissus* blooms in July.

Santolina chamaecyparissus

The silver-grey, feathery leaves of this hardy evergreen dwarf shrub, strongly aromatic when bruised, make it a natural garden companion for herbs. It is a native of Mediterranean hillsides and therefore, in Britain, needs full sun and perfect drainage if it is to maintain its typical compact habit, with a height and spread of 1½-2 ft.

In July, the shrub bears a mass of blooms, each a bright yellow button – rather like a daisy centre without the surrounding ray florets. There is much to be said for clipping the shrub all over in spring to make the growth denser and thus enhance the silveriness of its foliage. A line of clipped plants makes a lovely low hedge.

HOW TO GROW
Plant in autumn or spring, in ordinary, well-drained garden soil and in full sun. For hedging, set plants 15-18 in. apart. Propagate by cuttings under glass, in late summer. Trim hedges during summer.

If grown in the right conditions and trimmed in spring, the shrub makes a beautifully compact mound of foliage.

The dense growth of *S. confusa* makes it an especially robust hedge.

Sarcococca confusa (SWEET BOX)

Resembling a small box tree, this shrub is grown for its tiny but fragrant winter flowers. The specific name *confusa* denotes the uncertainty about the plant's country of origin, which is probably China. The shrub builds up a dome of little leathery evergreen leaves, some 4 ft high and wide, beneath which clusters of petal-less, creamy-stamened flowers hide from January to March. Their fragrance carries for yards on a mild, moist day.

Known sometimes as sweet box, the plant is valuable for its tolerance of shade, though in a shady position it is much less likely to produce the black, shining berries that normally appear from April to July.

HOW TO GROW
Plant in autumn or spring, in any good soil; particularly suitable for chalk. Thrives in shade beneath trees and is excellent for ground-cover. Propagation is easiest by removal of rooted suckers. Pruning seldom required.

The shrub's evergreen leaves, which are darker above than beneath, are adorned in winter with small cream flowers.

Senecio 'Sunshine'

The value of evergreen shrubs in the garden is self-evident. But just as necessary are 'evergrey' plants, to contrast with other foliage. *Senecio* 'Sunshine', hardy in all but the coldest winters, is a grey-leaved shrub from New Zealand that is usually sold inaccurately as *S. greyi* or *S. laxifolius*. It is a shapely, wide, spreading bush with soft leaves. These unfold snow white and, although the upper surfaces turn almost green as they age, the undersides remain brilliant and shimmer in a wind.

Profuse heads of bright yellow daisy-like flowers, opening from white-felted buds, develop in June. But they do so rather at the expense of the foliage, and a choice has to be made between the two. If the flowers are chosen, their heads must be cut off the moment their display is over in order to retain the neat shape of the bush through autumn and winter.

Height in this association is provided by a fast-growing evergreen tree, *Eucalyptus gunnii* (the cider gum), which may be cut down every April to within 12 in. of the ground. From this stump a cloud of blue-green leaves on wand-like stems develops each summer. A similar colour is produced at ground level by a foreground planting of the evergreen shrub *Hebe pinguifolia* 'Pagei', one of the finest and easiest-grown of ground-cover plants. Gaps in the hebe can be filled by a few clumps of blue or purple-flowering late spring and summer bulbs, such as *Fritillaria meleagris* and *Allium albopilosum*.

HOW TO GROW
Senecio 'Sunshine'*: plant in autumn or spring, in ordinary well-drained soil, and full sun. Suitable, with its associates, for windy seaside gardens in all but the coldest areas. Propagate by cuttings under glass, in late summer. Prune as desired, but in any case remove faded flower stems and any shoots which spoil the outline.*
Allium albopilosum: see p. 140.
Eucalyptus gunnii: see p. 339.
Fritillaria meleagris: see p. 153.
Hebe pinguifolia 'Pagei'*: see p. 285.*

In August, the evergreen *Senecio* 'Sunshine' is presided over by the tall *Eucalyptus gunnii*. This silver-grey scheme is fronted by *Allium albopilosum* and a carpet of *Hebe pinguifolia* 'Pagei'.

Skimmia japonica

The pale, lustrous, often markedly curved leaves of this evergreen shrub have a quiet beauty, and when crushed they exude a delightful scent of orange. The plant, which slowly forms a shallow dome, up to 5 ft high and 6 ft wide, is valuable in the garden for its tolerance of shade and lime, and also for its hardiness.

In April and May each shoot carries upright clusters of fragrant white flowers. On female plants these are succeeded by a splendid display of berries. By September they are fully formed and a brilliant scarlet. The fruits may last until beyond February, depending on whether the birds decide to plunder them or not. A male plant is needed if a female is to fruit.

HOW TO GROW
Plant in autumn or spring, in any soil and in light shade or sun. Protect young plants with straw in winter. Increase from cuttings, in late summer. No pruning necessary.

The brilliant clusters of berries put out by a female shrub sometimes persist until flowers appear the following spring.

Skimmia japonica thrives in the dappled shade cast by trees.

A mature kowhai can reach as high as 12 ft against a warm wall.

Sophora tetraptera (KOWHAI)

This delightful evergreen shrub, growing some 12 ft high and with a spread half as great, is the national flower of New Zealand. It has the happy attribute of looking distinguished all the year round. The long, narrow leaves, each made up of a dozen or so pairs of leaflets, are particularly elegant. Most of the old leaves fall in April, as the bunches of golden waxy flowers open.

When the flowers are over in May, the current year's leaves unfold from furry new shoots and the plant's seed pods develop, hanging in what look like strings of four-winged beads. In all but the mildest areas of Britain the plant needs the protection of a wall.

HOW TO GROW
Plant during mid or late spring, in good well-drained soil and in a sunny, sheltered site. Best trained against a warm wall. Propagate by ripe seeds under glass in spring. No pruning, except to remove frost-damaged shoots.

The pendulous clusters of golden bellflowers, borne in spring, eventually develop into curiously shaped seed pods.

Tiny white flowers on plume-like panicles, 18 in. long, appear in August.

Sorbaria aitchisonii

Looking rather like enormous clumps of meadow sweet, sorbarias are hardy, deciduous, easily grown shrubs. *Sorbaria aitchisonii* (syn. *Spiraea aitchisonii*) makes a bush 8-10 ft high and broad, with a fountain of red-tinged shoots. In August and September the light, ferny leaves set off the great white, fuzzy flower heads perfectly.

The floral display is, unfortunately, short-lived, but the shape of the flower heads is maintained through autumn and winter, since the flowers' myriad little seed capsules remain on the plant after the leaves have fallen.

HOW TO GROW
Plant between autumn and spring, in any well-drained soil. Best in full sun, but also suitable for light shade at the edge of woodland. Propagate by rooted suckers during the dormant season, or in late summer by heel cuttings under glass. In early spring, remove one or two older stems at ground level and prune laterals back to two buds from the base.

The fresh mid-green leaves of *Sorbaria aitchisonii* are slender, pointed, and grow from red-tinged stems.

Spartium junceum, bright as sunshine, blazes against a brick wall in July.

Spartium junceum (SPANISH BROOM)

One of the best of all summer shrubs, Spanish broom has been grown in British gardens for at least 400 years. The common name is inaccurate, since it grows wild not just in Spain but all round the Mediterranean, in the Crimea and now in this country, on many road embankments.

The shrub is leafless, the bright green twigs doing the work normally performed by leaves. From June to August, with July as a peak, it puts on a marvellous display of clearest gorse-gold flowers, which are almost the shape and size of sweet peas and just as deliciously fragrant. Attaining a height of 8-10 ft, and a slightly lesser spread, it is easy to grow but can be damaged by severe winter cold.

HOW TO GROW
Plant in autumn or spring, in any well-drained soil and in full sun. Propagate by seeds only. May be pruned back in spring, but cutting into old wood causes die-back.

A mass of green shoots takes the place of foliage on *Spartium junceum*, whose fragrant yellow flowers are rather like sweet peas.

With its profusion of white flowers, borne on arching stems, bridal wreath is one of the finest of garden shrubs.

Spiraea × arguta

(BRIDAL WREATH, FOAM OF MAY)

With its pure white flowers, handsome mid-green leaves and fountain shape, *Spiraea × arguta* is one of the most desirable shrubs in the garden. It is not only beautiful in flower and leaf for seven or eight months of the year, but is an ideal shrub for providing the dappled shade which many small flowers love. If the lowest branches are clipped so that the fountain sprays out 2 ft from the ground, there will be a wide circle of soil beneath that can be filled with a succession of flowers.

The shrub could be planted in a raised bed 5-6 ft back from the retaining wall, and the fountain shape repeated with the dwarf broom, *Genista lydia*, falling over the wall. A succession of flowers could start with the very early scilla, *Scilla tubergeniana*, of a light Cambridge blue, to bloom in February.

The spiraea itself will be massed with clusters of pure white flowers in April and May, followed by leaves which keep their freshness through the summer. The broom will produce its yellow pea-like flowers in June. It could be succeeded in autumn by a mass of *Cyclamen neapolitanum* in both pink and white flowers and with handsome marbled leaves.

These cyclamens are not easy to place in the garden, for they need shade and must not be disturbed by anybody deciding to clean up a mixed shrub bed with a fork or hoe. In a circle of soil that is carefully hand-weeded, the corms should enjoy a long, peaceful life.

If midsummer flowers are also wanted, a few seeds of a gossamer-like annual, such as *Nigella damascena* 'Miss Jekyll Blue', could be sprinkled round the spiraea during spring. But the soil beneath the shrub must be bare by September to show off the cyclamen.

HOW TO GROW

Spiraea × arguta: plant during the dormant season, in ordinary garden soil. Best in full sun. Propagate by cuttings, in summer or early autumn. Spring-flowering spiraeas form buds the previous year and should be pruned immediately after flowering; remove faded flowers and thin out old and spindly stems and branches.
Cyclamen neapolitanum: see p. 150.
Genista lydia: see p. 283.
Nigella damascena 'Miss Jekyll Blue': *see p. 47.*
Scilla tubergeniana: see p. 168.

The resemblance to an ornamental fountain and falling water in this association between the spiraea and dwarf broom is greatly enhanced by planting them in a raised bed. The spiraea is just coming into autumn leaf; the genista has already lost its leaves and forms a complex network of arching twigs. The effect of sparkling water drops on the surface of the pool beneath the fountain is created by an underplanting of *Cyclamen neapolitanum.*

Spiraea japonica

Named after the country where it was first collected, *Spiraea japonica* is by no means confined to Japan. It is also found in Korea, China and the eastern Himalayas. It is a bushy, twiggy shrub, 3-5 ft tall, with narrow, toothed, lance-shaped leaves that are grey to blue-white beneath. In late summer the tip of every erect stem carries a flattened head of tiny pink to red flowers.

In 1885 a dwarf version, *S. j.* 'Bumalda', bearing carmine-pink flowers above curiously and erratically cream-variegated leaves, was introduced to Kew Gardens. It is seldom seen now, having been superseded by its more vigorous and better-coloured sport, 'Anthony Waterer'. This is 4 ft or so high and has rich carmine flowers. Its leaves are variegated not only with cream but sometimes with pink.

Lovers of white-flowered plants should look out for *S. j.* 'Albiflora', introduced from Japan as long ago as 1864, or the superior seedling raised from it, 'Leucantha'. Both are rarely above 2 ft high and have a neat, erect habit.

Another striking cultivar is the fairly recent 'Goldflame'. All its shoots and young leaves are a bright coppery-red and gold, the flowers crimson.

Several smaller versions of *S. japonica* have arisen, the most dependable being *S. j.* 'Alpina' ('Nana'). It forms a wide hummock of slender stems, rarely more than 18 in. tall and not much more across, studded with rose-pink flowers. It is suitable for even the smallest garden.

S. j. 'Bullata' (*S. crispifolia*) is a curious but attractive mutant, stubby and erect in habit. It is slow growing and compact, eventually reaching a height of no more than 15-18 in. The leaves are small, broad and crinkled. During the flowering season, they are almost hidden by the rounded clusters of crimson blooms.

HOW TO GROW
Cultivation as for Spiraea × arguta (see p. 317). This spiraea may also be propagated by removal and replanting of rooted suckers. The plant flowers on current season's wood, and hard pruning should be done in early spring.

The broad panicles of 'Anthony Waterer' bring massed colour to the mixed border in late summer.

'Anthony Waterer' has toothed leaves and glowing crimson flowers.

Somewhat smaller than 'Anthony Waterer', 'Goldflame' earns its place principally by the rich colouring of its foliage.

Stephanandra tanakae

Some shrubs depend for their charm not on their flowers, leaves or fruits but simply on their habit. The hardy, deciduous *Stephanandra tanakae*, from mountain slopes in Japan, is such a plant. Its grace lies in its fountain of long, arching branches, which are a rich brown. At the tip of every shoot an open cluster of tiny yellow and white flowers appears in June and July. The shrub is 5-7 ft high and 6-7 ft broad.

The toothed leaves, which are rather like those of currant bushes, turn a clear yellow in autumn. After the leaves have fallen, the exposed brown stems provide a perfect complement to the bare red shoots of *Cornus alba* 'Spaethii' (p. 266).

HOW TO GROW
Plant between autumn and spring, in ordinary soil that is well drained but moisture retentive. Sun or partial shade. Propagate in autumn by rooted suckers, layering or cuttings in the open. Remove old or decayed wood in early spring.

Stephanandra tanakae resplendent in autumnal shades of yellow and orange.

The yellow and white star-shaped flowers, which are in terminal panicles 4 in. long, last for two months during the summer.

Stranvaesia davidiana undulata

Looking like some kind of distinguished cotoneaster, the key plant of this association, a hardy evergreen shrub, was one of the many fine discoveries of the plant collector Ernest Wilson. He introduced it to Britain from western China in 1901. The variety *undulata*, which is smaller than the species, still makes a robust shrub, ultimately 10 ft high and rather more across.

The plant's great attraction is the display of brilliant scarlet berries which hang in clusters along its branches from autumn to spring. Unlike the fruit of the closely related cotoneaster and firethorn, the berries are dry enough to be rather unpalatable to birds. The wide, spreading branches carry wavy-edged, leathery, dark green leaves, some of which – unusually in an evergreen – turn vivid red in autumn and contrast the following spring with the new green leaves.

Try planting the stranvaesia with *Mahonia japonica*, one of the finest of all garden shrubs. It has beautiful, glistening, deep green whorls of leaves, and its long, fragrant spikes of lemon-yellow flowers come out at the same time as the stranvaesia's red berries.

At the base of these two shrubs are thickly clustered two ferns: hart's-tongue (*Asplenium scolopendrium*) and lady fern (*Athyrium filix-femina*). The vivid green of their developing fronds announces the arrival of spring, when the shrubs renew their growth after their fine winter display.

HOW TO GROW
Stranvaesia davidiana undulata: plant in autumn or spring, in any type of well-drained soil, in sun or shade; excellent on chalk. Tolerant of air pollution and suitable for town gardens. Propagate by heel cuttings under glass in summer. No pruning.
Asplenium scolopendrium: see p. 128.
Athyrium filix-femina: see p. 130.
Mahonia japonica: see p. 295.

The white flowers of the stranvaesia (above) prophesy a bright display of red berries. The berries in autumn (left) are set off to perfection by starfish-flowered *Mahonia japonica*, and the ferns *Asplenium scolopendrium* and *Athyrium filix-femina*.

Symphoricarpos × doorenbosii 'Mother of Pearl'
(SNOWBERRY)

The crowning glory of this shapely, vigorous shrub is the snow-white, pink-cheeked, marble-sized fruits that weigh down each branch from October to February. Birds leave these alone, perhaps because they associate whiteness with unripeness. The shrub, which is deciduous and has a height and spread of 6 ft, makes a dense bush of smooth, blue-green leaves from spring to autumn, with little pink bell-shaped flowers appearing from July to September. One of the hybrid's parents, *Symphoricarpos orbiculatus*, is also a good garden shrub, especially *S. o.* 'Foliis Variegatus', which has purple-red fruits and golden-edged leaves.

HOW TO GROW
Plant between autumn and spring, in any well-drained soil. Highly accommodating and thrives in the shade of overhead trees. Propagate in autumn by hardwood cuttings in the open, or by rooted suckers. May be trimmed in early spring.

Symphoricarpos × doorenbosii 'Mother of Pearl', unlike some snowberries, produces dense clusters of berries every year.

The gold-rimmed foliage of *S. orbiculatus* 'Foliis Variegatus'.

Syringa microphylla (LILAC)

This elegant, hardy, small lilac, 4-5 ft high and wide, is for those who do not have space to grow a large hybrid syringa. And, unlike those many lilac species that smell rather like privet, this one has the typical lilac fragrance.

Growth is comparatively delicate, and in June the rose-lilac spires of flowers are heavy enough to cause the twigs to bow gracefully outwards. A bonus is often provided in September by a second flowering display. The plant is thus the perfect companion for those Old roses that also bloom in June and September.

HOW TO GROW
Plant between autumn and spring, in fertile, well-drained soil and a sunny site. Feed young shrubs each spring with an organic mulch. Propagate in summer by cuttings under glass, or in autumn by layering or hardwood cuttings in the open. For pruning, see Syringa vulgaris 'Madame Lemoine'.

Syringa microphylla, which is unusual in flowering twice during summer, is a graceful lilac with slender branches.

The pale rosy-lilac blooms of the shrub are deep mauve on the outside.

Syringa vulgaris 'Madame Lemoine' (LILAC)

The big hybrid lilacs are such an eagerly anticipated part of the early summer scene that few large gardens are without one. The flowering season is short and the shrubs are not elegant, but the heady fragrance of the great flower heads is as irresistible as the sight of them tossing lightly in the breeze above a sea of heart-shaped leaves.

'Madame Lemoine', up to 12 ft high and almost as wide, is a beautiful lilac that in May and June develops great clusters of creamy buds, which open to pure white flowers.

HOW TO GROW
Cultivation as for Syringa microphylla. Propagation is easiest by heel cuttings in late summer, or by layering. Pruning of all syringas consists of dead-heading after flowering; in early autumn remove weak and crossing branches. Old, over-grown plants may be cut back to 12 in. from the ground in winter, for flowering after three or four years. Remove suckers from cultivars of S. vulgaris at any time.

The dazzling white 'Madame Lemoine' is a popular hybrid of common lilac.

Left to grow unchecked, the spreading *Syringa vulgaris* 'Madame Lemoine' requires plenty of garden space.

Tamarix pentandra (TAMARISK)

There are some plants which not only do best in a certain habitat but seem to epitomise it. Such a plant is the hardy deciduous tamarisk, which thrives even when fully exposed to harsh salt winds and which somehow needs to be at the coast anyway to look fully at home.

The cascade of softest rose-pink blooms which *Tamarix pentandra* becomes in August and September is one of the gayest sights of late summer, especially if seen against a backdrop of sparkling sea. Out of flower, the shrub is still attractive, something like a delicate, showering cypress, with its tiny leaves lost in the general impression. Since the tamarisk flowers on the current year's shoots, the previous season's growth can be pruned hard in spring to one-third of its length, to keep the plant to manageable proportions.

Other shrubs which do well at the seaside can be planted with the tamarisk to add interest through summer and autumn. The display suggested here starts at the front with the Floribunda rose 'Iceberg', whose large trusses of white blooms appear on and off from June until late autumn. Also in the foreground is the low-growing *Hebe* 'Blue Gem', seldom out of flower.

At the rear is a Spanish broom (*Spartium junceum*). In July, big yellow flowers begin to appear on its leafless, wand-like stems. Giving bulk to the group is the evergreen *Bupleurum fruticosum*, which is rather like a shrubby cow parsley. Its narrow sea-green leaves and almost round heads of small green flowers are highly unusual – and flower arrangers love them.

HOW TO GROW
Tamarix pentandra: plant between autumn and spring, in any well-drained soil except shallow chalk. Full sun is ideal. Good for exposed sites by the sea. Propagate in summer by soft cuttings under glass, or in autumn by hardwood cuttings in the open. To prevent tamarisk from swamping its neighbours, prune in early spring, cutting the previous season's growths back to within 2-3 ft of their base.
Bupleurum fruticosum: see p. 255.
Floribunda rose, 'Iceberg': see p. 230.
Hebe 'Blue Gem': see Hebe salicifolia, p. 285.
Spartium junceum: see p. 316.

Fluffy tassels of pink flowers adorn *Tamarix pentandra* in late summer.

In August, the rose-pink blooms of tamarisk overhangs yellow Spanish broom *Spartium junceum* and white *Rosa* 'Iceberg'; at the front are yellow-flowered *Bupleurum fruticosum* and *Hebe* 'Blue Gem'.

The pea-like flowers of gorse produce a honeyed fragrance on warm days.

Ulex europaeus (GORSE, FURZE, WHIN)

There is an old adage that 'kissing is out of season when gorse is out of bloom'. More prosaically, this is a way of saying that although the shrubs are covered with fragrant golden flowers only from March until May, one plant or another can show a flash of colour most months of the year, except during the very coldest spells.

Throughout most of the year, gorse makes a dark green, thorny bush some 5-8 ft high and across. Only for a couple of weeks after flowering, as the new growth emerges, do both the green colour and the spininess soften.

HOW TO GROW
Set out pot-grown plants, between autumn and spring, in ordinary to poor, dry to well-drained soil. Good on acid soil, also suitable for shallow chalk. Full sun. Propagate by seeds in spring. Prune leggy specimens back to just above ground level in spring.

Gorse tolerates poor soil, except shallow chalk, and is therefore useful for covering dry banks and for exposed seaside gardens.

By September, the mid-green leaves start to turn vivid scarlet and bronze.

Vaccinium corymbosum (SWAMP BLUEBERRY)

The hardy deciduous swamp blueberry, growing up to 6 ft high and even more across, is a twin-purpose shrub. The white-bloomed berries, which are ripe by August, make delicious desserts and preserves; and in May and June the plant puts forth charming spikes of pink and white, heather-like flowers, the leaves providing further decoration with autumn scarlet. There are three essentials for success: planting in acid soil; selecting at least two distinct clones for cross-pollination; and protecting the fruit from birds.

HOW TO GROW
Plant two or three specimens together between autumn and spring, in moist, acid soil enriched with organic matter. Best in full sun. Keep these surface-rooting plants cool and moist with a peat mulch in summer. Propagate by soft cuttings under glass in summer, or hardwood cuttings in the open during autumn. Prune in spring to remove dead wood and old stems that have borne fruit.

Urn-shaped flowers in 2 in. long loose clusters are followed by blue-black berries the size of small grapes.

The plant does not reach flowering size until it is three or four years old.

Viburnum × bodnantense

Raised at Bodnant, in North Wales, this splendid hybrid has remarkable frost resistance – which extends even to the open flowers. It is a vigorous upright shrub, with a height and spread of some 8-10 ft. Its somewhat corrugated leaves often turn bronze from midsummer onwards. As the leaves fall in October, clusters of fragrant pink-tinted white flowers open on the bare wood. They continue to do so on and off until about February, with the most spectacular display usually occurring before Christmas or in mild spells soon afterwards. 'Dawn' is the form that is most seen in cultivation.

HOW TO GROW
Plant between autumn and spring, in any well-drained but moisture-retentive soil, and in full sun. The plant needs protection from north and east winds, in a site where morning sun after night frost will not damage the flower buds. Propagation: see Viburnum × burkwoodii.

There is every likelihood of the sweetly scented flowers appearing in profusion during the Christmas holiday period.

Viburnum × burkwoodii

This superb shrub starts to bloom just as the winter-
flowering viburnums are finishing. Rather as in
rhododendrons, the tips of the shoots have already borne
by the previous August heads of rusty, spherical flower
buds. When at last they unfold, the effect is entrancing: a
rounded cluster of pink buds that open to pure white, with
an overpowering scent of golden-rayed lilies. Some flowers
open in February, but the height of the display is in April.
The shrub is near-evergreen: up to one-third of its shining,
dark green leaves, which have a brown felt beneath, persist
through winter to be joined by new leaves in spring. It is
one of the easiest shrubs to grow, either as a free-standing
bush or loosely trained against a wall. It eventually grows
up to 8 ft high, with an equal spread.

HOW TO GROW
*Cultivation as for Viburnum × bodnantense, setting plants out
in autumn or spring. Prune after flowering if necessary.
Propagate all viburnums by semi-hardwood cuttings in late
summer under glass. They can also be increased by layering in
early autumn.*

Just as *V. × bodnantense* often graces the
Christmas garden, so *V. × burkwoodii* is
generally at its most beautiful over Easter.

'Park Farm Hybrid' is of more spreading habit and has larger flowers.

Viburnum opulus (GUELDER ROSE)

The guelder rose, a native of Britain, is here the star of a
group of plants that love moisture but do not demand
soggy ground. A tall, bushy, deciduous shrub, with a
height and spread of up to 12 ft, the guelder rose has two
seasons of beauty. In May and June it is covered with
blooms resembling those of a lacecap hydrangea: flat heads
of small white flowers are encircled by larger white
individual flowers, forming a striking contrast with the
deep green maple-like leaves.

In autumn there is a second performance: the shrub is
loaded with clusters of translucent, squashy-looking red
berries, and the leaves turn crimson. In the variety 'Sterile'
(Snowball bush), which is popular in cottage gardens, the
flower heads are as round as a ball, pale green in bud, and
snow white when they open; but there are no berries.
Guelder roses associate well with beardless irises and large-
leaved hostas.

In this grouping, clumps of the bearded iris 'Dancer's
Veil' are grown. In June, their tall stems, rising from bold
sword-shaped leaves, bear large white flowers etched with
blue-purple. Between them are drifts of the sumptuous
Hosta sieboldiana, which has the largest leaves of all the
hostas.

The hostas provide a ground-cover of rich blue-green
foliage from spring, when the leaves rise like furled flags
and open slowly, to autumn, when they turn yellow for a
week or two and then suddenly disappear.

HOW TO GROW
*Viburnum opulus: cultivation as for V. × bodnantense, but
tolerates damp soil provided this is not waterlogged. To ensure
mass production of berries, plant at least two shrubs. Prune
lightly after flowering to remove old wood. For propagation see
V. × burkwoodii.*
Hosta sieboldiana: see p. 95.
Iris, bearded hybrids: see p. 97.

Above: Copious bunches of red fruits persist
long into winter. The variety 'Xanthocarpum'
produces clear golden-yellow berries. Right:
The flowers of the guelder rose scent the air
in early summer. Here, planted around it, are
groups of *Iris* 'Dancer's Veil', in full bloom at
this time, and *Hosta sieboldiana*.

Even when the shrub is in flower, the leaves are its most striking feature.

White, arching 'Mariesii' is backed here by full-bloomed *Rosa moyesii*.

Vinca major 'Elegantissima' is not quite as hardy as the type plant.

Viburnum davidii

Some viburnums are grown for their flowers, others for their fruits – and this one is much in demand for its distinctive foliage and habit. It is a low, hardy, evergreen shrub, some 2-3 ft high and spreading to 5 ft, that makes excellent ground-cover in sun or shade. The long leaves, carried in pairs on warty twigs, are a glossy dark green with three conspicuous veins and a netted pattern.

If a group of these shrubs is planted, ensuring cross-pollination, the dull white heads of flowers that appear in June and July will be succeeded in autumn by turquoise-blue berries – which birds generally leave alone.

HOW TO GROW
Plant in autumn or spring, in groups of two or three as a specimen planting, or more for ground-cover. Any kind of moist soil, in sun or dappled shade. Pruning rarely necessary. For propagation see Viburnum × burkwoodii (p. 323).

Plants may be male, female or a combination of both, so a group planting is necessary to ensure reliable production of berries.

Viburnum plicatum tomentosum 'Mariesii'

This deciduous shrub's white floral display, which appears in May, could be likened to layers of lacework draped over the branches. The dull green, oval leaves form a perfect contrast to this white splendour, and in autumn they turn wine red, creating a fresh attraction in their own right.

The form 'Mariesii' (and 'Lanarth', which is similar) accentuates the tiered-branch structure of the species. Both have a height and spread up to 10 ft. 'Mariesii' needs an isolated position for its shape to be appreciated. Given space and suitable soil, the shrub extends itself indefinitely by layering.

HOW TO GROW
Plant between autumn and spring, in any well-drained but not dry soil, and in light shade or sun. Best as a solitary specimen plant by the side of a lawn; since it is sterile, no berries are produced. Propagate as for Viburnum × burkwoodii. If necessary, prune to shape after flowering.

The 2-3 in. wide white flowers of 'Mariesii' have a fragile, delicate appearance but are pleasingly long-lasting.

Vinca major, V. minor

(GREATER AND LESSER PERIWINKLE)

These are two lovely evergreen plants. *Vinca major* bears fine blue flowers from April to June and trails long leaf stems that root at the tips, quickly forming ground-cover 3-4 ft across. The foliage of the form 'Elegantissima' is green and creamy-yellow.

V. minor has smaller stems, leaves and flowers, roots at the stem joints and blooms longer – from March to July. However, it spreads just as quickly as its larger relative. Forms with variegated leaves or purple, white or double flowers are available.

HOW TO GROW
Plant between autumn and spring, in ordinary, well-drained, deep and moist soil, and in shade. Excellent ground-cover, if spaced 12-18 in. apart. Propagate, if necessary, by division during dormancy. No pruning is necessary, but the plants will tolerate hard clipping.

Vinca minor may continue to bear a few flowers until the autumn after the main display is over in early July.

Weigela florida 'Variegata'

Famed in particular for its beautiful, variegated foliage, this hardy, deciduous shrub also bears attractive flowers and is easy to grow. The glory of the plant is its spring leaves, but the mature foliage is also very striking.

The leaves that start the season are magnificent, unfolding in a medley of pink, white and pale: green. This is matched perfectly in May and June by sprays of small, foxglove-like pink and white flowers (which continue to appear in bursts well into autumn). When mature, the leaves are irregularly dark green in the centre with lime-green margins. Another, smaller cultivar, 'Foliis Purpureis', has purple leaves and pink flowers.

Around the foot of the 5-6 ft high weigela are clumps of the clear blue flowered *Iris pallida dalmatica*, which blooms when the shrub does and whose pronounced vertical line contrasts well with the diffused shape of the weigela. Intermingled with the iris is the white-flowered honesty, *Lunaria annua* 'Alba'.

The iris is best dead-headed as soon as it has finished flowering, to encourage good leaf growth. But the flowers of the honesty should be left to produce their paper-moon seed pods, which turn from green to white and provide interest into winter, after the weigela has lost its leaves.

Until the biennial honesty reproduces itself from seeds, it needs to be augmented with one-year-old seedlings planted in the autumn after flowering.

HOW TO GROW
Weigela florida: plant between autumn and spring, in fertile soil that is well drained but moisture retentive. Sun or light shade, and good in town gardens. Propagate in summer by heel cuttings under glass, or in autumn by hardwood cuttings in the open. Pruning should be done right after flowering, which takes place on the previous season's wood. Remove one or two older stems annually.
Iris pallida dalmatica: see p. 96.
Lunaria annua: see p. 41.

'Foliis Purpureis' is more compact, and grows more slowly, than 'Variegata'.

The frothy clusters of clear, pale pink blooms and attractive variegated leaves of a weigela in May overhang a group of blue *Iris pallida dalmatica* interspersed with a sprinkling of *Lunaria annua* 'Alba'.

Sculptural Plants

How shape and texture can add a spectacular new dimension to the garden

The plants recommended in this book have mostly been chosen for the beauty of their flowers, foliage, fruit or bark. But some plants have another valuable attribute: a sculptural quality – that is, a dramatic, graceful or otherwise interesting shape, or perhaps texture.

The sculptural plant has several functions. It may be needed in the centre of a formless planting of somewhat retiring plants to give it a strong focal point. It may, by its crisp, firm shape, be used to accentuate the soft flounces of its neighbours. It may have large, bold leaves which, especially in silhouette, can give a solid framework to a planting. Or it may simply be grown for its own sake, for its singular beauty.

In a warm, dry garden the softly rounded shapes of such sun-loving plants as lavender, santolina and helianthemum would benefit from a contrast with a group of the evergreen sub-shrub *Euphorbia characias*. This will provide an impressively dense, handsome mass with whorls of grey-green leaves building up to 4 ft high and across and lit from February to June with giant candles of almost luminous lime-yellow bloom.

In a sunny area of the rock garden or stone sink that is devoted to small houseleeks (*Sempervivum*), a few *S. tectorum*, with their fuller leaf rosettes and taller, thicker flower stems, will effectively break up the low, spreading clumps around them.

Bold leaves for shady spots

Many fine foliage plants thrive in shade, among them such charming ground-cover specimens as foam flower (*Tiarella cordifolia*) and crane's-bill (*Geranium endressii*). But such large expanses of small, uniformly sized leaves can look tedious without the intervention of some bold, large-leaved sculptural plants. One of the best of these in shade is the 2 ft tall plantain lily *Hosta sieboldiana*, whose broad, blue-green leaves are so deeply veined as to appear quilted. This texture is as striking as the sheer leaf size.

In small, shaded gardens, several dominant evergreen foliage plants should be grown to break up the straight lines of borders and paving when other greenery has died down. Excellent for this purpose is the stinking iris, *Iris foetidissima* 'Citrina', whose sizeable clumps of dark leaves rise like massed broadswords. Contrasting in habit, and ideal as a complement to the iris, are bergenias, whose large, oval, leathery leaves curve away from the plant in a delightfully lazy fashion.

For semi-shade the most impressive sculptural plants are ornamental rhubarbs (*Rheum*). The form *R. palmatum* 'Atrosanguineum' needs plenty of space: its huge, deeply cut leaves sprawl for several feet around. Purplish-red and crumpled when they unfold in March, they become smooth and green as they mature, showing only traces of red on their undersurfaces as a breeze ruffles them. Rising man-high from their centre, the stout red flower stems put out large clusters of raspberry-pink blooms in June. After the plant has flowered, its great leaves disintegrate untidily, but no matter – by then the space they have filled so impressively is being taken

Hosta sieboldiana, with its handsome, quilted leaves, adds a bold touch among small, uniformly sized leaves such as candytuft.

A fine specimen of *Phormium tenax* adds drama to a garden pool.

up by the foliage and flowers of summer plants.

Large fountain-like grasses also have panache, especially when seen rising above a group of heavy foliage plants. One of the best for a dry sunny garden is the feather grass *Stipa gigantea*. From its dense tussocks of narrow, arching leaves slender stems rise to 4 ft, each carrying a large, open plume of golden-bronze, oat-like flowers throughout the summer. As these catch the sun they glow magnificently, particularly when set against a dark background.

Molinia coerulea variegata is a grass for damper soil, on the edge of a border. It has dense tufts of arching green leaves, conspicuously striped with cream, from which there emerges in late summer a spray of small green and buff flowers. Finally, the whole plant fades to the colour of parchment and remains, a pale beauty, throughout winter.

Plants to enhance water

There are many fine waterside plants suitable for framing a pool or pond. *Gunnera manicata* is positively majestic, sometimes towering as high as 10 ft, its thickset prickly stems holding aloft, like huge upturned umbrellas, dark green lobed leaves that may be as wide as the plant is tall.

Almost as dramatically high are the great evergreen, sword-like leaves that the New Zealand flax (*Phormium tenax*) sends up against the sky. The leathery leaves are deep green in the species, suffused with bronze-purple in the form 'Purpureum' and striped yellow in 'Variegatum'. The forms are usually no more than 4 ft tall, just the right size for a small pool.

A truly theatrical as well as sculptural waterside plant is the wand flower, or angel's fishing rod (*Dierama pulcherrimum*). From its bulbous rootstock appear tall clumps of tough, grass-like leaves; from the midst of this foliage elegant wiry flower stems rise to a height of 6 ft before arching over like the top of a fountain. From their tips in late summer cascade slender red trumpet flowers, to be followed by strings of silvery bead-like seed cases.

Grown on the margin of a pool, the marsh marigold (*Caltha palustris*) will unite bank and pool by colonising a wide area of mud and water with its welter of deep green foliage, lit up in spring with large yellow saucer-like flowers.

On large ponds, water lilies (*Nymphaea*) provide interest not only with their lovely summer blooms but at all times with their large, leathery leaves, or pads – heart-shaped rafts that jostle one another and break up the sky-reflecting surface of the water with intriguing patterns.

The huge, lime-yellow blooms of *Euphorbia characias* rise majestically above the plant's spiky, grey-green leaves. The bold form of the euphorbia provides a strong contrast with the soft, feathery foliage of the prostrate juniper growing below it. The cup-shaped yellow-green flowers between the two are those of *Helleborus lividus corsicus*.

327

Trees

Trees can transform a plain garden into a place of fascination and beauty

———◆———

OF ALL PLANTS GROWN in the garden, trees have the greatest impact and appeal. A tree becomes a focal point and introduces a feeling of proportion and perspective to a bland or uninteresting aspect. And by virtue of their size, trees are the only living things that are able to dominate the man-made environment – they can enhance good buildings immeasurably, improve those that are mediocre and help to hide the bad.

But there are many other reasons for planting trees. For instance, they provide colour and form as their swelling buds are succeeded by leaves, flowers, fruit and, often, autumn colour. They also introduce sound and movement, act as windbreaks and stand as barriers to deaden unpleasant noise.

By careful selection, the gardener will find a tree for every situation. For example, in the smaller garden, tree height and spread without weight are the most important requirements. For this, some of the maples are ideal – *Acer japonicum* 'Aureum', for example, whose rounded head of soft yellow spring foliage flares into orange, red and gold in autumn. Near to windows, where light is all important, it is wise to choose a tree that comes into leaf late and meets autumn early – catalpa is an example.

Even in summer, choice of foliage colour is not restricted to green alone. There are trees that offer variegated, golden, purple or near-blue leaves. But these must be chosen with care so that they blend harmoniously with their surroundings. This is even more important in places where gardens abut on to the countryside. Here it is best to plant local native species or their close relatives, so that the move from cultivated to natural landscape is less abrupt.

Japanese cherries make a feather-light cavern of flowers – this symphony of white in May has a group of vigorous *Prunus* 'Tai-haku' framing the weeping variety 'Shirotae' behind.

329

Abies koreana (KOREAN FIR)

The silver firs are with few exceptions tall, noble trees that in the wild grow in mountainous areas. For the small garden, they generally grow too high too soon, and the dwarf forms lack the symmetry and presence of their parents. However, there is one species, *Abies koreana*, which, although it can ultimately reach 35 ft, is extremely slow growing. It produces its exquisite violet-blue to green-blue cones when it is still a young tree, no more than 3 ft tall.

HOW TO GROW
Plant young trees in autumn or in late spring. The tree does best in slightly acid, deep and moist but well-drained soil and in sun or light shade; it is not recommended for gardens exposed to air pollution. Propagation, if desired, is best by seeds sown in spring. Pruning is unnecessary as long as a single strong leader predominates.

The cones of the Korean fir appear on the uppermost branches in summer and remain until winter or the following spring.

The dense evergreen needles of *Abies koreana* gleam white underneath.

Acer japonicum 'Aureum' (MAPLE)

In Japan, where this maple originated, its broad rounded head of soft yellow foliage in spring and early summer justly earned it the title of golden full-moon maple. Its early years excepted, it is extremely slow growing, making it one of the most suitable of trees for town gardens. It is at its very best when planted as a displayed specimen in a raised bed, paved area or lawn; it is also excellent as a tub tree.

In spring, the yellow lobed leaves provide a soft setting for clusters of conspicuous purple-red flowers. As the yellow of the leaves deepens with the advance of summer, the flowers give way to red-winged fruits which, again, contrast vivaciously with the foliage. The mature leaves turn green, then in the autumn they flare into red, orange and gold. Even in winter, a full-grown tree is attractive, its many angular branches forming striking patterns against the sky.

The maple may be either pruned or disbudded to control size and shape or, if there is plenty of space, left to develop to an eventual height of 10-15 ft.

If other plants are grown in association with the tree, they should be low growing or prostrate, to avoid detracting from its splendour. A spectacular display may be achieved by underplanting it with the late spring-flowering blue or purple varieties of *Crocus vernus*.

A splendid longer-term companion, also from Japan, would be *Hosta fortunei* 'Albopicta', whose unfurling yellow leaves would echo those of the maple above before turning a sumptuous green for summer.

HOW TO GROW
Acer japonicum 'Aureum': *plant from autumn to spring, in any good, moisture-retentive soil. It tolerates lime but is best in a neutral to acid soil. Either sun or light shade is suitable, with protection from cold winds and late spring frosts. Propagation, which requires some skill, is by grafting in spring. Any pruning should be done in late summer to avoid bleeding.*
Crocus vernus: see p. 149.
Hosta fortunei 'Albopicta': *see p. 95.*

A mature *Acer japonicum* 'Aureum', about 35 years old, glows yellow in summer. To the right is a group of ligularias.

Acer griseum (CHINESE PAPER-BARK MAPLE)

Several maples are grown primarily for the beauty of their bark, seen at its loveliest in winter when the tree is bare. Perhaps the most remarkable of these is *Acer griseum*, the enchanting Chinese paper-bark maple, which has a rich cinnamon-coloured bark that peels away in long rolls, revealing the new coppery bark beneath. In autumn, the leaves, each composed of three leaflets, turn scarlet and orange. The tree reaches a height of up to 20 ft.

Slow growing and compact, this is the ideal maple for the small garden. It is also an easy-going tree, taking chalk or acid soil, sun or shade in its stride. However, it does best in a site sheltered from cold winds and frost.

HOW TO GROW
Plant as for Acer japonicum. Propagate by seeds in autumn, but be prepared for very poor germination and slow growth of seedlings. No pruning is required.

Acer griseum, underplanted here with rodgersia foliage, has bark that flakes off to reveal cinnamon-coloured underbark.

In autumn the foliage of *Acer griseum* turns orange and scarlet.

Acer pseudoplatanus 'Brilliantissimum'
(SYCAMORE)

Common sycamore maple (*Acer pseudoplatanus*) is something of a Jekyll and Hyde among trees. A well-grown specimen standing alone in a large lawn or meadow is a most majestic sight. On the other hand, the prolifically borne, wind-carried seeds, or keys, and the seedlings that follow make it a weed of forest and garden alike. In forests of valuable young timber trees it can be a real nuisance, when the fast-growing saplings with their big leaves block out valuable light.

Although much too big for all but the largest gardens, this common maple has produced several cultivars of lesser stature. Among these *A. p.* 'Brilliantissimum' is the smallest and most desirable, rarely exceeding 20 ft and therefore suitable for the average garden. The main attraction of this compact tree is its leaves, which open rich coral pink and gradually fade to pale green.

HOW TO GROW
Plant from October to March in well-drained but moist soil, in sun or partial shade. Propagate only by grafting on to the rootstock of the type species in March.

The young foliage of *Acer pseudoplatanus* 'Brilliantissimum' opens pink.

Aged about 25 years, this *Acer pseudoplatanus* 'Brilliantissimum' displays a shapely crown of pale golden-green leaves.

Acer palmatum 'Senkaki' (JAPANESE MAPLE)

This ornamental maple has coral-red branches and shoots, whose glow intensifies as winter progresses. But almost as striking is its foliage. When the neatly lobed leaves emerge in spring they are a bright green delicately rimmed with red. This red margin disappears by summer. Then, as autumn approaches, they slowly fade to pale green before turning to a warm golden-yellow tinged with paler yellow and pink.

In winter and spring the brilliant red growth of this maple, which rarely exceeds 20 ft in height, can be enhanced by an underplanting of early flowering bulbs.

HOW TO GROW
Plant in autumn or spring, ideally in neutral to acid, moist soil, in a site sheltered from direct sun and east winds. The young foliage of this and other Asiatic maples may scorch in exposed positions. No pruning needed.

The bare winter bark of 'Senkaki', one of the most commonly grown ornamental maples, glows an intense coral red.

In autumn *Acer palmatum* 'Senkaki' becomes a giant golden torch.

Arbutus unedo (STRAWBERRY TREE)

Strawberry trees are among the loveliest of all evergreens. Their red or orange fruits look like strawberries – they are edible too, though insipid – and stand out brilliantly against the lustrous dark green foliage, as do the clusters of creamy-white, urn-shaped flowers.

Arbutus unedo, which reaches a height of 15-20 ft, takes on a splendidly gnarled appearance when mature. The flowers, white or pink, appear in autumn, at the same time as the previous year's fruits turn bright red. For earlier colour, you might also plant *A. andrachne*, which is roughly the same height but blooms in spring and bears orange-red fruits. It has the added attraction of a liver-red bark that peels away to reveal new pea-green bark beneath.

A. × andrachnoides, the superior child of these two strawberry trees, has a sinuous trunk and branches clad with cinnamon-red bark, and its ivory-white flowers open in autumn and winter. It will thrive even in thin chalky soils.

HOW TO GROW
Plant in autumn or spring, in any well-drained soil. Arbutus unedo is lime-tolerant, but A. andrachne does best in a neutral to acid soil. Full sun is essential for all, as is shelter from north and east winds. Propagate in summer by tip cuttings under glass. Prune lightly to shape in early summer.

Brilliant fruits and flowers decorate *Arbutus unedo* 'Rubra' in autumn.

Sunlight makes the bark of a 25-year-old strawberry tree, *Arbutus × andrachnoides*, gleam brilliant red.

Betula pendula 'Youngii'

(YOUNG'S WEEPING BIRCH)

Ornamental bark and graceful habit are the two qualities for which birches are renowned. From the gardener's point of view, the most versatile is the silver birch, *Betula pendula* – sometimes called the lady of the woods – which has glistening white bark and elegantly curved branches. Of the various forms available, 'Youngii' is one of the most suitable for small gardens, since it grows to no more than 10-18 ft high – a mere toy when compared with the 50-60 ft of the silver birch itself.

The branches of 'Youngii' develop horizontally, then curve gracefully towards the ground, giving the tree a weeping habit and its characteristic mushroom-shaped head. An old tree left to itself will create around it a dark space densely curtained with mid-green foliage, which in autumn turns to butter yellow. But careful, intelligent pruning of the birch will produce an arbour suffused with sunlight.

Young's weeping birch is usually grown by itself, to draw the eye to a lawn or paved area. But in gardens where there is space, several trees planted in a group can look very handsome – an effect that has been achieved at Westonbirt Arboretum in Gloucestershire.

The shade cast by the birch is too deep to allow much to be planted beneath it other than small early spring bulbs, though it looks very well with a surrounding group of heathers. Try planting the tree in mown grass and casting a drift of the trumpet daffodil 'Golden Harvest' around it. This will create a lovely spring scene for many years to come.

HOW TO GROW

Betula pendula 'Youngii' : *plant in autumn or spring, in ordinary soil. It grows most happily in sun or light shade, but looks at its best in a site where winter sun can emphasise the silvery bark and silhouette the intricate patterning of the branches. Propagate by grafting on to B. pendula in spring. Pruning, if necessary, should be done in summer or autumn to avoid bleeding.*
'Golden Harvest' *daffodil: see Narcissus pseudonarcissus, p. 165.*

An ideal setting for a beautiful tree – *Betula pendula* 'Youngii' (sometimes known as the weeping lady of the woods) stands amid March-flowering trumpet daffodils, spread like golden tears beneath the graceful drooping branches.

Carpinus betulus (HORNBEAM)

A mature hornbeam is a beautiful tree, with its elegant habit, muscular grey trunk and prominently ribbed leaves which in autumn turn a clear yellow. It is a tree for very large lawns only, however, since it eventually reaches a height of about 60 ft.

For a slightly smaller garden there is the form 'Fastigiata' (syn. 'Pyramidalis'), a conical, more erect tree that grows to 35-50 ft high. Allowance should be made for the broadening of its crown, which with age widens to about half the height of the tree. Both trees are best grown in a place where they can stand on their own.

HOW TO GROW

Plant these trees from autumn to spring, in any type of well-drained soil, in sun or shade. Propagate by seeds in autumn, 'Fastigiata' by grafting in spring. They rarely need pruning, but wayward shoots can be cut hard back at any time.

A group of *Carpinus betulus* 'Fastigiata' shows the erect, densely conical form that characterises the tree in its early years.

A magnificent 50-year-old hornbeam dominates a lawn.

Catalpa bignonioides (INDIAN BEAN TREE)

Despite its name and its tropical air, the tree comes not from India but from North America. The bright green leaves grow to 12 in. long – longer still on young trees – and in July they are glorified by large clusters of white foxglove-like flowers marked inside with yellow and purple. In autumn, the flowers are replaced by bunches of long, drooping seed pods shaped like narrow beans. They remain for months, to rattle in the winds of winter.

This catalpa rarely exceeds 40 ft in height, but it needs plenty of space, since it eventually spreads to 15-20 ft. There is an outstanding, slower-growing form called 'Aurea' with soft-textured, golden-yellow leaves.

HOW TO GROW
Plant during the dormant season, in any type of soil, dry or moist, alkaline or acid, but out of direct wind exposure. It is tolerant of air pollution, and looks most impressive against a backdrop of dark green conifers. Propagate in late summer by heel cuttings under glass. No pruning is required.

The bean tree bears delicately tinted foxglove-like flowers.

A 15-year-old Indian bean tree spreads its golden-green foliage. On the right is *Hydrangea quercifolia*.

Cercis siliquastrum (JUDAS TREE)

This is one of at least half-a-dozen trees – including the fig and the elder – on which Judas is said to have hanged himself. True or not, it is among the most unusual of all Mediterranean ornamental plants. In May, the first of its attractive, rounded, blue-green deciduous leaves are joined by hanging clusters of purplish-rose flowers that not only grow along the branches but also appear from the bark of the main stems. During this time, the flowers outweigh the foliage. Later, from July into autumn and winter, masses of red-brown, 3-4 in. long seed pods provide quiet colour. 'Alba' is a white-flowered form with pale green leaves.

The Judas tree usually develops into a sprawling tree 15-20 ft high and 10-15 ft across, with several of its main boughs rising almost from ground level. It can also be grown against a wall as an unusual espalier.

HOW TO GROW
Plant in autumn or spring; the trees resent root disturbance, and only young plants establish themselves easily. Suitable for any fertile, well-drained soil in full sun. Shelter the tree from spring frosts. In northern gardens, it is best grown against a wall for protection. Propagate by layering in autumn or from seeds in spring. Pot grown seedlings should be planted out in their permanent positions when they are two years old. Prune by cutting out dead or damaged shoots in early summer.

In spring *Cercis siliquastrum* bursts into pink blossom.

A Judas tree makes a fine decorative feature in a lawn.

Chamaecyparis obtusa (HINOKI CYPRESS)

In its native Japanese forests, the Hinoki cypress attains great heights, but in British gardens it rarely grows taller than 25 ft. Like the American Lawson cypress, it has evergreen scale-like leaves densely packed in large, flat, horizontal sprays.

Probably the tree is best known through cultivars, such as the slow-growing 'Tetragona Aurea', which is one of the most useful of the many garden forms; even in maturity it is not much more than 15 ft in height.

If something taller is required, then *Chamaecyparis obtusa* 'Crippsii' should be considered. It forms a conical tree of open habit, up to 25 ft or so tall, with plume-like sprays of rich yellow leaves.

HOW TO GROW
Plant in autumn or spring, in well-drained to moist, fertile and neutral to acid soil and, for the golden-leaved cultivars, a position in full sun. Propagate in autumn by cuttings under glass. The trees respond well to topiary pruning, which can be done at any time during the growing season.

A ten-year-old specimen of *Chamaecyparis obtusa* 'Crippsii' flaunts its beautiful feathery foliage of golden-yellow.

'Tetragona Aurea' looks splendid grown in a heather garden.

Chamaecyparis lawsoniana

(LAWSON CYPRESS)

The Lawson cypress, a North American evergreen, has been grown in Britain for more than a century. Forming a broad column that after 30-40 years can reach to about 60 ft high, it has tiny, scale-like, green or blue-green leaves carried in dense, flattened, overlapping sprays.

'Kilmacurragh' has dark green foliage and a tighter, more narrow habit, while rich blue-green foliage characterises 'Triomphe de Boskoop', a bold, fast-growing tree. The leaves of the broad, conical 'Pembury Blue' are a more delicate soft blue-grey, as are those of 'Grayswood Pillar', which rises as a narrow, graceful column. Then there is 'Wisselii', which has dark green, grey-tinted foliage that is borne along the branches in moss-like clusters. The bright green 'Erecta Viridis' is extremely narrow and erect, but it is easily spoiled by a heavy snowfall. 'Green Pillar' is a similar colour but less severely erect and more weather-resistant.

There is also a range of forms with yellow or golden leaves. Four of the best are the conical 'Stewartii', the dense, broadly columnar 'Winston Churchill', the rather similar 'Lutea' and the conical 'Lanei'.

Bearing in mind the heights to which these trees may eventually soar, it is important to give some thought to their siting. Make use of perspective by planting a group at a fair distance from the house; mixed plantings of differently coloured forms can be spectacular, while a gathering of columnar forms might be grown with heathers and low-growing conifers at their feet.

HOW TO GROW
Plant in autumn or spring, in any ordinary soil, including chalky ones. For group planting, space vigorous forms such as 'Winston Churchill', 'Lutea' and 'Triomphe de Boskoop' about 8 ft apart. The smaller and slow-growing cultivars can be set at 3 ft intervals. Propagate and prune as for Chamaecyparis obtusa.

Chamaecyparis lawsoniana 'Pembury Blue'.

Chamaecyparis lawsoniana 'Kilmacurragh' is a magnificent conifer. Here twin pillars rise amongst *Erica carnea* 'Winter Beauty'.

A 15-year-old specimen of 'Lutea' dominates a planting of mixed shrubs.

Cornus nuttallii (DOGWOOD, CORNEL)

This is the noblest of dogwoods and one of the loveliest of flowering trees. In May and June the tips of the shoots unfold into large creamy-white bracts – petal-like leaves. After a while they turn pure white, then become flushed with pink. In autumn the foliage flares into yellow or sometimes red.

The tree prefers woodland but also looks well on its own on a lawn, where it will eventually reach a height of 30 ft and a spread of about half as much. It is, however, slow growing and for many years is no more than a large bush. Indeed, in the drier areas of Britain it rarely ever becomes a true tree.

HOW TO GROW
Plant in autumn, in well-drained but moisture-retentive fertile soil, neutral to acid. Dappled shade and full sun are equally suitable as long as there is shelter from east and north winds. Propagate in late summer by heel cuttings under glass. Pruning should be kept to a minimum.

The 'flowers' of *Cornus nuttallii* consist in fact of petal-like leaves.

With its creamy-white blooms in spring, *Cornus nuttallii* lights up any garden. This tree is about 20-25 years old.

A fully grown *Crataegus laciniata* smothers itself in dazzling blossom.

Basking in sunlight, the colourful fruits of the ornamental thorn bring a warm glow to the autumn garden.

Crataegus laciniata (ORNAMENTAL THORN)

In Turkey the red and orange fruits of this ornamental thorn (also listed as *Crataegus orientalis*) are used to make sweetmeats. They make a bright splash of colour before they fall to the ground in November.

It is a well-shaped tree, erect when young but after many years developing a rounded crown as it gradually reaches towards its maximum height of about 18 ft. The young shoots are grey and hairy, as are the deeply cut leaves which stay on the tree until well into autumn. Clusters of large white flowers are borne in June, making it quite dramatic enough to grow alone on a lawn or patio.

HOW TO GROW
Plant in the same way as for Crataegus × prunifolia. Propagate by seeds sown in spring. For a year before sowing stratify the seeds – that is, mix them with sand or peat kept moist in containers placed in a cold frame. Pruning is rarely necessary, but crossing branches should be cut out in late winter; side branches can also be removed at this time if a clear trunk is wanted.

× *Cupressocyparis leylandii*
(LEYLAND CYPRESS)

The Leyland cypress is probably the most widely planted evergreen in Britain. It is generally cultivated as a fast-growing hedge, screen or windbreak (it grows 2-3 ft a year) but, where there is space, it is also worth considering as a single tree for a large lawn or border that needs a vertical accent. For this, choose forms such as 'Leighton Green', which has a compact columnar shape. Unrestricted and in good growing conditions, it can reach a stately 60 ft in perhaps as many years. There is also a golden-leaved form, known as 'Castlewellan', which is pyramidal in habit and takes on bronze tints in winter.

HOW TO GROW
Plant in late spring, in any – even poor – soil with good drainage. It does equally well in sun or light shade and withstands a fair amount of wind. For hedge and screen planting, set young plants 2 ft apart; in groups allow 8 ft intervals. Propagate in early autumn by cuttings set in a cold frame. Prune to shape in late summer.

Here the golden form 'Castlewellan' is grown as a hedge.

Leyland cypresses make a superb backing to a rose border.

Crataegus × prunifolia (ORNAMENTAL THORN)

When most gardeners consider planting an ornamental thorn, it is to the common hawthorn (*Crataegus monogyna*) that their thoughts turn. This is indeed a lovely tree, but the genus as a whole contains several other species with equally decorative flowers, leaves and fruits and – of at least equal importance in a small garden – of a considerably more compact habit. One of them that meets all these requirements is *C.* × *prunifolia*.

This is a small tree of garden origin that reaches up to 15 ft in height and has a dense, rounded head of branches 10-15 ft across, armed with savage thorns that are particularly noticeable in winter when the tree is bare. The leathery leaves, downy on the underside, have an upper surface of polished dark green, and this remains until mid-autumn, when suddenly they change to a rich crimson, seemingly turning the whole tree to flame.

In June, rounded clusters of white flowers cover the branches and are set off to perfection by the tree's glistening dark foliage. The blossom is followed by rounded red haws, or fruits, which generally fall with the leaves in autumn.

The tree is extremely hardy and is indifferent alike to the pollution of towns and to the salt winds of the coast. It is best planted singly in a lawn or courtyard, where its handsome foliage can be admired without distraction; but it also fits well into the mixed border, especially in company with shrubs whose foliage colours richly in autumn – for example, the guelder rose (*Viburnum opulus*) and *Euonymus europaeus* 'Red Cascade'.

HOW TO GROW
Crataegus × prunifolia: plant from autumn to spring, in ordinary, ideally well-drained soil; it is, however, tolerant of both drought and wet conditions. Best in an open, sunny position. Propagation is usually by budding or grafting on to the common hawthorn. No regular pruning is required.
Euonymus europaeus: see p. 279.
Viburnum opulus: see p. 323.

A mature *Crataegus × prunifolia*, such as this 30-year-old specimen, bears a profusion of brilliant red haws.

These stately twin *C.g.* 'Pyramidalis' are between 15 and 20 years old.

Cupressus glabra 'Pyramidalis' (CYPRESS)

Cypresses occur naturally in many of the warmer, non-desert areas of the Northern Hemisphere. *Cupressus glabra* 'Pyramidalis' (also known at nurseries as *C. arizonica* 'Pyramidalis') comes from Arizona. It is a narrow, conical tree growing to about 30 ft high and has branches densely covered with blue-grey scale-like leaves.

Also, by way of contrast, you might grow the slower-growing golden form of the Mediterranean cypress, *C. sempervirens* 'Swane's Golden'. This develops into a neat, narrow 25 ft high column that goes well with slow-growing dwarf conifers – such as junipers – or with heathers.

HOW TO GROW
Plant young cypresses, which should be container-grown, in late spring; they thrive in ordinary, well-drained soil, preferably in full sun. For the first few years give winter protection to C. sempervirens. Propagate in early autumn by cuttings under glass. Prune only lightly, in late spring.

A young specimen of *C. sempervirens* 'Swane's Golden', about five years old, planted among pink *Calluna vulgaris*.

The creamy petal-like leaves of *Davidia involucrata* emerge in May.

Davidia involucrata (DOVE TREE, GHOST TREE, POCKET-HANDKERCHIEF TREE)

This tree rarely puts forth its exquisite creamy-white bracts (petal-like leaves) before it is ten years old, but when it does the effect is truly astonishing. The bracts occur in pairs, one bract larger than the other, resembling, according to one's imagination, a loosely folded handkerchief or the drooping wings of a dove.

The tree is erect when young, then gradually expands until its spread equals its height – an eventual 40-50 ft. It should be grown in the centre of a large lawn or courtyard, so that its beauty can be fully appreciated.

HOW TO GROW
Plant in autumn or spring, in fertile, moisture-retentive soil. It does best in dappled shade on quick-draining soils in areas of high rainfall. Propagate in late summer by heel cuttings under glass, or in autumn by layering. Any pruning should be done in late winter.

The pocket-handkerchief tree shown here is the form *Davidia involucrata vilmoriniana*, which has smoother, paler leaves.

Embothrium coccineum lanceolatum is more slender and hardy than the species. This specimen is about 20 years old.

Embothrium coccineum (CHILEAN FIRE BUSH)

Few heads fail to turn when this Chilean fire bush is in bloom in May and June. The loose spikes of brilliant orange-scarlet flowers that crowd the slender branches produce an effect like blazing torches.

Except in mild western areas, the tree is tender and it is advisable to grow the hardy form 'Norquinco Valley'. This takes many years to reach a height of 20-30 ft. It is excellent in company with heathers or azaleas.

HOW TO GROW
Plant in spring, in moist soil, acid to neutral, and in a sheltered, lightly shaded site. Away from western gardens it is better grown against a south or west-facing wall, and should be given plenty of water in summer. Propagate in late spring by seeds, or suckers rooted in a cold frame. In late spring, cut out any frost-damaged shoot tips. If necessary, prune to shape after flowering.

Embothrium coccineum can look startlingly tropical in a British garden.

Eucalyptus gunnii (CIDER GUM)

For a touch of far-away places in the garden, try growing *Eucalyptus*, a genus of handsome-leaved evergreens from Australia. Unfortunately, only a few of the many species, varieties and hybrids are hardy in Britain. The most commonly grown is the cider gum, from Tasmania.

As with most gum trees, the leaves of this one change considerably with age. When young they are rounded and blue-grey to silvery, but with maturity they become lance-shaped and turn to blue-green or dark green.

HOW TO GROW
Set out young container-grown plants in early summer and keep them staked until fully established. Plant in good, ordinary or acid soil, well drained but moist; it does best in full sun. Shelter from strong winds is advisable. Propagate in spring by seeds under glass. Prune as for Eucalyptus niphophila. To obtain permanent juvenile foliage, cut all stems back to near ground level in late spring.

In the smaller garden *Eucalyptus gunnii* needs to be cut back hard. It then puts out suckers covered with silvery-blue juvenile leaves.

A ten-year-old cider gum with red-brown bark rises above a bed of shrubs.

Eucalyptus niphophila (ALPINE SNOW GUM)

What a variety of virtues the alpine snow gum possesses – striking bark, evergreen foliage, attractive flowers, unusual habit, hardiness and a height of only 15-20 ft. Perhaps the most outstanding feature is the bark that clothes the sometimes oddly leaning main stems. When old it flakes away in irregular patches, creating smooth-edged, python-skin patterns. These are basically of cream and grey, but many other colours appear at different times of day and in different weather. For example, after rain the bark glistens wondrously with silver, pink, green, brown, grey, cream and white – in contrast with the young branches, whose bark is a dark polished red, overlaid in spring with a white, waxy bloom.

When the glossy leaves emerge in spring they are a plain green, sometimes tinted with bronze, that matures to a leathery almost grey-green. In June, clusters of white flowers appear, each bloom having a tuft of delicate stamens. The flowers are replaced by tiny, woody, urn-shaped seed capsules that cling to the growth like limpets to a rock. The tree gives pleasure not only to the eye but also to the ear; the loud rustling of its leaves, even in the lightest breeze, is the voice of the garden.

To do justice to this unique tree, grow it as a single feature in a lawn or paved area. If an underplanting is wanted, this should consist of plants with grey or silver foliage or with purple, pink or blue flowers. A simple but effective combination might be a bush of *Euphorbia characias* beside the eucalyptus, both surrounded by *Lamium maculatum* 'Beacon Silver'.

HOW TO GROW
Eucalyptus niphophila: plant and propagate in the same way as for E. gunnii. Left to its own devices, this and other gum trees will grow as a single trunk with fairly sparse side branches. This habit can be broadened by cutting the leading shoot back to vigorous sideshoots in early summer and subsequently pinching out strong-growing laterals.
Euphorbia characias: see p. 86.
Lamium maculatum: see p. 99.

The alpine snow gum needs subtle harmonies when associated with other plants. Grey or silver foliage is ideal; likewise purple, pink or blue flowers. The combination seen here in May is with *Euphorbia characias* and a sea of silver lamium.

A ten-year-old weeping purple beech graces a lawn with its dark foliage.

Fagus sylvatica 'Purpurea Pendula'
(WEEPING PURPLE BEECH)

Slow growing and reaching a height of only 6-10 ft, the weeping purple beech is eminently suitable for the smaller garden. The leaves are of such a deep rich purple that they look almost black at a distance. Before falling in autumn, they briefly turn orange and gold.

By way of illustrating the enormous differences that can exist within a single species, there is *Fagus sylvatica* 'Dawyck', a splendid, green-leaved columnar tree that slowly but eventually grows to a height of 60 ft. This makes it suitable only for larger gardens.

HOW TO GROW
Plant from autumn to spring, in any kind of soil provided that this is well drained. Beeches will not thrive in wet or compacted soil; all kinds do best in an open, sunny site. Propagation of the purple beech is by grafting in spring. Prune young trees to shape in late summer.

The tall, columnar *Fagus sylvatica* 'Dawyck', here seen in its autumn colouring, provides a lawn with a bold, vertical accent.

The fresh green leaves of *Ginkgo biloba* are set off by its grey trunk.

Ginkgo biloba (MAIDENHAIR TREE)

The ginkgo is a remarkable tree whose ancestors, according to fossil evidence, looked exactly the same when they grew 180 million years ago. It is one of the few 'conifers' that are deciduous, and its fan-shaped leaves, which resemble the leaflets of a maidenhair fern, are unique. In autumn the yellowish-green of these leaves turns to a lovely clear yellow that remains after they have fallen, to make a golden pool beneath the tree. The ginkgo is suitable only for a large garden, in a lawn or paved area.

HOW TO GROW
Set out young container-grown plants in late spring, in fertile, moist but well-drained soil. It does best in full sun, with shelter from strong winds; it is not recommended for exposed northern gardens but will do well in large town gardens. Propagation is from seeds when ripe, in a cold frame. Any pruning to shape should be done in autumn.

The fast-growing maidenhair tree reaches a height of 40 ft in 30-40 years. To be seen at its best, it needs plenty of space.

The form 'Sunburst' was so named because of its yellow spring foliage.

Gleditsia triacanthos (HONEY LOCUST)

The honey locust, a native of the rich, moist soils of central USA, is a large, thorny deciduous tree with light green frond-like leaves. There are several named forms for the garden. 'Sunburst', which grows to over 30 ft, is actually thornless, and its young leaves are golden-yellow in spring and summer. Another thornless variety is 'Inermis', a small tree no more than 20 ft high in maturity with a dense, rounded, compact crown ideally suited to a formal setting. 'Sunburst' is a splendid tree for the smaller lawn. Its yellow-green autumn leaves make a fine accompaniment for the autumn crocuses *Crocus speciosus* or *Colchicum speciosum*, while daffodils make a fine spring accompaniment.

HOW TO GROW
Plant from autumn to spring, in ordinary, well-drained soil in full sun; once established, it is tolerant of short spells of drought. Propagate named cultivars by budding in summer. Prune only to remove dead and damaged shoots in spring.

In spring, the tracery of fine twigs of the honey locust contrasts charmingly with the golden trumpet daffodil 'Dutch Master'.

Halesia monticola (SNOWDROP TREE)

This beautiful snowdrop tree from the United States is a joy to behold when its bell-shaped white flowers drape the branches in May; these are followed by winged, pear-shaped, pale brown fruits. In fact, it would be a perfect tree in every way were it not for one thing: it grows to a height of 40 ft and spreads wider and sprawls even in its youth. However, the branches are generally few and loosely arranged, so that the tree has an open crown and lightly shades the ground beneath.

In May it looks especially lovely flowering with azaleas, rhododendrons and camellias, or with an underplanting of bluebells or other bulbs.

HOW TO GROW
Plant from autumn to spring, in moist but well-drained acid soil enriched with manure. It does best in the light shade and shelter of woodland edges. Propagate by layering in autumn. Young trees can be pruned to shape after flowering.

With its wide, open crown, *Halesia monticola* casts only light shade.

A soft down covers the undersides of the leaves of *Halesia monticola vestita*. The bell-shaped flowers resemble snowdrops.

Ilex aquifolium (ENGLISH OR COMMON HOLLY)

Holly is one of the most popular of evergreens and is represented in gardens by a host of cultivars. Even without regular clipping, they are of fairly compact habit and grow reasonably slowly, eventually reaching a height of 10-30 ft. The female forms are the most colourful, for it is these that bear the berries. Most of the cultivars are column-like or cone-shaped and their many branches are crowded with spine-toothed leaves.

'Pyramidalis' is the best of the self-fertile green-leaved female forms, standing sturdily erect and carrying, in season, an abundance of red fruit. There is also an equally impressive yellow-berried version, 'Pyramidalis Fructoluteo'.

The finest of the variegated forms is 'Madame Briot', whose leaves are a mixture of yellow and pale green with bold, irregular gold margins. Bright red berries and purple shoots add sparkle to the general effect. Then there is 'Handsworth New Silver', with narrow, dark green leaves margined in white; this form also has purple shoots and red berries.

In most cases, male hollies are required to pollinate the females, and should be planted within a few yards of them – though it is surprising how often female trees become pollinated when, seemingly, there are no males within miles. One of the best pollinating hollies is the silver-splashed, hostile-spined 'Ferox Argentea'.

Hollies make superb formal trees for lawns and edges of drives, especially the large-leaved cultivars known collectively as *Ilex × altaclarensis*. One of the most distinctive of these is 'Camelliifolia', which has virtually spineless leaves up to 5 in. long.

HOW TO GROW
Plant all hollies as young pot-grown specimens in autumn or spring. Any well-drained soil will do, in sun or shade, though variegated forms look best in full light. Avoid soils that are wet or dry out quickly. Propagate in late summer or autumn by cuttings in a cold frame. Little pruning is necessary except for shaping during summer. On variegated forms, remove shoots that are reverting to green.

Ilex × altaclarensis 'Camelliifolia' is a splendid female holly with almost spineless leaves and plenty of lustrous berries.

The sparkling foliage of the female *Ilex aquifolium* 'Handsworth New Silver' is both grey-splashed and white-margined.

A good example of *Ilex aquifolium*, Aureomarginata group

A ten-year-old *Juniperus chinensis* 'Aurea' shows off its golden cone against a dark background. Beneath is a pink heather.

A Juniperus chinensis 'Aurea' is here overhung by Catalpa bignonioides.

Juniperus chinensis 'Aurea'
(YOUNG'S GOLDEN JUNIPER)

With its handsome, flowing lines, *Juniperus chinensis* 'Aurea' is one of the best-looking of all junipers, and its conical form makes it ideal for smaller gardens and for other restricted planting areas. Comparatively slow growing and compact, it rarely exceeds 25 ft in height.

The tree's main attraction is its pale olive summer shoots, which last well into winter when they look best providing a warm contrast to a background of darker evergreens, buildings or deciduous trees. For this reason, the juniper should be planted on its own in a lawn. It also looks well when grown as a highlight in a winter garden, underplanted with heathers and dwarf or prostrate conifers.

HOW TO GROW
Plant in spring, in any kind of well-drained soil, acid or alkaline, chalk or gravel. Wind and drought-resistant, junipers thrive in sun or light shade. 'Aurea' does best in partial shade. Propagate in early autumn by heel cuttings under glass. Prune as for Juniperus virginiana.

Juniperus virginiana (PENCIL CEDAR)

The many forms of this American species can be grown in the garden either as a handsome backdrop to set off other plants or as beautiful trees in their own right. Most develop into a columnar shape, are hardy and are easy to grow. Some forms, such as 'Canaertii', make sombre columns 30 ft or so high, providing a permanent backdrop to the constantly shifting scenery of the seasons. They also look impressive when planted in groups of at least five at 6-10 ft intervals.

Equally impressive, though lighter in hue, are those with grey or blue-green foliage, such as the popular 'Glauca'. This is a compact tree when young, broadening somewhat and becoming more open when mature, with delicate shoots arching over at the tips. It reaches a height of 20 ft. 'Burkii' too is widely grown; this is a tightly packed form with blue-grey foliage that turns to a striking steel blue in autumn and purplish in winter. Grown with other blue or silver conifers, it makes a splendidly imperial scene.

Perhaps the best-known form, however, is 'Skyrocket', a name that vividly describes the streamlined habit of this tree – pencil-slim when young and no more than 2 ft thick in maturity. At all stages of its growth, the erect, grey-leaved branches taper to a fine spire that eventually reaches a height of almost 20 ft. There is no other conifer so slender as this, and not surprisingly it is used for a wide range of effects. It is particularly useful in the restricted space of a town garden, there contrasting splendidly with the glossy deep green leaves and fragrant white flowers of Mexican orange blossom (*Choisya ternata*) and the pink-flowered, also sweetly scented, *Daphne* × *burkwoodii*.

HOW TO GROW
Juniperus virginiana: plant and propagate in the same way as for J. chinensis. All junipers tolerate light pruning and can be clipped to shape in late spring.
Choisya ternata: see p. 263.
Daphne × burkwoodii: see p. 273.

The slender form 'Skyrocket' needs little space and is suitable for small gardens. It contrasts effectively with white-flowered choisya and pink *Daphne* × *burkwoodii*. The time of year for this setting is May.

Koelreuteria paniculata (PRIDE OF INDIA, CHINA-TREE, GOLDENRAIN-TREE)

Once it has reached maturity, there are few more decorative trees than this one from northern China. In spring and summer the branches of its rounded or spreading crown are densely covered with handsome, deeply divided mid-green leaves which turn bright yellow before falling in autumn. Rich yellow flowers are carried in bold terminal heads in July and August. After a hot summer they are followed by bladder-like, pale green red-flushed seed capsules. The tree, which eventually grows to a height of 40 ft, loves full sun.

HOW TO GROW
Plant in autumn or spring, in ordinary, fertile and well-drained soil. Sun is essential, as well as shelter in exposed gardens; warm town gardens are perfect. Propagate in autumn or spring by seeds. If necessary, trim young trees to shape in spring.

A 40-year-old *Koelreuteria paniculata* is here seen decked with red-tinted green seed capsules. It does best in warmer areas.

Another tree of the same age lights up in high summer with yellow blooms.

Laburnum × watereri 'Vossii'

(GOLDEN RAIN TREE)

The Victorians used to plant laburnums in the grander suburbs and, where they still survive, there is something about their brilliant golden flowers – booming with bees in May and June – that evokes an image of nannies pushing high-wheeled perambulators along the avenues.

The hybrid *Laburnum × watereri* 'Vossii', less often seen than the common laburnum (*L. anagyroides*), is more ornamental. Reaching a height of 15-20 ft, it is a majestic sight in a largish lawn or shrub border. This hybrid is partly sterile and therefore produces fewer of the poisonous seed pods for which laburnums are infamous.

HOW TO GROW
Plant laburnums from autumn to spring, in ordinary, moist but well-drained soil, and in sun or light shade. Stake young plants until they are established. Propagate species by seeds in autumn, named forms by grafting in spring.

With more and larger yellow flower clusters, *Laburnum × watereri* 'Vossii' is more ornamental than common laburnum.

Larix (LARCH)

The larch is one of the most elegant and lovely of trees, though if it is allowed to reach maturity – it will grow to over 50 ft – only large gardens can accommodate it.

Like many other conifers, the European larch (*Larix decidua*), produces its main branches in whorls with upward-curving tips and long slender branchlets that hang down in an ever-shifting curtain.

Similar, and equally charming, is the Japanese larch (*L. kaempferi*, syn. *L. leptolepis*), which, however, has leaves delightfully tinted with grey-blue. The hybrid between them, *L. × eurolepis* – sometimes called Dunkeld larch, from the estate in Scotland where it was raised – is a more vigorous tree and varies in its foliage colour.

HOW TO GROW
Plant all larches in late autumn or spring, in ordinary soil, well drained but moist and deep. They do best in sunny, open sites. Propagate by sowing seeds in the open during spring.

In splendid autumn foliage, a ten-year-old *Larix × eurolepis* (known also as Dunkeld larch) reaches about 15 ft high.

The hanging branches of *Larix decidua* 'Pendula' create an arbour within.

This 15-year-old sweet gum has turned in autumn to a sheet of flame, against which show the cool plumes of pampas grass.

Liquidambar styraciflua (SWEET GUM)

The genus is named after the amber-like resin the trees exude; but of greater joy to the gardener are the glossy, five-lobed, maple-like leaves that in autumn blaze into brightest orange, crimson and purple. After the leaves have fallen, the corky bark of the older twigs and branches often provides an interesting feature during the winter months, with their deeply fissured and textured surfaces. In March, inconspicuous green-yellow flowers are produced.

The tree, which eventually reaches a height of 50 ft or more, is robust and, once established, soon builds into a graceful cone with either ascending or spreading branches. However, since these are liable to break off in strong winds, it is not advisable to plant the tree in an exposed position, and it may in fact do best as part of a small ornamental wood.

Seed-raised plants are not reliable in their autumn colouring, so it is best to buy a young plant in late October when its autumn foliage can be seen.

In its North American homeland, *Liquidambar styraciflua* inhabits damp to swampy land. This preference could be used to greater advantage than it is in gardens, for there are not many first-rate ornamental trees suitable for wet sites.

Because of its leaf shape, the sweet gum is sometimes confused with the maples, but it can be differentiated from them by the alternate arrangement of its leaves.

HOW TO GROW
Plant container-grown seedlings from autumn to spring, in fertile soil, moist to wet, and in full sun or light shade. Young plants are prone to frost damage during severe winters and need protecting with bracken or polythene. Shelter the trees from strong winds. Propagate by layering or seeds in autumn or spring. Prune in winter, removing lower side branches and any crossed shoots.

'Fastigiatum', here ablaze in autumn, is a smaller form of the tulip tree.

In summer mature tulip trees produce unusual yellow-green flowers to grace the equally distinctive saddle-shaped leaves.

Liriodendron tulipifera (TULIP TREE)

The noble tulip tree, which can reach a height of 90 ft, should be grown in every garden where space is not a problem. Both its flowers and its foliage are unusual: the leaves are saddle shaped, and the yellow-green, orange-marked blooms, which appear in June and July, look something like tulips. They are followed by slender, cone-shaped, dark brown fruits. In autumn the foliage turns a rich deep yellow and the tree resembles a giant flame. It needs to be planted in a large lawn, where it can be admired from all sides.

There is also a smaller, columnar form, 'Fastigiatum', suitable for permanent residence in more modest plots. It is especially useful in a formal setting, to provide a clean vertical contrast to a horizontal planting.

Rarely seen but highly desirable is 'Aureomarginatum', whose leaves are boldly margined with pale yellow.

HOW TO GROW
Plant from autumn to spring, in any fertile soil, well drained yet moist, and in full sun or light shade out of strong winds. Layering gives quicker results than seeds, but, even so, few tulip trees flower before they are 20 years old. Any pruning should be done in summer.

Magnolia grandiflora

This fragrant-flowered evergreen tree thrives in a warm, sunny position – which is why it is so often grown against the south or west wall of a house or courtyard. It can also, however, be planted in a sheltered lawn or walled garden, where eventually it will reach a height of up to 25 ft, with a handsome rounded crown.

In late summer and autumn large, bowl-shaped, creamy-white flowers are produced from the ends of the shoots and, as the fleshy concave petals open, they release a rich spicy fragrance. The blooms are set among leathery leaves that are polished green above and, when they are young, rust-coloured beneath.

HOW TO GROW

The tree does not normally flower until mature, so it is usually sold as a layered plant that will bloom at an earlier age. Plant in spring or autumn. Grow in ordinary, moist, well-drained soil, in a sunny site sheltered from cold winds and from morning sun in spring. Magnolia grandiflora will tolerate a limy soil.

The magnificent, richly scented blooms of *Magnolia grandiflora*, which are borne from July to September, are up to 8 in. across.

The magnolia thrives against a warm wall. This plant is about 25 years old.

Magnolia kobus

Magnolias are named in honour of Pierre Magnol (1638-1715), Director of the Botanic Gardens at Montpellier, in France. The genus consists of some 80 species whose ancestors came from North and Central America, East Asia and the Himalayas; almost all produce superb, waxy flowers.

Magnolia kobus is a native of Japan. In winter, its smooth, dark branches are decorated with downy buds, which, with the arrival of spring, burst into 4 in. wide creamy-white flowers with the faintest touch of purple at the base. From then until autumn the tree carries a mass of mid-green leaves with pale undersides. After about 30 years the tree grows to as many feet high and spreads widely; but there is a dwarf mutant form, usually known as *M. stellata*, that grows to a height and spread of no more than 8-10 ft. There are also one or two cultivars with pink flowers.

In the wild, the magnolia enjoys moist but well-drained sites, so in cultivation it makes a good tree for the side of a pond or any other moist site. It can be enhanced by an underplanting of low-growing, large-leaved perennials, such as *Hosta plantaginea*, and, for winter foliage and spring flowers, *Bergenia*.

HOW TO GROW

Magnolia kobus: cultivate and propagate as for M. × soulangiana. If the site restricts the tree's roots, apply a mulch of organic matter annually in spring.
Bergenia: see p. 72.
Hosta plantaginea: see p. 94.

Magnolia kobus is decorated with flowers in April, when the dark branches are devoid of leaves. Trees from seed do not normally flower until they are at least ten years old. Here the magnolia is underplanted with bergenias.

Magnolia × soulangiana

The various forms of this magnolia make a magnificent spectacle in May and June when, before the leaves unfurl, purple-stained white goblet flowers crown each bare twig.

When young, the magnolia can be accommodated in any garden, but once established it grows vigorously and gradually spreads its limbs 10-18 ft – too much perhaps for many small gardens. To be seen at its best, it needs to be planted in a bed in a lawn, though a large border is nearly as good. By early pruning it can be trained to grow as a single-stemmed tree, which at flowering time will make a breathtaking sight when grown against a dark backdrop.

HOW TO GROW
Plant in spring. This magnolia is one of the easiest to grow, accepting any well-drained soil, even a chalky one if it is enriched with humus. It needs full sun and protection from north and east winds and from morning sun in spring. Propagate in summer by heel cuttings under glass. Prune only to remove dead or untidy stems.

In spring the magnolia becomes a mass of gleaming blooms.

Magnolia × soulangiana (right) flowers beside a wall bordering a semi-wild garden containing a white *Amelanchier lamarckii*.

Malus 'John Downie' (CRAB APPLE)

In spring the branches of this ornamental crab apple foam with purest white blossom. Then in autumn they blaze with orange and scarlet fruit that can be made into splendid crab-apple jelly. Though the tree can grow to a stately 35 ft, it will do so only after many years; 20 ft is probably closer to the average height. The tree is slender when young, but later builds up a crown. This is only modest though, and *Malus* 'John Downie' is eminently suitable for the smallish garden, where its frothy blossom and colourful fruit provide a superb display.

HOW TO GROW
Plant in the same way as for Malus tschonoskii. Although self-fertile, flowering and fruiting crab apples produce heavier crops if several are grown together. Propagation, by the skilled amateur, is by budding in summer or grafting in spring on to the appropriate Malling rootstock. Pruning depends on the tree form. Standard trees are usually supplied already trained; any young stems on the trunk should be removed during summer. On bush trees, maintain the goblet shape by shortening lateral branches, if necessary, in spring; then, too, remove dead and crossing branches.

The crown of a 'John Downie' crab apple spreads with age.

In flavour, brilliant colouring and size, *Malus* 'John Downie' bears the finest fruit of all the crab apples.

The magnificent foliage of *Malus tschonoskii* sets the October garden ablaze. For a striking setting, grow the tree on a bank planted with *Cotoneaster horizontalis* – another brilliant autumn beauty.

Malus tschonoskii (CRAB APPLE)

Ornamental crab apples (*Malus* species) are among the most attractive of small deciduous flowering and fruiting trees. Some are noted not for their spring blossom or colourful, ripening fruit but for their pleasing shape and brilliant autumn foliage. Of these *Malus tschonoskii* is the most popular and most easily obtained.

In October and November the large, round green leaves of summer are suffused by yellow, orange, bronze, purple and finally crimson, which make an established tree resemble a giant flaming torch. The sparsely produced dull red fruits are not very decorative and do not stay long on the tree.

When this tree is young, the ascending branches form a rather narrow crown. This gradually fills out to create the broad cone shape of the mature form. The branches of an old tree, which will reach a height of 20-30 ft, tend to spread, producing a rounded or loose crown.

The neat habit of all but old trees makes the crab apple suitable for small gardens and other restricted areas. It is a good tree for a lawn but looks even better in a bed or border grown with low shrubs, either flowering ones or those that have richly coloured autumn foliage. *Cotoneaster horizontalis* provides a splendid underplanting. It has red leaves and berries in autumn and its horizontal herring-bone shoots form a striking contrast to the upswept branches of the crab apple.

HOW TO GROW
Malus tschonoskii: plant from autumn to spring. All crab apples are fully hardy and easy to grow. They thrive in ordinary, well-drained but moist soil and do best in full sun. They are sold as either bush or standard trees. The latter need staking until well established. Propagate and prune as for M. 'John Downie'.
Cotoneaster horizontalis: see p. 269.

Metasequoia glyptostroboides
(DAWN REDWOOD)

This deciduous conifer caused something of a stir when it was discovered in China in 1941. It should have been long extinct and in fact was previously known only from fossils dating back at least 120 million years – hence the poetic common name, dawn redwood.

Despite its ancient lineage, it looks at home in quite modest gardens. It is extremely decorative: spring brings feathery pale green leaves that in summer deepen in colour before turning in autumn first to a delightful pink, then to a warm red-brown. The main stem soars skywards straight as a gun barrel and can reach 50 ft in less than 30 years; however, since the tree forms a slim cone, its height is not so obtrusive as might be thought.

HOW TO GROW
Plant from autumn to spring, in any fertile, moist but well-drained soil, ideally in full sun. Chalk is satisfactory, although growth rate will then be slower. Propagate by cuttings, ideally with a heel, in late summer or autumn, under glass. Pruning is not normally needed, but cut any damaged leading stem back in spring to a strong shoot lower down.

Set in a lawn, a twin-trunked dawn redwood, about 15 years old, flares softly in autumn against a background of dark conifers.

A young dawn redwood displays its spring foliage in a setting of spruces.

Parrotia persica

In any 'top ten' of trees notable for their autumn foliage, *Parrotia persica* would find a certain place. For several weeks before they fall, the leaves turn to a symphony of purple, gold and crimson. Tiny red flowers, consisting of stamens only, stud the naked winter branches.

The tree is as broad as it is high, reaching 15-20 ft in both directions. Therefore, it is best suited to larger gardens, where it should be grown in a lawn or border. Several stems develop near the base, but early pruning can train the tree to a single trunk.

HOW TO GROW
Plant from autumn to spring, in fertile, well-drained soil, ideally slightly acid - though the tree is lime-tolerant. For the best autumn colours, site in full sun. Propagate in autumn by seeds in a cold frame, or by layering. For a single-stemmed tree, remove side branches during winter.

On older trees the bark flakes away, creating an attractive pattern. This is best shown if the lower branches are removed.

Few small trees put on a richer autumn apparel than *Parrotia persica*.

Paulownia tomentosa

In its native China this magnificent deciduous flowering tree is known as the goddess tree. In May, before the large, downy, heart-shaped leaves unfurl, blue-purple, foxglove-shaped flowers are borne in large heads at the tips of the bare shoots. The flower buds are formed the previous summer and autumn; sadly, they are unlikely to survive prolonged severe frosts.

Paulownia tomentosa (syn. *P. imperialis*) is fast growing, especially when young, and eventually reaches a height of 30 ft. It has a wide-spreading crown and needs plenty of room for development.

HOW TO GROW
Set out young container-grown specimens from autumn to spring, in well-drained, even limy but moist soil, and in full sun with shelter from north and east winds. The tree is unsuitable for cold exposed gardens but it is tolerant of town pollution. Propagate in summer by heel cuttings under glass. No pruning is necessary.

The buds of the flowers that grace the tree in spring are susceptible to hard frosts, and the tree is unsuitable for cold areas.

A *Paulownia tomentosa*, about 35 years old, spreads its magnificent crown.

Photinia villosa

This native of China, Japan and Korea is a deciduous tree grown mainly for its autumn foliage. The leaves turn as bright a red as the small oval fruits which follow the white spring flowers. The tree, which grows to a height of 15 ft and has a spreading, often multi-stemmed crown, does best of all in the very acid soil of a woodland garden but will succeed in any acid to neutral site.

Although not a superlative ornamental, this small tree provides elegance and distinction, especially in autumn.

HOW TO GROW
Plant in late spring or autumn, in well-drained, acid to neutral soil. The tree needs full sun and shelter from north and east winds. Propagate in spring by seeds under glass. Thin wall shrubs to shape in winter. For a tree-like habit with a single main stem, prune off side branches flush with the trunk as growth progresses.

The leaves of *Photinia villosa* turn such a brilliant red and gold in autumn that the tree seems to catch fire.

Bright orange-red autumn foliage is the main asset of *Photinia villosa*.

Picea omorika (SERBIAN SPRUCE)

If you want to add a touch of elegance to your garden, consider this tall, slender, symmetrical evergreen conifer. It is equally impressive standing alone, or planted in a group with dwarf conifers or heathers.

If space allows only one tree, it should be sited with care so that its classical line can be fully appreciated. After many years the tree can reach a height of 60 ft in cultivation, but will be only about 10 ft across.

The Serbian spruce tolerates pollution and can be successfully grown in towns. The cultivar 'Pendula' is even more slender and has graceful weeping branches.

HOW TO GROW
Plant in late spring or autumn, in any moist but well-drained soil, in full sun or light shade. The tree does well in town gardens. Propagate in spring by seeds. There is no need to prune.

The dark green needles covering the gently curving, symmetrical branches of *Picea omorika* have a bright grey underside.

The Serbian spruce is a graceful tree that deserves to stand alone.

The startling blue-white leaves of *Picea pungens glauca* 'Hoopsii' are given added emphasis by the clear bright green of *Chamaecyparis lawsoniana* 'Erecta Viridis'. The combination looks best when placed in a natural setting on a grassy bank with, for example, the fern *Dryopteris filix-mas.*

Picea pungens glauca (BLUE SPRUCE)

Sharp blue needles crown the handsome branches of this ornamental spruce. On established trees, purplish-brown cones, ripening to grey-brown, are produced on the uppermost shoots in hanging clusters.

The main stem rises straight as an arrow, with the branches carried in layers and finishing in a rigid spire. The overall shape is that of a slender cone that in average soil reaches no more than 30-40 ft.

Picea pungens glauca looks splendid grown in a lawn, singly or in a group, or on its own in a bed surrounded by heathers such as varieties of *Erica carnea*. An alternative for those with enough garden room is to grow it with other trees. It is most effective planted in an island bed or on a steep bank with other conifers – its relatives, perhaps: *P. p. g.* 'Hoopsii', which has vivid blue-white leaves, and *P. p. g.* 'Spekii', whose foliage is pale blue-grey. Another suitable companion would be *Chamaecyparis lawsoniana* 'Erecta Viridis', a very erect bright green cultivar of the Lawson cypress.

HOW TO GROW
Picea pungens glauca: plant in the same way as for P. omorika, but do not grow the tree on shallow chalky soil. Propagation of the cultivars consists of grafting in spring, but is difficult. It is easy to raise plants from seeds, but with this method their blueness varies. The only pruning needed is to reduce forked trees to a single leader.
Chamaecyparis lawsoniana: see p. 335.
Erica carnea: see p. 277.

Pinus mugo (MOUNTAIN PINE)

The mountain pine varies considerably in its habit, but for the most part seems to be content as a low, shrubby, spreading plant that seldom exceeds 6 ft high and across. Its growth develops from several main stems that spring from the base of the tree, and these in turn produce shoots that are covered with dense bunches of dark green needles. Glossy brown cones cling singly or in clusters to the tips of the branches and, altogether, the tree has a charmingly tangled 'wild-wood' appearance. However, if your garden requires a more disciplined tree, prune the young pine into a single main stem. It will then grow to a slim column, of at least 20 ft.

From this, it is apparent that the mountain pine is valuable for its toughness and adaptability, a plant that will adjust as readily to poor, dry soils as to rich, wet ones. It is indifferent to harsh conditions and, if planted young enough, will accustom itself to all but the most massive doses of industrial pollution.

Just as tough, and of similar appearance, is the dwarf Siberian pine, *Pinus pumila*. Like the mountain pine it is normally spreading and bushy, but can be trained to form a single main stem that grows up to about 10 ft. The cones are dull and unexceptional, but the needles, carried in fives, are an attractive silvery blue-green.

Trained as small trees, both these pines are ideal for the smaller garden, where they can be planted with great effect in a bed between paving stones or in a large container.

A most effective planting that adds sparkle to the setting can be achieved by surrounding a single tree with a small drift of a low, bright plant such as the golden-flowered *Hypericum olympicum*.

HOW TO GROW
Plant in autumn or spring, in any soil. Propagate by seeds in spring under glass. No pruning is needed.
Hypericum olympicum: see p. 209.

Here seen growing in a large rock garden, the mountain pine usually forms more of a shrub than a tree.

Pinus sylvestris (SCOTS PINE)

The Scots pine is the only member of its genus native to Britain. Once, it clothed most of the Highlands, but forest fires and demands for timber and grazing land took their toll until it was nearly eradicated.

Since it grows to 100 ft high, it is not often thought of as a garden tree. However, it can be restricted by training when young, and there is no doubt that, with its grey-green leaves and its orange-red bark that glows like fire in the light of dawn or sunset, it is a most handsome tree. There are also a number of smaller forms whose growth is not so awe inspiring. 'Aurea', for example, which seldom reaches 20 ft, and whose foliage is blue-green in spring, yellow in summer and old-gold in winter; the silver-needled 'Argentea'; and the 30 ft columnar 'Fastigiata'.

HOW TO GROW
Plant in autumn or spring in any soil – though preferably deep, well drained and neutral or alkaline – and in full sun. Propagate as for Pinus mugo; graft named forms in spring. To contain spreading, pinch back new growth in late spring, and remove lower branches flush with trunk.

When summer comes, *Pinus sylvestris* 'Aurea' turns from green to yellow.

The beautiful foliage of *Pinus sylvestris* 'Argentea' reaches a colourful peak in winter when it is at its most silvery.

PRUNUS

In gardens up and down the land the foaming blossom of ornamental prunus trees, bursting forth in pink or white against a blue sky, is one of the surest and loveliest signs that spring has arrived. Botanists classify plants by the structure of their flowers, and so alike are those of plum, cherry, peach and almond that the 18th-century Swedish botanist Linnaeus classified them together, using *Prunus* – the Latin name for 'plum' – as the generic name.

Best known of all the ornamental prunus trees is the group of cultivars known as Japanese cherries, most of which originated in Japan as hybrids from *Prunus serrulata* and allied species. They vary in shape and size, but all have sharply toothed, handsome leaves, often coppery or flushed with red when young, and a profusion of single to double blossom. This ranges from white through pink to carmine and appears from November to May, according to cultivar.

Perhaps the Sargent cherry, *P. sargentii*, is the finest of the wild species. Large, clear pink flowers burst into bloom against red-tinged leaves, which in autumn turn bright shades of red and orange. Sadly, the tree eventually grows too big for the small garden, and it might be better to plant its smaller hybrid 'Accolade', which is of very nearly equal merit.

Among the ornamental plums, *P. cerasifera* is the best known, particularly in its purple-leaved form 'Pissardii' ('Atropurpurea'). The pink-budded flowers open on bare twigs, to be followed by red-purple leaves. The common peach (*P. persica*) and the common almond (*P. dulcis*, syn. *P. amygdalus*) produce large pink flowers on bare twigs. The hybrid between them, the ornamental almond *P. × pollardii* (syn. *P. × amygdalo-persica* 'Pollardii'), is an especially fine tree.

HOW TO GROW
Plant in early autumn while the ground is still warm – though in mild winters planting may be continued until March. Any ordinary, well-drained soil, preferably with a trace of lime, will do. Standard trees require staking until established. Propagate species by sowing seeds outdoors immediately after gathering them; named forms must be propagated by grafting or cuttings. Pruning is unnecessary.

About 25-30 years old, this ornamental cherry, *Prunus* 'Accolade', spreads its blossom above an underplanting of camellias.

A common almond, surrounded by daffodils, in full spring bloom.

Prunus cerasifera 'Pissardii' has rich purple leaves.

Japanese cherry blossom makes a dazzling show.

Prunus subhirtella 'Pendula Rubra'

(ORNAMENTAL WEEPING CHERRY)

All ornamental weeping cherries are glorious, but to the medium-sized garden *Prunus subhirtella* 'Pendula Rubra' brings a special blessing. Its slender, wand-like branches arch above the main stem, then curve sharply downwards to brush the ground, forming a curtain that sways gracefully in the breeze.

In April, before the leaves emerge, crimson buds appear, soon opening into flowers of the deepest rose, each one backed by a contrasting purple-red calyx – the outer part of the flower. In autumn, the foliage often flares into a brilliant display of crimson and orange before falling.

The tree is broader than it is tall – it has an eventual spread of 20 ft and a height of 10-15 ft – so requires a reasonable amount of space in which to develop. It looks at its best in a position where the branches do not trail but are able to hang down to their full length without touching

the ground – say, on a steep bank or in the centre of a raised bed. If these sites are not available, it deserves a prominent position on the lawn or in a border where it will create a focal point for the garden.

Like most flowering cherries, it harmonises well with an underplanting of spring bulbs, such as *Scilla sibirica* or one of the forms of narcissus.

HOW TO GROW
Prunus subhirtella 'Pendula Rubra': *plant and propagate as for other Prunus (see p. 351). Keep pruning of ornamental cherries to a minimum and carry it out in early summer when bleeding is unlikely. Prune crossing and badly placed branches cleanly back to their base and treat the cuts with a protective wound sealer. Bullfinches may strip developing buds in hard winters, so protect trees with fine netting.*
Scilla sibirica: see p. 167.

The weeping branches of *Prunus subhirtella* 'Pendula Rubra', wreathed in spring blossom, reach down to brush the ground.

In summer the prunus forms a dense drapery of graceful foliage.

Above a sea of narcissi, *P. s.* 'Pendula' flourishes its dazzling blossom.

In bloom, *Prunus subhirtella* 'Pendula Rubra' combines exquisitely with the spring bulb *Scilla sibirica*.

Pyrus salicifolia 'Pendula'
(WILLOW-LEAVED PEAR)

This weeping, willow-leaved pear is fast becoming a
favourite in small gardens. Rarely exceeding 15 ft in height,
it develops a crown of hanging branches densely clothed
with narrow, downy leaves – silvery when young, grey when
mature.

Like the weeping cherry, the weeping pear is at its
grandest in an elevated position, but is remarkable
anywhere. Left to itself, the crown tends to become dense
and tangled, but it is easily pruned into an open, elegant
shape by an occasional thinning of crooked shoots. This
is a practice that should be started when the tree is still
young.

HOW TO GROW
*Plant from autumn to spring, in full sun and in any fertile,
well-drained soil. Ornamental pears are tough, taking cold
winds, drought and air pollution in their stride. Propagate by
grafting in spring. Prune in late winter to early spring,
cutting out crowded branches at their base.*

In April *Pyrus salicifolia* 'Pendula' is studded with creamy blossom.

A 15-year-old willow-leaved pear, *Pyrus salicifolia* 'Pendula', lets hang its great drapery of silvery foliage.

Rhus typhina (STAG'S HORN SUMACH)

Stag's horn sumach is one of the trees that contribute to
the glory of autumn in New England and eastern Canada;
now it has brought something of the same splendour to
gardens of the Old World. Beginning in September, the
foliage puts on a firework display of colour that begins
with vivid yellow, then runs through a flare of orange-red
to purple. It remains attractive in summer, with its dipping
branches of fern-like leaves bearing tiny red flowers that are
followed on female trees by dull crimson fruits.

Once established, the tree, which grows to a height of
20 ft, produces many suckers.

HOW TO GROW
*Plant from autumn to spring in ordinary, well-drained, even
chalky soil. The tree is excellent for town gardens, in sun or
partial shade. Propagate by rooted suckers. The foliage is most
outstanding if, annually or every two years in late winter to
early spring, side branches are cut back to two or three buds
from their base, and crossing branches removed.*

The foliage of *Rhus typhina* 'Laciniata' is
deeply cut, fern-like and more elegant than
that of the parent species.

The autumn leaves of stag's horn sumach blaze brilliantly.

The robinia lights up a garden like a great splash of sunshine.

A ten-year-old *Robinia pseudoacacia* 'Frisia' is here seen in May, backed by conifers and with Floribunda roses in the foreground.

Robinia pseudoacacia 'Frisia'
(COMMON OR FALSE ACACIA, BLACK LOCUST)

The species to which 'Frisia' belongs contains some of the most elegant of deciduous garden trees. Their drawbacks are that they need full sun to flower freely and a position that protects their brittle branches from strong winds. However, they are easy to grow, and extremely vigorous. Once established, they put out large quantities of suckers.

Robinia pseudoacacia 'Frisia' is a lovely golden-leaved tree, 30-40 ft high, that in June carries hanging clusters of fragrant, creamy-white blooms.

HOW TO GROW

Plant from autumn to spring, in any – even poor – well-drained soil, and in full sun. The tree tolerates polluted air but is prone to wind damage in exposed sites. Propagate by grafting in spring. Do not prune, but cut out unwanted suckers before they form thickets.

'Kilmarnock' in October with a variegated holly and *Skimmia japonica*.

The great umbrella of a *Salix caprea* 'Weeping Sally', aged about 10-15 years, covered with grey-green catkins.

Salix caprea 'Kilmarnock' (WEEPING SALLOW)

Weeping trees of all kinds have a wide appeal, even to those not normally tempted to plant a tree. The well-known weeping willow, *Salix babylonica*, is an old favourite but it is ultimately too large for all but the biggest gardens. On the other hand, the weeping sallow, *S. caprea* 'Kilmarnock' – also known as 'Pendula' – is perfectly tailored for the small garden, forming a narrow head of hanging stems. These are clothed with big, wrinkled, grey-backed leaves and in early spring with silvery catkins that turn gold with pollen. *S. caprea* 'Weeping Sally' is the female form, which has grey-green catkins.

HOW TO GROW

Plant from autumn to spring, in any ordinary soil, not necessarily moist provided that young plants are watered until established. Site in full sun. Propagate in late spring by grafting on to an erect sallow stem. Prune while dormant, removing dead wood and shortening trailing branches.

Downy male catkins decorate the violet willow before its foliage appears.

The stems of this tree were cut hard back to promote the present two-year-old waxy-bloomed purple growth.

Salix daphnoides (VIOLET WILLOW)

The violet willow's natural habitat extends from northern Europe to deep into central Asia, making it a fairly undemanding tree for British gardens. In fact, if you have room for only one willow, this might be the one to grow. Its strong, upright shoots, reaching up to 15 ft and spreading the same distance, are purple and covered by a plum-like bloom. They are decorated in late winter or early spring, before the leaves appear, by yellow male catkins, up to 2 in. long.

The foliage is a lustrous dark green above and blue-white below, producing an effect like cool, whirling water as the leaves dance, lift and spin in the breeze.

HOW TO GROW

Plant as for Salix caprea. Propagate by hardwood cuttings in autumn or winter. Prune the young shoots hard back in late winter or early spring to create a fine display of stems in future winters.

Salix matsudana 'Tortuosa'

(PEKIN WILLOW, DRAGON'S CLAW WILLOW)

One of the toughest of willows, the Chinese and Korean *Salix matsudana* will thrive in all conditions from drought to flood to the worst of urban pollution. The Chinese call 'Tortuosa' the dragon's claw willow, because its branches and shoots are contorted, especially in young trees. In British gardens it is a curiosity, reminiscent of willow pattern, particularly in winter when the tortured spirals of its limbs are fully revealed. It is also ornamental in its summer livery of long, slender green leaves that show their greyish undersides in the breeze.

Because of its invasive roots, *S. matsudana* should be planted well away from buildings. It looks well grown as the main feature in a dramatic winter association with trees that have coloured bark, such as *Cornus alba* 'Sibirica' (coral red) and *C. stolonifera* 'Flaviramea' (bright greenish-yellow).

If 'Tortuosa' is grown as a specimen in the lawn, an enchanting picture can be produced by planting beneath it late winter or spring bulbs – crocuses, scillas and snowdrops.

HOW TO GROW

Salix matsudana: plant and propagate in the same way as for S. daphnoides (see p. 354). No pruning is required.
Cornus alba: see p. 266.
C. stolonifera: see p. 266.

'Tortuosa' stands starkly outlined in the snow among red *Cornus alba* 'Sibirica' and yellow *Cornus stolonifera* 'Flaviramea', beneath which are clumps of winter-flowering bulbs.

Sorbus aria (COMMON WHITEBEAM)

Whitebeam is a native of the southern chalk downs of Britain – a tough, round-headed tree that will put up with gales off the Channel in winter and atmospheric pollution. Its oval, toothed leaves are covered with a brilliant white down when they emerge in spring, and form a delicate background to the creamy-white flowers in May. Later the foliage fades to grey-green before it bursts into red and gold in autumn, a blaze that is intensified by large bunches of deep crimson berries speckled with brown.

The species is splendid, but one or two cultivars are particularly suited to the garden. *Sorbus aria* 'Lutescens', for example, is an erect, compact tree that eventually grows to about 30 ft high and is especially valued for its bright spring foliage.

'Decaisneana' (syn. 'Majestica') is more robust than the species and bears larger leaves and fruits.

Another form of *S. aria* is 'Pendula', a small, weeping variety that is splendid for the small garden. Growing to no more than 10 ft high, it has slender branches and long, narrow leaves.

One of the finest of all whitebeams, which was raised from Himalayan seeds, is sold by nurserymen under the name *S.* 'Mitchellii' syn. 'John Mitchell'. More robust than *S. aria*, it bears handsome broad leaves up to 8 in. long.

HOW TO GROW

Plant from autumn to spring in any well-drained soil, in full sun or light shade. The trees are ideal for almost any situation, accepting cold, strong winds, salt-laden sea spray and air pollution with equanimity. Propagate and prune as for Sorbus aucuparia.

A *Sorbus aria* 'Lutescens', aged about 30-40 years, unfurls its spring leaves, revealing their gleaming white upper surfaces.

In May and June the whitebeam bears 4-5 in. wide clusters of creamy-white flowers that resemble those of the hawthorn.

The whitebeam, 15-20 ft high, has an attractively compact crown.

Sorbus hupehensis

Whitebeam and rowan are our native and much-loved representatives of the genus *Sorbus*. However, since the other 90-odd species come from very similar habitats in the chilly-to-temperate parts of northern Europe and Asia, most of these, too, will settle down in this country. They can stand the worst in the way of frost, cold winds and atmospheric pollution, yet retain a delightful hint of faraway places.

One such is *Sorbus hupehensis*, which came originally from central China. It is a robust tree, growing to 25 ft or so and offering a great deal to the gardener. Its dark purple branches and shoots are clothed in summer with deeply divided leaves of a most unusual sea-green that in autumn can turn shades of yellow or red. In May or June, it produces clusters of white flowers that pave the way for the October spectacle of large, drooping bunches of white fruits, often borne on contrasting red stalks; this display may easily last through until Christmas, as may that of *S. h. obtusa*, whose fruits are pink. Very similar, but only half the size, is *S. vilmorinii*, which is more suitable for small gardens. It has drooping clusters of rose-red fruit, which gradually turn pink and finally white flushed rose.

All three trees are ideal for growing alone in a lawn or paved area, but a very attractive association can be created by underplanting any one of them with small colourful shrubs such as *Berberis × rubrostilla* or *Cotoneaster dammeri*; or with a dwarf rhododendron, such as *Rhododendron yakushimanum*, provided you have acid soil.

HOW TO GROW
Sorbus hupehensis: plant in the same way as for S. aria. The trees described here look their best where the autumn sun can illuminate them from behind. Propagate all Sorbus species by seeds in autumn; named forms should be grafted in spring, or budded in summer, on to rootstocks of the appropriate species. Prune as for S. aucuparia.
Berberis × rubrostilla: see p. 253.
Cotoneaster dammeri: see p. 269.
Rhododendron yakushimanum: see p. 309.

In October and November the white berries of *S. hupehensis* contrast superbly with the coral-red fruits of *Berberis × rubrostilla*, here underplanted with dwarf rhododendrons in foliage and *Cotoneaster dammeri* providing ground-cover in front.

Ripe fruits hang among the summer foliage of *Sorbus aucuparia* 'Beissneri'.

Sorbus aucuparia 'Beissneri'

(ROWAN, MOUNTAIN ASH)

'Beissneri', a most handsome form of our native rowan, or mountain ash, *Sorbus aucuparia*, is prized for its light coppery or orange-brown bark. The white flowers, which are borne in May or June, are followed in autumn by large red fruits that sometimes persist into winter.

If you have room, it would make a brave contrast to grow *S.* 'Joseph Rock' near by. Matching the 30 ft of 'Beissneri', it is nearly as attractive throughout spring and summer, but is at its finest in autumn when its crown turns to a brilliant ball of purple, crimson and scarlet foliage cushioning the ripening yellow fruits.

HOW TO GROW
Plant as for Sorbus aria (see p. 355). Propagate as for S. hupehensis. Pruning is rarely required, except to remove damaged and spindly shoots and to trim young trees to shape. Carry out all pruning in late winter or early spring.

The main attraction of 'Beissneri', apart from its handsome foliage and fruits, is its warmly coloured bark.

Stewartia pseudocamellia

This is a most spectacular tree, especially suited to gardens whose soil is acid. One attraction is the flaking piebald bark on the main stem and branches; another is the autumn foliage, which, after a good summer, is tinted with rich reds and yellows. In summer, too, the tree looks lovely, when satiny, cup-shaped white flowers with yellow centres adorn the branches during July and August. The tree generally grows to a height of 20-30 ft. However, there is also a smaller form, *Stewartia malacodendron*, which grows to only 15 ft, has autumn foliage that is just as vivid, and white flowers that are highlighted by purple anthers. The blooms, like those of *S. pseudocamellia*, appear in July and August.

HOW TO GROW
Set out young, container-grown plants in spring, in moist, acid to neutral soil enriched with peat. The trees are not recommended for cold, exposed gardens. They do best in the light shade and shelter of shrub borders or woodland edging. Propagate in summer by heel cuttings under glass. No pruning is needed.

This mature *Stewartia pseudocamellia* is smothered in buds that will soon open to join the flowers already in bloom.

Strikingly flaking bark adds to the tree's attractions.

A fine summer produces richly coloured autumn foliage.

The first flowers open on a young tree.

The spreading snowbell makes a superb specimen tree for a paved area.

Styrax japonica (SNOWBELL)

The common name of this lovely deciduous tree is justly earned, and its generic name recalls storax, the fragrant resin yielded by the tree that was once used in the manufacture of perfumes. In June, amid the small, neat, oval, green leaves, snowbell puts out exquisite star-shaped white flowers, with yellow-beaked centres, to crowd the undersides of the branches. The tree, which rarely tops 20 ft, will, if left to itself, often produce several spreading main stems.

HOW TO GROW
Plant from autumn to spring, in fertile, neutral to acid, well-drained but moist soil, preferably in a sheltered site in sun or light shade. Propagate in summer by heel cuttings under glass or by seeds. Prune young trees in late spring, removing all but the strongest stem at ground level. On established trees, shorten side branches if necessary and thin out crowded shoots to keep the crown open.

Restricting *Styrax japonica* to a single stem from an early age raises the crown, so that the flowers can be admired from below.

A mature *T. plicata* 'Zebrina' makes a compact cone.

Thuja occidentalis 'Rheingold' is here backed by a juniper.

The foliage of *Tilia mongolica* turns warm yellow in autumn.

Tilia petiolaris leaves are green above, silver beneath.

The Western hemlock is among the most beautiful conifers.

A 30-year-old *Tsuga mertensiana* spreads over a lawn.

Thuja plicata (WESTERN RED CEDAR)

The aristocrat of its genus, this fine timber tree, sometimes listed as *Thuja lobbii*, comes from the western side of North America. As it will grow to 60 ft or more high, it is suitable only for the largest garden, but if it is kept firmly in check it makes a fine windbreak or hedge for a garden of any size. Its branches, curving delicately upwards at their tips, are covered in rich, yellow-green foliage.

Much smaller is the white cedar (*T. occidentalis*). This has several good cultivars, including 'Rheingold', a shrub up to 4 ft high, with bronze-yellow young foliage.

HOW TO GROW
Plant from late autumn to spring, in ordinary, moisture-retentive soil. Single trees do best in full sun. For screening, space trees 6-8 ft apart; for hedging, space them 2 ft apart. Propagate species by seeds in spring, named cultivars by semi-hardwood cuttings in early autumn.

Tilia mongolica (MONGOLIAN LIME)

The Mongolian lime is one of the few members of its genus suited to the smaller garden. *Tilia mongolica* seldom climbs to much above 30 ft, and in maturity produces a compact rounded crown of arching branches that in July are smothered with clusters of fragrant, creamy flowers. The coarsely toothed, vine-like leaves turn to a warm yellow in autumn.

For those with more room, and a taste for the spectacular, there is the weeping silver lime (*T. petiolaris*), whose graceful, drooping branches show first green, then silver-white as they stir in the breeze. The tiny flowers are deliciously scented.

HOW TO GROW
Plant all lime trees from autumn to spring, in ordinary, moist but well-drained soil, and in sun or light shade, out of strong winds. Propagate in autumn by layering or by seeds. Pruning is unnecessary – although limes do tolerate hard cutting back.

Tsuga heterophylla (WESTERN HEMLOCK)

The hemlock firs are elegant evergreen conifers usually of vigorous growth. In ideal woodland conditions the Western hemlock, which has dark green leaves banded with white beneath, will eventually tower to a height of 100 ft, but it is unlikely to achieve this in domesticity. It forms a symmetrical cone with wide-spreading lower branches.

Its relative, *Tsuga mertensiana*, the mountain hemlock, which grows to a height of 70-100 ft, is an elegant tree that does particularly well in the wetter western areas of Britain. It is cone-shaped, sometimes narrowly so, with blue-grey foliage.

HOW TO GROW
Plant from autumn to spring, in moist but well-drained, neutral to acid soil. Hemlocks thrive in cool, shady situations with high rainfall and are not suitable for towns or exposed seaside gardens. Propagate from seeds in spring. Pruning is rarely needed, but the foliage responds well to clipping.

Trachycarpus fortunei

(CHUSAN PALM, FAN PALM)

The Chusan or fan palm, from China, is the only palm tree that is hardy in Britain; or, at least, it is in the balmier parts of the south and west. It is a slow-growing evergreen that can reach a height of about 25 ft in warm, sheltered conditions, but this is rare and the average is likely to be closer to half that height. Fan-shaped, beautifully pleated leaves, 2½-4 ft across, arise from the summit of the stout stem and are carried horizontally on long, sharply toothed stalks.

Established specimens have a main stem thickly covered with the dark fibrous remains of old leaf sheaths and, in a warm summer, produce drooping clusters of small yellow flowers. Even a young tree provides a bold display and brings a welcome touch of the tropics to our gardens.

The young tree can be damaged by a severe winter and should be protected with bracken or polythene. But, once established, the palm stands up well to harsh weather. It does best, however, in positions sheltered from cold north and east winds.

Exotic as it is, the Chusan palm needs careful siting in the garden if it is not to look out of place. The best way to grow it is to set it standing by itself in a paved patio or courtyard, or, somewhat less effectively, in a lawn. A striking effect can be achieved by adding a surrounding growth of sword-leaved plants, such as New Zealand flax (*Phormium tenax*) or *Iris foetidissima*, with its dark, evergreen leaves and scarlet autumn seeds. Young palms look very well when planted in tubs, and are then of course easily transportable if the weather turns savage.

HOW TO GROW

Trachycarpus fortunei: set out container-grown palms in late spring, in fertile, well-drained soil. Full sun and a sheltered site are essential, even in milder regions, with winter protection until the palm is established. Propagate by seed in spring, under glass. Do not prune, but remove dead leaves from the trunk if desired.
Iris foetidissima: see p. 96.
Phormium tenax: see p. 300.

Phormium tenax 'Purpureum' and the scarlet-berried *Iris foetidissima* provide bold accompaniment for the striking *Trachycarpus fortunei*.

The leaf fans of a ten-year-old Chusan palm, *Trachycarpus fortunei*, backed by Spanish broom, *Spartium junceum*.

The Plant Hunters

Explorers of old whose finds have enriched the gardens of today

We have come to think of the gloriously wide range of plants that adorn British gardens as traditional, stretching back over the centuries. But in fact most of them were introduced here only within the last 200 years by men whose searches took them to unmapped and often dangerous lands.

Previously plants had come into Britain only incidentally, as part of the assorted treasures brought back by, among others, crusaders and court ambassadors. It was not until the 17th century that men travelled abroad specifically to find new flora. The first of these early collectors were the Tradescants, father and son.

John Tradescant the Elder (c. 1567-1637), gardener to Charles I, journeyed widely – through America, Russia and Europe and around the Mediterranean seaboard – and bequeathed to the British garden some of its best plants, including the Persian lilac (*Syringa* × *persica*), the false acacia (*Robinia pseudoacacia*), *Hypericum* and the European larch (*Larix decidua*). His son John (1608-62), who succeeded him as royal gardener, made three adventurous trips around North America, where he discovered the true Virginia creeper (*Parthenocissus quinquefolia*), the tulip tree (*Liriodendron tulipifera*), the red maple (*Acer rubrum*), and the border perennial *Tradescantia virginiana*.

Plants from the New World

Collecting plant seeds was how the Reverend John Banister (1650-92), a missionary in Virginia, spent his time when he was not saving souls. He gave us the beautiful *Magnolia virginiana (glauca)*; *Rhododendron viscosum*; the scarlet hawthorn (*Crataegus coccinea*); several silver firs (*Abies*); the autumn-brilliant sweet gum (*Liquidambar styraciflua*); and the honey locust tree (*Gleditsia triacanthos*).

The American John Bartram (1699-1777) travelled throughout his homeland collecting plants. He became official American botanist to George III and also supplied plants and seeds to English patrons. Without his efforts our gardens would not be glorified with the lilies *Lilium superbum* and *L. philadelphicum*, *Phlox maculata* and *P. subulata*, sweet bergamot (*Monarda didyma*), *Magnolia acuminata* and several rhododendrons. He also introduced the bizarre insect-eating plants, *Sarracenia*.

Perhaps the man all British gardeners should bless more than any other is someone who did not himself introduce many plants, but ensured that others did – Sir Joseph Banks (1743-1820), whose eyes had been opened to the richness of the world's flora when he was botanist on Captain Cook's first voyage round the world (1768-71). Soon after he returned he became director of Kew Gardens, and in this position was able to send plant hunters all over the world.

One of them was Francis Masson (1741-1805), who spent a total of ten years at the Cape. There he found a wealth of plants, among them geraniums (*Pelargonium*), heaths (*Erica*), *Dimorphotheca*, *Protea*, *Watsonia* and the magnificent bird of paradise flower (*Strelitzia reginae*). In the Canary Islands he also discovered *Cineraria cruenta*, the progenitor of all modern cinerarias.

William Kerr (d. 1814) was the second of Banks' protégés. He was sent to China where he was confined for most of the time to the nursery gardens of Canton. But this proved an acceptable restriction, for the gardens contained an abundance of exciting new plants and Kerr shipped home some of the finest exotica that grace the modern garden: the tiger lily (*Lilium tigrinum*), the rose *Rosa banksiae*, the lovely bamboo *Nandina domestica*, the water lily *Nymphaea pygmaea* and the double-flowered form of the shrub named after him, *Kerria japonica* 'Pleniflora' ('Flore Pleno').

The greatest influx of exotic plants came in the 19th century, when the rhododendron genus was especially enriched. Boldest in this field was Sir Joseph Hooker (1817-1911). From the Himalayas he sent home many highly coloured rhododendrons, which, with their hybrids, were to set British woodland gardens aglow. Hooker's discovery, *R. griffithianum*, became one of the parents of 128 hardy hybrids, including 'Pink Pearl'.

It was obvious to the botanical world that, despite the work of the early adventurers, the plant riches of North America were as yet hardly tapped. In 1820 the Royal Horticultural Society sent the Scot, David Douglas (1798-1834), to the continent. There he scoured primitive forests in conditions of great hardship. But it was all worth it – to British gardeners, at any rate. The various species of silver fir (*Abies*), Douglas fir (*Pseudotsuga*) and pine (*Pinus*) that he discovered were to revolutionise the British landscape, just as his finds among herbaceous plants – lupins, penstemons, echiums, arabis, clarkias,

Namaqualand in South Africa was a paradise for plant collectors like Francis Masson. Among the many plants growing naturally in the wild are Cape marigolds, blue flax and arum lilies.

Francis Masson (1741-1805).

Sir Joseph Hooker's *Himalayan Journals* (1854) pictures rhododendrons in bloom among snowfields in the Himalayas.

The Wardian case, invented by A. A. Maconochie and Nathaniel Ward about 150 years ago, made it possible to bring plants alive from abroad.

phacelias, *Limnanthes douglasii* and the Californian poppy (*Eschscholzia californica*) – were to transform the garden border.

Other plant collectors followed Douglas to North America. One was William Lobb (1809-63), who while collecting found the massive coniferous Wellingtonia (*Sequoiadendron giganteum*). Before this he had crossed the forbidding plains and Andes of South America into Chile, where he had discovered the magnificent flowering shrubs *Escallonia macrantha*, *Desfontainea spinosa*, *Lapageria rosea* and *Berberis darwinii*, and the flame-bloomed tree, the Chilean fire bush, *Embothrium coccineum*.

In 1842 the Treaty of Nanking at last opened up China to British travellers, and in that year Robert Fortune (1812-80) was sent there by the Royal Horticultural Society. Off and on he was to spend almost 20 years in the Far East, and his rewards were great: 126 new species of flora. They included many of the most lovely shrubs and herbaceous plants of the modern garden: honeysuckles (*Lonicera*), many chrysanthemums, winter-flowering jasmine (*Jasminum nudiflorum*), *Weigela*, bleeding heart (*Dicentra spectabilis*), the Japanese anemone (*A.* × *hybrida*), *Forsythia viridissima*, *Mahonia japonica*, *Skimmia* and the ornamental almond (*Prunus triloba*).

Fortune's successes made other botanists realise just what a treasure-house of plants the Far East was. Ernest Henry Wilson (1876-1930) made four journeys to China, Japan and Formosa from 1899 to 1911 and brought back one of the finest harvests of plants ever. In 1976 the Royal Horticultural Society calculated that 600 of his discoveries were still being grown today – among them the beauty bush (*Kolkwitzia amabilis*), *Lilium regale*, the dogwood (*Cornus kousa*), *Acer griseum*, *Clematis montana rubens*, *Buddleia davidii*, the primrose jasmine (*Jasminum mesnyi*) and 50 Kurume azaleas.

George Forrest (1873-1932) found so many new rhododendrons on his seven trips to Yunnan, a mountainous region now in south-west China, that the whole genus had to be revised. One species, *R. griersonianum*, is now a parent of 122 hybrids. Forrest introduced altogether about 300 new plants.

Two more notable plant collectors who visited China were William Purdom (1880-1921) and Reginald Farrer (1880-1920), who on their joint expedition in 1914 discovered the shrubs *Viburnum farreri*, *Rosa farreri* and *Buddleia alternifolia*. Other splendid plants were found in China, and in Assam, Burma and Tibet, by Frank Kingdon-Ward (1885-1958), who is best remembered for giving us the exquisite Himalayan blue poppy (*Meconopsis betonicifolia*). He also introduced to Britain many new rhododendrons, as well as the lily *Lilium wardii*, the giant cowslip (*Primula florindae*) and such trees and shrubs as *Acer wardii*, *Cotoneaster wardii* and *C. conspicuus*. Tibet yielded further treasures to Frank Ludlow (1885-1972) and George Sherriff (1898-1967): *Meconopsis sherriffii*, *Paeonia lutea ludlowii*, and the lily *Lilium sherriffii*.

Water garden plants

A water garden provides an opportunity to grow many beautiful and unusual plants

THROUGHOUT THE AGES, the fascination of water – be it still, reflective pools, running rills or splashing fountains – has shown itself in gardens all over the world. Its appeal is no less today. Water in a garden adds movement, light and sound; it also makes it possible to grow plants which are otherwise utterly out of the question.

Adaptation to a watery environment has encouraged the evolution of two particularly distinct habits, the strong vertical one of irises and rushes and the horizontal one of floating lilies. Their juxtaposition in carefully thought out groupings is the essence of successful water gardening.

Only with pools in a formal garden does a drawn line show where water stops and dry land begins. In nature and the best informal pools the two merge. Aquatics growing in the water link with bog plants, which require less free moisture at their roots and flourish in the wet margins. Within this group are many beauties. Carefully selected, they will provide a show of foliage and flowers from early spring to late autumn.

However, the attractively lush growth of plants adapted for waterside conditions can sometimes prove a disadvantage. When planning a water or bog garden, account must be taken of the vigorous growth of plants like *Ranunculus lingua* which can easily get out of control and swamp smaller neighbours. A water garden requires commitment, but any time spent is repaid many times in pleasure.

In this water garden, horizontal and vertical balance is created by the flat leaves of the lily *Nymphaea* × *marliacea* 'Albida' and the spiky grass *Glycerium maxima* 'Variegata'.

363

Aponogeton distachyos leaves and white flowers float in the water, with irises behind and pink arabis on the bank.

Aponogeton distachyos (CAPE PONDWEED)

The Cape pondweed or water hawthorn is something of a curiosity in British gardens. It was one of the first Southern Hemisphere water plants to be used here as an outdoor plant, being introduced as long ago as 1788. It is also one of the few water plants that tolerate shade.

To be sure that it survives winter ice, give it at least 18 in. of water. In spring, it puts up its oval, floating leaves. Soon after, the flowers appear in a display that may continue from April until December.

The floral effect is made up of a V-shaped grouping of white, petal-like leaves half enclosing purple stamens, all of which stand above the water's surface. It puts forth a delicate scent of hawthorn.

HOW TO GROW
Plant the tubers in mud at the bottom of the pond, or in pots of loam, in spring. Propagate by division in spring.

The flowers may be cut, and will last in water for several days.

Acorus calamus 'Variegatus' (SWEET FLAG)

Strewing rushes and herbs on the stone floor of medieval halls, castles and churches was a way of combating the bitter chill of such places in winter, and incidentally helped to conceal the remains of weeks-old meals from the nostrils of the more sensitive. *Acorus calamus*, the sweet rush or sweet flag, was one of the most desirable plants for this purpose.

Its vernacular names describe it well, looking as it does like a 3 ft high yellow flag iris that apparently fails to flower. Obviously it does flower, but rather insignificantly. It is a member of the arum family, but as it lacks the wide-spreading spathe borne by most of the others, there is little to be seen; in June and July the yellow-green horn-like spadix pushes out from the side of a flattened stem, and that is all.

The form 'Variegatus', however, has leaves striped with cream. It should be placed in a few inches of water or by the waterside, where the leaves can be crushed in the hand, so releasing their sweet-cinnamon aroma.

HOW TO GROW
Plant during late March or April in shallow water or moist, loamy soil by the waterside. Propagate by division in spring.

Acorus calamus 'Variegatus'.

The delicate flowers of *Butomus umbellatus*.

Butomus umbellatus (FLOWERING RUSH)

The flowering rush is one of the most beautiful of waterside plants, a beauty that is said to be nourished by the blood of Acis, a Sicilian shepherd-lad slain by Polyphemus or Cyclops.

It is all rather unlikely, but then so is this whole group; there are only seven members in the entire family *Butomaceae*.

Having a liking for muddy stream or pond banks, butomus pushes up spears of purple-tinged leaves in spring. They grow up to some 3 ft in length, rush-like and triangular in section, with sharp edges. Then, in June and July, the tall flower spikes begin to overtop the leaves, slender wands carrying open heads of inch-wide, cup-shaped flowers of clear rose-pink. The effect is rather like that of a large-flowered allium. Doubled by reflection in still water, it is lovely indeed.

Though it is a wild plant, it does need care to prevent its being swamped by more exuberant neighbours.

HOW TO GROW
Plant in late March or April on the margins of pools or on the muddy banks of slow-flowing streams. Propagate by dividing the rootstocks in spring.

Caltha palustris (KINGCUP, MARSH MARIGOLD)

In late winter, by the poolside, few sights are more encouraging than the new heart-shaped leaves of kingcups pushing through the sere leaves of last year's rushes. The great golden-buttercup heads follow in April and May on stems that are thick, fleshy and full of substance. The native species is a fine garden-worthy plant; especially the interesting old double-flowered form, 'Flore Pleno', which makes a glowing centrepiece for a green-and-gold early spring association.

This double kingcup develops into a 12 in. high hummock of glossy green leaves with golden, regularly rosetted flowers. Planted at the water's edge, it can be joined on nearby solid land by the giant yellow bog arum, *Lysichiton americanus*, whose waxy spathes palely reflect the green flower spikes within.

As a background, plants of the tufted sedge (*Carex elata*) would be a good choice to provide contrasting shape and texture. Before the slender, grassy leaves of the dense tufts are fully grown, they are accompanied by erect, catkin-like flower spikes with pale yellow stamens. After flowering, the foliage continues to lengthen and arches over, creating broader clumps.

As the sedge leaves expand to their full size, so do those of the kingcup and giant bog arum. The association of these three widely differing types of foliage, and their water-mirrored reflections, provides an ever-changing delight until autumn.

HOW TO GROW
Plant from March to September in neutral or slightly acid, loamy soil and in sun or light shade. If planted above the water's edge it must be in a place that is continuously moist. Calthas planted in water should be grown in containers at least 6 in. deep.

Yellow double kingcup blooms (left), fleshy leaved *Lysichiton americanus* and tall tufted sedge lie mirrored in a pool.

Calla palustris (BOG ARUM, CALLA LILY)

Perhaps to make up for the fact that this is the only plant in its genus, *Calla palustris* has a whole range of common names, calla lily and bog arum among them. The most suitable name for it would be bog beauty, a direct translation of the Latin, but in fact it seems never to be used.

However, it is a lovely little plant for a pond where the water merges imperceptibly with the land. There, its creeping stems will grow through the marshy soil and through the shallow water, from its fleshy rhizomes, and produce thick, glossy, heart-shaped leaves.

The summer display of small, white arum flowers is full of charm, each lasting for a couple of weeks so that the effect goes on for some time. Flowering starts in May and continues through June. Sometimes there may be a second show of blooms in August. Though the calla is perfectly hardy and robust, the leaves of larger waterside plants, such as *Lysichiton*, should not be allowed to overwhelm it.

HOW TO GROW
Plant in late spring in fertile soil at the very edge of the water, in full sun or partial shade. Propagate by division in April.

The heart-shaped leaves and white flowers of bog arum are backed by hostas and sweet flag (*Acorus calamus*).

Filipendula rubra (QUEEN OF THE PRAIRIE)

It seems odd that one of the finest spiraeas for pondsides or boggy gardens should be called queen of the prairie, but perhaps it was culled from some vague association with the plant's North American ancestry. However, regal it certainly is, most especially in July and August when, from the summit of its 4-7 ft high stems, it sends forth plumes of elegantly bowing flower heads in the most exquisite shade of deep peach-pink. Reflected in the still, dark waters of a marsh, or even of a little artificial pool, *Filipendula rubra* (also listed as *Spiraea lobata*) has the precise delicacy of a painting on a Chinese vase.

There are several fine forms, including *F. r. albicans*, with white or pale pink flowers, and *F. r.* 'Venusta', whose blooms are deep carmine. 'Venusta' is the form that is most commonly cultivated. Filipendulas associate well with purple loosestrife (*Lythrum salicaria*) and yellow loosestrife (*Lysimachia punctata*).

HOW TO GROW
Plant between October and March in ordinary soil, and in a sunny or partly shaded position that does not dry out in summer. Mulch with compost or old manure in April or May, and cut the stems down in late autumn. Propagate by dividing and replanting the crowns between October and March. Alternatively, sow seeds in pans under glass in February or March. Prick off the seedlings into larger boxes when they are big enough to be handled. In June or July set the young plants in a nursery bed; they should be large enough to plant out between October and March.

The flowers of *Filipendula rubra* 'Venusta' are a darker pink. This is the most commonly cultivated form.

Glyceria maxima 'Variegata'

(MANNA GRASS, REED SWEETGRASS)

The bright green, 4-6 ft high reed grass, *Glyceria maxima*, a plant of wet meadows and watersides, abounds in the fens of East Anglia, where it was once cut to provide winter fodder for farm animals and also, mingled with other grasses and sedges, was used in thatching. However, it is far too robust for the usual garden scene. The form 'Variegata' is a beautiful and most valuable plant, being a little shorter and less likely to take over the pond.

It will, in fact, grow in dry positions, though it tends to lose its colour there as summer progresses. The waterside, or even shallow water, is its true element. In spring, it puts forth young leaf shoots of green, striped with pink-flushed white. As the long narrow leaves open out, the pink fades from the white and grassy sprays of cream flowers wave above.

Though the garden form 'Variegata' is not quite so invasive as the species, you must still keep an eye on it to ensure that it does not encroach on or overwhelm less vigorous plants, as it certainly will in moist soils.

HOW TO GROW
Plant in September or spring in a sunny position by the waterside, or in pots in up to 6 in. of water, or in soils to which leaf-mould and other moisture-retentive material has been added. The rootstocks spread very quickly and soon become invasive, so the plant needs to be kept within bounds. Propagate by division in spring.

Glyceria maxima 'Variegata' lies in the foreground of this setting with other variegated-leaved plants.

Hottonia palustris (WATER VIOLET)

The water violet actually looks much more like a
candelabra primula that has been overtaken by a serious
flood. The plant's other name, featherfoil, is more suitable,
since the submerged foliage has a feathery appearance.
These long, lacy underwater leaves are particularly
attractive. From them grow the 1-2 ft high leafless flower
stems that in June lift whorls of pale lilac blooms, each
with a yellow eye, above the surface of the pond.

This charming native of Europe, including Britain, is
happy in water depths ranging from a few inches to 2 ft. It
is, incidentally, an excellent plant for an outdoor aquarium,
since its foliage oxygenates the water – one of the few,
really good, flowering species to do so.

HOW TO GROW
Plant in good soil on the edge of a pond or place in a wire
basket and site in deeper, calm water in spring. Propagate by
division and replant in May. Alternatively, sow seeds in pans
of muddy soil in summer.

When the plant is growing in mud, the lacy foliage is stiff, like parsley. The flowers are scented.

Iris kaempferi

There is a species of iris for almost every possible garden
use; this one was recognised long ago in Japan as being
ideal for the waterside. It is something of a cult in its
country of origin where, since its introduction to the
Western world about 130 years ago, a great many hybrids
and cultivars have been introduced.

These include a number of double forms, and others
with great flat flowers almost a foot across. Best for garden
use are the simpler types close to the original species.
Typically, they are 2 ft or more tall and have small upper
petals and wide, flaring lower ones that range from white
through every shade of blue to deepest purple. A lot of
water is needed when the plants are growing, but not so
much in winter. (The Japanese often flood the beds during
flowering, for both aesthetic and horticultural reasons.)

The related, and similar, *Iris laevigata* likes its feet to be
constantly wet and is therefore excellent if you have the
kind of pond that permits plants to emerge straight from
the water.

I. kaempferi is at its best in July, when, for a midsummer
flowering display, it might be backed by the great horse-
chestnut-like leaves and pink flower spikes of *Rodgersia
pinnata* 'Superba' and fronted by clumps of *Astilbe*, delicate
in leaf and flower.

HOW TO GROW
Iris kaempferi: plant during March and April or in August
and September in lime-free, rich soil, in full sun and in water
up to 6 in. deep. Propagate by dividing the rhizomes after
flowering, or at planting time. Replant immediately, and
mulch annually with humus.
Astilbe: see p. 71.
Rodgersia aesculifolia and R. pinnata 'Superba'*: see p. 118.*

A mass of pink *Astilbe × arendsii* forms the foreground to this poolside
group in early July. A cloud of *Rodgersia aesculifolia* fills the background.
Royal-blue *Iris laevigata* grow to the right, and a rose-purple form of *Iris
kaempferi* flourishes on the far side of the water.

The bright flowers of 'Variegata' appear in late May and early June.

Iris pseudacorus (YELLOW FLAG, FLAG IRIS)

The yellow flag is the fleur-de-lys, originally the fleur de Louis, the emblem of the kings of France, whose three points are said to signify faith, wisdom and valour. Much later on, it became the badge of the Boy Scout movement.

Most valuable for the waterside is *Iris pseudacorus* 'Variegata', one of the best of all moisture-loving plants grown for foliage effect, from the moment the first brilliant yellow spears pierce the mud in spring, until autumn.

After flowering, ornamental brown seed capsules make a fine pattern but, sadly, the seeds will not breed true.

HOW TO GROW
Plant after flowering in late autumn, or in April. Set the rhizomes 1 in. deep in good moist garden soil, near the water's edge or in shallow water. Propagate every three to five years or so by cutting clumps into four or five pieces and replanting them in autumn or in spring.

Branching shiny stems carry five or more of the yellow flowers, 3-3½ in. across, which are sometimes veined with brown.

Lysichiton americanum
(GREAT BOG ARUM, SKUNK CABBAGE)

Abundance of water promotes growth, so that many waterside plants are on a large scale. The great bog arum (or, less happily, skunk cabbage) is one such.

The huge, waxy arum flowers that appear in early spring have yellow spathes, often a foot high. But the leaves may grow to 4 ft long, perhaps a bit much for a small garden – but magnificent in the right surroundings.

HOW TO GROW
Plant two or three-year-old bog arums between April and June in full sun or partial shade. They do best in deep, humus-rich soil by a poolside. Prepare the site first with rich loam to a depth of at least 12 in. Propagate by sowing seed when ripe in trays of wet soil. Pot the seedlings in rich compost and stand them in a tray of water. Plant out when the rootstock is a finger thick. Alternatively, divide established clumps and replant immediately.

The flowers of *Lysichiton americanum* consist of a clear, deep, golden-yellow open spathe, enclosing a thick green spadix.

Bog-bean, rooted under water, flowers in front of *Astilbe × arendsii.*

Menyanthes trifoliata (BOG-BEAN)

The bog-bean grows wild in Britain, most commonly in the north. However, it is well worth cultivating, even in the most sophisticated of collections. It grows best in mud just covered with water.

Thick green, horizontal stems carry the three-lobed leaves from which the Latin specific name is derived. From the stems, bare flower stalks arise in early summer, bearing whorls of pink-flushed white flowers. They make a charming effect when massed, and the plants nearer the pondside can be admired for their prettily fringed petals as well. Menyanthes looks especially fine when grown with *Iris laevigata* 'Variegata'.

HOW TO GROW
Menyanthes trifoliata: plant the rhizomes horizontally in spring, in boggy soil at the pool's edge, so that their roots can grow into the water. Propagate in spring by dividing the roots into lengths, each with a growing tip, and planting in situ.

Native to Britain, *Menyanthes trifoliata* will grow in wet mud or deep water. It will spread, though not uncontrollably.

Lythrum salicaria (PURPLE LOOSESTRIFE)

As long ago as Elizabeth I's reign, it was noted that purple loosestrife grew by 'the Bishop's house-wall at Lambeth, near the Thames', and to this day the 4 ft high spikes of vivid magenta flowers, at their best in July and August, lend their magnificence to watersides all over the country. 'The Beacon' is a deep rose-crimson; 'Robert' is nearer to pink and 'Rose Queen' is paler, but even this is of a strength of colour which makes association with other plants flowering at the same time decidedly difficult.

Perhaps it is better to allow the purple loosestrife to blaze away alone, especially the vivid cultivar 'Fire Candle', surrounded and cooled by a selection of foliage shapes and colours.

Alternatively, you might combine it with an equally brightly coloured plant, so that one complements the other and there is no danger of either looking faded. Try also to achieve a definite contrast of leaf size and shape. You could plant as a background an elegant, clump-forming grass such as *Miscanthus sinensis* 'Gracillimus', which differs from the usual *M. sinensis* by having slim, densely crowded leaves and which seldom exceeds 5 ft in height. In the foreground, have a smaller plant with bushy foliage. Study the flowering periods of the plants you choose, and the seasonal colour changes made by the foliage, and try to achieve an integrated effect of changing colours. *Lythrum salicaria* foliage turns attractive shades of orange and yellow in the autumn.

HOW TO GROW
Plant during October or in spring, in sun or semi-shade, preferably in a wet situation though it will do almost as well in any ordinary garden soil. Propagate by dividing the roots in October or spring.

In the background, *Miscanthus sinensis* 'Gracillimus' is just visible above the *Lythrum salicaria* 'Fire Candle'. This side of the water are a pink polygonum and, in the foreground, *Euphorbia palustris*.

Mimulus cardinalis (MONKEY FLOWER)

It seems that the open-mouthed, snapdragon-like flowers typical of the genus reminded someone of a monkey, so the plants were named *Mimulus*, from the Greek *mimo*, 'an ape'. Not many people have detected the resemblance since, but there is no doubt about the derivation of *cardinalis*, for the blazing red of this species does indeed precisely match the robes of a Prince of the Church.

Raising its brilliant heads some 2 ft high, it looks almost garish among the generally more muted hues of waterside plants, but its flowering season from June to September ensures that the eye will be drawn to the site the whole summer through. In its natural American habitat *Mimulus* is a bog plant; some species, in fact, will grow contentedly in up to 6 in. of water. Most, however, will do just as well in any damp soil.

HOW TO GROW
Plant between March and May in sun or light shade and in any situation that is perpetually moist, though not actually in water. Cut down old flower stems in November, and in very cold districts overwinter the plants under cloches. Propagate by division in March or April, or by taking 2 in. cuttings in April. Alternatively, sow seeds under glass in April for planting out the following spring.

Mimulus cardinalis flourishes at the brink of a garden pond; *Nymphaea* × 'James Brydon' grows in the water alongside.

Nymphaea Hardy hybrids (WATER LILY)

Water lilies are, of course, the classic plants for pools. The great, many-petalled stars, each with a centre of stamens like a sea anemone which has taken to fresh water, are one of the marvels of the aquatic garden.

Monet's studies of water lilies, painted by the pool in his garden at Giverney, were largely inspired by the genius of his compatriot and contemporary J. B. Latour-Marliac, who, in the last quarter of the 19th century, produced a brilliantly coloured range of hardy water lilies bred to succeed at all reasonable water depths.

The first water lilies flower in June, and in the right conditions will continue to bloom throughout the summer. It is therefore vital to choose those that will be happy in the size of pool you can provide. Leaves should be able to spread out with no overlapping and with plenty of water all round; they cannot achieve their full beauty without it. For example, the huge white hybrid 'Gladstoniana', often recommended, needs a couple of feet in depth and at least 10 ft on each side to spread.

For a small, formal garden pool of, say, 10 ft × 8 ft, you might do well to choose the medium-sized water lily *Nymphaea* × 'James Brydon'. Most water lilies close up on sunless days, but this one makes a little more effort and can even on occasion take light shade. It has rounded flowers of clear crimson that would be set off splendidly by the creaminess of Cape pondweed (*Aponogeton distachyos*). Then, for vertical emphasis emerging from the water, add the sword-shaped leaves of variegated sweet flag (*Acorus calamus*).

Not everyone has the space or the inclination to build and maintain an ornamental pool, yet almost all gardeners have, at one time or another, experienced the odd yearning for an aquatic garden. The answer is to create a tiny pool by filling a tub or half a beer barrel with water. One need not be without a water lily in such a miniature garden, for there is a hybrid ideal for the purpose. This is N. × 'Helvola', a plant with attractively red-blotched leaves only 2½-4 in. wide and thriving in only 6 in. of water.

The container should be placed, in full sun, where it can often be visited and the succession of flowers appreciated. Each is pale yellow and about the size of a 50p piece.

HOW TO GROW
Nymphaea: plant during April in water 6 in. to 3 ft deep, either directly into rich soil at the bottom of the pool or in 12 in. square containers enclosing an 8 in. depth of good humus, which should be saturated before planting. Propagate by division or by detaching offsets in April.
Acorus calamus: see p. 364.
Aponogeton distachyos: see p. 364.

Nymphaea × 'Helvola' – a miniature hybrid.

The crimson beauty of 'James Brydon' makes an attractive centrepiece for the small garden pool in late July. The lily's brilliant blooms are a splendid foil for the soft, cream-coloured flowers of Cape pondweed. The flat, floating leaves of both plants need vertical contrast, so plant sweet flag with its variegated, sword-shaped leaves.

Orontium aquaticum (GOLDEN CLUB)

Golden club came from the new-born United States in the 1770s and has been endearing itself to British gardeners ever since. If grown in waterside mud, it carries many of its leaves on stalks up to 12 in. high before leaning outwards to rest upon the ground or other foliage. However, it is much more ornamental when planted in a few inches – up to 12 in. – of water. Then the oval, bright, grey-hued green leaves float on the surface in nearly concentric rings. The flower stalks arise from the centre, topped with bright golden spikes, before falling outwards.

The flowering period extends from April until June, and the leaves remain ornamental until autumn.

HOW TO GROW
Plant between March and June either in rich loam, in water no more than 12 in. deep, or at the boggy edge of a pool. Make sure the rootstock is deeply buried. Propagate by dividing the roots in autumn or spring.

Yellow *Orontium aquaticum* grows in a pool; behind, left, is *Mimulus luteus*, which will flower as the orontium fades.

Pontederia cordata (PICKEREL-WEED)

There are very few blue aquatic plants, and for this reason alone pickerel-weed is well worth growing – at least in largish ponds. True, it will grow well in a really moist border, but it prefers, and certainly looks best, coming out of a few inches of open water. In such a position the blue of the flowers is patterned with light reflected from the ripples below.

Pickerel-weed roots in mud, from which its smooth and fleshy stems grow strongly to a height of 2-3 ft, carrying upward-pointing, heart-shaped leaves. Flower spikes push through the membranes at the leaf bases and come into full colour in July, often continuing until autumn.

HOW TO GROW
Plant in spring, in fertile soil and in water 6-12 in. deep. Spread by creeping rhizomes is usually rapid, and propagation by division in spring provides a ready means of increase.

Pontederia cordata has spikes of purple-blue flowers, each with a yellow eye on the uppermost petal.

Its leaves, each a perfect ace of spades, are a deep, glossy green.

Potamogeton crispus (CURLED PONDWEED)

None of the two dozen or so native potamogetons (pondweeds) can truly be called beautiful, but in small pools, in particular, they are valuable oxygenators and provide shelter for fish.

One of the most decorative is *Potamogeton crispus*, aptly known as the curled pondweed. A completely aquatic species, it has branched stems ranging from 1 to 3 ft, according to water depth and richness of mud or compost, and narrow wavy-edged leaves that are a beautiful bright, translucent green. It is an exuberant grower, especially in the year or two immediately after planting, but slows down later and is easily reduced with a rake.

HOW TO GROW
Plant in spring, in mud at the bottom of a pond or in containers of potting compost. Propagate by inserting small bunches of cuttings in situ in spring.

The leaves of *Potamogeton crispus* open out from its branching stems into loose, curly, feathery fronds in still water.

A spreading mass of *Potamogeton crispus* swirls around *Nymphaea* leaves.

Primula florindae (GIANT COWSLIP)

A watery site is not essential for this Tibetan giant, and it will thrive in a moist border. However, there is little doubt that it is happiest by the pondside, where it will grow to its full and impressive size.

The fat, overwintering buds remain at ground level until well into spring, when leaf growth starts. By May, long-stalked, trowel-shaped leaves have appeared, and from their centre the flower stems shoot up to a height of 3 ft or more, smooth and thickly coated with the waxy white dust (farina) characteristic of primulas. A great mop-head of wide-open, cowslip-like bells breaks out at the top; the flowers are deliciously scented and the display lasts for two months. Easy to grow, *Primula florindae* has been a favourite ever since its introduction in 1926.

Since it flowers when the most distinctive water-garden plants are at their best, you can partner it with almost anything. But for striking contrast, grow it with a shoreside clump of elegant blue Jacob's ladder (*Polemonium caeruleum*). The blue and yellow association could be repeated slightly later in the season with a nearby planting of pickerel-weed (*Pontederia cordata*) and monkey musk (*Mimulus luteus*).

HOW TO GROW
Primula florindae: plant between September and March in moist soil and sun or partial shade. Mulch with fresh compost in February. Propagate by division soon after the plants have ceased flowering, or by seeds sown either when they are ripe or in spring.
Mimulus luteus: see p. 105.
Polemonium caeruleum: see p. 112.
Pontederia cordata: see p. 371.

In this early summer group of water-loving plants, the blue *Polemonium caeruleum* at the back are in full bloom, as are also the tall *Primula florindae* and the *Mimulus luteus* in the foreground. The glossy, heart-shaped leaves of *Pontederia cordata* adorn the middle of the pond; its purple-blue flowers will not appear until August.

Ranunculus lingua (GREATER SPEARWORT)

Though the greater spearwort is one of the most poisonous of our native plants, there is no colourful fruit to attract children, and it can safely be grown in the garden. It is a stately and highly ornamental species.

Rising from a few inches of water, it puts up stout stems to a height of 4-5 ft, carrying narrow, blue-green leaves often as much as a foot long. Flowering is usually rather late – August and September. The flowers are shining buttercups, almost the size and texture of kingcups, and are carried in elegant leafy sprays. *Ranunculus lingua* is particularly valuable for the vertical lines it provides in a water planting.

Like all robust semi-aquatics, it spreads quickly, but it is easily controlled and unlikely to get out of hand.

HOW TO GROW
Plant between September and April in soil that is continuously wet, or in water up to 6 in. deep. Propagate – if necessary – by dividing the rhizomes in spring. However, drastic thinning in autumn or spring is the more usual need.

Ranunculus lingua (Greater spearwort).

Stratiotes aloides (Water-soldier).

Stratiotes aloides (WATER-SOLDIER)

One of the most extraordinary plants in the water garden is the water-soldier.

The plant closely resembles the top of a pineapple that has been cast into the water – a clump of 12 in. long, sword-like leaves sitting on the bottom of the pool. In summer it secretes oxygen, rises to the surface and puts forth white, three-petalled flowers to be pollinated. After pollination, the whole plant sinks again into the depths. In view of its largely submarine existence, it cannot be said that water-soldier makes much of a show – but it is an interesting plant to grow, and also provides a home for all kinds of useful pond creatures.

HOW TO GROW
Place on mud at the bottom of the pond in water up to 2 ft deep. It can reproduce rapidly by means of its offsets, so should therefore be kept under control in small ponds. Propagate by separating offset plants in October. Pond snails can be a nuisance when the plants are small, as they love to eat the young leaves.

Primula japonica (JAPANESE PRIMROSE)

The lovely Japanese primrose is perhaps the best of that marvellous group of candelabra primulas which came from the Himalayas, China and Japan. Though their leaves are much like those on our own hedgebank primroses, their flowers grow in separate, and progressively smaller, cartwheel whorls up the stems.

Candelabra primroses range over the spectrum, excepting only clear blue. *Primula japonica* itself is basically near crimson but, being the easiest of all to grow and seeding itself around like mustard and cress, it is not surprising that wide variations occur. Distinctive named forms include 'Miller's Crimson' and 'Postford White'.

HOW TO GROW
Plant between October and March, in full sun or partial shade, in any fertile garden soil or pondside site that never dries out. To preserve moisture, mulch with peat or well-rotted manure. Propagate by division and replanting after flowering or by seeds sown when ripe or in spring.

Primula japonica 'Postford White' surrounded by *Hosta sieboldiana*.

Magenta flowers of *Primula japonica*, dotted along the side of a stream, add a colourful touch from May to July.

Sagittaria sagittifolia

(COMMON ARROWHEAD, WATER-ARCHER)

The generic and specific names merely insist that this elegant aquatic plant has arrow-shaped leaves. But arrowhead is a highly distinctive plant for still or slow-moving water up to 18 in. deep. Beneath the surface it produces long, grass-like leaves which are almost translucent, but as the season progresses the typical triangular arrow leaves rise in a quiver up to 2 ft in height.

Flower stems stand above, carrying in July and August white, purple-blotched whorls of three-petalled flowers, each the size of a 10p piece. If you have only a small pool with room for just a couple of plants, you could do no better than to choose arrowhead.

HOW TO GROW
Sagittarias require full sun and 6-8 in. of fertile soil covered by up to 18 in. of water. Push the tubers 2-3 in. into the mud in March or April, or set out young growing plants in June. Propagate in June or July by replanting the smallest of the young plants rising round the parent growth.

Small, purple-centred white flowers appear in July and August among the light green, arrow-shaped surface leaves.

PLANTS FOR SPECIAL PURPOSES

The categories listed below are intended as a quick guide for the gardener who is looking for plants with special characteristics, such as colourful autumn foliage or fruits. For detailed advice on the suitability of a plant for a given location, consult the main entry.

Key to letters: A–Annual/biennial; P–Perennial; B–Bulb/corm/tuber; C–Climber; S–Shrub; T–Tree; R–Rock plant; W–Water/bog plant

Plants for autumn colour

Acer griseum T 331
A. japonicum 'Aureum' T 330
A. palmatum 'Senkaki' T 332
Ginkgo biloba T 340
Hamamelis mollis 'Pallida' S 284
Larix decidua T 343
L. × eurolepis T 343
L. kaempferi T 343
Liquidambar styraciflua T 344
Liriodendron tulipifera T 344
Osmunda regalis P 131
Parrotia persica T 348
Parthenocissus henryana C 187
Rhus typhina T 353
Vitis coignetiae C 190

Plants with red, purple or copper leaves

Ajuga reptans 'Purpurea' P 65
Cotinus coggygria 'Royal Purple' S 268
Epimedium × rubrum P 82
Sedum maximum 'Atropurpureum' P 121
Sempervivum tectorum R 218

Plants with grey or silver leaves

Alchemilla mollis P 66
Artemisia absinthium 'Lambrook Silver' P 69
Centaurea dealbata P 74
Cupressus glabra 'Pyramidalis' T 338
Eucalyptus gunnii T 339
Euphorbia characias P 86
Salvia farinacea A 54
S. officinalis S 313
Santolina chamaecyparissus S 314
Saxifraga Kabschia group R 216
S. longifolia R 215
Sedum cauticolum R 217
S. spathulifolium R 217
Stachys olympica P 122
Zauschneria californica R 221

Plants with yellow or gold leaves

Acer japonicum 'Aureum' T 330
Calluna vulgaris 'Beoley Gold' and C. v. 'Gold Haze' S 256
Catalpa bignonioides 'Aurea' T 334
Chamaecyparis lawsoniana 'Lanei' T 335
C. l. 'Lutea' T 335
C. l. 'Minima Aurea' R 201
C. l. 'Stewartii' T 335
C. l. 'Winston Churchill' T 335
C. obtusa 'Crippsii' T 335
C. o. 'Nana Aurea' R 201
Cupressus sempervirens 'Swane's Golden' T 338

Juniperus chinensis 'Aurea' T 342
Ligustrum ovalifolium 'Aureum' S 292
Robinia pseudoacacia 'Frisia' T 354
Thuja occidentalis 'Rheingold' T 358
Thymus × citriodorus 'Aureus' R 219
T. × c. 'E. B. Anderson' R 219

Plants with ornamental fruits

Arbutus unedo T 332
Aucuba japonica S 252
Berberis darwinii S 252
B. rubrostilla S 253
B. × stenophylla S 254
B. thunbergii 'Atropurpurea' S 253
Celastrus orbiculatus C 176
Cotoneaster dammeri S 269
C. horizontalis S 269
C. salicifolius floccosus S 269
C. × watereri S 270
Crataegus laciniata T 336
C. × prunifolia T 337
Hippophae rhamnoides S 284
Hypericum × inodorum 'Elstead' S 288
Ilex × altaclarensis T 341
I. 'Camelliifolia' T 341
I. 'Handsworth New Silver' T 341
I. 'Madame Briot' T 341
I. 'Pyramidalis' T 341
I. 'Pyramidalis Fructoluteo' T 341
Lunaria annua A 41
Mahonia aquifolium S 295
Malus 'John Downie' T 346
Pyracantha 'Orange Glow' S 304
Rosa S 227-45
Ruscus aculeatus S 311
Skimmia japonica S 315
Sorbus aria T 355
S. aucuparia 'Beissneri' T 356
S. hupehensis T 356
Symphoricarpos × doorenbosii 'Mother of Pearl' S 320
Vaccinium corymbosum S 322
Viburnum davidii S 324
V. opulus S 323

Plants with fragrant flowers

Aponogeton distachyos W 364
Buddleia alternifolia S 255
B. fallowiana 'Lochinch' S 254
Cheiranthus × allionii A 21
C. cheiri A 20
Chimonanthus praecox S 262
Convallaria majalis B 147
Daphne blagayana R 202
D. × burkwoodii S 273
D. cneorum R 203
D. mezereum S 273
D. odora 'Aureomarginata' S 274

D. retusa S 274
Dianthus barbatus A 26
D. chinensis A 25
D. Modern pinks P 80
D. Old-fashioned pinks P 80
Erica arborea 'Alpina' S 276
Genista aetnensis S 283
Hamamelis mollis 'Pallida' S 284
Heliotropium × hybridum A 34
Hyacinthus orientalis hybrids B 157
Iris Bearded hybrids P 97
I. bucharica B 157
I. pallida dalmatica P 96
I. reticulata B 158
Jasminum officinale C 184
Lathyrus odoratus A 37
Lavandula angustifolia S 291
Ligustrum ovalifolium S 292
Lilium Aurelian hybrids B 161
L. candidum B 161
L. regale B 162
Lonicera japonica 'Halliana' C 186
L. periclymenum C 186
Magnolia sinensis S 294
M. soulangiana T 346
Malcolmia maritima A 42
Matthiola bicornis A 43
M. incana A 42
Myrtus communis S 296
Narcissus poeticus B 165
Nicotiana alata A 46
N. sylvestris A 47
Philadelphus × 'Beauclerk' S 299
P. coronarius 'Aureus' S 299
Primula florindae P 372
P. vulgaris P 114
Reseda odorata A 53
Robinia pseudoacacia 'Frisia' T 354
Rosa S (note that not all cultivars are fragrant) 227-45
Syringa microphylla S 320
S. vulgaris 'Madame Lemoine' S 320
Verbena × hybrida A 58
Viburnum × bodnantense S 322
V. × burkwoodii S 323
V. opulus S 323

Plants for hedges

Berberis darwinii S 252
B. × stenophylla S 254
B. thunbergii 'Atropurpurea' S 253
Buxus sempervirens S 255
Cornus stolonifera 'Flaviramea' S 266
× Cupressocyparis leylandii T 337
Elaeagnus × ebbingei S 275
E. pungens 'Maculata' S 276
Escallonia 'Langleyensis' S 278
Euonymus japonicus 'Ovatus Aureus' S 279
Hippophae rhamnoides S 284
Lavandula angustifolia S 291
Ligustrum ovalifolium 'Aureum' S 292
Olearia macrodonta S 297
× Osmarea burkwoodii S 297

Prunus × cistena S 302
P. laurocerasus S 303
P. lusitanica S 303
Rosa 'Roseraie de l'Hay' S 239
R. 'Sarah van Fleet' S 240
Rosmarinus officinalis S 310
Santolina chamaecyparissus S 314
Tamarix pentandra S 321
Thuja plicata T 358

Plants with aromatic foliage

Dictamnus albus P 81
Laurus nobilis S 290
Lavandula angustifolia S 291
Lippia citriodora S 293
Monarda didyma 'Cambridge Scarlet' P 106
Myrtus communis S 296
Rosmarinus officinalis S 310
Salvia officinalis S 313
Santolina chamaecyparissus S 314
Thymus × citriodorus R 219
T. drucei R 219

Plants for cut flowers

Achillea filipendulina P 64
Agapanthus × 'Headbourne Hybrids' B 140
Alstroemeria 'Ligtu Hybrids' B 142
Anaphalis cinnamomea P 67
Anemone coronaria 'De Caen' B 144
Antirrhinum majus A 15
Aster frikartii P 70
A. novae-angliae P 70
A. novi-belgii P 70
Calendula officinalis A 18
Callistephus chinensis A 18
Catananche caerulea P 74
Centaurea cyanus A 21
C. dealbata P 74
Cheiranthus × allionii A 21
C. cheiri A 20
Chrysanthemum carinatum A 21
C. maximum P 76
C. parthenium A 22
C. rubellum P 75
Clarkia elegans A 22
Coreopsis drummondii A 24
C. verticillata P 77
Cortaderia selloana P 132
Cosmos bipinnatus A 24
Dahlia variabilis A 25
Delphinium ajacis A 24
D. Belladonna varieties P 78
D. Large-flowered varieties P 79
Dianthus barbatus A 26
D. Modern pinks P 80
D. Old-fashioned pinks P 80
Digitalis grandiflora P 81
D. purpurea A 27
Doronicum plantagineum P 82
Echinops ritro P 83
Erigeron speciosus P 84

Gaillardia aristata P 87
Gladiolus 'Albert Schweitzer' B 156
G. byzantinus B 155
G. Small-flowered B 156
Gypsophila elegans A 33
G. paniculata P 90
Helenium autumnale P 91
Helichrysum bracteatum A 28
H. petiolatum A 33
Heuchera sanguinea P 93
Iberis umbellata A 34
Iris Bearded hybrids P 97
I. kaempferi P 367
I. pallida dalmatica P 96
I. pseudacorus W 368
I. xiphioides B 159
I. xiphium B 159
Lathyrus odoratus A 37
Lilium Asiatic hybrids B 160
L. candidum B 161
L. regale B 162
L. tigrinum B 163
Limonium latifolium P 100
L. sinuatum A 28
Lupinus Russell strain P 102
Lychnis chalcedonica P 103
L. coronaria P 103
Matthiola bicornis A 43
M. incana A 42
Narcissus poeticus B 165
N. pseudonarcissus B 165
Nigella damascena A 47
Paeonia lactiflora P 107
P. officinalis P 108
Phlox drummondii A 51
P. maculata P 111
P. paniculata P 110
Physostegia virginiana P 111
Reseda odorata A 53
Rudbeckia laciniata P 118
Scabiosa atropurpurea A 55
S. caucasica P 120
Schizostylis coccinea B 167
Trollius × hybridus P 125
Tulipa Cottage group B 171
T. Darwin group B 169
T. Lily-flowered group B 170
Verbascum × hybridum P 126
Zantedeschia aethiopica 'Crowborough' P 127
Zauschneria californica R 221

Plants for winter interest

Arum italicum 'Pictum' P 69
Betula pendula 'Youngii' T 333
Chimonanthus praecox S 262
Cornus alba S 266
Cornus stolonifera S 266
Corylus avellana 'Contorta' S 267
Daphne mezereum S 273
Daphne odora 'Aureomarginata' S 274
Hamamelis mollis 'Pallida' S 284
Helleborus lividus corsicus P 92
Iris foetidissima P 96
Salix matsudana 'Tortuosa' T 355

INDEX AND PLANT SELECTION CHART

This combined index and chart can be used in two ways. Firstly, it is a conventional index. Page numbers in bold type identify main entries; page numbers in ordinary type indicate a mention elsewhere, usually in an association with another plant or plants. Secondly, the plant selection chart provides an at-a-glance reference for the gardener seeking a plant that will suit a particular situation in his garden. Most plants will tolerate a wide range of conditions; many will grow well in extremes. For more detailed information on how to grow each plant, read the main entry. For common names see page 383.

KEY TO SYMBOLS USED IN THE CHART

Type of plant This column identifies each plant with one of the nine section headings used within the book.

Ann — Annuals and biennials
Per — Perennials
Bulb — Bulbs, corms and tubers
Clmb — Climbing plants
Rock — Rock plants
Rose — Roses
Shrb — Shrubs
Tree — Trees
Wtr — Water plants

Soil Most plants will grow in any ordinary fertile soil. However, some do best in certain types of soil or will tolerate them better than other plants. The following letters indicate the preferences as listed.

O — Grows in ordinary fertile soil
D — Tolerates dry soil
M — Does best in moisture-retentive to wet soil
L — Needs or will tolerate chalky, or alkaline, soils
A — Needs an acid soil

Situation The symbols below show the most suitable site for each plant or the conditions which it will tolerate.

☼ — Does best in full sun
● — Does best in shade or dappled shade
◑ — Grows well in either sun or light shade
🌬 — Will tolerate exposed, windy sites
🏛 — Plant does best on a sheltered site

Flowering time Taking January as month 1, the numbers 1-12 indicate the months of the year when each plant is in flower. For example, 6-8 indicates that a plant blooms from June to August. If no numbers occur, flowering is insignificant.

Height The maximum likely to be obtained by a mature plant under ideal growing conditions. For trees and shrubs, 'mature' is taken to be 20 years old.

A

Name	Type of plant	Soil	Situation	Flowering time	Height
Abelia × grandiflora 251	Shrb	O	☼	7-10	5 ft
Abies koreana 330	Tree	A	◑	5	15 ft
Abutilon × hybridum 12	Ann	O	☼🏛	5-10	6 ft
striatum 'Thompsonii' 12	Ann	O	☼🏛	5-10	6 ft
vitifolium 250	Shrb	O	☼🏛	5-10	8 ft
Acanthus spinosus 64, 121	Per	D	☼	7-8	4 ft
Acer griseum 331	Tree	ML	◑	4-5	20 ft
japonicum 'Aureum' 330	Tree	ML	◑🏛	3-5	15 ft
palmatum 'Senkaki' 146, 332	Tree	O	●🏛	4-5	20 ft
pseudoplatanus 'Brilliantissimum' 331	Tree	ML	◑🏛	4-5	20 ft
Achillea × argentea 196	Rock	O	☼	5-6	6 in
filipendulina 64, 118, 140, 304	Per	DO	☼	6-9	4 ft
× 'King Edward' 196	Rock	O	☼	5-9	6 in
taygetea 'Moonshine' 65	Per	DO	☼	6-9	2 ft
tomentosa 196	Rock	O	☼	7-9	9 in
Aconitum napellus 65	Per	O	●	7-8	5 ft
Acorus calamus 'Variegatus' 364, 370	Wtr	M	☼		3 ft
Acrolinium roseum: see Helipterum roseum					
Actinidia kolomikta 176	Clmb	O	◑	6	12 ft
Adiantum pedatum 129	Per	O	●		15 in
Aesculus parviflora 251, 253	Shrb	O	◑	7-8	8 ft
Aethionema grandiflorum 196	Rock	D	☼	5-6	9 in
× 'Warley Rose' 195	Rock	D	☼	5	6 in
Agapanthus × 'Headbourne Hybrids' 117, 140, 147, 162, 298	Bulb	O	●	7-9	3 ft
Ageratum houstonianum 12	Ann	O	◑	6-10	12 in
mexicanum: see A. houstonianum					
Agrostemma coronaria: see Lychnis coronaria					

Name	Type of plant	Soil	Situation	Flowering time	Height
githago 'Milas' 12	Ann	O	☼	6-9	3 ft
Agrostis nebulosa 31	Ann	O	☼	7-8	15 in
Ajuga reptans 65, 107, 308	Per	O	◑	6-7	9 in
Akebia quinata 176	Clmb	O	◑	4	15 ft
Alcea: see Althaea rosea					
Alchemilla mollis 66, 98, 119	Per	O	◑	6-8	12 in
Allium albopilosum 140, 181, 315	Bulb	DO	☼	6	18 in
karataviense 122, 141	Bulb	DO	☼	5-6	12 in
moly 132, 141	Bulb	DO	☼	6-7	12 in
siculum 141, 264	Bulb	DO	☼	5-6	4 ft
Aloysia citriodora: see Lippia citriodora					
Alstroemeria aurantiaca 143	Bulb	DO	☼	6-9	3 ft
Ligtu hybrids 142	Bulb	DO	☼	6-9	3 ft
Althaea chinensis: see A. rosea					
frutex: see Hibiscus syriacus					
rosea 13	Ann	M	☼	7-9	9 ft
Alyssum saxatile 44, 52, 145, 151, 163, 197, 199	Rock	D	☼	4-6	12 in
Amaranthus caudatus 14, 15	Ann	O	☼	7-10	4 ft
Amaryllis belladonna 143	Bulb	DL	☼	9-10	2½ ft
Amelanchier lamarckii 251	Shrb	O	◑	4	10 ft
Anaphalis cinnamomea 67, 88	Per	O	◑	7-9	2 ft
triplinervis 67	Per	O	◑	8	12 in
yedoensis: see A. cinnamomea					
Anchusa azurea 'Loddon Royalist' 66	Per	D	☼	6-8	5 ft
capensis 14	Ann	O	☼	7-8	18 in
italica: see A. azurea					
Andromeda japonica: see Pieris japonica					
Androsace carnea 196	Rock	OL	☼	5-6	3 in
sarmentosa 196	Rock	OL	☼	5-6	4 in

Name	Type of plant	Soil	Situation	Flowering time	Height
Anemone blanda 115, 143, 274	Bulb	OL	◑	2-4	6 in
coronaria 'De Caen' 144	Bulb	DL	☼	3-4	12 in
× hybrida 67, 70, 287	Per	O	●	8-10	4 ft
japonica: see A. × hybrida					
nemorosa 128, 144, 152	Bulb	ML	●	3-4	8 in
Anthemis cupaniana 68, 88, 159	Per	O	☼	4-8	12 in
Anthericum liliago 145, 203	Bulb	O	◑	5-6	2 ft
Antirrhinum majus 15	Ann	D	☼	7-10	4 ft
Aponogeton distachyos 364, 370	Wtr	M	●	4-12	18 in
Aquilegia bertolonii 197, 209	Rock	O	◑	5-6	6 in
flabellata 197	Rock	O	◑	5-7	10 in
vulgaris 68	Per	O	◑	5-6	2 ft
Arabis caucasica 14	Ann	DL	☼	2-6	9 in
ferdinandi coburgii 'Variegata' 198, 209	Rock	D	☼	2-6	3 in
Aralia elata 252	Shrb	O	◑🏛	8	10 ft
japonica: see Fatsia japonica					
sieboldii: see Fatsia japonica					
Arbutus andrachne 332	Tree	D	◑🏛	3-4	15 ft
× andrachnoides 332	Tree	DL	◑🏛	3-4	15 ft
unedo 332	Tree	DL	◑🏛	10-12	15 ft
Armeria caespitosa 198	Rock	DL	☼	5-6	3 in
maritima 198	Rock	DL	☼	5-7	12 in
Artemisia absinthium 'Lambrook Silver' 69, 74, 80, 99, 156, 230	Per	D	☼	7-8	2½ ft
Arum italicum 'Pictum' 69, 128, 157	Per	M	◑	4-5	12 in
Asplenium scolopendrium 128, 319	Per	O	●		2 ft
Aster alpinus 198, 219	Rock	O	☼	7	6 in
× frikartii 70, 121	Per	O	☼	8-10	3 ft
novae-angliae 70, 112	Per	O	☼	8-11	5 ft
novi-belgii 70, 167	Per	O	☼	9-11	4 ft

	Type of plant	Soil	Situation	Flowering time	Height
Astilbe × arendsii **71**, 151, 280, 367, 368	Per	M	●	6-8	3 ft
Astrantia major 71	Per	O	●	6-7	2 ft
Athyrium filix-femina **130**, 163, 197, 319	Per	M	●		3 ft
Atriplex hortensis 16	Ann	O	☀◔		4 ft
Aubrieta deltoidea 14, 171, 197, **199**	Rock	D	☀	3-6	4 in
Aucuba japonica 252	Shrb	O	●	3-4	10 ft
Azalea: see *Rhododendron*					

B

	Type of plant	Soil	Situation	Flowering time	Height
Bartonia aurea: see *Mentzelia lindleyi*					
Begonia semperflorens 17, 34	Ann	O	☀	6-10	12 in
× *tuberhybrida* 16	Ann	O	◑	6-9	18 in
Bellis perennis Monstrosa 16, 220	Ann	O	◑	4-7	6 in
Berberis darwinii 252, 254	Shrb	OL	◑	4-5	8 ft
× *rubrostilla* 253, 356	Shrb	OL	☀	5	4 ft
× *stenophylla* 254	Shrb	OL	☀	4	8 ft
thunbergii 'Atropurpurea' 65, 227, 253	Shrb	OL	☀	5	4 ft
'Atropurpurea Nana' 205	Shrb	OL	☀	5	4 ft
Bergenia cordifolia 72, 133, 135, 345	Per	OL	◑	3-4	12 in
purpurascens × 'Admiral' 72	Per	OL	◑	4-5	15 in
× 'Silberlicht' 72, 99, 190, 292	Per	OL	◑	4-5	15 in
Betula pendula 308	Tree	O	◑	4-5	50 ft
'Youngii' 333	Tree	O	◑	4-5	10 ft
Bocconia cordata: see *Macleaya cordata*					
Briza maxima 24, 31	Ann	DO	☀	5-7	18 in
Brodiaea uniflora: see *Ipheion uniflorum*					
Buddleia alternifolia 255	Shrb	OL	☀	6	15 ft
davidii 254, 255	Shrb	DL	☀	7-10	10 ft
fallowiana 'Lochinch' 254	Shrb	DL	☀▥	7-10	8 ft
Bupleurum fruticosum 255, 321	Shrb	DL	☀▥	7-9	6 ft
Butomus umbellatus 364	Wtr	M	◑	6-7	4 ft
Buxus sempervirens 48, 255	Shrb	O	◑	4	10 ft

C

	Type of plant	Soil	Situation	Flowering time	Height
Calceolaria integrifolia 17	Ann	OD	☀	7-9	2 ft
mexicana 17	Ann	OD	☀	7-9	10 in
Calendula officinalis 18	Ann	D	☀	5-9	2 ft
Calla palustris 365	Wtr	M	◑	6-7	9 in
Calliopsis drummondii: see *Coreopsis drummondii*					

	Type of plant	Soil	Situation	Flowering time	Height
Callistephus chinensis 18	Ann	O	☀	7-10	2½ ft
Calluna vulgaris 211, **256**, 265, 337, 342	Shrb	DA	☀	7-11	2 ft
Caltha palustris 159, 365	Wtr	M	◑	4-5	12 in
Camassia leichtlinii 21, **145**	Bulb	M	◑	6-7	3 ft
Camellia 257-8					
japonica 257	Shrb	OA	●▥	2-5	12 ft
'Adolphe Audusson' 258	Shrb	OA	●▥	2-5	12 ft
reticulata 257	Shrb	OA	●▥	2-4	15 ft
saluenensis 257	Shrb	OA	●▥	3-4	15 ft
sasanqua 257	Shrb	OA	●▥	11-2	15 ft
× *williamsii* 257	Shrb	OA	●▥	11-4	8 ft
'J. C. Williams' 258	Shrb	OA	●▥	11-4	8 ft
Campanula cochleariifolia **200**	Rock	DL	☀	7-9	6 in
garganica 200	Rock	DL	☀	6-9	6 in
lactiflora 73, 79, 83, 124	Per	O	☀	6-9	5 ft
medium 19	Ann	D	◑	5-7	3 ft
muralis: see *C. portenschlagiana*					
persicifolia 72, 108, 181, 238, 270	Per	O	☀	6-8	4 ft
portenschlagiana 30, 41, 49, **200**, 211, 218	Rock	DL	◑	7-9	6 in
Campsis grandiflora 176	Clmb	O	☀▥	8-9	20 ft
Canna × *generalis* 19, 35	Ann	O	☀	7-11	4 ft
× *hybrida*: see *C.* × *generalis*					
indica: see *C.* × *generalis*					
Carex elata 365	Per	M	◑	5-6	3 ft
Carpenteria californica 259	Shrb	DL	☀	6-7	8 ft
Carpinus betulus 333	Tree	D	◑	4-5	20 ft
Caryopteris × *clandonensis* 143, 238, **259**	Shrb	O	☀▥	8-9	2 ft
Catalpa bignonioides **334**, 342	Tree	O	☀	7	15 ft
Catananche caerulea 74	Per	D	☀	6-8	2 ft
Ceanothus × 'Delight' 260	Shrb	D	☀▥	5	10 ft
× 'Gloire de Versailles' 260	Shrb	D	☀▥	7-9	8 ft
thyrsiflorus 'Repens' 260	Shrb	DL	☀▥	5-6	4 ft
Celastrus orbiculatus 176	Clmb	O	◑		40 ft
Centaurea cyanus 21	Ann	D	☀	6-9	3 ft
dealbata 'John Coutts' 74	Per	D	☀	6-10	18 in
moschata 21	Ann	D	☀	6-9	2 ft
Centranthus ruber 66, 75	Per	DL	☀	6-8	3 ft
Cerastium tomentosum 197, **200**	Rock	DL	☀	5-6	6 in
Ceratostigma willmottianum 120, **261**	Shrb	D	☀▥	7-9	4 ft
Cercis siliquastrum 334	Tree	DL	☀	5	20 ft
Chaenomeles speciosa 172, **261**	Shrb	O	☀	1-4	6 ft
Chamaecyparis (Dwarf forms) 201	Rock	O	☀		
lawsoniana 147, 245, **335**, 349	Tree	OL	☀		60 ft
obtusa 201, **335**	Tree	OA	☀		25 ft
pisifera 'Boulevard' 167, 201	Rock	O	☀		15 ft
Cheiranthus × *allionii* 21, 145	Ann	DL	☀	5-7	18 in
cheiri 20, 171	Ann	DL	☀	4-6	2 ft
Chimonanthus praecox 149, **262**	Shrb	OL	☀▥	12-2	10 ft

	Type of plant	Soil	Situation	Flowering time	Height
Chionodoxa luciliae 145, 164	Bulb	D	☀	2-4	6 in
Choisya ternata 55, **263**, 342	Shrb	O	☀▥	4-5	8 ft
Chrysanthemum carinatum 21	Ann	D	☀	6-9	2 ft
coccineum 75	Per	O	☀	6-7	3 ft
maximum 76, 118	Per	O	☀	6-8	3 ft
parthenium 16, 22	Ann	D	☀	7-9	18 in
rubellum 75	Per	O	☀	9-10	2 ft
tricolor: see *C. carinatum*					
Cistus 86, 263	Shrb	DL	☀▥		
corbariensis 159, 263	Shrb	DL	☀▥	5-7	4 ft
crispus 86, 168, **264**	Shrb	DL	☀▥	7	2 ft
× *cyprius* 263	Shrb	DL	☀▥	5-7	6 ft
× *purpureus* 55, 68, **264**, 300	Shrb	DL	☀▥	5-7	4 ft
'Silver Pink' 263	Shrb	DL	☀▥	5-7	3 ft
Clarkia elegans 12, **22**, 31, 34	Ann	D	☀	7-9	2 ft
unguiculata: see *C. elegans*					
Clematis 177					
armandii 177, **178**	Clmb	OL	☀▥	4-5	30 ft
× 'Ernest Markham' 177, 178	Clmb	OL	◑	6-9	12 ft
× 'Huldine' 177	Clmb	OL	◑	7-10	12 ft
× *jackmanii* 177	Clmb	OL	◑	7-10	13 ft
× 'Jackmanii Superba' 179	Clmb	OL	◑	7-10	12 ft
Large-flowered hybrids 178	Clmb	OL	◑	5-11	12 ft
× 'Lasurstern' 177, 178	Clmb	OL	◑	5-9	12 ft
macropetala 180	Clmb	OL	◑	5-6	12 ft
montana 177, **180**, 184	Clmb	OL	◑	5-6	40 ft
× 'Mrs Cholmondeley' 178, 187	Clmb	OL	◑	5-8	12 ft
× 'Nellie Moser' 177, 178	Clmb	OL	◑	5-9	12 ft
× 'Perle d'Azur' 177, 243	Clmb	OL	◑	6-8	12 ft
tangutica 181	Clmb	OL	◑	8-10	20 ft
viticella 177, **181**, 242, 262, 267, 268	Clmb	OL	◑	7-9	12 ft
Cleome pungens: see *C. spinosa*					
spinosa 22	Ann	O	☀	7-9	4 ft
Clerodendrum trichotomum 265	Shrb	O	☀	8-9	10 ft
Clethra alnifolia 265	Shrb	MA	◑	8-10	8 ft
Cobaea scandens 182	Clmb	O	☀▥	8-10	12 ft
Colchicum agrippinum 146	Bulb	O	◑	9-11	6 in
autumnale 74, 101, **147**	Bulb	O	◑	9-10	10 in
speciosum 67, **146**, 239, 290	Bulb	O	◑	9-11	16 in
Coleus blumei 23, 35, 54	Ann	O	◑		18 in
Colutea arborescens 265	Shrb	D	☀	6-9	10 ft
Convallaria majalis 147	Bulb	ML	●	4-5	8 in
Convolvulus tricolor 'Blue Ensign' 23	Ann	D	☀	7-9	10 in
Coreopsis drummondii 24	Ann	D	☀	7-9	2 ft
verticillata 76, 77	Per	O	☀	6-9	2 ft
Cornus alba 'Sibirica' **266**, 355	Shrb	M	◑	5-6	10 ft
'Spaethii' 103, 125, 163, **266**, 280, 318	Shrb	M	◑	5-6	10 ft
kousa chinensis 266	Shrb	M	◑	6	15 ft

Type of plant: Ann – annual, biennial; Per – perennial; Bulb – bulb, corm, tuber; Clmb – climber; Rock – rock plant; Rose – rose; Shrb – shrub; Tree – tree; Wtr – water plant
Soil: O – ordinary fertile; D – tolerates dry; M – moisture-retentive to wet; L – needs or tolerates chalk and lime; A – needs acid soil
Situation: ☀ – best in full sun; ● – best in shade or dappled shade; ◑ – sun or light shade; ◔ – tolerates exposed, windy sites; ▥ – needs sheltered site
Flowering months: Represented by the numbers 1–12   **Height:** Maximum, mature plant (or 20 years for trees and shrubs)

Name	Type of plant	Soil	Situation	Flowering time	Height
nuttallii **336**	Tree	M	☼▦	5-6	20 ft
stolonifera 'Flaviramea' **266**, 355	Shrb	M	☼	5-6	8 ft
Coronilla glauca **267**	Shrb	D	☼▦	3-4	6 ft
Cortaderia selloana **132**, 259	Per	O	☼	9	8 ft
Corydalis lutea 77, **152**	Per	D	●	4-11	8 in
Corylopsis willmottiae 88, **268**, 295	Shrb	M	☼▦	3-4	10 ft
Corylus avellana 'Contorta' **267**	Shrb	D	☼	1-2	20 ft
Cosmos bipinnatus **24**	Ann	D	☼	8-9	4 ft
sulphureus **24**	Ann	D	☼	8-9	2½ ft
Cotinus coggygria 'Royal Purple' 94, 143, **268**	Shrb	D	☼	6-7	10 ft
Cotoneaster dammeri **269**, 356	Shrb	O	☼	6	3 in
horizontalis 21, **269**, 303, 308, 347	Shrb	D	☼	5-6	2 ft
salicifolius floccosus **269**	Shrb	O	☼	6	12 in
× *watereri* **270**	Shrb	O	☼	6	15 ft
Crambe cordifolia 13, **78**	Per	D	☼	6	6 ft
Crataegus laciniata **336**	Tree	D	☼	6	18 ft
orientalis: see *C. laciniata*					
× *prunifolia* **337**	Tree	D	☼	6	15 ft
Crinodendron hookerianum **271**	Shrb	OA	☼▦	5	15 ft
Crinum × *powellii* 117, **147**, 254	Bulb	O	☼▦	8-9	3 ft
Crocosmia × *crocosmiiflora* 19, 78, 134, **148**	Bulb	D	☼	7-9	2 ft
Crocus aureus 'Dutch Yellow' **148**, 153, 164, 168	Bulb	O	☼	2-3	5 in
luteus: see *C. aureus*					
speciosus **149**	Bulb	O	☼	10	5 in
tomasinianus **149**, 243	Bulb	O	☼	3	3 in
vernus 148, **149**, 164, 266, 330	Bulb	O	☼	3	5 in
Cryptomeria japonica (Dwarf forms) **202**	Rock	O	☼		3 ft
× *Cupressocyparis leylandii* **337**	Tree	O	☼●		50 ft
Cupressus arizonica 'Pyramidalis': see *C. glabra* 'Pyramidalis'					
glabra 'Pyramidalis' **338**	Tree	D	☼		30 ft
sempervirens 'Swane's Golden' **338**	Tree	D	☼		25 ft
Cyclamen coum 149, **150**, 158	Bulb	DL	●▦	12-3	3 in
hederifolium **150**, 213, 295, 317	Bulb	DL	●	8-10	4 in
ibericum: see *C. coum*					
neopolitanum: see *C. hederifolium*					
orbiculatum: see *C. coum*					
vernum: see *C. coum*					
Cynoglossum nervosum **78**	Per	D	☼	6-7	2 ft
Cytisus battandieri **271**, 281	Shrb	D	☼	5-6	15 ft
× *beanii* **202**	Rock	D	☼	5	12 in
× *kewensis* **202**	Rock	D	☼	5	2 ft
× *praecox* **272**	Shrb	D	☼	5	6 ft
scoparius 'Andreanus' **271**	Shrb	D	☼●	5-6	8 ft

D

Name	Type of plant	Soil	Situation	Flowering time	Height
Daboecia cantabrica **273**	Shrb	MA	☼	6-11	18 in
polifolia: see *D. cantabrica*					

Name	Type of plant	Soil	Situation	Flowering time	Height
Dahlia variabilis **25**, 87, 106	Ann	O	☼	7-10	2 ft
Daphne blagayana **202**	Rock	O	●	4-5	6 in
× *burkwoodii* **273**, 342	Shrb	O	☼	5-6	4 ft
cneorum **203**	Rock	OL	☼	5-6	6 in
collina 202	Rock	O	☼	5-6	2 ft
mezereum 167, **273**	Shrb	OL	☼	2-4	4 ft
odora 'Aureomarginata' 188, **274**	Shrb	O	☼▦	2-4	5 ft
retusa **274**	Shrb	O	☼▦	5-6	2 ft
tangutica **274**	Shrb	O	☼▦	3-4	4 ft
Davidia involucrata **338**	Tree	O	●▦	5	20 ft
Delphinium (Large-flowered hybrids) 79, 123, 238	Per	O	☼	6-7	5 ft
ajacis 24, 33, 43	Ann	D	☼	6-8	3 ft
Belladonna varieties 78, 107, 123	Per	O	☼	6-7	4½ ft
Deutzia × *hybrida* 'Mont Rose' **275**	Shrb	D	☼	6-7	6 ft
Dianthus 90, 99, 103, 119, 120, 313					
alpinus **203**	Rock	DL	☼	5-8	4 in
barbatus **26**, 43, 66	Ann	D	☼	6-7	2 ft
chinensis **25**	Ann	D	☼	7-10	12 in
deltoides 59, **204**	Rock	DL	☼	6-7	9 in
Modern pinks **80**	Per	DL	☼	6-7	15 in
Old-fashioned pinks 28, **80**, 120, 146, 230, 236	Per	DL	☼	6	15 in
Diascia × 'Ruby Field' **204**	Rock	D	☼	5-8	12 in
Dicentra formosa **81**	Per	O	●▦	5-6	18 in
Dictamnus albus **81**	Per	DL	☼	6-7	3 ft
fraxinella: see *D. albus*					
Dierama pulcherrimum **151**	Bulb	OM	☼▦	8-10	6 ft
Digitalis ambigua: see *D. grandiflora*					
grandiflora **81**	Per	OL	☼	7-8	3 ft
purpurea 27, **81**, 290	Ann	O	☼	6-7	5 ft
Dimorphotheca aurantiaca **27**	Ann	D	☼	6-9	18 in
Doronicum plantagineum **82**, 199, 261	Per	OM	☼	4-6	2 ft
Dorotheanthus bellidiformis: see *Mesembryanthemum criniflorum*					
Draba aizoides **204**, 215	Rock	D	☼	3-4	4 in
bryoides **204**	Rock	D	☼	3-4	2 in
rigida bryoides: see *D. bryoides*					
Dryas octopetala 127, 199, **205**	Rock	DL	☼	5-6	3 in
Dryopteris borreri: see *D. pseudomas*					
dilatata 129	Per	O	●		4 ft
filix-mas **129**, 163, 197	Per	O	●		4 ft
pseudomas 129	Per	O	●		3 ft

E

Name	Type of plant	Soil	Situation	Flowering time	Height
Eccremocarpus scaber 176, **182**	Clmb	D	☼▦	6-10	10 ft
Echinacea purpurea **82**	Per	O	☼	7-9	4 ft
Echinops ritro **83**	Per	D	☼	7-8	4 ft
Echium lycopsis **29**, 31	Ann	D	☼	6-8	3 ft
vulgare: see *E. lycopsis*					

Name	Type of plant	Soil	Situation	Flowering time	Height
Elaeagnus angustifolia **275**	Shrb	O	☼●	6	15 ft
× *ebbingei* **275**	Shrb	D	☼	10	15 ft
pungens 'Maculata' **276**	Shrb	D	☼	10-11	12 ft
Embothrium coccineum **338**	Tree	MA	☼▦	5-6	20 ft
Endymion campanulatus: see *E. hispanicus*					
hispanicus **151**, 274, 278, 309	Bulb	OL	●	4-6	12 in
Epimedium × *rubrum* **82**	Per	O	●	5	12 in
Eranthis hyemalis 149, **153**, 168	Bulb	O	☼	1-3	4 in
Erica arborea 'Alpina' **276**	Shrb	DL	☼▦	3-4	10 ft
carnea 150, 165, 203, 211, 256, 277, 335, 349	Shrb	DL	☼	11-4	12 in
vagans 203, **277**	Shrb	DA	☼	7-10	2 ft
Erigeron speciosus **84**	Per	O	☼	6-8	2 ft
Erinus alpinus **206**	Rock	D	☼	3-7	3 in
Eryngium × *oliverianum* **84**, 121, 134	Per	D	☼	7-9	2 ft
variifolium 44, **84**, 107	Per	D	☼●	7-8	2 ft
Erythronium revolutum **152**	Bulb	O	●	4-5	12 in
tuolumnense 144, **152**	Bulb	O	●	4-5	12 in
Escallonia Donard Hybrids **278**	Shrb	OL	☼▦	6-9	8 ft
× *iveyi* **276**, 278	Shrb	O	☼▦	7-10	10 ft
× 'Langleyensis' **278**	Shrb	OL	☼▦	6-7	8 ft
Eschscholzia californica 14, 23, **29**, 51, 135	Ann	D	☼	6-10	15 in
Eucalyptus gunnii 230, 315, **339**	Tree	O	☼	7-8	45 ft
niphophila **339**	Tree	O	☼	6	20 ft
Eucryphia × *nymansensis* **278**	Shrb	OA	☼▦	8	15 ft
Euonymus europaeus 'Red Cascade' **279**, 337	Shrb	DL	☼	5	12 ft
fortunei 'Silver Queen' **279**, 308	Shrb	O	☼	5-6	4 ft
japonicus **279**, 284	Shrb	O	☼	5-6	6 ft
Eupatorium purpureum **85**	Per	O	☼	8-10	7 ft
Euphorbia characias **86**, 326-7, 339	Per	DL	☼▦	3-7	4 ft
wulfenii **86**, 168	Per	DL	☼▦	3-7	4 ft
epithymoides: see *E. polychroma*					
griffithii 'Fireglow' **85**	Per	O	☼	5-6	2½ ft
polychroma 85, **86**, 261	Per	D	☼	3-5	18 in
veneta: see *E. characias wulfenii*					
Euryops acraeus 203, **206**	Rock	D	☼▦	5-6	12 in
evansii: see *E. acraeus*					
Everlasting flowers 28	Ann	D	☼	7-9	2½ ft
Exochorda giraldii **280**	Shrb	O	☼	5	12 ft

F

Name	Type of plant	Soil	Situation	Flowering time	Height
Fagus sylvatica **340**	Tree	DL	☼		30 ft
Fatsia japonica 101, **280**	Shrb	D	●	10	10 ft
Felicia amelloides **29**	Ann	D	☼●	6-8	18 in
bergeriana **29**	Ann	D	☼	6-9	6 in
Ferns 128					
Festuca glauca 44, **132**, 140, 144, 221	Per	O	☼	6-7	9 in
Filipendula 94					
hexapetala: see *F. vulgaris*					

Filipendula (continued)

	Type of plant	Soil	Situation	Flowering time	Height
rubra 366	Wtr	M	◐	7-8	7 ft
ulmaria 86	Per	OM	◐	6-8	18 in
vulgaris 'Flore Pleno' 86	Per	OL	☼	6-7	2½ ft
Foeniculum vulgare 'Purpureum' 87	Per	D	☼	7-8	6 ft
Forsythia suspensa 272, 281	Shrb	D	◐	3-4	10 ft
Fothergilla major 282, 309	Shrb	MA	☼	5	6 ft
Fritillaria imperialis 154	Bulb	O	◐	4	3 ft
meleagris 115, 153, 315	Bulb	M	◐	4-5	12 in
Fuchsia (Hybrids) 30, 34	Ann	O	◐▦	6-9	2 ft
magellanica gracilis 30, 74, 281	Shrb	D	◐	6-10	6 ft

G

	Type of plant	Soil	Situation	Flowering time	Height
Gaillardia aristata 87	Per	D	☼	6-10	2 ft
Galanthus elwesii 155	Bulb	O	●	2-3	10 in
nivalis 69, 88, 92, 150, 153, **155**, 158, 168, 243, 262	Bulb	O	●	1-3	8 in
Galtonia candicans 155, 188, 278	Bulb	O	☼▦	7-10	4 ft
Garrya elliptica 282	Shrb	D	☼▦	1-3	15 ft
Gazania × hybrida 32	Ann	D	☼⚘	7-10	9 in
× splendens 32	Ann	D	☼⚘	7-9	9 in
Genista aetnensis 283	Shrb	D	☼	7	15 ft
lydia 140, 211, **283**, 317	Shrb	D	☼	5-6	3 ft
Gentiana acaulis 207, 219	Rock	O	☼	5-6	3 in
asclepiadea 89, 160, 190	Per	M	●	7-8	3 ft
septemfida 206	Rock	M	◐	7-8	12 in
verna 207	Rock	O	☼	5-6	3 in
Geranium armenum: see G. psilostemon					
dalmaticum 59, **207**, 219	Rock	O	☼	6-8	5 in
endressii 73, **89**, 236	Per	O	◐	5-8	18 in
'Johnson's Blue' 88, 93	Per	O	◐	7-8	15 in
psilostemon 27, 88	Per	O	◐	6-7	2½ ft
Geum × borisii 90	Per	O	◐	6-9	12 in
Ginkgo biloba 340	Tree	O	☼		20 ft
Gladiolus byzantinus 155'	Bulb	D	☼	6-7	2 ft
Large-flowered 156	Bulb	D	☼▦	7-9	4 ft
Small-flowered 156, 188	Bulb	D	☼	7-8	3 ft
Gleditsia triacanthos 340	Tree	D	☼		30 ft
Glyceria maxima 'Variegata' 366	Wtr	M	☼	8	6 ft
Grasses (Annual) 31					
(Perennial) 132					
Gunnera manicata 89, 313	Per	M	◐▦	4-5	10 ft
Gypsophila elegans 19, **33**, 42	Ann	DL	☼	5-9	2 ft
paniculata 90	Per	DL	☼	6-8	3 ft
prostrata: see G. repens					
repens 'Dorothy Teacher' 208	Rock	D	☼	6-8	6 in
fratensis 208	Rock	D	☼	6-7	4 in

H

	Type of plant	Soil	Situation	Flowering time	Height
Halesia monticola 341	Tree	AO	●	5	20 ft
Hamamelis mollis 'Pallida' 284	Shrb	O	☼	1	10 ft
Hebe 'Blue Gem' 321	Shrb	DL	◐▦	5-9	4 ft
pinguifolia 135, 202, 256, **285**, 315	Shrb	DL	☼	5	9 in
salicifolia 285	Shrb	DL	◐▦	6-8	6 ft
Hedera colchica 'Dentata Variegata' **183**	Clmb	D	☼		30 ft
helix (Cultivars) 92, 161, 183	Clmb	D	☼		30 ft
'Goldheart' 178, **183**	Clmb	D	●		30 ft
'Jubilee' see H. h. 'Goldheart'					
Helenium autumnale 91	Per	O	◐	8-10	5 ft
Helianthemum nummularium 86, 142, 151, 166, 179, 198, 199, **208**, 211	Rock	DL	☼	6-7	6 in
Helianthus annuus 32	Ann	D	☼	7-9	10 ft
× multiflorus 91	Per	D	☼	7-9	5 ft
Helichrysum bracteatum 28	Ann	D	☼	7-9	4 ft
macranthum: see H. bracteatum					
microphyllum 33	Ann	D	☼▦		18 in
petiolatum 33	Ann	D	☼▦		2 ft
Heliotropium arborescens 34	Ann	O	☼	5-10	2 ft
Helipterum manglesii 28	Ann	D	☼	7-9	15 in
roseum 28	Ann	D	☼	7-8	15 in
Helleborus argutifolius: see H. lividus corsicus					
foetidus 90, **92**, 262	Per	DL	●	3-5	2 ft
lividus corsicus 92, 231, 292, 327	Per	O	●	3-4	2 ft
orientalis 69, **93**, 141, 153	Per	O	●	2-3	18 in
Hemerocallis flava 93, 261	Per	O	◐	5-7	2 ft
fulva 93	Per	O	◐	6-7	3 ft
Hepatica nobilis 160, **208**, 213	Rock	OL	●	2-4	6 in
Heuchera sanguinea 27, **93**, 106	Per	O	◐	6-9	18 in
Hibiscus (Hybrids) 35	Ann	O	☼	8-9	5 ft
syriacus 284	Shrb	D	☼	7-10	8 ft
trionum 35	Ann	O	☼	8-9	2½ ft
Hippeastrum equestre: see Amaryllis belladonna					
Hippophae rhamnoides 284	Shrb	D	☼		10 ft
Hoheria glabrata: see H. lyallii					
lyallii 230, 286	Shrb	O	◐	7	20 ft
Hordeum jubatum 21, **31**	Ann	D	☼	6-8	12 in
Hosta crispula 94, 113, 155, 281	Per	M	●	8	2 ft
fortunei 'Albopicta' 15, **95**, 105, 108, 161, 308, 330	Per	M	●	7	2 ft
plantaginea 94, 345	Per	M	☼▦	8-9	2 ft
sieboldiana 65, 88, **95**, 103, 141, 243, 280, 306, 323, 326, 373	Per	M	●	8	2 ft
Hottonia palustris 367	Wtr	M	◐	6	12 in
Hyacinths, Dutch: see Hyacinthus orientalis (Hybrids)					
Hyacinthus candicans: see Galtonia candicans					
orientalis (Hybrids) 157, 230	Bulb	D	☼	4	9 in
Hydrangea hortensis: see H. macrophylla					
macrophylla 85, 245, 278, **286**	Shrb	M	●▦	7-9	6 ft
opuloides: see H. macrophylla					
petiolaris 182	Clmb	O	◐	6	30 ft
quercifolia 287, 333	Shrb	O	●▦	7	6 ft
scandens: see H. petiolaris					
villosa (aspera) 70, **287**	Shrb	M	●▦	8	8 ft
Hypericum coris 209	Rock	O	☼	7	6 in
elatum: see H. × inodorum					
'Hidcote' 287, **289**	Shrb	O	☼	6-9	5 ft
× inodorum 'Elstead' 288	Shrb	O	☼	8-9	4 ft
olympicum **209**, 220, 350	Rock	D	☼	7-8	12 in

IJK

	Type of plant	Soil	Situation	Flowering time	Height
Iberis amara 34	Ann	DL	☼	6-9	15 in
umbellata 12, 19, **34**, 42	Ann	DL	☼	6-9	15 in
Ilex aquifolium 59, 341	Tree	O	◐		
Impatiens walleriana 35	Ann	O	◐	4-10	9 in
Incarvillea delavayi 96, 297	Per	O	☼	5-7	2 ft
Ionopsidium acaule 36	Ann	O	◐	3-11	3 in
Ipheion uniflorum 157	Bulb	O	◐▦	4-5	8 in
Ipomoea tricolor 184	Clmb	D	☼	7-9	9 ft
Iris (Bearded hybrids) 46, **97**, 134, 234, 311, 323	Per	OL	☼	6	3½ ft
bucharica 157	Bulb	OL	☼	4-5	18 in
English: see I. xiphioides					
foetidissima 92, **96**, 267, 359	Per	D	●	6	20 in
histrioides 132, **158**, 267	Bulb	DL	☼	1-3	18 in
kaempferi 367	Wtr	MA	☼	6-7	3 ft
laevigata 367	Wtr	M	☼	6	2 ft
pallida dalmatica 96, 102, 141, 155, 250, 281, 325	Per	OL	☼	5-6	2½ ft
pseudacorus 159, 368	Wtr	M	☼	5-6	4 ft
reticulata 92, 155, **158**, 205	Bulb	DL	☼	2-3	6 in
Spanish: see I. xiphium					
xiphioides 125, **159**	Bulb	O	◐	6-7	2 ft
xiphium 159	Bulb	O	☼	6-7	2 ft
Jasminum nudiflorum 158, **185**, 187	Clmb	D	◐	11-3	10 ft
officinale 184	Clmb	D	◐	6-10	10 ft

Type of plant: Ann – annual, biennial; Per – perennial; Bulb – bulb, corm, tuber; Clmb – climber; Rock – rock plant; Rose – rose; Shrb – shrub; Tree – tree; Wtr – water plant
Soil: O – ordinary fertile; D – tolerates dry; M – moisture-retentive to wet; L – needs or tolerates chalk and lime; A – needs acid soil
Situation: ☼ – best in full sun; ● – best in shade or dappled shade; ◐ – sun or light shade; ⚘ – tolerates exposed, windy sites; ▦ – needs sheltered site
Flowering months: Represented by the numbers 1–12 **Height:** Maximum, mature plant (or 20 years for trees and shrubs)

L

Type of plant	Soil	Situation	Flowering time	Height
Juniperus chinensis 'Aurea' 342	Tree	D	☼	15 ft
communis 'Compressa' 198, **209**	Rock	DL	☼	2 ft
virginiana 342	Tree	D	◐	20 ft
Kalmia latifolia 289	Shrb	MA	● 6	10 ft
Kerria japonica 172, **289**, 292	Shrb	O	◐ 4-5	6 ft
Kniphofia caulescens 99	Per	D	☼ 9	2 ft
'Maid of Orleans' **98**, 140, 156	Per	D	☼ 7-9	2½ ft
northiae 99	Per	D	☼ 7-9	6 ft
Kochia scoparia 36, 51	Ann	D	☼⌐	3 ft
Koelreuteria paniculata 343	Tree	O	☼ 7-8	20 ft
Kolkwitzia amabilis 290	Shrb	O	☼ 6	10 ft
Laburnum × watereri 'Vossii' **343**	Tree	O	◐ 5-6	20 ft
Lagurus ovatus 31	Ann	D	☼ 6-9	12 in
Lamium maculatum 76, **98**, 116, 141, 339	Per	O	◐ 5	9 in
Larix decidua 343	Tree	O	☼	55 ft
× eurolepis 343	Tree	O	☼	65 ft
kaempferi 343	Tree	O	☼	60 ft
leptolepis: see L. kaempferi				
Lathyrus odoratus 185	Clmb	O	☼ 6-9	7 ft
Dwarf varieties 37	Ann	O	☼ 6-9	12 in
Laurus nobilis 142, 290	Shrb	D	◐▥ 5	15 ft
Lavandula angustifolia 68, 80, 168, 184, 228, 231, 264, **291**, 300	Shrb	DL	☼ 7-9	3 ft
spica: see L. angustifolia				
Lavatera olbia 254, **291**	Shrb	O	☼▥ 5-11	8 ft
rosea: see L. trimestris				
trimestris 38, 87	Ann	D	☼ 7-9	3 ft
Layia elegans 37, 74	Ann	D	☼⌐ 6-10	18 in
Leontopodium alpinum 210	Rock	O	☼ 6-7	9 in
Leptosiphon hybridus 39	Ann	D	☼ 6-9	6 in
Leucojum aestivum 147, **159**	Bulb	M	◐ 3-5	2 ft
vernum 88, **160**	Bulb	M	◐ 2-3	8 in
Leucothoe fontanesiana 258, **291**	Shrb	MA	● 5	4 ft
Lewisia cotyledon (Hybrids) **210**	Rock	O	☼ 5-6	12 in
Leycesteria formosa 292	Shrb	D	◐ 7-8	6 ft
Liatris spicata 99	Per	M	☼ 8-9	3 ft
Ligularia clivorum: see L. dentata				
dentata 'Desdemona' **100**, 313	Per	M	● 7-8	4 ft
Ligustrum ovalifolium 'Aureum' 66, 288, **292**	Shrb	D	◐ 7	12 ft
Lilium (Aurelian hybrids) **161**	Bulb	O	● 8-9	6 ft
'Bright Star' (Trumpet hybrids) **160**	Bulb	O	● 7-8	6 ft
candidum 79, **161**, 268	Bulb	OL	☼ 6-7	5 ft
martagon 128, **163**, 258	Bulb	OL	● 7	5 ft
regale 73, 126, **162**	Bulb	O	☼▥ 7	6 ft
'Shuksan' (Bellingham hybrids) **160**	Bulb	O	● 7	7 ft
tigrinum 95, **163**	Bulb	O	☼ 8-9	3½ ft
Limnanthes douglasii 38, **45**, 85	Ann	D	☼ 5-8	6 in
Limonium latifolium 100	Per	O	☼ 7-9	2 ft

Type of plant	Soil	Situation	Flowering time	Height
sinuatum 28	Ann	O	☼ 7-9	18 in
Linaria maroccana 39	Ann	D	☼ 6-7	15 in
Linum flavum 210, 220	Rock	DL	☼ 6-8	18 in
grandiflorum 40	Ann	DL	☼ 6-8	18 in
narbonense 101	Per	DL	☼ 6-8	2 ft
perenne 101	Per	DL	☼ 6-8	18 in
salsoloides 210	Rock	DL	☼ 6-7	8 in
usitatissimum 40	Ann	DL	☼ 6-7	2 ft
Lippia citriodora 293	Shrb	D	☼▥	8 ft
Liquidambar styraciflua 344	Tree	O	◐▥	20 ft
Liriodendron tulipifera 344	Tree	O	◐ 6-7	25 ft
Liriope muscari 101, 120, 256	Per	O	☼ 9-10	18 in
Lithodora diffusa 211, 217	Rock	O	☼▥ 6-10	4 in
Lobelia cardinalis 101	Per	M	◐ 7-8	2½ ft
erinus 17, 30, 37, **40**, 46, 49, 57	Ann	O	● 5-10	9 in
fulgens 101	Per	M	◐ 8-10	4 ft
splendens: see L. fulgens				
Lobularia maritima 29, **41**	Ann	D	☼ 6-9	6 in
Lonicera × americana 186	Clmb	OD	◐ 4-10	30 ft
japonica 'Aureoreticulata' 186	Clmb	O	◐ 6-10	20 ft
'Halliana' 111, 176, **186**	Clmb	O	◐▥ 6-10	20 ft
periclymenum 186	Clmb	O	◐ 6-10	20 ft
pileata 293	Shrb	O	● 4-5	2 ft
× tellmanniana 105, **187**	Clmb	O	◐ 6-7	15 ft
Lunaria annua **41**, 164, 325	Ann	D	● 4-6	2½ ft
biennis: see L. annua				
Lupinus arboreus 76, 250, **293**	Shrb	O	☼ 6-8	4 ft
hartwegii 'Pixie Delight' 39, **42**	Ann	DA	◐ 7-10	18 in
Russell strain 102	Per	OA	◐ 5-7	3 ft
Lychnis chalcedonica 103	Per	O	☼ 7-8	4 ft
coronaria 83, **103**, 140, 220	Per	O	☼ 6-9	2 ft
Lysichiton americanum 100, 109, 313, 365, **368**	Wtr	M	◐ 3-5	4 ft
Lysimachia punctata 103, 142	Per	M	◐ 6-8	3 ft
Lythrum salicaria 100, **369**	Wtr	M	◐ 7-8	4 ft

M

Type of plant	Soil	Situation	Flowering time	Height
Macleaya microcarpa 104	Per	M	☼▥ 6-8	8 ft
Magnolia grandiflora 345	Tree	OL	☼▥ 7-9	15 ft
kobus 41, **345**	Tree	OL	◐▥ 3-4	20 ft
× loebneri 294	Shrb	OL	☼ 4	20 ft
sinensis 294	Shrb	O	☼ 5	10 ft
× soulangiana 144, 151, 294, **346**	Tree	OL	◐▥ 5-6	18 ft
stellata 152, 345	Tree	OL	◐▥ 5-6	10 ft
Mahonia aquifolium 99, **295**	Shrb	O	● 3-4	5 ft
× 'Charity' 294	Shrb	O	●▥ 11-2	10 ft
japonica 92, 149, 294, **295**, 319	Shrb	O	● 12-5	10 ft
Malcolmia maritima 42	Ann	O	☼ 4-9	8 in
Malus 'John Downie' **346**	Tree	O	☼ 4-5	35 ft
tschonoskii 347	Tree	O	☼ 4-5	30 ft
Malva moschata 13, 100, **104**	Per	D	◐ 6-9	3 ft
Matricaria eximia: see Chrysanthemum parthenium				

Type of plant	Soil	Situation	Flowering time	Height
Matteuccia struthiopteris 130, 306	Per	M	●	5 ft
Matthiola bicornis 43, 80	Ann	ML	◐ 7-8	15 in
incana 42	Ann	ML	◐ 6-7	2½ ft
Meconopsis baileyi: see M. betonicifolia				
betonicifolia 105	Per	O	● 6-7	4 ft
cambrica 81, 88, **104**	Per	O	◐ 6-9	12 in
Mentzelia lindleyi 36, 43	Ann	D	☼⌐ 6-8	18 in
Menyanthes trifoliata 368	Wtr	M	☼ 5-6	9 in
Mesembryanthemum criniflorum 44	Ann	D	☼ 6-8	6 in
Metasequoia glyptostroboides 347	Tree	O	◐	40 ft
Mille uniflora: see Ipheion uniflorum				
Mimulus cardinalis 369	Wtr	M	◐ 6-9	2 ft
× hybridus 45	Ann	M	◐ 7-10	12 in
luteus 105, 371, 372	Per	M	◐ 5-8	2 ft
Miscanthus sinensis 120, 132, **133**, 369	Per	O	☼	6 ft
Monarda didyma 'Cambridge Scarlet' 106	Per	M	◐ 6-9	3 ft
Muscari armeniacum 115, **163**, 274	Bulb	D	☼ 4	8 in
Myosotis sylvatica 20, **44**, 153, 166, 171	Ann	O	● 4-6	12 in
Myrtus communis 296	Shrb	O	◐▥ 6-8	8 ft
tarentina 'Jenny Reitenbach' 296	Shrb	O	◐▥ 6-8	5 ft

N

Type of plant	Soil	Situation	Flowering time	Height
Narcissus cyclamineus 'February Gold' 147, 164	Bulb	O	◐ 2-4	15 in
poeticus 'Recurvus' 151, **165**	Bulb	O	◐ 4-5	18 in
pseudonarcissus 'Golden Harvest' 115, **165**, 295, 333	Bulb	O	◐ 3-4	15 in
triandrus 'Thalia' 165	Bulb	O	◐ 4	15 in
Nemesia strumosa 45	Ann	O	☼ 6-8	18 in
Nemophila insignis: see N. menziesii				
menziesii 45	Ann	O	◐ 6-8	9 in
Nepeta × faassenii 18, **106**, 146, 229, 234	Per	DL	☼⌐ 5-9	18 in
Nerine bowdenii 46, 70, 74, 99, 101, **166**	Bulb	D	◐▥ 9-11	2 ft
Nicotiana affinis: see N. alata				
alata 43, **46**, 79, 134, 183, 227	Ann	O	☼ 6-9	3 ft
sylvestris 47	Ann	O	☼ 8	5 ft
Nigella damascena 19, 33, 36, 40, **47**, 137	Ann	D	☼ 6-8	2 ft
Nymphaea (Hardy hybrids) 369, **370**	Wtr	M	☼ 6-9	

O

Type of plant	Soil	Situation	Flowering time	Height
Oenothera missouriensis 90, **107**	Per	D	☼ 6-8	6 in
Olearia macrodonta 297	Shrb	D	☼▥ 6-7	8 ft

	Type of plant	Soil	Situation	Flowering time	Height
Onoclea germanica: see Matteuccia struthiopteris					
Ornithogalum nutans 166	Bulb	D	☼	4-5	15 in
umbellatum 166	Bulb	D	◑	4-5	12 in
Orontium aquaticum 371	Wtr	M	☼	4-6	12 in
Osmanthus aquifolius: see O. heterophyllus					
heterophyllus 297	Shrb	O	◑	9-10	10 ft
ilicifolius: see O. heterophyllus					
× Osmarea burkwoodii 297	Shrb	DL	◑	4-5	10 ft
Osmunda regalis 100, 131	Per	M	●		6 ft

P

	Type of plant	Soil	Situation	Flowering time	Height
Paeonia albiflora: see P. lactiflora					
lactiflora 107, 133, 236	Per	O	◑	5-6	3 ft
lutea ludlowii 298	Shrb	O	◑▦	5	6 ft
mlokosewitschii 108	Per	O	◑	4	2 ft
officinalis 108	Per	O	◑	5	2 ft
suffruticosa 298	Shrb	O	◑▦	5	5 ft
Papaver nudicaule 47	Ann	D	☼	6-7	2 ft
orientale 22, 44, 109, 134, 234	Per	O	☼	6	3 ft
rhoeas 48, 135	Ann	D	☼	6-8	2 ft
Parrotia persica 348	Tree	OL	☼	3-4	20 ft
Parthenocissus henryana 187	Clmb	O	●▦		30 ft
Passiflora caerulea 117, 188	Clmb	O	◑▦	6-9	30 ft
Paulownia imperialis: see P. tomentosa					
tomentosa 348	Tree	O	☼▦	5	20 ft
Pelargonium peltatum 40, 48, 49, 183	Ann	O	☼	5-10	3 ft
zonale 48, 49	Ann	O	☼	5-10	6 ft
Peltiphyllum peltatum 109, 130, 131, 306	Per	M	◑	3	3 ft
Pennisetum longistylum: see P. villosum					
villosum 133	Per	O	☼	6-7	2 ft
Penstemon campanulatus 110	Per	O	◑	6-9	2 ft
× gloxinioides 23, 51	Ann	O	☼	7-9	2½ ft
roezlii 212	Rock	D	☼	5-7	6 in
scouleri 212	Rock	D	☼	6-7	12 in
Pernettya mucronata 299	Shrb	OA	☼	6	3 ft
Petunia × hybrida 36, 40, 42, 50, 183	Ann	D	☼	6-11	18 in
Phalaris arundinacea 'Picta' 132, 134	Per	O	☼		5 ft
Philadelphus × 'Beauclerk' 124, 299	Shrb	O	◑	6-7	8 ft
coronarius 'Aureus' 299	Shrb	D	●	6-7	8 ft

	Type of plant	Soil	Situation	Flowering time	Height
Phlomis fruticosa 300	Shrb	D	☼	6-7	5 ft
Phlox douglasii 199, 205, 212	Rock	O	☼	5-6	4 in
drummondii 51	Ann	D	☼	7-9	15 in
maculata 111, 133	Per	O	◑	7-9	3 ft
paniculata 110	Per	O	◑	8	3½
subulata 199, 212	Rock	D	☼	4-5	4 in
Phormium tenax 94, 300, 326, 359	Shrb	O	☼⊂	6	10 ft
Photinia villosa 348	Tree	O	●▦	5-6	10 ft
Phygelius capensis 111, 119, 298	Per	O	☼▦	7-10	4 ft
Phyllitis scolopendrium: see Asplenium scolopendrium					
Physostegia virginiana 111, 123	Per	M	◑	7-8	4 ft
Picea omorika 349	Tree	O	◑		45 ft
pungens glauca 306, 349	Tree	OA	◑		25 ft
Pieris formosa 'Forrestii' 301	Shrb	MA	●▦	4-5	10 ft
japonica 301	Shrb	MA	●▦	3-4	8 ft
Pinus mugo 350	Tree	O	☼		15 ft
pumila 350	Tree	O	◑		10 ft
sylvestris 350	Tree	DL	☼		35 ft
Pittosporum tobira 296, 301	Shrb	O	☼▦	4-7	8 ft
Platycodon grandiflorum 112	Per	D	☼	6-8	2 ft
mariesii 112	Per	D	☼	6-8	12 in
Polemonium caeruleum 94, 112, 372	Per	O	◑	4-7	2 ft
Polygonatum × hybridum 113, 270	Per	O	●	6	4 ft
Polygonum affine 112	Per	O	◑	7-9	9 in
baldschuanicum 189	Clmb	D	◑	7-9	40 ft
campanulatum 114	Per	O	◑	6-9	3½ ft
vaccinifolium 112	Per	O	◑	8-10	6 in
Pontederia cordata 371, 372	Wtr	M	☼	7-9	3 ft
Portulaca grandiflora 51	Ann	D	☼	6-9	9 in
Potamogeton crispus 371	Wtr	M	☼		3 ft
Potentilla atrosanguinea 114	Per	O	☼	6-9	2 ft
× 'Elizabeth' 188, 288, 302	Shrb	O	☼	5-11	4 ft
fruticosa 288, 302	Shrb	D	☼	6-9	4 ft
tabernaemontani 'Nana' 209, 212	Rock	D	☼	6-10	1 in
verna: see P. tabernaemontani					
Primula auricula (Hybrids) 59, 213	Rock	O	●	3-5	6 in
denticulata 115, 151	Per	M	◑	3-5	12 in
florindae 130, 131, 160, 372	Wtr	M	●	6-7	6 ft
frondosa 213	Rock	O	●	4	4 in
japonica 373	Wtr	M	◑	5-7	2½ ft
marginata 214	Rock	O	☼	4-5	4 in
Polyanthus group 52, 227	Ann	O	●	3-5	12 in
× pubescens 213	Rock	O	●	4-5	4 in
sieboldii 213	Rock	O	●	4-5	9 in
vulgaris 93, 114, 115, 163, 221	Per	O	◑	3-4	6 in
Prunella grandiflora 115	Per	O	◑	5-10	12 in
Prunus 351-2					
'Accolade' 163, 351	Tree	L	◑	3-4	30 ft
× amygdalo-persica: see P. × pollardii					

	Type of plant	Soil	Situation	Flowering time	Height
amygdalus: see P. dulcis					
cerasifera 'Pissardii', syn. 'Atropurpurea' 351	Tree	OL	◑	2-3	25 ft
× cistena 287, 302	Shrb	OL	◑	4	5 ft
dulcis 351	Tree	OL	◑	3-4	25 ft
laurocerasus 303	Shrb	DL	◑	4	15 ft
lusitanica 99, 169, 303	Shrb	DL	◑	6	15 ft
persica 351	Tree	OL	◑	4	25 ft
× pollardii 351	Tree	OL	◑	3-4	25 ft
sargentii 351	Tree	OL	☼	3	30 ft
serrulata 351	Tree	OL	☼	4-5	30 ft
subhirtella 'Autumnalis' 150	Tree	OL	☼	11-3	25 ft
'Pendula Rubra' 352	Tree	OL	☼	4	15 ft
Pulmonaria saccharata 92, 102, 115, 116, 135, 141	Per	O	●	3-4	12 in
Pulsatilla vulgaris 157, 171, 214, 219	Rock	DL	☼	4-5	12 in
Puschkinia libanotica: see P. scilloides					
scilloides 166	Bulb	O	◑	3-5	8 in
Pyracantha 'Orange Glow' 304	Shrb	O	☼	6-7	18 ft
Pyrethrum ptarmaciflorum 17, 49, 50, 52, 53	Ann	D	☼		15 in
'Silver Feather' 52	Ann	D	☼		15 in
ptarmicaefolium: see P. ptarmaciflorum					
roseum: see Chrysanthemum coccineum					
Pyrus salicifolia 'Pendula' 353	Tree	D	☼	4	10 ft

R

	Type of plant	Soil	Situation	Flowering time	Height
Ranunculus aconitifolius 'Flore-pleno' 116	Per	OL	◑	5-6	2 ft
lingua 372	Wtr	M	◑	8-9	4 ft
Reseda odorata 43, 53, 76, 236	Ann	DL	◑	6-10	2½ ft
Rheum palmatum 116	Per	M	☼	6	8 ft
Rhodanthe manglesii: see Helipterum manglesii					
Rhododendron 104, 163, 282, 291, 305-9, 341, 356					
arboreum 305	Shrb	MA	◑▦	3-4	15 ft
auriculatum 305	Shrb	MA	◑▦	8	10 ft
'Blue Tit' 152, 306	Shrb	MA	◑▦	4	3 ft
calophytum 306	Shrb	MA	◑▦	3-4	10 ft
× cilpinense 307	Shrb	MA	◑▦	3	3 ft
concatenans 305	Shrb	MA	◑▦	4-5	6 ft
fulvum 305	Shrb	MA	◑▦	3-4	10 ft
'Goldsworth Yellow' 113, 307	Shrb	MA	◑▦	6	10 ft

Type of plant: Ann – annual, biennial; Per – perennial; Bulb – bulb, corm, tuber; Clmb – climber; Rock – rock plant; Rose – rose; Shrb – shrub; Tree – tree; Wtr – water plant
Soil: O – ordinary fertile; D – tolerates dry; M – moisture-retentive to wet; L – needs or tolerates chalk and lime; A – needs acid soil
Situation: ☼ – best in full sun; ● – best in shade or dappled shade; ◑ – sun or light shade; ⊂ – tolerates exposed, windy sites; ▦ – needs sheltered site
Flowering months: Represented by the numbers 1–12   **Height:** Maximum, mature plant (or 20 years for trees and shrubs)

	Type of plant	Soil	Situation	Flowering time	Height
Sorbus aria 115, **355**	Tree	D	◑	5	20 ft
aucuparia 'Beissneri' **356**	Tree	D	◑	5-6	30 ft
hupehensis **356**	Tree	D	◑	5-6	25 ft
'Joseph Rock' 356	Tree	D	◑	5	25 ft
'Mitchellii' (John Mitchell) 355	Tree	D	◑	5-6	30 ft
vilmorinii **356**	Tree	D	◑	6	10 ft
Spartina pectinata 'Aureomarginata' 134, **261**	Per	M	☼		6 ft
Spartium junceum 316, **321**	Shrb	D	☼	6-8	10 ft
Spiraea aitchisonii: see *Sorbaria aitchisonii*					
× *arguta* 26, **317**	Shrb	O	☼	4-5	8 ft
japonica 165, **318**	Shrb	O	☼	7-8	5 ft
lobata: see *Filipendula rubra*					
Stachys lanata: see *S. olympica*					
olympica 43, **122**, 140, 230, 300	Per	O	☼	6-7	18 in
Stephanandra tanakae **318**	Shrb	O	◑	6-7	7 ft
Sternbergia lutea **168**	Bulb	O	☼	9-11	6 in
Stewartia malacodendron 357	Tree	MA	●▥	7-8	15 ft
pseudocamellia **375**	Tree	MA	●▥	7-8	20 ft
Stipa gigantea 135	Per	D	☼	6-8	6 ft
pennata **135**	Per	D	☼	6-8	2½ ft
Stokesia cyanea: see *S. laevis*					
laevis **123**	Per	O	☼	7-10	18 in
Stranvaesia davidiana undulata **319**	Shrb	DL	◑	6	18 ft
Stratiotes aloides **372**	Wtr	M	☼	6-7	12 in
Styrax japonica **357**	Tree	OA	◑▥	6	15 ft
Symphoricarpos × *doorenbosii* 'Mother of Pearl' **320**	Shrb	D	◑	7-9	6 ft
orbiculatus 320	Shrb	D	◑	7-9	6 ft
Syringa microphylla **320**	Shrb	D	◑	6	5 ft
vulgaris 'Mme Lemoine' **320**	Shrb	D	◑	5-6	12 ft

T

	Type of plant	Soil	Situation	Flowering time	Height
Tagetes erecta 23, **57**	Ann	D	☼	7-10	3 ft
patula 23, 40, 54, **56**, 57	Ann	D	☼	6-9	12 in
Tamarix pentandra **321**	Shrb	D	☼☞	8-9	15 ft
Teucrium chamaedrys **218**	Rock	D	◑▥	7-9	9 in
Thalictrum speciosissimum 79, **123**	Per	O	◑	7-8	6 ft
Thermopsis caroliniana 124	Per	O	☼	7	4 ft
montana **124**	Per	O	☼	5-6	3 ft
Thuja lobbii: see *T. plicata*					
occidentalis 'Rheingold' 358	Tree	O	☼		4 ft
plicata **358**	Tree	O	☼		40 ft
Thunbergia alata **58**	Ann	O	☼▥	6-9	10 ft
Thymus × *citriodorus* 73, 159, **219**, 220, 221	Rock	DL	☼	6-8	8 in

	Type of plant	Soil	Situation	Flowering time	Height
drucei 151, 209, **219**, 220	Rock	DL	☼	6-8	3 in
praecox arcticus: see *T. drucei*					
serpyllum: see *T. drucei*					
Tiarella cordifolia **221**	Rock	O	●	4-7	10 in
Tilia mongolica **358**	Tree	O	◑	7	30 ft
petiolaris **358**	Tree	O	◑	7-8	25 ft
Trachycarpus fortunei **359**	Tree	D	☼	5-6	10 ft
Tradescantia × *andersoniana* **124**, 238	Per	O	☼	6-9	2 ft
Trillium grandiflorum **125**, 144, 152	Per	O	●	4-6	15 in
Triteleia uniflora: see *Ipheion uniflorum*					
Trollius × *hybridus* **125**	Per	M	☼	5-6	2½ ft
Tropaeolum majus 37, **57**	Ann	D	☼	6-9	8 ft
speciosum 183, **190**	Clmb	MA	●▥	7-9	15 ft
Tsuga heterophylla 358	Tree	O	●		40 ft
mertensiana 358	Tree	O	●		40 ft
Tulipa 'Artist' 171	Bulb	D	☼	4-5	3 ft
'China Pink' 170	Bulb	D	☼	4	2 ft
clusiana **169**	Bulb	D	☼	4	12 in
Cottage group 171, 239	Bulb	D	☼	4-5	3 ft
Darwin group 169, 234, 239	Bulb	D	☼	5	2½ ft
dasystemon: see *T. tarda*					
'Dillenburg' 171	Bulb	D	☼	4-5	3 ft
'Fritz Kreisler' 170	Bulb	D	☼	3-4	10 in
'Golden Harvest' 157, 171	Bulb	D	☼	4-5	3 ft
greigii (Hybrids) **169**	Bulb	D	☼	4	18 in
'Halcro' 171	Bulb	D	☼	4-5	3 ft
'Heart's Delight' 170	Bulb	D	☼	3-4	10 in
'Jewel of Spring' 169	Bulb	D	☼	5	2½ ft
kaufmanniana (Hybrids) **170**	Bulb	D	☼	3-4	10 in
Lily-flowered group 82, **170**	Bulb	D	☼	4	2 ft
'Mariette' 170	Bulb	D	☼	4	2 ft
'Niphetos' 166, 169	Bulb	D	☼	5	2½ ft
'Purissima' 44	Bulb	D	☼	5	2½ ft
'Scarlett O'Hara' 169	Bulb	D	☼	5	2½ ft
'Stresa' 170	Bulb	D	☼	3-4	10 in
'Sulphur Triumph' 44	Bulb	D	☼	5	2½ ft
tarda 154, **171**	Bulb	D	☼	3	6 in
'The First' 170	Bulb	D	☼	3-4	10 in
'West Point' 170	Bulb	D	☼	4	2 ft

UV

	Type of plant	Soil	Situation	Flowering time	Height
Ulex europaeus **322**	Shrb	D	☼	3-5	8 ft
Ursinia anethoides **58**	Ann	D	☼	6-9	8 in
'Sunstar' 58	Ann	D	☼	6-9	8 in
Vaccinium corymbosum **322**	Shrb	MA	☼	5-6	6 ft

	Type of plant	Soil	Situation	Flowering time	Height
Verbascum × *hybridum* 'Gainsborough' **126**, 304	Per	OL	☼	6-8	4 ft
'Mont Blanc' 304	Per	OL	☼	6-8	4 ft
Verbena × *hybrida* **58**	Ann	O	☼	6-10	12 in
Veronica **220**	Rock	D	☼		
incana **127**	Per	O	☼	6-8	15 in
prostrata 220	Rock	D	☼	5-7	8 in
spicata incana: see *V. incana*					
teucrium 124, 220	Rock	D	☼	6-8	15 in
Viburnum × *bodnantense* 147, 168, 181, **322**	Shrb	O	☼	10-2	12 ft
× *burkwoodii* **323**	Shrb	O	☼	2-5	8 ft
davidii **324**	Shrb	O	◑	6-7	3 ft
opulus 323, 337	Shrb	O	☼	5-6	15 ft
plicatum tomentosum 'Mariesii' **324**	Shrb	O	●	5	10 ft
Vinca major **324**	Shrb	D	●	4-6	12 in
minor 324	Shrb	D	●	3-7	4 in
Viola biflora **221**	Rock	O	●	4-5	3 in
cornuta 126, 219	Per	O	●	5-7	12 in
'Alba' 126	Per	O	●	5-7	12 in
'Jersey Gem' 126	Per	O	●	5-7	12 in
labradorica 'Purpurea' 154, 166, **221**, 274	Rock	D	●	4-5	5 in
tricolor: see *V.* × *wittrockiana*					
× *wittrockiana* 59, 228, 236	Ann	O	☼	5-3	9 in
Vitis coignetiae 187, **190**	Clmb	O	☼		40 ft

WX

	Type of plant	Soil	Situation	Flowering time	Height
Weigela florida 'Foliis Purpureis' 325	Shrb	O	◑	5-6	6 ft
'Variegata' 36, **325**	Shrb	O	◑	5-6	6 ft
Wisteria floribunda 191	Clmb	O☞	☼	5-6	50 ft
'Macrobotrys' 191	Clmb	O	☼	5-6	50 ft
sinensis 191, 244	Clmb	O	☼	5-6	50 ft
Xeranthemum annuum 28	Ann	D	☼	7	3 ft

Z

	Type of plant	Soil	Situation	Flowering time	Height
Zantedeschia aethiopica 'Crowborough' **127**, 177	Per	M	◑	6-7	2½ ft
Zauschneria californica 140, **221**	Rock	D	☼▥	9-10	18 in
cana 221	Rock	D	☼▥	9-10	18 in
Zinnia elegans **59**	Ann	O	☼	7-9	2½ ft

Type of plant: Ann – annual, biennial; Per – perennial; Bulb – bulb, corm, tuber; Clmb – climber; Rock – rock plant; Rose – rose; Shrb – shrub; Tree – tree; Wtr – water plant

Soil: O – ordinary fertile; D – tolerates dry; M – moisture-retentive to wet; L – needs or tolerates chalk and lime; A – needs acid soil

Situation: ☼ – best in full sun; ● – best in shade or dappled shade; ◑ – sun or light shade; ☞ – tolerates exposed, windy sites; ▥ – needs sheltered site

Flowering months: Represented by the numbers 1–12   **Height:** Maximum, mature plant (or 20 years for trees and shrubs)

DICTIONARY OF COMMON NAMES

The preceding index identifies plants by their botanical names; however, some seed and plant catalogues may give only the common name. To help you find the plant when you do not know its botanical name, the common names of plants described in this book are listed below. Alongside, in italics, are the botanical names of the species, varieties or genera (indicated by the letters 'spp') to which the common names relate.

A

Acacia, Common *Robinia pseudoacacia*
Acacia, False *Robinia pseudoacacia*
Acacia, Rose *Robinia hispida*
Aconite, Winter *Eranthis hyemalis*
Agrimony, Hemp *Eupatorium* spp
Alyssum, Sweet *Lobularia maritima*
Anemone *Hepatica nobilis; Anemone*
Angelica tree, Japanese *Aralia elata*
Angel's fishing rod *Dierama pulcherrimum*
Apple, Crab *Malus* spp
Arbor-vitae *Thuja* spp
Arrowhead, Common *Sagittaria sagittifolia*
Arum, Bog *Calla palustris; Lysichiton americanus*
Ash, Mountain *Sorbus aucuparia*
Aster, China *Callistephus chinensis*
Aster, Stokes' *Stokesia laevis*
Avens *Geum* spp
Avens, Mountain *Dryas octopetala*

B

Baby blue eyes *Nemophila menziesii*
Baby's breath *Gypsophila elegans*
Bachelor's buttons *Kerria japonica 'Pleniflora'*
Balloon flower *Platycodon grandiflorum*
Barberry *Berberis* spp
Barberry, Chilean *Berberis darwinii*
Barrenwort *Epimedium* spp
Bay, Sweet *Laurus nobilis*
Bean tree, Indian *Catalpa bignonioides*
Bear's breeches *Acanthus* spp
Beauty bush *Kolkwitzia amabilis*
Bee balm *Monarda didyma*
Beech, Weeping purple *Fagus sylvatica 'Purpurea Pendula'*
Bellflower *Campanula* spp
Bellflower, Peach-leaved *Campanula persicifolia*
Bergamot, Sweet *Monarda didyma*
Berry, June *Amelanchier* spp
Birch, Silver *Betula pendula*
Birch, Young's weeping *Betula pendula 'Youngii'*
Bishop's hat *Epimedium* spp
Bittersweet, Climbing *Celastrus* spp
Black-eyed Susan *Thunbergia alata*
Blanket flower *Gaillardia* spp
Blazing star *Liatris* spp
Blossom, Blue *Ceanothus* spp
Blossom, Creeping blue *Ceanothus thyrsiflorus 'Repens'*
Bluebell, Spanish *Endymion hispanicus*
Blueberry, High-bush *Vaccinium corymbosum*
Blueberry, Swamp *Vaccinium corymbosum*
Bog bean *Menyanthes trifoliata*
Bog beauty *Calla palustris*
Bottlebrush buckeye *Aesculus parviflora*
Box, Common *Buxus sempervirens*
Box, Sweet *Sarcococca confusa*
Bridal wreath *Spiraea × arguta*
Broom *Cytisus* spp
Broom, Bulgarian *Genista lydia*
Broom, Butcher's *Ruscus aculeatus*
Broom, Common *Cytisus scoparius*
Broom, Moroccan *Cytisus battandieri*
Broom, Mount Etna *Genista aetnensis*
Broom, Spanish *Spartium* spp
Broom, Warminster *Cytisus × praecox*
Buckthorn, Sea *Hippophae rhamnoides*
Bugle *Ajuga reptans*
Burning bush *Dictamnus* spp; *Kochia scoparia 'Trichophylla'*
Busy Lizzie *Impatiens walleriana*
Buttercup *Ranunculus* spp
Butterfly flower *Schizanthus* spp

C

Calico bush *Kalmia latifolia*
Camellia, Common *Camellia japonica*
Campion *Lychnis* spp; *Silene* spp
Candlemas bells *Galanthus nivalis*
Candytuft *Iberis* spp
Canterbury bell *Campanula medium*
Carnation *Dianthus* spp
Castor oil plant *Ricinus communis*
Catchfly *Silene* spp
Cathedral bell *Cobaea scandens*
Catmint *Nepeta × faassenii*
Cedar, Japanese *Cryptomeria japonica*
Cedar, Pencil *Juniperus virginiana*
Cedar, Western red *Thuja plicata*
Cherry, Ornamental *Prunus* spp
Cherry, Ornamental weeping *Prunus subhirtella 'Pendula'*
Cherry pie *Heliotropium* spp
Chestnut, Horse *Aesculus* spp
China-tree *Koelreuteria paniculata*
Cinquefoil *Potentilla* spp
Cob-nut *Corylus avellana*
Columbine *Aquilegia* spp
Cone flower *Rudbeckia* spp
Cone flower, Purple *Echinacea* spp
Coral flower *Heuchera* spp
Cornel *Cornus* spp
Cornflower *Centaurea cyanus*
Cowslip, Giant *Primula florindae*
Crane's-bill *Geranium* spp
Creeper, Chinese Virginia *Parthenocissus henryana*
Creeper, Flame *Tropaeolum speciosum*
Creeper, Trumpet *Campsis* spp
Cress, Violet *Ionopsidium acaule*
Crocus, Autumn *Colchicum* spp
Crown imperial *Fritillaria imperialis*
Cup and saucer plant *Cobaea scandens*
Cupid's dart *Catananche* spp
Currant, Flowering *Ribes* spp
Cydonia *Chaenomeles* spp
Cypress *Chamaecyparis* spp; × *Cupressocyparis* spp; *Cupressus* spp
Cypress, Hinoki *Chamaecyparis obtusa*
Cypress, Lawson *Chamaecyparis lawsoniana*
Cypress, Leyland × *Cupressocyparis leylandii*
Cypress, Summer *Kochia scoparia*

DE

Daffodil, Wild *Narcissus pseudonarcissus*
Daisy, African *Dimorphotheca* spp
Daisy, Common *Bellis perennis*
Daisy, Double *Bellis perennis* Monstrosa
Daisy, Livingstone *Mesembryanthemum criniflorum*
Daisy, Michaelmas *Aster* spp
Daisy, Shasta *Chrysanthemum maximum*
Daisy bush *Olearia* spp
David's harp *Polygonatum × hybridum*
Devil-in-a-bush *Nigella damascena*
Dogwood *Cornus* spp
Dove tree *Davidia involucrata*
Dropwort *Filipendula vulgaris*

Edelweiss *Leontopodium* spp
Elder, American *Sambucus canadensis*
Elder, Red-berried *Sambucus racemosa*
Everlasting flowers *Helichrysum* spp; *Helipterum roseum; Limonium* spp; *Xeranthemum* spp

F

Fair maids of February *Galanthus nivalis*
Fair maids of France *Ranunculus aconitifolius*
Fair maids of Kent *Ranunculus aconitifolius*
Fennel, Common *Foeniculum vulgare*
Fern, Broad buckler *Dryopteris dilatata*
Fern, Buckler *Dryopteris* spp
Fern, Flowering *Osmunda regalis*
Fern, Golden-scaled male *Dryopteris pseudomas*
Fern, Hart's tongue *Asplenium scolopendrium*
Fern, Lady *Athyrium filix-femina*
Fern, Maidenhair *Adiantum pedatum*
Fern, Male *Dryopteris filix-mas*
Fern, Ostrich plume *Matteuccia struthiopteris*
Fern, Royal *Osmunda regalis*
Fern, Shuttlecock *Matteuccia struthiopteris*
Feverfew *Chrysanthemum parthenium*
Fir *Abies* spp
Fir, Korean *Abies koreana*
Fir, Silver *Abies koreana*
Fire bush, Chilean *Embothrium coccineum*
Firethorn *Pyracantha* spp
Flag *Iris pseudacorus*
Flag, Yellow *Iris pseudacorus*
Flag, Sweet *Acorus calamus*
Flax *Linum* spp
Flax, New Zealand *Phormium tenax*
Fleabane *Erigeron* spp
Flower-of-an-hour *Hibiscus trionum*
Foam flower *Tiarella cordifolia*
Foam of May *Spiraea × arguta*
Forget-me-not *Myosotis* spp
Foxglove *Digitalis* spp
Foxglove, Common *Digitalis purpurea*
Foxglove, Fairy *Erinus alpinus*
Fuchsia, Californian *Zauschneria californica*
Furze *Ulex* spp

G

Gardener's garters *Phalaris arundinacea 'Picta'*
Garland flower *Daphne cneorum*
Garlic, Golden *Allium moly*
Gayfeather *Liatris* spp
Gentian *Gentiana* spp
Gentian, Trumpet *Gentiana acaulis*
Gentian, Willow *Gentiana asclepiadea*
Geranium *Pelargonium zonale*
Geranium, Ivy-leaved *Pelargonium peltatum*
Germander, Wall *Teucrium chamaedrys*
Ghost tree *Davidia involucrata*
Globe flower *Trollius* spp
Glory flower, Chilean *Eccremocarpus* spp
Glory of the snow *Chionodoxa* spp
Goat's beard *Aruncus* spp
Gold dust *Alyssum saxatile*
Golden chain *Laburnum* spp
Golden club *Orontium aquaticum*
Golden-rain tree *Koelreuteria paniculata; Laburnum* spp
Golden rod *Solidago* spp
Gorse *Ulex* spp
Granny's bonnet *Aquilegia vulgaris*
Grape, Oregon *Mahonia aquifolium*
Grass, Cord *Spartina pectinata*
Grass, Feather *Stipa* spp
Grass, Hare's tail *Lagurus ovatus*
Grass, Pampas *Cortaderia* spp
Grass, Pearl *Briza maxima*
Grass, Whitlow *Draba* spp
Gum, Alpine snow *Eucalyptus niphophila*
Gum, Cider *Eucalyptus gunnii*
Gum, Sweet *Liquidambar styraciflua*
Gum tree *Eucalyptus* spp

H

Harry Lauder's walking stick *Corylus avellana 'Contorta'*
Hawthorn, Water *Aponogeton distachyos*
Hazel, Corkscrew *Corylus avellana 'Contorta'*
Heath *Erica* spp
Heath, Connemara *Daboecia cantabrica*
Heath, Cornish *Erica vagans*
Heath, Irish *Daboecia cantabrica*
Heath, St Dabeoc's *Daboecia cantabrica*
Heath, Tree *Erica arborea*
Heather *Erica* spp; *Calluna* spp
Heliotrope *Heliotropium* spp
Hellebore *Helleborus* spp
Hellebore, Corsican *Helleborus lividus corsicus*
Hellebore, Stinking *Helleborus foetidus*
Hemlock, Western *Tsuga heterophylla*
Hibiscus, Syrian *Hibiscus syriacus*
Holly *Ilex* spp
Holly, Moroccan sea *Eryngium variifolium*
Hollyhock *Althaea* spp
Honesty *Lunaria* spp
Honeysuckle *Lonicera* spp
Honeysuckle, Himalayan *Leycesteria formosa*
Honeysuckle, Japanese *Lonicera japonica*
Hornbeam, Common *Carpinus betulus*
Houseleek, Common *Sempervivum tectorum*
Hyacinth, Common *Hyacinthus orientalis*
Hyacinth, Dutch *Hyacinthus orientalis*
Hyacinth, Grape *Muscari* spp
Hyacinth, Summer *Galtonia* spp
Hydrangea, Japanese climbing *Hydrangea petiolaris*

I

Iris, English *Iris xiphioides*
Iris, Flag *Iris pseudacorus*
Iris, Gladdon or Gladwyn *Iris foetidissima*
Iris, Spanish *Iris xiphium*
Iris, Stinking *Iris foetidissima*
Ivy *Hedera helix*
Ivy, Persian *Hedera colchica*
Ivy, Shield *Hedera helix 'Deltoides'*

J

Jacob's ladder *Polemonium caeruleum*
Japonica *Chaenomeles japonica*
Jasmine, Common white *Jasminum officinale*
Jasmine, Rock *Androsace* spp
Jasmine, Winter-flowering *Jasminum nudiflorum*
Jew's mallow *Kerria japonica*
Judas tree *Cercis siliquastrum*
Juniper *Juniperus* spp

KL

Kingcup *Caltha palustris*
Knotweed *Polygonum* spp
Kowhai *Sophora tetraptera*

Laburnum, New Zealand *Sophora tetraptera*
Lady's mantle *Alchemilla* spp
Lamb's tongue *Stachys olympica*
Lantern tree *Crinodendron hookerianum*
Larch *Larix* spp
Larch, Dunkeld *Larix × eurolepis*
Larkspur, Rocket *Delphinium ajacis*
Laurel, Cherry *Prunus laurocerasus*
Laurel, Common *Prunus laurocerasus*
Laurel, Mountain *Kalmia latifolia*
Laurel, Portugal *Prunus lusitanica*
Laurel, Spotted *Aucuba japonica*
Lavender, Cotton *Santolina chamaecyparissus*
Lavender, Old English *Lavandula angustifolia*
Lavender, Sea *Limonium* spp
Leopard's bane *Doronicum* spp
Lilac *Syringa* spp
Lilac, Californian *Ceanothus* spp
Lily *Lilium* spp
Lily, African *Agapanthus* spp
Lily, American trout *Erythronium revolutum*
Lily, Arum *Zantedeschia aethiopica*
Lily, Calla *Calla palustris*
Lily, Chinese trumpet *Lilium × aurelianense*
Lily, Day *Hemerocallis* spp
Lily, Kaffir *Schizostylis coccinea*
Lily, Lent *Narcissus pseudonarcissus*
Lily, Madonna *Lilium candidum*
Lily, Peruvian *Alstroemeria* spp
Lily, Plantain *Hosta* spp
Lily, Regal *Lilium regale*
Lily, St Bernard's *Anthericum liliago*
Lily, Sword *Gladiolus byzantinus*
Lily, Tiger *Lilium tigrinum*
Lily, Torch *Kniphofia* spp
Lily, Turf *Liriope muscari*
Lily, Turk's cap *Lilium martagon*
Lily, Water- *Nymphaea* spp
Lily of the valley *Convallaria majalis*
Lime, Mongolian *Tilia mongolica*
Ling *Calluna vulgaris*
Locust, Black *Robinia pseudoacacia*
Locust, Honey *Gleditsia triacanthos*
London pride *Saxifraga × urbium*
Loosestrife, Purple *Lythrum salicaria*
Loosestrife, Yellow *Lysimachia punctata*
Lords and ladies *Arum italicum 'Pictum'*
Love-in-a-mist *Nigella damascena*
Love-lies-bleeding *Amaranthus caudatus*
Lungwort *Pulmonaria* spp
Lupin *Lupinus* spp
Lupin, Tree *Lupinus arboreus*

M

Maidenhair tree *Ginkgo biloba*
Mallow *Lavatera* spp
Mallow, Jew's *Kerria japonica*
Mallow, Musk *Malva moschata*
Maltese cross *Lychnis chalcedonica*
Maple *Acer* spp
Maple, Chinese paper-bark *Acer griseum*
Maple, Coral-bark *Acer palmatum 'Senkaki'*
Maple, Japanese *Acer palmatum*
Maple, Sycamore *Acer pseudoplatanus*
Marguerite, Blue *Felicia amelloides*
Marigold *Tagetes* spp
Marigold, African *Tagetes erecta*
Marigold, Cape *Dimorphotheca* spp
Marigold, French *Tagetes patula*
Marigold, Marsh *Caltha palustris*
Marigold, Pot *Calendula officinalis*
Masterwort *Astrantia* spp
Mespilus, Snowy *Amelanchier* spp
Mexican orange *Choisya ternata*

Mezereon *Daphne mezereum*
Mignonette *Reseda* spp
Monkey flower *Mimulus* spp
Monkey musk *Mimulus luteus*
Monkshood *Aconitum* spp
Montbretia *Crocosmia × crocosmiiflora*
Morning glory *Ipomoea* spp
Mullein *Verbascum* spp
Myrtle, Common *Myrtus communis*

N

Narcissus, Poet's *Narcissus poeticus*
Nasturtium *Tropaeolum majus*
Nettle, Dead *Lamium* spp
Noah's Ark tree *Juniperus communis* 'Compressa'

O

Obedient plant *Physostegia virginiana*
Oleaster *Elaeagnus angustifolia*
Orach, Purple *Atriplex hortensis*
Orange, Mexican *Choisya* spp
Orange, Mock *Philadelphus* spp
Oswego tea *Monarda didyma*

P

Paeony *Paeonia* spp
Palm, Chusan *Trachycarpus* spp
Palm, Fan *Trachycarpus* spp
Pansy *Viola* spp
Pansy, Garden *Viola × wittrockiana*
Pasque flower *Pulsatilla vulgaris*
Passion flower *Passiflora* spp
Peach, Ornamental *Prunus persica*
Pear, Willow-leaved *Pyrus salicifolia*
Pearl everlasting *Anaphalis* spp
Peony *Paeonia* spp
Peony, Apothecaries' *Paeonia officinalis*
Peony, Tree *Paeonia lutea*
Pepper bush, Sweet *Clethra alnifolia*
Periwinkle, Greater *Vinca major*
Periwinkle, Lesser *Vinca minor*
Pickerel-weed *Pontederia cordata*

Pincushion flower *Scabiosa* spp
Pine *Pinus* spp
Pine, Mountain *Pinus mugo*
Pine, Scots *Pinus sylvestris*
Pink *Dianthus* spp
Pink, Indian *Dianthus chinensis*
Pink, Maiden *Dianthus deltoides*
Pink, Sea *Armeria maritima*
Plum, Ornamental *Prunus* spp
Poached egg flower *Limnanthes douglasii*
Pocket-handkerchief tree *Davidia involucrata*
Polyanthus *Primula*: polyanthus group
Pondweed, Cape *Aponogeton distachyos*
Pondweed, Curled *Potamogeton crispus*
Poppy *Papaver* spp
Poppy, Californian *Eschscholzia californica*
Poppy, Field *Papaver rhoeas*
Poppy, Himalayan blue *Meconopsis betonicifolia*
Poppy, Iceland *Papaver nudicaule*
Poppy, Oriental *Papaver orientale*
Poppy, Plume *Macleaya* spp
Poppy, Tree *Romneya* spp
Poppy, Welsh *Meconopsis cambrica*
Potato-tree, Chilean *Solanum crispum*
Pride of India *Koelreuteria paniculata*
Primrose *Primula vulgaris*
Primrose, Drumstick *Primula denticulata*
Primrose, Evening *Oenothera missouriensis*
Primrose, Japanese *Primula japonica*
Primula, Bog *Primula florindae*
Privet, Golden *Ligustrum ovalifolium* 'Aureum'

QR

Quamash *Camassia* spp
Queen of the prairie *Filipendula rubra*
Quince, Japanese *Chaenomeles speciosa*

Red hot poker *Kniphofia* spp
Redwood, Dawn *Metasequoia glyptostroboides*
Rhubarb, Ornamental *Rheum* spp

Rose, Apothecary's *Rosa gallica* 'Officinalis'
Rose, Guelder *Viburnum opulus*
Rose, Lenten *Helleborus orientalis*
Rose, Rock *Cistus* spp; *Helianthemum nummularium*
Rose, Sun *Cistus* spp
Rose of Lancaster, Red *Rosa gallica* 'Officinalis'
Rosemary *Rosmarinus* spp
Rowan *Sorbus aucuparia*
Rue *Ruta* spp
Rue, Meadow *Thalictrum* spp
Rush, Flowering *Butomus umbellatus*

S

Sage *Salvia officinalis*
Sage, Jerusalem *Phlomis fruticosa*
St John's wort *Hypericum* spp
Sallow, Weeping *Salix caprea* 'Kilmarnock'
Saxifrage *Saxifraga* spp
Scabious *Scabiosa* spp
Scabious, Sweet *Scabiosa atropurpurea*
Self-heal *Prunella* spp
Senna, Bladder *Colutea* spp
Skunk cabbage *Lysichiton americanum*
Smoke tree *Cotinus coggygria*
Snake's head *Fritillaria meleagris*
Snapdragon *Antirrhinum* spp
Snowball bush *Viburnum opulus* 'Sterile'
Snowbell *Styrax japonica*
Snowberry *Symphoricarpos* spp
Snowdrop *Galanthus* spp
Snowdrop, Common *Galanthus nivalis*
Snowdrop tree *Halesia* spp
Snowflake *Leucojum* spp
Snowflake, Summer *Leucojum aestivum*
Snow-in-summer *Cerastium tomentosum*
Solomon's seal *Polygonatum* spp
Spearwort, Greater *Ranunculus lingua*
Speedwell *Veronica* spp
Spider flower *Cleome* spp
Spiderwort *Tradescantia × andersoniana*
Spikenard, False *Smilacina racemosa*

Spindle tree *Euonymus* spp
Spleenwort *Asplenium* spp
Spruce *Picea* spp
Spruce, Colorado *Picea pungens*
Spruce, Serbian *Picea omorika*
Squill, Striped *Puschkinia scilloides*
Star of Bethlehem *Ornithogalum* spp
Star of Bethlehem, Drooping *Ornithogalum nutans*
Star of the veldt *Dimorphotheca aurantiaca*
Statice *Limonium* spp
Stock *Matthiola* spp
Stock, Night-scented *Matthiola bicornis*
Stock, Virginian *Malcolmia maritima*
Stonecrop *Sedum* spp
Strawberry tree, Chinese *Cornus kousa*
Strawberry tree, Killarney *Arbutus unedo*
Straw flower *Helichrysum* spp
Sumach, Stag's horn *Rhus typhina*
Sunflower *Helianthus* spp
Sun plant *Portulaca grandiflora*
Sweet pea *Lathyrus odoratus*
Sweet sultan *Centaurea moschata*
Sweet William *Dianthus barbatus*
Sycamore *Acer pseudoplatanus*

TU

Tamarisk *Tamarix* spp
Thistle, Globe *Echinops ritro*
Thorn, Ornamental *Crataegus* spp
Thrift *Armeria* spp
Thyme, Lemon-scented *Thymus × citriodorus*
Thyme, Wild *Thymus drucei*
Tickseed *Coreopsis drummondii*
Tidy tips *Layia elegans*
Toadflax, Moroccan *Linaria maroccana*
Tobacco plant *Nicotiana* spp
Trinity flower *Tradescantia × andersoniana*
Tulip, Lady *Tulipa clusiana*
Tulip, Water-lily *Tulipa kaufmanniana*
Tulip tree *Liriodendron* spp

Umbrella plant *Peltiphyllum peltatum*

V

Valerian *Centranthus* spp
Valerian, Greek *Polemonium caeruleum*
Verbena, Lemon-scented *Lippia citriodora*
Veronica *Hebe* spp
Veronica, Shrubby *Hebe* spp
Vine, Japanese crimson glory *Vitis coignetiae*
Vine, Kolomikta *Actinidia kolomikta*
Vine, Russian *Polygonum baldschuanicum*
Vine, Staff *Celastrus* spp
Vine, Trumpet *Campsis* spp
Violet *Viola* spp
Violet, Water *Hottonia palustris*

WY

Wake Robin *Trillium grandiflorum*
Wallflower *Cheiranthus* spp
Wallflower, Siberian *Cheiranthus × allionii*
Wand flower *Dierama* spp
Water-archer *Sagittaria sagittifolia*
Water-soldier *Stratiotes aloides*
Whin *Ulex* spp
Whitebeam, Common *Sorbus aria*
Willow *Salix* spp
Willow, Dwarf *Salix reticulata*
Willow, Jerusalem *Elaeagnus angustifolia*
Willow, Kilmarnock *Salix caprea* 'Kilmarnock'
Willow, Pekin *Salix matsudana*
Willow, Violet *Salix daphnoides*
Willow, Woolly *Salix lanata*
Windflower *Anemone* spp
Winter sweet *Chimonanthus* spp
Wisteria, Chinese *Wisteria sinensis*
Witch hazel, Chinese *Hamamelis mollis*
Wood anemone *Anemone nemorosa*
Woodbine *Lonicera periclymenum*
Wormwood, Common *Artemisia absinthium*

Yarrow *Achillea* spp

PAPER, PRINTING AND BINDING BY: C. Townsend Hook Paper Co. Ltd. Sprint Ltd, London EC2 Brown Knight & Truscott Ltd, Tonbridge

Filmtype Services Ltd, Scarborough Grafascan, Dublin BPCC Hazell Books Ltd, Aylesbury